KELSEN'S LEGACY

This volume offers a comprehensive examination of Hans Kelsen's legal and political philosophy, focusing on four central themes.

The first part analyses Kelsen's theory of norms, including its periodisation and concepts of validity and coercion. The second part explores his perspectives on international law, addressing its structural analysis, primitive law characterisation, and teleology. The third part examines Kelsen's theory of democracy, its relationship with the pure theory of law, collective will, and democratisation of the administration. The final part discusses Kelsen's influence on the Vienna School of Legal Theory and its impact on case law and jurisprudence beyond Europe. This collection is essential for scholars and practitioners seeking to understand Kelsen's legacy.

Kelsen's Legacy

Legal Normativity, International Law and Democracy

Edited by
Gonzalo Villa-Rosas
Jorge Luis Fabra-Zamora
and
Jorge Emilio Núñez

with an Introduction by Stanley L Paulson

•HART•
OXFORD • LONDON • NEW YORK • NEW DELHI • SYDNEY

HART PUBLISHING

Bloomsbury Publishing Plc

Kemp House, Chawley Park, Cumnor Hill, Oxford, OX2 9PH, UK

1385 Broadway, New York, NY 10018, USA

Bloomsbury Publishing Ireland Limited, 29 Earlsfort Terrace, Dublin 2, D02 AY28, Ireland

HART PUBLISHING, the Hart/Stag logo, BLOOMSBURY and the Diana logo are trademarks of Bloomsbury Publishing Plc

First published in Great Britain 2025

A catalogue record for this book is available from the British Library.

A catalogue record for this book is available from the Library of Congress.

Library of Congress Control Number: 2024949196

ISBN: HB: 978-1-50996-580-9
ePDF: 978-1-50996-582-3
ePub: 978-1-50996-581-6

Typeset by Compuscript Ltd, Shannon

For product safety related questions contact productsafety@bloomsbury.com

PREFACE

Over 50 years after his death, Hans Kelsen (1881–1973) remains one of the most influential and discussed legal scholars. Although best known for his pure theory of law, he made substantive contributions on virtually every major legal topic. His widely translated work has extensively influenced a wide range of legal scholars and practitioners from all major legal traditions worldwide. This collection brings together leading scholars to discuss the lasting impact of Hans Kelsen's work and attempts to serve as a point of departure for further research on theory of norms, international law and democracy.

Chapters are divided into four parts. The chapters collected in the first part examine Kelsen's theory of norms by analysing its periodisation, the various answers Kelsen formulated to the question of the ultimate foundation of the normativity of law, and the intricate concepts of validity and coercion. The second part expands on Kelsen's theoretical positions on international law, addressing key issues such as the structural normative analysis of international law, its characterisation as primitive law, and the teleological aspects underpinning its development. The third part is devoted to an examination of Kelsen's theory of democracy. This part considers the relation between this theory and pure theory of law, the constructive approach to the collective will, and the problem of democratisation of the administration. The final part of the volume discusses the reception of Kelsen's theory, highlighting its profound influence on the Vienna School of Legal Theory and its significant contributions to the development of case law and jurisprudence in some states outside the European orbit.

In preparing this volume, we incurred in numerous debts. Jorge Fabra-Zamora expresses his gratitude to the University at Buffalo School of Law. Gonzalo Villa-Rosas would like to express his gratitude to Professor Robert Alexy and Professor Stanley L Paulson for their encouragement and support. Jorge Núñez donates his share of royalties from the sales to the Fundação Angelica Goulart in Pedra de Guaratiba, Rio de Janeiro, Brazil. For up-to-date details about the Fundação Angelica Goulart, see: drjorge.world.

Some of the chapters in this book are drawn from papers presented at the online Roundtables on Kelsen's work organised by 'Juris North' on 24–25 September 2021. Juris North is a legal and political discussion group led by chairs of academic institutions in Aberdeen, Durham, Hull, Lancashire, Liverpool, Manchester, Newcastle, Surrey and Westminster. Juris North was launched in 2015 and now has over 2,000 members worldwide.

The online Kelsen Roundtables organised by Juris North in 2021 featured speakers from virtually every corner of the world, from Canada to Australia and from Argentina to China, including contributions from Austria, Barbados, Brazil,

Colombia, England, Germany, Italy, Poland, Russia, the United Kingdom and the United States. The tremendous enthusiasm that these conferences generated in the international academic community demonstrates the timeliness and global reach of the legacy of Hans Kelsen's work. The organisers of this event and the editors of this volume would like to thank all the speakers and participants at the 2021 online Kelsen Roundtables, in particular Cristiano de Aguiar, Andrés Botero Bernal, Wei Feng, Carlo Garbarino, Maris Köpcke Tinturé, Portela Moita, Rubin Assis da Silveira Souza, Anna Taitslin and Jingshu Wang.

This volume honours the memory of the late Professor Ernesto Garzón Valdés (University of Mainz, Germany), Professor María Teresa López (UNLP, Argentina), Professor John Gardner (Oxford, UK), Professor Eugenio Bulygin (UBA, Argentina) and Professor Roberto Vernengo (UBA, Argentina), all of whom made important contributions to the study of Kelsen's work.

Gonzalo Villa Rosas
Jorge Luis Fabra-Zamora
Jorge Emilio Núñez
June 2024

CONTENTS

PART III
DEMOCRACY

PART IV
KELSEN'S LEGACY

CONTRIBUTORS

Robert Alexy is Senior Professor at the University of Kiel.

Mikhail Antonov is Professor of Legal Theory at the Law Faculty of the Higher School of Economics in St Petersburg.

Rodrigo Cadore is Research Assistant and Lecturer at the Faculty of Law, University of Freiburg, and Senior Member of the Hans Kelsen Research Group in Freiburg.

Phil Edwards is Research Fellow at Manchester Metropolitan University.

Jorge Luis Fabra-Zamora is Associate Professor at the University at Buffalo School of Law, State University of New York.

Carsten Heidemann is a Schleswig-Holstein Bar Association Lawyer.

Jörg Kammerhofer is Senior Research Fellow and Senior Lecturer, University of Freiburg, and Senior Lecturer for International Law and Legal Theory at the Vienna University of Economics and Business.

Jorge Emilio Núñez is Reader in Legal Philosophy (Jurisprudence), Political Philosophy and International Relations at Manchester Metropolitan University.

Thomas Olechowski is Full Professor for Austrian and European Legal History at the University of Vienna.

Asya Ostroukh is Senior Lecturer at the Faculty of Law, Cave Hill Campus, University of the West Indies.

Stanley L Paulson is Research Fellow at the Hermann Kantorowicz Institute of the University of Kiel.

Julieta A Rabanos is Postdoctoral Fellow in Theory and Philosophy of Law at the University of Belgrade.

Iain Stewart is Associate Professor at Macquarie Law School.

Gonzalo Villa-Rosas is Research Fellow at the Department of Legal and Constitutional History at the Faculty of Law of the University of Vienna.

Lars Vinx is Associate Professor at the Faculty of Law of the University of Cambridge.

Tomasz Widłak is Associate Professor at the Faculty of Law and Administration of the University of Gdańsk.

Monika Zalewska is Assistant Professor at the Department of Theory and Philosophy of Law at the Faculty of Law and Administration of the University of Lodz.

Introduction*

STANLEY L PAULSON

Arguably, Hans Kelsen's greater legacy comprises no fewer than five fields:

- Legal philosophy
- Norm theory
- Constitutional law
- Public international law
- Ethnologico-sociological studies

While this list cannot be understood in any sense as definitive, other lists will overlap with it to a considerable degree.[1]

Legal philosophy and norm theory. In this short introduction, I prioritise the first two fields. This tack is scarcely controversial vis-à-vis the first field, the entire juridico-philosophical colossus of – as many profess – the twentieth century's greatest legal philosopher. But the second field? Can norm theory be anything other than a sideshow?

To draw this conclusion would be, I think, a mistake. The field that we may be inclined to belittle as a free rider is introduced by Kelsen, as early as his first major treatise *Main Problems in the Theory of Public Law* (1911), as a field of inestimable significance:

> Owing to the extraordinary significance that the theory of the legal norm and of its logical form has for the entire system of the perception of the law, the concept of the legal norm … must be characterised as the central problem of constructive jurisprudence.[2]

The subtitle of Kelsen's *Main Problems* is telling: *Developed from the Theory of the Legal Norm.*

* Special thanks to Bonnie Litschewski Paulson for good suggestions and rewarding discussions on the text.

[1] The list could easily be expanded. Additions might include election law, critique of Marxism, the theory of democracy, Greek philosophy (especially Plato), critique of ideology, and the philosophy and sociology of religion.

[2] H Kelsen, *Hauptprobleme der Staatsrechtslehre* (Tübingen, JCB Mohr, 1911) 378 repr in M Jestaedt (ed), *Hans Kelsen Werke Vol 2* (hereafter: HKW, with volume number) (Tübingen, Mohr Siebeck, 2008) 512. There is no English translation of *Hauptprobleme*, but *Main Problems in the Theory of Public Law* has established itself as an accurate rendition of the title. See, eg, SL Paulson and B Litschewski Paulson (eds), *Normativity and Norms. Critical Perspectives on Kelsenian Themes* (Oxford, Clarendon Press, 1998) 3–22.

In 'Legal Science and the Law' (1922), Kelsen is engaged in outspoken criticism of Fritz Sander.[3] In the course of his response to Sander, he underscores the significance of the legal norm, writing of

> a legal theory that comprehends all law simply as legal norm and, accordingly, develops from the theory of the legal norm all juridico-theoretic problems – as I have already done in my *Main Problems*.[4]

Kelsen's claim deserves emphasis. *All* juridico-theoretic problems are developed from the theory of the legal norm.

Five years later, in the first of his autobiographical sketches (1927), Kelsen emphasises yet again the priority of the legal norm over everything else in his conceptual repertoire.

> I arrived at the decisive standpoint of *Main Problems* by way of the insight that the essence of the law is norm. Thus, all legal theory must be norm theory, the theory of the legal norm, and as such the theory of the objective law.[5]

Then, as if this outspoken case on behalf of the significance of the legal norm were not enough, Kelsen, in the 1930s, stands traditional norm theory on its head. In a little-known but extraordinary development, he introduces empowerment as the fundamental modality of legal norms, relegating the deontic modality to a derivative status.[6] What is more, Kelsen's radical norm theory, as I call it, is evident in the treatises[7] he wrote in the last two decades of his classical phase.[8] Readers of these treatises, unaware of Kelsen's radical norm theory, were not looking for it and so did not find it either.

A brief observation on the first field listed, Kelsen's legal philosophy: his truly creative work in the field takes place in a relatively compressed period, the 1920s. In a string of treatises, beginning with *The Problem of Sovereignty and the Theory of*

[3] H Kelsen, 'Rechtswissenschaft und Recht. Erledigung eines Versuchs zur Überwindung der "Rechtsdogmatik"' (1922) 3 *Zeitschrift für öffentliches Recht* 103 in HKW9, 75–190. On Sander, see T Olechowski, *Hans Kelsen. Biographie eines Rechtswissenschaftlers* (Tübingen, Mohr Siebeck, 2020) 317–41, 563, 568, 620–22; R Cadore, *Rechtswidriges Recht* (Tübingen, Mohr Siebeck, 2024).

[4] Kelsen, 'Rechtswissenschaft und Recht' (n 3) 124 in HKW9, 95.

[5] H Kelsen, 'Selbstdarstellung' in M Jestaedt (ed), *Hans Kelsen Werke, Vol 1 Veröffentliche Schriften 1905 und Selbstzeugnisse* (Tübingen, Mohr Siebeck, 2007) 19–27, 20.

[6] See H Kelsen, 'Recht und Kompetenz. Kritische Bemerkungen zur Völkerrechtstheorie Georges Scelles' in K Ringhofer and R Walter (eds), *Auseinandersetzungen zur Reinen Rechtslehre. Kritische Bemerkungen zu Georges Scelle und Michel Virally* (Vienna, Springer Verlag, 1987) 1–108, 75 *et passim*. This little known publication stems from a manuscript that Kelsen drafted a half-century earlier. A French translation, also from the 1930s (which Kelsen apparently sent to Scelle), has been published under the title 'Droit et competence. Remarques critiques sur la théorie du droit international de Georges Scelle'. See H Kelsen, *Controverses sur la Théorie pure du droit*, C Leben (ed) (Paris, Editions Panthéon-Assas, 2005) 63–161, 130 *et passim*.

[7] See H Kelsen, *General Theory of Law and State*, trans A Wedberg (Cambridge, MA, Harvard University Press, 1945) 59; H Kelsen, *Reine Rechtslehre*, 2nd edn (Vienna, Franz Deuticke, 1960) § 4(b) (4–5), § 5(a) (26); English: H Kelsen, *Pure Theory of Law*, M Knight trans (Berkeley, University of California Press, 1967) 15, 25.

[8] Kelsen's classical phase, running from 1920 to 1960, begins with his treatise *Das Problem der Souveränität und die Theorie des Völkerrechts. Beitrag zu einer Reinen Rechtslehre* (Tübingen, JCB Mohr, 1920) (hereafter: PSTVR) in HKW4, 263–572; an English translation by Paul Silverman is forthcoming with Oxford University Press. Kelsen's earlier, constructivist phase runs from 1911 through 1919; *Main Problems* (n 2) is the representative work. The 'late theory' (*Spätlehre*), representing Kelsen's dramatic shift in 1960 and following, is a different theory, not a part of and not to be confused with the pure theory of law. See n 30.

International Law (1920),[9] Kelsen broaches what would become an abiding commitment to Immanuel Kant,[10] and he introduces the basic norm, which he goes on to develop as his vehicle for bringing the Kantian argument to bear on his legal theory.[11] Matthias Jestaedt has noted that Kelsen's treatise of 1925, *A General Theory of Law*,[12] represents a comprehensive statement of the pure theory of law, largely complete at that point in time.[13]

Constitutional law.[14] At the end of World War I, the various nationalities of the former Austro-Hungarian monarchy declared their independence as individual nation states. So too, in the case of Austria.[15] Karl Renner, the chancellor of the immediate post-War Austrian state, directed Kelsen, his legal adviser, 'to prepare, together with the constitutional department of the state chancellery, a draft of the federal constitution'.[16] The guidelines – federalism and a democratically elected parliament – had been established by Renner.[17] His directive came in early May of 1919, and between May and September of that year, Kelsen produced six drafts,[18] whose differences were for the most part modest. After a good bit of pulling and hauling, including negotiations that Kelsen conducted with various political factions, a draft was ready in September of 1920 for submission to the constituting National Assembly. Kelsen was active at every stage of the process that culminated in the Austrian Federal Constitution of October 1920.

Kelsen took special satisfaction in the role he played in bringing centralised constitutional review into the new constitution. That the laws of the *Länder* were to be subject to constitutional review is an issue on which Kelsen won agreement at an early stage.[19]

[9] Kelsen, PSTVR (n 8).

[10] See H Kelsen, *Die philosophischen Grundlagen der Naturrechtslehre und des Rechtspositivismus* (Charlottenburg, Verlag Rolf Heise, 1928); English: *Natural Law Doctrine and Legal Positivism*, WH Kraus trans as an appendix to Kelsen, *General Theory of Law and State* (n 7) 389–440.

[11] For serious doubts about whether the Kantian argument, understood as undergirding Kelsen's legal theory, is defensible, see H Dreier, *Hans Kelsen zur Einführung* (Hamburg, Junius, 2022) 87–93; SL Paulson, 'Immanuel Kant, Hans Kelsen und Hermann Cohen' in A Funke et al (eds), *Rechtskonflikte – Festschrift für Horst Dreier zum 70. Geburtstag* (Tübingen, Mohr Siebeck, 2024) 223–41, 223–29.

[12] H Kelsen, *Allgemeine Staatslehre* (Berlin, Julius Springer, 1925). There is no English translation. What is more, the translation of Kelsen's title presents problems. A perfectly literal translation, 'General Theory of Law and State', would have the 1925 work bearing the very same title as his treatise of 1945 (see n 7). They are altogether different works.

[13] See M Jestaedt, 'Vorrede zur Studienausgabe' in H Kelsen, *Allgemeine Staatslehre. Studienausgabe*, M Jestaedt (ed) (Tübingen, Mohr Siebeck, 2019) vii–x, vii–viii.

[14] See T Olechowski, 'Der Beitrag Hans Kelsens zur österreichischen Bundesverfassung' in R Walter et al (eds), *Hans Kelsen: Leben – Werk – Wirksamkeit* (Vienna, Manz Verlag, 2009) 211–30; Olechowski, *Hans Kelsen* (n 3) 271–305; E Wiederin, 'Grundlagen und Grundzüge staatlichen Verfassungsrechts. Österreich' in A von Bogandy et al (eds), *Handbuch Ius Publicum Europaeum* (Heidelberg, CF Müller, 2007) 389–449; E Wiederin, 'From the Federalist Papers to Hans Kelsen's "Dearest Child": The Genesis of the Austrian Constitutional Court' (2021) 76 *Zeitschrift für öffentliches Recht* 313; R Cardore, 'Editorischer Bericht: Die Verfassungsgesetze der Republik Österreich' in HKW9, 505–73, 520–73.

[15] Initially 'German-Austria' (*Deutschösterreich*), owing to the widespread assumption that the post-war Austrian state would be merged with Germany, a move precluded by the Treaty of St Germain.

[16] H Kelsen et al (eds), *Die Verfassungsgesetze der Republik Österreich Teil 5: Die Bundesverfassung vom 1. Oktober 1920* (Vienna and Leipzig, Franz Deuticke, 1922) 54 in HKW8, 38–502, 93, quoted in Olechowski, *Hans Kelsen* (n 3) 271.

[17] See Wiederin, 'Genesis' (n 14) 322.

[18] See G Schmitz, *Die Vorentwürfe Hans Kelsens für die österreichische Bundesverfassung* (Vienna, Manz Verlag, 1981).

[19] See H Kelsen, 'Die Stellung der Länder in der künftigen Verfassung Deutschösterreichs' (1919) 1 *Zeitschrift für öffentliches Recht* 98 in HKW4, 115–46.

The later development – that federal laws were also to be subject to constitutional review – was taken up by the *Länder* and the political parties, winning approval at the Salzburg Conference of the *Länder* in February 1920. And at that point Kelsen, too, was on board.[20]

Public international law. Writing in 1914, Alfred Verdross, Kelsen's colleague in what would become the Vienna School of Legal Theory, sets out the possibilities for resolving the problem of the relation between public international law and municipal law. In a dualistic theory, the systems of international law and municipal law are understood to be altogether disparate and independent of one another, whereas, in a monistic theory, either municipal law is brought within the system of international law or international law is brought within one system of municipal law.[21]

Kelsen, too, addresses the issue in 1914. He gives the impression that he would like to leave open the question of whether the dualistic solution is defensible,[22] but his later argument against the very possibility of dualism[23] is already discernible here. He asks whether it would be warranted to characterise as 'law' – on a univocal reading – two fully independent normative systems. And in the case of a conflict of obligations, where the conflicting norms belong to different, fully independent normative systems, would it make sense to treat both norms as legal norms?[24] Kelsen has grave doubts, which lead to his defence of legal monism, a staple in his long career. Scholars who have grappled with Kelsen's ambitious programme of legal monism have not had an easy time of it. 'Cognitive unity' proves to be one of the stumbling blocks, reflected in Kelsen's counter-intuitive notion that legal validity – analogous to truth? – reaches beyond the boundaries of a given legal system.[25]

Leaving aside the puzzles that arise here, I confine myself to a textual detail. As Verdross notes in his paper, legal monism comes in two forms – either municipal law is brought within international law or international law is brought within one system of municipal law. Kelsen, far from violating his purity thesis by offering policy (value-laden) grounds for choosing one form or the other, claims – and this is boilerplate – that we are free to choose either form. In the first work in which he examines legal monism at length, however, he undermines the boilerplate, contending that the priority of municipal law is subjectivistic and leads to solipsism.[26]

Ethnologico-sociological studies. Relatively early in his career, Kelsen began collecting material on indigenous communities. The results of his investigations, tracing the

[20] See Wiederin, 'Grundlagen und Grundzüge (n 14) 395–96; Wiederin, 'Genesis' (n 14) 325.

[21] A Verdross, 'Zur Konstruktion des Völkerrechts' (1914) 8 *Zeitschrift für Völkerrecht* 329, 336.

[22] See H Kelsen, 'Über Staatsunrecht' (1914) 40 *Grünhuts Zeitschrift für das Privat- und öffentliche Recht der Gegenwart* 1, 100–01 *et passim* in HKW3, 439–531, 519–20 *et passim*.

[23] See Kelsen, PSTVR (n 8) 102–320 in HKW4, 367–572.

[24] See n 22.

[25] As Kelsen writes in the first edition of his standard work, the dualistic theory 'is not tenable even on purely logical grounds if the norms of international law as well as those of the state legal systems are to be regarded *as simultaneously valid norms*'. H Kelsen, *Reine Rechtslehre*, 1st edn (Leipzig and Vienna, Deuticke, 1934) § 50(a) (135); English: *Introduction to the Problems of Legal Theory*, SL Paulson and BL Paulson trans (Oxford, Clarendon Press, 1992) 111 (emphasis added).

[26] See Kelsen, PSTVR (n 8) § 63 (314–17) in HKW4, 567–69. I am indebted to Paul Silverman for helpful discussion on the text. Solipsism, from *solus ipse* (I alone with my consciousness exist), stems from Schopenhauer.

transformation from retribution to causality, appear in a large volume that Kelsen completed in 1940.[27] Perhaps not surprisingly, this work of Kelsen's was not well received.[28] After all, he was not an ethnologist, and his work was confined to an examination of bits and pieces that he drew from the literature in the field. Still, in one respect Kelsen's effort is of great interest. In what counts as the first upheaval in his legal theory, Kelsen abandons his earlier commitment to Kant and endorses David Hume, the celebrated empiricist.[29] To be sure, the first upheaval was short-lived, coming to an end in 1941, but an intriguing question arises: is Kelsen's late theory, the second upheaval,[30] a repeat performance of the first?

A sampler. This brief introduction is a sampler, inviting attention to significant fields that figure in Kelsen's monumental *œuvre*. For the greater spectrum of his bequest, see the contributions in *Kelsen's Legacy*.

[27] See H Kelsen, *Vergeltung und Kausalität. Eine soziologische Untersuchung* (The Hague, WP Van Stockum & Zoon). The book bears a copyright of 1941, but owing to the Second World War it did not appear until 1946. The English edition, *Society and Nature* (Chicago, University of Chicago Press, 1943), is shorn of the tell-tale signs in the German original that point to Kelsen's abandonment of Kant and his endorsement of David Hume.

[28] See, above all, T Parsons, 'Review: Kelsen, *Society and Nature*' (1944) 58 *Harvard Law Review* 140.

[29] See Kelsen, *Vergeltung und Kausalität* (n 27) 275–77 *et passim*.

[30] In so far as the beginning of the second upheaval – the late theory (*Spätlehre*) – can be established on the basis of Kelsen's writings, the point of departure is Kelsen's letter of 4 July 1960 to Ulrich Klug. Kelsen, reacting sharply to Klug's unsuccessful attempt to resolve the problem of norm conflicts, draws far-reaching conclusions. See H Kelsen and U Klug, *Rechtsnormen und logische Analyse. Ein Briefwechsel 1959 bis 1965* (Vienna, Franz Deuticke, 1980) 42–50.

1

Reading 'Kelsen's Legacy'

GONZALO VILLA-ROSAS*

As Thomas Olechowski has argued, it is no exaggeration to say that Kelsen was the 'architect of the Austrian federal constitution'.[1] His contributions were not limited to the drafts that served as the basis for the final version adopted on 1 October 1920,[2] nor to his participation as an impartial expert adviser on constitutional matters to various political leaders and to the Constitutional Sub-Commission of the National Constituent Assembly.[3] His principal contribution was the fact that he belonged to the select group of academics[4] whose opinions influenced not only the development of the 'guarantee

* The author would like to express gratitude to Mikhail Antonov, Phil Edwards, Jorge L Fabra-Zamora, Carsten Heidemann, Thomas Olechowski, Assya Ostroukh, Monika Zalewska, and most especially Stanley L Paulson and Iain Stewart for their suggestions.

[1] T Olechowski, *Hans Kelsen. Biographie eines Rechtswissenschaftlers*, 2nd edn (Tübingen, Mohr Siebeck, 2021) 923. Following the dissolution of the Austro-Hungarian monarchy in October 1918, Chancellor [*Staatskanzler*] Karl Renner tasked Kelsen with the drafting of a federal constitution in collaboration with the Constitutional Department of the State Chancellery [*Verfassungsabteilung der Staatskanzlei*] (see ibid 271). Olechowski states that 'Kelsen later asserted that he had prepared his work in accordance with Renner's instructions, namely, "with the support of the Constitutional Department". In any case, he was assisted by his superior, Section Councillor Georg Froelich, and by Ministerial Secretary Egbert Mannlicher. It is likely that he also received assistance from Adolf J Merkl, although the nature and extent of this assistance is not known' (ibid). For further information on Kelsen's role as the creator of the Austrian Federal Constitution [*Verfassungsmacher*], please refer to ibid 271–305. Furthermore, Olechowski has employed the term *spiritus rector* to describe Kelsen's role in the drafting of the Austrian Federal Constitution of 1920 (see T Olechowski, 'Hans Kelsen und die Bundesverfassung' (2022) 3 *Austrian Law Journal* 28, 28). For further information on Kelsen's role in the construction of the Austrian Federal Constitution of 1920, please refer to T Olechowski, 'Der Beitrag Hans Kelsens zur österreichischen Bundesverfassung' in R Walter, W Ogris and T Olechowski (eds), *Hans Kelsen: Leben – Werk – Wirksamkeit* (Vienna, Manz Verlag, 2009) 211–30.

[2] The six drafts prepared by Kelsen and his colleagues, only made available to the public again in 1981, following their editing by Georg Schmitz (see G Schmitz, *Die Vorentwürfe von Hans Kelsen für die österreichische Bundesverfassung*, Hans Kelsen Institut Series Vol 6 (Vienna, Manz Verlag, 1981)) can be regarded as the basis for the Federal Constitution, in particular what is known as Draft II [*Entwurf II*] (see ibid 273).

[3] For further details on Kelsen's involvement in the Constitutional Sub-Commission of the National Constituent Assembly [*Verfassungsunterausschuss der Konstituierenden Nationalversammlung*], see Olechowski, *Hans Kelsen* (n 1) 291–95.

[4] As part of the influence of the Vienna School of Legal Theory on the development of Austrian public law (see, eg, E Wiederin, 'Über den modus austriacus in der Staatsrechtslehre' (2007) 7 *Die Verwaltung. Zeitschrift für Verwaltungsrecht und Verwaltungswissenschaft. Staatsrechslehre als Wissenschaft* 293) Kelsen's contributions to the shaping of the constitutional control of laws in the Federal Constitution of 1920 undoubtedly constitute a definitive link in its historical development however, this is the fruit of various strands. The Kremsier and Frankfurt constitutional projects of 1848 and 1849 represent important historical precursors

of the Constitution by the judiciary',[5] but above all the creation of the concrete review of norms [*konkrete Normenkontrolle*].[6] Kelsen had a decisive influence not only on the

of the concept of centralised control (see J Osterkamp, *Verfassungsgerichtsbarkeit in der Tschechoslowakei (1920–1939)*, Studien zur europäischen Rechtsgeschichte, Veröffentlichungen des Max-Planck-Instituts für europäische Rechtsgeschichte Frankfurt am Main, Vol 243 (Frankfurt am Main, Vittorio Klostermann, 2009) 8). It is also important to consider the contributions of Heinrich Jaques and Edmund Bernatzik, as well as those of Karl Renner, who repeatedly advocated for establishing a constitutional court. (For further insight, see K Heller, *Der Verfassungsgerichtshof: die Entwicklung der Verfassungsgerichtsbarkeit* (Vienna, Verlag Österreich, 2010) 117–35; K Renner, *Das Selbstbestimmungsrecht der Nationen* (Vienna, J Deuticke, 1917) 292–93; K Renner [R Springer], *Der Kampf der Österreichischen Nationen um den Staat. Erster Theil: Das nationale Problem als Verfassungs- und Verwaltungsfrage* (Vienna, Franz Deuticke Verlag, 1902) 241.) It is similarly clear that the work of Georg Jellinek is of great significance. With the publication of his book *Ein Verfassungsgerichtshof für Österreich* [*A Constitutional Court for Austria*] (Vienna, Alfred Hölder, 1885), he became one of the most renowned advocates of the centralised model of constitutional control.

[5] The expression is employed by Kelsen (see H Kelsen, 'Mitbericht von Professor Dr. Hans Kelsen in Wien' in H Triepel, E von Hippen, H Kelsen, M Layer, *Wesen und Entwicklung der Staatsgerichtsbarkeit. Berichte: Verhandlungen der Tagung der deutschen Staatsrechtslehrer zu Wien am 23. Und 24. April 1928: mit einem Auszug aus der Aussprache* (Berlin, De Gruyter, 1929) 88–123, 101). The constitutional jurisdiction proposed by Kelsen, which is centralised, specialised and institutionally independent with competence for an abstract control of the legislative activity of the federal and state parliaments, differs from the decentralised – also called diffuse – control of constitutionality that characterises the legal system of the United States. For further reading, see, for example, M Tushnet, 'Comparative Constitutional Law' in M Reimann and R Zimmermann, *The Oxford Handbook of Comparative Law*, 2nd edn (Oxford, Oxford University Press, 2019) 1194–221; D Lustig and JHH Weiler, 'Judicial review in the contemporary world – Retrospective and prospective' (2018) 16 *International Journal of Constitutional Law* 315; AS Sweet, 'Constitutional Courts' in M Rosenfeld and A Sajó (eds), *The Oxford Handbook of Comparative Constitutional Law* (Oxford, Oxford University Press, 2012) 816–30; M Cappelletti, *Judicial Review in the Contemporary World* (Indianapolis, Bobbs-Merrill, 1971). Following the dissolution of the Austro-Hungarian Empire and the collapse of the Habsburg monarchy, the Republic of Czechoslovakia adopted a model of centralised control of constitutionality of legislative activity. This was first established in the Czechoslovak Constitutional Charter of 29 February 1920, and six months later in the Austrian Federal Constitution of 1 October 1920. As Osterkamp has argued, the impetus for the creation of centralised constitutional control in Czechoslovakia did not originate with the representatives of the pure theory of law, as represented by the Brno School of Legal Theory. Instead, the driving force behind this development was Jiří Hoetzel, one of the school's most vocal critics. In fact, the founder of the school, František Weyr, expressed his scepticism of the centralised constitutional control, as evidenced by Osterkamp (n 4) 10. Heller has contributed to the debate against Osterkamp by arguing that although the Czechoslovak Constitutional Charter is a few months older than its Austrian counterpart, the Constitutional Court established under the Austrian Constitution issued its first judgment on 14 December 1920, whereas the Constitutional Court provided for in the Czechoslovak Constitution did not issue its first judgment until 7 November 1922. Furthermore, in contrast to the position proposed by Osterkamp, Heller has underscored the influence of František Weyr on Czechoslovak constitutional design. Weyr was personally close to Kelsen, to the University of Vienna, and to the circle of Pure Legal Theory. This would explain the creation of an Austrian-inspired constitutional design (see Heller (n 4) 188–89). For further information on the relationship between Kelsen and Weyr, please refer to ch 13 by Cadore in this volume. Notwithstanding the aforementioned disputes, it is evident that the most noteworthy aspect of this phenomenon is the fact that two of the principal inheritors of the Austro-Hungarian monarchy's collapse developed a model of constitutional control that ultimately influenced the constitutional development of numerous European states and states across the globe. For further insight into the expansion of the centralised model of constitutional review in comparison to the decentralised model of constitutional review, please refer to AHY Chen and M Poiares Maduro, 'The Judiciary and Constitutional Review' in M Tushnet, T Fleiner and C Sounders (eds), *Routledge Handbook of Constitutional Law* (New York, Routledge, 2013) 97–109, esp 97–101. Regarding the development of the centralised model, in particular in European constitutional law, and the influence of Kelsen, it is worth noting the recent contribution of P Cruz Villalón, 'The Evolution of Constitutional Adjudication in Europe' in A von Bogdandy, PM Huber and C Grabenwarter (eds), *Constitutional Adjudication: Common Themes and Challenges*, Max Planck Handbooks in European Public Law Vol IV (Oxford, Oxford University Press, 2023) 1–50.

[6] A concrete review of norms [*konkrete Normenkontrolle*] is the remedy whereby the Constitutional Court on its own initiative can initiate a review procedure of the law when, having to apply it in another procedure, it has doubts about the conformity of such a law with the Constitution. For further details, see Olechowski,

establishment of the German-Austrian Constitutional Court,[7] but also on numerous decisions of the Constitutional Court[8] of the Republic of German-Austria and of the Republic of Austria[9] during his tenure as a judge from May 1919 to February 1930. At that time, as a result of the escalation of political conflicts that had begun in the second half of the 1920s, he and the other members of the Constitutional Court were removed from their lifetime appointments as judges.[10]

Nevertheless, as Christoph Schmetterer observes, Kelsen's contributions as a constitutional expert within the Austrian sphere were not limited to his contributions to the Federal Constitution and the Constitutional Court's decisions, they also included the five memoranda written between 1917 and 1918, in which Kelsen, as legal adviser to the last (joint) Minister of War of the Austro-Hungarian monarchy, offered his expert opinion on the domestic political situation of the monarchy and the possibilities of

Hans Kelsen (n 1) 924; 190; G Bongiovanni, *Reine Rechtslehre e dottrina giuridica dello Stato* (Milano, Giuffrè, 1998) 190. §140b Austrian Federal Constitution (B-VG): www.ris.bka.gv.at/Dokumente/Erv/ERV_1930_1/ERV_1930_1.pdf.

[7] As Olechowski has argued (T Olechowski, 'Von Georg Jellinek zu Hans Kelsen. A contribution to the history of political theory at the University of Vienna around 1900' in E Röhrlich and A Meisinger (eds), *Migration und Innovation um 1900. Perspektiven auf das Wien der Jahrhundertwende* (Vienna, Böhlau Verlag, 2016) 375–98, 398) Kelsen prepared a counter-draft bill to the bill submitted by the State Office for Justice [*Staatsamt für Justiz*] to transfer the competences of the former Imperial Court of Justice [*Reichsgericht*] to the new German-Austrian Constitutional Court [*Deutsch-österreichischer Verfassungsgerichtshof*]. (Kelsen's counter-draft was published under the name *Entwurf eines Gesetzes über die Errichtung eines Verfassungsgerichtshofes* [*Bill to establish a Constitutional Court*]. See Schmitz (n 2) Appendix 1, 308–10) Kelsen's counter-draft was submitted to the Provisional National Assembly for Germany-Austria [*Provisorische Nationalversammlung für Deutschösterreich – ProvNV*] on 23 January 1919. Following its discussion by the Constitutional Committee, the Assembly passed the draft into law on 25 January 1919 without substantial changes. (Olechowski, *Hans Kelsen* (n 1) 246–47.) Subsequent reforms extended the competences of the Constitutional Court. (For further information on the history of the Austrian Constitutional Court, see, eg, Olechowski, *Hans Kelsen* (n 1) 244–47; Heller (n 4) 141–50.).

[8] For further insight, see Olechowski, *Hans Kelsen* (n 1) 255–62; I Stewart, 'Hans Kelsen, Legal Scientist' (2023) 48 *Journal of Legal Philosophy* 119, 186.

[9] For an analysis of the effects of the Treaty of Saint-Germain-en-Laye of 10 September 1919 on German unification as proposed in the Law on the Form of Government and State of Austria-Germany of 12 November 1918 [*Gesetz vom 12. November 1918 über die Staats- und Regierungsform von Deutschösterreich*] and the adoption of the official name Republic of Austria, see JW Boyer, *Culture and Political Crisis in Vienna: Christian Socialism in Power, 1897–1918* (Chicago, University of Chicago Press, 1995) 437–43.

[10] As Dreier has argued, the primary source of contention for the conservative forces was the liberal stance of the Constitutional Court on the question of so-called dispensation marriages, which was largely shaped by Kelsen and for which he was responsible (H Dreier, 'Hans Kelsen (1881–1973)' in H Dreier, *Kelsen im Kontext. Beiträge zum Werk Hans Kelsens und geistesverwandter Autoren*, M Jestaedt and SL Paulson (eds) (Tübingen, Mohr Siebeck, 2019) 1–26, 3). As Olechowski has elucidated, the concept of civil marriage and divorce, irrespective of the religious denomination of the spouses, was not introduced in Austria until the enactment of the Marriage Act of 1938 by the Nazi regime. The legal solution to authorise a new marriage, namely, to grant a dispensation or permission, involved the application of the civil code. The application of civil law gave rise to numerous legal problems. The Constitutional Court's attempts to resolve such legal problems from 1926 onwards resulted in a greater degree of conflict and opposition. For further reading, see T Olechowski, 'The Controversy Surrounding Marriage Law in 20th Century Austria with a Special Emphasis on Constitutional Court Decisions Regarding the "Dispensation Marriages"' (2017) 10(1) *Krakowskie Studia z Historii Państwa i Prawa* 97; Olechowski, *Hans Kelsen* (n 1) 437–55. For an analysis of Kelsen's role in the constitutionality of dispensation marriages, see C Neschwara, 'Kelsen als Verfassungsrichter. Seine Rolle in der Dispensehen-Kontroverse' in SL Paulson and M Stolleis (eds), *Hans Kelsen: Staatsrechtslehrer und Rechtstheoretiker des 20. Jahrhunderts* (Tübingen, Mohr Siebeck, 2005) 353–84. Only two of the 14 judges of the Constitutional Court dismissed in 1930 were re-elected. Kelsen received an offer from the Social Democrats to put himself forward as a candidate, but he rejected it because he wanted to preserve his party neutrality (see Olechowski, *Hans Kelsen* (n 1) 472–78; Stewart, 'Hans Kelsen, Legal Scientist' (n 8) 187).

constitutional reform.[11] At the European level too, once Kelsen's academic reputation as author of the Austrian Federal Constitution [*Verfassungsmacher*] had been established, he was commissioned to draft a Constitution for the Free State of Fiume[12] (now Rijeka, Croatia) in 1921.[13] His expert opinion was sought again in 1928 to settle the question of the competence of the Parliament of the Principality of Liechtenstein.[14] Similarly, beyond the borders of Europe, Kelsen's intervention was sought to define the competence of the Brazilian National Constituent Assembly in 1933.[15]

In addition, Kelsen contributed to the practice of international law in the inter-war period through his 1927 report on the creation of the Czechoslovak state and citizenship,[16] and in his 1939 memorandum to the League of Nations on the violation of the Munich Agreement by the German Third Reich.[17] Before the end of the war, Kelsen had given an expert opinion on the 'Present Status and Re-establishment as an Independent State of Austria' in 1944[18] and, once the conflict had concluded, gave opinions both on the 'Legal Status of the Continental Shelf in Positive International Law' in the Australia–Japan dispute in 1954[19] and on the eligibility of the future Republic of Cyprus as a member of the United Nations in 1959.[20] No less remarkable was Kelsen's

[11] C Schmetterer, 'Hans Kelsens Überlegungen zur Reform der Österreichisch-Ungarischen Monarchie' in C Jabloner, T Olechowski and K Zeleny (eds), *Das internationale Wirken Hans Kelsens*. Schriftenreihe des Hans Kelsen-Instituts 38 (Vienna, Manz, 2016) 1–24, 1.

[12] The 1921 draft Constitution of the Free State of Fiume, as proposed by Kelsen, was never implemented due to the overthrow of the government of this Free State by the Italian Fascists the following year. See Olechowski, *Hans Kelsen* (n 1) 304; S Wedrac, 'Hans Kelsens Arbeiten an der Verfassung des Freistaats Fiume (Rijeka): eine Spurensuche' in C Jabloner, T Olechowski and K Zeleny (eds), *Das internationale Wirken Hans Kelsens*. Schriftenreihe des Hans Kelsen-Instituts 38 (Vienna, Manz, 2016) 25–42; RA Métall, *Hans Kelsen: Leben und Werk* (Vienna, Deuticke, 1969) 47.

[13] On the legal framework of the city of Fiume between 1918 and 1924, see A Agrì, 'Lo "Stato di Fiume" e il suo diritto (1918–1924)' (2021) 19 *Rivista di storia giuridica dell'età medievale e moderna* 1.

[14] See Olechowski, *Hans Kelsen* (n 1) 425–26.

[15] See ibid 593–95. On Kelsen's opinion on Decree No 22.621 of 5 April 1933 on the procedure rules of the Brazilian National Constituent Assembly of 1933 and 1934, see MG Losano, 'Kelsens Gutachten von 1933 über die konstituierende Nationalversammlung Brasiliens' in C Jabloner, T Olechowski and K Zeleny (eds), *Das internationale Wirken Hans Kelsens*. Schriftenreihe des Hans Kelsen-Instituts 38 (Vienna, Manz, 2016) 65–76; G Silveira Siquiera, 'O parecer de Kelsen sobre a Constituinte brasileira' (2015) 6 (11) *Dereito e Práxis. Rio de Janeiro* 348. In 1926, Kelsen published 'Bemerkungen zur chilenischen Verfassung' ['Comments on the Chilean Constitution'] ((1926) 5 *Zeitschrift für öffentliches Recht-(ZÖR)* 616). As Miriam Gassner has argued, 'the provenance of these comments remains uncertain. According to some South American researchers (eg, Agustín Squella of the University of Valparaíso), Chilean President Arturo Alessandri, who was in exile in France, Switzerland and Italy from September 1924 to March 1925, may have commissioned Kelsen to write an expert opinion on the Chilean Constitution of 1925. However, there is no record of this'. (M Gassner, 'Der Kreis um Hans Kelsen in Lateinamerika. Wie die Reine Rechtslehre Lateinamerika eroberte' (2014) 4 (1) *Beiträge zur Rechtsgeschichte Österreichs – BRGÖ – Zeitschrift der Kommission für Rechtsgeschichte Österreichs der österreichischen Akademie der Wissenschaften* 64, 64; see also Olechowski, *Hans Kelsen* (n 1) 395.

[16] See Olechowski, *Hans Kelsen* (n 1) 426–28.

[17] See J Kuklík and J Němeček, 'Memorandum by Hans Kelsen on the Breaking up of Czecho-Slovakia' in C Jabloner, T Olechowski and K Zeleny (eds), *Das internationale Wirken Hans Kelsens*. Schriftenreihe des Hans Kelsen-Instituts 38 (Vienna, Manz, 2016) 107–19.

[18] See Olechowski, *Hans Kelsen* (n 1) 732; T Olechowski, 'Hans Kelsens Gutachten zur Neugestaltung Österreichs und Deutschlands nach dem Zweiten Weltkrieg' in C Jabloner, T Olechowski and K Zeleny (eds), *Das internationale Wirken Hans Kelsens*. Schriftenreihe des Hans Kelsen-Instituts 38 (Vienna, Manz, 2016) 121–40.

[19] See Olechowski, *Hans Kelsen* (n 1) 855–57.

[20] See ibid 857–58; A Constantinides, 'Hans Kelsen's Opinion on the Eligibility of the future Republic of Cyprus as a Member of the United Nations' in C Jabloner, T Olechowski and K Zeleny (eds), *Das internationale Wirken Hans Kelsens*. Schriftenreihe des Hans Kelsen-Instituts 38 (Vienna, Manz, 2016) 169–200.

work as legal adviser to the US War Department in preparing for the war crimes trials at Nuremberg.[21]

Without a solid academic reputation, this influence would have been impossible for Kelsen.[22] According to Olechowski, Kelsen began his long teaching career in the summer semester of 1909 as a private tutor and lecturer in law at the Law Department of the Imperial and Royal Teresian Academy. In the winter semester of 1909 to 1910, Kelsen became the course director at the Imperial and Royal Export Academy, now the Vienna University of Economics and Business.[23] In May 1910, Kelsen was appointed a member of the Imperial and Royal State Examination Commission in Vienna.[24] On 10 July 1911, 'Dr Hans Kelsen completed the requirements for the *Habilitation* at the University of Vienna in general and Austrian constitutional law, philosophy of law and its history'[25] with his work *Hauptprobleme der Staatsrechtslehre, entwickelt aus der Lehre vom Rechtssatze* [*Main Problems in the Theory of Public Law, Developed From the Theory of the Legal Statement*].[26] On 21 July 1911, Kelsen was appointed part-time lecturer in constitutional theory at the Imperial and Royal Export Academy; on 23 December of the same year, he was appointed regular lecturer; and on 10 June 1914, he took up the post of full-time lecturer at the same academy.[27] Between 1911 and 1918 Kelsen taught as a private lecturer [*Privatdozent*] at the University of Vienna.[28] On 27 February 1918, Kelsen was appointed to the position of associate professor [*außerordentlicher Professor*].[29] Following the conclusion of hostilities, on 19 July 1919, he was elevated to the rank of full professor [*ordentlicher Professor*] of law and political science at the same university.[30] On 12 June 1920, Kelsen was elected Dean of the Faculty of Law and Political Science at the University of Vienna for the winter semester 1920 to 1921.[31]

A few months after his dismissal as judge of the Austrian Constitutional Court, on 11 August 1930, Kelsen was appointed Professor of Public Law, in particular Political Science and Philosophy of Law, and (co-)Director of the Faculty of Law and the newly established Faculty of International Law at the University of Cologne.[32] On 12 April 1933,

[21] See M García-Salmones Rovira, 'Not Just Pure Theory: Hans Kelsen (1881–1973) and International Criminal Law' in F Mégret and I Tallgren (eds), *The Dawn of a Discipline. International Criminal Justice and Its Early Exponents* (Cambridge, Cambridge University Press, 2020) 174–204; Olechowski, *Hans Kelsen* (n 1) 745–50.

[22] For information on Kelsen's origins and family background see, inter alia, Olechowski, *Hans Kelsen* (n 1) 27–90; H Kelsen, 'Autobiographie (1947)' in M Jestaedt (ed), *Hans Kelsen Werke, Vol 1 Veröffentlichen Schriften 1905 und Selbstzeugnisse* (hereafter HKW1) (Tübingen, Mohr Siebeck, 2007) 30–91, 30–33.

[23] Olechowski, *Hans Kelsen* (n 1) 119–23.

[24] ibid 123.

[25] See *Österreichisches Staatsarchiv* [*ÖStA*], *Allgemeines Verwaltungsarchiv* [*AVA*], *Unterricht Allgemein, Universität Wien*, 4 Jus, Personalakt Hans Kelsen, Z. 30728/1911.

[26] Kelsen's *Habilitation* work was written under the supervision of Edmund Bernatzik and Adolf Menzel, as outlined by Olechowski, *Hans Kelsen* (n 1) 144. The work of Hans Kelsen, *Hauptprobleme der Staatsrechtslehre, entwickelt aus der Lehre vom Rechtssatze* (hereafter HPSL1), is cited according to the pagination in the margin taken from the original published in Hans Kelsen, *Hans Kelsen Werke, Vol 2, Veröffentlichte Schriften 1911*, M Jestaedt (ed) (hereafter HKW2) (Tübingen, Mohr Siebeck, 2008) 49–878.

[27] Olechowski, *Hans Kelsen* (n 1) 144.

[28] ibid 144–50. On Kelsen's teaching at the University of Vienna during the war, see ibid, 185–86.

[29] ibid 204–05.

[30] ibid 260.

[31] ibid 307.

[32] ibid 492.

during his term of office as Dean, Kelsen was dismissed from his post at the University of Cologne on the authority of the Law for the Restoration of the Professional Civil Service, which had been enacted on 7 April.[33] As Horst Dreier has explained, this dismissal was followed by difficult times.[34] In 1933, Kelsen accepted the chair of international law at the Graduate Institute of International Studies in Geneva.[35] As Olechowski reports, Kelsen worked at this institute from the winter semester between 1933 and 1934 until the summer semester of 1936.[36] From October 1936, Kelsen took up the chair of international law at the German University in Prague, where, as Dreier informs us, 'anti-Semitic propaganda campaigns were soon organised by the student body, so that his teaching activities at this university were terminated at the end of the winter semester between 1937 and 1938'.[37] From the summer term of 1938 to the summer term of 1940, Kelsen again worked for the Graduate Institute of International Studies in Geneva.[38]

[33] See Salzburger Zeitung, 28 September 1933, 2: anno.onb.ac.at/cgi-content/anno?apm=0&aid=sch&datum=19330928&seite=2; Olechowski, *Hans Kelsen* (n 1) 565. The Law for the Restoration of the Professional Civil Service [*Gesetz zur Wiederherstellung des Berufsbeamtentums*], enacted on 7 April 1933 by the National Socialist regime, saw the gradual removal of politically undesirable individuals, including Communists and Social Democrats, as well as those of Jewish descent, from the civil service (see: www.bundesarchiv.de/DE/Content/Virtuelle-Ausstellungen/NS-Digitalisierung/Berufsbeamtentum_virtuelle_ausstellung.html). Section 3(1) of the aforementioned legislation states that '[c]ivil servants who are not of Aryan descent must be retired (§8 et seq); if they are honorary civil servants, they must be dismissed'. For the text of the Act, see Österreichiche Nationalbibliothek: alex.onb.ac.at/cgi-content/alex?aid=dra&datum=1933&page=300&size=45. As Dreier has established, both elements described in the law for the Restoration of the Professional Civil Service applied to Kelsen. His removal from office was not only because of his political stance but also because of his Jewish origins. (See H Dreier, 'Festvortrag "Rezeption und Rolle der Reinen Rechtslehre"' in H Dreier, *Rezeption und Rolle der Reinen Rechtslehre. Festakt aus Anlaß des 70. Geburtstags von Robert Walter mit Laudationes von Clemens Jabloner und Ludwig Adamovich sowie einer Bibliographie des Jubilars* (Vienna, Manzsche Verlags- und Universitätsbuchhandlung, 2001) 17–36, 26.

[34] Dreier, *Kelsen im Kontext. Beiträge zum Werk Hans Kelsens und geistesverwandter Autoren* (n 10) 4.

[35] Olechowski, *Hans Kelsen* (n 1) 571. Documents discovered in the Historical Archives of the University of Barcelona in 2023 demonstrate that, in addition to the job offers received from Anglo-Saxon universities that Kelsen himself had previously disclosed (see Kelsen, 'Autobiography (1947)' (n 22) 80–81), the University of Barcelona appointed Kelsen Adjunct Professor [*Profesor encargado de curso*] on 22 June 1933 (for further details, see J Muñoz Almazán, 'Hans Kelsen, professor at the University of Barcelona' (2023) 50 *Cuadernos Electrónicos de Filosofía del Derecho* 86, 109). Muñoz Almazán asserts that José Ramón Xirau Palau (ibid 87), who served as Dean of the Law School at the University of Barcelona, was the primary motivating force behind Kelsen's appointment. Furthermore, Xirau played a leading role in the approval of the Statute of Autonomy [*Estatuto de Autonomía*] of the University of Barcelona in 1933 (ibid 95). The position of Adjunct Professor [*Profesor encargado de curso*] was the position of professors engaged on an annual basis to teach a particular course, who were permitted to extend their contracts beyond the initial teaching period (ibid 102). This position, to which Kelsen was appointed, was the same one through which other academics fleeing Nazi persecution were recruited to Spanish universities during the Second Spanish Republic – this was the case, for example, of James Goldschmidt (ibid 102–03) and Hermann Heller (see U Volkmann, 'Hemann Heller (1991–1933)' in M Kilian, HA Wolff and P Häberle (eds), *Staatsrechtslehrer des 20. Jahrhunderts. Deutschland – Österreich – Schweiz*, 2nd edn (Berlin, De Gruyter, 2018) 471–86, 474). A few years later, however, Spanish universities fell into the clutches of fascism (Muñoz Almazán, ibid, 102–03). The University of Barcelona was deprived of its autonomy as early as 1934 (ibid 103). Muñoz Almazán's research has yet to ascertain the reasons behind Kelsen's decision not to accept the appointment at the University of Barcelona, nor why he did not include this information in his autobiography (ibid 89). Nevertheless, Muñoz Almazán's research represents a significant contribution to the historical understanding of the Spanish educational system before the Civil War, as well as of the recognition that Kelsen was already receiving in Spain in the early 1930s. I am indebted to JJ Moreso for his guidance in writing this passage.

[36] Olechowski, *Hans Kelsen* (n 1) 571.

[37] Dreier, *Kelsen im Kontext. Beiträge zum Werk Hans Kelsens und geistesverwandter Autoren* (n 10) 4.

[38] This was also the case in the winter semester between 1952 and 1953 as well as in the summer semester of 1953 (see Olechowski, *Hans Kelsen* (n 1) 571).

In June 1940, Kelsen emigrated to the United States, 'already 60 years old and barely able to speak English'.[39] In the United States, Kelsen was appointed Oliver Wendell Holmes Lecturer at Harvard Law School and Research Associate in Comparative Law from 1940 to 1942. From 1942 Kelsen taught at the University of California at Berkeley, where he was appointed Professor of Political Science in 1945, a position he held until his retirement in 1952.[40]

This impressive academic life is the result of the echo of Kelsen's theoretical contributions, in which we can most clearly appreciate the magnitude of the impact of his work. This magnitude is partly the result of Kelsen's prolific intellectual activity, whose contributions during his lifetime ranged from the publication of *Die Staatslehre des Dante Alighieri* [*Dante Alighieri's Political Philosophy*] in 1905[41] to the publication of 'The Essence of International Law' in 1968.[42] More than 60 years of recognised[43] and uninterrupted academic contributions reveal an extensive and intense scholarly output the influence of which spanned continents and crossed oceans.[44] Indeed, Kelsen's theoretical contribution survived like no other the bloody vicissitudes of twentieth-century history, of which the author was both a victim and a witness. As Miriam Gassner has argued,[45] the enduring influence of Kelsen's work may be attributed not only to its extensive volume and the compelling force of its style, but also to the author's strenuous efforts to transmit his theory and methodology to mostly younger colleagues.[46] Certainly, despite the difficulties of his exiles,[47] Kelsen persevered in his attempt both to

[39] Dreier, *Kelsen im Kontext. Beiträge zum Werk Hans Kelsens und geistesverwandter Autoren* (n 10) 4.

[40] ibid.

[41] H Kelsen, *Die Staatslehre des Dante Alighieri* (Vienna, Deuticke, 1905). Reprinted in HKW1, 134–300. On the background of *Die Staatslehre des Dante Alighieri*, see Olechowski, *Hans Kelsen* (n 1) 80–85. For a discussion of this work see O Lepsius, 'Hans Kelsen on Dante Alighieri's Political Philosophy' (2016) 27 *European Journal of International Law* 1153.

[42] H Kelsen, 'The Essence of International Law' in KW Deutsch and S Hoffmann (eds), *The Relevance of International Law. Essay in Honour of Leo Gross* (Cambridge, MA, Schenkman, 1968).

[43] Kelsen's career was duly recognised by more than 10 honorary doctorates, including from the universities of Utrecht (1936), Harvard (1936), Chicago (1941), Berkeley (1952), Berlin (1961), Vienna (1961), Paris (1963), Salzburg (1967) and Strasbourg (1972). Additionally, he was bestowed with the highest honours, including the Austrian Decoration of Honour for Science and Art [*Österreichisches Ehrenzeichen für Wissenschaft und Kunst*] (1961) and the Ring of Honour of the City of Vienna [*Ehrenring der Stadt Wien*] (1966). See Dreier, *Kelsen im Kontext. Beiträge zum Werk Hans Kelsens und geistesverwandter Autoren* (n 10) 1.

[44] For further insight into the influence of the pure theory of law outside the Austrian orbit, see, among other sources, GA Ramírez Cleves (ed), *Kelsen en el mundo: la influencia de la Teoría pura del derecho en distintos lugares* (Bogotá, Universidad Externado de Colombia, 2024); R Walter, C Jabloner and K Zeleny (eds), *Hans Kelsen anderswo. Hans Kelsen abroad. Der Einfluss der Reinen Rechtslehre auf die Rechtstheorie in verschiedenen Ländern.* Teil III. Schriftenreihe des Hans Kelsen-Instituts, Vol 33 (Vienna, Manz Verlag, 2010); NN, *Der Einfluß der Reinen Rechtslehre auf die Rechtstheorie in verschiedenen Ländern.* Schriftenreihe des Hans Kelsen-Instituts, Vol 8 (Vienna, Manz Verlag, 1983); N Achterberg (ed), *Der Einfluss der Reinen Rechtslehre auf die Rechtstheorie in verschiedenen Ländern.* Schriftenreihe des Hans Kelsen-Instituts, Vol 2 (Vienna, Manz Verlag, 1978). On the reception of the Pure Theory of Law by authors outside the European orbit – more specifically: Eugenio Bulygin, Simeon McIntosh and various Soviet scholars – see, respectively, the contributions by Paulson (ch 2), Ostroukh (ch 14) and Antonov (ch 15) in this volume.

[45] Gassner, 'Der Kreis um Hans Kelsen in Lateinamerika' (n 15) 64.

[46] ibid.

[47] After the cessation of his office as a judge of the Austrian Constitutional Court in February 1930, Kelsen emigrated to Cologne, where he remained until 1933. Kelsen acquired citizenship of the State of Prussia and the German Empire [*die preußische Staats- und deutsche Reichsangehörigkeit*], which he retained alongside the Austrian citizenship he had obtained at birth (see Olechowski, *Hans Kelsen* (n 1) 493). In 1936, Kelsen

maintain contact with his former students and to win new followers.[48] Throughout his career, Kelsen organised private seminars,[49] corresponded with his students and made numerous academic visits.[50]

In particular, it was as a result of his private seminars that the Vienna School of Legal Theory [*Die Wiener rechtstheoretische Schule*][51] was founded around Kelsen, creating a network of scholars who not only contributed to the development of a particular strand of juridico-philosophical thought,[52] but also influenced the Austrian academy

acquired Czechoslovak citizenship, while simultaneously relinquishing his German and Austrian citizenship (Métall (n 12) 69 ff). In 1940, Kelsen emigrated to the United States, where he became a naturalised American citizen on 31 July 1945.

[48] Gassner, 'Der Kreis um Hans Kelsen in Lateinamerika' (n 15) 64.

[49] Olechowski informs us that Kelsen organised private seminars not only in Vienna but also in Cologne (see Olechowski, *Hans Kelsen* (n 1) 147–50, 520–22). On the private seminars organised by Kelsen in his flat at Wickenburggasse 23 in Vienna's 8th district, which were held on an almost continuous basis between 1913 and 1930, please refer to ch 13 by Cadore in this volume. In the following passage, Gassner elucidates the distinctive character of the private seminar convened by Kelsen: 'What distinguished the "Kelsen seminar" from similar events, which were a characteristic feature of the intellectual milieu of Vienna's "modernity", was the fact that it was frequented by many people who were experts not in legal theory but in neighbouring disciplines such as sociology or philosophy. These "outsiders" contributed fresh ideas to be discussed in a climate of intellectual freedom. No pressure of any kind was exerted on the participants to agree with Kelsen's views and Kelsen's "disciples" – were no sworn brotherhood. They were highly individualistic personalities, as was noted by Brno legal scholar František Weyr, one of Kelsen's lifelong friends. In the Preface to the first edition of the *Pure Theory of Law* Kelsen himself calls his "circle" a school "only in so far … as everyone here tries to learn from the others without therefore waiving the right to go their own way"' (M Gassner, 'The Distaff Side? – Hans Kelsen's Viennese Female Students' (2024) 1 *Journal on European History of Law* 2). This feature of the Vienna School is also reported by M Stolleis, *A History of Public Law in Germany 1914–1945* (Oxford, Oxford University Press, 2008) 151–60.

[50] Among Kelsen's most notable documented academic visits are his trips to Sweden in 1933 and Finland in 1953 (see U Bindreiter, 'Hans Kelsens Vortragsreisen nach Schweden (1933) und Finnland (1953)' in C Jabloner, T Olechowski and K Zeleny (eds), *Das internationale Wirken Hans Kelsens*. Schriftenreihe des Hans Kelsen-Instituts 38 (Vienna, Manz, 2016) 89–106); to Cuba in 1941 and 1949 (O Sarlo, 'Los viajes de Kelsen a Cuba' in A González Monzón and O Sarlo (eds), *Presencia y recepción de Kelsen en Cuba y otros ensayos sobre su pensamiento* (Santiago de Chile, Ediciones Olejnik, 2024) 151–182; O Sarlo, 'Kelsen en La Habana. El *intermezzo* tropical de la Teoría Pura' in GA Ramírez Cleves (ed), *Kelsen en el mundo: la influencia de la Teoría pura del derecho en distintos lugares* (Bogotá, Universidad Externado de Colombia, 2023) 293–344); to Argentina, Uruguay and Brazil in 1949 (see RA Guibourg, 'Kelsen en la Argentina' in ibid 63–78; D Luna, 'Kelsen en la Universidad Nacional de La Plata, 1949. El capítulo platense del debate Kelsen-Cossio' in ibid 79–132; Gassner, 'Der Kreis um Hans Kelsen in Lateinamerika' (n 15); O Sarlo, 'La gira suramericana de Hans Kelsen en 1949: el "frente sur" de la teoría pura' in GA Ramírez Cleves (ed), *Kelsen en el mundo: la influencia de la Teoría pura del derecho en distintos lugares* (Bogotá, Universidad Externado de Colombia, 2012) 97–123); to Spain in 1956 (see J Vega López, 'Una visita a España' in GA Ramírez Cleves (ed), *Kelsen en el mundo: la influencia de la Teoría pura del derecho en distintos lugares* (Bogotá, Universidad Externado de Colombia, 2023) 549–54); and to Mexico in 1960 (see IB Flores, 'Una visita a Hans Kelsen en Mexico' in ibid 409–40).

[51] On the Vienna School of Legal Theory, see ch 13 by Cadore in this volume. For a brief overview of the Vienna School, see Stolleis (n 49) 153–55.

[52] The definition of the pure theory of law as a legal philosophical approach corresponding to a collective intellectual enterprise is set out by Kammerhofer (ch 7) and Cadore (ch 13) in this volume. Jestaedt (M Jestaedt, 'Hans Kelsens Reine Rechtslehre. Eine Einführung' in H Kelsen, *Reine Rechtslehre. Studienausgabe der 1. Auflage 1934*, M Jestaedt (ed) (Tübingen, Mohr Siebeck, 2008) XI–LXVI, XXII) highlights the contributions to this particular legal philosophical approach of two of Kelsen's pupils and members of the Vienna School of Legal Theory. Adolf Julius Merkl's contributions to the theory of the dynamic dimension and hierarchical structure of the legal system [*Stufenbaulehre*], as well as to the theory of error calculation [*Fehlerkalkül*], are noteworthy. Similarly, Alfred Verdross's contributions to the hypothetical character of the basic norm and the doctrine of the systematic unity of law are worthy of mention. (See, eg, AJ Merkl, 'Das Recht im Lichte seiner Anwendung' in D Mayer-Maly, H Schambeck and W-D Grussmann (eds), *Adolf Julius Merkl. Gesammelte Schriften, Vol 1 Grundlagen des Rechts, Pt 1* (hereafter AJMGS 1.1) (Berlin, Duncker & Humblot, 1993–2009 (1916, 1917, 1919)) 85–146; AJ Merkl, 'Prolegomena einer Theorie des rechtlichen Stufenbaues'

and numerous academies worldwide.[53] As Rodrigo Cadore explains in his chapter in this volume, the appointment of several members of the Vienna School of Legal Theory as professors at the University of Vienna[54] was a crucial factor in securing the prestige and influence of the pure theory of law within the Austrian academy. This prestige and influence, in turn, attracted the attention of scholars from various countries[55] who subsequently headed their own home or host academies. These scholars[56] and their students subsequently developed their own theories in dialogue with, or even in opposition to, the theory developed by Kelsen. The leadership of these scholars further enhanced the prestige and influence of the pure theory of law in the Austrian academy and abroad.

in A Verdross (ed), *Gesellschaft, Staat und Recht. Untersuchungen zur Reinen Rechtslehre, Festschrift Hans Kelsen zum 50. Geburtstag gewidmet* (Vienna, Springer, 1931) 252–94 (reproduced in AJMGS 1.1, 437–92); AJ Merkl, *Die Lehre von der Rechtskraft. entwickelt aus dem Rechtsbegriff. Eine rechtstheoretische Untersuchung.* Wiener Staatswissenschaftliche Studien (Leipzig, Franz Deuticke, 1923); AJ Merkl, *Das doppelte Rechtsantlitz. Eine Betrachtung aus der Erkenntnistheorie des Rechts* (Vienna, Sonderabdruck aus den Juristischen Blättern. Selbstverlag des Verfassers, 1918) (reproduced in AJMGS 1.1, 227–52); AJ Merkl, 'Die gerichtliche Prüfung von Gesetzen und Verordnungen' in D Mayer-Maly, H Schambeck and W-D Grussmann (eds), *Adolf Julius Merkl. Gesammelte Schriften, Vol 2 Verfassungsrecht-Völkerrecht, Pt 1* (hereafter AJMGS 2.1) (Berlin, Duncker & Humblot, 1999 (1921)) 393–438; AJ Merkl, 'Justizirrtum und Rechtswahrheit' in AJMGS 1.1, 369–84. On the relevance of *Stufenbaulehre* for the history of the theory of legal power, see G Villa-Rosas, 'Merkl's Stufenbaulehre in the History of the Theory of Legal Power' in G Villa-Rosas and T Spaak (eds), *Legal Power and Legal Competence. Meaning, Normativity, Officials and Theories* (Cham, Springer, 2023) 289–303. On the incorporation of the *Stufenbaulehre* into the pure theory of law see, eg, SL Paulson, 'The Stufenbau Yields Legal Powers. Aspects of Hans Kelsen's Norm Theory (Manuscript)' Online Lecture, Juris North Kelsen's Roundtables. Session 3 on 25 June 2021: youtu.be/pwcF8nnZ-BU; SL Paulson, 'How Merkl's *Stufenbaulehre* Informs Kelsen's Concept of Law' (2013) 21 *Revus. Journal for Constitutional Theory and Philosophy of Law* 29; SL Paulson, 'Zur Stufenbaulehre Merkls in ihrer Bedeutung für die Allgemeine Rechtslehre' in R Walter (ed), *Adolf J. Merkl. Werk und Wirksamkeit. Ergebnisse eines Internationalen Symposions in Wien (22.–23. März 1990)* (Vienna, Manz, 1990) 93–105. On the contributions of Alfred Verdross see, eg, A Verdross, *Die Einheit des rechtlichen Weltbildes auf Grundlage der Völkerrechtsverfassung* (Tübingen, Mohr Siebeck, 1923); A Verdross, 'Zum Problem der Rechtsunterworfenheit des Gesetzgebers' (1916) 45 *Juristische Blätter* 471, 483). Kammerhofer has referred to the integration of the *Stufenbaulehre* into the pure theory of law as the 'dynamic turn', see ch 7 in this volume.

[53] In fact, Kelsen's most significant texts have been translated into more than 30 languages (see Olechowski, *Hans Kelsen* (n 1) 928).

[54] Cadore names a number of other notable figures, including Adolf Julius Merkl (Austria, Austro-Hungarian Empire 1890 – Austria 1970); Alfred Verdross (Austria, Austro-Hungarian Empire 1890 – Austria 1980); Felix Kaufmann (Austria, Austro-Hungarian Empire 1895 – the United States 1949); Walter Henrich (Romania, Austro-Hungarian Empire 1888 – Germany, Rep Fed 1955); and Josef Laurenz Kunz (Austria, Austro-Hungarian Empire 1890 – the United States 1970).

[55] Olechowski has identified the growing internationalisation of the Vienna School of Legal Theory from the second five years of the 1920s until 1930 (see Olechowski, *Hans Kelsen* (n 1) 390–95; Gassner, 'The Distaff Side?' (n 49)).

[56] This is exemplified by the cases of Kisaburo Yokota (Empire of Japan 1896 – Japan 1993); Shiro Kiyoumiya (Empire of Japan 1898 – Japan 1989); Julius Kraft (German Empire 1898 – the United States 1960); Alf Niels Christian Ross (Denmark 1899 – Denmark 1979); Artur-Tõeleid Kliimann (Estonia, Russian Empire 1899 – Estonia (Occupied) 1941); Saturo Kuroda (Empire of Japan 1900 – Japan 1990); Margit Kraft-Fuchs (Hungary, Austro-Hungarian Empire 1902 – the United States 1994); Luis Recaséns Siches (Guatemala 1903 – Mexico 1977); Charles Eisenmann (France 1903 – France 1980); Leo Gross (Galicia (Poland), Austro-Hungarian Empire 1903 – the United States 1990); Benjamin Akzin (Latvia, Russian Empire 1904 – Israel 1985); Helen Silving-Ryu (Poland, Austro-Hungarian Empire 1906 – Poland 1993); and Luis Legaz y Lacambra (Spain 1906 – Spain 1980). (See Olechowski, *Hans Kelsen* (n 1) 390–95.) For further information on the relationship between Luis Recaséns Siches and Luis Legaz y Lacambra and the Vienna School of Legal Theory, see Gassner, 'Der Kreis um Hans Kelsen in Lateinamerika' (n 15) 65–68. For details on Margit Kraft-Fuchs and Helen Silving-Ryu, see Gassner, 'The Distaff Side?' (n 49). For further information on the internationalisation of the pure theory of law and the Vienna School, please refer to ch 13 by Cadore in this volume.

This influence was jeopardised by the dark advances of National Socialism,[57] which ironically, by forcing the dispersal of the School's members, contributed to its international standing. That said, it certainly abruptly and painfully curtailed the intense academic exchange among its members,[58] whose main channels of dissemination were the *Zeitschrift für öffentliches Recht* [*Journal of Public Law*], the *Internationale Zeitschrift für Theorie des Rechts* [*International Journal of Theory of Law*] and the *Wiener Staats- und Rechtswissenschaftliche Studien* [*Viennese Papers in Public Law and Jurisprudence*].[59] As Matthias Jestaedt has explained, in the early 1940s '[t]he once localised cooperation in academic Vienna (Cologne and Geneva) was replaced by the "circle of like-minded people", who disseminated their ideas worldwide.[60]

It is these ideas that constitute Kelsen's most valuable and best-known legacy. The book before the reader addresses this legacy by bringing together chapters devoted not only to a careful analysis of its construction and reception, but also to the study of three fundamental themes of Kelsen's theoretical heritage: legal norms, international law and democracy.

I. Legal Norms

The long series of arguments with which Kelsen developed his theory of legal norms over more than six decades has led to a broadly accepted agreement[61] on the need to distinguish the phases of its development in order to avoid serious inconsistencies and to do justice to its philosophical fundamentals.[62] Despite this agreement, the diversity of

[57] For insights into the effects of the rise of National Socialism on the Vienna School of Legal Theory, see Cadore, ch 13 in this volume.

[58] Jestaedt, 'Hans Kelsens Reine Rechtslehre' (n 52) XXIV.

[59] For an overview of the dissemination vehicles of the Vienna School of Legal Theory, see ch 13 by Cadore in this volume. According to Jestaedt, the *Zeitschrift für öffentliches Recht* [*Journal of Public Law*] was initially called *Österreichische Zeitschrift für öffentliches Recht* [*Austrian Journal of Public Law*] and was co-edited by Kelsen between 1919 and 1934. The *Internationale Zeitschrift für Theorie des Rechts* [*International Journal of Theory of Law*] was established by Kelsen and edited by him from 1926 to 1939. The *Wiener Staats- und Rechtswissenschaftliche Studien* [*Viennese Papers in Public Law and Jurisprudence*] was co-edited by Kelsen between 1922 and 1937 (ibid XXIII). For a detailed account of the dissemination of the Vienna School of Legal Theory, see Olechowski, *Hans Kelsen* (n 1) 395–97; M Jestaedt, '"Kelsens Zeitschrift". Die Reine Rechtslehre im Spiegel der Zeitschrift für öffentliches Recht' (2014) 69 *Zeitschrift für öffentliches Recht* (*ZÖR*) 655.

[60] Jestaedt, 'Hans Kelsens Reine Rechtslehre' (n 52) XXIV; see also Stolleis (n 49) 154–55.

[61] Chiassoni noted that, while such exercises in periodisation are certainly worthwhile, as 'in the long run, there were indeed noteworthy changes in Kelsen's thought … there is a risk that the Pure Theory is thereby depicted as rife with instability and internally afflicted by conflicting pulls – an impression which is, I think, ultimately untrue, and which it is important to counterbalance'. (P Chiassoni, 'Wiener Realism' in L Duarte d'Almeida, J Gardner and L Green, *Kelsen Revisited. New Essays on the Pure Theory of Law* (Oxford, Hart Publishing, 2013) 131–62, 131).

[62] C Heidemann, *Hans Kelsen's Normativism* (Cambridge, Cambridge University Press, 2022) 23–24. Some have even warned that the changes in Kelsen's theory of norms are so abrupt that it is 'almost impossible to speak of *the* Pure Theory of Law; none of Kelsen's books, not even the monumental second edition of the *Reine Rechtslehre* (1960), published when he was nearly eighty, can be regarded as the final version of his thought' (E Bulygin, 'An Antinomy in Kelsen's Pure Theory of Law' in SL Paulson and B Litschewski Paulson (eds), *Normativity and Norms. Critical Perspectives on Kelsenian Themes* (Oxford, Clarendon Press, 1998) 297–315, 298).

interpretations of Kelsen's theory of norms[63] has also supported a plurality of perspectives in the interpretative construction of the phases of development of Kelsen's legal-theoretical writings.[64] Carsten Heidemann, for example, has distinguished four phases in the development of Kelsen's legal theory. These correspond, first, to the set of sources consisting of Kelsen's *Habilitation* and some writings after 1911, in which Kelsen does not achieve a coherent philosophical or epistemological foundation of his theory, although he does anticipate some of the theorems that will become part of what he himself called the 'pure theory of law'; second, to the writings published between 1916 and 1935, in which 'Kelsen develops most of the special tenets of the Pure Theory in full and grounds them in a specific neo-Kantian epistemology';[65] third, to the texts published between 1940 and 1960, which are based 'on a rather naive cognitive realism according to which the legal norm is an entity "given" to cognition';[66] and fourth, to the sources published from 1960 onwards, in which Kelsen 'introduces a rather heterogeneous jumble of philosophical conceptions into his theory – especially from linguistic philosophy – and couples them with a strict will-theory of norms'.[67] In contrast to Heidemann's perspective, Eugenio Bulygin, in his 1990 article 'An Antinomy in Kelsen's Pure Theory of Law',[68] distinguishes three main periods in Kelsen's thought. The first period is between 1911 and 1940, in which 'the Kantian and the positivistic

[63] As Paulson has argued, '[t]he interpretations of Kelsen's idea of normativity run the gamut, from a counter-factual interpretation of normativity (R Walter) to a "justified normativity" thesis. The justified normativity thesis is far and away the most ambitious reading of normativity in Kelsen's legal philosophy. It has been attributed to Kelsen in different forms with different sorts of argument by no fewer than four leading figures – Robert Alexy, Carlos Santiago Nino, Joseph Raz, and, a bit earlier, by Alf Ross – with, so far as I can tell, each writer developing his own case independently of the others' (SL Paulson, 'The Very Idea of Legal Positivism' (2011) 102 *Revista Brasileira de Estudos Políticos* 139, 153). To these interpretations must be added the profoundly realist orientation of the pure theory defended by Chiassoni (see Chiassoni, 'Wiener Realism' (n 61)). For Paulson's criticisms of Raz's 'justified normativity thesis', see below. For Eugenio Bulygin's and Alf Ross's critique of Kelsenian theory, see Antonov, ch 15 in this volume.

[64] On the periodisation of Kelsen's normative theory see, eg, Heidemann, *Hans Kelsen's Normativism* (n 62); Chiassoni, 'Wiener Realism' (n 61); C Heidemann, 'Noch einmal: Stanley L Paulson und Kelsens urteilstheoretischer Normbegriff' (2007) 93 *Archiv für Rechts- und Sozialphilosophie* 345; W Krawietz, 'Hans Kelsen – ein normativer Mastermind des Rechts und der Rechtstheorie für das 21. Jahrhundert' (2007) 38 *Rechtstheorie* 34, 37–52; SL Paulson, 'Arriving at a Defensible Periodization of Hans Kelsen's Legal Theory' (1999) 19 *Oxford Journal of Legal Studies* 351; C Heidemann, 'Norms, Facts, and Judgments. A Reply to SL Paulson' (1999) 19 *Oxford Journal of Legal Studies* 345; SL Paulson, 'Four Phases in Hans Kelsen's Legal Theory? Reflections on a Periodization' (1998) 18 *Oxford Journal of Legal Studies* 153; C Heidemann, *Die Norm als Tatsache. Zur Normentheorie Hans Kelsens* (Baden-Baden, Nomos Verlagsgesellschaft, 1997); D Beyleveld, 'From the "Middle-Way" to Normative Irrationalism: Hans Kelsen's General Theory of Norms' (1993) 56 *Modern Law Review* 104; SL Paulson, 'Toward a Periodization of Kelsen's Pure Theory of Law' in L Gianformaggio (ed), *Hans Kelsen's Legal Theory. A Diachronic Point of View* (Turin, G Giappichelli Editore, 1990) 11–47; D Beyleveld and R Brownsword, 'Normative Positivism: The Mirage of the Middle-Way' (1989) 9 *Oxford Journal of Legal Studies* 463; O Weinberger, *Normentheorie als Grundlage der Jurisprudenz und Ethik. Eine Auseinandersetzung mit Hans Kelsens Theorie der Normen* (Berlin, Duncker & Humblot, 1981) 168–77; E Bulygin, 'An Antinomy in Kelsen's Pure Theoy of Law' (1990) 3 *Ratio Juris* 29 reprinted in SL Paulson and B Litschewski Paulson (eds), *Normativity and Norms. Critical Perspectives on Kelsenian Themes* (Oxford, Clarendon Press, 1998). On Bulygin's reception of Kelsen's theory of norms, see SL Paulson, 'On Eugenio Bulygin's Kelsen', ch 2 in this volume. On what has been called the fiction turn in the conception of the basic norm in Kelsen's work, see Stewart, ch 4 in this volume. On the thesis of an evolutionary turn, see Edwards, ch 8 in this volume.

[65] Heidemann, *Hans Kelsen's Normativism* (n 62) 23–24.

[66] ibid.

[67] ibid.

[68] Bulygin, 'An Antinomy in Kelsen's Pure Theoy of Law' (n 62).

elements coexist more or less harmoniously, and Kelsen seems to be unaware of their antagonism';[69] the second period corresponds to a transitional phase between 1940 and 1960, in which Kelsen published his treatise *General Theory of Law and State* in 1945,[70] the French revision of the first edition of his *Reine Rechtslehre* [*Pure Theory of Law*] in 1953,[71] and the second edition of the same book in 1960;[72] and finally the third period is characterised by Bulygin as 'predominantly positivistic in spirit',[73] in which he groups works such as 'Derogation', published in 1962,[74] 'Recht und Logik' ['Law and Logic'], published in 1965,[75] and the unfinished treatise entitled *Allgemeine Theorie der Normen* [*General Theory of Norms*], published in 1979.[76]

In the chapter that opens this collection, Stanley L Paulson responds to Bulygin's position that there are two Kelsens: the Kantian Kelsen and the positivist Kelsen. Paulson argues that Bulygin's position presupposes a particular interpretation of the stages of development of Kelsenian theory, which is incorrect. In the first part of his chapter, Paulson outlines his own periodisation, according to which it is possible to distinguish three phases in the development of Kelsenian norm theory. The first phase termed 'constructivist' comprises the Kelsenian sources published between 1911 and 1919. In them, Kelsen reacts against to the German positivist jurisprudence of the nineteenth century and attempts to construct new concepts that do not turn on psychologism or legal naturalism. This methodology used by Kelsen is by no means based on a particular philosophical approach. Nonetheless, this philosophical approach will be the object of Kelsen's research in the transitional period that Paulson locates in Kelsen's writings published between 1914 and 1919. The second, so-called 'classical', phase, which Paulson locates between 1920 and 1960, is characterised by the generally explicit use of neo-Kantian foundations. From 1960 onwards, however, Kelsen contributes to the collapse of his own theory by endorsing a kind of legal empiricism. In the second part of his chapter, Paulson presents the reasons why he considers that the extremes of the time spectrum of the periodisation of Kelsen's work proposed by Bulygin are erroneous. On the one hand, the characterisation of the initial year is incorrect, because the coexistence of neo-Kantian and positivist elements does not begin before 1920. On the other hand, the determination of the final year is arbitrary, because Bulygin does not give us a good reason to place the end of the first period of development of the Kelsenian theory in 1940. In the third part of his chapter, Paulson presents a condensed version of his account of the development of Kelsenian theory of norms, according to which,

[69] ibid 298.

[70] H Kelsen, *General Theory of Law and State* (New Brunswick, 2007 (1945)).

[71] H Kelsen, *Théorie pure du droit. Introduction a la science du droit*, H Thévenaz trans (Neuchâtel, Éditions de la Baconniére, 1953).

[72] H Kelsen, *Reine Rechtslehre*, 2nd edn (Vienna, Deuticke, 1960) (hereafter RR2); H Kelsen, *Pure Theory of Law*, M Knight trans (hereafter PTL2) (Berkeley, University of California Press, 1967).

[73] Bulygin, 'An Antinomy in Kelsen's Pure Theoy of Law' (n 62) 298.

[74] H Kelsen, 'Derogation' in RA Newman (ed), *Essays in Jurisprudence in Honor of Roscoe Pound* (Indianapolis, Bobbs-Merrill, 1962) 339–95.

[75] H Kelsen, 'Recht und Logik' (1965) 12 *Forum* 421, 495. The English version was published as H Kelsen, 'Law and Logic (1965)' in O Weinberger (ed), *Hans Kelsen. Essays in Legal and Moral Philosophy*, P Heath trans (Dordrecht, D Reidel, 1973) 228–53.

[76] H Kelsen, 'Allgemeine Theorie der Normen' (Vienna, Manzsche Verlags- und Universitätsbuchhandlung, 1979). The English translation was published as H Kelsen, *General Theory of Norms*, M Hartney trans (Oxford, Clarendon Press, 1991).

the earliest development of this theory can be found in Kelsen's *Habilitation* of 1911. In this work, the search for the ideal form of the legal norm led Kelsen to formulate the sanction-norm as a hypothetical norm rejecting the imperative form. A second development occurred in the 1920s, when Kelsen, moving away from the positivist current which regarded the statute as the only form of law, adopted the *Stufenbaulehre* proposed by Adolf Julius Merkl. A third development occurred in the 1930s, when empowerment became the basic form of the sanction-norm. The fourth and last development occurred in the 1950s in two phases. On the one hand, this was through the introduction of the distinction between the dependent legal norms – comprising three types of legal norms: positive permissions, empowerments of norm issuance and commands – the independent legal norms – corresponding to a generic 'ought' embedded in the sanction-norm – and the complete legal norms – reflecting the pattern of the *Stufenbau* in miniature by including the highest-level empowerments of norm issuance and, at the ground level, the independent legal norm. On the other hand, the fourth and final development occurred through Kelsen's work on conflicts between legal norms, the study of which led him to abandon the applicability of logic to law and to discard the pure theory of law in favour of the late theory [*Spätlehre*]. To analyse the positions defended by Bulygin regarding the late theory, Paulson relies on the analysis of Bulygin's article 'Zum Problem der Anwendbarkeit der Logik auf das Recht' ['On the problem of the applicability of logic to law'], published in 1983.[77] As a result of his analysis, Paulson informs us about Bulygin's acceptance of Kelsen's theory of normative conflicts; that Bulygin is willing to attribute an expressive theory of norms to the late theory; and of his sceptical reaction to Kelsen's conclusions on derogation.

As the chapter by Paulson illustrates, a particular neo-Kantian-inspired method of approaching law[78] gives Kelsenian theory its uniqueness compared to other

[77] E Bulygin, 'Zum Problem der Anwendbarkeit der Logik auf das Recht' in G Kohlmann (ed), *Festschrift für Ulrich Klug zum 70. Geburtstag*, 2 vols (Cologne, Peter Deubner, 1983) Vol 1, 19–31.

[78] In contrast to other contemporary authors of Kelsen who were also influenced by Neo-Kantianism – among whom we can include Rudolf Stammler and Gustav Radbruch – Kelsen adopted a sceptical stance with regard to Kantian practical reason (see n 113 below). Nevertheless, as Dreier has argued, '[t]he precise determination of Kelsen's relation to neo-Kantianism is a (broad and complicated) question in itself' (Dreier, *Kelsen im Kontext. Beiträge zum Werk Hans Kelsens und geistesverwandter Autoren* (n 10) 7, fn 29). For an analysis of the neo-Kantian influence on Kelsen's legal philosophical thought, see, eg, Heidemann, *Hans Kelsen's Normativism* (n 62); C Heidemann, 'Facets of "ought" in Kelsen's Pure Theory of Law' (2013) 4 *Jurisprudence* 246; SL Paulson, 'Hans Kelsen und Gustav Radbruch. Neukantianische Strömungen in der Rechtsphilosophie' in C Krijnen and AJ Noras (eds), *Marburg versus Südwestdeutschland. Philosophische Differenzen zwischen den beiden Hauptschulen des Neukantianismus* (Würzburg, Königshausen & Neumann, 2012) 141–62; A Carrino, *Das Recht zwischen Reinheit und Realität. Hermann Cohen und die philosophischen Grundlagen der Rechtslehre Kelsens* (Baden-Baden, Nomos Verlagsgesellschaft, 2011); SL Paulson, 'Konstitutive und methodologische Formen. Zur Kantischen und neukantischen Folie der Rechtslehre Hans Kelsens' in M Heinz and C Krijnen (eds), *Kant im Neukantianismus. Fortschritt oder Rückschritt?* (Würzburg, Königshausen & Neumann, 2007) 149–65; SL Paulson, 'Zwei radikale Objektivierungsprogramme in der Rechtslehre Hans Kelsens' in SL Paulson and H Stolleis (eds), *Hans Kelsen-Saatsrechtslehler und Rechtstheoretiker des 20. Jahrhunderts* (Tübingen, Mohr Siebeck, 2005) 191–200; C Heidemann, 'Geltung und Sollen. Einige (neu-)kantische Elemente der Reine Rechtslehre Hans Kelsens' in R Alexy, LH Meyer, SL Paulson and G Sprenger (eds), *Neukantianismus und Rechtsphilosophie* (Baden-Baden, Nomos Verlagsgesellschaft, 2002) 223–52; SL Paulson, 'Faktum/Wert-Distinktion, Zwei-Welten-Lehre und immanenter Sinn. Hans Kelsen als Neukantianer' in R Alexy, LH Meyer, SL Paulson and G Sprenger (eds), *Neukantianismus und Rechtsphilosophie* (Baden-Baden, Nomos Verlagsgesellschaft, 2002) 223–51; S Hammer, 'A Neo-Kantian Theory of Legal Knowledge in Kelsen's Pure Theory of Law?' in SL Paulson and B Litschewski Paulson (eds), *Normativity and Norms. Critical Perspectives*

contemporary juridico-philosophical theories.[79] However, the magnitude of the legacy of Kelsen's contributions to general legal theory is undoubtedly not only due to the singular inspiration of his method but also the result of his stated ambitions. Indeed, as a reaction to the ideological[80] and methodological syncretistic tendencies of jurisprudence still present in his time,[81] which – openly or covertly – reduced legal thought almost entirely to considerations of legal policy,[82] Kelsen understood that the task of his theory was to provide a critical methodology of legal knowledge as early as his *Habilitation* in 1911.[83]

on Kelsenian Themes (Oxford, Clarendon Press, 1998) 188–94; SL Paulson, 'The Neo-Kantian Dimension of Kelsen's Pure Theory of Law' (1992) 12 *Oxford Journal of Legal Studies* 311; H Dreier, *Rechtslehre, Staatssoziologie und Demokratietheorie bei Hans Kelsen*, 2nd edn (Baden-Baden, Nomos Verlagsgesellschaft, 1990); SL Paulson, 'Zur neukantianischen Dimension der Reinen Rechtslehre' in F Sander and H Kelsen, *Die Rolle des Neukantianismus in der Reinen Rechtslehre*, SL Paulson (ed) (Aalen, Scientia, 1988) 7–22.

[79] Indeed, as Paulson has argued, the Kelsenian notion of legal knowledge itself is neo-Kantian in origin. Consequently, '[t]o excise the neo-Kantian dimension would be a mistake, I believe, removing far too much that is characteristic of Kelsen's legal theory. After all, even if no one nowadays is prepared to defend Plato's doctrine of forms or exemplars on the merits, no one, by the same token, is suggesting that the doctrine be excised from the Platonic dialogues. The very idea is fanciful, eliminating in one fell swoop a great deal of what is rightly associated with Plato. Similarly, *mutatis mutandis*, for Kelsen' (SL Paulson, 'Hans Kelsen on Legal Interpretation, Legal Cognition, and Legal Science' (2019) 10 *Jurisprudence* 188, 220).

[80] In various texts, Kelsen expresses his opposition to the ideological and political trends that he sees as dominant in the legal science of his time. For example, see H Kelsen, *Introduction to the Problems of Legal Theory. A Translation of the First Edition of the Reine Rechtslehre or Pure Theory of Law*, B Litschewski Paulson and SL Paulson trans (hereafter PTL1) (Oxford, Clarendon Press, 1992) §10, 22; H Kelsen, *Reine Rechtslehre: Einleitung in die rechtswissenschaftliche Problematik*, 1st edn (hereafter RR1) (Vienna, Verlag Franz Deuticke 1934) 19; H Kelsen, 'The Function of the Pure Theory of Law' in A Reppy (ed), *Law. A Century of Progress 1835–1935*, Vol 2 (New York, New York University Press, 1937) 231–41, 237. However, Kelsen not only declared himself against the dominant ideological positions of his time, but also accused nineteenth-century German positivist legal scholarship of not having completely renounced the legitimation of law on the basis of natural law. For further examples, see PTL1 §11(a), 23; §18, 37; RR1, 21, 39.

[81] Paulson has argued that the term 'methodological syncretism' was used in fin-de-siècle legal theory in the German-speaking countries to refer to an illegitimate combining or fusion of different methods (Paulson, 'Hans Kelsen on Legal Interpretation, Legal Cognition, and Legal Science' (n 79) 205, fn 83). Jellinek himself condemned this tendency as detrimental to the objectivity of scientific legal knowledge, stating that 'among the vices of the scientific enterprise of our day is the vice of methodological syncretism' (see, eg, G Jellinek, *System der subjektiven öffentlichen Rechte*, 2nd edn, J Kersten (ed) (Tübingen, Mohr Siebeck, 2011 (1905)) 17). However, Kelsen (see H Kelsen, *Das Problem der Souveränität und die Theorie des Völkerrechts. Beitrag zu einer Reinen Rechtslehre* (Tübingen, JCB Mohr, 1920) (hereafter PSTVR – to be cited according to the pagination in the margin taken from the original) in H Kelsen, *Hans Kelsen Werke, Vol 4 Veröffentlichte Schriften 1918–1920*, M Jestaedt (ed) (hereafter HKW4) (Tübingen, Mohr Siebeck, 2013) 11, 1) highlighted the lack of consistency in Jellinek's position, as elsewhere his methodological position contradicts the neo-Kantian postulate of the constitution of the object through method. For further insight into Jellinek's contributions, see, for instance, J Kersten, 'The Normative Power of the Factual: Georg Jellinek's Phenomenological Theory of Reflective Legal Positivism' in T Spaak and P Mindus (eds), *The Cambridge Companion to Legal Positivism* (Cambridge, Cambridge University Press, 2021) 248–71.

[82] Kelsen, PTL1, 1; RR1, III.

[83] Kelsen positioned his theory as a repository of the contributions of late nineteenth-century German positivist theories of public law (see H Kelsen, *Allgemeine Staatslehre* (Berlin, Verlag von Julius Springer, 1925) VII) and appreciated the various critical possibilities that the constructivism born of these positivist theories could offer, when such constructivism was founded on the thesis of normativity that he himself developed. In his *Habilitation* work of 1911, Kelsen describes the concepts of legal science as 'formal categories' [*formale Kategorien*], derived from the elimination of all teleological substance – which is, however, the object of study of other disciplines such as sociology, history, politics or ethics (Kelsen, HPSL1, 92, 353–78). Kelsen directs the critical possibilities, for example, to the dissolution, through the concept of imputation [*Zurechnung*], of the anthropomorphic fictions of the will used by traditional jurisprudence – both those relating to legal persons and especially the state (see Kelsen, HPSL1, 145–46), and those relating to the concepts of subjective right and duty (HPSL1, 435–36, 447, 618–29). (On Kelsenian critical constructionism, see eg, SL Paulson, 'Konstruktivismus, Methodendualismus und Zurechnung im Frühwerk Hans Kelsens' (1999) 124

Such a critical methodology requires the search for objectivity[84] or, in other words, the development of a theory of law that is 'conscious, so to speak, of the autonomy of the object of its enquiry and thereby conscious of its own unique character'.[85] This demand for the independence of law as an 'object of scientific knowledge'[86] – which was to serve legal scholars[87] as a basis for critiquing existing legal theory[88] – led Kelsen to develop the normativity thesis in his *Habilitation* in 1911.[89] This thesis was not only a recurrent theme in Kelsen's research up to the beginning of his late period,[90] but it also embodied

Archiv des öffentlichen Rechts 631; Heidemann, *Die Norm als Tatsache: Zur Normentheorie Hans Kelsens* (n 64) 23–42, 221–22.) In his 1934 *Pure Theory of Law*, Kelsen explicitly outlines the critical function of his theory from the very first paragraphs. He states that the pure theory aims to free jurisprudence of all foreign elements, which he considers to be its fundamental methodological principle (PTL1 §1, 1; RR1, 1). (On this idea see C Heidemann, *Hans Kelsen's Normativism* (n 62) 33–34; C Heidemann, 'Das "Faktum der Rechtswissenschaft" bei Hans Kelsen' (2020) 163 *Archiv für Rechts- und Sozialphiosophie* 81.) In his 1934 *Pure Theory of Law*, Kelsen sought to overcome the dualisms that had become characteristic of traditional legal science. These included the dichotomy between objective and subjective law (see PTL1 §24, 43–45; RR1, 47–52), between physical person and legal person (see PTL1 §25, 46–51; RR1, 52–59), between objective law and the state (see PTL1 §VIII, 97–106, in particular §46, 97–98; RR1, 115–37, 115–17) and between national law and international law (see PTL1 §IX, 107–26, in particular §50, 111–26; RR1, 129–54, 135–54). Subsequently, Kelsen would also propose that this theory of positive law, which is aware of its assumptions and limitations, should be designated as critical positivism (Kelsen, *General Theory of Law and State* (n 70) 438). (A reconstruction of the critical function of Kelsen's theory can be found in I Stewart, 'The Critical Legal Science of Hans Kelsen' (1990) 17 *Journal of Law and Society* 273). Kelsen further develops the critical function of his theory by introducing a 'radical realist' function, which is aimed at the creation and application of law. He states that '[the pure theory of law] attempts, therefore, an aim wholly neglected by traditional jurisprudence: to make use of the results of theoretical cognition for the practical creation and application of the law. It is in this sense a radically realist theory of law. As a science, it sees its tasks exclusively in understanding the nature of the law through an analysis of its structure, and by doing so, in creating the possibility of an applied science of law' (Kelsen, 'The Function of the Pure Theory of Law' (n 80) 237).

[84] Indeed, in Kelsen's own words, from his *Habilitation* work of 1911, his aim 'was to raise [jurisprudence] to the level of a genuine science, a human science. The idea was to develop those tendencies of jurisprudence that focus solely on cognition of the law rather than on the shaping of it, and to bring the result of this cognition as close as possible to the highest values of all science: objectivity and exactitude' (Kelsen, PTL1, 1; RR1, III.) For a discussion of the postulate of purity as a constitutive methodological principle of the pure theory, see ch 13 by Cadore in this volume.

[85] Kelsen, PTL1, 1; RR1, III.

[86] H Kelsen, *Hauptprobleme der Staatsrechtslehre, entwickelt aus der Lehre vom Rechtssatze*, 2nd edn (hereafter HPSL2) (Tübingen, Mohr Siebeck, 1923) V.

[87] As Paulson has stated, '"legal cognition" is simply a label for the work of legal scholars' (Paulson, 'Hans Kelsen on Legal Interpretation, Legal Cognition, and Legal Science' (n 79) 203).

[88] Stewart, 'The Critical Legal Science of Hans Kelsen' (n 83) 276–77.

[89] Thus, Kelsen initially proposed his thesis of the sanction-norm as the sole type of legal norm in his *Habilitation* work (HPSL1, 21–432; see SL Paulson, 'The Makings of a Radical Norm Theory. Hans Kelsen's Sanction-Norm as Empowering Norm' in M Borowski, SL Paulson and J-R Sieckmann (eds), *Rechtsphilosophie und Grundrechtstheorie. Robert Alexys System* (Tübingen, Mohr Siebeck, 2017) 589–630, 595–600).

[90] Paulson has associated each of the three stages into which he has divided the development of Kelsen's theory with a representative work. Thus, *Hauptprobleme der Staatsrechtslehre*, published in 1911, would be representative of the critical constructivism extending to 1920; *Reine Rechtslehre* (first edn), published in 1934, would be representative of the classical or neo-Kantian stage extending to 1960; and *Allgemeine Theorie der Normen*, published posthumously in 1979, would be the representative work of his late theory or *Spätlehre* (SL Paulson, 'Der Normativismus Hans Kelsens' (2006) 11 *Juristen Zeitung – JZ* 529, 530 fn 11). This latter theory extended roughly from 1960 to 1971 (SL Paulson, 'Metamorphosis in Hans Kelsen's Legal Philosophy' (2017) 80 *Modern Law Review* 860, 860, fn 1). As Paulson has argued, this theory, 'which represents a kind of will theory of law, contrasts sharply with the first two phases and can be set aside in the presentation of the conception of [Kelsen's] normativism' (Paulson, 'Der Normativismus Hans Kelsens', ibid, 530, fn 11). Clearly, this does not mean that the *Spätlehre* is not a stage worthy of specific study on its own merits. For instance, see M Zalewska, *A Dynamic Approach to Hans Kelsen's General Theory of Norms* (Oxford, Hart Publishing, 2024); M Zalewska, 'Empowerment and the Act of Will in Hans Kelsen's General Theory of Norms' in G Villa-Rosas and T Spaak (eds), *Legal Power and Legal Competence. Meaning, Normativity, Officials and*

an impetus that encouraged the search for solutions to theoretical problems through the development of neo-Kantian-inspired foundations.[91] In accordance with these foundations, Kelsen is convinced that the achievement of objectivity in jurisprudence requires the avoidance of all possible biases, both from sociological and psychological positions that use the scientific causal method,[92] and from positions that he groups under the term 'natural law'.[93]

On the one hand, Kelsen includes under the umbrella of the scientific causal method all those empirical-positivist positions which regard law as part of the world of facts or nature.[94] In his 1911 work, Kelsen shows the inadequacy of all these positions to account for the normativity of law, for they all deny the world of 'ought' to which law belongs.[95] As Paulson has put it, 'Kelsen rightly assumes that legal norms are meaningful only if there can be a discrepancy between what actually happens according to the laws of nature and what is required by the norm',[96] and this discrepancy can only be explained by the strict separation between 'is' (*Sein*) and 'ought' (*Sollen*).[97] For Kelsen,

Theories (Cham, Springer, 2023) 305–16; M Zalewska, 'Imputation as a Supervenience in the General Theory of Norms' in G Villa-Rosas and JL Fabra-Zamora (eds) *Objectivity in Jurisprudence, Legal Interpretation and Practical Reasoning* (Northampton, Edward Elgar Publishing, 2022) 71–85; M Zalewska, 'Kelsen's Rejection of Logic in General Theory of Norms and its Impact on his Legal Science Project' in H Yoshino and G Villa-Rosas, Law and Logic – Making Legal Science a Genuine Science, Archiv für Rechts- und Sozialphilosophie, Supplement 166 (Stuttgart, Franz Steiner Verlag, 2021) 15–28. On the 'fiction turn' of the basic norm see ch 4 by Stewart in this volume.

[91] Paulson has identified the first textual evidence pointing to the explicit use of neo-Kantian arguments in the Foreword to PSTVR (see ch 2 by Paulson in this volume; SL Paulson, 'Hans Kelsen and Normative Legal Positivism' in T Baldwin (ed), *The Cambridge History of Philosophy 1870-1945* (Cambridge, Cambridge University Press, 2003) 739–43, 739).

[92] Kelsen HPSL2, V.

[93] See, eg, Kelsen HPSL2, V; H Kelsen, 'Zur Theorie der juristischen Fiktionen (1919)' in HKW4, 209–34, 229. As Paulson has elucidated, 'Kelsen, along with many others, understands the Western tradition in jurisprudence and legal philosophy in terms of two basic types of theory – natural law theory, and an empirical, sociological, or "positivist" theory of law. In natural law theory, the law is seen as necessarily subject to moral constraints; in the empiric-positivist theory, it is seen as part of the world of fact or nature' (SL Paulson, 'Introduction. On Kelsen's Place in Jurisprudence' in PTL1, xvii–xlii, xx). By defending a third normativist and positivist theoretical option which, however, does not admit the reduction of law to facts, Kelsen demonstrates the falsity of the belief of traditional jurisprudence in the exhaustive nature of the classification of the possible criteria for the foundation of law into the basic types of theory embodied by natural law and positivist factual-reductivist theories. The demonstration that these basic types of theory do not exhaust the possibilities for the foundation of law also implies, according to Kelsen, the relativisation of the absolute character of the distinction between value and reality that traditional jurisprudence associates with the contrast between natural law theories and positivist factual-reductivist theories. In fact, if we accept Kelsen's normativist thesis, 'the antithesis between value and reality becomes a relative one and the law becomes value and reality, according as it is considered as a *norm*, compared with the order of factual happenings, determined by the relation of causality, or as the *act* of creation or adherence to a norm, compared with the normative order of morals' (Kelsen, 'The Function of the Pure Theory of Law' (n 80) 235). In numerous writings, Kelsen refers to his own thesis as '*der richtige Mittelweg*' [the correct middle way] (see, eg, Kelsen, PTL2 § 34(g), 211; Kelsen, RR2, 215). Paulson has drawn a parallel between the Kelsenian philosophical-legal programme, with respect to reductivist factual positivism and natural law, and the Kantian epistemic programme, with respect to British empiricism and continental rationalism. (See Paulson, 'Hans Kelsen on Legal Interpretation, Legal Cognition, and Legal Science' (n 79) 189, fn 5.)

[94] Paulson, 'Introduction. On Kelsen's Place in Jurisprudence' (n 93) xx.

[95] Kelsen, HPSL2, VI.

[96] Paulson, 'Faktum/Wert-Distinktion, Zwei-Welten-Lehre und immanenter Sinn. Hans Kelsen als Neukantianer' (n 78) 237.

[97] Kelsen HPSL1, 7. On the neo-Kantian influence reflected in the two-world thesis (*Zwei-Welten-Lehre*), which postulates the dualism between the 'is' and the 'ought' see, eg, Heidemann, *Hans Kelsen's Normativism* (n 62); Paulson, 'Faktum/Wert-Distinktion, Zwei-Welten-Lehre und immanenter Sinn. Hans Kelsen als Neukantianer' (n 78).

this dualism corresponds to the most general determination of thought,[98] which is rooted in a certain world view,[99] in so far as this determination refers to indefinable original categories[100] that correspond to completely separate and irreducible worlds.[101] For in both cases we are dealing with logically independent and infinite chains, and it is only our psychological necessity demands that set limits.[102] This distinction between the two worlds underlies the division between explanatory and normative disciplines. Whereas the former are 'oriented to what is really given, to the world of "is", to *reality*',[103] the perspective of the latter 'refers to the world of "ought", to the *ideality*'.[104] Thus, '[w]hile the natural sciences set themselves the task of demonstrating and explaining the actual behaviour of things, of grasping their existence, other disciplines establish norms that prescribe behaviour, demand a state of being or non-being, i.e. an "ought"'.[105] Hence,

> logic, grammar, aesthetics, ethics and jurisprudence are the disciplines that deal with such 'norms'; their approach is therefore called normative. The laws of morality and of the state, the norms of logic, grammar and aesthetics, are not, like the laws of nature, explanations of what exists; they do not assert a real event, they merely demand such an event; they do not say that something has happened or is happening because it must happen that way, but that it should happen.[106]

Consequently, although the question of the origin of a norm naturally leads to the realm of 'is', ie, to the will of the one who dictates the norm,[107] the norm itself, considered as such, belongs to the world of 'ought', in as much as it is the objectification of a will.[108]

On the other hand, for Kelsen, the doctrine of natural law[109] succumbs to subjectivism, as it is nothing more than a form of 'philosophical absolutism',[110] for its essence

[98] Kelsen, HPSL1, 7.
[99] Kelsen, HPSL1, VI.
[100] Kelsen, HPSL1, 7.
[101] Kelsen, HPSL1, 8.
[102] Kelsen, HPSL1, 9–10.
[103] Hans Kelsen, 'Über Grenzen zwischen juristischer und soziologischer Methode (1911)' in H Kelsen, *Hans Kelsen Werke, Vol 3 Veröffentlichte Schriften 1911–1917*, M Jestaedt (ed) (hereafter HKW3) (Tübingen, Mohr Siebeck, 2010) 22–56, 29.
[104] ibid 30.
[105] Kelsen, HPSL1, 5.
[106] Kelsen, HPSL1, 5.
[107] For will belongs to the world of 'is' inasmuch as it is a psychological event and therefore in essence something different from the 'ought'. Thus, according to Kelsen: 'It should be pointed out right here that the object of psychological observation, which is a purely explicative one, is exclusively the real being – and never the ought – and that one must not be embarrassed enough to beware of the obvious conflation of the two points of view in the problem of the will' (Kelsen, HPSL1, 115).
[108] H Kelsen, 'Rechtswissenschaft und Recht. Erledigung eines Versuchs zur Überwindung der "Rechtsdogmatik"' (1922) 3 *Zeitschrift für öffentliches Recht* (*ZÖR*) 103, 182. As Paulson has argued, the distinction between 'is' and 'ought' is reflected in the Kelsenian distinction between two concepts of law: 'The first concept, which has as its focus legal science, is *the law qua object of legal cognition*. The second concept, which has as its focus the social sciences, is *the law qua acts of will* or, as I prefer to call it, *the law qua politics*' (Paulson, 'Hans Kelsen on Legal Interpretation, Legal Cognition, and Legal Science' (n 79) 190) (emphasis in original).
[109] For a reconstruction of the arguments used by Kelsen to characterise the positions he groups under the term 'natural law' [*Naturrecht*] and his criticisms against these positions, see ch 10 by Zalewska in this volume. Further reading includes P Chiassoni, 'Kelsen on Natural Law Theory. An Enduring Critical Affair' (2014) 23 *Revus. Journal for Constitutional Theory and Philosophy of Law* 135.
[110] Kelsen defines 'philosophical absolutism' as 'the metaphysical view that there is an absolute reality, that is, a reality that exists independently of human knowledge. Hence its existence is objective and unlimited in,

lies in the fact that the inherent, objective and necessary validity of the higher order that this doctrine defends is based on the absolute value of justice that such an order embodies.[111] For Kelsen, however, justice in its absolute validity is beyond our possible experience, just as Platonic ideas are beyond natural reality.[112] Since justice is beyond the limits of our possible experience, its content cannot be rationally determined,[113] and therefore both it and the positions on which it is based succumb to subjectivism as they can only be expressed in terms of mere value judgements.[114]

While Kelsen locates the purifying task of his philosophy in the application of the transcendental method to jurisprudence,[115] he considers the task of Kantian philosophy against metaphysics as an unfinished critical undertaking to which his purifying theory must contribute.[116] For Kelsen, the metaphysical dualism implicit in the formulation of

or beyond, space and time, to which human cognition is restricted' (H Kelsen, 'Absolutism and Relativism in Philosophy and Politics (1948)' in H Kelsen, *What is Justice? Justice, Law, and Politics in the Mirror of Science* (Berkeley, University of California Press, 1971) 198–209, 198). In his campaign against 'philosophical absolutism', Kelsen categorises a diverse range of positions under the term 'natural law', which postulate a static normative order (Kelsen, *General Theory of Law and State* (n 70) 399–400) that claims to have validity over positive law (ibid 12, 438). According to Kelsen, natural law positions ground the objective validity of the higher normative order they defend on the basis that this higher order has not been created by any artificial will – that is, it has not been created arbitrarily (H Kelsen, 'The Idea of Natural Law (1928)' in O Weinberger (ed), *Hans Kelsen. Essays in Legal and Moral Philosophy*, P Heath trans (Dordrecht, D Reidel, 1973) 27–60, 28–30; H Kelsen, 'The Natural-Law Doctrine before the Tribunal of Science (1949)' in H Kelsen, *What is Justice? Justice, Law, and Politics in the Mirror of Science* (Berkeley, University of California Press, 1971) 137–73, 142). Furthermore, natural law positions ground the necessity of such a higher normative order in the fact that its validity is self-evident, since it can be understood and recognised by all. Consequently, such a higher normative order must be universally obeyed (H Kelsen, 'The Idea of Natural Law (1928)' in O Weinberger (ed), *Hans Kelsen. Essays in Legal and Moral Philosophy*, P Heath trans (Dordrecht, D Reidel, 1973) 27–60, 37–38).

[111] Kelsen, PTL1 §8, 15–16; RR1, 12; Kelsen, 'The Natural-Law Doctrine before the Tribunal of Science (1949)' (n 110) 141; Kelsen, 'The Idea of Natural Law (1928)' (n 110) 56–57; Kelsen, *General Theory of Law and State* (n 70) 8; H Kelsen, 'Natural Law Doctrine and Legal Positivism (1928)' in Kelsen, *General Theory of Law and State* (n 70) 391–446, 435.

[112] Kelsen, PTL1 §8, 15–16; Kelsen, *General Theory of Law and State* (n 70) 13. For a discussion of the rejection of the 'thing-in-itself' as a legacy of the neo-Kantian movement embraced by Kelsenian theory, see ch 5 by Heidemann in this volume.

[113] According to Kelsen, '[j]ustice *qua* absolute value is irrational. However indispensable it may be for human will and action, it is not accessible to cognition. Only positive law is given to cognition, or, more accurately, is given to cognition as a task'. (Kelsen, PTL1 §8, 17–18; RR1 16; see also Kelsen, *General Theory of Law and State* (n 70) 13). It should be noted that according to Kelsen, 'even the categorical imperative is entirely without content' (Kelsen, PTL1 §8, 17; RR1 15). Despite Paulson's assertion that 'it is necessary to acknowledge Kelsen's appeal to Kant's doctrine of freedom and his even more profound acceptance of a second normative sphere or validity, which is to be considered alongside that of the external world, presupposes the grasp of some essential elements of Kantian practical philosophy' (see Paulson, 'Faktum/Wert-Distinktion, Zwei-Welten-Lehre und immanenter Sinn. Hans Kelsen als Neukantianer' (n 78) 236, fn 55), Kelsen maintained a sceptical position towards the possibility of Kantian practical reason in general (see, eg, H Kelsen, *Die philosophischen Grundlagen der Naturrechtslehre und des Rechtspositivismus* (Charlottenburg, Verlag Rolf Heise, 1928) §39, 75–76). Kelsen limited the scope of rationality to theoretical rationality in Kant's sense. For further insight, see A Wilson, 'Is Kelsen Really a Kantian?' in R Tur and W Twining (eds), *Essays on Kelsen* (Oxford, Clarendon Press, 1986) 37–64, 38.

[114] Kelsen, *General Theory of Law and State* (n 70) 6–11.

[115] In several passages, Kelsen explicitly acknowledges the influence of Kantian epistemological theory on his contributions. For instance, see HPSL2, VI; Kelsen, *Allgemeine Staatslehre* (n 83) VII; H Kelsen, 'The Pure Theory of Law, "Labandism" and Neo-Kantianism. A Letter To Renato Treves', SL Paulson and B Litschewski Paulson trans in SL Paulson and B Litschewski Paulson (eds), *Normativity and Norms. Critical Perspectives on Kelsenian Themes* (Oxford, Clarendon Press, 1998) 171–75, 171.

[116] Kelsen states that '[t]he final type [of dualism] developed here, which differs from metaphysical dualism and is therefore termed epistemological-critical dualism, exhibits characteristics similar to those of Kant's

'philosophical absolutism' is overcome 'when man, especially through the advance of the empirical science, finds the courage to discard the realm of the transcendent, which is beyond his experience, because it is an unknowable, uncontrollable, and therefore a scientifically useless hypothesis'.[117] However, Kelsen points out to us that in becoming aware that we have lost the rational basis for our belief in transcendent existence,[118] we necessarily also become aware of the fact that it is our cognition that plays 'an active and productive role in relation to its objects'.[119] Indeed, the merely passive role of our cognition is based on the belief that our cognition is limited to reflecting things that are somehow given in themselves.[120] Thus, the denial that such things can exist independently of our cognition implies a denial of the merely passive role of our cognition in relation to its objects. Our cognition, Kelsen tells us, 'creates its objects out of the materials provided by the senses'.[121]

Nevertheless, Kelsen warns us that when we are aware of the fact that we have no rational basis for our belief in a transcendent existence, and are thus forced to accept the active and productive role of our cognition in relation to its objects, we renounce the absolute character of our ontological judgements, in as much as the truth of such judgements can no longer be maintained on the basis of their relation to an absolute existence, but only on the basis of cognition.[122] The truth, Kelsen informs us, 'which is asserted within the system is never more than a relative truth, and it appears, therefore, in comparison with the metaphysical-absolute truth, as a merely formal one'.[123] Thus,

> [i]t might appear that a cognition which produces its own objects can only claim subjective validity for its judgments. Actually, there is the danger that, if we fail to anchor truth in a

transcendental philosophy or critical idealism. However, it becomes evident that Kant's philosophical doctrinal system also diverges somewhat from the ideal. This is already evident in the field of natural philosophy. In the battle which this philosophical genius waged against metaphysics, based on the tenets of science, and which earned him the name of "crusher of all", he did not really go all the way. After all, according to the disposition of his character, he probably did not have a markedly combative character at all, but was rather inclined towards a mediating equalisation of opposites. There is still much of metaphysical transcendence in the role that the "thing-in-itself" plays in his work. Therefore, one will look in vain for an open and unreserved commitment to relativism, which is the inevitable consequence of any real overcoming of metaphysics' (Kelsen, *Die philosophischen Grundlagen der Naturrechtslehre und des Rechtspositivismus* (n 113) §39, 75–76).

[117] Kelsen, *General Theory of Law and State* (n 70) 433.

[118] It is evident that a fundamental aspect of Kelsen's work is the acceptance of the Kantian distinction between the transcendental and the transcendent. (For further discussion of the use of these terms in RR1 and RR2, see Paulson, 'Der Normativismus Hans Kelsens' (n 90) 530, fn 19.) According to Kant, 'I call all cognition transcendental that is occupied not so much with objects but rather with our mode of cognition of objects insofar as this is to be possible *a priori*. A **system** of such concepts would be called **transcendental philosophy**' (I Kant, *Critique of Pure Reason*, P Guyer and AW Wood trans (hereafter KrV) (Cambridge, Cambridge University Press, 2000) (hereafter cited according to *Akademieausgabe* – KPAW-KGS: KrV A/B) Kant, KrV A12/B25) Kant employs the term 'transcendent' to signify that which transcends the limits of possible experience (Kant, KrV A296) (emphasis in original).

[119] Kelsen, *Die philosophischen Grundlagen der Naturrechtslehre und des Rechtspositivismus* (n 113) §34, 62; According to Kelsen, the 'thing-in-itself' can be maintained, but only as a sign of the limitation of the knowable. This awareness of the unreality of what lies beyond the senses enables us to maintain that phenomena do not exist, because the phenomenal is the only real thing (Kelsen, *General Theory of Law and State* (n 70) 434).

[120] Kelsen, *General Theory of Law and State* (n 70) 434; Kelsen, *Die philosophischen Grundlagen der Naturrechtslehre und des Rechtspositivismus* (n 113) §34, 62.

[121] Kelsen, *Die philosophischen Grundlagen der Naturrechtslehre und des Rechtspositivismus* (n 113) §34, 62.

[122] ibid.

[123] ibid.

> transcendent realm above all human cognition, we fall into the bottomless pit of subjectivism, into a boundless solipsism.[124]

Kelsen's philosophy, however, defends itself against such attacks by emphasising that although our cognition creates its objects from the material provided by the senses, it does so in accordance with their immanent laws, and it is this conformity with the laws that guarantees the objective validity of the results of the processes of cognition.[125] Thus, the establishment of laws – ie, the determination of 'the objective conditions under which the process of cognition occurs'[126] – is one of the main tasks of understanding. For in this task our understanding replaces metaphysical speculation with epistemic normativity, so that a critical theory of knowledge takes the place of metaphysics[127] – or, as Kelsen puts it, in the sense of Kant's philosophy, the transcendental then replaces the transcendent.[128] Kelsen thus accepts that the philosophy on which his theory of jurisprudence is based is also dualistic.[129] However, the dualism on which it is based is no longer a metaphysical, 'but an epistemological, epistemocritical dualism'.[130]

Thus, although it is correct to say that the theoretical rationality defended by Kelsen – at least as far as its classical phase is concerned[131] – is based on the normativist epistemological theory of Kantian origin,[132] it is also true that the theoretical rationality defended by Kelsen deepens the Kantian critical tasks as it dissolves the metaphysical dualism on which the defence of natural law normativism rests, making Kelsen's pure theory of law inevitably a theory of positive law.[133] That is, a theory which, in seeking to answer questions about what law is and how it is made – and 'not the questions of what the law ought to be or how the law ought to be made'[134] – necessarily grants that law can have any content.[135] For, according to Kelsen, by drawing an analogy[136] between the method by which natural science creates its object and the method by which jurisprudence creates its object,[137] it can be concluded that, just as natural science constitutes a cosmos which we call nature,[138] that is, a system of synthetic judgements determined

[124] ibid.
[125] Kelsen, *Die philosophischen Grundlagen der Naturrechtslehre und des Rechtspositivismus* (n 113) §34, 62.
[126] Kelsen, *General Theory of Law and State* (n 70) 435.
[127] ibid.
[128] ibid.
[129] Kelsen, *Die philosophischen Grundlagen der Naturrechtslehre und des Rechtspositivismus* (n 113) §34, 63.
[130] ibid.
[131] On the periodisation of Kelsen's works on the theory of norms, see ch 2 by Paulson in this volume.
[132] See, eg, Heidemann, *Hans Kelsen's Normativism* (n 62).
[133] As Kelsen himself wrote, '[c]ognition can only deal with positive law' (Kelsen, 'The Function of the Pure Theory of Law' (n 80) 236).
[134] Kelsen, PTL1 §1, 7; RR1, 1. See also Kelsen, PTL1 §9, 18; RR1, 17.
[135] Kelsen, PTL1 §28, 56; RR1, 64.
[136] In opposition to Sander, Kelsen is unequivocal in maintaining that it is only logical to present an analogy, but not to affirm the identity between the science of law and the natural sciences with respect to the process of unification through synthetic judgements of the material they unify. (See Kelsen, 'Rechtswissenschaft und Recht Erledigung eines Versuchs zur Überwindung der "Rechtsdogmatik"' (n 108) 109, 133.) For an analysis of the relationship between legal norms [*Rechtsnormen*] and legal propositions [*Rechtssätze*] understood as a cognitive judgement of legal science in the context of the problem of validity, see Heidemann, ch 5 in this volume.
[137] Kelsen, 'Rechtswissenschaft und Recht Erledigung eines Versuchs zur Überwindung der "Rechtsdogmatik"' (n 108) 181.
[138] Kelsen, *Théorie pure du droit* (n 71) §3(d) 42–45, 45.

by the empirical material which these judgements unify, so jurisprudence constitutes a legal order, that is, a system of synthetic judgements[139] – called legal propositions [*Rechtssätze*][140] – whose content corresponds to the material – that is, statutes, ordinances, court decisions, administrative acts, etc – which such judgements unify.[141] It is clear that natural science can only and exclusively process the data provided by perception in order to formulate its judgements.[142] In the same manner – since the metaphysical dualism on which natural law normativism rests has been dissolved by the theoretical rationality defended by Kelsen – jurisprudence can only and exclusively process the positive material given to it to formulate its judgements.[143] However, unlike the empirical material with which natural science formulates its judgements, the material with which jurisprudence formulates its judgements corresponds to acts of will [*Willensakte*].[144] Consequently, whereas the judgements formulated by natural science aim to explain 'one event as a necessary consequence of another in a group of similar sequences',[145] the judgements formulated by jurisprudence prescribe a certain fact as the result of a certain behaviour that must occur according to a will 'objectified in the sphere of the judgement'.[146]

Hence, the answer to the question of how it is possible to make the subjective meaning of certain acts objective in the sphere of law[147] is found in the epistemic-normativist foundation of Kantian origin on which the theoretical rationality defended by Kelsen rests.[148] Indeed, for Kelsen, legal propositions guarantee 'the independence of their validity from all subjective wishes and desires'[149] because they unify the positive legal material in accordance with the transcendental presuppositions that guarantee the objectivity of the results of our processes of legal cognition.[150] In this manner, the transcendental

[139] Kelsen, PTL2 §16, 72; RR2, 74; Kelsen, 'Rechtswissenschaft und Recht Erledigung eines Versuchs zur Überwindung der "Rechtsdogmatik"' (n 108) 182.

[140] ibid 181–82.

[141] ibid 181.

[142] ibid 181–82.

[143] Kelsen, HPSL1, 510–14.

[144] Kelsen, 'Rechtswissenschaft und Recht Erledigung eines Versuchs zur Überwindung der "Rechtsdogmatik"' (n 108) 182.

[145] As Kelsen himself states, '[o]nly positive law is given to cognition, or, more accurately, is given to cognition as a task'. (Kelsen, PTL1 §8, 17–18; RR1, 28).

[146] Kelsen, 'Rechtswissenschaft und Recht Erledigung eines Versuchs zur Überwindung der "Rechtsdogmatik"' (n 108) 182.

[147] Kelsen, PTL2 §34(d), 202; RR2, 205. Kelsen emphasises the distinction between the subjective meaning of an act (*Willensakt*) and the objective meaning ascribed to it by law (see Kelsen, *Théorie pure du droit* (n 71) §3(b), 35–40). Kelsen developed various versions of the question concerning the transcendental presuppositions of legal knowledge, particularly in relation to the fundamental norm (see, eg, Kelsen, *Die philosophischen Grundlagen der Naturrechtslehre und des Rechtspositivismus* (n 113) §36, 66).

[148] See also Heidemann, *Hans Kelsen's Normativism* (n 62).

[149] Kelsen, 'Rechtswissenschaft und Recht Erledigung eines Versuchs zur Überwindung der "Rechtsdogmatik"' (n 108) 205.

[150] In his text against Sander, Kelsen maintains the analogy between jurisprudence and natural science. Kelsen posits that in the synthetic judgements of natural science, the unification (*Einheitsbeziehung*) occurs through which the concept of understanding (*Verstandesbegriff*) is related to sensory perceptions (ibid 127). Such unification as a process of cognition in its systematic context represents experience in the scientific sense according to Kant (ibid). Transcendental philosophy analyses synthetic judgements, establishes the synthesis that exists in them between the concept of understanding and perception, and distinguishes its two components (ibid 127–28). Accordingly, Kelsen posits that the analysis of synthetic judgements represents

presuppositions are necessary conditions for legal validity and thus serve as the basis for the critical or purifying task of jurisprudence,[151] for transcendental presuppositions enable us to identify which components of our experience are to be unified in legal propositions as legal material[152] in such a manner that it corresponds to jurisprudence to 'attribute to certain acts the objective meaning of legal norms'.[153] This leads to the conclusion that without the fact of legal science [*Faktum der Rechtswissenschaft*],[154] there would be no such thing as law.

Chapters three and four of this volume focus on two of these transcendental presuppositions that correspond to Kelsen's possible answers to the question of the ultimate foundation of the normativity of the law[155] – ie, the question of the ultimate foundation that enables us to render the subjective meaning of certain acts as objective

a foundational approach to comprehending the transcendental presuppositions of natural science (ibid). Although an explicit revelation of the nature of synthetic judgements with respect to the transcendental presuppositions of legal propositions is absent from the 1922 text, it is evident that for Kelsen legal propositions are synthetic judgements and, as such, functions of cognition (ibid 181–82.).

[151] Heidemann, 'Das "Faktum der Rechtswissenschaft" bei Hans Kelsen' (n 83) 90–91.

[152] Kelsen, *Théorie pure du droit* (n 71) 45. See ch 3 by Alexy in this volume.

[153] Kelsen, *Théorie pure du droit* (n 71) 45. The postulate of the constitutivity of the understanding with respect to its object – which corresponds to the identification of the correctness of the hypothetical judgement of legal science with the validity of the legal norm – constitutes the unmistakable sign of Kelsen's neo-Kantian phase. As Heidemann has demonstrated, this identification is not only absent in the phase of critical constructivism (Heidemann, *Hans Kelsen's Normativism* (n 62) 34) but also in Kelsen's late theory (see Kelsen, *Allgemeine Theorie der Normen* (n 76) 123–24). The lengthy process of revision of the neo-Kantian inspiration that Kelsenian norm theory underwent commenced with the introduction of the descriptive function of legal propositions [*Rechtssätze*] with respect to norms [*Rechtsnormen*] in 1941. (H Kelsen, 'The Pure Theory of Law and Analytical Jurisprudence' (1941) 55 *Harvard Law Review* 44; see also Kelsen, *General Theory of Law and State* (n 70) 45–47). The introduction of this function led to the thesis of the indirect application of logic to the relations between legal norms (see PTL2 §16, 74; RR2, 76–77) and subsequently to the complete decoupling of the correctness of legal propositions and the validity of legal norms. This decoupling is implied in the sceptical thesis about the application of logic to the relation between norms in 1960 (H Kelsen and U Klug, *Rechtsnormen und logische Analyse. Ein Briefwechsel 1959 bis 1965* (Vienna, Franz Deuticke, 1981) ms 4 July 1960, 42–50). As Paulson has elucidated, this scepticism subsequently led to the ultimate dismantling of the 'Kantian edifice' of Kelsen's late normative theory (Paulson, 'Metamorphosis in Hans Kelsen's Legal Philosophy' (n 90) 875).

[154] Kelsen, PTL1 §16, 34; RR1, 37; H Kelsen, 'Was ist die Reine Rechtslehre? (1953)' in HR Klecatsky, R Marcic and H Schambeck (eds), *Die Wiener rechtstheoretische Schule: Schriften von Hans Kelsen, Adolf Merkl, Alfred Verdross* (Vienna, Verlag Österreich, 2010) 499–514, 499–500. On the neo-Kantian background to the notion of the fact of science [*Faktum der Wissenschaft*] and Kelsen's reception of this notion, see eg, Heidemann, 'Das "Faktum der Rechtswissenschaft" bei Hans Kelsen' (n 83) 81; SL Paulson, 'The Great Puzzle: Kelsen's Basic Norm' in L Duarte d'Almeida, J Gardner and L Green (eds), *Kelsen Revisited. New Essays on the Pure Theory of Law* (Oxford, Hart Publishing, 2013) 43–61, 53–57.

[155] As previously stated (n 153), the identification of the correctness of the hypothetical judgement of legal science with the validity of the legal norm is a clear indication of Kelsen's neo-Kantian phase. Consequently, in the classical period of Kelsen's theory of norms, the transcendental question concerning the ultimate foundation of the normativity of the law corresponds to the epistemic question concerning what is the transcendental category that makes it possible for positive law to be the object of cognition. Kelsen explicitly elaborates the latter question in his 1928 paper: 'How is positive law – as an object of cognition, as an object of jurisprudence – and therefore: how is it possible?' (Kelsen, *Die philosophischen Grundlagen der Naturrechtslehre und des Rechtspositivismus* (n 113) §36, 66). In light of the aforementioned considerations, Alexy maintains in the chapter he has devoted to this compilation that: 'Two questions need to be linked. The first is what Kelsen means when he describes Ought as a "relatively a priori category". The second is whether he can solve the problem of the normativity of law with this idea'. In contrast, Kelsen's late doctrine is characterised by the decoupling of the correctness of legal propositions and the validity of legal norms (n 153). For a detailed analysis of the descriptive character of the science of law in Kelsen's late doctrine, please refer to ch 4 by Stewart in this volume.

in the sphere of law.[156] As early as his *Habilitation* in 1911, Kelsen describes the concepts of jurisprudence as 'formal categories' [*formale Kategorien*] resulting from the elimination of all teleological substance.[157] Thus, on the basis of such concepts, it is impossible to find a substantive answer to the reason for the normative character or objective validity of legal norms. Consequently, according to Kelsen, the jurist must accept this normative character as 'an unshakeable presupposition, beyond dispute',[158] for to doubt this character would mean for the jurist '[sawing] off the very branch on which he sits'.[159] This is because the normative character of legal norms is a 'self-sufficient and independent quality which does not derive from any other'.[160] However, if the legal scholar were to disregard Kelsen's injunction and enquire as to the ultimate basis of the normativity of the law, Kelsen's 1911 work could not provide him with an answer, for, as Kelsen said there, law belongs to the world of 'ought', and this world corresponds to a logically independent and infinite chain of 'ought' [*unendliche Kette des Soll*].[161] A few decades later, however, Kelsen argued that 'the search for the reason of a norm's validity cannot go on indefinitely like the search for the cause of an effect'.[162] In numerous writings following his *Habilitation*, Kelsen formulated various answers to the question of the ultimate reason for the validity of legal norms,[163] to the point that this question became a cardinal issue in his theory.[164] On the basis of these various answers, as Paulson has observed,[165] Kelsen's system encompasses diverse approaches to normativity, some of which may even be perceived as competing interpretations of his own legal doctrine.

According to Paulson, two of these approaches are of particular interest: 'The first focuses on the thesis of substantive normativity, the second on the thesis of modal normativity'.[166] The substantive normativity thesis assumes that the reconstruction of the legal system proposed by Kelsen is to be interpreted on the basis of the deontic modality of obligation, understood as the 'duty of the subject of law to obey the law'.[167] Paulson contrasts this thesis with the thesis of modal normativity, which argues that the reconstructive programme of the legal system advocated by Kelsen corresponds to a methodological approach in which the basis of the reconstruction corresponds to the deontic modality of empowerment [*Ermächtigung*], understood as 'the capacity

[156] Kelsen, PTL2 §34(d), 202; RR2, 205.
[157] Kelsen, HPSL1, 92, 353–78.
[158] Kelsen, HPSL1, 353.
[159] ibid.
[160] ibid 352.
[161] ibid 9–10. On the problem of infinity and the ultimate foundation of the normativity of the law, see ch 4 by Stewart in this volume.
[162] Kelsen, PTL2 §34(a), 195; RR2, 197.
[163] Paulson has identified the genesis of this investigation in Kelsen's 1914 publication 'Rechtsgesetz und Landesgesetz nach österreichischer Verfassung'. (See Kelsen, HKW3, 359–425) cited in Paulson, 'The Great Puzzle: Kelsen's Basic Norm' (n 154) 48. For a discussion of the change of course after 1914, see also Olechowski, *Hans Kelsen* (n 1) 266, fn 281.
[164] T Olechowski, 'Kelsens Rechtslehre im Überblick' in T Ehs (ed), *Hans Kelsen. Eine politikwissenschaftliche Einführung* (Baden-Baden, Nomos, 2009) 47–65, 58.
[165] Paulson 'Der Normativismus Hans Kelsens' (n 90) 530.
[166] ibid.
[167] ibid.

to bring about certain legal changes by means of behaviour'.[168] Paulson posits that an exemplar of the first approach is found in the thesis of justified normativity put forth by Joseph Raz.[169]

It is sufficient to note, for the purposes of this introductory overview, that the complex argumentative mechanism proposed by Raz aims to present an argument based on the postulation of the analytical relation between the normativity of the law and obligation as a fundamental deontic modality.[170] On these bases, Raz introduces the hypothetical standpoint of the legal man. This is to say that the perspective of he 'who endorses the basic norm and all that follows from it and nothing else'.[171] According to Raz, such a man can inform us of the nature of law through normative statements. However, the normative statements issued by such a man from his perspective will be morally committed to law, for the legal man morally believes in the binding force of the basic norm.[172] Raz asserts that Kelsen posits that, although the legal scientist assumes the hypothetical perspective of the legal man, this nonetheless results in the scientist's detachment from the moral commitment to the basic norm.[173] Raz then elucidates that the legal scientist, as conceived by Kelsen, does not merely describe the perspective of the legal man – ie, he does not merely describe what would be valid if the basic norm were valid – but rather, the legal scientist presupposes the basic norm by issuing normative statements about a legal system that he presupposes to be valid, but without making a moral commitment to it.[174] In this manner, Raz introduces the hypothetical perspective of the legal man as an epistemological tool with the aim of explaining the Kelsenian aspiration to found a genuine legal science. That is, a jurisprudence that, on the one hand, dispenses with any axiological and causal commitment by constituting itself as a science of positive law and, on the other, understands law from its internal perspective by conceiving legal statements as normative statements.

In contrast to Raz, Paulson rules out the possibility that the normativity of the law is based on the analytical relation between the normativity of the law and the modality of obligation. In light of Guastini's contributions, Paulson posits that what distinguishes normativism is its non-reductive programme. This entails a conception of the norm as a peculiar entity inhabiting the world of 'ought'.[175] Therefore, the link that the norm exhibits with a deontic modality is contingent on its nature as a peculiar entity and therefore dependent on the interpretation that grounds such a link. Furthermore,

[168] H Kelsen, 'Recht und Kompetenz. Kritische Bemerkungen zur Völkerrechtstheorie Georges Scelles' in K Ringhofer and R Walter (eds), *Hans Kelsen. Auseinandersetzungen zur Reinen Rechtslehre. Kritische Bemerkungen zu Georges Scelle und Michel Virally* (Vienna, Springer Verlag, 1987) 1–108, 72.

[169] Paulson, 'Der Normativismus Hans Kelsens' (n 90) 530.

[170] J Raz, 'Kelsen's Theory of the Basic Norm' in SL Paulson and B Litschewski Paulson (eds), *Normativity and Norms. Critical Perspectives on Kelsenian Themes* (Oxford, Clarendon Press, 1998) 47–67, 60.

[171] J Raz, 'The Purity of the Pure Theory' in SL Paulson and B Litschewski Paulson (eds), *Normativity and Norms. Critical Perspectives on Kelsenian Themes* (Oxford, Clarendon Press, 1998) 237–61, 246.

[172] ibid 247.

[173] ibid; Raz, 'Kelsen's Theory of the Basic Norm' (n 170) 58.

[174] ibid; ibid.

[175] R Guastini, 'Normativism or the Normative Theory of Legal Science: Some Epistemological Problems' in SL Paulson and B Litschewski Paulson (eds), *Normativity and Norms. Critical Perspectives on Kelsenian Themes* (Oxford, Clarendon Press, 1998) 317–30, 318. See SL Paulson, 'The Weak Reading of Authority in Hans Kelsen's Pure Theory of Law' (2000) 19 *Law and Philosophy* 131, 136.

Paulson posits that 'if there is an argument that can be used to support the substantive normativity thesis, then this argument must be a transcendental argument that is based solely on the condition of possibility of the normativity of law, independently of morality and facticity'.[176] Paulson notes that certain passages in Kelsen's writings indicate that Kelsen is attempting to present a transcendental argument.[177] However, Paulson states that if the term 'transcendental' is to be understood in a Kantian sense, Kelsen's efforts to offer a transcendental argument are unsuccessful, for his argument fails to prove why his theory is the only defensible alternative to natural law and reductive causal positivist theories.[178] Consequently, Paulson concludes that:

> Neither from a systematic perspective nor from a historical perspective does it seem justified to attribute [the substantive normativity thesis] to Kelsen. The juridico-theoretic instruments that are necessarily associated with the substantive normativity thesis cannot be reconciled with Kelsen's system. Moreover, the substantive normativity thesis does not reflect the central concern of Kelsen's engagement with the problems of general jurisprudence, namely, his struggle against naturalism. The conclusions of the modal normativity thesis are exactly the opposite. They directly address Kelsen's central concern of elaborating a response to naturalism. With its help, [Kelsen] can find exactly what he so urgently seeks: a means of preserving the autonomy of law.[179]

It would be of interest to enquire whether Paulson's arguments could be extended to other attempts to interpret the Kelsenian reconstruction of the legal system on the basis of the deontic modality of obligation. While the answer to this enquiry must remain open for the present, this compilation offers us another interpretation of the Kelsenian reconstruction on the basis of this deontic modality.

In his *Reine Rechtslehre* [*Pure Theory of Law*] of 1934, Kelsen proposed the 'ought' as a relative a priori category as the ultimate foundation of the normativity of the law.[180] According to Robert Alexy, Kelsen's solution amounts to 'nothing less than an ambitious attempt to add another category to the table of categories that Kant declared complete'.[181] In Alexy's chapter in this collection, he analyses this Kelsenian proposal, clarifying its meaning in the first part of his chapter and assessing its plausibility in the second. To clarify what Kelsen means when he describes the 'ought' as a 'relative a priori category', Alexy first explains the Kelsenian notion of norm. For Kelsen, norms have the ontological status of semantic content. Thus, Alexy argues that three candidates could bear the title of transcendental categories of the normativity of the law: imputation, the basic norm and the 'ought'. Alexy dismisses the first two candidates by arguing that their grounding depends precisely on the 'ought'. Nevertheless, Kelsen uses the 'ought' as a collective concept which includes (positive) permission, competence and obligation. On the basis of the fundamental character inherent in the concept of transcendental category, Alexy rules out the possibility that these three modalities can be interpreted simultaneously

[176] Paulson, 'Der Normativismus Hans Kelsens' (n 90) 530.
[177] ibid.
[178] ibid 532.
[179] ibid 536. Paulson's criticisms of Raz's justified normativity thesis were also presented, albeit inconclusively, in Paulson, 'The Weak Reading of Authority in Hans Kelsen's Pure Theory of Law' (n 175) 131.
[180] Kelsen, PTL1 §11(b), 23–25; RR1, 22–24.
[181] Alexy, ch 3 in this volume.

as relative a priori categories. Consequently, the key question is which of these modalities has the status of being fundamental. Since there is virtually no argument for the fundamental status of (positive) permission, only competence and obligation could have such a status. According to Alexy, however, competence can only be defended as a transcendental category on the basis of its actual exercise. Therefore, to avoid the factual argument concerning such an exercise and thus maintain the purity of the analysis, the only possible solution is to interpret the 'ought' in terms of obligation. However, can the interpretation of the 'ought' as obligation be the ultimate basis of the normativity of the law? To assess the plausibility of the 'ought' as an answer to this transcendental question, Alexy seeks to elucidate the two characteristics that Kelsen attributes to the 'ought' as a category – namely, its a priori character and relative character. Alexy argues that the 'ought' has an a priori character because it constitutes the norm as an abstract object and thus constitutes law by allowing empirical data from objects already constituted by other categories, such as causality, to be processed as legal. In our experience, however, the empirical data that the 'ought' allows us to process are called norms, so it seems superfluous to speak of the category of 'ought' as norms are already present in our experience. To counter this objection, Alexy argues that the concept of correctness is key to understanding the role of the deontic modality of 'ought' in legal norms. For Alexy, we experience law as an objective 'ought', which ultimately corresponds to correctness, because someone who expresses a judgement about an objective 'ought' is making a claim that their judgement is correct. Alexy argues that the Kelsenian 'ought' has a relative character because, unlike the Kantian transcendental categories necessary for all possible experiences, the Kelsenian 'ought' is the ultimate foundation that enables the interpretation of empirical data as empirical data of a legal character, and this interpretation is, from an external perspective, one possible interpretation among many others. Despite this relative character of the Kelsenian 'ought', Alexy warns us that it would be wrong to ascribe an arbitrary character to it. First, because the Kelsenian a priori remains tied to the concept of cognition; second, because it is inconceivable that empirical legal data could lead to a change in the category of 'ought'; and third, because the concept of the necessity of 'ought', as a transcendental category underpinning the normativity of the law, is open to various interpretations such as expediency, cultural identity and practical necessity – even if the latter cannot be shared by Kelsen because it leads to the field of morality.

Although Alexy's arguments that the 'ought' as a relative a priori category constitutes the ultimate foundation of the normativity of the law are convincing, the richness of the argumentative strategies employed in his text also highlights the notorious complexity of the definition of the transcendental category of the normativity of the law in Kelsen's theory. Indeed, if we were innocently to embark on a search for Kelsen's answer to the question of the definition of such a transcendental category, we would face two obvious difficulties. On the one hand, Kelsen did not explain in detail the method necessary to reveal the transcendental presuppositions of jurisprudence.[182] On the other hand,

[182] Heidemann, 'Das Faktum der Rechtswissenschaft" bei Hans Kelsen' (n 83) 89. As previously stated, the lack of a detailed explanation of the transcendental method of Kelsenian philosophy, which should fulfil the basic requirement of offering a proof that would make it possible to rule out any alternative to the pure theory of law as a science, has led Paulson to assert the failure of Kelsen's transcendental enterprise

this methodological gap makes it possible to argue for the suitability of more than one candidate for the transcendental category of the normativity of the law, which simultaneously appears to contradict its fundamental character.[183] As Alexy indicates in his chapter, in addition to the 'ought' as a relative a priori category, imputation and the basic norm are plausible candidates for qualifying as the ultimate ground of the normativity of the law. Of these possible candidates, it is perhaps the basic norm that is Kelsen's best known, but perhaps also most frequently misunderstood doctrine.[184] The obscure character sometimes attributed to this doctrine[185] is undoubtedly because Kelsen's texts contain different formulations of it.[186] Moreover, as Iain Stewart argues in his chapter in this volume, its obscure character also stems from the fact that Kelsen paid more attention to the functions of the basic norm than to its definition. However, that is not all; according to Stewart, the picture becomes more complicated when one considers that Kelsen used both the term 'hypothesis' and the term 'presupposition' in order to bring the meaning of the basic norm into conformity with the Kantian terminology of a logico-transcendental condition, without which subjective meanings could not be understood as legal norms, and thus the observed phenomena could only be interpreted as power relations.

In addition, this obscure character is reinforced by the fact that the concept of a basic norm was the protagonist of one of the 'turns' of Kelsen's theory from 1960 onwards. In this turn, Kelsen no longer defined a basic norm as a hypothesis, but as a 'fiction' in the strong sense given to this term by Hans Vaihinger – a postulate that may be scientifically useful although not only false but also self-contradictory. As Stewart argues in chapter four of this volume, positions on the fiction turn have been mixed. Either it has been regarded as insignificant or it has been used to diagnose a collapse of the Kelsenian theory of legal norms. It is possible, however, that Kelsen's redefinition of the 'basic norm' concept responds to a need in his theory and that its introduction does not have the dire consequences attributed to it. According to Stewart, when claiming that the basic norm is a 'fiction' in Vaihinger's strong sense, Kelsen is attempting to resolve a problem of inconsistency in his theory. In 1962, Kelsen recognised that defining the basic norm as a hypothesis implies creating an unjustifiable exception to his definition of a norm,

(see Paulson, 'Der Normativismus Hans Kelsens' (n 90) 530; Paulson, 'Metamorphosis in Hans Kelsen's Legal Philosophy' (n 90) 880–81; Paulson, 'The Great Puzzle: Kelsen's Basic Norm' (n 154) 51–52, 51). Paulson (Paulson, 'Metamorphosis in Hans Kelsen's Legal Philosophy' (n 90) 878–79; Paulson, 'The Great Puzzle: Kelsen's Basic Norm' (n 154) 53–57) has identified a regressive form of the Kantian transcendental argument (I Kant, *Prolegomena to Any Future Metaphysics*, G Hatfield trans (Cambridge, Cambridge University Press, 2004) 27 (hereafter cited according to *Akademieausgabe* – KPAW-KGS: Pro 4) Pro 4: 276) in the Kelsenian strategy based on the neo-Kantian conception, which starts from the *Faktum der Wissenschaft* for the proof of transcendental presuppositions (see Kelsen, PTL1 §29, 58; RR1, 67 in relation to the basic norm). The Kelsenian strategy, however, does not include a progressive form of the transcendental argument (see Kant, Pro 4: 274), which, in contrast, Kant did use in his KrV (Kant KrV A84/B116–B169).

[183] For further insight, please refer to Alexy, ch 3 in this volume.

[184] Olechowski, 'Kelsens Rechtslehre im Überblick' (n 164) 58.

[185] For an analysis of the conceptual ambiguity of Kelsen's basic norm, see Stewart, ch 4 in this volume.

[186] Paulson has identified 10 different formulations of the basic norm in Kelsen's texts, in addition to the formulations of the late theory. For further details, please refer to SL Paulson, 'Die unterschiedlichen Formulierungen der "Grundnorm"' in A Aarnio, SL Paulson, O Weinberger, GH von Wright and D Wyduckel (eds), *Rechtsnorm und Rechtswirklichkeit. Festschrift für Werner Krawietz zum 60. Geburtstag* (Berlin, Duncker & Humblot, 1993) 53–74, 58–62.

since a basic norm would no longer correspond to the meaning of an act of will, but to an act of thought.[187] Such an exception would lead to interpreting the relation between the elements that make up his definition of a norm – that is, on the one hand the objective meaning of the act of will, on the other the act of will and the volitional subject – as logically contingent. However, by defining a legal norm as the objective meaning of an act of will, Kelsen establishes a logically necessary relation between these elements. Moreover, jurisprudence cannot fail to presuppose a basic norm, required to support the objective validity of the meanings composing the legal order. Yet then an infinite chain of norms is irremediably produced. Thus, if the pure theory postulates the existence of a basic norm for any legal order, that postulate will be self-contradictory in being infinitely regressive. It cannot be a 'hypothesis', yet it can be a 'fiction' in Vaihinger's strong sense. Stewart suggests that associated with the fiction turn lie two deeper turns. One is a 'closure turn', which appears in 1959 – although in Kelsen's conception of justice according to natural law and not in the pure theory itself. However, closure of positive law can be found early in the development of the pure theory: a closure of a state legal order, manifested in relations between states and manageable (if at all) only if each state legal order is subsumed within a perhaps also closed international legal order. The other is an 'independence turn', which moves the pure theory towards an external descriptive perspective, with which the pure theory might become a social science of law. Stewart extrapolates the closure and independence turns in Kelsen's thought – beyond relevance only to Kelsen – to suggesting a concept of law simply as closed norms. This concept includes both natural law and positive law, as observably practised beliefs.

As should now be clear, validity is a transcendental presupposition of Kelsen's theory of norms. However, as Heidemann argues in chapter five of this collection, determining the precise meaning of the term 'validity' in this theory is a singularly difficult undertaking, compounded by Kelsenian scholarship's use of this term to refer to various normative properties such as the existence, binding force, applicability, membership of a legal system, or even the efficacy of legal norms. Despite all these uses, Heidemann emphasises that the Kelsenian sources, which belong to the neo-Kantian phase,[188] show a clear central meaning of the term 'validity'. To explain this meaning, in the first part of his chapter Heidemann traces not only its philosophical genesis in Kant's *Critique of Pure Reason*, but also its development in the neo-Kantian sources of the Baden School, preceded by the contributions of Rudolf Hermann Lotze. According to Heidemann, Kantian epistemology replaces the traditional object-centred model of cognition with a normativist model, according to which a cognitive judgement is universal or objectively valid if it is correctly constituted according to the immanent rules of understanding. As Heidemann further explains, for Lotze validity is an indefinable basic concept that corresponds to the timeless way of being of values, which guide human cognition and subjectivity and thus condition the way of being of objects as a precondition of their very existence. Wilhelm Windelband and Heinrich Rickert, for their part, as representatives of the Baden School, combined the Lotzean approach with their interpretation of Kantian philosophy. Indeed, according to Heidemann these authors argued that validity

[187] This position was maintained by Kelsen in the second edition of the 1960 *Pure Theory of Law* (see Kelsen, PTL2 §4 b) 9–10; RR2 9).

[188] See initial paragraph of this section and above (n 64).

is a metaphysical concept that allows the immanent content of subjective cognitive acts to be grounded in the norms derived from the transcendental values that govern them. In the second part of his chapter, Heidemann analyses the development of the central meaning of the concept of validity in Kelsenian sources from the *Habilitation* thesis of 1911 onwards, focusing especially on the most relevant works that Kelsen published between 1920 and 1934. According to Heidemann, the incorporation of a neo-Kantian philosophical foundation enabled Kelsen to clarify the relationship between norms and legal propositions, the differentiation of which he had introduced in his 1911 work. According to this transcendental idealist foundation, in so far as legal norms are identical with legal propositions – ie, with the judgements of jurisprudence – the validity of legal norms is identical with the validity of such propositions. Thus, the legal proposition according to which '*a* must φ' is valid if the norm which commands that *a* must φ is valid – ie, if every rational being must think that *a* ought to φ. However, Heidemann warns us of an ambiguity in Kelsen's thesis. In any juridico-normative judgement, two kinds of normativity are involved: one is part of the judgement itself, its modality – that which makes it a normative judgement – the 'normativity-"ought"'. The other is a rule external to the judgement saying that one ought to think that way, the 'validity-"ought"' which is only given with 'true' judgements, no matter whether they are 'is'-judgements or 'ought'-judgements. Kelsen sometimes seems to argue that the validity-'ought' follows from the normativity-'ought' – when arguing against Weber – sometimes, that the normativity-'ought' follows from the validity-'ought' – when dealing with Windelband. Two objections, which Heidemann rejects, add to this reservation. According to the first objection, in upholding this notion of validity, Kelsen promoted a notion of 'justified legal normativity'. Nevertheless, as Heidemann argues, this reading does not consider the status that Kelsen attributes to jurisprudence in his neo-Kantian phase. According to the second objection, the various uses that Kelsen attributes to the term 'validity' deny the possibility of a central meaning of this term. However, as Heidemann claims, such uses refer either to criteria or conditions of validity, but not to its concept.

In chapter six of this collection, Julieta Rabanos proposes four theses that explore the relation between law and coercion in Kelsen's theory. The first thesis emphasises that for Kelsen, law is a coercive social normative order, since law is a system of norms whose unity is given by the fact that they all have the same source of validity – ie, the basic norm – which aims to regulate human behaviour – when this behaviour occurs in a direct or indirect relation to other human beings – and which regulates sanctions – ie, acts against the will of the subjects and even acts involving the use of physical force in the event of resistance. Unlike other social orders, legal sanctions have their source in human authority and are socially organised. According to the second thesis, coercion determines the hypothetical form that corresponds to the ideal linguistic form that distinguishes legal norms from moral norms. This ideal form contains in its antecedent the necessary conditions whose occurrence determines that the sanction described in its consequent ought to take place. Coercion thus serves as a criterion for classifying legal norms. Thus, for example, while the object of a primary legal norm corresponds to the sanction described in its consequent, which must be imposed by the empowered subject to whom the norm is addressed if the conditions foreseen in its antecedent are fulfilled, a secondary legal norm is a mere correlate of a primary legal norm, imposing duties on the non-empowered subject. According to the third thesis, the effectiveness of legal systems is defined by reference to sanction-norms. Thus, regarding coercion, if the norm is effective it has direct effects on the subject producing the behaviour – corresponding to the sanction – and indirect effects on the other subjects – due to the threat of sanction. The indirect effects refer to the psychological pressure exerted on subjects by both the existence of a system of sanction-norms and the direct application of sanctions. Thus, the more plausible the application of sanctions, the greater the motivation of non-empowered subjects to comply with the norms. According to Rabanos, this psychological pressure is intrinsically linked to a characteristic feature of legal coercion, and manifests itself in the form of an objective sense of duty to refrain from behaviour that serves legal norms as a condition for the imposition of sanctions. Consequently, the indirect effects of coercion are necessary for normative effectiveness for they constitute a motivation to comply with legal norms in the absence of sanctions. However, indirect effects are also necessary for normative production. By generating a sense of duty, these effects motivate the empowered subjects themselves to impose sanctions. In this manner, indirect effects make it possible to explain the reason why empowered subjects ascribe validity to sanction-norms and to the legal system as a whole. Thus, the indirect effects of coercion can empirically explain the conceptual link that Kelsen proposed between primary and secondary legal norms. The fourth thesis postulates that coercion is a necessary condition for the validity of law. As Rabanos explains, there are two ways to demonstrate this thesis: first, in so far as coercion is a necessary condition for the effectiveness of a legal order, coercion is also a necessary condition for the basic norm; second, the content of at least some characterisations of the basic norm is intrinsically based on the notion of coercion.

II. International Law

In the wake of the whirlwind of war that threatened to engulf every vestige of European culture in the second decade of the twentieth century, the modernising movement of international law was born.[189] This movement sought to address the inability of international law as it had hitherto been configured to respond to the challenges of peacekeeping in the new post-war scenario. This scenario was characterised not only by the gradual fading of civilisational ideology, but also by a new balance of forces, which reflected the slow dissipation of continental European influence and the advent of an international system dominated by the Anglo-Saxon powers.[190] As Wilhelm G Grewe has argued,[191] the system of international law based on the existence of a disorganised multitude of sovereign states gave way to an international law inclined, on the one

[189] For an analysis of the term 'modernising' as it is used to describe this movement, see J von Bernstorff, *The International Law Theory of Hans Kelsen. Believing in Universal Law*, J Dunlap trans (Cambridge, Cambridge University Press, 2010) 6, fn 12. For an examination of the legal dimension of war, see eg, JW Garner, *International Law and the World War*, 2 Vols (London, Longmans, Green and Co, 1920). For an analysis of international law in the interwar period, see WG Grewe, *The Epochs of International Law*, M Bryers trans (Berlin, Walter de Gruyter, 2000) 573–636.

[190] Grewe, ibid 581. Grewe identifies the distinguishing features of this new system of international law and refers to it as post-classical. See ibid 581–88.

[191] ibid 581–88.

hand, to protect the rights of minorities and, on the other, to indiscriminately extend the international legal order to the entire globe. These objectives led to the establishment of the League of Nations and the creation of instruments to regulate relations between states through conflict prevention and peaceful conflict resolution. This modernising movement was thus born from the necessity to acknowledge that the very principles on which nineteenth-century international law had been founded had allowed and even promoted the detonation of the world conflict.[192] Among the most visible representatives of this modernising movement[193] were prominent members of the Vienna School of Legal Theory,[194] including the irreplaceable figure of Hans Kelsen.

Although the 1950 publication of *The Law of the United Nations. A Critical Analysis of Its Fundamental Problems*[195] and the 1952 publication of *Principles of International Law*[196] are considered important contributions to the development of contemporary international law,[197] the 1920 publication of *Das Problem der Souveränität und die Theorie des Völkerrechts. Beitrag zu einer Reinen Rechtslehre* [*The Problem of Sovereignty*

[192] For an analysis of the use of international law as a rationale for justifying aggression among the powers of the time, see IV Hull, *A Scrap of Paper. Breaking and Making International Law during the Great War* (Ithaca NY, Cornell University Press, 2014); von Bernstorff, *The International Law Theory of Hans Kelsen* (n 189) 6 ff.

[193] *Staatswillenspositivismus* can be seen as a common feature of international law in the second half of the nineteenth century, represented in particular in the work of authors such as Carl Bergbohm, Georg Jellinek and Heinrich Triepel, who, despite their differences, postulated the will of the state as the source of international law (see, eg, J von Bernstorff, 'German intellectual historical origins of international legal positivism' in J Kammerhofer and J D'Aspremont (eds), *International Legal Positivism in a Post-Modern World* (Cambridge, Cambridge University Press, 2014) 50–80, esp 62–63; von Bernstorff, *The International Law Theory of Hans Kelsen* (n 189) 15–43). If we adopt as a common characteristic of the authors belonging to the modernising movement of international law their reaction against *Staatswillenspositivismus*, then we can group together, in addition to the authors associated with the Vienna School of Legal Theory, others who, by advocating the revival of iusnaturalist positions, gave an important impulse to this movement, among them Léon Duguit (L Duguit, *Traité de droit constitutionel*, Vol 1, 2nd edn (Paris, Fontemoing & Cie, 1911)); Rudolf Stammler (R Stammler, *Theorie der Rechtswissenschaft* (Halle, Buchhandlung des Waisenhauses, 1911)); Heinrich Hugo Edwin Lammasch (HHE Lammasch, *Das Völkerrecht nach dem Kriege. Publication de l'Institut Nobel, 3* (Oslo, Kristiania, H Aschehoug & Co (W Nygaard), 1917)); Leonard Nelson (L Nelson, *Die Rechtswissenschaft ohne Recht. Kritische Betrachtungen über die Grundlagen des Staats- und Völkerrechts, insbesondere über die Lehre von der Souveränität* (Leipzig, Verlag von Veit & Comp, 1917)); Hugo Krabbe (H Krabbe, *Die Moderne Staatsidee* (Aalen, Scientia Verlag, 1969) (originally published Den Haag, 1918)); Hersch Lauterpacht (H Lauterpacht, *Private Law Sources and Analogues of International Law* (with special reference to International Arbitration) (London, Longmans Green, 1927)); James Leslie Brierly (JL Brierly, *The Law of Nations: An Introduction to the International Law of Peace* (Oxford, Clarendon Press, 1928)); Georges August Jean Joseph Scelle (GAJJ Scelle, *Précis de droit des gens. Principes et systématique*, Vol 1 (Paris, Recueil Sirey, 1932)); as well as authors representing Soviet Leninist Marxism, such as Aleksandrovič Evgenij Korovin (AE Korovin, *Das Völkerrecht der Übergangszeit*, H Kraus trans (Berlin, Rothschild, 1929)).

[194] In ch 7 by Kammerhofer in this volume, he describes the pure theory as a collective scientific enterprise and explores the contributions of representatives of the Vienna School of Legal Theory to international law, including Alfred Verdross, Josef Laurenz Kunz and Rudolf Aladár Métall. For a biographical summary, see von Bernstorff, *The International Law Theory of Hans Kelsen* (n 189) 272–85.

[195] H Kelsen, *The Law of the United Nations. A Critical Analysis of its Fundamental Problems* (London, Stevens and Sons, 1950).

[196] H Kelsen, *Principles of International Law* (New York, Rinehart & Co, 1952).

[197] As von Bernstorff has argued, several factors influenced the difficult reception of Kelsen's contributions to the dogmatics of international law in the post-1945 period. These include, on the one hand, the predominance of Anglo-American pragmatism and realism in the field of international law and, on the other, the renewed interest in natural law. Furthermore, it is necessary to consider the growing pessimism about the rationalisation of international relations that was characteristic of the first decades of the Cold War. This is evidenced by von Bernstorff, *The International Law Theory of Hans Kelsen* (n 189) 9.

and the Theory of International Law. Contribution to a Pure Theory of Law][198] had already established Kelsen as a pivotal figure in the modernising movement of international law during the interwar period.[199] As previously discussed, the years following the dissolution of the Austro-Hungarian monarchy saw Kelsen engaged in a period of intense activity, focused on the tasks of his constitutional law expertise. Nevertheless, the demands of these tasks did not prevent Kelsen from pursuing his academic endeavours, which led him to identify international law as one of the most fruitful areas for the further development of his own theory. As previously mentioned, Kelsen subsequently devoted a significant portion of his legal practice to the field of international law.[200] In his monograph published in 1920, Kelsen presents the philosophical foundations of his theory by critically confronting the most relevant theoretical approaches to international law developed in the German cultural milieu since the second half of the nineteenth century.[201] At the centre of his attacks is the dogma of sovereignty, which constituted the central axis that enables the distinction between the relations of the state to its subjects – which are defined as sovereignty under state law [*staatsrechtliche Souveränität*] – and the relations of the state to other states – which are defined as state sovereignty under international law [*völkerrechtliche Souveränität*].[202]

This latter concept of sovereignty enabled the restrictive nature of the binding of states to international law to be justified for such law was then conceived as the product of the exercise of the subjective right of each state 'to bind itself and to be bound only by its own will'.[203] Accordingly, this concept of sovereignty[204] implied the negation of any form of limitation imposed on the power of the state.[205] As Kelsen observed, this constituted a *contradictio in adiecto*, given that 'the state is, on the most profound interpretation of its essence, order, barrier and restraint in itself'.[206] Nevertheless, an alternative argument could be made against Kelsen's position; specifically, the restrictive power of the state is not affected by the concept of sovereignty for this concept merely

[198] Kelsen, PSTVR (n 81).
[199] von Bernstorff, *The International Law Theory of Hans Kelsen* (n 189) 6.
[200] Olechowski, *Hans Kelsen* (n 1) 265.
[201] As Rigaux has argued, Kelsen's critiques were not limited to the dualism of Triepel, who espoused irreconcilable views of the state by identifying it with both the legal order and the anthropomorphic figure of a subject of law acting in the international legal order. In addition to challenging the dualism of Triepel, Kelsen also opposed the influence of Hegelianism, which advocated a kind of monism. This view held that international law was merely a branch of state law [*äußeres Staatsrecht*] whose binding force derived from the convergent will of the states [*Völkerrecht als gemeinsames Recht*] (F Rigaux, 'Hans Kelsen on International Law' (1998) 9 *European Journal of International Law* 325, 326, 330). Nevertheless, Kelsen's criticism was also directed against Jellinek, arguably the most influential author of the second half of the nineteenth century in the German-speaking world. As von Bernstorff has observed, Jellinek's influence was pervasive in the development of major theoretical frameworks for international law, extending from the period preceding the First World War to the Weimar era (von Bernstorff, 'German intellectual historical origins of international legal positivism' (n 193) 62).
[202] Kelsen, PSTVR, 37–38.
[203] G Jellinek, *Die Lehre von den Staatenverbindungen* (Vienna, Alfred Hölder, KK Hof- und Universität-Buchhändler, 1882) 55. Similarly, Jellinek states in *Allgemeine Staatslehre* that 'sovereignty is the quality of a state authority by virtue of which it has the exclusive capacity for legal self-determination and self-binding force' (G Jellinek, *Allgemeine Staatslehre*, 3rd edn (Berlin, Verlag von O Häring, 1914) 481).
[204] Kelsen posits that Bodin is the founder of the doctrine of sovereignty and suggests that Bodin may have employed it primarily to defend the French kings' claim to political independence against the German emperors' empire (see Kelsen, PSTVR, 2).
[205] ibid 44.
[206] ibid.

indicates that the sovereign can limit itself.[207] In response to this argument, however, Kelsen argued that this conception of sovereignty is inherently anthropomorphic, since it fails to recognise the normative foundation that prevents anarchy. This normative foundation underlies both the very existence of the sovereign and their power of self-limitation.[208]

Kelsen further argues that on the basis of the empirical scientific approach,[209] sovereignty has been conceptualised as a mere natural fact, analogous to 'freedom or independence from one power or from domination by another'.[210] Against such 'monstrous nonsense',[211] Kelsen demonstrates that, even if we were to accept such a concept for the sake of discussion, we would then be giving sovereignty a meaning without any basis in reality. First, it is evident that the concepts of power, domination and violence in the context of social facts cannot be reduced to a simple causal relation. Instead, they are better understood as motivations.[212] Second, it is evident that no state could be considered sovereign in a factual sense.[213] According to Kelsen, every state, even the most politically powerful great power, is determined, dependent and not free from others in all aspects of economic, legal and cultural life.[214]

In this context, Kelsen also employs his theoretical apparatus to challenge the view that the state is both a natural entity and a legal person.[215] According to Kelsen, this two-pronged conception, comprising two distinct forms of cognition – namely, the sociological-natural-scientific approach and the normative-legal approach – contravenes the fundamental theorem of epistemology, which stipulates that 'the object of knowledge is determined by the direction of knowledge'.[216] According to this fundamental theorem,

> two different methods, such as the natural-scientific-causal and the legal-normative, must not produce one and the same object. For example, the state 'in itself' cannot be the object of both methods. Instead, two objects must be produced that are at the same time different. When designated by the same name, 'state', these two objects can only lead to a misleading error.[217]

[207] ibid.

[208] ibid. As previously discussed (n 83), in his 1911 *Habilitation* work, based on the normativity thesis, Kelsen describes the concepts of jurisprudence as 'formal categories' [*formale Kategorien*] resulting from the elimination of all teleological substance. In this context, Kelsen directs the critical possibilities of his theory towards the dissolution of anthropomorphic fictions of the will employed by traditional jurisprudence through the concept of imputation. In particular, the concept of central imputation (on the difference between central and peripheral imputation see, eg, P Langford, I Bryan, 'Hans Kelsen's Concept of Normative Imputation' (2013) 26 *Ratio Juris* 85; SL Paulson, 'Hans Kelsen's Doctrine of Imputation' (2001) 14 *Ratio Juris* 47) enables the linkage of certain external facts with a subject [*Subjekt der Zurechnung*], namely a person which constitutes the endpoint of imputation [*Endpunkt der Zurechnung*] as defined in the legal norm. For Kelsen, 'person' is simply an expression for the unity constituted by the legal positions defined by the norms in the form of rights, obligations and competences. It is therefore entirely at the discretion of the norm-issuer to confer the status of person on an individual human being or on a different entity (Kelsen, HPSL1, 145–46; Kelsen PTL1 §25, 46–52; RR1, 52–60; Kelsen, PSTVR, 45–46; Kelsen, PTL2 §33, 168–92; RR2, 172–95).

[209] Kelsen, PSTVR, 6–7.

[210] ibid.

[211] Kelsen, PSTVR, 7.

[212] ibid.

[213] Kelsen makes it clear that a truly naturalistic view could not refer to the state, but only to 'persons exercising the power of the will, ie [to] governing and governed persons' (Kelsen, PSTVR, 7).

[214] ibid.

[215] Kelsen, PSTVR, 9–10.

[216] ibid 10–11. As previously discussed, this theorem is the result of Kelsen's denial of transcendent existence and his conviction of the activity of the understanding in the generation of its objects.

[217] ibid.

Consequently, if one accepts that the object of knowledge is determined by the direction of knowledge, the state as an object of jurisprudence can only be considered as a normative order.[218] Therefore, from the perspective of jurisprudence the normative order that is commonly referred to as the state is, in fact, identical to the normative order commonly referred to as law.[219] Thus, sovereignty can be defined as a characteristic of that legal order which is not derived from any higher legal order because it is supposed to be supreme, from the perspective of jurisprudence.[220] Accordingly, the question of the sovereign character of a legal order is equivalent to the question of its supreme norm, or, in more common parlance, its basic norm.[221]

It can therefore be asserted that among the dualisms dissolved by the pure theory[222] is also that which refers to the dualism between national law and international law. As Phil Edwards reminds us in chapter eight in this volume, the unity assured by the basic norm corresponds to an epistemic requirement. This is because if international law is also the object of jurisprudence, then it must be represented by jurisprudence together with national law, as a unified and non-contradictory system of legal propositions.[223] Moreover, as Jörg Kammerhofer states in his contribution to this collection, the pure theory, by incorporating the *Stufenbaulehre*, identified the rationale for the dissolution of the dualism between national and international law in a theory of the validity of legal norms. This theory posits that the totality of what we call law must refer to norms whose validity is grounded in some constitutive segment of the chain of normative foundation, which finds its ultimate reason in the basic norm.

Consequently, the epistemic requirement of the unity of the object proposed by the pure theory[224] dissolves the restrictions on which the binding nature of international law was based. For it is no longer possible to argue that there is any difference between the object of international law and the object of national law. In conclusion, as François Rigaux has stated, 'Kelsen's theory brought into focus an idea largely accepted nowadays and which the contemporary evolution of international law has overwhelmingly confirmed: international law is not confined to relations among states, it can encompass all human activities. The clearest example of such an evolution is the international protection of human rights: while the relations between a state and its own nationals were viewed in the past as a purely domestic question, protected by the concept of state sovereignty within its frontiers, such relations have acceded to the international legal sphere'.[225] As Tomasz Widłak argues in chapter nine in this collection, the Kelsenian model thus expresses the hopes of an underlying

[218] ibid 37.
[219] ibid.
[220] ibid 10, 37.
[221] ibid 94–101. As previously discussed, the question of the ultimate normative basis represents a departure from the position espoused by Kelsen in his 1911 *Habilitation*, see (n 163).
[222] See above (n 83).
[223] As Kelsen himself stated: 'The unity of the cognitive standpoint imperatively demands a monist view' (Kelsen, PSTVR, 104, 120).
[224] Accordingly, Kelsen posits that '[t]he postulate of the unity of knowledge also applies without restriction to the normative plane and finds its expression here in the unity and exclusivity of the system of norms that is assumed to be valid. This is synonymous with the necessary unity of the point of view of observation, evaluation or interpretation' (Kelsen, PSTVR, 105).
[225] Rigaux (n 201) 332.

cosmopolitan project, which sees in the creation of an institutionalised legal community of global scope the guarantee of peace.[226]

The chapters included in the second section of this volume address three fundamental themes of the pure theory of international law; specifically: the normative structural analysis of international law; the definition of international law as primitive law; and the teleological question of international law.

In chapter seven of this volume, Jörg Kammerhofer states that the pure theory corresponds to a collective intellectual enterprise that constitutes a particular stream of juridico-philosophical thought. The pure theory offers a methodology of analysis that can be used to propose solutions to current legal problems, including those posed by international law. Kammerhofer states that the pure theory asserts that all normativity, including the normativity of the law, responds to the same fundamental mechanisms. Consequently, the pure theory is a general theory of norms. However, the pure theory is also a general theory of law, for the formal analysis it offers enables the explanation of all possible legal orders, without differentiating between the scope of their validity or the subject matter they regulate. Kammerhofer coined the term 'nomomechanics' to refer to the pure theory as a theory concerned with the morphology and functions of both legal norms and legal systems. In this context, nomomechanics encompasses a theory of normativity and validity, which is aimed at elucidating, among other things, the interrelation between normative orders and the legal operations that explain the creation, derogation and solution of conflicts of norms. Kammerhofer situates the genesis of nomomechanics within the 'dynamic turn' of the pure theory, which was precipitated by the reception of the *Stufenbaulehre*, a theoretical framework developed primarily by Merkl. Given the strict separation between 'is' (*Sein*) and 'ought' (*Sollen*), the *Stufenbaulehre* postulates that, from a static perspective, only one norm can serve as the foundation for the validity of another norm. Consequently, no norm can be valid without its validity being founded on another norm. From a dynamic perspective, the *Stufenbaulehre* maintains that a norm is valid as long as it has been created in the predetermined form according to another norm. Therefore, the latter norm constitutes the immediate source of validity of the former. Thus, to determine the validity of a norm it is necessary to ascertain the norm that enabled its creation. The set of norms that enable the creation of other norms allows us to speak of a normative order and analyse its structure. The initial section of Kammerhofer's chapter is dedicated to an examination of the contributions of Hans Kelsen, Alfred Verdross, Josef L Kunz and Rudolf Aladár Métall – representatives of the Vienna School of Legal Theory – to the field of structural analysis of international law, with a particular focus on two key questions. The first is how the sources of international law are constituted and ordered, and the second concerns the relation between national law and international law. The second part of the chapter examines the author's recent efforts to develop a theoretical substratum based on nomomechanics that enables a review of the viability of the arguments proposed by

[226] cp von Bernstorff, *The International Law Theory of Hans Kelsen* (n 189). Von Bernstorff has argued that an adequate reconstruction of the Kelsenian doctrine of international law must reflect the tension between its two structural goals. These are, first, the definition of a pure method for understanding international law and, second, the promotion of a cosmopolitan and enlightenment-based political project underlying the interwar period.

the orthodox position regarding the force of precedents in international law. To this end, the author assumes judgements and arbitral awards as sources and employs international investment law as a case in point. Kammerhofer draws on the contributions of the authors of the Austrian public law doctrine of the second half of the twentieth century, who were strongly influenced by the pure theory of law. Contending on the basis of these figures and of the research on empowerment norms, Kammerhofer argues against the orthodox position that there is no legal basis for granting the status of general norms to precedents in international law.

In chapter eight of this compilation, Edwards states that the pure theory of law encounters theoretical challenges when it engages with the study of international law. From the perspective of national legal systems, international law is perceived as a normative entity characterised not only by its diffuse codification, but also by imperfect and decentralised adjudication, and normative enforcement. Despite the relatively anarchical conditions that characterise international law, Kelsen argued that it is, nevertheless, a legal system. Moreover, as previously discussed, Kelsen posited a normative continuity between international law and national legal systems. In his chapter, Edwards recalls that, during his neo-Kantian phase, Kelsen maintained that legal cognition has the same task as cognition in natural science. Kelsen further argued that the epistemic representation of the object of jurisprudence must comply with the principle of non-contradiction as a negative criterion of unity. Consequently, if international law is to be considered a subject of study within the field of jurisprudence, it must be represented in conjunction with national law as a unified and non-contradictory system. Monism thus emerges as a result of the epistemic demands of the Kelsenian theory. However, Edwards directs two questions to this position. The first concerns the object of Kelsen's presupposition. This leads to the question of whether Kelsen is referring to a theoretical construct or an observable entity when he states that international law is a legal system. The second question concerns the conditions of Kelsen's presupposition. That is to say, if international law is indeed a system in accordance with Kelsen's position, what could be the basic norm of this system? Edwards states that the concept of the primitive legal system, as expounded by Kelsen in his work *Society and Nature* (1943),[227] is the key concept that allows us to resolve not only the question of the existence of international law as a legal system, but also the question of its ultimate normative foundation. In Edwards' view, the concept of the primitive legal system, as developed in the 1943 text, provides the simplest and most logical explanation for the argument that, despite its diffuse, imperfect and decentralised character, international law is an observable entity. According to Edwards' account, the reason for the ontological status of international law is that, for Kelsen, both primitive law and international law obey the same core meaning of the term 'law'. In other words, they are normative orders of a coercive nature, aimed at achieving socially desired conduct through the threat of sanction, which is in turn socially accepted. Regarding the second question, Edwards reminds us that Kelsen, in his 1920 monograph[228] proposed that the maxim *pacta sunt servanda* constituted the legal proposition underlying the binding nature of international law. Nevertheless,

[227] H Kelsen, *Society and Nature* (Chicago, University of Chicago Press, 1943).
[228] Kelsen, PSTVR, 171.

in his 1934 *Pure Theory of Law* and in the second edition of the same work in 1960, Kelsen stated that the status of the ultimate normative foundation of international law belonged to custom. However, according to Edwards the primitive law model offers a more satisfactory response to the functions that the ultimate normative foundation of international law is supposed to fulfil. Indeed, the basic norm of the primitive legal order is based on the retributive principle, according to which collectivities are entitled to respond to external influences, returning good for good and evil for evil. This norm, which underlies the doctrine of *bellum justum*, also underpins the basic doctrine of customary international law, namely the principle of *pacta sunt servanda*.

Finally, Widłak devotes chapter nine, which concludes this section, to showing the relation of complementarity and dependence between the views of international law from the theory and philosophy of law in Kelsen's contributions. In their 1926 preface to the first volume of the *Internationale Zeitschrift für Theorie des Rechts* [International Journal for the Theory of Law], Hans Kelsen, Leon Duguit and Francis Weyr introduced the distinction between these two views. They argued that whereas the theory of law is concerned with the study of the basic concepts and methods of legal cognition regarding the relations between the various orders of state law, as well as between the orders of state and international law, the philosophy of law is concerned with the speculative solution of the problem of the aims of law.[229] According to Widłak, the postulate of purity and the distinction between 'is' (*Sein*) and 'ought' (*Sollen*) cause the theory of law to exclude any consideration of the aims of international law. However, the philosophical view of international law follows Kelsen in the formulation of arguments that are at least partially teleological in character. Widłak categorises these arguments into two groups. On the one hand, critical-reflexive arguments are employed to elucidate the distinctive characteristics of international law as a legal order. On the other hand, normative arguments are employed to define the further development of this law. The critical-reflexive arguments are based on a teleological thesis that postulates peace as the aim of law. The achievement of this aim is contingent upon the political community's organs acting in accordance with the law and being empowered to intervene in the interests of its members to the extent necessary to ensure the community's freedom from a state of generalised violence. According to Widłak, the neo-Hobbesian thesis states that although war and the use of force in international relations cannot be eliminated, it is possible for violence to be monopolised by the community and bring it under judicial control. According to Widłak, this teleological thesis serves as the basis for Kelsen to propose an evolutionary theory of international law. The evolutionary theory comprises three theses: the first proposes that legal systems evolve in an evolutionary manner, with the degree of their advancement corresponding to the level of centralisation; the second states that international law in its current form can be considered a primitive legal system; and the third maintains that international law must progress towards centralisation, in a manner similar to the evolution of national legal systems. Normative arguments state that the centralisation of international law is a desirable aim in overcoming the current primitive state of international law. The centralisation of international law is achieved

[229] L Duguit, H Kelsen and F Weyr, 'Préface – Vorwort' (1926/27) 1 *Internationale Zeitschrift für Theorie des Rechts* 1, 1–4.

both through rendering it subject to adjudication and through the development of the international criminal responsibility of individuals. On the one hand, adjudication is not only necessary to preserve the principle of legality in the application of the law, but also to guarantee the principle of objectivity in proceedings. The principle of legality is safeguarded by the institutionalisation of the sanctioning process, whereas the principle of objectivity is safeguarded by precluding states from simultaneously recognising both the role of judge and party in conflicts. Conversely, for Kelsen, the principle of individual criminal responsibility represents a more advanced degree of the application of justice than the primitive technique of collective responsibility. In conclusion, Widłak asserts that, based on the aforementioned arguments, Kelsen expressed his frustration that the Nuremberg trials should be interpreted as a missed opportunity for the reform of international law.

III. Democracy

As previously shown, following the dissolution of the Austro-Hungarian monarchy, Kelsen played a pivotal role in the establishment and evolution of Austrian democratic and constitutional institutions. Moreover, by the late 1920s, Kelsen had already become one of the most renowned protagonists of the controversies surrounding the Weimar Constitution.[230] In the early 1930s, Kelsen argues on behalf not only of electoral reform in Germany[231] but also of the defence of the first German democracy. Even shortly before the fateful Prussian state elections of 1932,[232] Kelsen, sensing the death throes of the German republic,[233] called on the few who had managed to keep their heads

[230] As Mathias Jestaedt and Oliver Lepsius argue, Hans Kelsen (1881–1973), alongside Rudolf Smend (1882–1975), Carl Schmitt (1889–1985) and Hermann Heller (1891–1933) were the most prominent theorists of the so-called 'Weimar debate on the tasks, aims, and methods of the theory of the law of the state' [*Weimarer Methoden- und Richtungsstreit der Staatsrechtslehre*]. This is the name given to the series of debates that took place in the third decade of the twentieth century around the understanding and interpretation of the first German democratic Constitution. (See M Jestaedt and O Lepsius, 'Der Rechts- und der Demokratietheoretiker Hans Kelsen: Eine Einführung' in H Kelsen, *Verteidigung der Demokratie*, M Jestaedt and O Lepsius (eds) (Tübingen, Mohr Siebeck, 2006) VII–XXIX, IX; S Korioth, 'Introduction' in AJ Jacobson and B Schlink (eds), *Weimar. A Jurisprudence of Crisis* (Berkeley, University of California Press, 2000) 41–50; M Gangl (ed), *Die Weimarer Staatsrechtsdebatte. Diskurs- und Rezeptionsstrategien* (Baden-Baden, Nomos, 2011); Stolleis (n 49) 139–97.) On Kelsen's debates with Smend and Schmitt, see Olechowski, *Hans Kelsen* (n 1) 501–04, 507–13, 530–36.

[231] See Olechowski, *Hans Kelsen* (n 1) 504–05.

[232] The elections of 24 April 1932, which resulted in the electoral success of the NSDAP, can be considered a foretaste of the *Reichstag* elections of 31 July 1932, which also gave a majority to the National Socialist Party. (See Olechowski, *Hans Kelsen* (n 1) 536–40, 536; HA Winkler, *Weimar 1918–1933. Die Geschichte der ersten Deutschen Republik* (München, Verlag CH Beck, 2018 (1993)) 477–616, 503–20.)

[233] In fact, Kelsen explicitly laments that, 'today, scarcely more than a decade after the historic deed of Weimar, there is no constitution in the world so alien to its people as this one, none before which so large a part of the people is so cold and indifferent, and an even larger part so hateful and contemptuous. It appears that the Germans no longer appreciate the freedom they have bestowed upon themselves. However, other peoples also seek to extinguish the light that once shone brightly with the idea of freedom. The ideal of democracy is fading, and on the dark horizon of our time a new star is rising, towards which the hope of the masses becomes all the brighter the more bloodily its splendour shines: dictatorship'. (H Kelsen, 'Verteidigung der Demokratie (1932)' in H Kelsen, *Verteidigung der Demokratie*, M Jestaedt und O Lepsius (eds) (Tübingen, Mohr Siebeck, 2006) 229–37, 229–30).

'free from the *obfuscation of political ideologies*',[234] to publicly defend democracy, before its extinction taught others the meaning of having lost it.[235] Nevertheless, Kelsen was compelled to acknowledge that this form of government was on the precipice of a tragic fate, having nurtured its most formidable adversary within its own bosom. Indeed, by adhering to its principles, the first German democracy had permitted a movement destined to destroy it by affording it the same opportunity to flourish as any other political conviction.[236]

Despite his own pessimism, Kelsen maintained that the defence of democracy is the duty of every democrat, even if any attempt to save it is utterly futile.[237] Years earlier, Kelsen had postulated the value of individual political freedom[238] as the foundation of the democratic social order.[239] Now, in the face of impending disaster, Kelsen consistently held that '[*a*] *democracy which attempts to impose itself against the will of the majority, even by force, has ceased to be a democracy*'[240] and, consequently, its supporters must not allow themselves to be dragged into this disastrous contradiction and resort to dictatorship to save it.[241] The democrat, Kelsen maintained, 'must remain faithful to his flag, even if the ship sinks; and he can only carry with him into the depths the hope that the ideal of freedom is indestructible and that the deeper it sinks, the more passionately it will rise again'.[242]

The events that transpired subsequent to 1932 served to substantiate Kelsen's most dire apprehensions. As David Dyzenhaus has argued,[243] the wounds resulting from the devastation of much of Europe still stand today as a historical warning of the outcome of the failure of the first German democratic experiment. This failure was the consequence not only of the efforts of supporters of the radical Left to destroy the Weimar Constitution, which they regarded as a veiled defence of the interests of the bourgeoisie,[244] but also of the effective activity of the radical Right which, with the support of a section of the leading intellectuals,[245] regarded the German Constitution, born from the bloody chaos of war, as a corrupt[246] and weak[247] political mechanism

[234] ibid 231 (emphasis in original).
[235] ibid.
[236] ibid 237.
[237] ibid.
[238] Indeed, in response to the objection raised by socialists that 'democracy, which stands for the principle of equality, has in reality only brought about a formal equality', Kelsen states that 'democracy, properly understood, does not so much want to realise the principle of equality as that of freedom, that of political self-determination. The real democracy, especially in Germany, fully realises this political self-determination, indicating that it has not promised anything that it has not also realised' (ibid 231).
[239] I refer to Kelsen's essay published in 1920 entitled 'Vom Wesen und Wert der Demokratie' ['On the Essence and Value of Democracy'], see below (n 251).
[240] Kelsen, 'Verteidigung der Demokratie (1932)' (n 233) 237 (emphasis in original).
[241] ibid.
[242] ibid.
[243] D Dyzenhaus, *Legality and Legitimacy. Carl Schmitt, Hans Kelsen and Hermann Heller in Weimar* (Oxford, Oxford University Press, 2003 (1997)) 17.
[244] Kelsen, 'Verteidigung der Demokratie (1932)' (n 233) 231.
[245] Against such a bourgeoisie, Kelsen's warning is particularly strong: 'The intellectuals who today fight against democracy and thus saw off the branch on which they are sitting will curse the dictatorship they advocate once they have to live under it, and will long for nothing else but a return to the democracy they so despise' (ibid 236–37).
[246] ibid 234.
[247] ibid.

incapable of guaranteeing the 'correct' formation of the national will.[248] The profound hatred and contempt for democracy held by the antagonistic groups led Kelsen to conclude that, regardless of which of them emerged triumphant from the conflict, their flag would be raised 'over the grave of democracy'.[249]

In contrast, Kelsen believed that the solution to the conflicts between the opposing sides could be found in the respect for the Weimar Constitution. The democratic principles enshrined in the Constitution offered the prospect of avoiding a revolutionary catastrophe by means of a peaceful and gradual resolution of the considerable contradiction surrounding the organisation of the economic system.[250] This position reflected Kelsen's own conception of democracy, which he had previously endorsed in his 1920 work 'Vom Wesen und Wert der Demokratie' ['On the Essence and Value of Democracy'][251] and subsequently expanded upon in his 1955 article 'Foundations of Democracy'.[252]

In the latter, Kelsen presents democracy as opposed to autocracy,[253] as a procedure aimed at the creation and application of a social order[254] that guarantees the principle of freedom understood as political self-determination through the representation of the governed in government.[255] To elucidate the aforesaid principle, Kelsen directs our

[248] ibid 234–35.

[249] ibid 230.

[250] As Vinx has shown (L Vinx, *Hans Kelsen's Pure Theory of Law. Legality and Legitimacy* (Oxford, Oxford University Press, 2007) 133), Schmitt considered it a mistake that in the Weimar Constitution he had left it up to Parliament to decide on the economic system that should govern Germany (see C Schmitt, *Legalität und Legimität*, 8th edn (Berlin, Duncker & Humblot, 2012 (1932)) 82–91). Kelsen, however, regarded such openness as a virtue of the Constitution (see H Kelsen, 'Vom Wesen und Wert der Demokratie (2. Aufl. 1929)' in H Kelsen, *Verteidigung der Demokratie*, M Jestaedt und O Lepsius (eds) (Tübingen, Mohr Siebeck, 2006) 149–228, 204). This position reflects Kelsen's conception according to which, while democracy corresponds to a form of government, that is, to a 'procedure or method for the creation and implementation of a social order', economic systems correspond to the content of such an order (H Kelsen, 'Foundations of Democracy' (1955) 66 *Ethics* 1, 68 (hereafter 'Foundations')).

[251] Two different versions of Kelsen's lecture delivered at the plenary meeting of the *Wiener Juristische Gesellschaft* [Vienna Legal Society] on 5 November 1919 were published. The first corresponds to H Kelsen, 'Vom Wesen und Werte der Demokratie' (1919) 63 *Gerichtshalle* 292 and 304. The second corresponds to H Kelsen, 'Wesen und Wert der Demokratie. Vortrag vor der Wiener Juristischen Gesellschaft am 5. November 1919' (1919) 48 *Juristische Blätter* 378. The latter version is a literal transcription of Kelsen's lecture (M Jestaedt, 'Editorischer Bericht "(Vom) Wesen und Wert(e) der Demokratie"' in HKW4, 700–62, 713). The first version corresponds to a preliminary version of it (ibid 714–15). The finalised version of the lecture was subsequently published as H Kelsen, *Vom Wesen und Werte der Demokratie* (Tübingen, JCB Mohr (Paul Siebeck), 1920). The expanded version of this work was published in 1929 as H Kelsen, *Vom Wesen und Wert der Demokratie*, 2nd edn (Tübingen, JCB Mohr, 1929). This version was subsequently republished by Aalen, Scientia Verlag, in 1963. The English version was published in H Kelsen, 'On the Essence and Value of Democracy', B Cooper trans, in AJ Jacobson and B Schlink (eds), *Weimar. A Jurisprudence of Crisis* (Berkeley, University of California Press, 2000) 84–109. The quotations from this work in the present text are taken from Kelsen, 'Vom Wesen und Wert der Demokratie (2. Aufl. 1929)' (n 250).

[252] Kelsen continued to contribute to the development of the theory of democracy with numerous writings. Two compilations of his writings on the subject being available: H Kelsen, *Verteidigung der Demokratie*, M Jestaedt and O Lepsius (eds) (Tübingen, Mohr Siebeck, 2006); H Kelsen, *Demokratie und Sozialismus. Ausgewählte Aufsätze*, N Leser (ed) (Vienna, Verlag der Wiener Volksbuchhandlung, 1967).

[253] Kelsen, 'Foundations' (n 250) 1, 2, 68. Indeed, Kelsen presents the oppositional relation between democracy and autocracy, for example, in Kelsen, 'Vom Wesen und Wert der Demokratie (2. Aufl. 1929)' (n 250) 155.

[254] Kelsen, 'Foundations' (n 250) 68.

[255] ibid 2.

attention to one of his most perspicacious passages, in which he elucidates his epistemological position. As previously discussed, Kelsen argues that in acknowledging the absence of a rational basis for our belief in transcendent existence, we are compelled to accept that our cognition is the primary creator of its objects through sensory data and in accordance with immanent and universal laws. Conformity to such laws guarantees the objective validity of the results of our cognitive processes and establishes a level playing field for access to knowledge.[256] Such egalitarian conditions preclude the possibility of arguing on behalf of a privileged access to truth.[257] According to Kelsen, this impossibility in turn implies the necessity of resolving a contradiction in relation to our freedom.

Kelsen states that freedom and equality are inherent to our human condition as social beings, forming part of our instinctual make-up.[258] To counter our discomfort with heteronomy [*Qual der Heteronomie*] – that is, our primary reaction against any outside will that seeks to impose itself on our own – we require reasons.[259] The impossibility of arguing for a privileged access to truth implies that we can confront the rational justification of the will that seeks to impose itself on ours.[260] Concurrently, however, as Kelsen states, our social nature renders domination an unavoidable consequence.[261] Thus, a contradiction arises between our freedom as instinct and the demands of domination that constitute the social order. According to Kelsen, democracy is the only form of social order that offers an egalitarian solution to this contradiction by universally granting the possibility of participating in the creation of the norms imposed on us.[262] As Kelsen further expounds, participation in government is the defining characteristic of democracy.[263]

Therefore, as Dreier has argued, Kelsen's conceptualisation of democracy does not originate from the collective subject but rather from the notion of individual freedom.[264]

[256] ibid 18.

[257] As Raz has warned us, we should not confuse Kelsen's relativism with scepticism: '[F]or the most part Kelsen adopts a cognitive view and regards every normative statement, legal or otherwise, as a statement of a binding norm or of the value it institutes. Such a semantic view is of course consistent with value-scepticism. It will merely lead the sceptic to the belief that all normative statements are false. Kelsen, however, is not a sceptic. He is a subjectivist or a relativist. Normative statements can be true or false. It is merely that their truth depends on the existence of relative rather than absolute values' (Raz, 'The Purity of the Pure Theory' (n 171) 244.

[258] Kelsen, 'Foundations' (n 250) 18.

[259] Kelsen, 'Vom Wesen und Wert der Demokratie (2. Aufl. 1929)' (n 250) 154; Kelsen, 'Foundations' (n 250) 18.

[260] Kelsen, 'Foundations' (n 250) 18.

[261] ibid 19.

[262] Kelsen posits that social or political freedom is the consequence of the transformation of the meaning of natural freedom. He asserts that those who are subject to their own will but not to the will of others are politically free. (Kelsen, 'Vom Wesen und Wert der Demokratie (2. Aufl. 1929)' (n 250) 155). As Vinx has argued, this idea resonates with the aspiration raised by Rousseau, who advocated the social contract in order to find an answer to the fundamental problem of '[f]inding a form of association which defends and protects with all common forces the person and property of each associate, and by means of which each, while joining all, nevertheless obeys only himself and remains as free as before' (JJ Rousseau, 'On the Social Contract' in ML Morgan (ed), *Classics of Moral and Political Theory*, 5th edn (Indianapolis, Hackett, 2011) 882–941, 887. See Vinx (n 250) 113).

[263] Kelsen, 'Foundations' (n 250) 3.

[264] H Dreier, 'Kelsens Demokratietheorie: Grundlegung, Strukturelemente, Probleme' in R Walter and C Jabloner (eds), *Hans Kelsens Wege sozialphilosophischer Forschung: Ergebnisse eines internationalen Symposions in Wien (14.–15. Oktober 1996)* (Vienna, Manz Verlag, 1997) 79–102, 80.

According to Kelsen, this integration of political freedom into the concept of democracy corresponds to a modification of the pre-modern concept of democracy originating in liberalism.[265] In this manner, Kelsen emphasises that the concept of democracy that he defends, is characterised by its attempt to harmonise two principles that have antagonistic origins:[266] on the one hand, democracy in its classical sense, and on the other, liberalism. Whereas democracy was initially conceived in Greek philosophy and even reflected in the French Declaration as the unlimited power of the people,[267] liberalism was subsequently defined by modern authors as the restriction of governmental power based on the individual's rights of defence.[268] However, Kelsen's intention to harmonise democracy and political freedom corresponds to the recognition that

> [i]f we define democracy as a political method by which the social order is created and applied by those subject to the order, so that political freedom, in the sense of self-determination, is secured, then democracy necessarily, always and everywhere, serves this ideal of political freedom.[269]

Hence, as Lars Vinx has argued, the Kelsenian conception of democracy assumes that the interest in freedom 'is an interest that is shared even by members of groups that are radically divided in their ideals of social justice'.[270] Accordingly, Kelsen argues that, in so far as the democratic process of social order creation is justified on the basis of the value of freedom, it will be able 'peacefully to arbitrate conflicts about justice amongst ideologically divided groups'.[271] In this manner, Kelsen justifies the objective validity of the social order, that is, the validity of the norms to be imposed on the will of the individual,[272] in the application of majority rule. This rule is the most effective method of articulating collective decision-making processes[273] while simultaneously guaranteeing the freedom of the greatest possible number of people, in so far as their will is reflected in the general will of the social order expressed in the rule.[274] Therefore, the most likely approximation of the realisation of the principle of political freedom is achieved when

[265] Kelsen, 'Foundations' (n 250) 3.

[266] ibid. For further insight into the differences between liberalism and democracy, see eg, S Lagi, *Democracy in its Essence. Hans Kelsen as a Political Thinker* (Lanham, Lexington Books, 2021) 1–15; N Bobbio, *Liberalism and Democracy*, M Ryle and K Soper trans (London, Verso, 1990 (1985).

[267] Kelsen, 'Foundations' (n 250) 3.

[268] ibid 4.

[269] ibid.

[270] Vinx (n 250) 26.

[271] ibid.

[272] eg, see Kelsen, 'Vom Wesen und Wert der Demokratie (2. Aufl. 1929)' (n 250) 158; Kelsen, 'Foundations' (n 250) 24; Kelsen, PTL2 §4(b), 8–9; RR2, 7.

[273] In his rationale for majority rule, Kelsen highlights the practical difficulties in terms of the effectiveness of decision-making mechanisms and guarantees of individual political freedom presented by collective decision-making processes based either on a qualified majority (see Kelsen, 'Vom Wesen und Wert der Demokratie (2. Aufl. 1929)' (n 250) 158; Kelsen, 'Foundations' (n 250) 24–25) or on the rule of unanimity – which was, however, proposed by Rousseau (see Kelsen, 'Vom Wesen und Wert der Demokratie (2. Aufl. 1929)' (n 250) 156–157; Kelsen, 'Foundations' (n 250) 22).

[274] Accordingly, Kelsen posits that majority rule is a reasonable consequence of the idea that individuals should be free, as long as the number of those who are not free is minimal. This is evident in Kelsen's assertion that '[o]nly the idea that – if not all – *at least as many people as possible should be free, i.e. as few people as possible should come into conflict with the general will of the social order*, leads reasonably to the majority principle' (Kelsen, 'Vom Wesen und Wert der Demokratie (2. Aufl. 1929)' (n 250) 159) (emphasis in original).

majority rule is applied on the basis of the closest possible approximation of the realisation of the principle of equality – or, in other words, when the application of majority rule is based on the condition that 'all individuals are of equal political value and everybody has the same claim to freedom, ie, the same claim that the collective will be in concordance with his individual will'.[275] Consequently, Kelsen states that a synthesis of freedom and equality lies at the very foundation of the idea of democracy.[276] Finally, as the chapters in this section demonstrate, for Kelsen, the implementation of majority rule necessitates not only the organisation of political parties, but also the constitutional guarantee of 'certain intellectual freedoms, such as freedom of conscience, freedom of press, etc'.[277] In addition, it requires respect for political minorities[278] and the principle of tolerance,[279] without which the very existence and promotion of democracy would be impossible.[280] In this manner, Kelsen offers us a description of an ideal type of government,[281] which, as Vinx argues, corresponds to

> a political system based on a universal franchise, in which general legislative decisions are taken by majority vote of the people or by majority vote of their elected representatives, that is committed to the rule of law, and that includes a written constitution protecting individual rights and rights of minority groups.[282]

The description of this ideal type of government thus corresponds to a theory the aim of which is to study the legitimacy of law from an axiological perspective, committed to the defence of the central values of political freedom and equality.[283] Thus, Kelsen's theory of democracy appears hardly compatible with his pure theory of law, for, as previously shown, Kelsen's pure theory is designed to achieve the objectivity of jurisprudence. This is achieved by avoiding any potential bias that may arise from sociological or psychological positions that employ the scientific causal method, as well as from axiologically committed positions, which Kelsen categorises under the term 'natural law'.[284] The comprehensive overview of Kelsen's intellectual legacy presented in this collection prompts us to examine the relationship between Kelsen's pure theory of law and his theory of democracy. Although the results of this examination are beyond the scope of this introductory overview, it is possible to note that an adequate response must begin by distinguishing two opposing interpretative positions.

[275] Kelsen, 'Foundations' (n 250) 25.

[276] Kelsen, 'Vom Wesen und Wert der Demokratie (2. Aufl. 1929)' (n 250) 155.

[277] Kelsen, 'Foundations' (n 250) 4.

[278] Kelsen asserts that '[i]t is significant that experience has shown that majority rule is compatible with the protection of *minorities*. The majority, by its very nature, presupposes the existence of a *minority*, and therefore the right of the majority presupposes *the right of a minority* to exist. This, however, does not imply the necessity of *protecting the minority* from the majority. Rather, it demonstrates the possibility of such *protection. This protection of the minority* is the essential function of the so-called *fundamental rights and freedoms, or human and civil rights*, which are guaranteed in all modern constitutions of parliamentary democracies' (Kelsen, 'Vom Wesen und Wert der Demokratie (2. Aufl. 1929)' (n 250) 193–94) (emphasis in original).

[279] Kelsen, 'Foundations' (n 250) 27–29.

[280] ibid 4.

[281] Vinx (n 250) 103.

[282] ibid.

[283] Dreier, 'Kelsens Demokratietheorie' (n 264) 80.

[284] See above (n 93).

The first position is that there is no inherent connection between the pure theory of law and Kelsen's theory of democracy. This stance asserts that the epistemological objectives of the former are safeguarded even if one accepts Kelsen's political writings as an account of the conditions of the normative justification of law. The formal nature resulting from the elimination of all teleological substance from the categories used by the pure theory[285] renders this theory impervious to any answer to the question of the conditions of the substantive justification of law.[286] Consequently, from the perspective of pure theory, Kelsen's theory of democracy represents a theory of the substantive justification of the law pertaining to a specific form of government, among others.[287] The study of each form of government would also offer a theory of the normative legal justification of each of them. Accordingly, the choice of democracy for Kelsen cannot be resolved entirely rationally.[288] Thus, Dreier is correct in stating that although this fact does not preclude Kelsen's aims of determining the internal functional laws of democracy, of identifying its structural elements, and of demonstrating the value premises on which it rests,[289] the very choice of political freedom as the founding value of this form of government is, to some extent, axiomatically presupposed by Kelsen in his theory.[290]

In contrast, the second of these positions asserts a necessary link between the pure theory of law and Kelsen's theory of democracy. As Vinx posits, the foundational tenets of the normativity of the law, which underpin the pure theory as a theory of law, are intelligible only when read as part of the broader politico-theoretical project aimed at developing an explanation of legal legitimacy.[291] This explanation is inextricably linked to a democratic constitution,[292] for only a democratic constitution can outline 'the institutional conditions under which the positive legality of political decisions can exercise a legitimizing force over the content of those decisions, a force strong enough to motivate

[285] The position that denies the existence of a necessary link between pure legal theory and Kelsen's theory of democracy is supported by its exegetical adequacy: see above (n 83); see Paulson, 'Der Normativismus Hans Kelsens' (n 90).

[286] On Paulson's conclusion that the substantive normativity thesis advocated by Raz is an interpretative thesis that is not adequate to the Kelsenian theory of norms, see ibid 536.

[287] Dreier, 'Kelsens Demokratietheorie' (n 264) 80. As Dreier argues, 'as much as Kelsen appears as a committed democrat and a profound theorist of democracy, Kelsen's construction of his doctrine of the state and law depends very little on the nature of the state, whether it is a democracy or a dictatorship, a monarchy or a republic. According to Kelsen, the neutral description of a positively valid law says nothing about its moral dignity or its internal responsibility towards the individual' (Dreier, 'Festvortrag "Rezeption und Rolle der Reinen Rechtslehre"' (n 33) 24).

[288] Dreier, 'Kelsens Demokratietheorie' (n 264) 80.

[289] ibid.

[290] ibid 81.

[291] Vinx (n 250) 208. Dyzenhaus must be included in the same current of thought as those who intend to understand the pure theory as nested within a broader political philosophy on the justification and proper functioning of liberal democracy (Dyzenhaus (n 243) 102–60, 104). For an interpretation of Kelsenian theory as an axiologically committed theory, see ch 15 by Antonov in this volume. The thesis of justified normativity has been defended by authors such as Robert Alexy, Carlos Santiago Nino, Joseph Raz, Alf Ross and Eugenio Bulygin: see above (n 63). For a synthesis of Raz's thesis of justified normativity and Paulson's reaction, please refer to section I on Legal Norms of this introductory overview.

[292] Vinx acknowledges that the fundamental tenet of the Kelsenian programme is the identity between law and state (see, for instance, Vinx (n 250), 208).

the adoption of the point of view of the law-abiding citizen'.[293] According to Vinx, the assertion that pure theory is not ideological can only be upheld

> once the normative aspiration to create a decent and stable society minimally dependent on myth is openly acknowledged as the motivation for the pure theory of law and once that aspiration, even though practical, is recognized as something other than the expression of a subjective will to power.[294]

The perspective offered by Monika Zalewska in chapter ten of this volume is found in the second of these two positions. According to Zalewska, unravelling the relativistic world-view and the congruent set of values underlying Kelsen's theories of norms and democracy reveals both theories to be components of the same project. As Zalewska further explains, examining the foundations of such a project requires, first, reconstructing Kelsen's theory of norms to make explicit the structural purposes that led Kelsen to formulate the theory; second, studying Kelsen's theory of democracy, the fundamental value of which is social freedom understood as political self-determination; and third, explaining the relation between the foundations common to Kelsen's theory of norms and of democracy. First, on the basis of a study of the 1934 *Reine Rechtslehre* [*Pure Theory of Law*], Zalewska argues that when Kelsen's normativism is interpreted in its historical context, the purity thesis appears not only as an epistemic strategy, but also as a political one aimed at creating a theory capable of securing the constitutional conception of the legal order in the face of the challenges posed by the emergence of totalitarian movements. This analysis explains Kelsen's underlying reasons for rejecting the doctrines of natural law and defending normativist legal positivism. According to Kelsen, normativist legal positivism, in contrast to the doctrines of natural law, by postulating validity on the basis of formal concepts, makes it possible to establish the appropriate legal institutions to end disputes and guarantee social peace by justifying the state's monopoly on force, expressed in the form of sanctions. Second, according to Zalewska, the Kelsenian theory of democracy holds that individuals, through the exercise of political self-determination, contribute to the creation of positive law and thus to the legitimacy of the coercive norms through which the state's monopoly of force is exercised. However, political self-determination alone cannot fully explain the phenomenon of democracy. The democratic regime is also based on the complementarity and limitation that the defence of equality and tolerance implies for political freedom. The democratic pillars of debate and compromise, through which the positive legal order is articulated, are based on these values. Third, according to Zalewska, relativism, peace and legality are the common foundations of Kelsen's theories of norms and democracy.

[293] ibid.

[294] Vinx identifies three distinct paradigms of legal positivism: methodological positivism, Razian positivism and political positivism (ibid 3). After ruling out the possibility of classifying the pure theory within the first two paradigms, he argues that it falls under the mantle of the third. Vinx argues that political positivism asserts that 'our understanding of legal practices shapes the nature of our law. Choices between different concepts of law that meet basic standards of descriptive adequacy are not perfectly determined by objective matters of fact beyond our control. Hence, such choices should reflect our ideal of good law. The separation of law and morality, the political positivist goes on to argue, can be defended on the ground that adopting a positivist standard of legality will have morally beneficial consequences for a society' (ibid 4).

Indeed, the denial of the existence of absolute values implies the denial of privileged access to truth. Since there is no privileged access to truth, subjects have only interests. Thus, if peace is considered the highest social value, debate and compromise will serve as methods of resolving conflicts of interest, the resolution of which will be supported by the coercive power of the state. Such coercion thus enables the coexistence of individuals who hold different views of what is just and who, by recognising and tolerating each other's views, seek to arrive at compromises for the sake of a greater good, which is only possible within the framework of the doctrine of the hierarchical structure of law, with the constitution at its apex and the constitutional court as its guardian.

In chapter eleven of this collection, Vinx suggests that as a strategy for responding to the populism that characterises the contemporary crisis of democracy, we should prioritise the distinction between the expressive and the constructive conception of the collective will – which emerged from Kelsen's contributions – over the distinction between purely electoral democracy and liberal democracy. According to Vinx, this crisis differs from previous episodes in that contemporary detractors do not express their explicit repudiation of democracy; instead, they exploit the ambiguity that results from the discourse in favour of democracy. Indeed, many contemporary subverters of democracy declare themselves to be democrats by appealing to a rhetoric that not only imposes descriptive and voluntarist demands for the identification of their sympathisers, but also characterises those who do not meet such demands as internal enemies. This rhetoric leads to the conclusion that those who espouse these views arrogate to themselves the right to be the authentic members of the political community. They thus claim to be the true representatives of the will of the people denouncing constitutional gains and their judicial protection as a triumph of an elite servicing its own hegemonic preservation. Consequently, by invoking the distinction between electoral democracy and liberal democracy, populists can always argue that either they are defenders of democracy or that constitutional gains are undemocratic because they do not align with the will of the people. Accordingly, Vinx states that to respond to contemporary populist rhetoric, it is necessary to examine Kelsen's contributions more closely. These reveal that populist rhetoric undermines the foundations of democracy by undermining the conditions through which majority rule can be translated into genuine collective self-government. For Kelsen, a social order must be objective in the sense that its demands must be enforced even on those members of the community who reject them. The justification for these demands can be found, according to Kelsen, in majority rule. Nevertheless, the application of law to minority groups does not appear to be justified by this rule. To address this concern, Vinx examines the dimensions of democratic equality as conceptualised by Kelsen, concluding that, in contrast to the expressive conception that underpins the democratic order in the absolute homogeneity of the community prior to the organised political process, Kelsen is instead sympathetic to a constructive approach to the collective will that underpins the democratic order in the relative homogeneity of the community. This approach enables the emergence of an inclusive common will that encourages the peaceful resolution of conflicts by being based on the free, fair and peaceful competition of political options. In conclusion, Vinx asserts that this constructive approach justifies the application of the law to minority groups because, in its extended temporal dimension, it provides the opportunity for these groups to become majorities through the persuasion of other members of the political community. Conversely, majority rule appears at odds with the protection of a formal constitution subject to judicial review as this can ensure the preservation of legal content that may not align with the political preferences of the majority. However, according to Kelsen such a constitutional order does not undermine majority rule if, when properly designed, it facilitates the identification of all citizens with the temporally extended collective will and protects the integrity of the democratic process.

In the final chapter of this section, Thomas Olechowski shows that juridico-historical factors were the main driving force behind the doctrinal shift in Kelsen's research on the democratisation of administration in the 1920s. According to Olechowski, by contrasting the traditional image of the principle of the separation of powers as a democratic guarantee with the doctrine of the hierarchical structure of the legal system, Kelsen and Merkl concluded that the administration, or executive, was not only at a lower level than the legislature but had a power comparable to that of the legislature, since its function was also to issue general norms. This conclusion prompted Kelsen to argue on behalf of the extension of Parliament's own democratic guarantees to the administration. However, the experience of the democratisation of the Tsarist bureaucracy, which had led to its complete fragmentation after the reform of the Soviets, led Kelsen to modify his position on the demand for the democratisation of the Austrian administration. In his 1921 article 'Demokratisierung der Verwaltung' ['Democratisation of the Administration'], Kelsen argues that the primary function of the administration is to apply the law. He further asserts that the most effective guarantee of the proper application of the law is the presence of officials who are subject to instructions and not democratically elected. According to Kelsen, the democratic principles of the whole must take precedence over those of the parts. Consequently, in the interest of preserving democratic principles, the administration should not be democratised.

IV. Kelsen's Legacy

In the German context, the theory developed by Kelsen appears to have been consistently under attack.[295] Although the reception of Kelsen's *Habilitation* work, published in 1911, reflected its independent and original character,[296] it also led to criticism from representatives of sociology of law, who perceived this work as an anaemic enterprise devoid of any contact with reality.[297] In contrast to the internationalisation of

[295] See Jestaedt, 'Hans Kelsens Reine Rechtslehre' (n 52) XII–XVIII; Dreier, 'Festvortrag "Rezeption und Rolle der Reinen Rechtslehre"' (n 33).

[296] Dreier, 'Festvortrag "Rezeption und Rolle der Reinen Rechtslehre"' (n 33) 19.

[297] E Ehrlich, *Grundlegung der Soziologie des Rechts* (Munich and Leipzig, Verlag von Duncker & Humblot, 1913) 6: archive.org/details/grundlegungderso00ehrl/page/6/mode/2up. The polemic between Eugen Ehrlich and Hans Kelsen took place through various exchanges, see: H Kelsen, 'Eine Grundlegung der Rechtssoziologie' (1914/15) 39 *Archiv für Sozialwissenschaft und Sozialpolitik* 839; HKW3 317–58); E Ehrlich, 'Entgegnung' (1916) 41 *Archiv für Sozialwissenschaft und Sozialpolitik* 844; H Kelsen, 'Replik' (1916) 41 *Archiv für Sozialwissenschaft und Sozialpolitik* 850; E Ehrlich, 'Replik' (1916/17) 42 *Archiv für Sozialwissenschaft und Sozialpolitik* 609; H Kelsen 'Schlußwort' (1916/17) 42 *Archiv für Sozialwissenschaft und Sozialpolitik* 611 (HKW3, 613–14). For further details on the controversy, see S Baer, *Rechtsssoziologie. Eine Einführung in die interdisziplinäre Rechtsforschung*, 4th edn (Baden-Baden, Nomos, 2021) 38–39. For a detailed account of the controversies between Kelsen and representatives of legal sociology, see SL Paulson, *Hans Kelsen und die*

the Vienna School of Legal Theory[298] and the growing influence of the pure theory of law in various parts of the world,[299] Kelsen's fame as a constitutionalist in the German sphere was accompanied by debates surrounding the interpretation and understanding of the first German democratic Constitution.[300] As Dreier has noted, during the era of National Socialism, the mere mention of Kelsen's Jewish heritage was frequently sufficient to discredit his theory,[301] which was also described as destructive and nihilistic.[302] Following the Second World War, the resurgence of rehabilitative currents of natural law led to a backlash against positivist legal theories, including the pure theory of law.[303] Furthermore, the reception of this theory also suffered the consequences of the attacks on some positions defended by Kelsen.[304] Only time seems to have allowed prejudices to be overcome, paving the way for a quiet growth of interest in Kelsen's legacy, to which this volume bears witness.

The final section of this book addresses the reception of Kelsen's theory in terms of its influence not only on the development of the Vienna School of Legal Theory, but also on the development of the case law and jurisprudence of non-European states. To analyse this latter influence, this collection has considered two examples seldom dealt with in Kelsenian scholarship. The first concerns the analysis of a case involving the use of the interpretation of Kelsen's norm theory in postcolonial jurisdictions belonging to the former British Empire. The second concerns the analysis of the reception of the Kelsenian theory by its opponents in the Soviet state.

In the initial chapter of this section, Rodrigo Cadore states that, although Kelsen is undoubtedly the driving force behind the Vienna School of Legal Theory, his prominence has overshadowed the broader theoretical potential of the School, limiting it to the 'Kelsenian' variant of the pure theory of law. To give expression to this potential, Cadore proposes that the pure theory should be regarded as the product of a collective scholarly enterprise. To demonstrate this, Cadore examines the evolution of the theory since the late 1910s, highlighting how it emerged from the initial inspiration provided by Kelsen's 1911 *Habilitation* thesis as a metatheory of legal knowledge. The insights of this metatheory were shaped by a set of theses about the structure of statically observed positive legal norms. Consequently, the creation, application

Rechtssoziologie: Auseinandersetzung mit Hermann U. Kantorowicz, Eugen Ehrlich und Max Weber (Aalen, Scientia-Verlag, 1992).

[298] See above (n 55) and (n 56).

[299] See above (n 44).

[300] See above (n 230).

[301] Dreier, 'Festvortrag "Rezeption und Rolle der Reinen Rechtslehre"' (n 33) 26.

[302] K Larenz, *Rechts- und Staatsphilosophie der Gegenwart*, 2nd edn (Berlin, Junker und Dünnhaupt Verlag, 1935) 49.

[303] Dreier, 'Festvortrag "Rezeption und Rolle der Reinen Rechtslehre"' (n 33) 29–30.

[304] As Dreier reports ('Festvortrag "Rezeption und Rolle der Reinen Rechtslehre"' (n 33) 27–29), Kelsen's involvement as legal adviser to the US War Department in the preparation of the Nuremberg Trials, see above (n 21), as well as the defence of his thesis on the 'international legal status of Germany to be established immediately after the end of the war' (H Kelsen, 'The Legal Status of Germany according to the Declaration of Berlin' (1945) 39 *American Journal of International Law* 518), which was part of his 1944 opinion on the 'Present Status and Re-establishment as an Independent State of Austria', see above (n 18), could cause suspicions. In particular, in this last opinion, Kelsen defended a thesis grounded in the concept of *debellatio*. Based on this thesis, Kelsen concluded that the unconditional surrender of the German *Wehrmacht* should result in the disappearance of the German state (Dreier, 'Festvortrag "Rezeption und Rolle der Reinen Rechtslehre"' (n 33) 27). (On the *debellatio* thesis and Kelsen's opinion, see Olechowski, *Hans Kelsen* (n 1) 735–39.)

and derogation of law were perceived as meta-legal phenomena that exist outside the realm of jurisprudence. As an expression of the cultural avant-gardism of Viennese modernism, the Vienna School of Legal Theory emerged from the private seminar organised by Kelsen at the beginning of 1914. The seminar served as the foundation for the formation of a network of researchers, who collectively refined the theoretical framework to the point of establishing it as an academic enterprise. As part of the network of Viennese cultural circles, the School founded by Kelsen benefited from the transfer of knowledge that occurred between groups from different disciplines and backgrounds. Moreover, the School exerted considerable influence on academies in Central Europe beyond the University of Vienna, particularly the Brno School of Legal Theory. In the second part of his chapter, Cadore discusses the common research programme developed by the Vienna School of Legal Theory, outlining the core elements that were shared by its different members and that characterised their unique approach to legal science. The pure theory of law offers both an epistemic model and a metatheory, of how legal theory and doctrine should be structured. Regarding the epistemic model, it seeks to establish an autonomous jurisprudence that deals with legal processes and examines their inner workings. In this manner, pure theory endeavours to both describe the normative practice of legal authorities and formulate appropriate categories for its description from an internal perspective. This endeavour is intended to demythologise legal thought. Regarding legal theory, the School's debates led to the definition of law as a coercive and generally effective normative order of human behaviour, as well as to the dynamic conception of law. The explanatory potential of pure theory was then found in the particular ways in which law normatively seeks to regulate its own reproduction. Consequently, pure theory posits that the creation, application and derogation of law are also subject to legal norms and thus also the subject matter of jurisprudence. Consequently, law is regarded as a social normative process that is perpetually undergoing restructuring as a result of an uninterrupted series of self-referential operations. The model of the pure theory of law is thus predicated on the centrality of the figure of the competent organs in charge of legal decisions. The moments of cognition and decision, of definiteness and indeterminacy, of bindingness and discretion, are present in all normative operations of law. Although the scope of the limits of decision-making powers is always indeterminate, the allocation and limitation of these powers result in law presenting itself as an order of power and violence. Cadore states that the Vienna School of Legal Theory was essential for the development of a theory of the dynamics inherent in positive law. Consequently, although the Vienna School was, to a significant extent, the work and legacy of Kelsen, the absence of the Vienna School would have resulted in the absence of the pure theory of law.

In chapter fourteen of this volume, Asya Ostroukh analyses the Grenada High Court's attempt to apply Kelsen's theory of revolutionary legality in the 1985 *Mitchell* case (*Andy Mitchell et al v Attorney General and Director of Public Prosecutions*). This case forms part of a body of decisions that collectively constitute a form of transnational case law from various postcolonial jurisdictions on the validity of revolutionary regimes that were established during the decolonisation movements in the former British Empire throughout the twentieth century. According to Ostroukh, the very name 'Kelsen's theory of revolutionary legality' gained its worldwide popularity due to the writings of the famous Caribbean legal philosopher of the natural law school, Simeon McIntosh. McIntosh's interpretation of Kelsenian theory addresses the problem of the creation of new legal orders by means not provided for in existing constitutions. From this perspective, Kelsen's theory of revolutionary legality establishes a connection between the validity of a legal order and its effectiveness. This connection is created by emphasising that, as a legal order is considered valid if its norms are generally effective, a legal order as a whole, and an individual legal norm, can no longer be considered valid when they cease to be effective. This theory, in conjunction with the doctrine of (public) necessity, are the legal strategies most commonly employed by postcolonial common law jurisdictions to justify the establishment of new political regimes, and the Commonwealth Caribbean country of Grenada is no exception. In accordance with the doctrine of necessity, that competes with Kelsen's theory in judicial reasoning, courts may validate unconstitutional acts of the state when extraordinary circumstances and the good of society that this state promotes overweigh the negative consequences of such unconstitutional acts. In the 1985 *Mitchell* case, the High Court of Grenada had to consider both theories, trying the 1984 assassination of the prime minister and other ministers, committed in the aftermath of a 'palace coup' that overthrew the People's Revolutionary Government (PRG). The appeal filed by the accused before the High Court was unsuccessful. Although the trial judge employed the rhetoric that ostensibly applied Kelsenian theory, he nevertheless used the doctrine of necessity to justify the establishment of the High Court by the PRG, which was in power from 1979 to 1983, and its retention by the Governor General, who was exercising full power in the country after the US intervention in the island in 1983. Similarly, the Court of Appeal judges ruled that Kelsen's theory of revolutionary legality had only non-binding authority in Grenada and refused to apply it to validate the PRG regime on the grounds that there was insufficient evidence that the revolutionary government had become a *de jure* government in the Kelsenian sense. Thus, the Court of Appeal based its decision exclusively on the doctrine of necessity. It was recognised that the West Indies Associated Supreme Court was no longer operational in Grenada following the 1979 revolution. Consequently, the PRG was compelled to establish its own judicial system to address public necessity. McIntosh provided a comprehensive analysis of the *Mitchell* case, identifying the circularity of the reasoning employed by the courts. McIntosh's position is that a court cannot determine the legitimacy of a new political regime because in such a case the court serves as an instrument of that regime and cannot validate itself in a legal sense. Furthermore, McIntosh criticised the application of the doctrine of necessity, arguing that it can only be applied in a situation of continuity of a legal regime and not in situations of rupture. Finally, although McIntosh based his own reasoning on Kelsen's theory (or rather its interpretation provided by common law courts and legal philosophers), he criticised its merely formal conception of validity, which leads to the consideration of any effective regime as legal and, by implication, legitimate. In addition to its efficacy, McIntosh asserts that a legal order must also be morally justified to be considered legitimate. Such addition of a moral justification criterion (as expressed in Acquinas' and Fuller's jurisprudence) to Kelsen's formal test of validity, according to Ostroukh, constitutes the most important contribution that McIntosh made to Kelsenian studies in postcolonial common law jurisdictions.

In the concluding chapter of this collection, Mikhail Antonov seeks to elucidate the reasons that led Kelsen to publish *The Communist Theory of Law* in 1955[305] and the reasons for the reaction of his Soviet opponents to the pure theory of law. Antonov's account indicates that both Kelsen and his Soviet opponents shared a common aim of achieving scientific objectivity, understood as axiological neutrality, in their positivist methodological approach to law, as evidenced by their critique of the schemas of traditional jurisprudence. Indeed, both Kelsen and his Soviet opponents were engaged in denying the existence of an ideal source of legal validity beyond positive norms. Their endeavours culminated in the use of the term 'ideology' to signify the set of biases that impede the realisation of scientific objectivity as the epistemic ideal that should guide jurisprudence. However, it was precisely their common approach to law that led to their mutual disqualification which was aimed at proving the axiologically compromised character of their counterpart's research. Kelsen denounced Marx's way of pursuing objectivity as an exercise in the self-projection of his own ideology and in his 1923 text Kelsen accused Marx's Soviet followers of ideological blindness and political servility.[306] In Kelsen's view, Soviet legal theory was merely a form of natural law that posited the realisation of a utopian society emerging from the class struggle and was based on the idea of a just order inherent in social reality. In response, the Soviet theorists of the 1920s and 1930s made every effort to demonstrate the bias of their bourgeois opponents. In particular, the Soviet authors had good reasons to accuse Kelsen of having elaborated a theory that sought not only to reduce legal analysis to mere form, but also to conceal under the cloak of a supposed science his real ideological preferences for the bourgeois values of democracy and liberalism. In this perspective, as even non-Soviet authors subsequently argued, Kelsen's theory corresponded to a disguised doctrine of natural law as it could only be vindicated on the basis of justified normativity. By equating legal positivism with the pursuit of axiological neutrality as the ideal of jurisprudence, Kelsen and his Soviet opponents were led down a cul-de-sac by accusing each other of promoting some form of natural law. Each side could demonstrate the unscientific character of their counterpart's theory, but only at the cost of concealing the bias of their own theory. Nevertheless, theoretical reasons only partially explain the reaction of Kelsen and his Soviet opponents. Antonov reminds us that the availability of sources, linguistic issues and political vulnerability were also significant factors in their dispute. On the one hand, Soviet critics had no direct access to Kelsen's works, but only to Pashukanis' reception of them in the 1920s. It was only from the 1950s and 1960s onwards that Soviet critics had access to recent texts of Kelsenian theory. However, such access was limited as there were few translated texts and few scholars remained who could read them in their original language. Conversely, the political persecution experienced during the McCarthy era may have prompted Kelsen to publish the 1955 text as a means of demonstrating his distance from his Austro-Marxist past. The eagerness to publish his text may be taken as an explanation for the carelessness of the details and sources used, as well as the superficiality of the analysis, which is atypical for his research.

[305] H Kelsen, *The Communist Theory of Law* (London, Stevens & Sons Ltd, 1955).

[306] H Kelsen, *Sozialismus und Staat. Eine Untersuchung der politischen Theorie des Marxismus*, 2nd edn (Leipzig, CL Hirschfeld, 1923).

PART I

Legal Norms

2

On Eugenio Bulygin's Kelsen*

STANLEY L PAULSON**

I. Introduction

Admirers of Eugenio Bulygin are inspired not only by his philosophical prowess but by a *joie de vivre* unique to him. Since the best form of admiration that can be accorded to a philosopher is serious criticism, I examine here, inter alia, certain claims of Bulygin's in one of his richest and most provocative statements on Hans Kelsen's legal theory, 'An Antinomy in Kelsen's Pure Theory of Law' (1990).[1] Bulygin writes that there are, in effect, two Kelsens, the Kantian Kelsen and the positivistic Kelsen:

> [W]e find in Kelsen's thought two groups of ideas that stem from quite different philosophical traditions. These ideas are not only difficult to reconcile but indeed are radically incompatible as I shall try to show in some detail. Both the Kantian and the positivistic persuasions are vividly present in Kelsen's works, and some of his main tenets can be traced back to these two greatly opposed philosophical traditions. Being incompatible, some of his ideas stemming from one of these traditions must be eliminated in order to render the Pure Theory of Law coherent.[2]

Several of Bulygin's motifs presuppose his periodisation of the phases of development in Kelsen's legal theory. With this in mind, I offer, in the first section of the

* Reprinted from JA Rábanos, GB Ratti and MC Redondo (eds), *Eugenio Bulygin en la Teoría del Derecho contemporánea*, Vol II (Madrid, Marcial Pons, 2022) 431–48, with the kind permission of the editors and the publisher.

** My thanks to another admirer of Eugenio Bulygin, Bonnie Litschewski Paulson, for, as always, discerning advice on matters of content and style, and to still another admirer, Pierluigi Chiassoni, for welcome comments. My thanks, too, to Gonzalo Villa-Rosas for kindly taking the initiative in having the essay reprinted.

[1] Bulygin's paper 'An Antinomy in Kelsen's Pure Theory of Law' (1990) first appeared in 3 *Ratio Juris* 29 and has been anthologised several times – first in SL Paulson and B Litschewski Paulson (eds), *Normativity and Norms. Critical Perspectives on Kelsenian Themes* (Oxford, Clarendon Press, 1998) 297–315, and more recently in E Bulygin, *Essays in Legal Philosophy*, C Bernal, C Huerta, T Mazzarese, JJ Moreso, PE Navarro and SL Paulson (eds) (Oxford, Oxford University Press, 2015) 234–51. Certain views of Bulygin's in his paper of 1990 are corrected in Bulygin 2015, see below (n 18). Citations to Bulygin's 'Antinomy' paper are to the reprinting of 2015.

[2] Bulygin, 'An Antinomy in Kelsen's Pure Theory of Law' (n 1) 236.

chapter, a sketch of my own periodisation, useful as a focal point in my criticism of aspects of Bulygin's periodisation.

Following the sketch of my own periodisation of Kelsen's phases of development, I turn, in the second section of the chapter, to some of the issues that arise in Bulygin's periodisation. He addresses both of the philosophical traditions that he finds in Kelsen's work, the Kantian and the positivistic, identifying and analysing various theses. The yield is instructive. Noteworthy on legal validity, for example, is Bulygin's sharp distinction between binding force and membership, along with his tidy characterisation of membership in terms of a recursive definition that dispenses with any need for Kelsen's notorious basic norm.[3]

Still, there is a fly in the ointment. In his periodisation, Bulygin employs as one of his criteria the idea that 'the Kantian and the positivistic elements coexist more or less harmoniously' during 'the first period' of Kelsen's legal theory, which, according to Bulygin, runs from 1911 to 1940.[4] But at both ends of Bulygin's temporal spectrum, this claim of his is mistaken. I return to the point below.

The first and second sections of the chapter, devoted to the periodisation of Kelsen's legal theory, are followed by two sections on aspects of Kelsen's *norm theory*. In the third section, I turn to a compressed statement of Kelsen's phases of development in norm theory. In the fourth section, I turn to Kelsen's *Spätlehre* or late theory, where Bulygin's rewarding paper 'On the Problem of the Applicability of Logic to the Law' (1983) plays a key role. So far as I can tell, the paper remains largely unknown, having appeared in German in a *Festschrift* for Bulygin's colleague and friend, Ulrich Klug. In the paper, Bulygin comments on Kelsen's work on norm theory during the last decade in Kelsen's career.

II. A Periodisation of the Phases of Development in Kelsen's Legal Theory

The outlines of my own periodisation can be summarised in terms of three phases: the constructivist phase (1911–19), including a transition period from 1914 to 1919; then the lengthy, classical phase (1920–60); and finally, the late phase or late theory, known in the literature as the *Spätlehre* (1960–71).[5]

'Construction' in the European jurisprudential literature of the nineteenth century refers to concept formation, a prominent motif in Kelsen's *Main Problems in the Theory*

[3] See ibid 243–46. Thanks to María Cristina Redondo, we now have a comprehensive statement on Bulygin's work on legal validity. MC Redondo, 'Bulygin's Analytical Legal Positivism' in P Mindus and T Spaak (eds), *Cambridge Companion to Legal Positivism* (Cambridge, Cambridge University Press, 2021) 371–93, 384–87.

[4] See Bulygin, 'An Antinomy in Kelsen's Pure Theory of Law' (n 1) 236.

[5] Hans Kelsen died on 19 April 1973. Kelsen's younger daughter, Maria Feder, who saw her father on virtually a daily basis during the last 20 years of his life, informed Bonnie and me during one of our visits with her in Kensington, California, that her father was not engaged in research or writing during the last 18 months of his life. For details on the last years of Kelsen's life, see T Olechowski, *Hans Kelsen. Biographie eines Rechtswissenschaftlers* (Tübingen, Mohr Siebeck, 2020) 910–17.

of Public Law (1911).[6] Kelsen makes a sustained effort in the treatise to provide new constructions of what are in part familiar legal doctrines, speaking, for example, of criminal liability as 'clearly [a] construction from a specifically *normative* point of view'.[7] Kelsen's constructions are new, for, as he argues, they do not turn on an appeal to psychologism or naturalism, the characteristic appeal of his predecessors in the nineteenth-century German *Staatsrechtslehre* or theory of public law. In *Main Problems* (1911) and in the major papers that Kelsen publishes shortly thereafter, no juridico-philosophical focus, *sensu stricto*, is to be found at all, as Gabriel Nogueira Dias makes clear in his outstanding treatise on Kelsen.[8] What is more, Kelsen is arguing in *Main Problems* that it would be folly to search for a grounding of the law, the very idea that emerges later as Kelsen's basic norm with its ostensibly juridico-philosophical grounding function.

In what I am calling the transition period of the constructivist phase, Kelsen raises the question of support for his constructions. How, without either psychologism or naturalism, can they be supported? Kelsen's answer is found in his effort to arrive at philosophical support for his constructions, specifically, Kantian support. The first textual evidence pointing to this quest of Kelsen's is found in the Foreword to *The Problem of Sovereignty*, published in 1920. There he announces his programme, a *pure* theory of law, and he refers to neo-Kantian philosophers with an eye to undergirding the programme.[9] This development has me designating 1920 as marking a point of departure and the period from 1920 to 1927 as marking the beginnings of the classical phase.

Then, starting with Kelsen's monograph of 1928, *The Philosophical Foundations of Natural Law Theory and Legal Positivism*, and running all the way up to and including the second edition of *Pure Theory of Law* in 1960, the Kantian dimension of Kelsen's legal theory is more or less explicit, notwithstanding the great variations in emphasis. This classical phase looms large in my periodisation.

In 1960 and the years immediately thereafter, Kelsen throws overboard the greater pure theory of law. He begins anew at this stage, and the result is the late theory or *Spätlehre*. In the last decade of his long life, Kelsen is endorsing what might be termed a species of legal empiricism.[10]

With this framework in mind, I turn to Bulygin's periodisation.

[6] H Kelsen, *Hauptprobleme der Staatsrechtslehre* (Tübingen, JCB Mohr, 1911) repr M Jestaedt (ed), *Hans Kelsen Werke* Vol 2 (hereafter: HKW, with volume number) (Tübingen, Mohr Siebeck, 2008) 49–878.

[7] Kelsen, *Hauptprobleme* (n 6) 142; HKW2, 249.

[8] See G Nogueira Dias, *Rechtspositivismus und Rechtstheorie. Das Verhältnis beider im Werke Hans Kelsens* (Tübingen, Mohr Siebeck, 2005) 148–50, 154, *et passim*.

[9] In the Foreword to Hans Kelsen, *Das Problem der Souveränität und die Theorie des Völkerrechts. Beitrag zu einer Reinen Rechtslehre* (Tübingen, JCB Mohr 1920) iii, vi, repr HKW4, 265, 267, Kelsen refers to Paul Natorp and Rudolf Stammler, both prominent neo-Kantians. Bulygin is entirely correct, however, in pointing to Kant as the philosophical source of some of Kelsen's ideas. Notwithstanding occasional references to the neo-Kantians, Kelsen did not in the main explore their writings.

[10] A species of legal empiricism is evident in Kelsen's first, albeit short-lived abandonment of the pure theory of law, 1939–40, with some indications of the dramatic shift coming earlier. Kelsen dismisses Kant *expressis verbis* and defends an empiricist view, accompanied by accolades for David Hume. The old regime was restored no later than 1941. See SL Paulson, 'Metamorphosis in Hans Kelsen's Legal Philosophy' (2017) 80 *Modern Law Review* 860, 885–92.

III. Aspects of Bulygin's Periodisation of Kelsen's Phases of Development

As noted in my introductory remarks, a major problem that I see in Bulygin's periodisation pertains to what he terms the first period, beginning in 1911 and running up to 1940. Bulygin claims that in this first period, 'the Kantian and the positivistic elements coexist more or less harmoniously'.[11] This claim of Bulygin's comes as a surprise, for in *Main Problems* (1911), Kelsen's major treatise at the beginning of the first period, there is no Kantian element at all. In *Main Problems*, Kelsen distinguishes carefully between formal and material questions, arguing that material questions, which reach both to explanatory and to *begründende* or Kantian issues – ie, issues that speak to the grounding of the law – play no role whatever in his legal theory. Legal science, he says, is concerned solely with formal questions,[12] many of which turn on enquiries into the nature of the legal norm.

Kelsen makes this point emphatically, contending that to ask why the legal norm *ought* to be complied with and applied is nonsense:

> Intrinsic to the concept of the legal norm … is that the legal norm *ought* to be complied with and applied. The idea of the legal norm qua 'norm' already contains this qualification that a norm *ought* to be complied with and applied, so that the question of why ought a norm be complied with would be tantamount to asking, say, why ought a norm that ought to be complied with be complied with.[13]

Having expressly precluded *begründende* issues, Kelsen has no occasion to draw on a Kantian element to undergird his legal theory. The search for such an undergirding is folly. It is precisely what Kelsen, in *Main Problems*, rejects.

Then, as I point out in the sketch of my own periodisation, Kelsen changes his mind. During the transition period (1914–19), he concludes that the enquiry into reasons for grounding the law may indeed be seen as posing what he calls a formal question, leading, then, to the basic norm and its Kantian support. These developments mark the beginnings of Kelsen's classical phase, running from 1920 up to 1960.

In summary, Bulygin errs when he claims that in what he is calling the first period, running from 1911 to 1940, 'the Kantian and the positivistic elements coexist more or less harmoniously.' The coexistence of these elements begins no earlier than 1920.

What is more, there is no good reason for Bulygin to terminate his first period with the year 1940. Why not go right up to the second edition of *Pure Theory of Law* in 1960? As I understand Bulygin, the only reason he has for terminating the long phase with the year 1940 is Kelsen's introduction (actually in 1941) of legal sentences (*Rechtssätze*) as a doctrinal notion to be sharply distinguished from legal norms (*Rechtsnormen*).[14] Legal

[11] See Bulygin, 'An Antinomy in Kelsen's Pure Theory of Law' (n 1) 236.

[12] See Kelsen, *Hauptprobleme* (n 6) 353; HKW2, 482.

[13] Kelsen, *Hauptprobleme* (n 6) 352; HKW2, 481.

[14] For the initial introduction of *Rechtssätze*, see H Kelsen, 'The Pure Theory of Law and Analytical Jurisprudence' (1941) 55 *Harvard Law Review* 44, 51. On *Rechtssätze* and *Rechtsnormen*, see the discussion in R Guastini, '"Sollsätze". An Exercise in Hard Legal Positivism' in P Chiassoni (ed), *The Legal Ought* (Torino, G Giappichelli Editore, 2001) 103–16.

sentences, according to Bulygin, serve to introduce legal science as an entirely descriptive enterprise, ostensibly displacing Kelsen's earlier view of a normative legal science. A central idea of Kelsen's earlier view, on Bulygin's interpretation, is the 'creation' of legal norms by legal science.[15] As Bulygin writes, it is only by means of legal science 'that certain acts, like those of the legislator, become law-creating acts and give rise to legal norms. This is why legal science is a normative science'.[16]

Bulygin claims that normative legal science, with its creative dimension, is characteristic of the *early* Kelsen. But this very dimension is especially conspicuous in Kelsen's later work, in particular, in the treatise of 1960, the second edition of *Pure Theory of Law*:

> It is ... correct that, in the sense of the Kantian theory of knowledge, legal science as cognition of the law is – as all cognition is – constitutive in character, therefore 'creating' its object in comprehending it as a meaningful whole. Just as the chaos of sensory perception first becomes a cosmos, that is, nature as a unified system, by means of the ordering cognition of science, so it is that the wealth of general and individual legal norms issued by legal organs – the material given to legal science – first becomes a unified system by means of the cognition of legal science, a system free from contradiction, that is, a legal order. This 'creation', however, is purely epistemological in character. It is altogether different from the creation of objects by means of human labour or the creation of the law by means of the legal authority.[17]

In a word, there is no basis for Bulygin's claim that Kelsen's Kantianism is characteristic solely of the 'early Kelsen'.

To be sure, in a later paper, 'Kelsen on the Completeness and Consistency of Law' (2013), Bulygin takes a different stance on some aspects of his periodisation. He still maintains that 'the first "period" of [Kelsen's] work' terminates in 1940,[18] but he is now contending that a 'second "Kantian" stage of Kelsen's development ... runs until 1960'.[19] Bulygin quotes from the second edition of *Pure Theory of Law*,[20] and then, in what he goes on to write, he includes a quotation from Kelsen's *Spätlehre*:

> In spite of the odd Kantian passage, then, we can say that with the publication of the second edition of the Reine Rechtslehre Kelsen rejects his earlier thesis that legal norms are the epistemological 'creation' of legal science. Indeed he comes to recognize that 'the science of law is just as incompetent to solve by interpretation existing conflicts between norms, or better, to repeal the validity of positive norms, as it is incompetent to issue legal norms'.[21]

[15] For a somewhat different view of the import of normative legal science, see R Guastini, 'Normativism or the Normative Theory of Legal Science: Some Epistemological Problems' in SL Paulson and B Litschewski Paulson (eds), *Normativity and Norms* (Oxford, Clarendon Press, 1998) 317–30.

[16] Bulygin, 'An Antinomy in Kelsen's Pure Theory of Law' (n 1) 242.

[17] H Kelsen, *Reine Rechtslehre*, 2nd edn (Vienna, Franz Deuticke, 1960) § 16, 74–75.

[18] E Bulygin, 'Kelsen on the Completeness and Consistency of Law' in E Bulygin, *Essays in Legal Philosophy*, C Bernal, C Huerta, T Mazzarese, JJ Moreso, PE Navarro and SL Paulson (eds) (Oxford, Oxford University Press, 2015) 337–53, 338.

[19] ibid 339.

[20] A directly comparable text appears in H Kelsen, *Théorie pure du droit. Introduction a la science du droit*, H Thévenaz trans (Boudry-Neuchâtel, Éditions de la Baconnière, 1953) 53–54.

[21] Bulygin, 'Kelsen on the Completeness and Consistency of Law' (n 18) 343, quoting H Kelsen, 'Derogation' in RA Newman (ed), *Essays in Jurisprudence in Honor of Roscoe Pound* (Indianapolis, Bobbs-Merrill, 1962) 339–55, 355.

Here, according to Bulygin, Kelsen 'rejects his earlier thesis that *legal norms* are the epistemological "creation" of legal science'. But Bulygin's interpretation cannot be squared with what Kelsen actually writes in the second edition of *Pure Theory of Law*, where he endorses both the Kantian notion of cognition as constitutive and the ordinary creation of the law by legal authorities.[22] Only by attributing to Kelsen's earlier work a view that Kelsen first endorses in his *Spätlehre* is Bulygin able to proceed as though the Kantian notion of cognition as constitutive were not a proper part of the second edition of *Pure Theory of Law*. What Bulygin refers to as an 'odd Kantian passage' (see footnote 21) is in fact an integral part of Kelsen's lengthy classical phase, running up to and including the second edition of *Pure Theory of Law*.

IV. Kelsen's Phases of Development in Norm Theory

The earliest development in Kelsen's norm theory goes back to his first major treatise in legal theory, *Main Problems in the Theory of Public Law* (1911).[23] Here Kelsen dismisses the familiar imperative and goes to considerable lengths to establish the sanction-norm in its peculiarly Kelsenian form as the sole norm-type. A second development comes in the mid-1920s, to wit: Kelsen's adoption of Adolf Julius Merkl's *Stufenbau*, the legal system as hierarchical construction. This development is portentous in that it invites Kelsen's attention to the central role of *empowerment* in norm theory. A third development is Kelsen's drastic shift in the 1930s, his introduction of empowerment as the fundamental modality of the sanction-norm. The fourth and last development takes place during the 1950s, the last decade of Kelsen's work before the *Spätlehre*, and comes in two very different rounds. One of these is what I am calling Kelsen's composite norm theory, with the basic distinctions captured by what he terms *dependent legal norms* (positive permissions, empowerments of norm issuance, and commands); *independent legal norms* (with a generic 'ought' embedded in the sanction-norm); and finally, *complete legal norms* (including the highest-level empowerments of norm issuance and, at the ground level, the independent legal norm). The greater scheme reflects the pattern of the *Stufenbau*, albeit in miniature. The other round in the fourth development is Kelsen's well-known work on conflicts between legal norms. Thanks to a good bit of pulling and hauling on this front, including questions about the applicability of logic to the law,[24] Kelsen, as noted above, is led to throw overboard the entire pure theory of law, supplanting it with the *Spätlehre*.

Here, in this section on Kelsen's norm theory, I turn to a handful of details from the first three developments and from one of the rounds that make up the fourth development. In my final section, I return to the other round, with special attention to Bulygin's commentary on aspects of Kelsen's *Spätlehre*.

[22] As I have written elsewhere, cognition as constitutive reflects the ideal dimension of the law in Kelsen's legal theory, whereas ordinary lawmaking by legal authorities – legislators and the like – reflects the empirical dimension of the law.

[23] Kelsen, *Hauptprobleme* (n 6).

[24] On the issues that arise here, see generally, PE Navarro and JL Rodríguez, *Deontic Logic and Legal Systems* (Cambridge, Cambridge University Press, 2014); Bulygin, *Essays in Legal Philosophy* (n 1).

A. The First Development: Kelsen's Sole Norm-Type

In *Main Problems*, Kelsen, looking to the nineteenth-century tradition in legal theory, assumes that there are two norm-types in play, which are together exhaustive of the possibilities, *tertium non datur*. The *sanction-norm* directs officials to carry out sanctions, and the *imperative* imposes obligations on legal subjects. Kelsen's argument is clear: if the imperative can be eliminated as untenable, what remains is the sanction-norm as the sole norm-type.

Kelsen proceeds by taking aim at the well-known imperative theory of Karl Binding (1841–1920), which Binding had developed for the criminal law.[25] Binding's position, a reflection of the nineteenth-century imperative theory of law, comprises the traditional two norm-types, the first of which is indistinguishable from Kelsen's own sanction-norm in *Main Problems*. Kelsen says as much in a statement summarising Binding's position:

> It is well known that the core of Binding's theory is the distinction between the criminal law norm (*Strafrechtssatz*) and what Binding terms, by way of contrast, the 'norm'. Binding's criminal law norm has the very form that, according to the view I have presented here, is essential to the [sanction-]norm; it is a hypothetical judgment about … the will of the state, indeed – since Binding is focused only on the criminal law – the will of the state … to punish. Binding believes, however, that, alongside this norm of the criminal law, a second legal norm must be assumed. It is the 'imperative' or the 'you ought …', requiring the subject to behave in accordance with the law. Binding dubs this the 'norm'.[26]

Kelsen's arguments on behalf of the sanction-norm *qua* sole norm-type are, without exception, unpersuasive,[27] but my present concern is simply to set out his position.

B. The Second Development: The *Stufenbau* (ca 1925)

In Kelsen's early treatise, *Main Problems* (1911), he is wedded – quite apart from his work here on norm theory – to a doctrine known as statutory legal positivism, according to which the statute is the only type of law. To interpret the doctrine literally would of course be absurd. Still, in fin-de-siècle public law theory in the German-speaking countries and elsewhere in Europe, statutory legal positivism shaped the conception of the law, and Kelsen's conception follows suit.

[25] K Binding, *Die Normen und ihre Übertretung*, Vol 1, 2nd edn (Leipzig, Wilhelm Engelmann, 1890).

[26] Kelsen, *Hauptprobleme* (n 6) 270–71; HKW2, 390, quoting from Binding, *Die Normen und ihre Übertretung* (n 25) §1 (7).

[27] eg, there is the 'argument from "choice"'. Binding (n 25) § 6 (37) distinguishes (1) 'You ought not to kill!' from (2) 'You ought not to kill on pain of punishment', and argues that to recognise (2) would be tantamount to giving the legal subject a choice, thereby undermining the import of the command. Kelsen contends that the possibility of choice can never be withdrawn from the subject: '[Binding's] argument is rendered untenable by the knowledge that no command of whatever type can absolutely deprive someone of the possibility of a choice' (Kelsen, *Hauptprobleme* (n 6) 277; HKW2, 397). Here Kelsen confuses law and fact. That the commandee will as a matter of fact always have a choice does not, from Kelsen's own standpoint, bear on the question of law.

In the mid-1920s, Kelsen is emancipated from statutory legal positivism by his adoption of Adolf Julius Merkl's *Stufenbau* doctrine.[28] The doctrine served to relativise the difference between law creation and law application and thereby to relativise the standing of the different types of law – constitutional law, statutory law, administrative law, and the like. Legislation, the standard-bearer of public law theory in Europe at the turn of the century, loses its privileged position, and statutory legal positivism loses whatever standing it may have had.

What is more, the significance of the *Stufenbau* doctrine for Kelsen's norm theory can scarcely be overestimated. In his early treatise, *Main Problems* (1911), Kelsen offers a tidy formulation of his overriding thesis, namely, that '[t]he question of whether the legal norm is to be understood as an imperative or as a hypothetical judgment is the question of the *ideal* linguistic form of the legal norm'.[29] Precisely the view that Kelsen takes up here in his reply to Binding has him theorising about the form of the legal norm *sans* any reference to the legal system.

But Kelsen's adoption of the *Stufenbau* in the mid-1920s stands his original view on its head. Alfred Verdross, Kelsen's colleague in the Vienna School of Legal Theory, gives expression to the significance of this development, noting that the legal system, the *Stufenbau*, serves as the basis for determining the form of the legal norm.[30] Legal powers – empowering norms – are now front and centre. Verdross's point is correct and serves to underscore the significance of Kelsen's shift. With the adoption of the *Stufenbau*, Kelsen is no longer theorising about the form of the legal norm in isolation from the legal system. On the contrary, he comes to appreciate the import of empowering norms.

C. The Third Development: Empowerment *qua* Modality of the Sanction-Norm (Mid-1930s)

This major development of the 1930s has Kelsen shifting to the modality of empowerment vis-à-vis the sanction-norm. In a lengthy paper,[31] he argues that the sanction-norm is now to be understood not as a hypothetically formulated *obligation* but as an *empowerment*, with obligation relegated to the status of a derivative concept.

To appreciate the significance of the shift, we have to return to the first development, where, as I noted, Kelsen eliminates the imperative addressed to the legal subject, arguing that the sanction-norm is the sole norm-type. He appears to suppose, at least for

[28] H Kelsen, 'Die Lehre von den drei Gewalten oder Funktionen des Staates' (1924) 17 *Archiv für Rechts- und Wirtschaftsphilosophie* 214; H Kelsen, *Allgemeine Staatslehre* (Berlin, Julius Springer, 1925) §§ 32–36 (229–55). For earlier statements of Merkl's *Stufenbau* doctrine, statements on which Kelsen drew, see AJ Merkl, 'Das Recht im Lichte seiner Anwendung' (1916–19) 8 *Deutsche Richterzeitung* 584; Vol 9, 162–76, 394–98, 443–50; Vol 11, 290–98; AJ Merkl, *Die Lehre von der Rechtskraft* (Vienna, Deuticke, 1923).

[29] Kelsen, *Hauptprobleme* (n 6) 237; HKW2, 353.

[30] A Verdross, 'Die Rechtstheorie Hans Kelsens' (1930) 59 *Juristische Blätter* 421, 421–22. See also, J Gardner, *Law as a Leap of Faith* (Oxford, Oxford University Press, 2012) 178–81; PE Navarro, 'Normative Systems and Legal Positivism: Eugenio Bulygin and the Philosophy of Law' in E Bulygin, *Essays in Legal Philosophy*, C Bernal, C Huerta, T Mazzarese, JJ Moreso, PE Navarro and SL Paulson (eds) (Oxford, Oxford University Press, 2015) 1–21, 3–5.

[31] See below (n 33).

the moment, that the imperative and, with it, legal obligation are eliminated altogether. But this supposition proves to be mistaken. After all, as we saw in *Main Problems*, Kelsen agrees with Binding on the character of the sanction-norm, a sanction-norm that includes imperatives addressed to legal officials, imposing obligations on them to carry out sanctions. Thus, in what I am calling the first development, Kelsen's effort to eliminate the imperative and its concomitant obligation as the fundamental modality of the legal norm is incomplete. Only now, in the 1930s, does Kelsen resolve this serious problem; empowerment now replaces obligation as found in the sanction-norm.

Commentators on Kelsen, without knowledge of this radical shift in his norm-theoretic position, speak invariably of officials being 'directed' to impose sanctions. Understandably, HLA Hart's role in giving voice to this view, accurate for Kelsen's work up to the shift in the 1930s, commanded widespread attention.[32] Indeed, Kelsen's shift to empowerment was unknown to all of us until the late 1980s, when his paper on empowering norms, drafted in the 1930s as a reply to Georges Scelle, was published.[33] The shift was of course there all along in *General Theory of Law and State* (1945) and in the second edition of *Pure Theory of Law* (1960). But until Kelsen's reply to Scelle emerged in the late 1980s, readers of Kelsen were not looking for a dramatic shift and so did not find one either.

Two moves of Kelsen's mark the breakthrough to empowerment as the modality of the sanction-norm. First, in his study of Scelle's theory of public international law, Kelsen introduces the hypothetically formulated sanction-norm as an empowering norm and characterises legal obligation in its terms, namely, as a function of the power or competence to impose sanctions. Specifically,

> [there is a possibility] of basing the concept of legal obligation … on the concept of competence, a possibility of tracing legal obligation back to competence. That is, if the legal obligation of an individual to behave in a certain way is recognized as given only if, in the event of the opposite behaviour, another individual is empowered by the legal system to impose a sanction on the first individual, and, furthermore, if the empowerment to impose a sanction counts as 'competence', then the legal obligation of the one individual rests on the sanction-imposing competence of the other.[34]

The second move comes in *General Theory of Law and State* (1945), where Kelsen brings his reading of 'ought' into line with his introduction of empowerment as the modality of the sanction-norm. Kelsen's 'ought' – what I shall call the *generic 'ought'* – takes as one of its readings the 'can' of empowerment. In a word, a sanction can be imposed under certain conditions, ie, an official is empowered to impose the sanction.

What of the case where there is an obligation to impose the sanction? Kelsen replies:

> Under this definition of legal duty, the legal norm which obligates the subject to refrain from the delict by attaching a sanction thereto does not stipulate any legal duty of executing the

[32] See HLA Hart, *The Concept of Law*, 2nd edn (Oxford, Clarendon Press, 1994) 35–36.

[33] H Kelsen, 'Recht und Kompetenz. Kritische Bemerkungen zur Völkerrechtstheorie Georges Scelles' in K Ringhofer and R Walter (eds), *Auseinandersetzungen zur Reinen Rechtslehre. Kritische Bemerkungen zu Georges Scelle und Michel Virally* (Vienna, Springer, 1987) 1–108. The publication stems from a manuscript of the 1930s.

[34] Kelsen, 'Recht und Kompetenz' (n 33) 75; and see generally 61–108.

> sanction, of 'applying' the norm itself. The judge – or, to use a more general expression, the law-applying organ – can be legally obligated to execute the sanction – in the sense in which the subject is obligated to refrain from the delict, to 'obey' the legal norm – only if there is a further norm which attaches a further sanction to the non-execution of the first sanction.[35]

These lines in *General Theory of Law and State* (1945) are a clear reflection of Kelsen's radical shift to empowerment. What is more, they serve to spell out the scope of the generic 'ought', which is akin to a variable expression ranging over the 'can' of empowerment and the specific 'ought' of obligation, namely, the official's obligation to impose the sanction.

The generic 'ought' is embedded in what Kelsen calls the primary legal norm, the hypothetically formulated sanction-norm addressed to the legal official, which is, Kelsen writes, 'the only genuine norm'. By contrast, the secondary norm, addressed to the legal subject, 'is certainly superfluous in an exact exposition of law'.[36]

Details of Kelsen's empowerment doctrine are not entirely clear in *General Theory of Law and State*,[37] but he pursues the doctrine further in the second edition of *Pure Theory of Law*:

> [I]f a delict specified by the legal system is committed, then a sanction specified by that legal system ought to be imposed; here the term 'ought' covers both the case in which [the official] is only empowered … to impose the sanction and the case in which [he] is commanded to do so.[38]

When is the modality of empowerment called for, and when the modality of the command? Kelsen answers:

> The imposition of a sanction is commanded, is the content of a legal obligation, if its omission is made the condition for a sanction. Where this is not the case, [the official] can be taken to be only empowered to impose the sanction, not commanded.[39]

Where an official's failure to impose a sanction is itself understood as the condition for a sanction, then 'condition' is shorthand for the antecedent of the completive hypothetically formulated sanction-norm empowering a still higher official to impose a sanction on the derelict official.

[35] H Kelsen, *General Theory of Law and State*, trans A Wedberg (Cambridge, MA, Harvard University Press, 1945) 59.

[36] ibid 61, 63. Without wanting to suggest that there is anything remotely like an isomorphic mapping of Kelsen's primary norm onto Hart's secondary rules, or for mapping Kelsen's secondary norm onto Hart's primary rules, the rough idea that Kelsen's complex is the inverse of Hart's is not incorrect. See M Kramer, *HLA Hart* (Cambridge, Polity, 2018) 70–78, who speaks of the 'general distinction' between primary and secondary in Hart's theory and follows up with a detailed exposition. For Kelsen's view, see the texts cited below (nn 41–42); see also, Kelsen, *Allgemeine Staatslehre* (n 28) § 10(d), 51–52; Kelsen, *Théorie pure du droit* (n 20) ch 4, § 4, 75–77.

[37] See Kelsen, *General Theory of Law and State* (n 35) 59–60.

[38] Kelsen, *Reine Rechtslehre*, 2nd edn (n 17) § 18 (82–83). At the point of the ellipsis, Kelsen adds 'or positively permitted', as though empowerments and positive permissions came to the same thing. See, correcting this oft-encountered mistake, E Bulygin, 'On Norms of Competence' in E Bulygin, *Essays in Legal Philosophy*, C Bernal, C Huerta, T Mazzarese, JJ Moreso, PE Navarro and SL Paulson (eds) (Oxford, Oxford University Press, 2015) 272–83, 275–76.

[39] Kelsen, *Reine Rechtslehre*, 2nd edn (n 17) § 5(a) 26. Kelsen requires *sensu stricto* a necessary condition at the end of the first line, that is to say, 'only if' rather than 'if' (Kelsen's *wenn*). This reading is confirmed by the import of the second sentence in the quotation.

D. The Fourth Development: Kelsen's Composite Norm Theory (1950s)

Kelsen's norm theory evolves in the 1950s in two very different rounds. In one of these, the norm-theoretic problems that occupy Kelsen in the 1950s are problems posed by *deontic* norms, best illustrated by looking to Kelsen's work on conflicts between legal norms, which leads ultimately to the so-called *Spätlehre* or late theory. I return to aspects of the late theory in the final section of the chapter.

In the other round on norm theory during this period, Kelsen works up the rudiments of a systematic norm theory. It is in fact cumulative, but its most complete statement is found, albeit piecemeal, in the second edition of *Pure Theory of Law*. I call it Kelsen's composite norm theory, which incorporates deontic norms into a scheme governed by the generic 'ought' of the sanction-norm *qua* empowering norm. I offer here a few lines on how this scheme of Kelsen's is to be understood.

A tripartite distinction is directed to the *standing* of legal norms as dependent, independent, or complete.[40] The dependent legal norm comprises three species, namely, command, positive permission, and empowerment.[41] Empowering norms turn up here as dependent legal norms that speak to *norm issuance* – Parliament's issuance of general legal norms as well as, in private law, an individual's power to initiate a legal proceeding by filing a legal complaint.[42] By contrast, an independent legal norm is represented by the empowering norm as understood in terms of the generic 'ought' of Kelsen's standard sanction-norm addressed to the legal official.[43] That is, the independent legal norm empowers the legal official to impose a sanction but does not obligate him to do so unless the official's failure to impose the sanction counts as the condition for a further sanction, for whose imposition a still higher-level official is empowered.[44]

Now, if the scheme is filled out with all of the conditions in place, the result is a complete legal norm. Merkl's example of a complete legal norm, stemming from Austrian law,[45] is a bit richer than Kelsen's examples.[46] In reproducing Merkl's example, I designate with lower-case letters between square-cornered brackets those dependent legal norms that qualify as empowering norms of issuance. At the base, at [g], we find

[40] The corresponding German-language terminology is *unselbständig, selbständig* and *vollständig*. Some of this terminology is familiar from the tradition, see eg, R Bierling, *Juristische Prinzipienlehre*, Vol 1 (Tübingen, JCB Mohr, 1894) §§ 4–5, 71–106.

[41] See, eg, Kelsen, *Reine Rechtslehre*, 2nd edn (n 17) § 4(b), 4–5; § 4(d), 15–16; § 6(e), 57 (these references are simply illustrative). Kelsen mentions derogating norms in the second edition of *Reine Rechtslehre* as a species of dependent legal norm, see Kelsen, *Reine Rechtslehre*, 2nd edn (n 17) § 6(e), 57. As a motif in Kelsen's work, however, derogating norms belong to the late theory; see Kelsen, 'Derogation' (n 21), and H Kelsen, *Allgemeine Theorie der Normen*, K Ringhofer and R Walter (eds) (Vienna, Manz, 1979) ch 27, 84–92.

[42] From among the many possible references, see eg, Kelsen, *Reine Rechtslehre*, 2nd edn (n 17) §31, 164; § 33(a), 172–73.

[43] Or it can be read as saying: 'If condition C obtains, the legal official ought to impose a certain sanction'. This formulation, but with my incorporation of the generic 'ought', stems from B Celano, *La teoria del diritto di Hans Kelsen* (Bologna, il Mulino, 1999) 205–06.

[44] See text quoted above (n 38).

[45] See Merkl's example of a complete legal norm, quoted below (n 47).

[46] See, eg, Kelsen, *Reine Rechtslehre*, 2nd edn (n 17) § 6(e), 57–58.

an independent legal norm. And, to repeat, the greater complex counts as a complete legal norm:

> [a] If an organ, called by the Federal Constitution to initiate legislation, has introduced a bill in the National Assembly to the effect that the seller of certain wares is to pay a tax amounting to a certain percentage of the proceeds from the sale, and, further, [b] if the National Assembly, first in committee and then in plenary session, in the procedure specifically prescribed by the parliamentary rules of order, has passed a bill to this effect, and, further, [c] if this legislation has been submitted to the Federal Assembly, which either raised no objection within eight weeks or decided before this deadline to raise no objection, and, further, [d] if the Federal President has signed this legislation, and the Federal Chancellor as well as the Federal Minister of Finance have countersigned the presidential signature, and, further, [e] if the Federal Chancellor has published the signed and countersigned legislation in the Federal Statute Book, and, further, [f] if, after the effective date of this legislation, the tax official designated in the statute has prescribed, in a certain procedure, payment of a certain tax by a certain person, and, finally, [g] if this certain person has not paid the prescribed amount within the prescribed period, then the tax penalty ought to be imposed on this person.[47]

The complete legal norm can be understood as a mirror image in miniature of the *Stufenbau*, the hierarchical structure of the legal system. The complete legal norm, moving downwards through the hierarchy of dependent legal norms, culminates in a single independent legal norm whose formulation, including Kelsen's generic 'ought', is found at [g]. The command, a dependent legal norm leading to and analysed in terms of the independent legal norm at [g], is found at [f].

A closer look at Merkl's language in his example is illuminating. At [b], the procedure set out in the parliamentary rules of order is 'prescribed' (*vorgeschrieben*) in the sense of being stipulated, which is to say that failure to follow this procedure could well mean that the National Assembly does not succeed in doing what it has been empowered to do, namely, pass legislation, but no sanction is attached to its failure. Its failure is simply a matter of failing to observe the conditions of the empowerment norm *qua* means of norm issuance.

By contrast, at [f], payment of a certain tax is 'prescribed' in the standard sense of being commanded, which is to say that failure to pay the tax is the condition for the imposition of a sanction; it affirms the antecedent of the hypothetically formulated empowering norm, namely, the independent legal norm at [g]. In other words, the generic 'ought' in the independent legal norm at [g] flags an empowerment to impose a tax penalty; the prescription that a tax be paid is found in the dependent legal norm at [f].

The other clauses in the complete legal norm also give expression to empowerments addressed to norm issuance. For example, in [a], to say that an organ is called by the Federal Constitution to initiate legislation is to say that the organ is empowered to do so by the Constitution. Similarly for the remaining clauses. None of these empowering norms stands alone. They are dependent legal norms in the hierarchy of the complete legal norm, culminating in an independent legal norm that empowers an official to impose a sanction.

[47] AJ Merkl, 'Prolegomena einer Theorie des rechtlichen Stufenbaues' in A Verdross (ed), *Gesellschaft, Staat und Recht. Festschrift für Hans Kelsen zum 50. Geburtstag* (Vienna, Springer, 1931) 252–94, 274.

V. Kelsen's Late Theory (*Spätlehre*): The Applicability of Logic to the Law

Three views of Kelsen's on the applicability of logic to the law are of interest here. There is Kelsen's very early view, where he sometimes speaks as though logic were directly applicable to legal norms.[48] There is his view in 1959 and again in 1960, where he indirectly applies logic to legal norms.[49] And there is his view, beginning – at least in so far as the published record is concerned – in July of 1960, where he rejects the applicability of logic to the law.

The first clear indication of this rejection, a sharp break in Kelsen's thinking, comes in his letter of 4 July 1960 to Ulrich Klug, with whom Kelsen had been corresponding about the applicability of formal logic to the law.[50] Kelsen, in the correspondence, in letters from 1959, and in the second edition of *Pure Theory of Law* (1960), a work completed at the end of the 1950s, argues that the principles of logic have no direct application to norms, which, unlike statements, are neither true nor false. In these writings, he does endorse, however, an indirect or *per analogiam* application of logic to norms by way of the corresponding legal sentences.[51] This is well-trodden ground, and I need not rehearse the details here.[52]

Klug, in a letter to Kelsen on 26 April 1960, attempts to save the idea of applying formal logic to the law by resorting to 'validity-values' of legal norms as a surrogate for the rejected truth-values. As Klug writes:

> The familiar two-valued calculus of statements (*Aussagenkalkül*) can easily be interpreted as a calculus of norms (*Normenkalkül*). One need only establish that the symbols hitherto employed as statement variables are now to be read as norm variables and that the two admissible values are no longer the values 'true' and 'not true' ('false') but are, instead, the values 'valid' and 'not valid' ('invalid'). One is concerned, then, no longer with statements, which can be true or false, but with norms, which can be valid or invalid.[53]

Of course, Kelsen could reply that if the validity-values are to function in the same way as the rejected truth-values were supposed to function, nothing is gained, and Klug's proposed change is merely terminological.

Kelsen, however, does not reply in this way. Rather, Klug's letter prompts him to answer along very different lines – with radical consequences. Far from endorsing a

[48] See H Kelsen, 'Reichsgesetz und Landesgesetz nach österreichischer Verfassung' (1914) 32 *Archiv des öffentlichen Rechts* 202–45, 390–438, 206–09, repr HKW3, 359–425, 364–66. The claim that Kelsen, in early work, applies logical principles directly to legal norms is not entirely supported in his text. Merkl, however, interprets Kelsen in this way, see eg, AJ Merkl, *Allgemeines Verwaltungsrecht* (Vienna and Berlin, Julius Springer, 1927) 211.

[49] See the references below (n 51).

[50] H Kelsen and U Klug, *Rechtsnormen und logische Analyse. Ein Briefwechsel 1959 bis 1965* (Vienna, Franz Deuticke, 1981); Kelsen's Letter of 4 July 1960, 42–50.

[51] See Kelsen and Klug (n 50); Kelsen's Letter of 15 May 1959 (including 'Manuskript') and his Letter of 18 July 1959, 34–35 and 37, respectively; Kelsen, *Reine Rechtslehre*, 2nd edn (n 17) § 16, 76–77.

[52] See, eg, Paulson, 'Metamorphosis in Hans Kelsen's Legal Philosophy' (n 10) 872–74.

[53] Kelsen and Klug, *Rechtsnormen und logische Analyse* (n 50); Klug's Letter of 26 April 1960, 39.

logic that serves to govern relations between norms, Kelsen now argues that the validity of a norm runs parallel to the existence of a fact:

> The validity of a norm is … the specific existence of a norm, that is, the validity of a norm runs parallel to the existence of a fact, not to the truth of a statement.[54]

The upshot of Kelsen's argument is an altogether contingent field. Beginning with 'parallel to the existence of a fact', we may assume for the sake of Kelsen's argument that two facts are in play. Kelsen, now taking his cues from the contingent field, follows through with the parallel case vis-à-vis conflicting norms. As he writes:

> Logic says that if one of two contradictory statements (*Aussagen*) is true, then the other is false … [O]ne of the two statements … must be true, and then the other must be false. It is not possible that both are true or both false. If, now, the validity-value replaces the truth-value, then the difference in the relation between the two conflicting norms appears first of all not to be the question of which is valid and which is not – *both norms are valid norms*.[55]

In resolving a norm conflict, the question for lawmakers is which of the conflicting norms loses its validity.[56] This, Kelsen adds, is the only question that remains.

Beyond the specifics in his reply to Klug, Kelsen goes on to reject the very idea of applying formal logic to the law, be it a direct application, be it an application by analogy:

> It is entirely possible that *neither of the two norms is valid*. That means, however, that the law of the excluded middle has no application to the relation between the two norms, not an application by analogy either.[57]

If the law of the excluded middle does not apply to norms, then formal logic has no application to norms at all.

Kelsen neatly summarises his new position as follows:

a. The validity-value does not correspond to the truth-value.
b. The logical law of non-contradiction and the logical law of the excluded middle have no application to the relation between positive norms.
c. The validity of a norm means its specific existence, and – in so far as a parallel is possible at all – the parallel here is to the existence of a fact.[58]

In his letter of 4 July 1960, Kelsen also addresses questions pertaining to derogation:

> A very important difference exists between positive norms that set down certain behaviour as obligatory and positive norms that do not set down certain behaviour as obligatory but simply rescind the validity of another norm or, as the technical expression runs, derogate another norm.

[54] Kelsen and Klug (n 50); Kelsen's Letter of 4 July 1960, 43–44. Also from the late phase, on validity as 'specific existence', but without the telling reference to 'the existence of a fact', see Kelsen, 'Derogation' (n 21) 351.

[55] Kelsen and Klug (n 50); Kelsen's Letter of 4 July 1960, 44 (emphasis added); see also 46.

[56] See Kelsen and Klug (n 50); Kelsen's Letter of 4 July 1960, 44, 46–47.

[57] See Kelsen and Klug (n 50), Kelsen's Letter of 4 July 1960, 45 (emphasis added).

[58] See Kelsen and Klug (n 50); Kelsen's Letter of 4 July 1960, 49.

Kelsen pursues the derogation motif further:

> Such a derogating norm has simply the function of rescinding the validity, that is, the 'ought' [*das Sollen*] of another norm, invalidating the existence of the norm. Such a merely derogating norm can be valid only if another norm, a norm setting down certain behaviour as obligatory – the norm whose validity is being rescinded – is already valid … The norm rescinding the validity of a norm automatically loses its validity as soon as its function, the rescinding of the validity of the other norm, has been accomplished.[59]

Bulygin, in his critical examination of aspects of the correspondence between Kelsen and Klug, emphasises Kelsen's significant letter of 4 July 1960. As my first quotations from this letter of Kelsen's make clear,[60] it is at this point in Kelsen's work that we have his rejection of the applicability of formal logic to the law and thereby his ushering in of the *Spätlehre*.[61]

Bulygin begins with a summary statement on Kelsen's position, including what Kelsen says about derogation. The summary comprises seven theses and three conclusions that Bulygin draws from Kelsen.

1. For a conflict of norms to arise, both norms must be valid or there would be no conflict.
2. The question is not which of the two norms is valid and which not but, rather, which of the two should lose its validity.
3. When a loss of validity transpires, it is not based on reasons of logic but on the basis of a third norm, which derogates one of the two (or both). But derogation is not a logical principle, and in the relation between statements there is nothing at all analogous.
4. Derogation can but need not take place; if there is no derogating norm such as, say, the rule *lex superior* or *lex posterior*, then both conflicting norms remain valid and the conflict is not resolved.
5. These derogating norms are not necessary, for positive norms are at issue.
6. A fundamental distinction exists between truth and validity: for validity, an act of issuance is necessary; for truth, no speech act is required.
7. In the end, it is also possible that neither of the two conflicting norms is valid, and so the law of the excluded middle is not applicable.

From these seven theses, Bulygin draws out three conclusions:

a. The validity value does not correspond to the truth value.
b. The logical principles of non-contradiction and of the excluded middle are not applicable to positive norms.
c. A logical contradiction arises only between two statements, one of which claims the validity of a norm and the other the lack of validity of this norm.[62]

[59] See Kelsen and Klug (n 50); Kelsen's Letter of 4 July 1960, 42–43.

[60] See the quotations in the text (nn 54, 55, 57).

[61] To be sure, there were other developments, too, that played a role in bringing about the *Spätlehre*. See Paulson, 'Metamorphosis in Hans Kelsen's Legal Philosophy' (n 10) 872–74, 882–85.

[62] See E Bulygin, 'Zum Problem der Anwendbarkeit der Logik auf das Recht' (hereafter 'Anwendbarkeit') in G Kohlmann (ed), *Festschrift für Ulrich Klug zum 70. Geburtstag*, 2 vols (Cologne, Peter Deubner, 1983) Vol 1, 19–31, 24–25.

What Kelsen has to say about norm conflicts in his *Spätlehre* is, according to Bulygin, 'in principle correct'.[63] What is more, Bulygin is prepared to attribute to Kelsen's *Spätlehre* the expressive theory of norms, developed a few years earlier by Bulygin with his colleague and good friend Carlos E Alchourrón.[64]

By contrast, Bulygin is sceptical about some of Kelsen's conclusions respecting derogation. Unpersuasive in particular is Kelsen's basis for including derogation in his family of norms, namely, not only as derogating norms but also as commanding, forbidding, or permitting various forms of behaviour. Derogation does not address behaviour. Bulygin suggests that Kelsen has simply brought derogating norms into the family by fiat.[65]

Following up, Bulygin characterises as erroneous Kelsen's claim that a derogating norm can attain validity only if another norm, the norm to be rescinded, is already valid.[66] For, Bulygin asks, is it not the case that, say, the derogating norms *lex posterior* and *lex superior* are valid quite apart from the validity of whatever norms they may derogate?

In a line near the end of his paper, Bulygin underscores his admiration for Hans Kelsen, writing that '[i]t is really a pity that Kelsen was only marginally conversant with modern logic, for even without this logical apparatus, he arrived at insights of exceptional value'.[67]

[63] Bulygin,'Anwendbarkeit' (n 62) 25.

[64] ibid 26–27. With respect to the paper on the expressive theory of norms, see E Bulygin and CE Alchourrón, 'The Expressive Conception of Norms' in E Bulygin, *Essays in Legal Philosophy*, C Bernal, C Huerta, T Mazzarese, JJ Moreso, PE Navarro and SL Paulson (eds) (Oxford, Oxford University Press, 2015) 146–70. Later Bulygin writes that he is no longer prepared to defend the expressive theory of norms. See E Bulygin, 'Lógica deóntica' in CE Alchourrón, JM Menéndez and R Orayen (eds), *Enciclopedia Iberoamericana de Filosofía*, Lógica Vol 7 (Madrid, Trotta, 1995) 139–40; E Bulygin, *Lógica deóntica, normas y proposiciones normativas*, PE Navarro, JL Rodríguez and GB Ratti (eds) (Madrid, Marcial Pons, 2018) 43. I wish to thank Giovanni Battista Ratti (Genoa) for these details.

[65] Bulygin, 'Anwendbarkeit' (n 62) 25.

[66] ibid 25.

[67] ibid 30.

3

Hans Kelsen's Concept of the Relative A Priori*

ROBERT ALEXY**

I. The Normativity Problem

One of Hans Kelsen's most frequently quoted statements is as follows: 'Any content whatever can be law'.[1] This assertion is the antithesis of Gustav Radbruch's famous formula, according to which positive law that 'intolerably' contradicts justice is to be denied legal validity or the character of law.[2] This formula excludes extreme injustice as a possible content of law. Anyone who advocates Radbruch's formula establishes a connection between morality and the concepts of law or legal validity, at least where extreme injustice is concerned.[3] This puts him on the side of the non-positivists. On the other hand, those who adopt Kelsen's statement are committed to the positivist thesis of separability; they are therefore positivists.

* Translated from the German by Gonzalo Villa-Rosas. English editing and proofreading by Jorge Fabra-Zamora. We are very grateful to Professor Stanley L Paulson and Bonnie Litschewski Paulson for the great care they took in suggesting improvements in our first draft of the translation. The original version of this chapter was published as R Alexy, 'Hans Kelsen's Begriff des relativen Apriori' in R Alexy, LH Meyer, SL Paulson and G Sprenger (eds), *Neukantianismus und Rechtsphilosophie* (Baden-Baden, Nomos Verlagsgesellschaft, 2002) 179–202. It is published with the permission of *Nomos Verlagsgesellschaft*, the author and the editors of the original version of the chapter.

** The author would like to thank Stanley L Paulson for many extremely valuable suggestions.

[1] H Kelsen, *Introduction to the Problems of Legal Theory. A Translation of the First Edition of the Reine Rechtslehre or Pure Theory of Law*, B Litschewski Paulson and SL Paulson trans (hereafter PTL1) (Clarendon Press, Oxford, 1992) §28, 56; H Kelsen, *Reine Rechtslehre: Einleitung in die rechtswissenschaftliche Problematik*, 1st edn (hereafter RR1) (Vienna, Franz Deuticke 1934) 63. This sentence is something of a constant in Kelsen's otherwise richly varied work. It appears almost unchanged in the second edition, published 26 years later. cp H Kelsen, *Pure Theory of Law*, M Knight trans (hereafter PTL2) (Berkeley and Los Angeles, University of California Press, 1967) 198 (H Kelsen, *Reine Rechtslehre*, 2nd edn (hereafter RR2) (Vienna, Franz Deuticke, 1960) 201): 'Therefore any kind of content might be law'.

[2] G Radbruch, 'Gesetzliches Unrecht und übergesetzliches Recht' in A Kaufmann (ed), *Gesamtausgabe*, Vol 3 (Heidelberg, CF Müller Juristischer Verlag, 1990) 83–93, 89. Only the first part of this formula – the so-called 'Radbruch's intolerability formula' – is referred to here.

[3] cp R Alexy, *The Argument from Injustice. A Reply to Legal Positivism*, B Litschewski Paulson and SL Paulson trans (Oxford, Clarendon Press, 2004) 28 f.

We might think that the main problem of all positivists is the dispute with the non-positivists. However, Kelsen shows that this is clearly not the case. As Stanley L Paulson has observed with great clarity,[4] in addition to the division between positivism and non-positivism, there is a second division that runs right through the field of positivism; namely, between the advocates of the reductionist thesis and those of the normativity thesis. The reductionist thesis holds that law can be traced back to empirical facts. An important proponent of this argument is Karl Olivecrona, who described the reductionist programme unmistakably on his banner: 'My purpose is to reduce our picture of the law in order to make it tally with existing objective reality'.[5] Thus, the rules of law are declared to be natural causes: 'The rules of the law are a *natural cause* – among others – of the actions of the judges in cases of litigation as well as of the behaviour in general of people in relation to each other'.[6] Kelsen opposes such reductionism with the same vigour as he opposes any connection between law and morality. In the preface to the second edition of his '*Hauptprobleme der Staatsrechtslehre*',[*] he emphasises that he is waging a war on two fronts. The purity of legal theory in the form of the 'independence of law as an object of scientific cognition' must be defended not only against the 'doctrine of natural law', by which he means connections between law and morality of any kind, but also against 'the claims of a so-called "sociological" view which wants to grasp law as a piece of natural reality according to the causal scientific method'.[7] Such reductionism cannot grasp the nature of law, which lies in its normativity. This can only be understood by those who grasp 'the norm or the "ought" with which the law represents itself and is represented by jurisprudence'.[8] This is how Kelsen's programme is formulated: normativity without any morality and positivity without mere factuality. Is this possible? Can there be a normativity of law that is not based on morality and a positivity that cannot be based on empirical facts? In short, is normativity without morality and positivity without factuality conceivable?

The key to Kelsen's answer to this question, which is decisive for the whole programme of the *Pure Theory of Law*, is the idea of Ought as a 'relatively a priori category'[9] [*eine relativ apriorische Kategorie*] alongside the idea of the basic norm. This idea is at the centre of the classical, neo-Kantian phase of his work and forms the subject of this chapter. Two questions need to be linked. The first is what Kelsen means when he describes Ought as a 'relatively a priori category'. The second is whether he can solve the problem of the normativity of law with this idea.

Before answering these questions, it is necessary to clarify the text to be interpreted. As we have just seen, in the first edition of the '*Reine Rechtslehre*',[**] one of the main

[4] SL Paulson, 'The Neo-Kantian Dimension of Kelsen's Pure Theory of Law' (1992) 12 *Oxford Journal of Legal Studies* 311, 318.

[5] K Olivecrona, *Law as Fact* (London, Wildy & Sons, 1962) 27.

[6] ibid 16. Emphasis added by Robert Alexy.

[*] Translator's note (hereafter TN): Main Problems in the Theory of Public Law. The treatise has been translated into Polish, Spanish and Italian. See SL Paulson, 'How Merkl's *Stufenbaulehre* Informs Kelsen's Concept of Law' (2013) 21 *Revus. Journal for Constitutional Theory and Philosophy of Law* 29, fn 5.

[7] H Kelsen, *Hauptprobleme der Staatsrechtslehre*, 2nd edn (Tübingen, JCB Mohr (P Siebeck) 1923) v.

[8] Kelsen, PTL1 §§15–16, 33; Kelsen, RR1, 34.

[9] Kelsen, PTL1 §11(b), 24; Kelsen, RR1, 23.

[**] TN: PTL1.

works of his main – neo-Kantian – period, Kelsen writes of a 'relatively a priori category' [*eine relativ apriorische Kategorie*]. In this formulation, 'relatively' appears as an adverb related to the adjective 'a priori', which makes a priori a matter of degree. If we take Kelsen's formulation literally, it says that Ought is an approximately or proportionally a priori category. Well, not only are there general arguments in favour of the fact that a priori is not a matter of degree or a matter of more or less, but Kelsen himself indicates this when he writes of a 'relative' a priori in his work *Das Problem der Souveränität*.[10] There are, therefore, good reasons to regard the formulation contained in the first edition of the *Pure Theory of Law* as ephemeral and imprecise.[11] Instead of a 'relatively a priori category [*eine relativ apriorische Kategorie*]', we should therefore read it is a 'relative a priori category [*eine relative apriorische Kategorie*]'.[12]

II. Ought as Category

To answer our first question – what Kelsen means when he categorises Ought as a relative a priori category – we must first enquire what Kelsen means by Ought, which is supposed to have the property of being both a priori and relative. This question can also be formulated in terms of what the category that gives normativity to law should consist of. Kelsen is a clear writer. Nevertheless, this question is difficult to answer. There are three candidates: imputation, Ought and the basic norm. All three are concerned with the norm or its validity in a sense that remains to be determined. Before asking which of these three candidates deserves the title 'category', we will first examine the general ontological status of what Kelsen understands by 'norm'. Again, the consideration will be confined to the classical neo-Kantian period.[13]

A. Norm

Reductionist theories tend to ground the concept of norm in some individual or collective mental act, state or disposition, or even to physical events such as the exercise of coercion. Kelsen is vehemently opposed to such reductionist naturalism. Whoever

[10] H Kelsen, *Das Problem der Souveränität und die Theorie des Völkerrechts. Beitrag zu einer Reinen Rechtslehre* (Tübingen, JCB Mohr, 1920) viii: 'The only thing that matters is to become aware of the – relative – a priori of this system [*Worauf es allein ankommt ist: sich des – relativen – a priori dieses Systems bewußt zu werden*].' [TN: For an English translation see H Kelsen, *The Problem of Sovereignty and the Theory of International Law: A Contribution to a Pure Theory of Law*, P Silverman trans (Oxford, Oxford University Press, 2021)].

[11] Instead of an ephemeral and imprecise formulation, one could also think of a typographical error. However, the fact that the expression 'relatively a priori category' [*relativ apriorische Kategorie*] does not only appear in the first edition of the *Pure Theory of Law* argues against this. This expression can also be found in H Kelsen, 'Allgemeine Rechtslehre im Lichte materialistischer Geschichtsauffassung' (1931) 66 *Archiv für Sozialwissenschaft und Sozialpolitik* 449, 463 reprinted in H Kelsen, *Demokratie und Sozialismus. Ausgewählte Aufsätze*, N Leser (ed) (Vienna, Verlag der Wiener Volksbuchhandlung, 1967) 81.

[12] cp Kelsen, PTL1 §11(b), 24 fn 23.

[13] On Hans Kelsen's concept of norm in general cp C Heidemann, *Die Norm als Tatsache. Zur Normentheorie Hans Kelsens* (Baden-Baden, Nomos Verlagsgesellschaft, 1997).

wishes to understand something legally should 'not look to mental processes or physical events'. Rather, to comprehend something legally means comprehending it as law. To comprehend something as law is to comprehend it as a norm. However, a norm is a 'meaning'.[14] As a meaning, a norm does not belong to natural reality, but to ideal reality.[15] As an element of ideal reality, the norm, unlike anything that exists in nature, 'does not exist in space and time'.[16] Physical and psychological phenomena associated with the norm are not part of the norm itself, but are only 'parallel phenomena in nature'.[17]

These statements by Kelsen clearly reveal the three-tiered physical–psychological–ideal scheme. This suggests that the norm, as meaning, should be assigned to a 'third realm' in Frege's sense,[18] ie, a world of abstract entities. The neo-Kantian Kelsenian concept of norm is thus a semantic concept of norm. This is defined by the parallelism of statement and normative statement on the one hand, and proposition and norm on the other. Just as statements express propositions or – in Frege's terminology – thoughts, normative statements express norms.[19] Norms as 'meanings' in Kelsen's sense thus have the ontological status of semantic content [*Bedeutungsgehalten*]. Kelsen's neo-Kantian concept of norm is thus caught up in the maelstrom of the general metaphysical question of whether a world of abstract or ideal entities can exist or be constituted alongside the physical and psychological world. Kelsen himself assumes that this is the case.

B. Imputation

With the classification of the norm as meaning or semantic content, naturalism is averted, but the specific properties of the norm remain to be elucidated. What distinguishes the meaning of a statement, ie, a thought in Frege's sense, from a norm as the meaning of a normative statement? This question is aimed at the *differentia specifica* that distinguishes a norm from other meanings or semantic content. To answer this question, Kelsen could have returned directly to the Is–Ought dichotomy[20] to use it as a basis for enquiring into the specific character of the legal Ought. This does happen in some places. Thus, Kelsen writes that

> [t]he formal category of norm – the category designated by "ought" – yields only the genus, not the *differentia specifica*, of the law.[21]

Here, Ought is clearly classified as a genus for all possible kinds of norms. Such a classification of Ought means that Ought is the *differentia specifica* that distinguishes the norm as meaning from all other meanings or semantic content, notably from Frege's notion of the meaning of a statement. In a second step, then, coercion is introduced as

[14] Kelsen, PTL1 §5, 11; Kelsen, RR1, 6.
[15] Kelsen, PTL1 §8, 15; Kelsen, RR1, 12.
[16] Kelsen, PTL1 §6, 12; Kelsen, RR1, 7.
[17] Kelsen, PTL1 §7, 14; Kelsen, RR1, 10.
[18] G Frege, 'Der Gedanke. Eine logische Untersuchung' in G Frege and G Patzig (eds), *Logische Untersuchungen* (Göttingen, Vandenhoeck & Ruprecht, 1966) 30–53.
[19] cp in this regard R Alexy, *A Theory of Constitutional Rights*, J Rivers trans (Oxford, Oxford University Press, 2010) 21 f.
[20] cp Kelsen, PTL1 §§14(c)–15, 32; Kelsen, RR1, 33.
[21] Kelsen, PTL1 §12, 26; Kelsen, RR1, 25.

a second *differentia specifica* to distinguish the legal norm from other norms, especially moral norms. Thus, Kelsen writes

> the legal norm is a coercive norm (a norm providing for coercion), and that precisely thereby the legal norm is distinguished from other norms.[22]

Elsewhere, however, it sounds different. Here, it appears Kelsen wanted at all costs to avoid including morality in a common genus by separating law from morality, again after a logical second, as it were, by means of a *differentia specifica*. Even such brief contact seems too much for him in his war on two fronts. Therefore, he arrives at the idea of complete detachment [*zur Idee einer völligen Loslösung*].[23] This consists in separating law from morality not only materially or substantially, but also formally or structurally. The material separation is achieved by severing all connections between the concept of justice or the idea of a 'social ordering that is absolutely right'[24] and the concept of law. However, this is not enough for Kelsen. Rather, the formal separation should lead to

> Free[ing] the conceptual characterization of the law from this ideological element by *completely* severing the concept of the legal norm from its source, the concept of the moral norm, and by securing the autonomy of the law even vis-à-vis the moral law.[25]

For this reason, Kelsen does not want formally to unite law and morality under a common formal category, ie, independently of all content, in order then, in a second step (as in the first passage quoted) to separate them again not only by material but also by formal differences. Rather, the 'autonomy of law' is to be secured by the direct application of a specific legal category.[26] Kelsen presents imputation as such a category.[27]

[22] ibid.

[23] Kelsen, PTL1 §11(a)–(b), 23; Kelsen, RR1, 21.

[24] Kelsen, PTL1 §8, 16; Kelsen, RR1, 13.

[25] Kelsen, PTL1 §11(a)–(b), 23; Kelsen, RR1, 21. Emphasis added by Robert Alexy.

[26] In the text under consideration here, Kelsen helps to comprehend the complete detachment of the law by choosing not morality as Ought, but 'the moral norm, as an imperative' [*Moralnorm als Imperativ*] as the object of detachment (Kelsen, PTL1 §11(a)–(b), 23 f; Kelsen, RR1, 22 f).

[27] Kelsen distinguishes between 'peripheral' and 'central' imputation. Central imputation – apart from the aspect of imputation to a 'legal subsystem or comprehensive legal system' (Kelsen, PTL1 §25(c)–(d), 50; RR1, 57), which dominated Kelsen's early writings – is concerned with the imputation of acts and conditions to a legal subject; peripheral imputation is concerned with the linking of a fact to a legal consequence (cp Kelsen, PTL1 §25(b)–(c) 49 f; RR1, 56 f; cp also Kelsen, PTL2 150; RR2, 154, where the terminology is changed in favour of the distinction between imputation [*Zurechnung*] and attribution [*Zuschreibung*]). Only what Kelsen calls 'peripheral imputation' is of interest here. This is fundamental in the sense that, first, without the linking of facts and legal consequences there is – at least according to Kelsen – no legal norm at all, and secondly, without legal norms there can be no central imputation. Where there is central imputation, there is always peripheral imputation. Without peripheral imputation there can be no central imputation. Whether the reverse is also true is not so easy to say. The answer to this question presupposes a distinction between concrete and abstract peripheral imputation. A concrete peripheral imputation exists when the facts and legal consequences of a norm are not only abstractly related to each other, but are also related to a concrete legal subject. If, on the other hand, a legal norm refers to a specific legal subject (ie, according to Kelsen, to the common point of reference for all legal rules which 'have as their content … the behaviour of a human being'. (H Kelsen, *Allgemeine Staatslehre* (Berlin, Julius Springer, 1925) 63), then there is also a central imputation. The concrete peripheral imputation thus includes the central imputation. This is different in the case of abstract peripheral imputation, because its abstractness consists precisely in the fact that any reference to any subject is excluded. Abstract peripheral imputation could also be called 'pure peripheral imputation' because of the exclusion of any subjectivity. In this sense, concrete peripheral imputation could be characterised as 'subjective' and abstract or pure peripheral imputation as 'objective'.

The concept of imputation is a typical parallel concept. For Kelsen, the parallel to imputation is causality:

> Just as laws of nature link a certain material fact as cause with another as effect, so positive laws [in their basic form] link legal condition with legal consequence (the consequence of a so-called unlawful act). If the mode of linking material facts is *causality* in the one case, it is *imputation* in the other, and imputation is recognized in the Pure Theory of Law as the particular lawfulness, the autonomy, of the law.[28]

This general parallelism thesis can be divided into two specific parallelism theses: transcendental and logical parallelism. The former is concerned with the role of causality and imputation as an a priori category. The latter is limited to logical structure in the broader sense of what functions as a parallel category. Only this is of interest here.

A comprehensive comparison of the link between cause and effect with that between fact and legal consequence quickly concludes that things are quite complicated on both sides. Mackie's theory of INUS-conditions[29] is a good example of this, as is the debate about *defeasibility*, ie, ruling out, overturning or overruling in the law.[30] Of course, complexity as such is neutral with respect to the parallelism thesis. Even the complicated can have parallel structures. However, this is not the place to discuss it. The simplifications made by Kelsen in the context of his theory of norms[31] will serve as a starting point. In light of this, we can identify both a similarity and a difference.

Common ground is found in what Kelsen alludes to when he describes the norm as a 'hypothetical judgement'.[32] The proximity to Kant is obvious. According to Kant, the category of causality as a pure concept of understanding corresponds to the logical function of hypothetical judgement.[33] Kant explains this in terms of the relation 'of the ground to the consequence'.[34] This relation is indeed causality, but it goes further. The connection between the facts [*Tatbestand*] and the legal consequence [*Rechtsfolge*] is, therefore, found in Kant's table of forms of judgement,[35] even if it is difficult to find it in the table of categories. Kelsen's parallelism thesis is thus well-founded on the grounds of the 'logical function of understanding'.

Kelsen grasps the similarity between causality and imputation in terms of ground and consequence just as sharply as the difference. In doing so, he distinguishes between 'Ought' [*Sollen*] and 'Must' [*Müssen*]. Ought and Must are meant to express the respective 'functional connection'. They are meant to capture the 'specific way'[36] of the connection, the 'specific sense' in which the condition and the consequence 'belong together'.[37]

[28] Kelsen, PTL1 §11(a)–(b), 23; RR1, 22 (emphasis added by Robert Alexy).

[29] cp JL Mackie, *The Cement of the Universe* (Oxford, Oxford University Press, 1980) 62.

[30] cp D Nute (ed), *Defeasible Deontic Logic* (Dordrecht, Kluwer Academic Publishers, 1997).

[31] That Kelsen was aware of the complexity of the structure of causality becomes clear as soon as he not only deals with the parallelism of imputation and causality from the point of view of the theory of norms, but also considers causality as such. cp in particular H Kelsen, *Vergeltung und Kausalität. Eine soziologische Untersuchung* (The Hague, WP van Stockum, 1946 (first pub 1941)) 259 f.

[32] Kelsen, PTL1 §11(a)–(b), 23; RR1, 22.

[33] I Kant, *Critique of Pure Reason*, Paul Guyer and AW Wood trans (hereafter KrV) (Cambridge, Cambridge University Press, 2000) (*Akademieausgabe* – KPAW-KGS) A70, 79.

[34] Kant, KrV, A73.

[35] Kant, KrV, A70.

[36] Kelsen, PTL1§11(b)–(c), 25; RR1, 23.

[37] Kelsen, PTL §11(b)–(c), 25; RRI, 24.

This clarifies that a second element is added to the hypothetical or conditional structure in the form of the 'specific sense' of the link. In the case of causality, this should be the classical modality of necessity with 'Must'. In the case of imputation, this is a deontic modality with Ought. However, this brings us back to Ought as the old generic term that, at least formally, unites law and morality, and the question arises as to whether the attempt to establish 'the particular lawfulness, the autonomy, of the law' by means of the concept of imputation has failed. Is imputation nothing more than a conditional plus deontic operator? That depends on what Kelsen understands by 'Ought'.

C. Ought

The concept of Ought can be understood in two ways: as a fundamental or as a collective concept. As a fundamental concept, it is introduced by Alf Ross, who argues that the obligation formalised by the obligation operator '*O*'[38] is 'the fundamental directive category in which any norm may be expressed',[39] 'the single and irreducible normative category'.[40] For Ross, the obligation modality as a category – certainly in a non-transcendental sense – is a 'true ancestral concept' [*wahre(r) Stammbegriff(e)*], ie, a 'predicament [*Prädikament(e)*]',[41] and in this respect it fulfils the requirements for a category, while all other deontic modalities of this 'original and primitive concept' are only derived concepts and therefore only 'predicables [*Prädikabilien*]'.[42] Kelsen sees things differently. He uses the concept of Ought as a collective concept that simply summarises all deontic modalities:

> [I]f the connection brought about by a legal norm, establishing certain material facts as condition and consequence, is expressed in the legal proposition by the connective 'ought', this word is not being used in the ordinary sense, which was noted earlier and must be emphatically restated. With 'ought', one usually expresses the idea of a command, not that of an empowerment or a permission. The legal ought, that is, the connective that links condition with consequence in the legal proposition, encompasses all three senses: that of command, of empowerment, and of (positive) permission. That is, with the 'ought' expressed in the legal proposition, all three normative functions are designated.[43,*]

[38] A Ross, *Directives and Norms* (London, Routledge & Kegan Paul, 1968) 120, 155.
[39] ibid 117.
[40] ibid 118.
[41] cp Kant, KrV, A81.
[42] Kant, KrV, A82.
[43] RR2, 80 f. (English translation of the German text by Stanley L Paulson and Bonnie Litschewski Paulson.) The concept of Ought as a collective concept appears with the clarity of the quotation here only in Kelsen's later writings. Essential elements can already be discerned, however, ahead of their explicit formulation. In the first edition of *Pure Theory of Law*, for example, Kelsen writes: 'If one deprives the norm or the 'ought' of meaning, then there will be no meaning in the assertions that something is legally allowed, something is legally proscribed, this belongs to me, that belongs to you, *X* has a right to do this, *Y* is obligated to do that, and so on' (Kelsen, PTL1 §16, 33; RR1, 35). The Ought refers here to the whole range of deontic modalities. Although empowerment, unlike permission and prohibition, ie, the command to forbear from doing something, is not mentioned, nevertheless, in light of the thesis that without Ought 'all the thousands of statements in which the life of the law is manifest daily' would lose their significance (ibid), empowerment may lie somewhere in Kelsen's phrase 'and so on'.
* TN: Two decades before the publication of the work quoted here, the second edition of *Pure Theory of Law*, Kelsen, in 'The Pure Theory of Law and Analytical Jurisprudence' (1941) *Harvard Law Review*

In terms of category, this opens up three possibilities. The first is that Kelsen genuinely intends to introduce three relative a priori categories. However, in view of the idea of originality and primitiveness – in short: fundamentality – inherent in the concept of category, this could only be accepted if Kelsen did not consider one of the three modalities he mentions as being the fundamental one. In light of the postulate of simplicity that applies to categories, this would also only be possible if none of the three modalities could be characterised as an 'ancestral concept',[44] ie, as fundamental in relation to the others. Therefore, the key question is whether one of the three modalities has the status of fundamentality. As there is virtually no argument for the fundamentality of (positive) permission from the outset, this leads to a competition between obligation and empowerment for the status of category.

The question of whether obligation or empowerment deserves the title of true fundamentality can only be answered by considering Kelsen's distinction between primary and secondary norms. It is common terminology to refer to those norms that command or prohibit certain behaviour as 'primary',[45] and to call norms that impose a sanction for non-compliance with a primary norm 'secondary'.[46] For Kelsen, this is exactly the opposite. For him, norms that state a behaviour as commanded or prohibited, such as saying that it is prohibited to steal, are secondary norms. This is because, according to Kelsen, such norms are legal norms only if they are linked to a second norm that says that

> given, as condition, behaviour opposite that which the norm establishes as sanction-avoiding, then a coercive act is to be forthcoming as consequence. This reconstructed legal norm is the legal norm in its primary form.[47]

If we qualify the deontic modality in the secondary norm defined in this manner as a legal deontic modality, we can establish an equivalence relation between primary and secondary norms: whenever it is *legally* prohibited to steal, it is commanded that a coercive act ought to occur as a consequence of theft, and whenever it is commanded that a coercive act ought to occur as a consequence of theft, it is *legally* forbidden to steal. However, this equivalence does not mean they have the same status. The legal aspect is only represented in the secondary norm by the predicate 'legal,' ie, it remains completely unanalysed. In contrast, it is reflected in the structure of the primary norm. This is why Kelsen regards it as the original norm. For him, it is the only adequate answer to the question he posed early on: 'the question of the ideal linguistic form of the legal proposition', which he purposely equates with the question 'of the essence of objective law'.[48] The secondary norm is, therefore, only a convenient means of representation;[49]

44, 55, introduces a systematic distinction between the legal norm [*Rechtsnorm*] and the legal proposition [*Rechtssatz*]. He devotes a section of the work being quoted here, namely §16, 73–77, to the distinction, which is observed in the translation of this passage.

[44] Kant, KrV, A81.

[45] cp, eg, HLA Hart, *The Concept of Law*, 2nd edn (Oxford, Oxford University Press, 1994) 81.

[46] cp, eg, H Nawiasky, *Allgemeine Rechtslehre als System der rechtlichen Grundbegriffe* (Köln, Benziger, 1941) 12 f, 76 f.

[47] Kelsen, PTL1 §14(b), 30; RR1, 30.

[48] Kelsen, *Hauptprobleme der Staatsrechtslehre* (n 7) 237.

[49] Kelsen, PTL1 §14(b), 30; RR1, 30.

it cannot reveal[50] the essence of the law, which Kelsen calls 'the particular lawfulness, the autonomy, of the law'.[51]

With the primacy of the primary norm, only the location for the competitive struggle between obligation and empowerment has been determined. Now everything depends on which modality is the actual modality of the primary norm. According to Stanley L Paulson, it is that of empowerment or competence.[52] Paulson relies on impressive textual evidence.[53] These are the words of the treatise 'Recht und Kompetenz',* written in the early 1930s but not published until 1987:

> [The possibility] of basing the concept of obligation … on the concept of competence, a possibility of tracing legal obligation back to competence. That is, if the legal obligation of an individual to behave in a certain way is recognized as given only if, in the event of the opposite behaviour, another individual is empowered by the legal system to impose a sanction on the first individual, and, furthermore, if the empowerment to impose a sanction count as a competence, then the legal obligation of the one individual is based on the sanction-imposing competence of the other.[54]

This consideration can be supplemented by a systematic argument.[55] If we equate the legal obligation, which Kelsen aptly defines as the legal command of certain behaviour,[56] with the competence to impose sanctions, then, according to Kelsen, if we go back further and further, we eventually arrive at a norm behind which there is no further norm that empowers a subject to impose a sanction. The final sanctioning body is, therefore, only to be regarded as empowered, but in the absence of a further sanctioning authority above it, no longer as obliged (in the sense of subjection to a sanctioning competence): 'the last sanction in this chain can only be authorized, not commanded'.[57]

Does this prove the fundamentality of the modality of empowerment or competence? Of the numerous arguments relevant here, we will consider only one, which accepts both Kelsen's not unquestionable premise that the legal command is generally equivalent to the norm providing for a sanction, and the not entirely certain premise

[50] Whether or not one agrees with Kelsen's thesis of the coercive or sanctioning norm as an actual legal norm, one advantage cannot be denied: it makes it possible to distinguish between legal and moral norms on the level of meaning, ie, on the semantic level. Anyone who imagines a primary norm in the form of a coercive or sanctioning norm imagines a legal norm, regardless of whether this norm is valid or not, no longer valid or not yet valid.

[51] Kelsen, PTL1 §16(b), 23; RR1, 22.

[52] SL Paulson, 'An Empowerment Theory of Legal Norms' (1988) 1 *Ratio Juris* 58, 69 f.

[53] SL Paulson, 'The Weak Reading of Authority in Hans Kelsen's Pure Theory of Law' (2000) 19 *Law and Philosophy* 131, 139 f.

* TN: Law and Competence.

[54] H Kelsen, 'Recht und Kompetenz. Kritische Bemerkungen zur Völkerrechtstheorie Georges Scelles' in K Ringhofer and R Walter (eds), *Auseinandersetzungen zur Reinen Rechtslehre. Kritische Bemerkungen zu Georges Scelle und Michel Virally* (Vienna, Springer, 1987) 75. [TN: I have taken over the translation by SL Paulson in SL Paulson, 'A "Justified Normativity" Thesis in Hans Kelsen's Pure Theory of Law? Rejoinders to Robert Alexy and Joseph Raz' in M Klatt (ed), *Institutionalized Reason. The Jurisprudence of Robert Alexy* (Oxford, Oxford University Press, 2012) 61–111, 83.].

[55] SL Paulson, 'Introduction' in SL Paulson and B Litschewski Paulson (eds), *Normativity and Norms. Critical Perspectives on Kelsenian Themes* (Oxford, Clarendon Press, 1998) XXIII–LIII, XLIX f.; Paulson, 'The Weak Reading of Authority in Hans Kelsen's Pure Theory of Law' (n 53) 148.

[56] Kelsen, PTL2 §27(a), 108; RR2, 12.

[57] Kelsen, PTL2 §5(a), 25; cp also §28(b), 117; RR2, 26, cp also 124.

that there must be a final instance in the chain of sanctioning competence as in the chain of lawmaking competence,[58] in addition to the not unquestionable premise that the final instance can only have a legal sanctioning competence and not a legal sanctioning obligation. We can imagine any number of long chains of levels of sanctioning competences. For the sake of simplicity, we consider a series of three levels here: K_1, K_2, and K_3. K_1 is the competence of a court of first instance to impose sanctions for criminal offences. K_2 is the competence of a court of second instance to impose a sanction on the judge(s) of first instance if K_1 is not exercised, although the conditions for exercising K_1 are met. Finally, K_3 is a corresponding power of the highest court. Now suppose that not only the court of first instance does not exercise its competence K_1 against an offender, but also the court of second instance does not exercise its competence K_2 against the court of first instance, and the highest court does not exercise its competence K_3 against the court of second instance. From the perspective of competence, however, everything should still be in order, because it is part of the concept of competence that this does not include the concept of obligation or command.[59] Anyone who fulfils the relevant conditions has the competence to marry, but no one has to make use of it. Does this purity of competence from de facto use also apply to sanctioning competence? Can it really be said that the prohibition of theft addressed to the citizen is the same as a pure sanctioning competence or a chain of sanctioning competences, regardless of whether these competences are ever used?

Of course, we could attempt to find a solution with the help of effectiveness. We could say that competences that are not exercised have no effect and thus lose their legal validity. The secondary norm would then not correspond to any valid primary norm at all if the competence were not exercised, which is why the secondary norm would no longer be valid. This step, however, leads from the realm of normative modalities to the realm of factuality, irrespective of whether the exercise of a competence is really a condition for its validity. This is not a problem in itself, since it is easy to say that a criminal norm in the form of a secondary prohibition that is 'never being applied or obeyed' loses its validity.[60] However, it is then a question of effectiveness as a condition of validity in the relation between norms of command and norms of prohibition on the one hand and norms of competence on the other, and in this sense of a relation of effectiveness and not of a purely logical relation between norms as semantic content with different normative modalities. If the equivalence of norms of command and norms of prohibition as secondary norms with norms of competence as primary norms is made dependent on the fact that norms of competence are effective in the sense that they are exercised, then effectiveness becomes a condition not only for the validity of norms of command and norms of prohibition, but also for norms of competence. Effectiveness also becomes a condition for the existence of equivalence – and that is a problem. The reason why the logical relation has to be extended to an effectiveness relation to establish equivalence is because Kelsen introduces the primary norm in order to connect the legal Ought necessarily and strictly generally with the concept of coercion, but mere, ie, unexercised, sanctioning competence is something that does not yet include coercion. However, if

[58] Nawiasky (n 46) 14.
[59] Alexy, *A Theory of Constitutional Rights* (n 19) 149 f.
[60] Kelsen, PTL2 213; RR2, 220.

the equivalence between secondary norms of command and norms of prohibition, on the one hand, and primary norms of competence, on the other, is to depend on the fact that the norms of competence have a certain relation to reality, ie, that coercion is actually exercised, then the purity of the relation between the modality of obligation at the level of the secondary norm and the modality of competence at the level of the primary norm is lost. This creates a phantom that should have been banished long ago: the phantom of realism or naturalism.

This intrusion of factuality into the relation between primary norms as norms of competence and secondary norms as norms of command and prohibition lies ultimately in the fact that competences do not represent an actual Ought, but only a potential Ought. A potential Ought is an Ought that is conditioned by the actual exercise of competence.[61] No matter how comprehensive a system of competence norms may be, as long as no competence belonging to it is ever exercised, then although it may contain an enormous amount of potential instances of Ought, it nonetheless contains nothing in the way of actual Ought. Normativity exists in it only in a state of pure latency. The same is true of sanctioning and lawmaking competences. The resulting dependence of the relation between primary and secondary norms on the factuality of the actual exercise of the competence can be avoided if we dispense with the fundamental nature of the competence and also demand a command for the primary norms, ie, the sanction norms, which is linked to the competence. The secondary norm as a command for a certain behaviour can then be considered equivalent to the primary norm as a sanction command for the failure to act. In this manner, the primary norm defines the legal command contained in the secondary norm by incorporating the modality of obligation into the structure of (peripheral) imputation. Neither the hypothetical nor the normative structure of imputation would be affected. Although this brings us closer to morality than with purely empowering norms, we would still remain quite far from it owing to imputation, which in Kelsen's model occur at the level of sanctioning norms and not at the level of behavioural norms, which is central to moral norms. Above all, however, the relation between primary and secondary norms can be understood as a purely semantic one. Of course, this does not solve all the problems. That said, it has been shown that the modality of obligation in favour of competence cannot be dispensed with in imputation if the equivalence of primary and secondary norms is not to depend on the factuality of the exercise of the sanctioning competence, ie, the actual exercise of coercion. This is certainly not a weighty argument for the fundamental nature of the modality of obligation in all aspects. Nevertheless, this argument grows in significance once we attach fundamental importance to the distinction between the legal system as a system of semantic content and its factuality. In any case, this importance will be insisted upon by those who do not want to commit themselves from the outset to the factuality of social facts as the sole criterion of legal validity. In this light, we will regard the modality of obligation as the fundamental normative modality.[62]

[61] cp R Alexy, 'Ross on Competence', Lecture (Alf Ross Conference, Copenhagen, June 1999). Published as R Alexy, 'Alf Ross' Begriff der Kompetenz' in A Hoyer, H Hattenhauer, R Meyer-Pritzl and W Schubert (eds), *Gedächtnisschrift für Jörn Eckert* (Baden-Baden, Nomos Verlagsgesellschaft, 2008) 43–64.

[62] The argument for the fundamentality of the modality of obligation has a systematic character. It is concerned with the question of which modality is rightly to be classified as the most fundamental modality of Ought. This systematic question must be distinguished from the interpretive question. It is about which

D. The Basic Norm

There are other candidates for the title of a relative a priori category constituting law and legal cognition. In addition to imputation and Ought, the basic norm represents a third candidate. A precondition for the triumph of this third candidate is that the concept of the basic norm is associated with something that, first, has a categorical character for the problem of normativity and, second, goes beyond the Ought incorporated in imputation. However, this is not the case. If the basic norm is considered solely from the perspective of normativity, then it is, in short, nothing other than Ought in a systematic form. This becomes particularly clear in the formulation that comes closest to our formula of the relative a priori, namely that of the first edition of the *Pure Theory of Law*. Kelsen gives the basic norm the form of 'the basis of the validity of the constitution' and thus of all laws and legal acts based on it:

> Coercion is to be applied under certain conditions and in a certain way, namely, as determined by the framers of the first constitution or by the authorities to whom they have delegated appropriate powers.[63]

This 'schematic formulation of the basic norm of a legal system'[64] clearly refers to the 'basic form of positive laws [*Grundform des Gesetzes*]'.[65] Its hypothetical or conditional character appears when the condition with the legal consequence is linked to the form of the imposition of coercion. The modality of this connection is Ought. This corresponds exactly to the imputation which contains Ought. The basic norm now adds a dynamic element to this static element. This consists in the competence of the framers of the first constitution and the authorities empowered by them to establish norms corresponding to the basic form. As in the case of the sanctioning or coercive competence we considered above, the problem of the relation between obligation and competence also arises in the case of lawmaking and norm-setting competence. Irrespective of the difference between sanctioning and lawmaking, the relation between the modalities of obligation and competence is analogous in both cases.[66] If, on the one hand, we begin from the factuality of the exercise of lawmaking or norm-setting competence and, on the other hand, we are guided by the assumption that issuance in accordance with the legal system [*ordnungsgemäße Gesetzheit*]* and thus

modality was the more fundamental for Kelsen. According to Stanley L Paulson, the stronger textual evidence suggests that the fundamentality of competence corresponds to Kelsen's true intentions. However, Paulson also identifies an opposing line. His conclusion is: 'I think Kelsen can be understood as defending both views' (Paulson, 'The Weak Reading of Authority in Hans Kelsen's Pure Theory of Law' (n 53) 168). Suffice it to say here that there is at least one line in Kelsen's work that corresponds to the thesis of the fundamentality of the modality of obligation. It is expressed in basic norm formulations such as: 'Behave as the legal authority: the monarch, the people's assembly, the parliament, etc. commands [*Verhaltet euch so wie die Rechtsautorität: der Monarch, die Volksversammlung, das Parlament etc. befiehlt*]' (Kelsen, *Allgemeine Staatslehre* (n 27) 99) or '[o]ne ought to behave as the constitution prescribes [*Man soll sich so verhalten, wie die Verfassung vorschreibt*]' (Kelsen, PTL2 §34(c), 201; RR2, 205).

[63] Kelsen, PTL1 §28, 57 f; RR1, 65 f.

[64] Kelsen, PTL1 §28, 57; RR1, 66.

[65] Kelsen, PTL1 §28, 23; RR1, 22.

[66] The difference is essentially between potentiality for effectiveness and potentiality for norm-setting.

* TN: On the use of the term 'issuance in accordance with the legal system', see Alexy, *The Argument from Injustice* (n 3) 3 f, fn 3.

in accordance with the competence [*kompetenzgemäße Gesetztheit*] is both a necessary and a sufficient condition for legal validity, then we quickly arrive at the following equivalence: if the norm is legally valid, the competence has been exercised in accordance with the legal system, and if the competence has been exercised in accordance with the legal system, then the norm is legally valid. Transferred to the level of normative modalities, this means that a norm-setting competence is the same as the class of commands and prohibitions that are directly or indirectly possible according to it. In short, competences are potential Ought. We can thus reduce the concept of competence to that of potential Ought.[67] On the other hand, a reduction of the concept of Ought to that of competence is possible only if that which is the result of the exercise of competence can be Ought. Beginning from this basic positivist assumption, the modalities of obligation and competence can be considered equally fundamental and mutually definable with assistance from the concept of potentiality regarding norm-setting competence and on the basis of established and applicable norms of competence. The problem here is that such an equal fundamentality of the modality of competence only exists under the condition that only those norms that have been set on the basis of a competence can be legally valid. This excludes the existence of norms whose *legal* validity is based not on their issuance in accordance with the legal system, but on their substantive correctness. This shows that the problem of the fundamentality of obligation or competence is much more than mere logic. It is related to the problem of positivism in the form of the classical problem of the relation between law and morality. This connection does not mean that the decision in favour of the fundamentality of the modality of obligation is necessarily a decision against positivism. It is easily possible to associate commands exclusively with positivist criteria of validity. The modality of command as such is therefore neutral regarding the alternative of positivism or non-positivism. Rather, the crucial point is that the modality of obligation is open to morality in the sense of legal validity based on substantive correctness. Whoever opts for this, therefore, opts for a kind of normativity which does not have to be extended to morality, but which can be extended to morality. Those who do not want to exclude the possibility of legal validity on the basis of substantive correctness from the outset will, therefore, assume the fundamental nature of the modality of obligation and only concede the possibility of the same fundamentality for the field of what is issued in accordance with the legal system. We must concede that from the perspective of the defence of positivism, the fundamental nature of the modality of competence has the advantage that, on its basis, there is no temptation to extend legal normativity beyond the realm of what is issued in accordance with the legal system into the realm of morality. As Kelsen pursues a clear positivist programme, this argues in favour of giving priority to the modality of competence within the framework of his interpretation. However, such a priority would make Kelsen's conception of normativity dependent on Kelsen's positivist programme, which would mean a systematic weakening of Kelsen's central ideas. To avoid this, we will continue to regard obligation as the fundamental normative modality – perhaps against Kelsen's essential

[67] Alexy, 'Alf Ross' Begriff der Kompetenz' (n 61).

intentions – which does not exclude the use of the concept of Ought in the broad sense defined by Kelsen in most texts.

From the perspective of normativity, ie, that of Ought as a category, the significance of the basic norm is thus limited to the fact that the conferral of normativity does not have to occur for each norm, ie, individually as it were, but only once at the top of the tiered structure of the legal system. The basic norm feeds normativity in one act, ie, generally, down to the mot minute ramifications of the legal system. This is the meaning of the thesis that the basic norm, concerning normativity, is nothing other than the category of Ought in systemic form. More precisely, we can state that the application of the basic norm to a legal system is nothing other than the systemic presupposition of the category of Ought in the process of cognition of positive law. Of course, the basic norm has other functions under different aspects.[68] For Kelsen, for example, it is not only the gate to the realm of legal Ought, but also the guardian of this gate, letting through only that which corresponds[69] to the positivist criterion of issuance in accordance with the legal system – combined with the condition of a certain social efficacy.[70] However, this is of no further interest to us.

III. Ought as a Relative A Priori Category

Having identified Ought as the type of link between legal condition and legal consequence in the legal norm as the most promising candidate for what Kelsen means by a normative category, we must now enquire as to what Kelsen means and can mean by labelling this category as both a priori and relative.

A. A Priori

Kelsen's use of the concept of the a priori is an expression of his attempt to apply the basic ideas of Kant's transcendental philosophy, as he saw them represented in his time primarily by Hermann Cohen, to law. This is particularly clear in a letter to Renato Treves in 1933, shortly before the first edition of the *Pure Theory of Law* appeared. In this letter, Kelsen explains the pure legal theory of law as an attempt to apply the 'transcendental method' to a theory of positive law.[71]

In contrast to Cohen, Kelsen emphatically emphasises that his attempt is not concerned with any substantive principles of practical reason, ie, not with a priori

[68] cp in this regard SL Paulson, 'Die unterschiedlichen Formulierungen der 'Grundnorm'' in A Aarnio, SL Paulson, O Weinberger, GH von Wright and D Wyduckel (eds), *Rechtsnorm und Rechtswirklichkeit. Festschrift für Werner Krawietz zum 60. Geburtstag* (Berlin, Duncker & Humblot, 1993) 58 f.

[69] Alexy, *The Argument from Injustice* (n 3) 105 f.

[70] Kelsen, PTL2 §34(g), 213; RR2, 220.

[71] H Kelsen, 'Reine Rechtslehre, 'Labandismus' und Neukantianismus' in SL Paulson (ed), *Hans Kelsen – Renato Treves. Formalismo giuridico e realtà sociale* (Napoli, Edizioni Scientifiche Italiane, 1992) 56; in English see H Kelsen, 'The Pure Theory of Law, "Labandism" and Neo-Kantianism. A Letter To Renato Treves', SL Paulson and B Litschewski Paulson trans in SL Paulson and B Litschewski Paulson (eds), *Normativity and Norms. Critical Perspectives on Kelsenian Themes* (Oxford, Clarendon Press, 1998) 171–75, 171.

postulates of the law of reason [*Vernunftrecht*] as set out by Kant in the '*Metaphysik der Sitten*',[72] but with a purely formal a priori which provides an answer to the question 'how is positive law – as an object of cognition, as an object of jurisprudence – and thus: how is this possible'.[73] This is the question of the conditions of the possibility of cognition, and thus a transcendental question.[74] Kelsen's a priori therefore aims to be a transcendental a priori. Kelsen's interpretation of Ought as a relative a priori category is, therefore, nothing less than an ambitious attempt to add another category to the table of categories that Kant declared complete.[75]

This project has a certain intuitive plausibility. Kant limited his transcendental programme to the natural sciences and mathematics. If something like 'empirical cognition'[76] is to be possible in the humanities, then the transcendental programme – if it can be applied to anything at all – must also be applicable to them. The attempt to interpret Ought as a relative a priori category can thus be considered an exemplary attempt to apply the transcendental programme beyond the natural sciences and mathematics to the field of the humanities.

The parallel between causality and imputation, which Kelsen has already discussed above, can serve as a touchstone for such an extension. Kant speaks of categories, and thus of causality, as 'pure concepts of synthesis'. The understanding 'by these concepts alone can it understand something in the manifold of intuition, i.e. think an object for it'.[77]

This 'by these concepts alone' does not apply to the category of Ought. Ought is not a category of which it is true that 'only by means of them can any object of experience be thought at all'.[78] The work of the category of Ought begins only after the other categories, including that of causality, have already done their work and constituted objects of experience. It is these categories that, first and foremost, produce the 'empirical legal data' that are transformed into law by the category of Ought. The category of Ought is thus a second-level category.[79] Ought does not 'work up the raw material of

[72] cp, eg, I Kant, *The Metaphysics of Morals*, M Gregor trans (Cambridge, Cambridge University Press, 1991) 69; Königlich Preußische Akademie der Wissenschaften (ed), *Metaphysik der Sitten, Kant's gesammelte Schriften* Vol VI (hereafter MdS) (Berlin, Druck und Verlag von Georg Reimer, 1907) (*Akademieausgabe* – KPAW-KGS) 247.

[73] H Kelsen, *Die philosophischen Grundlagen der Naturrechtslehre und des Rechtspositivismus* (Charlottenburg, Verlag Rolf Heise, 1928) §36, 66; reprinted in H Kelsen, 'Die philosophischen Grundlagen der naturrechtslehre und des Rechtspositivismus (1928)' in HR Klecatsky, R Marcic und H Schambeck (eds), *Die Wiener rechtstheoretische Schule*, Vol 1 (Stuttgart, Franz Steiner Verlag, 1968) 339.

[74] I Kant, *Prolegomena to Any Future Metaphysics*, G Hatfield trans (Cambridge, Cambridge University Press, 2004) 125; Königlich Preußische Akademie der Wissenschaften (ed), *Prolegomena, Kant's gesammelte Schriften*, Vol IV (Berlin, Druck und Verlag von Georg Reimer, 1911) (*Akademieausgabe* – KPAW-KGS) 4, 373: '[T]he word: transcendental … does not signify something that surpasses all experience, but something that indeed precedes experience (a priori), but that, all the same, is destined to nothing more than solely to make *cognition from experience possible*'. Emphasis added by Robert Alexy.

[75] Kant, KrV, A79/B105.

[76] Kant, *Prolegomena* (n 74) 373.

[77] Kant, KrV, A80.

[78] Kant, KrV, A93.

[79] cp S Hammer, 'A Neo-Kantian Theory of Legal Knowledge in Kelsen's Pure Theory of Law?' in SL Paulson and B Litschewski Paulson (eds), *Normativity and Norms. Critical Perspectives on Kelsenian Themes* (Oxford, Clarendon Press, 1998) 177–94, 186; A Wilson, 'Is Kelsen Really a Kantian?' in R Tur and W Twining (eds), *Essays on Kelsen* (Oxford, Clarendon Press, 1986) 37–64, 52.

sensible impressions into a cognition of objects that is called experience',[80] but rather it links up with the results of such processing by giving them a 'specifically legal sense … [that is] their own peculiarly legal meaning'.[81] In this context, Kelsen uses the term 'scheme of interpretation [*Deutungsschema*]'. Although he applies this term directly to the norm, it can also be applied to Ought in general, in which case we can say that the use of the category Ought consists in the interpretation of what is already constituted by other categories. As a scheme of interpretation, however, the category of Ought fulfils the most fundamental requirement for the transcendental a priori: it constitutes an object. This object is the norm. The fact that this object is an abstract object in the sense described above would only constitute an objection if there could be no abstract objects. An intermediate result is thus established: Ought has the character of a transcendental a priori category in so far as it constitutes an abstract object, namely the norm, and thus the law.

Of course, objections remain, one of which is that to speak of a category of Ought that transforms empirical data into norms is too transcendental: norms are not first constituted by a category of Ought but are already present in reality. Thus, the legislator constantly uses the concept of Ought and related concepts, including the conditional structure of legal condition and legal consequence, in the formulation of his laws. The theory of legal cognition, therefore, finds its Ought already in reality and thus does not need to impose it on reality by means of any transcendental methods.

To counter this objection, it is necessary to determine the role that the modality of Ought plays in norms or in connection with norms. The starting point may be its weakest role. This role is played by the deontic modality of Ought in merely conceived norms. Kelsen often writes of merely conceived norms.[82] In the first edition of *Pure Theory of Law*, he expresses this idea by writing of legal norms as '(intended or imagined) meaning'.[83] Anyone can imagine any legal norm. However, such ideas only acquire legal significance – at least from the perspective of pure positivism – when an empowered body expresses the will to implement these norms. Before the decision of the empowered body, the norm is merely a thought containing a deontic modality. After the decision, three concepts compete for the ability to best describe the situation. It is these concepts that are important in answering the question of the transcendental status of the category of Ought. They are the concepts of validity, objective Ought and correctness.

i. Validity

All three concepts lead to a two-level structure of normativity. The first level is the norm as mere content of thought, ie, as a semantic entity. In it, Ought is found in a form free

[80] Kant, KrV, B1.

[81] Kelsen, PTL1 §4, 10; RR1, 5.

[82] cp, eg, Kelsen, PTL2 §4(b), 9; RR2, 9; H Kelsen, 'Vom Geltungsgrund des Rechts' (1960) in HR Klecatsky, R Marcic and H Schambeck (eds), *Die Wiener rechtstheoretische Schule. Schriften von Hans Kelsen, Adolf Merkl und Alfred Verdross* (München, Europa-Verlag, 1968) 1417–27, 1418; original printed in FAF von der Heydte, I Seidl-Hohenveldern, ST Verosta and K Zemanek (eds), *Völkerrecht und rechtliches Weltbild. Festschrift für Alfred Verdross* (Vienna, Springer Verlag, 1960) 157–65; translated into English as 'On the Basis of Legal Validity', S L Paulson trans (1981) 26 *American Journal of Jurisprudence* 1, 178.

[83] Kelsen, PTL1 §7, 14; RR1, 11.

of validity. We could also term this a 'neutral Ought'. A prime example is a bill. The door to the second stage is opened when the bill is enacted by the legislature. The law as a mere thought becomes the object of a will. Following Kelsen's distinction between the subjective and objective meaning of a legislative act, this can be described as 'subjective validity'. Once the norm is endowed with subjective validity, the Ought contained in it is no longer neutral in the sense just described. We can call it a 'subjective Ought'. The step through the door to the second stage, which is opened by the legislative decision, is finally completed when the enactment of the law is interpreted as the exercise of a competence that derives directly or indirectly from a constitution to which the basic norm gives validity. This leads to what Kelsen calls 'objective validity'.[84] Thus something is added to the Ought which, as a mere content of thought, is neutral regarding validity, and as an object of the legislative will is only subjectively valid, namely objective validity. We can also speak of an 'objective Ought'. If we note '*Op*' for 'It is commanded that *p*' and '*G*' as 'It is objectively valid that', we can consider the objective validity of a norm as '*GOp*'.

The concept of validity has been raised because the Ought contained in the merely conceived norm, in addition to that contained in the decision of the legislature, is not sufficient to constitute what is experienced as law. However, what is the category capable of constituting this experience? The concept to which we initially turned to solve our problem, that of validity in the form of objective validity, certainly cannot be it. It is precisely the task of the transcendental category to take the step from the subjective to the objective,[85] to 'objective validity' in the Kantian[86] or Kelsenian sense.[87] As a result of the application of the category, validity cannot therefore be the category itself.

ii. *Objective Ought*

Thus, from the validity at which we have arrived, we must somehow return to the concept of Ought. Kelsen's definition of validity as bindingness makes this easy. It reads:

> A norm referring to the behaviour of a human being is 'valid' means that it is binding – that an individual *ought* to behave in the manner determined by the norm.[88]

Validity is here defined as bindingness and bindingness as Ought. It follows that validity is Ought. This is formulated with great acuity, not tempered by the concept of bindingness, in the 1960 essay 'Vom Geltungsgrund des Rechts'.*

> To say that a valid norm commands, permits, or empowers a certain behaviour is to say that one should behave in the way prescribed by the norm, i.e. it is an *ought*-judgement [*Soll*-Urteil].[89]

[84] cp Kelsen, PTL2 §34(d), 202; RR2, 205.
[85] Kant, KrV, B127.
[86] Kant, KrV, A202. [TN: In the original text, the author quotes the expression '*objective Gültigkeit*' from the Kantian source.]
[87] Kelsen, PTL2 §34(d), 204; RR2, 207. [TN: In the original text, the author quotes the expression '*objective Geltung*' from the Kelsenian source.]
[88] Kelsen, PTL2 §34(a), 193; RR2, 196 (emphasis added by Robert Alexy).
* TN: On Reasons for the Validity of the Law.
[89] Kelsen, 'Vom Geltungsgrund des Rechts' (n 82) 1418.

This '*Ought*-judgement' is explicitly opposed to the '*Is*-judgement', which takes the form of stating that a fact exists.[90]

Referring to Oughtness [*Gesolltsein*], on what determines a norm appears to amount to an iteration of Ought. This can be noted as '*OOp*'. What, however, does an iterated Ought mean? And does not the interpretation of validity as bindingness or Ought lead dangerously close to the field that should be avoided at all costs, that of morality?[91]

iii. Correctness

The term Ought-judgement used in the above quotation indicates the third candidate for solving our problem, the concept of correctness. We may speak of 'truth' instead of 'correctness', but this is inadvisable owing to the problems of practical cognition, which cannot be excluded from the outset even in the case of legal cognition. If a law has been passed, drafted and promulgated in accordance with the legal system, and is otherwise formally and materially constitutional, and if it orders the legal consequence *R* under the condition *T* such that ($T \rightarrow OR$), then the jurist who repeats the proposition '$T \rightarrow OR$' with the intention of expressing his cognition of the legal order for himself or of communicating it to others is not simply repeating the text of the law. Even if he syntactically and semantically only reproduces what Kelsen calls 'empirical data',[92] his statement goes far beyond this. He is expressing a judgement about what, according to his legal system, should be done (*OR*) under certain conditions (*T*). This judgement, like every judgement, is linked to a claim to correctness. Like any judgement, it can be right or wrong. The judgement is correct, and the claim to correctness associated with it is thus fulfilled if the norm $T \rightarrow OR$ as a semantic entity fulfils the validity criteria of the legal system in question, which are to be noted here as 'S_1, S_2, … S_n'. According to Kelsen, these validity criteria are of a purely positivist nature. For him, what is decisive is the issuance in accordance with the legal system, ie, compliance with the norms of competence or empowerment in the act of norm-setting, and – as a condition of validity – a certain degree of effectiveness.[93] This is where the old argument about legal positivism is applicable, which ultimately revolves around the question of whether legal correctness can be defined by more criteria than the two of compliance with the legal system and social efficacy.[94] However, not only can this not be pursued here, it need

[90] ibid.

[91] According to Alf Ross, it is impossible to avoid this danger if one wants to interpret the law as normative. For any validity in the normative sense can only be a moral validity. Ross therefore thinks that it is inevitable for Kelsen, who fights for the normativity of law, to assume a moral duty to obey any positive law, which excludes him from the club of true positivists and makes him a 'quasi-positivist' (Alf Ross, 'Validity and the Conflict between Legal Positivism and Natural Law' in SL Paulson and B Litschewski Paulson (eds), *Normativity and Norms. Critical Perspectives on Kelsenian Themes* (Oxford, Clarendon Press, 1998) 146–63, 159 f). Of course, Ross assumes that the dispute over the problem of normativity has already been decided in his favour, namely in the sense of the thesis that normativity is impossible without morality, ie, that there is only the alternative of factuality or morality. Whoever regards this as a foregone conclusion is not only incapable of engaging with Kelsen's programme of normativist positivism, but is also incapable of continuing it in the direction of not linking normativity to either social facts (factuality) or moral arguments (morality).

[92] Kelsen, PTL1 §29, 58; RR1, 66.

[93] Kelsen, PTL2(g), 213; RR2, 220.

[94] cp Alexy, *The Argument from Injustice* (n 3) 20.

not be. The greatness of Kelsen's idea of Ought as a relative a priori is shown not least by the fact that the idea of Ought as an a priori category can survive even if the positivist criteria of legal validity, which rule out legal correctness and limit the criteria to issuance according to the legal system and effectiveness, do not apply.[95] It could still be the case that the category of Ought constitutes the norm in the act of legal cognition.[96] What is decisive is that the objectivity of such a constitutivity presupposes in any case the fulfilment of the criteria of legal validity S_1, S_2, … S_n, whatever they may be. The objective Ought is thus possible because three aspects are combined – synthesised – in a judgement that aims at cognition[97] of the law: the legal condition (T), the legal

[95] For this reason, Horst Dreier's thesis that Kelsen's interpretation of Ought as a relative a priori category is a cognitive quandary [*Verlegenheitsbestimmung*] cannot be accepted. (H Dreier, *Rechtslehre, Staatssoziologie und Demokratietheorie bei Hans Kelsen*, 2nd edn (Baden-Baden, Nomos Verlagsgesellschaft, 1990) 49, fn 130.).

[96] If we pursue this further, we come to the conclusion that there is no specific legal category of Ought. There is only one category of Ought. This extends beyond the realm of law and includes, in particular, the realm of morality. This single Ought is, of course, unsaturated in terms of the criteria of validity and unweighted in terms of its relation to the subject. This can be illustrated by Joseph Raz's 'legal man'. Raz's legal man is a pure construction invented to capture the legal point of view. According to Kelsen, lawyers have 'always' adopted this point of view, but 'mostly unconsciously', 'when they consider as law exclusively positive law' (Kelsen, PTL2 §34(d), 205; RR2, 209). What is special and unusual about Raz's legal man is that he combines the positivist criteria of validity with personal and, in this sense, moral acceptance (J Raz, 'Kelsen's Theory of the Basic Norm' in SL Paulson and B Litschewski Paulson (eds), *Normativity and Norms. Critical Perspectives on Kelsenian Themes* (Oxford, Clarendon Press, 1998) 47–68, 63). The jurist is thus a positivist 'whose moral convictions are identical with the law. He neither adds nor subtracts an iota from it'. He achieves this by being someone who 'endorses the basic norm and all that follows from it, and nothing else' (J Raz, 'The Purity of Pure Theory' in SL Paulson and B Litschewski Paulson (eds), *Normativity and Norms. Critical Perspectives on Kelsenian Themes* (Oxford, Clarendon Press, 1998) 236–52, 246). In terms of criteria of validity, then, the jurist is a strict positivist, in Raz's terminology: a strict adherent to the 'source thesis' (ibid 239). He saturates Ought with issuance in accordance with the legal system and social efficacy, and nothing else. Even when it comes to the weighting of Ought in relation to one's own person, the jurist cannot be surpassed as a positivist. Positive law is fully morally binding for him. Of course, the jurist is not Kelsen's positivist jurist. His point of view only emerges when the moral commitment to the positivist criteria of validity is cancelled and replaced by a distanced attitude, which is defined by the fact that the basic norm is not accepted, but merely assumed by adopting the point of view of the positivist jurist, which can be revoked at any time. The committed statements of the jurist are thus downgraded to the detached statements of the positivist jurist (ibid 247). Within the positivist standpoint, despite this downgrading, they cannot, by definition, be cancelled out by moral assertions of greater weight. The situation is different, however, when the positivist standpoint is extended to a comprehensive normative or practical standpoint, which is impossible in the case of a jurist because of his construction, but quite natural in the case of a human as a rational being. Here, regardless of Hart's position on the relation between law and morality, his dictum applies: 'No human being is just a lawyer' (HLA Hart, 'Kelsen Visited' in HLA Hart (ed), *Essays in Jurisprudence and Philosophy* (Oxford, Oxford University Press, 1983) 286–308, 306). From this comprehensive normative or practical point of view, Ought, and thus normativity is, on the one hand open to criticism' and on the other only definitive after all criteria have been weighed. For normative reasons such as legal certainty and, in the case of parliamentary laws, the separation of powers and democratic legitimacy, the positivist validity criteria of issuance in accordance with the legal system and social efficacy play a very important role in this weighing up, but they do not exhaust the canon of criteria for the correctness of legal decisions. All this falls under the category of Ought, because as such it is both unsaturated and unweighted. According to Ralf Dreier, 'it is part of the tragedy of Kelsen's work that its author, fixated on the dualism of Is and Ought, radically deepens the rift between jurisprudence and sociology and does not … contribute to overcoming this rift' (R Dreier, 'Sein und Sollen. Bemerkungen zur Reinen Rechtslehre Kelsens' in R Dreier (ed), *Recht-Moral-Ideologie*, 2nd edn (Berlin, Suhrkamp Verlag, 1981) 225). The above considerations show that Kelsen's insistence on the normativity of law at least ensured the connection of pure legal theory to a more comprehensive normative theory of law.

[97] What is said here applies both to the cognition of the law by jurisprudence – Kelsen speaks of a cognition 'as it were from the outside' – and to the cognition of the law by the organs applying the law – Kelsen describes

consequence including the modality of Ought (*OR*), and the criteria of legal validity (S_1, S_2, … S_n). If the judgement is correct, its object is an objective Ought. It is precisely in this sense that we can conclude that Kelsen's programme is successful from the perspective of what constitutes law – independently of the problem of positivism and without prejudice to numerous individual questions.

Assertions and judgements tend not to make explicit their claim to truth or correctness. Explicitness, however, benefits analysis everywhere. If we use '*R*' for 'It is correct that', the basic form of the judgement expressing legal cognition can be written as '*ROp*'. '*ROp*' expresses what '*GOp*' and '*OOp*' attempt to express – with limited success: the objectivity of the legal Ought. This justifies – whatever the outcome of the dispute over legal positivism – speaking of Ought as correctness. The key to law is, therefore, the concept of correctness.

B. Relative

The a priori as an element of transcendental philosophy is characterised by two dimensions in Kant. The first is that of constitutivity in the sense of transcendental philosophy, which is concerned with the conditions of the possibility of experience. So far, only this aspect has been considered, and we have established that Kelsen's discussion of Ought as an a priori category is plausible. Difficulties arise, however, with the second dimension essential to Kant, that of necessity. For Kant, the concept of necessity is necessarily linked to the concept of a priori: '[n]ecessity and strict universality' are 'secure indications of an *a priori* cognition'.[98] According to him, experience is not possible without space and time as a priori forms of perception and without a priori categories such as causality.[99] This should apply not only to any experience, but to 'all experiential cognition'. Without the categories, not less but 'nothing is possible as object of experience'.[100] In this respect, the categories claim universal validity, at least as far as human beings are concerned.[101] Transcendental apriority in Kant's sense is, therefore, a necessity relative to the possibility of experience in general.

With Kelsen, the situation is quite different, at least initially. His a priori is expressly intended to be only a relative one. This means that the interpretation of 'empirical data'[102] as law is only a possible interpretation and by no means a necessary one. Thus, an anarchist could refuse 'to see anything but naked power where jurists

it as a cognition 'as it were from the inside' (Kelsen, PTL2 §16, 72; RR2, 74). Differences arise from the competence of the courts to determine the law in a legally binding way and to interpret it in a legally binding way. Neither the findings of legal scholars on the applicable law nor its interpretation by legal scholars are legally binding.

[98] Kant, KrV, B4.

[99] Kant, KrV, A93.

[100] ibid.

[101] Kant, KrV, A26; cp also B72. In B72 Kant considers possible extensions: '[I]t may well be that all finite thinking beings must necessarily agree with human beings in this regard (though we cannot decide this)'. According to Schnädelbach, Kant thus gave the cue to an anthropological interpretation and relativisation of the a priori that he himself rejected. cp H Schnädelbach, 'Was ist eigentlich ein relatives Apriori?' in H Schnädelbach, *Philosophie in der modernen Kultur* (Berlin, Suhrkamp, 2000) 189 f.

[102] Kelsen, PTL1 §29, 58; RR1, 66.

speak of the law'.[103] Regarding Kant's sentence: 'One can never represent that there is no space',[104] the following negated parallel can be formulated with regard to Kelsen: 'One can always maintain that there is no law'. Is such a relativised a priori still an a priori? We could consider this question a pure problem of definition and decide that constitutivity is sufficient for a priori. Kelsen's concept of the a priori would then be a weak concept because of the absence of necessity, while Kant's would be a strong concept of the a priori because of the inclusion of necessity. We could even claim that everything that is somehow constitutive has an a priori character. Even the rules of chess would then have an a priori status. However, such an extension would not only unnecessarily devalue the concept of the a priori, but it is also not the basis of Kelsen's idea of a relative a priori. It is anything but an arbitrary a priori. This can be seen in three characteristics of Kelsen's concept of the a priori, which do not eliminate relativity but rather bring about a certain de-relativisation.

The first is that Kelsen's concept of the a priori remains tied to the concept of cognition, irrespective of relativisation. Thus, for Kelsen too, the concept of the a priori is a concept that belongs to the dimension of correctness or truth.

Second, Kelsen follows Kant in that a distinction must be made in the system of cognition between a priori and a posteriori elements. Thus, like Kant, Kelsen constructs a dividing line in cognition that a radical holist must doubt.[105] Such a line can be drawn in two ways, resulting in two kinds of a priori relativity: an internal and an external kind. An example of an internal relative a priori can be found in Reichenbach's early work *Relativitätstheorie und Erkenntnis Apriori*.* According to Reichenbach, Kant's transcendental aesthetics is refuted by Einstein's theory of relativity.[106] Nevertheless, he clings to the idea of a priori cognition. This is because experience is not possible without constitutive principles.[107] However, such an a priori as a constitutive principle can be refuted by experience.[108] For Reichenbach, therefore, the relativity of the a priori means that within the realm of natural cognition, changes in the system of categories may become necessary for the sake of truth.[109] This is different for Kelsen and Kant. For Kelsen, it is inconceivable that the 'empirical legal data'[110] could at some point lead to a change in the category of Ought or the 'basic form of positive laws'.[111] If we wish to recognise law as law, then this is only possible by means of the category of Ought. According to Kelsen, there is no alternative. In this respect, the category is internally necessary and only externally relative. Internally, then, Kelsen's a priori is a genuine a priori, linking constitutivity with necessity. What we do not find in Kelsen, however, is

[103] Kelsen, PTL1 §16, 34; RR1, 36.
[104] Kant, KrV, A24.
[105] cp in this regard M Friedman, *Reconsidering Logical Positivism* (Cambridge, Cambridge University Press, 1999) 67 f.
* TN: For an English translation see H Reichenbach, *The Theory of Relativity and A Priori Knowledge*, M Reichenbach trans (Berkeley, University of California Press, 1965).
[106] H Reichenbach, *Relativitätstheorie und Erkenntnis Apriori* (Berlin, Verlag von Julius Springer, 1920) 3 f.
[107] ibid.
[108] ibid 89, 100.
[109] ibid 3.
[110] Kelsen, PTL1 §11(b)–(c), 24–25; RR1, 23.
[111] Kelsen, PTL §11(a)–(b), 23; RR1, 22.

an attempt to prove necessity, ie, an attempt to produce something like a transcendental deduction of the category of Ought.[112]

The third peculiarity of Kelsen's a priori, which leads to a certain de-relativisation, is the question of how relative external relativity is. Kelsen writes not only of the possibility but also of the 'necessity' of a normative theory of law, which is 'shown by the very existence of legal science over a millennium'.[113] The concept of necessity is open to several interpretations; we consider three here. The first focuses on expediency. We need only think beyond the existence of law to appreciate the importance of its necessity in terms of expediency. There are few human ends for which the abolition of law would not be detrimental. The second interpretation of necessity concerns cultural identity. Replacing law with brute force would mean abandoning correctness in social and political life, which would profoundly alter our cultural identity. This leads to a third interpretation, which reads the necessity of law as a practical necessity. This interpretation leads to a new realm of the a priori, that of the practical a priori, among the laws of which Kant undoubtedly includes the obligation of transition to the rightful condition [*der rechtliche Zustand*].[114] However Kelsen, who fought on two fronts, would not allow himself to be drawn into this path for the sake of a possible de-relativisation of his a priori. It leads directly into the field that Kelsen wants to avoid at all costs, that of morality. The relativity that remains because Kelsen does not morally justify the necessity of law is not only somehow intentional, but it is rather part of the basic architecture of his system and, therefore, for him a necessary relativity.

[112] To do this, Kelsen, following Kant, would have had to choose a method 'that takes no foundation as given except reason itself, and that therefore tries to develop cognition out of its original seeds without relying on any fact whatever' (Kant, *Prolegomena* (n 74) 274). Kant contrasts this method, which he calls 'synthetic' or 'progressive,' with the analytic or regressive method: '[I]t signifies only that one proceeds from that which is sought as if it were given, and ascends to the conditions under which alone it is possible' (Kant, *Prolegomena* (n 74) 276). This is precisely Kelsen's way: 'With the doctrine of the basic norm, the Pure Theory analyses the actual process of the long-standing method of cognizing positive law, in an attempt simply to reveal the transcendental logical conditions of that method' (Kelsen, PTL1 §29, 58; RR1, 67. cp Paulson, 'The Neo-Kantian Dimension of Kelsen's Pure Theory of Law' (n 4) 328 ff).

[113] Kelsen, PTL1 §16, 34; RR1, 37.

[114] Kant, MdS, 306 f.

4

Kelsen the Outsider

IAIN STEWART

I. Introduction

In the preface to the second version of his book *Reine Rechtslehre*,[1] which would be the final full statement of his 'pure theory of law (*Reine Rechtslehre*)', the almost

[1] The two principal versions of the book titled *Reine Rechtslehre*, in 1934 and 1960, will be referred to here as 'first' and 'second' *Reine Rechtslehre* – hereafter, respectively, as 'RR1' and 'RR2', their English translations as 'RR1en' and 'RR2en', and the French and Italian translations similarly with 'fr' and 'it'.

- RR1: H Kelsen, *Reine Rechtslehre. Einleitung in die rechtswissenschaftliche Problematik. Studienausgabe der 1. Ausgabe 1934*, M Jestaedt (ed and intro) (Tübingen, Mohr Siebeck, 2008); cited according to its in-margin pagination from the 1934 text.
- RR1en: H Kelsen, *Introduction to the Problems of Legal Theory*, B Litschewski Paulson and SL Paulson trans, with a long introduction by the latter (Oxford, Clarendon Press, 1992) (Oxford Scholarship Online 2012). The title of RR1en was originally the subtitle for RR1, now used to distinguish RR1en from RR2en.
- RR1fr: H Kelsen, *Théorie pure du droit. Introduction à la science du droit*, H Thévenaz trans (Neuchâtel, Éditions de la Baconnière, 1953).
- RR2: H Kelsen, *Reine Rechtslehre. Mit einer Anhang: Das Problem der Gerechtigkeit. Studienausgabe der 2. Ausgabe 1960*, M Jestaedt (ed and intro) (Tübingen, Mohr Siebeck, 2017); cited according to its in-margin pagination from the 1960 text. Differs importantly from the 1960 text in that it tracks changes made for the Italian translation (RR2it).
- RR2en: H Kelsen, *Pure Theory of Law*, M Knight trans (Berkeley, University of California Press, 1967).
- RR2fr: H Kelsen, *Théorie pure du droit*, C Eisenmann trans (Paris, Dalloz, 1962).
- RR2it: H Kelsen, *La dottrina pura del diritto*, MG Losano trans (Turin, Einaudi, 2021) (translation originally published 1966).

Separately, 'RR2App' will refer to the essay 'Das Problem der Gerechtigkeit' ('The Problem of Justice') which is appended to RR2 at 355–444 (but is omitted by RR2en, RR2fr and RR2it). It was first published in French translation, as the article 'Justice et droit naturel', É Mazingue trans (1959) 3 *Annales de philosophie politique* 1, and has not been translated into English.

Other abbreviations for works by or involving Kelsen:

- 'ATN': H Kelsen, *Allgemeine Theorie der Normen*, K Ringhofer and R Walter (eds) (Vienna, Manz, 1979).
- 'ATNen': English trans of ATN by M Hartney as *General Theory of Norms* (Oxford, Clarendon Press, 1991) (Oxford Scholarship Online 2012).
- 'ATNfr': French trans of ATN by Olivier Beaud and Fabrice Malkani as *Théorie générale des normes* (Paris, Presses universitaires de France, 1996).
- 'ATNit': Italian trans of ATN by M Torre as *Teoria generale delle norme*, MG Losano (ed) (Turin, Einaudi, 1985).

octogenarian Hans Kelsen avows that he is laying down his pen. This book, he says, 'is to be regarded not as a presentation of final results but as an enterprise needing to be continued by supplementation and other kinds of improvement'; it will have achieved its aim if continuation of that enterprise were to be considered worthwhile by others than an author 'already at the end of his life'.[2] That might be taken as just a farewell gesture,[3] but this old man would not keep still. From 1962 to 1965, he made three major corrections to the pure theory, which I will refer to as 'turns': a 'constitution' turn, a 'logic' turn and a 'fiction' turn.

The constitution turn and the logic turn could be regarded as belated refinements of the pure theory. Not so, the fiction turn. In converting a 'basic norm' (*Grundnorm*) from a 'hypothesis' of some sort into a 'fiction', and moreover a 'fiction' in a dubiously extended sense that involved a self-contradiction or something similar, Kelsen has seemed to some to have shattered the keystone of the pure theory and, in doing so, to have brought down the pure theory itself.

One could have expected opinion on the fiction turn to be keenly divided. Rather, there has mostly been bewilderment.[4] Most supporters of the pure theory either have

- 'FV' etc: see below (n 7).
- 'GNRL': H Kelsen, 'Die Grundlage der Naturrechtslehre' in F-M Schmölz (ed), *Das Naturrecht in der politischen Theorie* (n 46) 1–37; in *Die Wiener rechtstheoretische Schule* (n 7) 869–912 (misspelling the title with 'Grundlagen (Foundations)').
- 'GNRLen': English trans of GNRL as 'The Foundation of the Theory of Natural Law' in Kelsen, *Essays in Legal and Moral Philosophy*, O Weinberger sel and intro, P Heath trans (Dordrecht, Reidel, 1973) 114–53.
- 'GTLS': *General Theory of Law and State*, A Wedberg trans (New York, Russell & Russell, 1945).
- 'HKW': *Hans Kelsen Werke* – Kelsen's collected works, edited by Matthias Jestaedt of the Hans-Kelsen-Forschungsstelle (Hans Kelsen Research Centre) based at the Universities of Freiburg and Frankfurt, in collaboration with the Hans Kelsen-Institut in Vienna. Published in Tübingen by Mohr Siebeck and appearing in roughly chronological order, the *Werke* have got up to 1923 in nine volumes (*Bände*), of which Bd 9 will soon appear. Bde 1–5 can be downloaded free online: kelsen.online/digitale-baende.

'HPS', 'HPS1', 'HPS2', 'HPS2en'. HPS: H Kelsen, *Hauptprobleme der Staatsrechtslehre: entwickelt aus der Lehre vom Rechtssatze* (*Main Problems in Theory of Public Law: Explained from Theory of the Legal Statement*) (Tübingen, Mohr, 1911 – hereafter, in the text, *Main Problems*). Had two printings, in 1911 and 1923. The first and second printings are identical except for their prefaces. The first printing forms HKW2; the preface to the second printing (Mohr 1923; republished by Scientia Verlag in 1984) is to appear in HKW9. The preface from the first printing will be cited as 'HPS1' (there is no translation of it) and the remainder of the HKW text as 'HPS'. The substituted preface in the second printing will be referred to as 'HPS2', with 'HPS2en' for its English translation as '"Foreword" to the Second Printing of *Main Problems in the* [sic] *Theory of Public Law*' (various trans) in SL Paulson and B Litschewski Paulson (eds), *Normativity and Norms. Critical Perspectives on Kelsenian Themes* (Oxford, Clarendon Press, 1998) (Oxford Scholarship Online 2012) 3–22. The text in HKW2 (as with other major works so far included in HKW) will be cited according to the in-margin pagination taken from the original as well as with the pagination of HKW itself.

- 'PSTV': H Kelsen, *Das Problem der Souveränität und die Theorie des Völkerrechts* (Tübingen, Mohr Siebeck, 1920) (HKW4, 235–572).
- 'SHKI': Schriftenreihe des Hans Kelsen-Instituts.

References to works in German for which there is an English translation are to the German original; citation of the translation is added for anglophone readers' convenience.

[2] RR2, vii; RR2en omits (although it is paraphrased in the translator's preface, v–vi).

[3] It appeared so to his disciple Josef L Kunz, who referred to it as the 'definitive formulation of the Pure Theory of Law': 'Die definitive Formulierung der Reinen Rechtslehre' (1961) 11 *Zeitschrift für öffentliches Recht* (n.F.) 375.

[4] cp N Duxbury, 'Kelsen's Endgame' (2008) 67 *Cambridge Law Journal* 51, 54.

ignored the fiction turn altogether or have minimised it by ignoring the extension as to self-contradiction – which surely is not a legitimate response. Even opponents of the pure theory, who might have been expected to seize upon a moment of self-injury, have paid little attention to the fiction turn. Both supporters and opponents have been faced with the threshold problem: what does this turn mean? Various 'takes' on the fiction turn are summarised in the Appendix below.

Troubled by this predicament, two of Kelsen's admirers have enquired further: myself in the 1980s[5] and then the doyen of Kelsen studies, Stanley L Paulson.[6] Both of us have concluded that the fiction turn is a failure and that this failure seems to be fatal to the pure theory. Paulson explores whether the pure theory can be saved in neo-Kantian terms. I have, more simply, remained anxious: if the fiction turn threatens dire consequences for the pure theory, how does Kelsen appear never to see them? Perhaps he has perceived something that others have not yet noticed and that could be of greater importance. This is the matter that I will now investigate.

It will be suggested that behind the fiction turn – and not only as to its content, but also as to the way in which it was announced – lie two other turns, both of them very general, which operate partially separately from each other and partially in conjunction. These I will call an 'independence turn' and a 'closure turn'. I will understand these as turns in the direction of converting the pure theory into a social-scientific theory of law, committed to an 'outsider' perspective on law. I will term that development a 'social-scientific shift', but I stress: only 'in the direction'. My initial focus will be very specific: to ascertain how it was that, during a balmy August of 1962, in a congenial seventeenth-century Austrian hilltop residence, Hans Kelsen suddenly informed a small workshop, which he knew to be composed of opponents and even enemies, that he had been talking fiction.

II. Three Late Turns

A. The Constitution Turn

Of the three turns made soon after second *Reine Rechtslehre*, the simplest is the *constitution turn*, of 1964. A specifically 'constitutional' sector is removed, as unnecessary, from the concept of a positive legal order; instead, every relatively 'higher' norm is to be a 'constitution' in relation to a norm below it. 'The concept of a constitution is thus relativized'.[7] The pure theory is now to be read – which previously had been considered

[5] I Stewart, 'The Basic Norm as Fiction' [1980] *Juridical Review* 199; I Stewart, 'Kelsen and the Exegetical Tradition' in R Tur and W Twining (eds), *Essays on Kelsen* (Oxford, Clarendon Press, 1986) 123–47; with a response by Tur, 'The Kelsenian Enterprise' in Tur and Twining, ibid, 149–83.

[6] SL Paulson, 'Ralf Dreiers Kelsen' in R Alexy (ed), *Integratives Verstehen. Zur Rechtsphilosophie Ralf Dreiers* (Tübingen, Mohr Siebeck, 2005) 159–97; 'Metamorphosis in Hans Kelsen's Legal Philosophy' (2017) 80 *Modern Law Review* 860; 'The Basic Norm' in C Bezemek, M Potacs and A Somek (eds), *Vienna Lectures on Legal Philosophy*, vol 2 'Normativism and Anti-normativism in Law' (Oxford, Hart Publishing, 2020) 41–90. Also Duxbury in 2008, but his analysis is not so extensive: 'Kelsen's Endgame' (n 4).

[7] H Kelsen, 'Die Funktion der Verfassung' in *Verhandlungen des Zweiten Österreichischen Juristentages Wien 1964*, Bd II, Tl 7 (hereafter 'FV1') (Vienna, Manz, 1964) 65–76, 71–73; republished with layout changes and omitting material towards the end on norms and logic, as 'Die Funktion der Verfassung' (1964) 11 *Forum*

exceptional[8] – by taking the theoretically presupposed basic norm of a positive-legal order to refer to whatever are the highest norms of that order.[9] The pure theory is thereby relieved of the task of constructing a consistent concept of a 'constitution' – very difficult for domestic law and barely possible, if at all, for international law.[10] No change of principle is involved.[11]

B. The Logic Turn

The *logic turn*[12] does involve principle. For Kelsen, because norms are not statements of what is, they cannot be true or false. Then, since the logical law of non-contradiction applies only to statements that can be true or false, a conflict between norms cannot be a contradiction. However, statements that *describe* norms can be true or false, and so a conflict between such statements can be a contradiction. Then, to register a contradiction between statements that describe norms might be to say 'indirectly' that there is a contradiction between those norms.[13]

In 1962, Kelsen instead holds that the laws of logic are entirely inapplicable to norms, even by analogy; all that can be said about the norms themselves is that they 'conflict'. Two norms 'conflict' when it is in fact impossible to comply with both. Whether that is so for legal norms can be determined only by a judicial decision and not by legal science.[14]

The logic turn touches on the sense in which a legal science grounded in the pure theory is 'descriptive'. It is a stage in Kelsen's gradual differentiation between a legal norm and a statement that describes a legal norm – in second *Reine Rechtslehre*, between

583, 585–86 (hereafter 'FV2'). FV2 is reprinted in H Klecatsky, R Marcic and H Schambeck (eds), *Die Wiener rechtstheoretische Schule. Schriften von Hans Kelsen, Adolf Merkl, Alfred Verdross* (Vienna, Europa Verlag, 1968) 1971–79. I have translated FV2 as H Kelsen, 'The Function of a Constitution' (hereafter 'FV2en') in R Tur and W Twining (eds), *Essays on Kelsen* (n 5) 109–19; this translation supersedes that in I Stewart, 'The Basic Norm as Fiction' (n 5). Quotations in the present work contain some improvements to FV2en.

[8] RR2, 204 fn *; RR2en, 201, fn 70.

[9] RR2, 232–33; RR2en, 226.

[10] On the other hand, almost all positive-legal orders include a constitution and most if not all of its norms are entrenched, so the pure theory would still need to take account of that difference from the lower norms.

[11] In 1966 Kelsen writes as though this turn had not occurred: 'On the Pure Theory of Law' (1966) 1 *Israel Law Review* 1, 6. This appears to be just an aberration, however, since the constitution turn will remain fully in the general theory of norms: ATN, 207–08; ATNen, 257–58.

[12] Called the 'normological turn' by J Kammerhofer: 'Kelsen – Which Kelsen? A Reapplication of the Pure Theory to International Law' (2009) 22 *Leiden Journal of International Law* 225, 235, fn 69, 240.

[13] RR2, 77, 209–10; RR2en, 74, 205–06 (where legal propositions are 'rules of law').

[14] H Kelsen, 'Derogation' in RA Newman (ed), *Essays in Jurisprudence in Honor of Roscoe Pound* (Indianapolis, Bobbs-Merrill, 1962) 339–55; reprinted in *Essays in Legal and Moral Philosophy* (n 1) 261–75. The logic turn is set out fully in H Kelsen, 'Recht und Logik' (1965) 12 (nos 142 and 143) *Forum* 421 and 495; reprinted in *Die Wiener rechtstheoretische Schule* (n 7) 1469–97; translated as 'Law and Logic' in *Essays in Legal and Moral Philosophy* (n 1) 228–53. Kelsen had persuaded himself of this during argument by correspondence, beginning in 1959, with legal logician Ulrich Klug: H Kelsen and U Klug, *Rechtsnormen und logische Analyse. Ein Briefwechsel 1959 bis 1965* (Vienna, Deuticke, 1981). The logic turn is foreshadowed in 1957 when Kelsen considers 'not in conformity with' as alternative to 'in contradiction to' a norm: 'Aristotle's Doctrine of Justice' in H Kelsen, *What is Justice? Justice, Law, and Politics in the Mirror of Science. Collected Essays* (Berkeley, University of California Press, 1957) 110–36, 119. Of course, legal science could still speculate on the options and likelihood of a judicial decision.

a legal norm (*Rechtsnorm*) and a legal proposition (*Rechtssatz*).[15] However, the textual changes required by the logic turn amount only to switching terminology of 'contradiction' to that of 'conflict'.[16]

C. The Fiction Turn

The 'constitution' and 'logic' turns demonstrate that, even at this late stage of its development, the pure theory was still malleable. In speaking of a task for a later generation, Kelsen had been entirely serious. Those two turns, however, can be seen as refinements of the Pure Theory. The *fiction turn* was something else.

i. What

The concept of a 'basic norm', although it is the keystone of the pure theory, had always been found obscure, partly because Kelsen had characterised a basic norm as a 'hypothesis' without clarifying in what sense. In 1962, however, he suddenly declared that a basic norm is not a 'hypothesis' at all but a 'fiction'. He could have meant 'fiction' in the most common scientific sense: a statement that is known to be false yet is considered to be useful. That actually would not have been a large change, since a basic norm was never intended to be a real norm.[17] In 1964, however, he explained that he meant 'fiction' in an extended sense: a statement that may be useful to enquiry although it is not only false but also self-contradictory. This looks like much more than a refinement. If the law of non-contradiction is taken seriously, as it is in the logic turn, this seems to threaten destruction of the pure theory's keystone and consequently a collapse of the whole theory.

ii. How

Kelsen also handled the fiction turn very oddly. His new position could have been announced in ordinary ways – in a paper for a seminar or a conference, or in a journal article or a book chapter. He announced it in 1962 in a workshop where he was the star participant, yet not in the paper that he delivered. Instead, he declared it by way of an intervention in a later discussion – out of the blue and hesitantly, with apparent embarrassment and, more oddly still, amid an audience that he knew to be unsympathetic, even hostile.[18] The fiction turn is elaborated in 1964, in a conference paper that Kelsen could not deliver in person but which was immediately published. The elaboration

[15] RR2, 73–77; cp RR2en, 71–75.

[16] Made in the Italian translation of second *Reine Rechtslehre* (RR2it) and registered in the 2017 text of RR2 (RR2, xciii, 759–71). And see below (n 23).

[17] 'To act as though it were something, about a thing that one knows does not exist, is to construct a fiction and not in any way a hypothesis. All these "basic norms" are nothing but fictions': R Horneffer, *Die Entstehung des Staates. Eine staatstheoretische Untersuchung* (Tübingen, Mohr, 1933) 63; quoted, A Carrino, *Das Recht zwischen Reinheit und Realität. Würzburger Vorträge zur Rechtsphilosophie, Rechtstheorie und Rechtssoziologie*, Bd 42 (Baden-Baden, Nomos Verlag, 2011) 29, fn 86.

[18] See below (n 46).

attributes the extended concept of fiction to philosopher Hans Vaihinger,[19] but only with his name and with no reference to his writings.[20]

In a further oddity, the translations of second *Reine Rechtslehre* that appeared after these three turns – the Italian and English translations[21] – deal with the turns inconsistently. The logic turn is registered with a 'translator's note' – actually written by Kelsen himself[22] – and some amendments to the text.[23] However, neither the constitution turn nor the fiction turn is mentioned.[24] For the constitution turn, that is understandable: a mere mention of it would have had to be loose-ended, while sufficient amendments to the text would have had to be extensive.[25] About the fiction turn there is also silence, even though it concerns the status and even the viability of the pure theory. That might be thought to indicate misgivings about this turn, yet Kelsen refers to it again in 1965[26] and 1966,[27] and it is still included, although not accompanied by much further elucidation, in the drafts published posthumously as *General Theory of Norms*.[28]

D. Assumptions

The present work forms a pair with my recent article 'Hans Kelsen, Legal Scientist',[29] which is a review-essay on the first and only extensive biography of Kelsen,

[19] H Vaihinger, *Die Philosophie des Als Ob. System der theoretischen, praktischen und religiösen Fiktionen der Menschheit auf Grund eines idealistischen Positivismus*, first published in 1911. In 1919 Kelsen cites the second printing (*Auflage*) 1913; in ATN he will cite the 'seventh and eighth' printing (Leipzig, Meiner, 1922). The printings of 1913 and 1922 appear to be identical at least for the main text and the latter (available online: archive.org/details/DiePhilosophieDesAlsOb) will be cited here (hereafter *Die Philosophie des Als Ob*). Also cited here will be the abridged English translation by CK Ogden, *The Philosophy of 'As if'. A System of the Theoretical, Practical and Religious Fictions of Mankind*, 2nd edn of translation (London, Routledge & Kegan Paul, 1935) (hereafter *The Philosophy of 'As if'*).

[20] FV1, 71.

[21] RR2it; RR2en. RR2fr appears to have been written before the fiction turn was announced; Kelsen's brief foreword is signed at 'spring 1962'.

[22] RR2it, 106, fn 9; RR2en, 74 fn *; now reproduced in the 2017 text of RR2: RR2, 77, fn 18; 760, fn 18). For Kelsen's authorship of the note, see R Erne, 'Eine letzte authentische Revision der Reinen Rechtslehre' in W Krawietz and H Schelsky (eds), *Rechtssystem und gesellschaftliche Basis bei Hans Kelsen. Rechtstheorie*, Beiheft 5 (Berlin, Duncker & Humblot, 1984) 35–62, 42–43.

[23] These amendments are tracked in the correspondence between Kelsen and his translator, Losano: Erne (n 22). All of these alterations, to both the main text and the appended essay on justice, have been incorporated in the 2017 text of RR2 by Jestaedt (n 1). The changes are principally exchanges of '*Widerspruch* (contradiction)' and cognates for '*Konflikt* (conflict)' and cognates. A few of the alterations might be understood as tweaking the text towards the fiction turn; such tweaking might also occasionally be traceable in the English translation (RR2en), but in that text it can be difficult to tell whether a discrepancy between the original and the translation may be for that reason. See also below (n 233).

[24] Not even in the Italian translator's extensive introduction: MG Losano, 'Saggio introduttivo' in RR2it, xxxi–lxxxii.

[25] RR1 had been extensively amended, mostly by reorganisation, in RR1fr. However, in general RR1fr may be put aside since RR2 is an expansion of RR1.

[26] H Kelsen, 'Zum Begriff der Norm' in R Dietz and H Hübner (eds), *Festschrift für Hans Carl Nipperdey zum 70. Geburtstag 21. Januar 1965* (Munich, Beck Verlag, 1965) vol 1, 57–70, 63; translated as 'On the Concept of Norm' in *Essays in Legal and Moral Philosophy* (n 1) 216–27, 220.

[27] Kelsen, 'On the Pure Theory of Law' (n 11) 6.

[28] ATN, 205–07; ATNen, 254–56; and see below (nn 158–59).

[29] I Stewart, 'Hans Kelsen, Legal Scientist' (2023) 48 *Journal of Legal Philosophy* 119.

Thomas Olechowski's *Hans Kelsen: Biographie eines Rechtswissenschaftlers*.[30] I agree with Olechowski that Kelsen is primordinately a legal scientist. He is often counted as a philosopher, but, if a philosopher is someone who pursues specialist philosophers' issues for their own sake, Kelsen did not join that club until, following second *Reine Rechtslehre*, he embarked upon a general theory of norms. The pure theory is an enterprise less in philosophy than in legal science; it is philosophical, and interesting to philosophers, mainly in that it draws upon philosophy for its own development. For Kelsen as legal scientist and for the pure theory, philosophical doctrines are ancillary in theory-construction, even if they become logically fundamental to the theory. By the end, however, Kelsen's relation to philosophical doctrines becomes so unstable that one might not wish to share a canoe with him. Olechowski copes with this by focusing on Kelsen's life rather than his thought; my review-essay explores some directions of the thought. The suggestions arising from those explorations are assumed here.

One of those suggestions is that the pure theory should not be taken in isolation from what I have identified as a broader Purification Project.[31] This project is a critique of legal science, which began with Kelsen's commitment in *Main Problems* to a reform of 'method' and can be seen as double-sided. There is a side of denial, consisting of arguments *against*; it is a process of 'purification'. And there is a side of affirmation, consisting of arguments *for*; it is 'pure theory' as an activity (which is an exact interpretation of the name *Reine Rechtslehre*). An advantage of the distinction between two sides of this critique is that important elements of Kelsen's thinking may be understood better as elements of the Purification Project than as components of the pure theory.

The pure theory is 'pure' in two ways, which are independent of each other. One of these is that, on analogy with Kant's conception of natural science, the pure theory is a 'pure part' of legal science, stating the fundamental components of the science, which would make an 'empirical part' of the science possible. This form of purity, which is essentially Kantian, has sometimes been misunderstood: it has been supposed that the pure theory is directly empirical, so that it is a 'theory of pure law'.

The other way is more familiar, in legal theory as well as elsewhere: an avoidance of confusion between Is (*Sein*) and Ought (*Sollen*). This follows two philosophical doctrines that the Purification Project has made fundamental to the pure theory:

- A *Positivity Principle*: that reality is solely sensuous and, obversely, there is no transcendent reality.
- A *Separation Principle*: that statements of what is and of what ought to be are different in kind, so that a statement that is of the one kind cannot be inferred from a statement that is of the other kind.[32]

Kelsen takes both of these principles to be self-evident.[33] He does not derive either of them from any particular philosopher, although he occasionally reflects on what

[30] T Olechowski, *Hans Kelsen. Biographie eines Rechtswissenschaftlers*, 2nd edn (Tübingen, Mohr Siebeck, 2021) (originally published 2020).

[31] I Stewart, 'Hans Kelsen, Legal Scientist' (n 29) 162–64.

[32] Distinct from, although a logical reason for, the 'separability thesis' – the 'separability' of legal and moral norms: eg, SL Paulson, 'Introduction' in RR1en, xvii–xlii, xxiv.

[33] HPS, 7 (HKW2, 86); 'Ought (*Sollen*) is an "original category" just like Is (*Sein*); and we can no more give a definition of Ought than we can describe what Being (*Sein*) is': ATN, 2; ATNen, 2 (modified); citing G Simmel,

particular philosophers have made of them. He seems to have found them both as debated in the general culture around him and as adopted in recent legal science and in the only other science with which he became closely familiar, psychoanalysis.

Implicit in Kelsen's late work, it will now be suggested, is a tendency towards another and potentially equally important principle:

- An *Independence Principle*: that an observer's frame of reference ought, as far as possible, to be independent of the frame of reference of the observed.

If this principle were adopted in legal science, it could rank with the Positivity Principle and the Separation Principle – although whether it would necessarily accompany either of them is debatable.

The concern here is with meanings and for the present purpose I will sketch some specifications of terms:[34]

- These meanings are, directly, the meanings of the Purification Project and the pure theory themselves and, indirectly, the meanings that are their subject matter, norms. All of them are communicated meanings and not private thoughts – they are in the first place material, *socio-historical* events.
- Those meanings are, to begin with, elements of *attitudes* – ways of holding and expressing doctrines, and not wholly reducible to doctrines but at large in the environing cultures.[35] A thinker's attitude, together with the doctrines that they hold, is their *way*.[36] A culture is a collective way.
- Kelsen's attitude is *relativist*. He emphasises this, but without expressing it as a doctrine.[37] To the extent that he expresses it, he does so mainly in opposing an attitude of relativism to an attitude of absolutism. This is 'relativism' not in the insouciant sense of 'well, everything's relative' but in the sense of anti-absolutism,[38] in which one can be firmly committed against something absolutistic even though not to any specific alternative.[39] It is not drawn from any particular philosopher,

Einleitung in die Moralwissenschaft. Eine Kritik der ethischen Grundbegriffe (Stuttgart, Cotta, 1892) vol 1, 8. Is and Ought are two modes of thought, resulting in what seem to be 'two worlds torn apart': HPS, 8 (HKW2, 86).

[34] Spelt out further in I Stewart, 'Hans Kelsen, Legal Scientist' (n 29).

[35] 'Attitude' is meant here in something like the aeronautical sense – as a presence in the world that, among other things, is a way of holding beliefs, which include philosophical doctrines. On 'belief' see B Good and A McDowell, 'Belief, Anthropology of' in *International Encyclopedia of the Social & Behavioral Sciences*, 2nd edn, vol 2 (Amsterdam, Elsevier, 2015) 493–97.

[36] Preferable to saying 'stances' or 'standpoints'; after all, our bodies and minds are never quite still. A 'way' here includes both thinking and acting.

[37] L Vinx, *Hans Kelsen's Pure Theory of Law. Legality and Legitimacy* (Oxford, Oxford University Press, 2007) 134–44, On varieties of 'relativism' as a doctrine, see briefly M Baghramian, 'Relativism: Philosophical Aspects' in *International Encyclopedia of the Social & Behavioral Sciences*, 2nd edn, vol 2 (Amsterdam, Elsevier, 2015) 233–38.

[38] JL Kunz, contrasting Kelsen's thought with Catholicism, describes him simply as 'a relativist': JL Kunz, 'Jean Dabin et Hans Kelsen' in *Mélanges en l'honneur de Jean Dabin* (Brussels, Bruylant, 1963) Vol 1, 149–69, 165.

[39] This is explored by two contributions in M Jestaedt, R Poscher and J Kammerhofer (eds), *Die Reine Rechtslehre auf dem Prüfstand. Hans Kelsen's Pure Theory of Law: Conceptions and Misconceptions. Archiv für Rechts- und Sozialphilosophie*, Beiheft 163 (Stuttgart, Steiner Verlag, 2020): U Wagrandl, 'Kelsen was No Relativist. Reading Hans Kelsen in the Light of Isaiah Berlin's Value Pluralism' 373–91; and F Lijoi, 'The Democratic Value of Law. Hans Kelsen on the Theory and Praxis of Relativism' 393–411.

but from Kelsen's cultural environment. Absolutism, similarly, is identified less as doctrine than by way of examples. Kelsen's principal example of absolutism had to be the main kind that already confronted him: Catholic Christianity. Within and around that example, he confronts particular doctrines of natural law.

- As to philosophy, Kelsen is inconstant in doctrine but constant in attitude. In a constantly relativistic attitude, he searches for relativistic doctrine to assist him in reconstructing legal science as well as in contributing to political theory.

E. 'The' Basic Norm

There is a grammatical difficulty, which is not only a matter of translation: Kelsen's predilection for the generic definite article. He is not alone in this, but it particularly affects his arguments.

In English, the definite article is always 'the'. The expression 'the dog' would usually refer to an individual creature, Fido-over-there. In 'the dog is a loyal creature', however, 'the dog' refers generically to all canines. In German, the definite article is principally *die*, *der* or *das*.[40] Then, when Kelsen speaks of '*die Grundnorm*', sometimes it is not immediately clear whether the reference is individual or generic. When using Kelsen's terminology, I will not speak generically but will speak individually of 'the' or 'a' basic norm and, for the general concept of a basic norm, of 'the basic norm concept'. In translating Kelsen, however, his generic usage sometimes can be elided[41] and sometimes has to be rendered as though it were a reference to multiple individuality.[42]

III. Making the Fiction Turn

The fiction turn was made at two events held in Kelsen's native Austria: in 1962 in Salzburg and in 1964 in Vienna.

A. The Salzburg Intervention

i. *Invitation to a Workshop*

The fiction turn was announced at a small but internationally composed workshop held in Salzburg in 1962.

[40] According to whether the associated noun is grammatically feminine, masculine or neuter.

[41] Thus, eg, Kelsen's title *Das Problem der Souveränität und die Theorie des Völkerrechts* (hereafter 'PSTV') should be translated as 'The Problem of Sovereignty and Theory of International Law'.

[42] In Kelsen's title 'Die Funktion der Verfassung' (n 7), the first definite article ('*Die*') refers to a particular *Funktion* (function) while the second definite article (*der*) refers to *Verfassung* (constitution) as a class. To translate the title as 'The Function *of the* Constitution' would make '*the*' appear to refer to a particular constitution, which will not be Kelsen's argument. To maintain a generic meaning there, I have resorted to '*of a* Constitution'.

The University of Salzburg was founded in 1622 as a Catholic institution, supported by Benedictine monasteries, but it was closed under Napoleonic rule in 1810. Following the Second World War, it was re-established; in 1962 it reopened as a formally secular university with two faculties, of Catholic theology and of politics, and it added a faculty of law in 1965. In 1961, the Catholic Church had founded in Salzburg its own multidisciplinary research institution, an Internationale Forschungszentrum für Grundfragen der Wissenschaften (International Research Centre for Fundamental Questions of Science), directed by social philosopher Franz-Martin Schmölz.[43] The Centre was intended to work closely with the new university and soon became affiliated with it, as part of an inter-faculty Institut für Politische Wissenschaften (Political Sciences Institute), headed by René Marcic,[44] which Schmölz joined. There appears to have been an intention to revive the Catholic university in substance.

From 1 to 5 August 1962, the Centre held an inaugural workshop, on the theme '*Das Naturrecht in der politischen Theorie* (Natural Law in Political Theory)'.[45] The workshop's proceedings were later published under that title, initially in the prominent *Österreichische Zeitung für öffentliches Recht* (*Austrian Journal of Public Law*) and then as a separate volume.[46]

ii. *The Workshop Participants*

There were ten participants, of whom eight would give papers. Those eight were, with their papers and in the order in which the papers are printed:[47]

Hans Kelsen (1881–1973) Paper: 'Die Grundlage der Naturrechtslehre' ('The Foundation of the Theory of Natural Law').

Eric Voegelin (1901–85): Austrian political philosopher; student and research assistant of Kelsen in Vienna;[48] an enthusiastic theorist of 'race' and the authoritarian state, but opposed to biological reductionism; dismissed from his post at the *Anschluss* in 1938 and migrated to the USA; became professor of political science at the University of Munich in 1958, then returned to the USA in 1969; developed his own theory of

[43] Internationales Forschungszentrum für Soziale and Ethische Fragen, 'Über uns': www.ifz-salzburg.at/; Österreichische Cartellverband (ÖCV), 'Präs. Univ.-Prof. Dr. P. Franz-Martin Schmölz, OP': oecv.at/Biolex/Detail/13100173.

[44] Österreichische Cartellverband (ÖCV), 'Univ.-Prof. Dr. René Marcic': oecv.at/Biolex/Detail/13100315.

[45] The Centre was then based in a large residence built at the end of the seventeenth century and today housing the Stefan Zweig Zentrum Salzburg: stefan-zweig-zentrum.at/das-zentrum/ueber-uns.

[46] F-M Schmölz, 'Das Naturrecht in der politischen Theorie' (1963) 13(1/2) *Österreichische Zeitschrift für öffentliches Recht*; republished as F-M Schmölz (ed), *Das Naturrecht in der politischen Theorie* (Vienna, Springer, 1963). References here are to the latter, which has textual corrections and a name index.

[47] The biographical details in this list include those given by Schmölz, together with information, including dates, drawn from other sources. My labelling of affiliations is intended only to indicate each participant's ideological orientation to Kelsen. For the complexity of then-recent Austrian political culture, see JW Boyer, *Austria, 1867–1955* (Oxford, Oxford University Press, 2022).

[48] E Arnold, 'Eric Voegelin' in R Walter, C Jabloner and K Zeleny (eds), *Der Kreis um Hans Kelsen. Die Anfangsjahre der Reinen Rechtslehre*. SHKI, Bd 30 (Vienna, Manz, 2008) 513–52; E Schmidt Passos, 'Eric Voegelin and the Natural Law Tradition' (2019) 48 *Perspectives on Political Science* 210. Voegelin was one of the first to make the pure theory known in the anglosphere: E Voegelin, 'Kelsen's Pure Theory of Law' (1927) 42 *Political Science Quarterly* 268.

the state; latterly opposed modern thinking as 'gnosticism', to which Kelsen strongly objected in tense correspondence during the 1950s[49] and eventually at book length although that work was not published in his lifetime.[50]

Paper: 'Das Rechte von Natur' ('The Right of Nature').

Franz-Martin Schmölz (1927–2003): Austrian social philosopher; Director of the Centre; previously research assistant to Voegelin; from 1965 associate professor[51] in social and political theory, University of Salzburg; Dominican priest (OP).

Paper: 'Der gesellschaftliche Mensch und die menschliche Gesellschaft bei Thomas von Aquin' ('The Individual in Society and Human Society according to Thomas Aquinas').

Albert Auer (1891–1973): Austrian Catholic philosopher with a specialisation in natural law; professor in the faculty of theology, University of Salzburg; Benedictine priest (OSB).

Paper: 'Elemente aus dem modernen Naturrecht für die demokratische Gesellschaftsordung' ('Elements of Modern Natural Law for Democratic Social Order').

René Marcic (1919–71): Austrian journalist, publicist and legal philosopher; from 1963 professor of law and state, University of Salzburg.[52]

Paper: 'Das Naturrecht als Grundnorm der Verfassung' ('Natural Law as Basic Norm of a Constitution').

Friedrich August Freiherr von der Heydte (1907–94): German (Bavarian) Catholic aristocrat; joined the Nazi Party in 1933; research assistant of Alfred Verdross in Vienna; a distinguished soldier in the Second World War and after; professor of international law and political science, University of Würzburg; conservative Catholic politician (CSU);[53] member of the Bavarian state parliament 1966–70.

Paper: 'Naturrecht und modernes Kriegsrecht' ('Natural Law and Modern Law of War').

Giorgio Del Vecchio (1878–1970): prominent Italian Catholic legal philosopher; professor at the University of Rome, specialising in theories of justice.[54]

[49] B Thomassen, 'Debating Modernity as Secular Religion: Hans Kelsen's Futile Exchange with Eric Voegelin' (review of Kelsen, *Secular Religion* (n 50)) (2014) 53 *History and Theory* 435; B Cooper, 'Hans Kelsen and Eric Voegelin: The History of a Divergence' (2023) 47 *Political Science Reviewer* 47; M Henningsen, 'The Kelsen–Voegelin Controversies: A Biopsy' (2023) 47 *Political Science Reviewer* 93.

[50] H Kelsen, *Secular Religion. A Polemic against the Misinterpretation of Modern Social Philosophy, Science, and Politics as 'New Religions'*, R Walter, C Jabloner and K Zeleny (eds) (Vienna, Springer, 2012); C Jabloner, T Olechowski and K Zeleny (eds), *Secular Religion. Rezeption und Kritik von Hans Kelsens Auseinandersetzung mit Religion und Wissenschaft*. SHKI, Bd 34 (Vienna, Manz, 2013); particularly E Arnold, 'Bedarf die politische Ordnung einer spirituellen Grundlage? Kelsens Kritik an Voegelins autoritärer politischer Theologie', 19–42. Also I Stewart, 'Kelsen, the Enlightenment and Modern Premodernists' in Jabloner, Olechowski and Zeleny, ibid, 179–201; reprinted from (2012) 37 *Australian Journal of Legal Philosophy* 251.

[51] *Ausserordentlicher Professor*, an academic rank similar to full professor but without an established chair.

[52] P Schneider, 'René Marcic' (1973) 59 *Archiv für Rechts- und Sozialphilosophie* 207.

[53] The Christian Social Union: a centre-right political party operating in Bavaria and partnered with the Christian Democratic Party of Germany (CDU), which operates in the other states of Germany.

[54] The only non-Germanic participant and the only participant older than Kelsen. See G Del Vecchio, *The Formal Bases of Law*, J Lisle trans (New York, Kelley, 1969) (originally published 1905–08).

Paper: 'Das Naturrecht als Basis für eine Theorie der Weltgesellschaft' ('Natural Law as Basis for a Theory of World Society').

Alfred Verdross[55] (1890–1980): Austrian Catholic aristocrat; diplomat and then professor of law, University of Vienna; as a member of Kelsen's circle in Vienna, one of the founders of the pure theory of law; initially conservative and nationalist, sympathising with Nazism; later a world-rank specialist on international law; a judge of the European Court of Human Rights 1958–77; Feltrinelli prize winner 1975.[56]

Paper: 'Die Einfluß der Naturrechtslehre auf Theorie und Praxis der internationalen Beziehungen' ('The Influence of Natural Law Theory on Theory and Practice of International Relations').

The other two participants were:

Gustav Eduard Kafka (1907–74): Austrian Catholic social scientist and jurist; associate professor[57] of public law, University for World Trade,[58] Vienna.[59]

Eberhard Welty (1902–65): German Dominican priest (OP); professor of social philosophy and social ethics at a Dominican institution in Wahlberg, Germany; during the Nazi period was a member of a Catholic circle working against the régime.

iii. Terms of the Invitation

The invitation to the workshop was selective. In his preface to the published proceedings, Schmölz records that it had been sent to 'scholars of high repute (*Gelehrte von hohem Rang und Namen*)'. World outlook, ideology or religion had not been criteria for the invitation: the focus of discussion was to be 'the truth – and nothing but the truth!'.[60] It happened, nevertheless, that of the ten participants all but Kelsen were Catholic and three were members of Catholic religious orders.[61] There is no indication of when the eventual participants discovered who their companions would be.

[55] Listed by Schmölz as 'Verdross-Drossberg' – his full surname after his father, Austro-Hungarian general Ignaz Verdroß von Droßberg.

[56] The same prize that Kelsen had won in 1960.

[57] See above (n 51).

[58] University for World Trade; now the Wirtschaftsuniversität Wien (Vienna University of Economics and Business). Kelsen had taught there during the First World War.

[59] Schmölz, *Das Naturrecht in der politischen Theorie* (n 46) vii, notes Kafka's authorship of *Der freiheitliche Sozialismus in Deutschland* (Liberal Socialism in Germany) (Paderborn, Bonifacius Verlag, 1959), omitting the informative subtitles: *Das Godesberger Grundprogramm der SPD aus katholischer Sicht. Hrsg. vom Sozialreferat des Zentralkomitees der deutschen Katholiken* (The SPD's [Social Democratic Party's] Godesberg Programme through Catholic Eyes. Social Report by the Central Committee of German Catholics).

[60] Schmölz, *Das Naturrecht in der politischen Theorie* (n 46) iii. It turned out that all participants were male and middle-aged or older, except for Schmölz in his mid-thirties; and all, so far as I am aware, were white.

[61] Auer (Benedictine); Schmölz and Welty (Dominican): ibid vii. On the other hand, I am working from a copy of the reprint of the proceedings, signed on the front cover by Schmölz 'In Verehrung und Dankbarkeit (In admiration and gratitude)', from the *Nachlass* of Julius Stone in Sydney and held in the Julius Stone Memorial Collection of the Law Library of the University of New South Wales. This indicates that Stone might have been invited; although, had he been invited, he would have had to decline since he did not speak German. He was no admirer of the pure theory. Involved with American legal realism, he would soon denounce the concept of a basic norm: J Stone, 'Mystery and Mystique in the Basic Norm' (1963) 26 *Modern*

Schmölz describes the invitation, at first, as an *Einberufung*: a 'summoning' to a meeting, where there may be an obligation to attend (for example, to a parliament); in a military context it can mean 'conscription' or 'call-up'. Only later does he use the academically usual term, referring to the participants being 'invited (*eingeladen*)'. This would evidently be a celebratory event and Catholics could have felt morally obligated to accept; for the same reason, others could have felt turned off. Kelsen was well qualified to be invited, of course, as an eminent scholar of theories of natural law and of political theory.[62] He was also, of course, the arch-critic of belief in natural law. His acceptance of the invitation would be a coup for the Centre;[63] even better, if during the workshop he could be persuaded to agree that Catholic legal doctrine had some advantages over the pure theory.[64]

In any case, Kelsen would be lending his remaining prestige to the event. In Austria, he was still personally revered as the principal creator in 1920 of a constitution that had now been more or less restored.[65] In Germanic jurisprudence generally, however, his reputation was at a low ebb. After Nazism, there had been a revival of belief in natural law and legal positivism stood accused of having weakened legal resistance to Nazi amorality.[66] That condemnation has now been refuted and it has been pointed out that Nazi doctrine tended towards natural law.[67]

Law Review 34. He later had a very personal fight with Kelsen, which ended with a public apology from Stone: see I Stewart, 'Coincidence or Derivation? When Julius Stone Accused Hans Kelsen of Plagiarism' (2008) 17 *Griffith Law Review* 203. There was a close connection between Stone and Marcic at least by 1971, when Marcic was a visitor to the University of Sydney law faculty: L Star, *Julius Stone. An Intellectual Life* (South Melbourne, Sydney University Press, 1992) 166.

[62] P Chiassoni, 'Kelsen on Natural Law Theory. An Enduring Critical Affair' (2014) 23 *Revus. Journal for Constitutional Theory and Philosophy of Law* 135. And not only overall but also recently, for he had scathingly reviewed a historian's book on Plato and natural law and been scathed by its author in return: H Kelsen, 'Platon und die Naturrechtslehre' (1957) 8 *Österreichische Zeitschrift für öffentliches Recht* 1, trans RN Porter as 'Plato and the Doctrine of Natural Law' (1960) 14 *Vanderbilt Law Review* 23; and see J Wild, 'Plato and Natural Law. An Answer to Hans Kelsen' (1961) 11 *Österreichische Zeitschrift für öffentliches Recht* 177. An extensive study of Plato's theory of justice would be published posthumously: H Kelsen, *Die Illusion der Gerechtigkeit. Eine kritische Untersuchung der Sozialphilosophie Platons* (*The Illusion of Justice: a Critical Investigation of Plato's Social Philosophy*) K Ringhofer and R Walter (eds) (Vienna, Manz, 1985).

[63] As was the prominent role accepted by Verdross.

[64] The workshop theme assumed an ordinary, broad meaning for 'natural law (*Naturrecht*)' and not the narrower sense given by Aquinas, following Justinian, to '*lex naturalis*' – as mainly instinct: *Summa Theologiae*, 1a2ae 94; Justinian, Institutes, 1.2pr; but see also below (n 119). The broad meaning, which was always Kelsen's, includes all law (*lex*) that Aquinas attributes to God as its author.

[65] Kelsen is sometimes referred to as the Constitution's 'father', but Olechowski finds 'architect' more accurate: *Hans Kelsen* (n 30) 296.

[66] Most prominently by G Radbruch, 'Statutory Lawlessness and Supra-Statutory Law (1946)' (B Litschewski Paulson and SL Paulson trans from selected original texts) (2006) 26 *Oxford Journal of Legal Studies* 1, 6.

[67] SL Paulson, 'On the Background and Significance of Gustav Radbruch's Post-War Papers' (2006) 26 *Oxford Journal of Legal Studies* 17; W Ott and F Buob, 'Did Legal Positivism Render German Jurists Defenceless during the Third Reich?' (1993) 2 *Social & Legal Studies* 91; W Ott and MA Rea-Frauchiger, *The Varieties of Legal Positivism. The Hitler Argument and Other Objections to Legal Positivism* (Zurich, Dike Verlag, 2018) 226–46; Ott, 'Report of a Visit to Prof. H.L.A. Hart in Oxford' (my trans) (2023) 14 *Jurisprudence* 254. See also I Müller, *Hitler's Justice. The Courts of the Third Reich*, DL Schneider trans (Cambridge, MA, Harvard University Press, 1991) and review by MD Dubber, 'Judicial Positivism and Hitler's Injustice' (1993) 93 *Columbia Law Review* 1807; also M Stolleis, 'Law and Lawyers Preparing the Holocaust' (2007) 3 *Annual Review of Law and Social Science* 213. Kelsen was also unpopular with conservatives for his advice to the American occupation authorities – consistently with the pure theory's understanding of state identity and legal revolution – that, after the ending of the Nazi government in Germany and Austria, the only sovereignty in those countries was

As of 1962, however, the Centre was riding the tide of the post-war natural law revival.[68] Kelsen's paper was carefully aimed: he would avoid historical territory; instead, he would engage the Catholics on their own legal-philosophical terrain.

Some of the other participants were very familiar to him. Verdross, Voegelin and von der Heydte had been his pupils or research assistants in Vienna, but had become Catholic critics of the pure theory. Verdross had been part of Kelsen's inner circle and in that period had contributed substantially to the development of the pure theory.[69] He would chair the discussions.[70]

iv. The Published Proceedings

The published proceedings of the workshop[71] are arranged in three parts – which unfortunately do not include the workshop's programme, so that one cannot be quite sure what took place on each day.

The first part consists of the eight papers, printed apparently in the order in which they were presented. The speakers seem to have been allowed to address the workshop theme as they wished. There is no indication that the papers had been circulated beforehand and they make very little reference to each other. There seems to have been an opportunity for revision prior to publication, but there is no sign of this for Kelsen's paper.

The second part contains verbatim records, presumably from tape, of the discussions. These appear not to have followed each paper, but to have taken place in a separate session following all of the papers.[72] The discussions roughly follow the order

that of the Allies: Olechowski, *Hans Kelsen* (n 30) 736–39; H Kelsen, 'The Legal Status of Germany According to the Declaration of Berlin' (1945) 39 *American Journal of International Law* 518; T Olechowski, 'Kelsens Debellatio-These. Rechtshistorische und rechtstheoretische Überlegungen zur Kontinuität von Staaten' in C Jabloner, T Olechowski and K Zeleny (eds), *Hans Kelsen in seiner Zeit*. SHKI, Bd 40 (Vienna, Manz, 2019) 275–96.

[68] Marcic would soon perceive a Kelsen 'renaissance': R Marcic, 'Die Reine Staatslehre: Der Hintergrund der Kelsen-Renaissance im deutsch-sprachigen Raum' in S Engel and RA Métall (eds), *Law, State, and International Legal Order. Essays in Honor of Hans Kelsen* (Knoxville, University of Tennessee Press, 1964) 197–208.

[69] S Verosta, 'Alfred Verdross – Leben und Werk' in FA von der Heydte, K Zemanek, I Seidl-Hohenveldern and S Verosta (eds), *Völkerrecht und rechtliches Weltbild* (Vienna, Springer, 1960) 1–29, 13–15, 21–23; HF Köck, 'Leben und Werk des österreichischen Rechtsgelehrten Alfred Verdross' (1991) 42 *Österreichische Zeitschrift für öffentliches Recht* 31; J von Bernstorff, *The Public International Law Theory of Hans Kelsen*, T Dunlap trans (Cambridge, Cambridge University Press, 2010) 281–83. Their relationship had been strained when Verdross had taken over after Kelsen was dismissed from editing the *Österreichische Zeitschrift für öffentliches Recht* in 1934, but in 1948 Kelsen had forgiven him completely: Olechowski, *Hans Kelsen* (n 30) 559–60, 775–76. Verdross maintained that a basic norm of a positive-legal order could only be a supreme value, drawn from natural law. Kelsen had recently contributed to a *Festschrift* for him: H Kelsen, 'Vom Geltungsgrund des Rechts' in FA von der Heydte, K Zemanek, I Seidl-Hohenveldern and S Verosta (eds), *Völkerrecht und rechtliches Weltbild* (above) 157–65.

[70] And see photograph of Kelsen, Verdross and Schmölz, facing the workshop venue, with Salzburg Cathedral in the background: *Der Staatsbürger*, 28 August 1962: epub.oeaw.ac.at/0xc1aa5576%200x00377190.pdf.

[71] Schmölz, *Das Naturrecht in der politischen Theorie* (n 46).

[72] The discussions are summarised in a review of the book by R Herzog in (1965) 12 *Zeitschrift für Politik* (n.F.) 95. Herzog mentions the 'fiction' moment without attaching any particular significance to it: 96. Other points that Kelsen makes are also in an article that he appears to have written at around the same time as the workshop: H Kelsen, 'Positivisme juridique et doctrine du droit naturel' in *Mélanges en l'honneur de Jean Dabin* (n 38) vol 1, 141–48.

of the papers, although the chair barely refers to the papers. Although the discussions are arranged under topics, these are different from those of the papers; they seem not to have been set beforehand and might have been inserted editorially after the whole event. In some cases, a discussion topic is linked by footnote to a particular paper, but the connection made is not always evident. The selection of topics has a Christian emphasis and some topics are drawn specifically from the Aristotelian-Thomist tradition: 'Existence and knowability of God' is followed by 'The problem of *participatio*', 'Interpretation of Aristotle' and 'Is "law" = "Is (*Sein*)" or "*aliquid rationalis*"?'. Other topics, however, are of general provenance: such as 'Law – a coercive order?', 'Atomic war' and several topics of international law.

The third part is by Schmölz himself and is titled a 'Summation (*Zusammenfassung und Ergebnis*)', although it does not refer to the other parts. It begins:

> Every discussion of natural law has, as its starting point, the question of the existence of God. Since this is a philosophical problem, the basic question of the existence of God cannot be answered through belief in the supernatural or by theology. It is clear, however, that we can come to know the existence of God with certainty through natural reason (*natürlicher Verstand*).[73]

Having assumed the old Aristotelian-Thomist differentiation between philosophy and theology, Schmölz goes on to offer his own Aristotelian-Thomist philosophical opinion on the general theme.[74]

This was emphatically a Catholic occasion, although Schmölz's assurance indicates that it had been intended to be an open and tolerant event.

v. *The Challenge*

For Kelsen, as will be seen, things worked out differently. Yet, if the workshop was a set-up, it was not an ambush, because Kelsen had already been challenged.[75] The challenge had been issued in 1961 in two articles by the dominant figure in the Salzburg circle, Marcic. I will focus on the longer and more scholarly of the two.[76]

In that article, Marcic takes Kelsen on philosophically. He proposes an 'ontological' theory of law, grounded in the Aristotelian-Thomist tradition and opposed to 'transcendental' philosophy in the manner of Kant, represented by the pure theory.

[73] Schmölz, *Das Naturrecht in der politischen Theorie* (n 46) 163.

[74] ibid 163–66. Schmölz dates his preface upon the Feast of St Thomas Aquinas, 1963: ibid iii.

[75] Kelsen might have warily declined Schmölz's invitation. In view of the challenge, however, that could have looked like weakness. In any case, a free trip from California to Austria and back – perhaps a leisurely journey by train and boat, since at that time air travel was still extremely expensive – was hardly to be sniffed at. Nor should one discount the possibility that Kelsen (more lively in person than one could suppose from his writings) looked forward to some fun.

[76] R Marcic, 'Reine Rechtslehre und klassische Rechtsontologie' (1961) 11 *Österreichische Zeitschrift für öffentliches Recht* 395. The journal's editor at the time was Verdross. Marcic could have counted on Kelsen seeing the article right away, since it appeared in a leading journal which Kelsen had founded (Olechowski, *Hans Kelsen* (n 30) 161–62) and of which he was still a co-editor, and this issue of it was one of four *Festschriften* celebrating Kelsen's eightieth birthday: RA Métall, *Hans Kelsen. Leben und Werk* (Vienna, Deuticke, 1969) 95. The other article was in a Viennese journal with a wider audience: R Marcic, 'Kelsen und das Naturrecht' (1961) 8 *Forum* 362.

A 'conversation between pure theory of law and legal ontology', Marcic proposes, is overdue.[77]

Marcic's style of argument is that of an ideologue. In his criticisms of the pure theory, he does not balance his opponent's view against his own and then seek a judicious conclusion. Rather, he stacks up supportive authorities (often quoted in Greek and in Latin, sometimes without translation) from many places in the Aristotelian-Thomist tradition and declares the opponent (sometimes misrepresented) wrong because they differ from his authorities.

A wide-ranging criticism of the pure theory in 1961 should have been directed at second *Reine Rechtslehre*, published in 1960. However, Marcic selects a target handier for him, a synopsis of the pure theory that Kelsen had published in 1953.[78] Marcic contends that a 'basic norm' for any positive-legal order, superordinate to its constitution, can and must be derived from natural law – at any rate as conceived within what he terms the 'classical' natural-law tradition, stemming from Aristotle and Aquinas. Centrally, Marcic challenges the pure theory from the standpoint of what he terms 'classical legal ontology', the 'Aristotelian-Thomist philosophy of order (*Ordnungsphilosophie*)' – from which, he claims, the pure theory goes awry into 'German idealism'.[79]

To make this argument, Marcic misrepresents Kelsen's views both methodologically and substantively. On the methodological plane, Marcic maintains that the pure theory pursues 'method' in the sense of Marburg neo-Kantianism, both in general and especially in subscribing to the notion of 'hypothesis' propounded by the leading figure in Marburg neo-Kantianism, Hermann Cohen (who is not mentioned in second *Reine Rechtslehre*). To demonstrate this, Marcic offers what he calls a 'bare outline (*schwacher Umriss*)' of Kelsen's philosophical position. Regarding Cohen, he does not quote Kelsen himself but only requotes a passage from Cohen that in 1953 Kelsen had quoted with approval. Then Marcic claims that therefore Kelsen subscribes to Cohen's special notion of 'hypothesis'.[80] However, in 1953 Kelsen had not referred to Cohen on 'hypothesis' but only to him on a necessary 'formalism', in its abstractness, of any general theory.[81] Cohen associates his notion of 'hypothesis' closely with '*Faktum der Wissenschaft* (fact of science)', proposing that philosophy should obtain factual knowledge not directly through observation but, for a non-scientist more reliably, from science – so that science itself becomes the primordinate 'fact' for philosophy. When Kelsen had used the expression '*Faktum der Wissenschaft*' in 1928, it had been with reference not to legal science but directly to Kant.[82] He referred to '*Faktum der Rechtswissenschaft* (fact of legal science)'

[77] Marcic, 'Reine Rechtslehre und klassische Rechtsontologie' (n 76) 396. He deems adherents of 'scientific socialism' (presumably Marxism) to be incapable of conversation: ibid 397, fn 7 (on 398).

[78] H Kelsen, 'Was ist die Reine Rechtslehre?' (1953) in *Die Wiener rechtstheoretische Schule* (n 7) 611–29.

[79] Marcic, 'Reine Rechtslehre und klassische Rechtsontologie' (n 76) 395–96, fn 6 (on 397). While Marcic barely references his criticism to the main body of RR2 (ibid 402, fn 28 (on 403)), he does refer (ibid 398) to its appendix, RR2App, where Kelsen stresses his distance especially from the Aristotelian-Thomist natural law tradition. Marcic also refers, obliquely, to a *Festschrift* chapter by Kelsen that had also appeared in 1960: Kelsen, 'Vom Geltungsgrund des Rechts' (n 69).

[80] Marcic, 'Reine Rechtslehre und klassische Rechtsontologie' (n 76) 398–99.

[81] Kelsen, 'Was ist die Reine Rechtslehre?' (n 78) 627.

[82] H Kelsen, 'Die philosophischen Grundlagen der Naturrechtslehre und des Rechtspositivismus' (first published as a monograph: Charlottenburg, Verlag Rolf Hesse, 1928) in *Die Wiener rechtstheoretische Schule*

in first *Reine Rechtslehre* in 1934[83] and again in 1953,[84] yet without stating that he meant the expression in Cohen's special sense.

Marcic presents a 'basic norm' concept as a concept of a real source norm, in order to contend that it would be better to find a source norm in natural law. Natural law, considered in its relation to positive law, he says is 'pre-positive law'. It is God's creative will, working through Nature. It establishes 'fundamental structures' that have priority over anything posited, even things posited (created) by God, but, even more, over acts of subjective, human will. What is called 'natural law', he suggests, would be better termed 'law of being'. It is 'legally normative (*rechtsnormativ*)', when the expression 'normative' is understood in its original Greek sense, as '"knowable", "trusted": what accords with *reason*'.[85]

Marcic now claims to take Kelsen's side against (Marcic clearly implies) Carl Schmitt. Norms set by arbitrary acts of human will cannot be binding, as in Schmitt's 'decisionism', because their irrationality makes them incompatible with the law of being. Thus, Marcic contends:

> This element of *being bound* (Gebundenheit), the moment of *binding* (Bindung) (of matter to form, of possibility to reality, of the material to spirit, of power to freedom, and so on and so forth) is, as a *binding to the order* (Bindung an die Ordnung), one of the core ideas of Hans Kelsen's theory of law: this makes completely evident the structural affinity (*Strukturverwandtschaft*) between the pure theory of law and legal ontology.[86]

This is quite a stretch. In the pure theory, emphatically, there is no natural law element in a norm's membership of a real legal order.

Once this alleged affinity of structures is noted, Marcic goes on, one can pinpoint their difference. Unlike the pure theory, 'classical' legal ontology in no way maintains the complete autonomy (*Eigenständlichkeit und Ursprünglichkeit*) of positive law. Aquinas has put it best: positive law is not independent of pre-positive law but stands in a conditional relationship to it. Then, as Marcic puts the issue: 'for any chosen part of positive law, the pre-positive basic norm is a *prius*, such that the creation of positive law – as with the pure theory's basic norm – provides, so to, speak, a blank authorisation (*Blanko-Vollmacht*)'.[87] To think of positive law as completely autonomous, leaving out of sight the law of being, is to acknowledge no 'boundary' to positive law.[88]

Back in 1928, Kelsen had acknowledged a *functional* affinity of his basic norm concept with natural law, since it was to replace natural law in the function of validating positive law.[89] In 1953 he had recognised an 'analogous function' of the pure theory's

(n 7) 281–350, 348; WH Kraus trans as 'Natural Law Doctrine and Legal Positivism' in GTLS, 389–446, 444 (says only 'science').

[83] RR1, 37; but only possibly equivalent phrases appear in RR1en, 34 ('the very existence of legal science') and in RR1fr, 84 ('Le fait qu'une science de droit existe').

[84] Kelsen, 'Was ist die Reine Rechtslehre?' (n 78) 611–12.

[85] Marcic, 'Reine Rechtslehre und klassische Rechtsontologie' (n 76) 408.

[86] ibid.

[87] ibid 409; referring to Aquinas, *Summa Theologiae*, 1a 21.1.3 and 1a2æ 95.2.

[88] ibid 409, fn 49a.

[89] Kelsen, 'Die philosophischen Grundlagen der Naturrechtslehre und des Rechtspositivismus' (n 82) 339; 'Natural Law Doctrine and Legal Positivism' (n 82) 437. Also, in 1924, a functional affinity with the doctrine of social contract: H Kelsen, 'Die Lehre von den drei Gewalten oder Funktionen des Staates' (1923) in *Die Wiener rechtstheoretische Schule* (n 7) 1625–60, 1652; and see (with some English translation) D Dyzenhaus, *The Long Arc of Legality. Hobbes, Kelsen, Hart* (Cambridge, Cambridge University Press, 2022) 161.

description of a norm, compared with a natural-scientific descriptive 'law'.[90] Marcic makes as much of these similarities as he believes he can.

Nonetheless, he contends, both theories recognise that positive law is 'contingent'; positive law (*positives Recht*), as posited law (*gesetztes Recht*), is conditional. Thus, he adds, it is 'forced to yield to the unconditionality of the first condition, the absoluteness of the basic norm as presupposition'. One can therefore, he concludes, raise against the pure theory the objection that 'it is dealing with a *hypothetical* absoluteness, while legal ontology presupposes *absolute* absoluteness'.[91]

His language is strong, although Kelsen's had been too. In 1955 Kelsen had written that 'what distinguishes a religious faith from secular opinions is just its claim to refer to the absolute'.[92] Before this, he had said that doctrines of natural law are found on the side of philosophical absolutism, as well as in alliance with political absolutism,[93] and: 'Philosophical absolutism may very well be characterized as epistemological totalitarianism'.[94]

In Marcic's case, evidence of such totalitarianism has been handed to Kelsen. The phrase, with its emphasis, '*absolute* absoluteness' is nonsense. Marcic must know that and he must be expecting to Kelsen to see it. Yet the phrase has some significance, in that it appears to be an answer to a question. An attempt at an answer appears to have led towards the sort of infinite regress to which a Christian would normally produce the universal solution 'God'. Marcic, instead, stands behind the regress, in an aggressive stance. Thus, while he proposes a 'conversation between pure theory of law and legal ontology', he declares an unwillingness to actually converse. It seems that, if there were to be a meeting, he would be interested solely in domination.

Kelsen would have to watch out for Marcic, and not only because Marcic was picking a fight but also because he had an unsavoury political record. Born in Vienna in 1919, Marcic was brought up in Slovenia and Croatia, and in 1942 he obtained a doctorate in law from the University of Zagreb. He then became a media officer in the Vienna consulate of the 'Independent State of Croatia', a Nazi puppet state run by the fanatically Catholic as well as genocidal Ustaše organisation. Despite that, after the war, the American-established newspaper *Salzburger Nachrichten* appointed him as a reporter.[95] He appears to have conformed to the new environment. Nevertheless, in the newspaper's Christmas supplement of 1949, Marcic wrote that a Jewish journalist and his wife were 'given to mocking God and prayer' and 'nothing worse' than such mockery 'could have been said even in the Nazi period'; people like them had forfeited their right to exist and deserved to be put in a gas chamber.[96] He publicly apologised for this in 1967

[90] Kelsen, 'Was ist die Reine Rechtslehre?' (n 78) 612.

[91] Marcic, 'Reine Rechtslehre und klassische Rechtsontologie' (n 76) 409.

[92] H Kelsen, 'Foundations of Democracy' (1955) 66 (no 1 pt 2) *Ethics* 1, 60 (misprint corrected).

[93] GTLS, 11.

[94] H Kelsen, 'Absolutism and Relativism in Philosophy and Politics' (1948) 42 *American Political Science Review* 906, 909; also, with significant changes in Kelsen, *What is Justice?* (n 14) 198–208, 202.

[95] Along with other journalists who had a far-Right history: O Rathkolb, *The Paradoxical Republic. Austria, 1945–2005*, O Binder trans (New York, Berghahn, 2010) 144–45. The American administrators in Austria would have favoured reliable anti-Communists.

[96] R Marcic, 'Strahlungen und Gegenstrahlungen', *Salzburger Nachrichten*, 23 December 1949, 22; quoted from Pinwinkler, below (n 98) and also found in other sources.

and in 2007 an inquiry exonerated him of having ever actually written in support of Nazism.[97] In 1960 he had become the newspaper's editor-in-chief.

He pursued a parallel career as a scholar, habilitating in legal philosophy and public law at the University of Vienna in 1949. He was active in the post-war re-establishment of the University of Salzburg, where he would become a full professor of law and state in 1963, soon afterwards dean of the law faculty and then rector of the university. He changed his political spots to become a leading Catholic proponent of human rights. In 1971 he was a guest in the law faculty at the University of Sydney, apparently invited by Zionist professor Julius Stone; he died in an air crash in Belgium on the way home. In Salzburg, although controversially, in 1979 a prize for journalism and in 1984 a street were named after him.[98]

Kelsen would likely have been acquainted with Marcic's career. After Marcic's challenging articles of 1961, he would surely have wanted to know about their author.[99]

vi. Kelsen's Paper

In the workshop, the ten participants presumably would have been seated around a large table or a group of tables put together.[100] A scene of scholarly intimacy.

Kelsen is honoured with the opening slot. He commences archly: 'I have accepted your invitation to speak on natural law – in this circle of *supporters* of that doctrine'. This is not, of course,

> with any intention of converting you to my point of view, namely that from a *scientifically* rational standpoint one *cannot accept* the validity of natural law. For I do not consider such a conversion possible, and that for a reason which follows precisely from what I wish to discuss: the foundation of a theory of natural law – that is, the answer to the question, on what presupposition alone can one assume the validity of an eternal, unchangeable law immanent in nature; so that anyone, like myself, who does *not* feel able to accept this presupposition is also unable to accept its consequence.[101]

[97] 'Marcic: "Keine Sympathie mit nationalsocialistem Regime"', *Salzburger Landeskorrespondenz*, 30 August 2007: service.salzburg.gv.at/lkorrj/Index?cmd=detail_ind&nachrid=39235.

[98] A Pinwinkler, 'René-Marcic-Strasse. Univ.-Prof. Dr. René Marcic. Publizist, Rechtsphilosoph, Rektor der Universität Salzburg' in Stadt Salzburg, 'Die Stadt Salzburg im Nationalsozialismus': www.stadt-salzburg.at/fileadmin/landingpages/stadtgeschichte/nsprojekt/strassennamen/biografien/marcic_rene-v1.pdf. René-Marcic-Strasse, 5020 Salzburg, is a nondescript suburban side-street (Google Earth, 13 February 2024). See also F Hausjell, 'Braune Federn. Zum Ende des Gedenkjahres. Wie Nazi-Journalisten nach dem Krieg in Österreich erstaunliche Karrieren machen konnten' ('Brown Pens. The End of a Year of Memories. How Nazi Journalists Were Able to Make Astonishing Careers in Post-war Austria'), *Die Zeit*, 50/2005, 8 December 2005: www.zeit.de/2005/50/oe_braune_federn; C Granbacher, 'René-Marcic-Preis: Die Fascistische Vergangenheit seines Namengabers' ('The René Marcic Prize: Named After Someone With a Fascist Past'), *GMX*, 6 March 2017: www.gmx.at/magazine/politik/rene-marcic-preis-faschistische-vergangenheit-namensgebers-32204182; 'Marcic, René', *Austria-Forum*: austria-forum.org/af/AEIOU/Marcic,_René; and above (n 61).

[99] Marcic presumably would have known that Kelsen was a Jew and likely that in 1905 (like many of his peers) he had converted to Catholicism, although switching to Lutheranism in 1912: Olechowski, *Hans Kelsen* (n 30) 87–88, 118–19. Marcic does not refer to these factors, but, given his history, they were further reasons for Kelsen to be wary of him.

[100] Microphones probably would not have been needed for amplification, but appear to have been used to tape the proceedings for transcription.

[101] A Kantian transcendental-logical argument: see SL Paulson, 'Introduction' in RR1en, xvii–xlii, xxix–xlii; 'The Basic Norm' (n 6) 77–86.

> This presupposition, as I shall try to show, is the *belief* in a just deity, whose will is not only transcendent, but also immanent, to the nature that it has created. To debate the truth of this belief is completely pointless. Neither someone who has this belief nor someone who does not have it can be persuaded of the opposite by rational arguments. But, in taking the view that this belief is the essential and unavoidable presupposition for a genuine (*echt*) theory of natural law, I find myself in a strange position vis-à-vis those among you who, despite this belief of yours, are of the widely-held opinion that the validity of natural law is independent of the will of an almighty and all-good deity.[102] I do not appear here – as perhaps you will expect of me – as an advocatus diaboli, but on the contrary as an advocatus *dei*.[103] But that, as I hope, will remove from the discussion that will follow any sting that might wound the feelings of either the one party or the other.[104]

On the strategy that the best defence is a bigger attack, he asks those who hold that natural law provides reasons for the validity of positive law (and who he knew would have been almost all, if not all, of his audience) to show reasons for the validity of natural law itself – a task which he supposes some of them might be prepared to attempt, and then their attempts could be rationally debated.

However, Kelsen does not remain conciliatory. His companions are unlikely to have enjoyed his attribution of belief in natural law to the fact that 'the subjectivity and relativity of value' is something that 'many people – though not all – find hard to bear'.[105] His main argument is that the assumption that norms can be immanent in nature involves two errors: (a) that a norm can be a product of reason (or thought),[106] whereas it can only be the meaning of an act of will (divine will, if you so believe); and (b) the fallacy of entelechy, that Ought can be logically derived from Is.[107]

A norm that is said to be grounded in all of Nature, he maintains, could proceed only from the will of a personified Nature, which would treat Nature as God, or from a will that transcends Nature, which would be the will of God. Also, this would be 'genuine (*echt*)' natural law only if it consisted of universal and unchangeable norms, which could be criteria for the justice of any positive law. However, Aristotle equates justice with positive law and consequently he does not have a genuine concept of natural law. Such a concept had first been proposed by Aquinas, Kelsen holds, although he also faults Aquinas for generally relying too much upon Aristotle. These arguments are supported by extensive references to Aristotle and Aquinas, with quotations in Greek and Latin.[108] Kelsen has responded to Marcic's ontological challenge, without mentioning him.[109]

[102] ie, that the validity of natural law can derive from human reason. Kelsen presumably knows (and he will be told) that this is assumed to be human participation in divine reason; it seems that he is being mischievous.

[103] '*dei*' as emphasis; indeed, he is being mischievous.

[104] GNRL, 1; in *Die Wiener rechtstheoretische Schule* (n 7) 869–912; GNRLen, 114 (modified); Kelsen's emphases.

[105] GNRL, 3; GNRLen, 117 (modified).

[106] Or 'thinking' – *Denken*.

[107] Entelechy might be possible if both statements contain referents of the same kind. For Aristotle, Ought can be inferred from Is because Ought and Is are not of wholly different kinds. Kelsen, however, always maintained that Ought and Is are obviously wholly different in kind: HPS, 7–8, 19 (HKW2, 86, 100).

[108] That homework went way back. In the early 1930s, Kelsen had embarked on a combined presentation of legal positivism and refutation of belief in natural law: Métall (n 76) 66–67. Arguments of the first component would become RR1. The second component, on law and justice in Plato and Aristotle, was cancelled at proof stage, although sections of it would see publication as articles.

[109] Whether Kelsen's argument against Aristotle succeeds need not be considered here; what matters here is that he believes that it succeeds.

vii. The Other Papers

Voegelin is next up.[110] The other participants might have expecting a champion performance, but they got a fizzler. Voegelin opens nicely, saying that Kelsen's paper had been 'so superbly argued that the only question can be: After this, what else is there to say on the subject?'.[111] Perhaps he would now slice the ground away from beneath Kelsen's whole argument. He seems to think that he does so by claiming that a conception of natural law is to be sought not in doctrine at all, but in experience. The distinctive experience is that of Aristotle's *spoudaios*, the 'mature' man, whose exemplary virtue is evident not in what he may say but in what he does. The virtue in his acts is different in each act, so it is important how the virtuousness of a particular act may be reliably determined. However, Voegelin does not show how this is to be done – or, therefore, who is to be respected as 'mature'.[112]

Neither Kelsen nor Voegelin mentions a basic norm concept. The idea of such a concept hangs in the air, like a leading actor waiting for a part. It is given a part later, in Marcic's paper,[113] but just by repeating his objections of the previous year.

viii. The Discussions

In the discussions, the first topic is 'Existence and knowability of God', which is footnoted 'In connection with the paper by Kelsen', although Kelsen had explicitly avoided that question.[114]

Verdross, chairing, begins the discussions by thanking Kelsen for his paper. He continues: 'Everybody, I am sure, agrees with his thesis that there can be no foundation of natural law without God (*dass Naturrecht ohne Gott nicht begründet werden kann*)'.[115] Verdross appears to be establishing neutral terms of debate. Or they would be neutral, if all participants were to restrict themselves to the *logical* issue of whether an idea of 'natural law' necessarily assumes divine authorship. There could then be debate on that issue and thereafter on whether the authorship can only be by will or, in addition or instead, by reason. Yet Verdross pre-empts the issue that he had stated, going on to define the main issue for discussion as whether the relation between a norm and a divine author involves knowledge of God through faith (*Glauben*) or through reason. This is not neutral, since the idea of faith makes sense only to those who believe in God. The discussion is already beginning to exclude Kelsen.

Auer takes up Verdross's theme as it had been left and asks Kelsen to resolve an ambiguity: whether in this context '*Glauben an Gott*' should be understood theologically, understanding '*Glauben*' to be a matter of faith, or philosophically, understanding

[110] E Voegelin, 'Das Rechte von Natur' in Schmölz, *Das Naturrecht in der politischen Theorie* (n 46) 38–51.
[111] ibid 38.
[112] Arnold, 'Eric Voegelin' (n 48) 549–50. Kelsen may have replied to Voegelin in 1963, when he argued that a 'recently proposed' doctrine of a relative and changeable natural law 'amounts to self-destruction of the original idea of natural law': 'Positivisme juridique et doctrine du droit naturel' (n 72) 147.
[113] R Marcic, 'Das Naturrecht als Grundnorm der Verfassung' in Schmölz, *Das Naturrecht in der politischen Theorie* (n 46) 69–90.
[114] Schmölz, *Das Naturrecht in der politischen Theorie* (n 46) 117, fn 1.
[115] ibid 117. Each in their own way. (In quotations, 'ß' modernised to 'ss'.)

it to be a matter of rational belief. Kelsen replies just that he is thinking only of rational belief. It is difficult to see a point in Auer putting that question to him, unless it had been to trap him into accepting the possibility of faith and, by so doing, presupposing the existence of the object of faith, God. Subsequently, on other points that Auer raises, he and Kelsen are inevitably at cross-purposes. And there ends the section of the discussion that had been specifically linked to Kelsen's paper.[116]

These themes, however, are continued in relation to the second topic for discussion, 'The problem of *participatio*', which is not linked by footnote to any paper.[117] To step aside for a moment: the doctrine of personal 'participation' derives from the Judaic and Christian belief that God has made human beings in his own 'image'.[118] Aquinas, drawing partly on the Platonic doctrine that sensuous reality both instantiates and participates in transcendent Forms, holds that all things 'participate' in the nature of God, as their creator.[119] Thus, human beings participate both in the eternal law (*lex aeterna*) by which God continues to rule the world and, as rational creatures, in divine reason. Accordingly, human beings are able rationally to grasp the eternal law, to a degree, and the eternal law as so grasped Aquinas calls the 'law of nature (*lex naturalis*)'[120] or natural law.

Auer and Schmölz understand the doctrine of participation to mean that natural law does not proceed from will, but is a human participation in divine reason;[121] natural law is therefore a rationally discovered *fact*.[122] Their argument (similar to Marcic's 'ontological' argument) appears to be that, although the eternal law is created by God's will, it exists for human beings only as they know it – that is, as natural law – and so, in effect, their knowing is a rational creation of natural law. Kelsen gives this short shrift, responding that it is impossible because any principle of law has to be expressed in an ought-statement (*Soll-Satz*) – a 'Thou shalt! Thou shalt not! (*Du sollst! Du sollst nicht!*)'. An 'Ought (*Sollen*)' is the correlate 'of a willing (*eines Wollens*)'. He insists: 'No command without a commander (*Keine Imperative ohne einen Imperator*[123])'. And he adds: 'How anybody can deny that is, to me, incomprehensible'.[124]

[116] ibid 117–18.

[117] ibid 118–22.

[118] Or 'likeness': Genesis 1.26–28, 5.1–3 and 9.6. In Latin, *imago dei*.

[119] Aquinas, *Summa Theologiae*, 1a 44.1; RA te Velde, 'Participation: Aquinas and his Neoplatonic Sources' in AJB Hampton and JP Kenney (eds), *Christian Platonism. A History* (Cambridge, Cambridge University Press, 2021) 122–39.

[120] Aquinas, *Summa Theologiae*, 1a2ae 91.2. But see also above (n 64): now Aquinas seems to be thinking less jurisprudentially than theologically. Kelsen, in referring to 'natural law (*Naturrecht*)' (both here and elsewhere), either does not make Aquinas's distinction between *lex aeterna* and *lex naturalis* or agrees (for the sake of argument) that the former is comprehensible only through the latter.

[121] F-M Schmölz, 'Der gesellschaftliche Mensch und die menschliche Gesellschaft bei Thomas von Aquin' in Schmölz, *Das Naturrecht in der politischen Theorie* (n 46) 52–59, 55–56, citing Aquinas, *Summa Theologiae*, 1a2æ 91.2. Kelsen may have been amused that in their papers Auer and Schmölz had disagreed on whether natural law is changeable.

[122] A Auer, 'Elemente aus dem modernen Naturrecht für die demokratische Gesellschaftsordnung' in Schmölz, *Das Naturrecht in der politischen Theorie* (n 46) 60–68, 63.

[123] Kelsen treats the expression as well known. He will later trace it to W Dubislav, 'Zur Unbegründbarkeit der Forderungssätze' (1937) 3 *Theoria* 330, 335: Kelsen, 'Recht und Logik' (n 14) 425 and in *Die Wiener rechtstheoretische Schule* (n 7) 1480–82; 'Law and Logic' (n 14) 237–38; also ATN, 161; ATNen, 54.

[124] Schmölz, *Das Naturrecht in der politischen Theorie* (n 46) 119. In RR2, however, an 'ought' (*Sollen*) had not been confined to commands but had included a 'may' (*Dürfen*) and a 'can' (*Können*): RR2, 4–5; RR2en, 5. When Kelsen now confines an 'ought' to a 'command (*Imperative*)', he seems to be focusing more generally.

By now, it must have been plain to all that Kelsen and his opponents, although talking much the same language, were not talking it in the same way.

ix. Announcing the Fiction Turn

As this discussion continues, Marcic says that he agrees with Kelsen that natural law is correctly characterised as 'norm (*Norm*)', but he contends that a norm is first of all a mode of being and may *in addition* be a product of will. (He comes back at Kelsen on the plane of ontology.) Drawing upon Aristotle, he says that a craftsman can derive from the known idea of what *is* a bed frame the norm that wood etc *ought* to be used in making a bed frame; and whether the craftsman decides (performing an act of *will*) to apply this norm in order to make a bed frame is something additional to that reasoning.[125] Has not Kelsen himself sometimes separated 'the normative from the volitional'?[126] Marcic has in mind that Kelsen had always presented a basic norm as the meaning not of an act of will but of an act of thought.

Kelsen's reply to Marcic begins:

> *Herr Kollege* Marcic, unfortunately I have to contradict you. In my earlier writings, I have spoken of norms that are not the meaning of an act of will. I have presented (*dargestellt*) my whole theory of the basic norm as a norm that is not the meaning of an act of will but, rather, is presupposed in thought.

Nothing new there. However, he continues in a surprising way:

> Now, gentlemen, unfortunately I must confess to you that I am no longer able to maintain this theory – I have had to abandon it (*ich diese Lehre aufgeben musste*). You can believe me when I say that it was anything but easy to abandon a theory that I have defended for decades. I have abandoned it in the knowledge that an Ought has to be the correlate of a Willing (*dass ein Sollen das Korrelat eines Wollens sein muss*). My basic norm is a *fictitious* (fiktive) norm, which presupposes a *fictitious* act of will that posits this norm. It is the fiction that some authority or other wills that something ought to be (*dass dies sein soll*).

There seem to have been some remarks that could not be transcribed,[127] for Kelsen goes on in a tone of response:

> You are right to reproach me for speaking against a theory that I myself have adopted and defended. That is entirely correct: I have had to modify my theory of the basic norm in its presentation (*in ihrer Darstellung modifizieren*). There cannot be norms that one merely thinks – that is, norms that are the meaning of an act of *thought*, not the meaning of an act of *will*. What one thinks, with a basic norm, is the fiction of an act of will that in reality does not exist.[128]

Kelsen is inconsistent. He says first that he has 'abandoned' the basic norm concept, but then that he has only 'modified' it. However, that works out: in 'modifying' the concept,

[125] Aristotle's doctrine of *prohairesis*: the craftsman example is in his *Nicomachean Ethics*, 1102–1103. A craftsman applying an idea or pattern to materials was a stock figure for creative activity: eg, Plato, *Timaeus*, 28–29; Aquinas, *Summa Theologiae*, 2a2æ 57.1.

[126] In several places, Marcic claims (without detailed citation, this being oral discussion), in H Kelsen, *Allgemeine Staatslehre*, M Jestaedt (ed) (Tübingen, Mohr Siebeck, 2019) (originally published 1925).

[127] Although the proceedings do not mention this.

[128] Schmölz, *Das Naturrecht in der politischen Theorie* (n 46) 119–20; Kelsen's emphases.

he has 'abandoned' it in its erstwhile form. Later in the workshop, he speaks of the concept as viable[129] – which it might be, in its modified form. But what is a modification of something 'in its presentation'? Why should a mere modification be 'anything but easy'? And, most importantly, Kelsen has explained how a basic norm in its new form will contain a fiction – 'an act of will that in reality does not exist' – but he has not yet shown, at least clearly, how this new creature will be viable.

Kelsen's intervention is astonishing in its content, manner and timing. His paper had not even alluded to the concept of a basic norm. Marcic's 'basic norm' was a different creature and the fiction turn does not seem to bear any relation to it. Now Kelsen looks like a soldier who, surrounded by enemies, shoots himself with 'friendly fire' and then points to a paper dressing as sufficient medical treatment. Or has he had a Damascene moment of revelation? That would be unlike the methodical Hans Kelsen. Yet the frailty of his supposed cure is also unlike the robust Hans Kelsen.

x. Further Discussion

He goes on to make two further but unrelated objections to what has been said. One involves a defiant reference to Cohen, perhaps as a response to Marcic's association of Kelsen with Cohen in 1961 (and one can imagine Kelsen glancing at Marcic while saying this): 'A very famous philosopher, from whom I have learned a great deal, Hermann Cohen, has spoken in his *Ethic of Pure Will* of an Is of Ought (*Sein des Sollens*)'. No contradiction is involved there, Kelsen says, because the Ought is referred to not prescriptively but as to its existence.[130] The other is that Marcic's bed-maker does not find an Ought but notes for himself a necessary means to an end.[131]

When he heard the 'fiction' admission, Marcic might have had trouble believing his apparent good fortune. He had challenged in 1961 what he had called Kelsen's 'hypothetical absoluteness' and Kelsen had now responded by not only abandoning 'hypothesis' but retreating further, into 'fiction'. Marcic later, in a tone of frustration, asks Kelsen: If your basic norm is 'a pure fiction' (Marcic's words), it is nothing and cannot even be named; your long-held doctrine that the basic norm is a Kantian 'transcendental schematism', providing the initial conditions for experience of objects,[132] now amounts to nothing. In response, Kelsen only confirms that his basic norm is transcendentally schematic (he is not going back on it being a transcendental-logical[133] presupposition)

[129] ibid 147–48, 155. Voegelin takes it to have been given a new 'form' – although he does not accept it in either form: ibid 148.

[130] It exists on an *ideell* (semantic) plane (ibid 120) – distinct from existence as *ideal* (ideal) or as *wirklich* (causally real): ATN, 22; ATNen, 28.

[131] ibid; ie, an operation of instrumental and thus of theoretical reason. 'Is of Ought' reappears in ATN, 132, cp 125; ATNen, 164, cp 155 – referring to H Cohen, *Ethik des reinen Willens* (Berlin, Cassirer, 1904) 13. Here Kelsen may at last be clarifying his declaration in 1923 that his habilitation thesis of 1911 had been deeply indebted to Cohen's thinking: HPS2, xvii; HPS2en, 15. However, this claim has been shown not to hold up: G Edel, 'The *Hypothesis* of the Basic Norm: Hans Kelsen and Hermann Cohen' in SL Paulson and B Litschewski Paulson (eds), *Normativity and Norms* (n 1) 195–219.

[132] See RR1, 66; RR1en, 57 – apparently in Kant's meaning of '*Schema*', a legal norm is a 'scheme of interpretation (*Deutungsschema*)': RR1, 4–5; RR1en, 10. cp RR2, 3–4; RR2en, 3–4.

[133] Kant distinguishes logic into 'general' logic, which (in summary) is 'the basic science of the forms of thought regardless of its object', and 'transcendental' logic, which is 'the science of the basic forms for the thought of objects': P Guyer and AW Wood, 'Introduction' in I Kant, *Critique of Pure Reason* (Cambridge, Cambridge University Press, 1998) 1–80, 4; and see I Kant, ibid 193–97 (*Akademieausgabe*, A50–57/B74–82).

and denies that he has nothing left.[134] Marcic also throws at him Isaac Newton's *'hypotheses non fingo'*,[135] implying that 'fictions' are even worse than 'hypotheses', but Kelsen does not bite.[136]

A little later, Kafka, who had declared himself a 'positivistic legal scholar' and sceptical of appeals to natural law (and so possibly a tactical ally for Kelsen), protests: 'What use to me is a succession of competences[137] if they only end in a fiction? Is it rational for me to recognise the historically first constitution-maker?'.[138] However – just as things are getting really interesting – Schmölz intervenes to change the subject.[139]

B. The Vienna Paper

The fiction turn was continued two years later at the Second Austrian Lawyers Day, held at the University of Vienna from 17 to 20 June 1964.[140] This was a major event, at which Kelsen would have been a (and probably the) star speaker, but he had caught a virus and was unable to travel. In the closing session, his paper was read on his behalf by Robert Walter, a specialist on his work,[141] and there was no discussion after it. The chair[142] only read out a letter of thanks that would be sent to Kelsen and added wryly: 'Since no contradiction has been offered, I can consider this address to have been accepted'.[143]

Kelsen had aimed not to disappoint: the version of his paper that appears in the conference proceedings[144] performs all three turns. According to the paper's title, 'The Function of a Constitution', its main theme is the concept of 'constitution' in the pure theory, and Kelsen makes the constitution turn.[145] The fiction turn is presented more

A proposition of transcendental logic is entirely a priori. It is a condition for the possibility of truth. The possibility, if any, of its own truth is not in question.

[134] Schmölz, *Das Naturrecht in der politischen Theorie* (n 46) 121–22.

[135] 'I frame no hypotheses': I Newton, *Principia* (originally published 1687), A Motte and F Cajori trans (Berkeley, University of California Press, 1971) 547 (and translator's commentary, 671–76). Marcic may have intended to be humorous, since the past participle of the Latin verb *fingere* is *fictum*, from which *fictus* (fictional) is derived. This had also been in Marcic's own paper, 'Das Naturrecht als Grundnorm der Verfassung' (n 113) 70.

[136] The published version of Marcic's paper only notes Kelsen's objection to his contention that Kant and Aquinas have much in common (ibid 77 and fn 34) and Kelsen's contribution to the discussions is followed up only by asserting that Kelsen had made a mistake about Aristotle (ibid 90, fn 62). Kelsen's views are still taken from lesser works than RR2, which is barely mentioned: ibid 74, fn 22 and 76, fnn 27–28.

[137] '*Zuständigkeiten*': for common-law systems sometimes 'jurisdictions'.

[138] Schmölz, *Das Naturrecht in der politischen Theorie* (n 46) 123–4.

[139] ibid 124.

[140] The Österreichischer Juristentag (ÖJT) is a non-profit association for all Austrian lawyers, founded in 1959 to promote the democratic restoration of Austrian law; its 'Juristentag' (Lawyers Day) is held every three years and the first of them took place in 1961: 'Österreichischer Juristentag (ÖJT)': www.juristentag.at/files/juristentag/pdf/ueber_den_oejt/Der%20Österreichische%20Juristentag-Entwicklung%20und%20Bedeutung.pdf.

[141] In 1971 Walter would become the founding Director of the Hans Kelsen-Institut in Vienna.

[142] Wilhelm Malaniuk, President of the ÖJT.

[143] FV1, 77.

[144] FV1.

[145] A similar turn had been suggested in Marcic's Salzburg paper, although Kelsen does not refer to him: Marcic, 'Das Naturrecht als Grundnorm der Verfassung' (n 113). Only similar, because Marcic's conception of a positive-legal order is imbued with natural law. Since Marcic might well have attended the Vienna conference, an opportunity for interesting debate was missed.

formally than in Salzburg, now adopting Vaihinger's extended conception of fiction – although this turn is still presented with reference to constitutions, as though the constitution turn were not taking place. Discussion of the logic turn follows, although Kelsen does not connect it to the other two turns. These non-connections, as well as the absence of any citations, suggest that the paper was unfinished. The later version published in a journal has been edited: it adds headings and some further paragraphing, it omits the material on logic and there are still no citations.[146] The passages that will now be discussed are identical in both versions.[147]

Kelsen first summarises the nature and function of a basic norm:

> Just as Kant asks how it is possible to have an interpretation, free from all metaphysics, of the facts given to our senses, in terms of laws of nature formulated by natural science, so a pure theory of law has asked how it is possible to have an interpretation of the subjective meaning of certain facts as a system of objectively valid legal norms, describable in legal propositions, without recourse to metalegal authorities such as God or Nature. The epistemological answer of a pure theory of law is, on the condition that one presupposes a basic norm: One ought to behave as the constitution prescribes – that is, in conformity with the subjective meaning of the act of will creating the constitution, the commands of the creator of the constitution. The function of this basic norm is to ground the objective validity of a positive legal order, ie the norms, posited by human acts of will, of a by and large effective coercive order – that is, to interpret the subjective meaning of these acts as their objective meaning.
>
> A basic norm may be termed a 'constitution in a transcendental-logical sense', as distinct from a constitution in a positive-legal sense. The latter is a constitution posited by human acts of will, whose validity is grounded by a presupposed basic norm.
>
> A basic norm may, but need not, be presupposed. What ethics and legal science say about it is: only if it is presupposed can the subjective meaning of acts of will directed towards the behaviour of others be interpreted also as their objective meaning, these meaning-contents be interpreted as binding moral or legal norms. Since this interpretation is conditioned by the presupposing of a basic norm, it must be granted that ought-propositions (*Soll-Sätze*) can be interpreted as objectively valid moral or legal norms only in this conditioned sense.[148]

This is the concept as it had appeared in second *Reine Rechtslehre*,[149] except that it is no longer characterised as a hypothesis. Now Kelsen characterises it as a fiction – this time in an extended sense, sourced to Vaihinger.[150] Kelsen, in effect, tries to explain what he had meant in Salzburg by 'modified':

> To the assumption (*Annahme*) of a norm not posited by a real act of will but only presupposed in legal thinking (*im juristischen Denken*[151]) one can validly object that a norm can be the meaning only of an act of will and not of an act of thinking, that there is an essential

[146] FV2.

[147] FV1 has not been translated into English. I will cite FV2en, with modifications: see above (n 7).

[148] FV2, 585; FV2en, 116.

[149] RR2, ch 5; RR2en, ch 5.

[150] No citation is given, but the reference to Vaihinger is evidently to his well-known book, *Die Philosophie des Als Ob*.

[151] cp KG Wurzel, *Das juristische Denken* (first published 1904), E Bruncken trans, 'Methods of Juridical Thinking' in *Science of Legal Method. Selected Essays by Various Authors* (New York, Kelley, 1969) 286–428. By '*juristiches Denken*' Wurzel means the intellectual skills of a legal practitioner.

> correlation between 'ought' and willing. One can meet this objection only by conceding that, along with a basic norm, presupposed in thought, one must also think of an imaginary (*imaginäre*) authority whose (imagined [*fingierter*]) act of will has the basic norm as its meaning.
>
> With this fiction, the assumption of a basic norm turns out to be contradictory to the assumption that the constitution, whose validity is grounded by the basic norm, is the meaning of an act of will of a supreme authority, over which there can be no higher authority. Thus, the basic norm becomes a genuine (*echte*[152]) fiction in the sense of Vaihinger's philosophy of 'as if'. A fiction in this sense is characterised by its not only contradicting reality, but also containing contradiction within itself. For the assumption of a basic norm – such as, for instance, the basic norm of a religious moral order, 'One ought to obey the commands of God', or the basic norm of a legal order, 'One ought to behave as the historically first constitution determines' – not only contradicts reality, since no such norm exists as the meaning of an actual act of will, but also contains contradiction within itself, since it represents empowerment by a supreme moral or legal authority, and hence it issues from an authority lying beyond that authority, even though the further authority is merely imagined.[153]

Despite its self-contradiction, he believes, the modified concept of a basic norm will still be helpful:

> For Vaihinger a fiction is an aid to thinking (*Denkbehelf*[154]), of which one avails oneself if the aim of one's thinking cannot be reached with the material available. The aim of one's thinking in presupposing a basic norm is: to ground the validity of the norms forming a positive moral or legal order; that is, to interpret the subjective meaning of the acts positing these norms as their objective meaning, ie as valid norms, and the acts in question as acts positing norms. This object can be attained only by way of a fiction. Therefore, one has to keep in mind that a basic norm in the sense of Vaihinger's 'as if' philosophy is not a hypothesis – as I myself have occasionally characterised it – but a fiction, which is distinct from a hypothesis in that it is or should be accompanied by an awareness that reality does not correspond to it (*ihr die Wirklichkeit nicht entspricht*).[155]

That is, in Vaihinger's terms: a hypothesis has a 'claim to facticity', which is considered to be worth investigating further, but a fiction has no such claim.[156]

C. Kelsen after Vienna

Later, 'as if' is heard again although Vaihinger is only fitfully attached to it.

[152] Vaihinger uses the word '*eigentlich*', which I am rendering as 'proper', but Kelsen's sense of '*echt*' is the same.

[153] FV2, 585; FV2en, 116–17 (modified).

[154] A legal fiction, with the example of legal personality, had been characterised similarly as an 'auxiliary concept (*Hilfsbegriff*)': RR2, 194; RR2en, 190; as in Vaihinger, *Die Philosophie des Als Ob* 19; *The Philosophy of 'As if* 12 (accessory concept).

[155] FV2, 585; FV2en, 117. It is unclear in what sense Kelsen speaks here of correspondence with reality, since he had long ago rejected an 'image' theory of truth ('Die philosophischen Grundlagen der Naturrechtslehre und des Rechtspositivismus' (n 82) 315–17; 'Natural Law Doctrine and Legal Positivism' (n 82) 419–20) and for Vaihinger truth is merely utility: 'only what is observed and unchangeable is real. Hence the whole framework in which we place what is perceived is only subjective: *subjective* is *fictional; fictional* is *false; falsehood* is *error*'; 'truth' is 'only the most expedient error' (*Die Philosophie des Als Ob* 192–93; *The Philosophy of 'As if* 108 (modified)).

[156] *Die Philosophie des Als Ob* 173; *The Philosophy of 'As if* 98 ('claim to actuality').

In a contribution to a *Festschrift* of 1965, Kelsen continues his view of a supposed natural-legal norm that it appears to be set by reason, as 'law of reason (*Vernunftrecht*)', yet this is impossible since there is no practical reason. He says that it is thought (*gedacht*), but is not the meaning of an act of thinking (*Denkakt*). It is indeed conceived as the meaning of an act of will (*Willensakt*), but this is not an act of will apparent in material reality (*Seins-Wirklichkeit*). One can, however, think (*denken*) it in the way that one can imagine (*vorstellen*) to be possible something that does not actually exist (and even if one is mistaken about its possibility). In the same way, then,

> I can think, to myself, a norm that has not actually been posited by any authority – that is not the meaning of any real act of will apparent in material reality. But I can think such a norm to myself only as the meaning of an act of will that I *think along with it*. I can think a norm to myself *as if* it were posited by an authority, although it has not actually been posited – and there is actually no act of will whose meaning it is. The principle 'no norm without a norm-positing authority' remains standing even though the authoritative act of will whose meaning the merely thought norm is, is imaginary (*fingiert*). A merely thought norm is the meaning of an imaginary act of will, in contrast to a positive norm, which is the meaning of a real act of will. To put this quite generally: no Ought (*Sollen*) without a Willing (*Wollen*), even if the willing is only imaginary.[157]

This contribution states in its first footnote that it is intended as the opening chapter of a work to be titled *Allgemeine Theorie der Normen* (*General Theory of Norms*), which the author 'hopes he will be able to complete in due course'. It will indeed form the first chapter of that work as left in draft; the section just discussed is altered only typographically[158] and there is still citation merely of a single paragraph of Vaihinger's book.[159]

In 1966, the fiction turn appears almost in passing during a routine-looking summary of the pure theory that graces the inaugural issue of the *Israel Law Review*:

> As a norm[,] the basic norm must be the meaning of an act of will. Hence it is not the *science* of law which presupposes the basic norm. The science of law, which is a function of cognition, not of will, only ascertains the fact[160] that if men consider a coercive order established by acts of will of human beings and by and large effective as an objectively valid order, *they*, in their juristic thinking, *presuppose* the basic norm as the meaning of an act of will. Since, however,

[157] Kelsen, 'Zum Begriff der Norm' (n 26) 63; 'On the Concept of Norm' (n 26) 220 (modified); Kelsen's emphases.

[158] ATN, 5–6; ATNen, 6.

[159] ATN, 186, fn *; ATNen, 256, fn 2; quoting respectively Vaihinger, *Die Philosophie des Als Ob* 24; *The Philosophy of 'As if'* 16. The drafts edited as ATN do not constitute a completed book. For one thing, they consist half of mere notes on reading, which would not normally be publishable. Its editors claim that the typescript 'had reached a high degree of completeness', although it was heavily amended and not finally organised: K Ringhofer and R Walter, 'Einleitung' in ATN, iii–v, iii; ATNen, lviii–lx, lviii. The French translators identify 'numerous repetitions, sometimes cumbersome style (systematically sacrificing clarity to precision), abnormally long sentences and even truncated sentences': 'Avant-propos des traducteurs', ATNfr, v–x, v. The editors' chosen arrangement has been challenged: K Opałek, *Überlegungen zu Hans Kelsens 'Allgemeiner Theorie der Normen'*. SHKI, Bd 4 (Vienna, Manz, 1980) 10. See further MG Losano, 'La dottrina pura del diritto dal logicismo all'irrazionalismo' in ATNit, xvii–lxi, xxxiii–xxxvi. It is possible that the sections of ATN now in question have been juxtaposed by the editors, but the arguments evidently belong together. There is no indication of whether these passages were written before or after 1966, but at any rate their arguments still have Kelsen's approval.

[160] Omitting intrusive colon.

> an act of will does not exist in reality, but only in the juristic thinking of men who interpret the coercive order as an objective valid legal order, the presupposition of the basic norm is the typical case of a *fiction* in the sense of Vaihinger's *Philosophie des Als-Ob*.[161]

The passage is footnoted to the journal version of the Vienna paper.[162] Regarding the fiction turn, there is nothing new here. Yet, saying that 'it is not the *science* of law which presupposes the basic norm' introduces what may be another turn, which will require further discussion.

D. Catholic Aftermaths

The Church did not leave Kelsen alone after he had introduced the fiction turn, although nothing was made of the turn itself.

i. The Challenger Returns

One could have expected Marcic, following his objections during discussion in Salzburg, to renew his challenge, now with the fiction turn as ammunition. He did renew the challenge, in 1965 with a further-lengthened version of his longer article of 1961.[163] In the 1965 work, he refers to the Salzburg workshop and to its published proceedings, but does not trouble to fully reference them.[164] This eccentricity continues when Marcic claims that during discussion in Salzburg Kelsen had admitted an '*Abstand*' (distancing from or perhaps abandonment) regarding one of his 'fundamental doctrines'.[165] But there is no page reference to the Salzburg discussions and the accompanying references to works by Kelsen do not clearly point to a particular doctrine; nor is there a reference to either version of Kelsen's Vienna paper.[166] Marcic states that he has made

[161] Kelsen, 'On the Pure Theory of Law' (n 11) 6; Kelsen's emphases.

[162] ie, to FV2. In the quotation, 'the typical case' presumably should have been 'a typical case'.

[163] R Marcic, 'Um eine Grundlegung des Rechts. Existentiale und fundamentalontologische Elemente im Rechtsdenken der Gegenwart' in A Kaufmann (ed), *Die ontologische Begründung des Rechts. Wege der Forschung*, Bd 22 (Darmstadt, Wissenschaftliche Buchgesellschaft, 1965) 509–65, particularly 562–65. In this revised treatment, Marcic bases his arguments more extensively upon Heidegger. He then finds Kelsen's transcendental argument to be – although he supposes that Kelsen might not be aware of it – a close match with the phenomenological arguments of Heidegger and himself (ibid 544). He also claims that, in recent work towards a general theory of norms, Kelsen 'gives up on many of his earlier positions, in particular the key notion that objective meaning is the essence of any norm, including of course the pre-positive basic norm – a retreat that, in the eyes of the present writer, is a step backward' (ibid 539, fn 28 (on 540)). The recent work by Kelsen is not named, but it is probably 'Zum Begriff der Norm' (1965) (n 26), translated as 'On the Concept of Norm' (n 26) (later it is ATN, ch 1; ATNen, ch 1). There Kelsen does say: 'the essential feature of a norm is that behaviour of some sort is decreed as obligatory (*als gesollt statuiert ist*)' (ibid 69; ibid 221–22; also ATN, 7; ATNen, 7). But 'is decreed as obligatory' does not give up, or suggest giving up, on the view that objectivity of meaning is essential to a legal norm. Moreover, a Kelsenian basic norm is not 'pre-positive' in Marcic's sense.

[164] Marcic, 'Um eine Grundlegung des Rechts' (n 163) 540 and fn 29; he mentions only the journal in which the proceedings have appeared and the editor of that journal (Verdross), although (despite meticulous referencing for other materials) without year, volume or page numbers.

[165] ibid 561, fn 96.

[166] Kelsen is several times referred to (it seems sneeringly) as 'the Master (*der Meister*)': ibid 539, 541, 548–49, 562.

'decisive' revisions to his 1961 article which, 'on the basis of private personal meetings with Kelsen and a debate (*Streitgespräch*) with [him] on the nature of natural law, proved to be inevitable'.[167] The 'debate' presumably is the discussion between them in Salzburg, which very likely had continued informally, but there are still no page references to the published Salzburg proceedings. The fiction turn is never specifically mentioned. Marcic is still interested only in attempting to demonstrate that Kelsen's kind of stairway theory (*Stufenbaulehre*) agrees with his own.

Kelsen was already defending the pure theory against this persistent claim, getting down with Marcic into interpretation of Aristotle.[168] Along that way, he also combated Marcic's attempt to find near the top of the stairway a judicially open 'vent' for natural law to enter.[169] Drafting a reaction to Marcic's reflection on their Salzburg encounter, Kelsen simply continued to consider 'pointless' Marcic's foundational belief that the Ought (*Sollen*) of law is grounded in a divinely inspired Is (*Sein*).[170]

ii. The Pope Attacks

In 2011, Pope Benedict XVI, addressing the German Parliament, defended natural law and human society against 'positivism' – essentially by rejecting the Positivity and Separation Principles.[171] He refers to only one modern thinker, Kelsen. Separation of Is and Ought, he says, wrongly supposes that Nature is merely (quoting Kelsen from 1965) 'an aggregate of objective data linked together in terms of cause and effect'.[172] But even Kelsen, he is glad to report, had learned the error of that way:

> The great proponent of legal positivism, Kelsen, at the age of 84 – in 1965 – abandoned the dualism of 'is' and 'ought'. (I find it comforting that rational thought is evidently still possible at the age of 84!) Previously he had said that norms can only come from the will. Nature therefore could only contain norms, he adds, if a will had put them there. But this, he says, would presuppose a Creator God, whose will had entered into nature. 'Any attempt to discuss the truth of this belief is utterly futile', he observed.[173]

[167] ibid 538, fn 28.

[168] H Kelsen, 'Professor Marcics Theorie der Verfassungsgerichtsbarkeit' (1965) 15 *Österreichische Zeitschrift für öffentliches Recht* 270.

[169] A 'vent function (*Veltilfunktion*)' in Marcic, 'Um eine Grundlegung des Rechts' (n 163) 538.

[170] ATN, 132, fn 102 (on 281–82); ATNen, 164, fn 102 (on 341–42). See Marcic, 'Um eine Grundlegung des Rechts' (n 163) 550 ('*Naturrecht*=SEINSRECHT' [his capitalisation and emphasis]') 550.

[171] Benedict XVI, 'Besuch des deutschen Bundestages' (2011) 42 *Rechtstheorie* 275 (original: www.vatican.va/content/benedict-xvi/de/speeches/2011/september/documents/hf_ben-xvi_spe_20110922_reichstag-berlin.html). Quotations here are from the official English translation, titled 'The Listening Heart. Reflections on the Foundations of Law': www.vatican.va/content/benedict-xvi/en/speeches/2011/september/documents/hf_ben-xvi_spe_20110922_reichstag-berlin.html. See further H Dreier, 'Benedict XVI. und Hans Kelsen' (2011) 66 *JuristenZeitung* 1151.

[172] ibid (*Rechtstheorie*) 278 (here quoting from the English translation); as quoted in W Waldstein, *Ins Herz geschrieben. Das Naturrecht als Fundament einer menschlichen Gesellschaft* (Augsburg, Sankt Ulrich Verlag, 2010) 19; quoting from Kelsen, 'Recht und Logik' (n 14), in *Die Wiener rechtstheoretische Schule* (n 7) 1474. Waldstein, a prominent Catholic philosopher of natural law, had been professor of Roman law and legal philosophy at the University of Salzburg from 1965 to 1991: Waldstein, *Mein Leben. Erinnerungen* (Illertissen, Media Maria Verlag, 2013).

[173] ibid (*Rechtstheorie*) 280 (quoting from the English translation); as quoted from Kelsen's Salzburg paper in Waldstein, *Ins Herz geschrieben* (n 172) ibid. Benedict was 84 years old at this time.

Kelsen's remark about futility is from the beginning of his Salzburg paper. However, as has been seen, it does not mean that presupposition of a Creator God is beyond discussion – so that Kelsen the arch-positivist would have returned to the fold. On the contrary, Kelsen was saying that there was no point in attempting to discuss it on that occasion. He did not change his position – he reserved it.

IV. More Vaihinger?

Neither of the two phases of the fiction turn, in Salzburg and in Vienna, is very plainly expressed, which begs for further exploration of Vaihinger's fictionalism. What was Kelsen getting at when he referred to Vaihinger?

Vaihinger is inspired by Kant's question 'How are synthetic judgements *a priori* possible?'[174] to ask: 'How does it happen, *that with consciously false ideas we can nonetheless come to an idea that is right?*'.[175] Vaihinger puts this question with regard to natural science (*Naturwissenschaft*) and human science (*Geistes-* or *Kulturwissenschaft*), including science of law. His answer is that two kinds of fiction are found useful.[176]

What he calls a 'half- or semi-fiction' (*Halbfiktion, Semifiktion*) is a 'fiction' in the most common scientific sense: a statement that is known to be false yet is considered to be useful; it can be useful in leading to a testable hypothesis. As he says, these are common in science: they can be handy for exposition, such as Maxwell's Demon; or they can be convenient as a placeholder along the way to a hypothesis. More difficult is his 'proper fiction': a statement that may be useful to enquiry although it is not only false but also self-contradictory. Such statements, he contends, are not always to be discarded; they too can lead to a testable hypothesis.

He accepts that a mere contradiction such as 'Here is a round square'[177] simply does not make sense; that, since it does not make sense, it cannot be true or false; and that therefore it cannot be either a hypothesis or a fiction. However, he sets out what in his view are many examples of self-contradiction, mostly from mathematics and natural science, that have made enough sense to facilitate and even stimulate scientific discovery by leading to a new hypothesis.

Vaihinger's 'philosophy of "as if"', first published in 1911, enjoyed a vogue when it was new[178] and Kelsen had noticed a kindred spirit. He had already committed himself in principle to the 'struggle against fiction', the pervasive and 'abominable white lie (*verwerfliche Notlüge*) of science'[179] and in 1920 he would aim to dispel fictions from science as 'veils' and 'ghosts'.[180] Vaihinger's attention to fictions regarding law is only to

[174] I Kant, *Critique of Pure Reason* (n 133) 146 (*Akademieausgabe*, B19).

[175] '*Wie kommt es, dass wir mit bewusstfalschen Vorstellungen doch Richtiges erreichen?*': *Die Philosophie des Als Ob* xii (Vaihinger emphasises the whole sentence); *The Philosophy of 'As if'* omits.

[176] Vaihinger, *Die Philosophie des Als Ob* 24; *The Philosophy of 'As if'* 16 ('half-fictions or semi-fictions' and 'real fictions'), 98 ('true fictions').

[177] My example.

[178] *The Philosophy of 'As if'* omits from the subtitle the promising further words '*auf Grund eines idealistischen Positivismus* (on the Basis of an Idealistic Positivism)'.

[179] HPS1, viii (HKW2, 56).

[180] PSTV, iv (HKW4, 265). Although eventually he will accept the legitimacy of scientific fictions, provided that the device is entirely conscious and that its function is strictly limited: RR2, 303; RR2en, 301.

fictions used in legal reasoning (ie, 'legal fictions'), which he classifies as semi-fictions. Kelsen's initial attention to Vaihinger is largely confined to this and he is not impressed by what Vaihinger says there.[181] More than four decades later, the fiction turn is a bigger issue: it concerns not fiction *in* law but fiction *about* law; and it involves, in Vaihinger's terms, not semi-fiction but proper fiction.

At this point it is necessary to focus on what Vaihinger means by '*Widerspruch* (contradiction)'. The English noun 'contradiction' and its cognates such as the verb 'to contradict' are rarely found to wander beyond breach of the law of non-contradiction in classical logic: that a proposition and its negation cannot both be true in the same sense at the same time. Vaihinger uses the noun *Widersprechung* and its cognates such as the verb *widersprechen*, and their meanings more readily depart from classical logic.

Proper fictions, he says, '*nicht nur der Wirklichkeit widersprechen, sondern auch in sich selbst widerspruchsvoll sind* (are not only in contradiction with reality but self-contradictory in themselves)'.[182] The translation looks fine, but how is a proposition 'in contradiction with reality' when the author is a Kantian and wants nothing to do with a Hegelian immanence of logic in material reality (*Wirklichkeit*)?[183] When Vaihinger says '*der Wirklichkeit widersprechen*', he cannot be speaking of classical logical contradiction. And then it must be questioned whether he is speaking of classical logical contradiction when he goes on to say '*in sich selbst widerspruchsvoll*'. A broader translation of *Widerspruch* is 'inconsistency'. Using that option, the passage may be reinterpreted as: 'are not only inconsistent with reality but [also] inconsistent within themselves'. One may now speculate whether this is Kelsen's understanding of Vaihinger; there does not seem to be any obstacle to supposing that it is.[184]

Kelsen appears to have been unaware of Jeremy Bentham's denunciation in 1776 of a 'pestilential breath of Fiction' pervading the law: J Bentham, 'A Fragment on Government' in his *A Comment on the Commentaries and A Fragment on Government*, JH Burns and HLA Hart (eds), *The Collected Works of Jeremy Bentham* (London, Athlone Press, 1977) 391–551, 411. And see HLA Hart, 'The Demystification of the Law' (1973) in his *Essays on Bentham* (Oxford, Clarendon Press, 1982) 21–39. Although Vaihinger had known of Bentham's philosophy, he had been unaware, until his English translator brought it to his attention, of the similarity between his philosophy of 'as if' and Bentham's theory of fictions: CK Ogden, 'Note' in Vaihinger, *The Philosophy of 'As if'* v–vi. Bentham proceeds beyond denouncing fictions, to accepting that at a deep level they may be a necessity of thought: CK Ogden (ed), *Bentham's Theory of Fictions*, 2nd edn (London, Routledge & Kegan Paul, 1951) (originally published 1932) xxxi–xxxii. At the same time, Ogden says, 'The chief defect of Vaihinger's monumental work was its failure to lay stress on the linguistic factor in the creation of fictions', as Bentham does (ibid).

[181] H Kelsen, 'Zur Theorie der juristischen Fiktionen. Mit besonderer Berücksichtigung von Vaihingers Philosophie des Als Ob' (1919) 1 *Annalen der Philosophie* 630 (HKW4, 209–34); 'On the Theory of Juridic [sic] Fictions. With Special Consideration of Vaihinger's Philosophy of the As-If' (C Kletzer trans) in M Del Mar and W Twining (eds), *Legal Fictions in Theory and Practice* (Cham, Springer, 2015) 3–22; C Kletzer, 'Kelsen on Vaihinger' in Del Mar and Twining, ibid, 23–29. See Vaihinger, *Die Philosophie des Als Ob* 46–49; *The Philosophy of 'As if'* 33–35. In 1923 Kelsen says that he was indebted to Vaihinger's discussion of personificatory fictions, as found in 'analogous situations' in other sciences: HPS2, xvii; HPS2en, 16. See Vaihinger, *Die Philosophie des Als Ob* 50–52; *The Philosophy of 'As if'* 36–38.

[182] *Die Philosophie des Als Ob* 24; *The Philosophy of 'As if'* 16.

[183] *Die Philosophie des Als Ob* 10–11; *The Philosophy of 'As if'* 8. Rather, the utility of factual research processes 'is manifested in the very fact that logical functions, operating according to their own laws, constantly eventually meet up with reality (*dem Sein*)': *Die Philosophie des Als Ob* 12; *The Philosophy of 'As if'* 8 (modified).

[184] In 1928, Kelsen denied that a basic norm can be a 'fiction' (Vaihinger's semi-fiction): because there is no suggestion that it is a real norm, since it is merely 'presupposed in thought', there can be no question of 'inconsistency with reality (*Widerspruch zur Wirklichkeit*)' – '*Behauptung einer Realität im Widerspruch zur Wirklichkeit, keine Rede sein kann*' – *Rechtsgeschichte gegen Rechtsphilosophie? Eine Erwiderung* (Vienna, Springer, 1928) 25.

Vaihinger has asked, with Kant, how it happens that with consciously false ideas one can nonetheless come to an idea that is right. His reply that this is done through fictions restates the question rather than answering it. Nonetheless, he restates it acceptably: false and inconsistent data should not always be rejected, but may be allowed to be a stimulus. A fiction can lead to a new hypothesis, although not logically but *causally*; that is, probably not by resolving the inconsistency but more likely, in struggle with the inconsistency, by coming upon a path where it ceases to arise. Then Vaihinger's enthusiasm carries him into thinking of this not only as a disposition but as a method – almost, at least temporarily, at the expense of the law of non-contradiction.[185] But Kelsen had lived by that law;[186] he does not become a Vorticist, but continues to rely upon the laws of classical logic.

In the fiction turn, a basic norm is no longer a hypothesis, but Kelsen does not indicate that he is stimulated in the direction of a fresh hypothesis.[187]

That may alleviate my anxiety about the fiction turn, as to *what*. It does nothing, however, to deal with my anxiety as to *how*. This will be found to contain a further *what* dimension.

V. What Has Been Turned?

In the fiction turn, what is it that has been turned? Kelsen's 'basic norm' is not a general tool that he has found in philosophy and then put to scientific work. It is from the start a scientific device, defined by the applications for which it has been invented. He is content to set out what a basic norm *does*, as a tool of legal science. He pays less attention to what it *is*, in the sense of what might be its philosophical status, and even to what it is called.

A. Name

It was born as an '*Ursprungsnorm*', an appellation couched in the traditional notion of legal 'sources' or 'founts' – German *Rechtsquellen*, from Latin *fontes iuris*.[188] These are material 'sources', in the sense of authoritative 'founts' that a legal decision-maker may draw from. An *Ursprungsnorm* is a formal sort of 'source'. The comparison with material sources, however, is strained: for those are tools for justification, whereas Kelsen and his circle were working on description.[189] This may be why, in 1922 and

[185] *Die Philosophie des Als Ob* 172–73; *The Philosophy of 'As if* 98.

[186] eg, GNRL, 5; GNRLen, 119; RR1, 136; RR1en, 112. For example, in 1963 Kelsen finds it a conclusive condemnation, to identify a self-contradiction by Aquinas: 'Positivisme juridique et doctrine du droit naturel' (n 72) 145.

[187] C Bouriau, *Les fictions du droit. Kelsen, lecteur de Vaihinger* (Lyon, ENS Éditions, 2013) 29–31, 37–49.

[188] CG Bruns, *Fontes Iuris Romani Antiqui*, 6th edn (Freiburg in Breisgau, Mohr, 1893) (originally published 1860).

[189] Kelsen eventually preferred not to speak of 'sources (*Quellen*)', to avoid confusion between legal and social-scientific uses of the term: RR2, 238–39; RR2en, 232–33.

again in 1925, '*Ursprungsnorm*' is only stumblingly transmuted through '*Grund- oder Ursprungsnorm*' into '*Grundnorm*'.[190]

B. Status

The picture is further complicated by Kelsen running in parallel – perhaps as alternatives or perhaps as mutual supplements – characterisation of a basic norm both as a 'hypothesis' (or as 'hypothetical') and as a 'presupposition (*Voraussetzung*)'.[191] His early usage was uncertain: in 1925, within a single page he jumps around among *Hypothese, hypothetisch, vorausgesetzt* and *Ursprungs–*.[192] In 1945, he appears to have settled (in English) upon 'hypothesis': 'The ultimate hypothesis of [legal] positivism is the norm authorizing the historically first legislator'.[193] By 1959, however, he says: 'The word "hypothesis" means originary presupposition (*Das Wort "Hypothese" bedeutet ursprüngliche Voraussetzung*)'.[194] This 'presupposition', however, is not 'categorical, ie unconditional', but only 'hypothetical (*hypothetisch*), ie conditional'.[195] We are (to employ a German idiom) just as clever as before.[196]

There have been two major meanings of 'hypothesis' (in German, *Hypothese* or *Hypothesis*), which may be distinguished as 'classical' and 'modern'. The modern meaning is familiar today from empirical science: 'A supposition or conjecture put forth to account for known facts'.[197] This cannot be what Kelsen intended, since he insists that a norm cannot be true or false and no empirical test of a basic norm is envisaged.[198]

[190] H Kelsen, *Der soziologische und der juristische Staatsbegriff. Kritische Untersuchung des Verhältnisses von Staat und Recht* (Tübingen, Mohr Siebeck, 1922); 2nd edn 1928, 94–104 (1922 edn, HKW7, 69–350, 194–202); *Allgemeine Staatslehre* (n 126) 104 (also '*Grundgesetz*' 575). There was also an '*Ursprungshypothese*': *Der soziologische und der juristische Staatsbegriff* 95, 102 (HKW7, 195, 201). The term '*Grundnorm*' had been used by Edmund Husserl, to designate a logical foundation but with a practical-rational role: E Husserl, *Logische Untersuchungen. I. Prolegomena zur reinen Logik* (Halle an der Saale, Niemeyer, 1900) vol 1, 45–46, 48; *Logical Investigations*, JN Findlay trans of 2nd German edn (London, Routledge & Kegan Paul, 1970) vol 1, 85–87. In an answer to Charles Boasson in 1966 (although not about this term), Kelsen said merely that Husserl's *Logische Untersuchungen* 'are not unknown to me': 'Recht, Rechtswissenschaft und Logik' (1966) 52 *Archiv für Rechts- und Sozialphilosophie* 545, 552; cp C Boasson, 'The Use of Logic in Legal Reasoning' (1966) 29 *Mededelingen der Koninklijke Nederlandse Akademie van Wetenschappen. AFD. Letterkunde* (n.r.) 61, 63–64.

[191] RR1, 66–67; RR1en, 58; RR2, 204–09; RR2en, 201–05. He also uses a variety of other classifications, but 'hypothesis' (or 'hypothetical') and 'presupposition' are the most frequent: U Bindreiter, *Why* Grundnorm? *A Treatise on the Implications of Kelsen's Doctrine* (The Hague, Kluwer, 2002) 75–85.

[192] Kelsen, *Allegemeine Staatslehre* (n 126) 256.

[193] GTLS, 116.

[194] 'Recht, Rechtswissenschaft und Logik' (n 190) 547.

[195] RR2App, 443.

[196] '*genauso klug wie befor*'. Because Kelsen did his serious theoretical thinking in German, I focus primarily on his German vocabulary. For general background, see J Ritter and K Gründer (eds), *Historisches Wörterbuch der Philosophie* (Basel, Schwabe Verlag, 1971–2007), '*Annahme*', '*Grundnorm*', '*Hypothese*', '*Hypothesis*' and '*Voraussetzungslosigkeit*' (literally 'presuppositionlessness'; incorporating discussion of '*Voraussetzung*').

[197] 'A supposition or conjecture put forth to account for known facts; *esp* in the sciences, a provisional supposition from which to draw conclusions that shall be in accordance with known facts, and which serves as a starting-point for further investigation by which it may be proved or disproved and the true theory arrived at': *Oxford English Dictionary* online, 'hypothesis' n 3.

[198] Nor, as has been seen (above (n 131)), despite an enthusiastic expression in 1923 of debt to Marburg neo-Kantian Hermann Cohen (HPS2, xvii; HPS2en, 15), can Kelsen be found to use the term 'hypothesis' in Cohen's special sense. (Cohen wrote '*Hypothesis*' as a transliteration from the Greek.)

He states relatively early that, while a basic norm is a hypothesis, 'it is not a hypothesis in the usual, ie natural-scientific, sense of the word'; however, he does not specify his preferred sense.[199] The classical meaning of 'hypothesis' is not, or not directly, empirical: 'A supposition in general; something supposed or assumed to be true without proof or conclusive evidence; an assumption'.[200] This is the meaning established by philosophers of Ancient Greece for the name *ὑπόθεσις* (*hypothesis*) and it was in common use from that time into the eighteenth century. Robert Walter has identified Kelsen's meaning of 'hypothesis' – or, more often, of 'hypothetical' – as the classical meaning.[201]

Thus, in 1966 and so after the fiction turn, Kelsen avers that he had always meant to say, and usually had said, not that a basic norm is a 'hypothesis' but that it is 'hypothetical (*hypothetisch*)', meaning that it is *conditional*.[202] He prefers what he had said in second *Reine Rechtslehre*: that a basic norm is conditional in that it '*may* but *need not* be presupposed'.[203] Norms as subjective meanings are understood as objective meanings – that is, as legal – only '*wenn* (if and when)' a basic norm is presupposed for them.[204] Otherwise, observed phenomena will appear only as power relations – which, although it would be true in a fashion, would be inadequate.[205]

A thread in this labyrinth is Kelsen's acquaintance, from his schooldays, with Ancient Greek philosophy and language. He was no doubt aware that *ὑπόθεσις*, combining ὑπό and θεσις, means literally 'what lies below'. In dialectic and mathematics it meant a presupposition.[206] Fast-forward to the Middle Ages and in Latin there is '*praesuppositio*', from which are derived English 'presupposition' and, with the same meaning, German '*Voraussetzung*'. It seems plausible to suppose that Kelsen meant 'hypothesis' as a synonym of 'presupposition' and '*Voraussetzung*'. Perhaps he then retained both 'hypothesis' and 'presupposition' in order for the latter to fit his meaning into Kant's terminology for the transcendental-logical. In that case, however, 'hypothesis' was already redundant.

[199] Kelsen, *Rechtsgeschichte gegen Rechtsphilosophie?* (n 184) 25.

[200] *Oxford English Dictionary* online, 'hypothesis' n 4.a.

[201] R Walter, 'Entstehung und Entwicklung des Gedankens der Grundnorm' in R Walter (ed), *Schwerpunkte der Reinen Rechtslehre*. SHKI, Bd 18 (Vienna, Manz, 1992) 47–59, 54–57; citing (54, fn 25) R Eisler, *Wörterbuch der philosophischen Begriffe*, 4th edn (Berlin, Mittler, 1927) (originally published 1899), '*Hypothese*'. Kelsen also cites this work, for '*Positivismus*': 'Was ist juristischer Positivismus?' (1965) 20 *JuristenZeitung* 465, fn 1; in *Die Wiener rechtstheoretische Schule* (n 7) 941–53, 941, fn 1. Eisler's dictionary was well known: the second edition 1904 and third edition 1910 are available online: archive.org/search?query=Rudolf+Eisler. It has been superseded by the much larger *Historisches Wörterbuch der Philosophie* (n 196); the latter's entry '*Hypothese, Hypothesis*' gives examples, particularly from Plato, with Greek text. Walter suggests other names for this meaning, principally *Annahme* (assumption). Kelsen had used *Annahme*, characterising a *Grundnorm* as a '*hypothetische Annahme*': *Allgemeine Staatslehre* (n 126) 251. However, the range of meanings of *Annahme* is so wide that the term is not very helpful without further qualification: *Historisches Wörterbuch der Philosophie* (n 196), '*Annahme*'. The same may be said about 'assumption': *Oxford English Dictionary* online, 'assumption' n.

[202] Kelsen, 'Recht, Rechtswissenschaft und Logik' (n 190) 547.

[203] RR2, 224; RR2en, 218.

[204] RR2, 47 (in 'Recht, Rechtswissenschaft und Logik' (n 190) Kelsen refers to RR2, 46 apparently in error for 47); RR2en, 46 (modified).

[205] RR2, 224; RR2en, 218.

[206] *Historisches Wörterbuch der Philosophie* (n 196), '*Hypothese, Hypothesis*'. What counted as before or after, or as above or below, depended on whether the direction of enquiry was progressive or regressive: Plato, *Republic*, 510.

At any rate, with the fiction turn Kelsen pushes the term 'hypothesis', in any sense, out of his game. 'Presupposition' remains – but now, he would have to acknowledge, somehow to be 'modified' into a Vaihingerian proper fiction with transcendental-logical application. He does not take his analysis that far: we are left with 'presupposition' (*Voraussetzung*) somehow in that sense.

C. What a Basic Norm Does

If a basic norm will be only a fiction, it will be weaker in its functions. Paulson finds that these are mainly functions of 'grounding (*Begründung*)' and he traces five. The basic norm of a particular positive-legal order will operate as:

(1) The ultimate (*letzter*) basis (*Grund*) of legal validity, by which the 'validity' of a legal norm is related to its membership of a legal order.[207]
(2) The ultimate basis of legal validity, by which the 'validity' of a legal norm is related to its bindingness.[208]
(3) The ultimate empowerment[209] to issue legal norms.
(4) The ultimate empowerment to impose sanctions.
(5) A presupposition for the transition from the subjective meaning of an act (of will)[210] to its objective – ie, legal – meaning.[211]

These are cognitive functions and are performed simultaneously. Presupposing a basic norm would be like switching on a bright light in a dimly lit furnished room.

Through function (1) a basic norm secures unity, the internal identity, of the scientific representation of the legal order; through functions (3) and (4) it secures differentiation, the external identity, of the legal order; and through functions (2) and (5) it acknowledges bindingness and objectivity as characteristics of legal norms, as well as passing bindingness and objectivity down to all the norms of the order as connotations of their validity.

Kelsen writes as though this collection of processes establishes, by itself, the 'legal' character of the norms, but that is difficult to discern. Function (2) may appear to do it, but suffices only to distinguish an order of positive law from an order of natural law or of moral norms; an order such as in function (2) can probably be found in any large

[207] eg, 'A plurality of norms forms a unity, a system, an order, if the validity of the norms can be traced back to a single norm as the ultimate basis of validity': RR1, 62; RR1en, 55.

[208] eg, 'That a norm referring to the behaviour of a human being is "valid" means that it is binding – that an individual ought to behave in the way determined by the norm': RR2, 196; RR2en, 193 (modified).

[209] Kelsen's term is *Ermächtigung*, which has been translated (eg, RR2en) as 'authorisation'. However, recent and more exact Kelsen translators have preferred the more literal rendering 'empowerment' (eg, RR1en). This is not to be confused with the political meaning of 'empowerment'.

[210] Adding 'of will' for clarification.

[211] SL Paulson, 'Die Funktion der Grundnorm: begründend oder explizierend?' in C Jabloner, D Kolonovits, G Kucsko-Stadlmayer, HR Laurer, H Mayer and R Thienel (eds), *Gedenkschrift Robert Walter* (Vienna, Manz, 2013) 553–73, 557. Later Paulson characterises these as 'forms': 'The Basic Norm' (n 6) 68–74. I will stick with 'functions': these are less things that a basic norm is (its theoretical status) than things that it does.

organisation.[212] Mainly regarding functions (3) and (4), Kelsen is at pains not to count coercion as the distinguishing feature of a legal norm; if it were so counted, he says, a demand for money, coupled with a threat, would be the same whether it came from a tax office or from a gang of robbers.[213] Nor will he accept justice as that criterion, even if the idea of justice were not transcendent, principally because a criterion of justice would lack scientific neutrality.[214]

In functions (2) and (5), a basic norm does not originate the characteristics of bindingness and objectivity but is simply assumed to possess them and to confer them upon lower norms through function (3). The bindingness appears to lie in the objectivity, so what is the 'objectivity' that is assumed, if it does not have a transcendent origin?[215] Kelsen's eventual account of objectivity is extraordinarily weak: it locates the 'objectivity' of legal norms in the supposedly 'objective' judgement of a 'disinterested third party (*unbeteiligten Dritten*)' to an individual dispute.[216] That may be a degree of value neutrality, but it does not come near to a reason for bindingness.[217] A source or sources for a legal norm's bindingness and objectivity, or at least its objectivity, will have to be available somewhere else.

D. What the Basic Norm Concept Does

The grounding functions had been performed by natural law (or at any rate by supposing that they were). In this way, as has been noted, a basic norm is a functional replacement for natural law.[218] Hence the idea of a basic norm,[219] Kelsen declares,[220] is not a great innovation. Rather, he writes in first *Reine Rechtslehre*:

> In formulating a basic norm, the pure theory of law is in no way attempting to inaugurate a new method for jurisprudence. It is aiming simply to raise to the level of consciousness (*Bewusstsein)* what all lawyers (*Juristen*) are doing (for the most part unwittingly (*unbewusst*))

[212] eg, 'a church is only a particular kind of state': Kelsen, 'Die philosophischen Grundlagen der Naturrechtslehre und des Rechtspositivismus' (n 82) 340, fn 17; 'Natural Law Doctrine and Legal Positivism' (n 82) 438, fn * (modified); see further Kelsen, *Allgemeine Staatslehre* (n 126) 133–36. This may be an exaggeration for many churches today, but it has much historical truth even on political-scientific criteria. FB Artz writes: 'The church was the true state of the Middle Ages; it not only commanded the first loyalty of the individual, which in modern times goes to the state, but it had, better than any state, the ability to collect its taxes and enforce its laws over a wide area. The mediaeval church was more like the Roman state and the modern state than was the mediaeval secular state.' – *The Mind of the Middle Ages A.D. 200–1500. An Historical Survey* (Chicago, University of Chicago Press, 1980 edn) 227.

[213] RR2, 8–9, 45–50; RR2en, 8, 44–49.

[214] RR2, 50–51; RR2en, 49–50.

[215] Kelsen addresses the idea of the 'objectivity' of a legal norm abstractly and not by asking what in ordinary language is meant by '*objektives Recht*', which refers to 'objectivity' in the sense of being 'in common'.

[216] RR2, 7; RR2en, 7.

[217] For instance, the third party could be an arbiter of the dispute only with the mutual agreement of the disputants.

[218] Above at (n 89).

[219] Paulson distinguishes an 'explicatory (*explizierend*)' function of a basic norm: 'Die Funktion der Grundnorm' (n 211).

[220] For I take him to be referring here to the basic norm concept.

> when, in conceptualising their object of enquiry, they reject any natural law as source of the validity of positive law, but nevertheless understand this positive law as a valid order – that is, as norm – and not merely as factual contingencies of motivation. With the theory (*Lehre*) of the basic norm, the pure theory of law tries simply, through analysing the actual process of a long-standing method of cognising positive law, to reveal the transcendental-logical conditions of that method.[221]

God, the author of the natural-legal norms, is shown a door and Jurisprudence is disenchanted. This is not a great innovation by specialist legal theory, because ordinary legal thinking has already run ahead of specialist theory. The change that has already occurred in legal thinking, however, is epochal.

VI. Finding Inconsistency

The ground here is now prepared for asking: what is the contradiction, or perhaps the inconsistency, within the fiction? It appears that, actually, two contradictions are involved, although only one of them is found within the fiction: these may be referred to as the Infinity Problem and the Synthesis Error. Both of these are contradictions and not just inconsistencies, but they are covered by Kelsen's recourse to Vaihinger's fictionalism even if it is only an inconsistency umbrella.

A. The Infinity Problem

In the pure theory, law is to be understood as norms and a norm is the meaning of an act of will directed towards the behaviour of another.[222] Legal norms are found not singly but in ordered groups, 'legal orders (*Rechtsordnungen*)'. The pure theory distinguishes two principles of ordering of norms. In 'static' ordering, the hierarchical relations between norms are of *logical* validity, established by kinds of deduction that could be performed in any individual's head. From the general norm 'Do not steal' may be deduced a particular norm such as 'Smith, do not steal from Jones'. The order is 'static' because creation of a norm requires only thought and not action. A moral order, including an order of so-called natural law, is of this kind. In 'dynamic' ordering, hierarchical relations will be of *legal* validity, created by use of empowerment; a norm is legally 'valid' when its creator has been so empowered[223] by another legal norm.[224] An order of positive law is primarily of this kind. For example, a constitution empowers the legislature to make laws with regard to 'taxation' and the legislature makes a law imposing a tax. The order is

[221] RR1, 67; RR1en, 58 (modified). Similarly: Kelsen, *Rechtsgeschichte gegen Rechtsphilosophie?* (n 184) 24; GTLS, 116–17; RR2, 209; RR2en, 204–05. Paulson, finding here an 'explicatory function' of a basic norm, wonders just what it manages to explicate: 'Die Funktion der Grundnorm' (n 211) 570–72; 'The Basic Norm' (n 6) 86–90.

[222] RR2, 1–9; RR2en, 1–10.

[223] '*ermächtigt*'; in RR2en translated as 'authorised' – cp above (n 209).

[224] RR2, 196–227; RR2en, 193–221.

'dynamic' because creation of a norm requires action, the use of an empowerment. The existence of a legal norm and its legal validity are one and the same.[225]

To ask why a legal norm is binding is, eventually, to ask for the ultimate source of its authority – that is, of its legal validity. In terms of the pure theory: by what norm, ultimately, has the creation of the norm in question been empowered? The pure theory's answer is guided by what Kelsen assumes to be two fundamental principles of any science. Following the Positivity Principle, the pure theory does not acknowledge the existence of natural law; hence the ultimate source of legal empowerment can only be human. Following the Separation Principle, an ultimate source of legal empowerment cannot be a fact (Is) and can only be a norm (Ought). The source, therefore, must itself be a norm whose human creation has been empowered. But by what norm, it has to be asked, has creation of *that* norm been empowered? And this line of questioning can, potentially, be continued infinitely. This potential of regression may be called the pure theory's Infinity Problem.

Kelsen's proposed solution to the Infinity Problem is to 'presuppose' in science an ultimate norm whose own validity is, by methodological fiat, not to be questioned.[226] That can be done for any order of norms regarded as binding, but most importantly for orders of positive law.[227] This ultimate norm, he says, is a 'basic norm (*Grundnorm*)'. It will not be a real norm: it will be 'transcendental-logical' in Kant's sense; that is, it will be supposed in order to make it possible to identify descriptively (in Kantian language, cognitively to construct) real norms.

Kelsen composed several template formulations (at different times, perhaps as many as ten) for the basic norm of a positive-legal order.[228] The formula in second *Reine Rechtslehre* may be taken as standard:

> Coercive acts ought to be performed under the conditions and in the way established by the historically first constitution of the state and the norms created according to it. (In short: One ought to behave as the constitution prescribes.)[229]

B. The Synthesis Error

In Salzburg, as has been seen, Kelsen states that he has abandoned his conception of a basic norm as a 'hypothesis'. He has done so, he says,

> in the knowledge that an 'ought (*Sollen*)' has to be the correlate of a 'willing (*Wollen*)'. My basic norm[230] is a *fictitious* (fiktive) norm, which presupposes a *fictitious* act of will that posits this norm. It is the fiction that some authority or other wills that something ought to be (*dass dies sein soll*).

[225] 'By the word "validity" we indicate the specific existence of a norm': RR2, 9; RR2en, 10 (modified).

[226] RR2, 200–09; RR2en, 198–205.

[227] RR2, 196–227; RR2en, 193–221.

[228] R Walter, 'Entstehung und Entwicklung des Gedankens der Grundnorm' (n 201); SL Paulson, 'The Basic Norm' (n 6) 61–68.

[229] RR2, 203–04; RR2en, 201 (modified). That is, of a state legal order; a basic norm for international law is a more complex case (RR2, 222–23; RR2en, 216), but it need not be considered for the present purpose. See also, in 1966: 'The basic norm says: We ought to obey the constitution and, consequently, the legal norms established in conformity with the constitution. Thus, the basic norm is the reason for the validity of the total legal order.' – Kelsen, 'On the Pure Theory of Law' (n 11) 6.

[230] The idea of a particular presupposed basic norm.

Yet, if previously it had been contradictory to suppose an Ought that is *not* the correlate of a Willing, to suppose instead that it *is* the correlate of a Willing could be just to resolve that contradiction. There would now be a fiction (a Vaihingerian semi-fiction), but no contradiction would remain; a Vaihingerian proper fiction would not be contemplated. However, Kelsen thinks that this track is not possible and that a proper fiction is needed.

In the Vienna paper, he states his position more informatively. The pure theory, he says, assumes that 'the constitution, whose validity is grounded by the basic norm, is the meaning of an act of will of a supreme authority, over which there can be no higher authority'.[231] For this to be conceivable, he had supposed, the basic norm of that legal order may be presupposed without identifying an author of it. He now seems to recognise that (in Kantian terms) he had identified as *synthetic* a relation that was actually *analytic*.[232] He had supposed that, in the series 'meaning/act-of-will/willer', the relation between 'act of will' and 'willer' could be synthetic – that is, optional – and so a specific willer would not always have to be considered. That would be possible for a basic norm, since a basic norm is the meaning not of an act of will but of an act of thought.

He now acknowledges that this thought is, after all, thought *of a norm*. To think of this norm is to imagine a meaning that has been created by an imaginary act of will of an imaginary willer. Whether the act of will and the willer are real or not, however, the relation between them is logically necessary – that is, it is *analytic*. Instead, that necessary relation had been believed to be unnecessary. This self-contradiction may be called the Synthesis Error.[233] But it is a self-contradiction in the pure theory as it had stood; it is not the self-contradiction in the proper fiction.

C. Revival of Infinity

In Salzburg, Kelsen confesses to the Synthesis Error. He has then to acknowledge that, in presupposing a basic norm, it would be necessary to identify both an act of will and a willer. His acknowledgement that it would be necessary to identify a willer revives the Infinity Problem. Then the Infinity Problem as resurrected is the contradiction in a particular basic norm as a Vaihingerian proper fiction. And, since the Infinity Problem would arise in presupposing any particular basic norm, it is restored as a flaw in the basic norm concept.

[231] For this argument, he does not catch up with the constitution turn.

[232] Kant, *Critique of Pure Reason* (n 133) 130–31 (*Akademieausgabe*, A6–8/B10–11).

[233] It is corrected by additions to the Italian and English translations of second *Reine Rechtslehre*: RR2it, 22, acknowledged in a footnote; and in RR2en, 9–10, without acknowledgement. It is also made, with acknowledgement, in the 2017 text of RR2: 2017, 35, 759 – reproducing the note as Kelsen had rewritten it for the Italian translator (see Erne, 'Eine letzte authentische Revision der Reinen Rechtslehre' (n 22) 39). The paragraph in that note and at 2017, 759 can be translated in its entirety as: 'Finally, it is to be noted that a norm need not be only the meaning of an actually (*real*) posited act of will (*Willensakt*). That is the case if the norm is only presupposed in our thinking, like the previously mentioned basic norm. Since there exists a correlation between the ought (*Sollen*) of a norm and a willing (*Wollen*) whose meaning it is, if in our thinking a norm is presupposed that is not the meaning of an actual (*realen*) act of will, along with it has to be thought an imaginary (*imaginäre*) act of will whose meaning is this norm that has merely been thought. Such a norm that has merely been thought is therefore not a *positive* norm – to be precise, not a norm posited by a *real* (realen) act of will – but a norm merely presupposed.' The clause that had been added in RR2en, 10, 'as is the basic norm of a positive legal order', is not included; however, the addition for RR2it of 'like the previously mentioned basic norm' may have been thought to have the same effect.

Revival of the Infinity Problem probably left Kelsen with three options: (a) to argue that an infinite regress is not necessarily fatal;[234] (b) to accept that it is fatal and abandon the basic norm concept; or (c) to find a rescue boat for the self-contradictory. He does not entertain (a); instead and hoping to avoid (b), he finds (c) in Vaihinger's notion of a proper fiction. But a Vaihingerian proper fiction is an unappealing sort of rescue boat.

D. Why the Rush?

A relatively specific *why*-question can be dealt with at this point, partly because its answer will have to remain speculative. At the time of the Salzburg workshop, the logic turn had been – or soon would be – made known by the leisurely route of a *Festschrift* chapter.[235] The fiction turn merited similar deliberation, yet Kelsen announced it with apparently barely considered haste. However, it seems hardly credible that the fiction turn was conceived only in Salzburg. In that case, the issue is not whether the fiction turn was hastily conceived but that it was hastily announced.

A possible explanation for this hurry may be that a workshop participant[236] might have informed Kelsen that his Synthesis Error could soon be exploited, the potential critic having noticed that second *Reine Rechtslehre* had pointed to it.

In 1953, Edwin W Patterson had objected to the basic norm concept that

> the assumption that the constitution is valid and that laws created pursuant to it are valid … depends ultimately upon the political authority not only of the officials who created the constitution, but also of those who maintain and uphold that constitution at the present time. This is something outside the constitution or the norms created pursuant to it.[237]

Kelsen's reply is almost buried within a long footnote in second *Reine Rechtslehre*:

> [T]he assumption that the constitution is valid is identical with the assumption that the creator of the constitution is an 'authority', the highest legal authority. The basic norm answers the question: What is the basis (*Grund*) of this authority? In this sense, it is indeed 'outside the constitution'.

[234] A possibility I must leave to logicians: see R Cameron, 'Infinite Regress Arguments', *Stanford Encyclopedia of Philosophy* (Fall edn, 2022): plato.stanford.edu/entries/infinite-regress/.

[235] The fiction turn, as has been seen, was announced in Salzburg in August 1962. The logic turn appeared in a chapter for a *Festschrift* celebrating the ninety-second birthday of Roscoe Pound on 27 October 1962: RA Newman (ed), *Essays in Jurisprudence in Honor of Roscoe Pound* (n 14) vii. Contributions to the volume would presumably have been due some months earlier. It therefore seems that the fiction turn and the logic turn happened, or in the case of the fiction turn commenced, at around the same time. There is no indication that the fiction turn influenced the logic turn. The other way around, however, is very possible.

[236] Perhaps Verdross, who had been among the designers of the basic norm concept, although he would come to disagree with Kelsen's more formal development of it. He would presumably have read RR2 immediately upon publication; very likely Kelsen had had a copy sent to him. The potential critic might have been Marcic, although Marcic's workshop paper did not include this point.

[237] EW Patterson, *Jurisprudence. Men and Ideas of the Law* (Brooklyn, NY, Foundation Press, 1953) 262. This is the 'first printed edition' of a student textbook, with copyright dates of mimeographed versions going back to 1940. It was called in 1957 'the leading American treatise on Jurisprudence': HW Jones, 'Edwin Wilhite Patterson: Man and Ideas' (1957) 57 *Columbia Law Review* 607, 608. Patterson was keen to introduce natural-scientific method to law and was a careful critic of the pure theory, although believing that it excluded all social reality and was about 'pure law': *Men and Ideas of the Law,* 91–92, 259–65, 390; 'Hans Kelsen and his Pure Theory of Law' (1952) 40 *California Law Review* 5.

Those who 'maintain and uphold' the constitution, he notes, are the individuals who have created it, who apply it in making laws pursuant to it and who apply those laws. 'Therein lies the effectiveness of the constitution and of the legal order created according to it. Clearly, Patterson is referring to this effectiveness.' The basic norm makes this effectiveness a condition for the validity of the constitution; it is a condition for the validity, not the basis of the validity.[238] But Patterson had said that 'the assumption that the constitution is valid' – that is, the basic norm – 'ultimately depends upon the political authority' of 'the officials who created the constitution'. This relation, he is saying, is analytic.[239]

In Salzburg, Kelsen appears to have come round to accepting Patterson's argument. He then appears to accept the consequence that presupposing a basic norm does not cut off the potentially infinite regress of norms and their authors. Removal of the Synthesis Error revives the Infinity Problem. Even worse, as the series of those authors ascended, it would soon either run out of lift or need to become supernatural. A description of a positive-legal order threatens to become, inversely to the legendary turtles, deities all the way up.[240] This would of course have been painful for Kelsen to admit, and partly because he was having to reverse his published reply to Patterson's criticism.[241]

This speculation might need to plead the maxim that 'when all other contingencies fail, whatever remains, however improbable, must be the truth'.[242] However, Kelsen showed later in the discussions that he was perfectly capable of stonewalling an objector. Might he have been playing a still deeper game?

VII. Description and Independence

A. The Pure Theory as 'Descriptive'

The pure theory is presented as an exercise in 'normative science' and Kelsen wrenches the word 'normative (*normativ*)' into meaning not 'prescriptive' but in a way 'descriptive' – that is, describing norms.[243] Then he says that a basic norm for a positive-legal order is

[238] RR2, 206, fn ** (on 207–08); RR2en omits. That is: legal validity exists within a legal order and a legal order exists when it is by and large effective.

[239] Ronald Moore would make this point in 1978 – see Appendix below – although without reference to Patterson.

[240] Kelsen does not contemplate the possibility of the legal scientist doing just that. After all, the deities (like Maxwell's Demon) would only be figments of a scientist's imagination ….

[241] Also perhaps in remembering his bitter conflict in 1928 with Viennese colleague and empiricistic legal historian (and anti-semite) Ernst Schwind, who had complained that Kelsen's basic norm was merely a fiction: *Grundlagen und Grundfragen des Rechts. Rechtstheoretische Betrachtungen und Erörterungen* (Munich, Hueber, 1928) 145–46. Kelsen had replied mockingly, accusing Schwind of assuming a 'right to self-contradiction': *Rechtsgeschichte gegen Rechtsphilosophie?* (n 184) 9. See further Olechowski, *Hans Kelsen* (n 30) 204–06, 399–400, 407–09.

[242] A Conan Doyle, 'The Adventure of the Bruce-Partington Plans' (originally published 1917) in *Sherlock Holmes. The Complete Novels and Stories* (New York, Bantam, 1986) vol 2, 398–428, 418–19.

[243] In contrast with causally 'explanatory' science: HPS, 42; cp GTLS, 163–64; RR2, 89–90; RR2en, 85–86. 'Normative (*normativ*)' cognition (cognition of norms) had been contrasted with causal cognition (cognition of causes), by Georg Jellinek: G Jellinek *Allgemeine Staatslehre*, 2nd edn (Berlin, Häring, 1905) 19.

not a real norm but a device to assist scientific description of the norms composing that order.[244] What Kelsen means by 'describe', however, is uncertain.

B. Dogmatics and Exegesis

Kelsen's Purification Project, which would give birth to the pure theory of law, commenced with *Main Problems* in 1911.[245] The Project was conceived as modernisation of legal dogmatics.[246] In this, Kelsen acknowledged, he would respectfully build upon the work of the previous generation of jurists – particularly Karl Friedrich von Gerber, Paul Laband and Georg Jellinek.[247] He would follow them in ripping out the current foundation of legal dogmatics in natural law. He appears to have chosen to couch his aims in disarmingly bland language, given that his academic career depended upon the thesis being accepted by a faculty that he knew to contain opposition. He aimed, he said, to construct 'a geometry of the entire phenomenon of law'; there was to be a 'stabilisation' of the fundamental concepts (*Grundbegriffe*) of 'dogmatic jurisprudence (*dogmatische Jurisprudenz*)' – that is, the core concepts in (although Kelsen rarely uses the name) legal 'doctrine (*Doktrin*)'.[248]

The characteristic method of legal dogmatics is exegesis. Drawn from theology, exegesis is the interpretation of an authoritative text as an expression of a priori truths and values.[249] In scriptural exegesis, where the author is supposedly divine, the a priori truths and values are necessarily elements of the authorial intention. With a view to applying the text, authorial intention may be supplemented by methods that establish a social or historical context. However, the core of the process remains – as Kelsen was told in Salzburg – *participation*. To know a legal norm exegetically is to seek to participate in its creator's intention. Kelsen declares a focus upon 'method'. He will not do methodology for its own sake, but will moderate the current 'hypertrophy' of conceptualist legal theory (*Begriffsjurisprudenz*). He plays upon the term 'construction', in effect bringing its traditional meaning as exegetical interpretation under the aegis of 'construction' in the sense of Kantian epistemology.[250] Who could object to him being 'constructive'? Yet he was not a free architect.

[244] RR2, 204–09; RR2en, 201–05.

[245] HPS; see above, section II.D.

[246] Legal dogmatics (*Rechtsdogmatik, dogmatique juridique* and so on) resembles what is called, in common law jurisdictions, 'legal formalism'.

[247] On the important extent to which Kelsen's project is a response to Jellinek, see N Wheatley, *The Life and Death of States. Central Europe and the Transformation of Modern Sovereignty* (Princeton, Princeton University Press, 2023) 4. Paulson suggests that the basic norm concept may have been invented by Walter Jellinek (son of Georg): 'Did Walter Jellinek Invent Hans Kelsen's Basic Norm?' in M Jestaedt, R Poscher and J Kammerhofer (eds), *Die Reine Rechtslehre auf dem Prüfstand. Hans Kelsen's Pure Theory of Law* (n 39) 351–59. If so, however, Kelsen has made it his own.

[248] HPS1; HPS, 34, 92–93 (HKW2, 51–64, 118, 185–86). To favour a 'geometrical' approach sounded safely Aristotelian in spirit; but Kelsen was later to denounce Aristotle's 'mathematical-geometrical' approach, especially in his doctrine of the 'golden mean', as reducing criteria of justice from qualitative to quantitative: Kelsen, 'Aristotle's Doctrine of Justice' (n 14) 117–18.

[249] cp A-J Arnaud, *Les juristes face à la société du XIXe siècle à nos jours* (Paris, Presses universitaires de France, 1975) 53–60.

[250] HPS1.

C. 'Describing' Law

Within the exegetical tradition, the relation between a legal norm and a statement that might be said to 'describe' it is a relation of authoritative to unauthoritative – in Kelsen's terminology, of empowered to unempowered.

i. *Of and About Law*

Any lawyer – and indeed anybody when they think of law – is familiar with the conceptual difference between a statement *of* law and a statement *about* law.[251] What is the criterion of that difference? When a polity's legislature makes a law 'Theft ought to be punished with imprisonment', this is a statement *of* law. Then others can say that, in this polity, 'Theft ought to be punished with imprisonment', which is a statement *about* law. The latter statement is about the former. The latter may use the same words as the former[252] or it may be a paraphrase (maybe 'If you nick stuff around here, they'll want to bang you up'), but it needs to have the same or much the same meaning as the former or it will be pointless. However, although the two statements are very alike in *meaning*, they are different in *status*. The difference of status is that the former statement is made with empowerment while the latter is not.[253] The criterion of the difference between the two statements is the presence or absence of empowerment.

Since the two statements have the same or much the same meaning and their difference of status is obvious, it can be convenient to refer to them with the same name. That name, in the usage orthodox when Kelsen began his Purification Project, was '*Rechtssatz*'.[254] *Rechtssatz*, in this sense, may be translated as 'legal statement'. The pure theory, however, is to emphasise that its statements about law differ from statements of law not only in status[255] but also, more specifically, in that statements about law *describe* statements of law. Accordingly, at least by 1934 in first *Reine Rechtslehre*, Kelsen finds a need to name a scientific statement about law differently from a statement of law.[256] He calls a statement *of* law a *Rechtsnorm* and for a statement *about* law he awkwardly

[251] HLA Hart, 'Legal Duty and Obligation' (1966) in his *Essays on Bentham* (n 180) 127–61, 144 ('of the law' and 'about the law'). cp RR2, 74; RR2en, 72; Kelsen, 'On the Pure Theory of Law' (n 11) 3.

[252] In effect, quoting the former: ATN, 149–50; ATNen, 187–88.

[253] cp J Bentham, *An Introduction to the Principles of Morals and Legislation* (1789) (ed) JH Burns and HLA Hart in *The Collected Works of Jeremy Bentham* (London, Athlone Press, 1970) 294; and identically in J Bentham, *Of the Limits of the Penal Branch of Jurisprudence* (ed) P Schofield in *The Collected Works of Jeremy Bentham* (Oxford, Oxford University Press, 2010) 16. Bentham distinguishes first between 'expository jurisprudence', which ascertains what the law is, and 'censorial jurisprudence', which ascertains what the law might morally be or become. Then he distinguishes expository jurisprudence into 'authoritative jurisprudence', which is written by a lawmaker, and 'unauthoritative jurisprudence', which can be written by anybody else. By 'authoritative' Bentham appears to mean what Kelsen will mean by 'empowered'. Kelsen will eventually refer to a statement of a legal or moral norm as '*echt* (authentic)' and to a statement about it as '*unecht* (inauthentic)': ATN, 125; ATNen, 155.

[254] Throughout HPS. Grammatically, *Rechtssatz* consists of *Satz* (statement) and *Rechts-* (legal/of law).

[255] A legal proposition is not a 'simple repetition' of a legal norm: RR2, 76; RR2en, 74.

[256] RR1, 22; cp RR1en, 23.

retains the name *Rechtssatz*.[257] *Rechtsnorm* translates into English easily as 'legal norm'; *Rechtssatz* in this revised sense has proved difficult to translate – to begin with, because in first *Reine Rechtslehre* the criterion of the difference is not yet clear.[258] The best option for translation of *Rechtssatz* now seems to be 'legal proposition'.[259] In this terminology, the pure theory says that a *legal norm* is described by a *legal proposition*.

ii. Mapping

For Kelsen, 'description' refers to a process akin less to photographing than to mapping, and it is interpretive mapping. The relations of legal validity presumably have been decided on through processes that have been partly logical, although those processes will not appear in the statements of law. The statements about law, however, may include those processes (or what they are thought to have been) in the map. Moreover, the statements about law will be assembled in terms of their own logical validity – for example, in a doctrinal treatise. The map will be a reproduction, but, as to logic, an enhanced reproduction. In displaying the logic employed (or thought to have been employed) in creating the relations of legal validity, the map might show faults in that reasoning. Such discrepancy could extend to the premises of the reasoning and even to its methods.

With the basic norm concept, the pure theory carries the mapping procedure up to the ultimate premise found, the criterion upon which a lawmaker has identified their statements as statements of law. Later, a logical flaw is found in the basic norm concept itself.

[257] RR2, 73–77; RR2en, 71–75. Here RR1en translates *Rechtssatz* as 'reconstructed legal norm' – on which see commentary in RR1en, 23, fn 20 and 132–34. The phrase is attributed there to Eugenio Bulygin, who elsewhere makes heavy weather of the issues: 'Norms, Normative Propositions, and Legal Statements' (1982) in his *Essays in Legal Philosophy*, several eds (Oxford, Oxford University Press, 2015) 188–206; 'An Antinomy in Kelsen's Pure Theory of Law' (1990) in Bulygin, ibid, 235–51, 241–43. It is true that around 1911 '*Rechtssatz*' was equivalent to '*Rechtsnorm*' (ibid 241): Kelsen says as much in RR2, 74, fn * (RR2en omits), citing Adolf Merkel, *Juristische Encyclopädie*, 2nd edn (Berlin, Guttentag, 1900) §12, where it is said that a judge can be 'bound by' either. Nevertheless, if the two expressions are found in the same place, they have not arrived at the same angle. *Rechtssätze* are a species of the genus *Satz* (statement), while *Rechtsnormen* are a species of the genus *Norm* (norm), and it is understood that the two specific meanings are exchangeable. Thus, with historical awareness, I have translated the subtitle of HPS with 'statements'.

[258] In English translations it has been a baffling 'rule of law in a descriptive sense': GTLS, 45; RR2en, 76–81 (cp RR2, 79–86). In RR1fr in 1953, *Rechtssatz* is obscurely '*règle de droit* (rule of law)': RR1fr, 42. In the long-delayed English translation of RR1, with the uncomfortable availability of hindsight B Litschewski Paulson and SL Paulson have found it necessary to adopt 'reconstructed legal norm' (RR1en, 23). RR2fr chooses the couple '*norme juridique* (legal norm)' and '*proposition de droit* (proposition of law)': RR2fr, 78. ATNfr, after toying with '*norme de droit*' (ATNfr, 28), also settles on '*norme juridique*' (ATNfr, 168), together again with '*proposition de droit*' (ATNfr, 28, 168). Translating ATN into English, M Hartney goes for 'proposition of law' (ATNen, 23). This is as accurate as 'legal proposition', but a reason not to use 'proposition of law' for Kelsen is that it is used by HLA Hart and R Dworkin with meanings different from Kelsen's and from each other's: Hart, 'Legal Duty and Obligation' (n 251) 145; for Dworkin, 'propositions of law' are 'the various statements lawyers make [when] reporting what the law is on some question or other': R Dworkin, *A Matter of Principle* (Cambridge, MA, Harvard University Press, 1985) 146. It is unnecessary here to do more than note Kelsen's characterisation of a *Rechtssatz* as a '*Rechtsgesetz*' in the sense of an analogy with a *Naturgesetz*, a 'law' in natural science: RR2, 79–86; RR2en, 76–81 ('legal law'); ATN, 18, 237–38; ATNen, 23, 290–91 ('legal law'). The analogy (besides being outdated in principle) is incomplete, since the essential generality of a natural-scientific 'law' is not replicated in a legal proposition that describes only an individual legal norm.

[259] Used predominantly in translations by B Litschewski Paulson and SL Paulson.

D. Legal Self-Knowledge

i. An 'External Point of View'

After moving to the United States and anxious to impress an American audience that he was both a proper 'lawyer' and as 'scientific' as them, Kelsen goes out of his way to explain that his descriptive standpoint is an 'external point of view'. He cites Joseph W Bingham, who had said that an 'external attitude' to law is not confined to study of the 'external phenomena' of law such as legislative and adjudicative processes:

> If we are to view the law as a field of study analogous to that of any science, we must look at it from the position of the law teacher, the law student, the legal investigator, or the lawyer who is engaged in searching the authorities to determine 'what the law is'. … They are studying that field from without and therefore from the position which will give a wholly objective and the least confusing view.[260]

Kelsen comments: 'This is exactly the standpoint of normative jurisprudence'. Bingham and others are, however, mistaken when they think that law can be described 'only by rules which have the same character as laws of nature'. The focus should instead be on 'the "ought"'. He ends: 'Normative jurisprudence describes law from an *external point of view* although its statements are ought-statements.'[261] One could now say: its statements are 'ought' propositions.

In these reflections, the word 'external' is used in two senses. One sense concerns the way in which physical phenomena are 'external' to an observer; Kelsen puts this aside. The other sense, which he adopts, is the way in which an observer's meanings may be 'external' to – that is, independent of – meanings observed.[262]

ii. 'Outside' and 'Inside' Views

In second *Reine Rechtslehre*, consistently with the latter sense, Kelsen says that legal science 'has to know the law – as it were, from outside – and on the basis of that knowledge to describe it'.[263] Then he adds: 'the law-applying organs also have first to know – as it were, from inside – the law that they are to apply'. A legislator has to know (which is, to describe) constitutional norms and a judge statutory norms. This knowing is 'preparation' for exercise of their specific function – for the legislator, creation of general

[260] JW Bingham, 'What is the Law?' (1912) 11 *Michigan Law Review* 1, 10.

[261] GTLS, 164; my emphasis.

[262] At the beginning of the first chapter of *Main Problems*, Kelsen writes: 'An inquiry into theory of the legal statement (*Rechtssatz*) has to begin by setting out the particular and characteristic relationships to be found between this concept and others of a similar kind. The common bond connecting the concept of a legal statement with certain other terms is, to begin with, purely external (*ein rein äusserliches*); it is the usage of the word (*Sprachgebrauch des Wortes*) "law (*Gesetz*)", which in the sense of a "law" of nature (*Naturgesetz*) is contrasted with a "law" in the moral sense (*Sittengesetz*) and is differentiated from a "law" in the legal sense (*Rechtsgesetz*).': HPS, 3 (HKW2, 80). Is this an early interest in an 'external' perspective? It seems, rather, only to be excusing a non-juristic step in preliminary clarification of terminology, before commencing a resolutely 'internal' refinement of legal dogmatics. Kelsen's publications show interest in linguistic expression, but little in theory of language. Towards the end, however, in the drafts for *General Theory of Norms*, JL Austin's theory of performative utterances gets brief attention: ATN, 87, fn 79 (on 265); ATNen, 108, fn 79 (on 322–23); see also below (n 350).

[263] RR2, 74; RR2en, 72 (modified).

norms and, for the judge, creation of individual norms.[264] This is an instance, he says, of what lawyers understand as 'interpretation'. Indeed, he places all knowledge of law – whether by a law-applying organ or by a private individual or a legal scientist – under the label of 'interpretation (*Interpretation*)'. Moreover, among interpretations by a law-applying organ, a judicial interpretation can itself be a norm; it will be an 'authentic, ie binding (*authentisch, d.h. verbindlich*)' interpretation. An empowered interpreter's statement about law can be a statement of new law.[265]

In terms of the stairway theory, it follows that a positive-legal order consists not only of norms, but also of empowered cognition of them. This is acknowledged in judicial reasoning and in legal science as one type of component of ratio decidendi. A legal order, therefore, includes its self-knowledge. A particular basic norm has to be understood as an attributed element of this self-knowledge.[266]

Having introduced a distinction between 'internal' and 'external', where the distinguishing criterion is the cognitive standpoint, Kelsen strives to sustain the older distinction, now under the labels 'inside' and 'outside', where the distinguishing criterion is the presence or absence of empowerment. Then he places both 'inside' and 'outside' under the rubric of legal interpretation, which itself appears to belong to an 'internal' standpoint. He seems to envisage, but then does not go to, a standpoint that would be 'external', like that of an observer, to legal meanings. That suggestion brings him almost to the place reached, at roughly the same time, by what HLA Hart too will call an 'external point of view'.[267] I will briefly characterise that place, then consider how and why Kelsen moves further.

E. Observation Frame and Observed Frame

Ordinary almost everywhere else in the humanities and the social sciences is a commitment to independence of perspective.[268] These disciplines follow a principle that for them is so obvious and banal that it usually need not be articulated, but for the present purpose I will spell it out.

A social-scientific investigator has to define their own frame of reference: let this be called here the *observation frame*. Using that frame, the investigator defines the frame of reference used by the people observed:[269] let this be called here the *observed frame*.[270]

[264] ibid; ibid.

[265] RR2, 346–54; RR2en, 348–56; Kelsen, 'Was ist die Reine Rechtslehre?' (n 78) 618–19.

[266] cp Kelsen, 'Was ist ein Rechtsakt?' (1951) 4 *Österreichische Zeitschrift für öffentliches Recht* 263, 264–65; in *Die Wiener rechtstheoretische Schule* (n 7) 1381–93, 1391; 'What is a Legal Act?' B Litschewski Paulson and SL Paulson trans (1984) 29 *American Journal of Jurisprudence* 199, 201–02.

[267] HLA Hart, *The Concept of Law*, 3rd edn (Oxford, Oxford University Press, 2012) (originally published 1961) 89. Although Hart is acquainted with Kelsen's *General Theory of Law and State*, he does not refer to Kelsen's use of the phrase 'external point of view'.

[268] Perhaps with the exception of theology, but, even there, only as to scriptural exegesis.

[269] It should not be assumed that the observed employ only a single frame; rather, the observer should be alert to differences and relations between observed frames.

[270] The two kinds of frame are variously named in different social sciences; the names employed here are chosen for present convenience. One inspiration for my distinction has been anthropologist Paul Bohannan's differentiation between an observer's 'analytical' frame and the 'folk' frame of the observed: *Social Anthropology* (New York, Holt, Rinehart and Winston, 1963) 12–14. He applied this to law: *Justice and Judgment among the Tiv* (London, Oxford University Press, 1968 reprint) (first published 1957).

It is important to remember that the observed frame is not necessarily a frame that the observed in fact possess or would acknowledge but a frame that, for the observer, they appear to possess.

The observation frame ought, as far as possible, to be constructed independently of the observed frame – let this be called the Independence Principle.[271] My interest here is in the extent to which Kelsen may have adopted this principle for description of law.

An indication to the contrary is his persistent resistance to sociology of law. He claims, early on, that sociology is confined to examining causal relations and that therefore it mistakes its own field when it attempts to deal with legal norms.[272] Actually, he alleges, the attempt fails: when sociology refers to law, what it deals with 'is not actually law itself, but certain parallel phenomena in nature'[273] (the perspective referred to earlier where law appears only as power relations). Kelsen finds no coherent sociological conception of the state; rather, he concludes, sociologists must accept a legal-scientific conception, in which the 'state' is a positive-legal order.[274] Otherwise, science of both law and state is infected with 'methodological syncretism'.[275]

While Kelsen does not directly discuss the Independence Principle, he was well aware of it – from psychoanalysis. There, separation of the observation and observed frames can be vital to the very task of observation; and sharpness in this separation permits the analyst to employ methods of natural science drawn from medicine. In *Main Problems* in 1911, Kelsen had already applied the psychoanalytical concept of projection to the allegedly suprahuman 'objectivity' of both the state and the laws attributed to it as their author.[276] He became acquainted with psychoanalysis in Vienna and no later than 1911, when he both completed *Main Problems* and attended several talks by Sigmund Freud.[277] He became a regular attender at meetings of Freud's circle, and he and Freud became close friends. Kelsen then applied psychoanalytical ideas in critical studies of state personification,[278] as well as later when using social-anthropological literature in studying a historical development of the idea of retribution to that of causation.[279] Nonetheless, despite identifying the state with a

[271] See further I Stewart, '"Le problème de l'identité du droit rend les juristes perplexes insomniaques". Entretien avec Iain Stewart' (2018) 100 *Droit et société* 799, 800; my English translation: '"The Problem of the Identity of Law Costs Perplexed Jurists a Lot of Sleep". Interview with Iain Stewart' (online only: f.hypotheses.org/wp-content/blogs.dir/1756/files/2018/12/Ian-Stewart.pdf) 2.

[272] Such work, he says, proceeds only from a 'so-called "*sociological*" point of view' (Kelsen's emphasis): HPS2, v; HPS2en, 3.

[273] RR1, 9–11; RR1en, 13–14 (modified); cp RR2, 108; RR2en, 101–02 (modified). Also cp GTLS, xv, 162 (rejecting the 'realist' jurisprudence of, in particular, Karl N Llewellyn).

[274] Kelsen, *Der soziologische und der juristische Staatsbegriff* (n 190). 'There is no sociological concept of the State besides the juristic concept.': GTLS, 188.

[275] RR1, 2; RR1en, 8; RR2, 1; RR2en, 1.

[276] HPS, 40–41 (HKW2, 125–26); see also I Stewart, 'Legal Obligation and Exclusion' in C Jabloner, D Kolonovits, G Kucsko-Stadlmayer, HR Laurer, H Mayer and R Thienel (eds), *Gedenkschrift Robert Walter* (n 211) 761–80.

[277] Olechowski, *Hans Kelsen* (n 30) 371.

[278] H Kelsen, 'Gott und Staat' (1922/1923) 11 *Logos. Internationale Zeitschrift für Philosophie der Kultur* 261 (HKW7, 435–58); in *Die Wiener rechtstheoretische Schule* (n 7) 171–93; translated as 'God and the State' in *Essays in Legal and Moral Philosophy* (n 1) 61–82; also 'The Conception of the State and Social Psychology with special reference to Freud's Group Theory', trans anonymous (1924) 5 *International Journal of Psycho-Analysis* 1 (this article corresponds to most of the first chapter of Kelsen, *Der soziologische und der juristische Staatsbegriff* (n 190)). See also GTLS, 191, 197–99.

[279] Principally H Kelsen, *Society and Nature. A Sociological Inquiry* (Chicago, University of Chicago Press, 1943).

positive-legal order, he refrained from applying psychoanalytical ideas directly to law. He continued to assume that positive law is characterised by an 'objectivity' in some non-personificatory sense.

Kelsen's rejection is not a failure to keep up with the development of social science since its early days of attempting to imitate natural science.[280] He did keep up, only he did not like what he saw. He refused to accept another development in social science which appeared to threaten legal thinking – the 'interpretive turn',[281] of which the best-known representative in Kelsen's early days was Max Weber.[282] Weber argues that, to explain regularities in social behaviour, it is necessary to understand interpretively the knowledge and values by which the actors are motivated.[283] With this approach, Weber produced an extensive although not highly systematic sociology of law.[284] He felt free to understand legal meanings differently from how they are presented by their makers – an application of the Independence Principle.[285] Kelsen, correctly, grasped this freedom as a threat to legal dogmatics. The Independence Principle was known to him then both as a foundation outside legal science and as a danger to legal science. One may therefore identify the change in his later work as an *independence turn*.

F. A Social-Scientific Shift

As has been seen, in 1934 Kelsen wrote in first *Reine Rechtslehre* that, with the basic norm concept, the pure theory aims to 'raise to the level of consciousness' what lawyers are doing when they think of law without natural law.[286] Here Kelsen locates the basic norm concept among unempowered statements about law. He finds it there through asking, in Kantian terms, what are the transcendental-logical conditions for those statements. This is to consider that sort of thinking comprehensively, but not necessarily from a standpoint outside it. Still less is it to do so in terms of an observation frame. The distinction between an observation frame and an observed frame is irrelevant to a science that still is not observational but participatory.

In 1966, however, as has been seen, along with a brief reference to the fiction turn Kelsen writes: 'it is not the *science* of law which presupposes the basic norm'; rather, if

[280] In the manner, for instance, of Émile Durkheim: *The Rules of Sociological Method*, S Lukes ed and intro, WD Halls trans (London, Macmillan, 1982) (originally published 1895).

[281] See, eg, RAW Rhodes, *Interpretive Political Science: Selected Essays*, vol 2 (Oxford, Oxford University Press, 2017).

[282] In that respect it differs from Kelsen's bitter contesting of the legal sociology of Eugen Ehrlich: see SL Paulson, 'The Basic Norm' (n 6) 57–61; H Rottleuthner, 'Rechtstheoretische Probleme der Soziologie des Rechts. Die Kontroverse zwischen Hans Kelsen und Eugen Ehrlich (1915/1917)' in W Krawietz and H Schelsky (eds), *Rechtssystem und gesellschaftliche Basis bei Hans Kelsen* (n 22) 521–51.

[283] Kelsen, *Der soziologische und der juristische Staatsbegriff* (n 190) 156–70 (HKW7, 253–67); GTLS, 175–78.

[284] AT Kronman, *Max Weber* (London, Edward Arnold, 1983); DM Trubek, 'Reconstructing Max Weber's Sociology of Law' (1985) 37 *Stanford Law Review* 919; DM Trubek, 'Max Weber's Tragic Modernism and the Study of Law in Society' (1986) 20 *Law & Society Review* 573.

[285] To speak of '*Verstehen* (understanding)' as though it were by itself a Weberian technical term is inappropriate – 'interpretive understanding' is more accurate. The interpretation, moreover, may be empathic yet not be intended to be sympathetic; the observer may want to 'get inside the head' of the observed, but presumably will not plan to migrate there.

[286] Above at (n 221).

people consider law as proposed in the basic norm concept, then '*they*, in their juristic thinking, *presuppose* the basic norm'. Thus, a basic norm is presupposed by anybody and everybody, whenever they are engaged in 'juristic thinking' – that is, thinking in legal terms – and legal science *observes* this social behaviour.[287] Maybe Kelsen is not looking beyond decisions made in legal terms.[288] At any rate, he now distinguishes between an observation frame and an observed frame. His observation frame is the pure theory. The pure theory seems to have been given what may be seen as a *social-scientific shift*.[289] What I have called 'turns' have been revisions of the pure theory; this is a shift of the whole theory to a new location.

Has Hans Kelsen really become, even in principle, a social scientist? If he has, that should hardly be surprising, because from 1942 to 1952 he had been employed as one – in the Department of Political Science at the University of California, Berkeley. He had taught law, but had researched and published on both law and political science. And, anyway, just by being a member of a social science department he would have been immersed in social-scientific culture. The relativistic predominant attitude[290] of social scientists would have been the cultural air that he breathed.

The social-science shift, therefore, might have commenced much earlier than 1966 and, importantly here, before the Salzburg incident.[291]

G. Imputation

In 1960, in second *Reine Rechtslehre*, Kelsen had said something that looks similar but which actually points in a different direction. He says that legal science may be classified as a 'social science' by virtue of its social subject matter – albeit that in the form of the pure theory it is a social science that applies a category parallel to that of causality.[292]

Description can conform to the Positivity Principle, Kelsen holds, not only (in Kantian terms) under the category of causality but also, when the description is of norms, under an additional category which he refers to as 'imputation (*Zurechnung*)'. In the application of both categories, there is a relation between condition and consequence. Under the category of causality, *if* event A happens *then* event B *will* happen. Under the category of imputation, *if* event X happens *then* event Y *ought to* happen – where 'ought' is descriptive, a reference to an existing norm which prescribes to somebody that,

[287] Above at (n 161).

[288] eg ATN, 197 and fn 169 (on 349); ATNen, 245 and fn 169 (on 415).

[289] Compare the social-scientific concept named 'legal consciousness': SS Silbey, 'After Legal Consciousness' (2005) 1 *Annual Review of Law and Social Science* 323; various, 'After Legal Consciousness Studies' (2018) 100 *Droit et société* 539–788. The concept of 'legal consciousness' is different from what is termed in German *Rechtsbewusstsein* – meaning a personal or collective sense of what is right or wrong, although that sense can be expressed with reference to law.

[290] cp Kelsen's reference to political or theoretical 'attitude (*Haltung*)': RR2, 224 fn **; RR2en, 218, fn 82.

[291] There is a hint of such an inclination as far back as 1951: Kelsen 'Was ist ein Rechtsakt?' (n 266); in *Die Wiener rechtstheoretische Schule* (n 7) 1381–93; 'What is a Legal Act?' (n 266). Although Kelsen had then withdrawn the suggestion: RR2, 208 fn *; RR2en, 204, fn 72. The 1951 article is muddled. It is a reply to Verdross and Kelsen goes along with Verdross's Aristotelianism in assuming that there is reality in a potential as well as in an actual constitution. Moreover, Kelsen takes an isolated act consistent with the terms of a constitution to be a 'recognition' of that constitution and even establishing it in potentiality ('*in statu nascendi*'). The idea of tacit recognition is also later withdrawn: RR2, 225 fn *; RR2en, 218, fn 83.

[292] RR2, 89–90; RR2en, 85–86.

if X happens, then they ought to make Y happen. As Kelsen pursues his reinvention of legal science on analogy with natural science, there might even be descriptive 'laws of law' of legal-phenomenal regularities.[293] However, although a statement of imputation is independent of a statement of law, it is not itself a reproduction thereof. Rather, it assumes a reproduction which it incorporates as an observable 'ought'.

VIII. The Closure Turn

What, in Salzburg and for Vienna, did Kelsen think he was doing? Before he got to Salzburg, and even before publishing second *Reine Rechtslehre*, he had made another and very deep turn, which may be called his *closure turn*.

A. Closure and Natural Law

Second *Reine Rechtslehre* is a treatise on Is of Ought. Appended to it is a long essay on Ought of Ought, 'Das Problem der Gerechtigkeit' ('The Problem of Justice'), which had appeared in French translation in 1959.[294] In this essay, Kelsen distinguishes 'norms of justice' into two types, which he labels 'metaphysical' and 'rational'. Norms of the first type are 'metaphysical' in the sense that they rest upon belief in a transcendent reality (contrary to the Positivity Principle). Their content, their ideal of justice, is claimed not to be fully or rationally comprehensible to human beings. The ideal of justice, as with the norm itself, is absolute. That is, Kelsen now explains: 'through its immanent meaning, it excludes (*schliesst aus*) in principle, fundamentally, the possibility of another ideal of justice'.[295] Kelsen does not explain 'immanent meaning', although he seems to refer not to the norm's specific content but somehow to its form. Nevertheless, some of his terminology is forthright: *schliesst aus* – literally 'shuts out'.

This interpretation of belief in natural law appears in the main text of second *Reine Rechtslehre* almost in passing. If a norm

> constituting a certain value and prescribing a certain behaviour is supposed to come from a suprahuman authority – from God or from Nature created by God – then this norm appears with a claim to exclude (*auszuschliessen*) the possibility that a norm prescribing the opposite behaviour could be valid. The value constituted by such a norm is described as 'absolute', in contrast to the value constituted by a norm posited by a human act of will.[296]

It has sometimes been convenient here to translate *ausschliessen* as 'to exclude', but as referring to an effect of a process to be referred to as 'closure'.[297] And we shall see in a moment that Kelsen employs the cognate noun *Ausschliesslichkeit*, meaning an effect.

[293] See above (n 258).
[294] RR2App; 'Justice et droit naturel' (n 1).
[295] RR2App, 365–66.
[296] RR2, 18; RR2en, 18 (modified).
[297] Kelsen distinguishes this from logical 'closure', at which he consistently aims: HPS1, xi (HKW2, 58–59). Also, 'closure' in the present sense is not entirely synonymous with 'exclusion': at least, a 'closure' in this sense

The turn to identifying closure appears to resolve the pure theory's Infinity Problem. Kelsen tries to explain how natural law could appear as binding. If there were a supreme norm 'One ought to obey the commands of God', who could be the author of that norm? A theology that assumed God to be the supreme authority would not admit the possibility of an authority higher than God. Or, as Kelsen says, if the norm 'were considered to be posited by God, it could not be the reason for the validity of norms posited by God, since it would itself be a norm posited by God'. The pure theory's answer is to presuppose a basic norm, 'One ought to obey the commands of God', which does not have these problems because it is not a real norm but exists only in (human) thought.[298] With the fiction turn, it would have to be admitted that this would not solve the Infinity Problem.

Identification of closure, however, offers a more promising path. This path begins with observing that, to a believer in God, the very possibility that an alternative to the norm could be legitimate is excluded. For the believer, *there is no alternative*[299] to 'the will of the Lord'. Justified disobedience of God's norms is *unthinkable*. The norm is therefore binding *by default*. It does not need support from any reason to obey it. The Infinity Problem does not arise.

B. The Closure Turn and Positive Law

In 'Das Problem der Gerechtigkeit' and briefly in the main text of second *Reine Rechtslehre*, the closure turn is applied only to belief in natural law. Much earlier, however, it had been applied to the state – and the state was already identified with positive law.

i. Theory of Sovereignty

In his 1920 book on theory of sovereignty, *Das Problem der Souveränität und die Theorie des Völkerrechts* (*The Problem of Sovereignty and Theory of International Law*),[300] Kelsen says much about the state, but he already assumes that a state and a positive-legal order are the same thing.[301] Later he will hold that, since they are the same, when speaking about a positive-legal order it is not necessary also to speak about the state.[302] Obversely, what is said about the state and sovereignty is also said about positive law.

Kelsen distinguishes two aspects of sovereignty: unity and closure. He holds that the legal order of a sovereign state, in its self-understanding (*ihrem eigenen Sinne*

is not the reason why I exclude uninvited others from my home by locking my front door. Nor is this 'closure' a species of rhetoric, if 'rhetoric' is an attempt to persuade.

[298] RR2, 206; RR2en, 203 (modified).

[299] I find apposite Herbert Spencer's mantra 'There is no alternative' (later adopted by Margaret Thatcher and truncated to 'TINA'): see I Stewart, 'Commandeering Time: the Ideological Status of Time in the Social Darwinism of Herbert Spencer' (2011) 57 *Australian Journal of Politics and History* 389, 391.

[300] PSTV. Already substantially completed, he says, by 1916, but publication had been delayed by his military duties: PSTV, vi (HKW4, 268).

[301] PSTV, 9–14 (HKW4, 280–84).

[302] GTLS, 192.

nach), is characterised by unity as a system (*Einheit des Systems*) and by closure (*Ausschliesslichkeit*). The legal order's closure, he says, is not derived from its historical practice of territorial – that is, spatial – exclusion. Rather, it is temporal, in that one state legal order cannot see both itself and any other state legal order as valid simultaneously.[303] That order regards itself as, like the 'God' of the Old Testament, the One-and-Only. There is exclusion (*Ausschluss*) of other sovereign legal orders, as well as of the possibility of subordinating domestic positive law to international law.[304]

If this behaviour, which Kelsen later labels 'state solipsism',[305] is to be controlled – and if recourse to natural law is no longer to be considered – the only remaining option is primacy of international law. That would be to maintain both unity and closure, elevated to the international level.[306] Kelsen recognised in 1920 that international monism was not a reality but, rather, an ethically motivated aspiration.[307] (In this respect his general ban on politics in science wavered.) He continued this hope through the 1930s[308] and 1940s,[309] and into the 1960s.[310] He also identified an alternative, perhaps more realistically related to state practice. The assumption that a legal order is marked by unity and closure remained, but as distributed. There would be unity and closure of each national legal order if primacy was supposed for national legal orders, each of them a grudging author of international law. There was, however, a general scientific reason to prefer international monism, that it was logically simpler; but in the pure theory the reality of a legal order lies not only in the existence of its norms but also in the order's effectiveness. Kelsen maintained the two pictures as scientific alternatives.

ii. Closure of Law

Kelsen understands closure as a process of semantic exclusion.[311] This process is a feature of the state's self-identification. Then, since Kelsen comes to equate the state with the positive-legal order, this closure must be considered to be a feature of positive law. Consequently, closure would have to be recognised as a component of the concepts of both natural law and positive law.

[303] PSTV, 74–75 (HKW4, 342).

[304] PSTV, 189 (HKW4, 449).

[305] RR2, 344; RR2en, 345. In 1928 he had sketched a 'psychological' (even psychoanalytical) explanation: 'Die philosophischen Grundlagen der Naturrechtslehre und des Rechtspositivismus' (n 82) 335–37; 'Natural Law Doctrine and Legal Positivism' (n 82) 434–35. By 1945, however, a philosophical perspective was preferred, apparently from critique of Arthur Schopenhauer's conception of the world as 'the will and idea of the subject': GTLS, 386–87; A Schopenhauer, *Die Welt als Wille und Vorstellung* (originally published 1818/19) had been translated by RB Haldane and J Kemp as *The World as Will and Idea*, 3 vols (London, Trübner, 1883–86).

[306] PSTV, 314–19 (HKW4, 567–71).

[307] PSTV, 319 (HKW4, 571).

[308] RR1, 134–54; RR1en, 111–25.

[309] GTLS, 382–88.

[310] RR2, 343–45; RR2en, 344–47. By this time, Kelsen wants to distinguish sharply between 'sovereignty' as a material and political fact and as a legal construct or 'presupposition': RR2, 334–35; RR2en, 334–35. This increases the significance of closure within legal construction.

[311] As I have suggested more generally: I Stewart, 'Closure and the Legal Norm: an Essay in Critique of Law' (1987) 50 *Modern Law Review* 908.

IX. 'Natural' Origins of Positive Law

In any case, Kelsen always speaks of natural law and positive law as 'law' in the same sense. This is, indeed, traditional: for, if a norm is to be considered valid as positive law only if it conforms to a norm of natural law, the two norms must be of much the same kind.

Perhaps, however, this tradition has been broken by 'legal positivism', if that name is taken to maintain that positive law is to be considered as involving a different sort of norm. This seems to be the tone of the opening words of both first and second *Reine Rechtslehre*: 'The Pure Theory of Law is a theory of positive law – of positive law as such, not of a specific legal order. It is general theory of law, not interpretation of particular national or international legal norms.'[312] In that case, what is said about closure and natural law might not apply, at all or at least in a similar way, to positive law.

A. Fact-Positivity and Will-Positivity; *ius positivum, lex positiva*

Yet the history of the idea of 'positive law' shows continuity, for the idea of 'positive law' is offspring of belief in natural law. The term 'positive law', with its equivalents such as German '*positives Recht*', can be traced to not one but two Latin origins and both of them arise in the heartland of Western natural-law thinking, scholasticism.

The first known use of the term 'positive law' in any Western language is as Latin *ius positivum*, by twelfth-century scholastic philosopher Peter Abelard.[313] He says: 'One kind of law is called natural and another kind positive (*Ius quippe aliud naturale, aliud positivum dicitur*)'. He defines natural law similarly to Justinian, as natural inclination of all creatures,[314] although with a higher profile for reason: 'A natural law (*ius naturale*) is one that reason itself, which is present in all people naturally and is therefore permanently in all people, persuades us must be fulfilled in practice'. Abelard does not define '*ius … positivum*', but what he means by '*positivum*' appears from his own characterisation of 'positive justice':

> [W]hat belongs to positive justice (*iustitia positiva*) is what is instituted by human beings to protect either usefulness or honour more surely, or to increase them. It depends either on custom alone or on written authority … Thus it comes about that, when we have to live with any other people, we conform to (*teneamus*) these laws (*instituta*) of theirs that we spoke of, just as we do to natural law.[315]

[312] RR1, 1; RR2, 1. cp RR1en, 7; RR2en, 1.

[313] E Pattaro, *A Treatise of Legal Philosophy and General Jurisprudence*, vol 1. *The Law and the Right. A Reappraisal of the Reality that Ought to Be* (Dordrecht, Springer, 2005) 80–82; J Marenbon, 'The Rise of Scholastic Legal Philosophy' in FD Miller and C-A Biondi (eds), *A Treatise of Legal Philosophy and General Jurisprudence*, vol 6. *A History of the Philosophy of Law from the Ancient Greeks to the Scholastics* (Dordrecht, Springer, 2nd edn, 2007) 267–83, 274–76; D van den Eynde, 'The Terms "Ius Positivum" and "Signum Positivum" in Twelfth-century Scholasticism' (1949) 9 *Franciscan Studies* 41; K Olivecrona, *Law as Fact*, 2nd edn (London, Stevens, 1971) (originally published 1939) 7.

[314] Institutes, 1.2.pr.

[315] Peter Abelard (Petrus Abelardus), *Dialogus inter Philosophum, Judaeum et Christianum* in J-P Migne (ed), *Patrologia Latina* (1136–39) (Turnhout, Brepols, 1979) vol 178, cols 1609–1683, 1656B–1656C: books.google.com.au/books?id=PndCAAAAcAAJ&pg=PA1611&source=gbs_toc_r&cad=3#v=onepage&q&f=false; *Ethical Writings: His 'Ethics' or 'Know Yourself' and His Dialogue between a Philosopher, a Jew and a Christian*, PV Spade trans (Indianapolis, Hackett, 1995) 117–18 (modified). See also S Kuttner, 'Sur les origines du terme "droit positif"' (1936) 15 *Revue historique de droit français et étranger* (4e s) 728, 730.

He has probably got the expression '*iustitia positiva*' from the fourth-century scholastic Calcidius.[316] Later in the twelfth century, the expression *ius positivum* is found in other Christian scholars, including a cardinal, and by the middle of the thirteenth century it had become, Stephan Kuttner states, 'quasi-officially' accepted.[317] It refers to observable operation of any type of law – divine (revealed) or human and, if human, legislated or customary. Kelsen does not seem to have become aware of this origin until quite late.[318] Here is an origin of *fact-positivity* of law.

A central idea of Roman law is *will-positivity* – especially in the foundation documents of the Western legal tradition, the *Corpus Iuris Civilis*. There Justinian instructs that a written law is a command of a state organ – including an imperial decree (*constitutio*), which is what the ruler wills ('*quod principi placuit legis habet vigorem*').[319] And each part of the *Corpus* is itself made law by an imperial decree. At least by the thirteenth century, this idea acquired a generic name: Aquinas refers to it both as *ius positivum* and as *lex positiva*.[320] However, Aquinas's mind is also on higher things: his *lex positiva* can be of divine creation, 'revealed' by God, especially in the Ten Commandments.[321] The idea of divine positive law, supplementing divinely rational natural law, was once in common use; it can be found, for example, in Grotius,[322] Hobbes[323] and Locke.[324] With present-day thinkers, including Kelsen,[325] it has fallen into desuetude.

Kelsen assumes that the fact-positivity and the will-positivity of deliberately created[326] human law generally coincide.[327] Sometimes he refers to both of them together; often he refers to only one of them, but apparently as standing for their combination.[328]

[316] Calcidius, *On Plato's* Timaeus, ed and trans J Magee (Cambridge, MA, Harvard University Press, 2016) 128–31, 725; A Somfai, 'The Eleventh-century Shift in the Reception of Plato's *Timaeus* and Calcidius's *Commentary*' (2002) 65 *Journal of the Warburg and Courtauld Institutes* 1.

[317] When it appeared in the commentary by Bernard of Botone on the Decretals (1234) of Pope Gregory IX: Kuttner, 'Sur les origines du terme "droit positif"' (n 315) 736. This commentary would later be printed with those Decretals, which were to form the principal part of the *Corpus Iuris Canonici* up to 1918.

[318] Kelsen, 'Was ist juristischer Positivismus?' (n 201) 943. Possibly first brought to his attention by a critic, Paul Amselek: ibid; P Amselek, *Méthode phénoménologique et théorie du droit* (Paris, Librairie générale de droit et de jurisprudence, 1964) 144, fn 122.

[319] Institutes, 1.2.3–8.

[320] Aquinas, *Summa Theologiae*, 2a2ae 57.2; vol 28 *Law and Political Theory*, T Gilby (ed) (Blackfriars, Eyre & Spottiswoode, 1966) 162–64 (Appendix 2: Gilby, 'The Theological Classification of Law').

[321] Aquinas, *Summa Theologiae*, 1a2ae 91.4.

[322] H Grotius, *The Jurisprudence of Holland*, RW Lee trans (Oxford, Clarendon Press, 1953) (originally published 1631) vol 1, 4–7; *De Iure Bellis ac Pacis*, FW Kelsey trans (Washington, Carnegie Institution, 1913–25 (originally published 1625) vol 1, 4 (Latin), vol 2, 39 (English) (bk 1, ch 1, X.2).

[323] Referring to Judaic revealed law: Thomas Hobbes, *Leviathan*, CB Macpherson (ed) (Harmondsworth, Penguin, 1968) (originally published 1651) 672 (in ch 45). See also LR Ford, 'Divine Positive Law. *Ancient Judaism* and Western Legality' in A Sica (ed), *The Routledge International Handbook on Max Weber* (Abingdon, Routledge, 2023) 261–73.

[324] John Locke refers to 'positive law' both human and divine: *Two Treatises of Government*, P Laslett (ed) (New York, New American Library (Mentor), 1963 edn) (originally published 1690) 322, 331, 350, 364, 376, 423 (human) and 307 (divine).

[325] Kelsen, 'Was ist juristischer Positivismus?' (n 201) 941–42.

[326] He struggles to provide a convincing will-theoretical account of what he eventually characterises as 'so-called' customary law, although it is required especially by his conception of international law: ibid 944–45; cp ATN, 114; ATNen, 140.

[327] PTSV, 92–94 (HKW4, 359–60). On 'will' theories of law in Kelsen's context, see J Schröder, 'Zur Geschichte juristichen Methodenlehre zwischen 1850 und 1933' (2008) 13 *Rechtsgeschichte* 160.

[328] On will-positivity: GTLS, 114; 'Science and Politics' (1951) in *What is Justice?* (n 14) 350–75, 364; 'Law and Logic' (n 14) 228–53, 231. On fact-positivity: 'Was ist juristischer Positivismus?' (n 201) 941.

B. Positivities and Absolutism

When Kelsen identifies closure in natural-law belief, he associates it with 'metaphysics', which for him is synonymous with philosophical 'absolutism'.[329] We find ourselves amid his central confrontation between relativist and absolutist attitudes.[330] In 1963 he still finds God to haunt the idea of law. There is still, he says, a basically religious absolutism of positive as well as of natural law:

> [T]he political necessity of an absolute justification of positive law – or, as it is usually formulated, the need for an absolute standard that may be referred to for evaluation of any positive law (*loi*) – can be satisfied by a doctrine of natural law only if the alleged natural law appears as an order of eternal, invariable justice. And this is possible only if that order is based on a transcendent, supra-empirical authority – indicating a religious belief.[331]

X. Closure and Kelsen's Starting Point

Perhaps, actually, Kelsen has not made a new turn but has only confirmed his starting point. In *Main Problems* in 1911, he wrote:

> to the concept of a legal norm it is intrinsic from the outset that it *ought* to be complied with and applied. The idea of a legal statement (*Rechtssatz*) as a 'norm (*Norm*)' already contains this characterisation as '*ought* to be complied with and applied'. Hence to question this would amount to asking: Why ought a statement that ought to be complied with and applied be complied with and applied?[332]

A moral philosopher, he says, may ask what is 'the normative nature of a legal statement *(die normative Natur des Rechtssatzes)*', but to a lawyer (*Jurist*) its 'normative nature' is 'an unshakeable presupposition, lying beyond all discussion'. In legal terms, to question the basis of the validity of law is to cut off the branch on which one is sitting.[333] Kelsen admits that a challenge to this 'presupposing' might come from a moral philosopher, but that would not have mattered greatly to him since he thinks that moral philosophers are a rather irrational bunch. Nor does he contemplate a challenge in terms of interdisciplinary description: that could just be some sociologist or psychologist straying out of their proper, causal province.[334] But a challenge in terms of legal-scientific description would be the question that the basic norm concept would be an attempt to answer.

Kelsen acknowledges that there are many kinds of 'norm (*Norm*)' in a prescriptive sense[335] and that some of them are sometimes called 'laws' – for example, those that are

[329] eg, Kelsen, 'Die philosophischen Grundlagen der Naturrechtslehre und des Rechtspositivismus' (n 82) 288; 'Natural Law Doctrine and Legal Positivism' (n 82) 396.
[330] I Stewart, 'Hans Kelsen, Legal Scientist' (n 29) 159–62.
[331] Kelsen, 'Positivisme juridique et doctrine du droit naturel' (n 72) 147.
[332] HPS, 352 (HKW2, 481) (Kelsen's emphases).
[333] HPS, 353 (HKW2, 481). See also SL Paulson, 'The Basic Norm' (n 6) 48.
[334] HPS, 353 (HKW2, 482).
[335] As against 'norm (*Norm*)' in the sense of a description of an observed regularity, as in 'it is the norm that' or 'this is normal': cp HPS, 4 (HKW2, 81).

moral, logical, grammatical or aesthetic.[336] Today's jurist would be likely to add table games and sport. Apart from 'moral' norms that amount to claims of natural law, all of them, as Kelsen says, 'ought to be obeyed and to be applied' under circumstances that are optional. Failure to conform to these norms can have a cost, but that cost can be avoided by choosing not to act so as to make the norm applicable. Some legal norms, by themselves, are like that: for example, laws for making a contract. Other legal norms, however, apply irrespective of choice – principally penal laws but also, for example, norms of citizenship by birth. Norms that may apply because of a choice may be backed up with norms that apply irrespective of further choice – for instance, rights and obligations of a spouse or of a naturalised citizen.

It seems to be in this sense that for Kelsen such unconditionality – one can also say closure – is 'intrinsic from the outset' to 'the concept of a legal norm'.[337]

XI. Turning to Fiction

So, what kind of thing did Kelsen do when he made the fiction turn?

A. Being Shut Out

Kelsen came to Salzburg willing to participate in rational discussion. Although he had anticipated that others would proceed upon an irrational foundation, he and they might have discussed what they had in common; after all, apart from that foundation the Aristotelian-Thomist tradition is deeply rational.

His paper begins by contrasting two views of natural law: whether it exists by dependence on the will of an 'almighty and all-good deity' or in some way without such dependence, perhaps through deriving from cosmic nature or from human reason. He argues that the second view does not hold up against the first, while the first is already

[336] HPS, 4, 6 (HKW2, 81, 84).

[337] cp Rudolf Stammler on '*Selbstherrlichkeit*'. In a political context, domestic or international, this term may mean 'sovereignty'. Stammler, however, goes wider, applying it to conceive law in general as an '*unverletzbar selbstherrlich verbindende Wollen* (inviolable *selbstherrlich* binding volition)': *Theorie der Rechtswissenschaft* (Halle an der Saale, Buchhandlung des Waisenhauses, 1911) 113. It is '*unverletztbar* (inviolable)' in that nothing can prevail against it. Although Stammler chooses to say that it is also '*selbstherrlich*', even he struggles to explain how that term should be defined. In considering alternatives, he finds '*autokratisch* (autocratic)' to be too political and '*autonom* (autonomous)' to have too much connection with ethics and with international law: ibid 96. He also emphasises that anybody might act in a *selbstherrlich* way. The meaning of *Selbstherrlichkeit* therefore includes somebody who does not actually possess authority but is 'lording it' (as with *Herr*, lord) over another, exercising domination (*Herrschaft*) by their own choice and not necessarily with legitimacy. Stammler's *Selbstherrlichkeit*, then, is characteristic of all law but not only of law. One could give '*selbstherrlich*' its ordinary meaning of 'self-aggrandising': cp *Deutsches Universalbuch*, 7th edn (Mannheim, Dudenverlag, 2011), '*selbstherrlich*'. I am tempted to translate *Selbstherrlichkeit* as 'bastardry'. Stammler comes to the rescue of positive law with the optimistic contention that '*Alles gestetzte Recht ist ein Versuch, richtiges Recht zu sein* (All positive law is an attempt to be just law)': *Die Lehre von dem richtigen Recht* (Berlin, Guttentag, 1902) 31; *The Theory of Justice*, I Husik trans (New York, Kelley, 1969) 24. Kelsen could respond that this might be closed justice.

unsustainable owing to its metaphysical presuppositions, which 'from a *scientifically* rational standpoint' are inadmissible. Ergo, there is no valid argument for the existence of natural law. He does not want to get into what would be a 'science *versus* religion' debate on this occasion, but to see what might be shared. His request is not empty: his opponents could accept the stairway theory, up to and including the constitutional level, and he has reason to believe that Marcic does so.

In the discussions, his invitation is ignored. His point of view is also ignored. The only interest shown even in his having a point of view is in whether he will participate in the Aristotelian-Thomist point of view. He is shut out – of and by it. That point of view is thoroughly imbued with a metaphysically grounded doctrine of natural law and he experiences the kind of closure that he has identified in that kind of belief. He is not alleged to have breached any norm of natural law: but, as he had implied, the closure lies in the form.

What was he to do? He was, after all, apparently an honoured guest. Complaint, silence or walking out would have been beneath his dignity and in any case pointless.

B. *De te fabula narratur*[338]

He responds, it seems, with his intervention. He shows them a map of themselves.

They have changed his role. His presence has been stripped of participation, so that he finds himself reduced to being an observer. Yet he is not then left alone. Natural law in its Aristotelian-Thomist conception jumps out of the books and confronts him – real as practised belief. Kelsen is brought literally face to face with natural-legal closure. During discussion in which he is involved, practitioners of the belief claim that, when they are productively discussing natural law, they are in effect making it. And their claim is correct: this is how the belief has been created and is maintained, even though they would not accept that this is all there is to it.

Very well: Kelsen as observer will show them how he has to alter his observation frame to make possible an observed frame that will fit them.

He is now distinguishing observation frame from observed frame. His observation frame is still the pure theory, but revised to include the concept of closure and its application to all law. The pure theory will still apply to statements *of* natural law and positive law. It will now also apply to statements *about* natural law and positive law, when those statements are now seen as 'internal' to legal orders – as not observational but participatory. This twofold application will create an enhanced observed frame. That frame will include the basic norm concept in its erstwhile form, now seen to be created by participants. The double inconsistency in the basic norm concept – inconsistency with reality as well as self-contradiction – will be attributed to adherents of internal legal science. In this way, the new, external legal science can supersede existing legal science, considering it to be 'internal'.

And that, now, is a modern hypothesis for Kelsen. In the Vienna paper he can add Vaihinger, since (although he does not spell this out) he actually satisfies Vaihinger's requirement of a fresh hypothesis.

[338] 'The story is told of you': Horace, *Sermones* (Satires) I.1.69.

In Salzburg he has also replied – to the man's face – to Marcic's contemptuous '*absolute* absoluteness'. On Kelsen's new hypothesis, so far as Marcic could express his absolutistic belief rationally this is the kind of nonsensical statement with which he would end up.

That is my hypothesis of what Kelsen has done.

XII. Conclusion

A. Puzzle, Turning and Shift

Kelsen's basic norm concept was always a 'puzzle';[339] the fiction turn made it bewildering. I have suggested, and Paulson has argued similarly, that the fiction turn appears to wreck the pure theory. Yet, if the pure theory is so much threatened, how does Kelsen seem not to see the danger? Has he been aware of something that has not yet been noticed? How was it, I have now asked, that in 1962, out of the blue and cryptically, he chose to inform a small workshop, which he knew to be at least unsympathetic, that for decades he had been talking fiction? And why did he dig himself deeper by adopting a dubiously extended conception of fiction? The published proceedings of the Salzburg workshop, with their apparently almost complete verbatim record of discussions, provide a rare opportunity to witness a major theoretical development as a socio-historical event. I have put the Salzburg material and the Vienna material together, and added to them mentions of the fiction turn in later work, to attempt to grasp what Kelsen thought he was doing. I have not tried to go beyond that, at the price of many a loose end, lest the enquiry get of hand.

My enquiry has identified five 'turns' and a 'shift', in an increasingly radical series. Three turns have been explicit: the constitution turn, the logic turn and the fiction turn. Two turns have been implicit: the independence turn and the closure turn. And then there has been the social-scientific shift – by which time, a new type of concept of law has begun to emerge on an unexpected horizon.

B. Consequences

The pure theory of law is a general theory, a theory of everything that in science of law ought to count as law. It presents analytical reasons, and Kelsen is also aware of historical reasons, why the term 'law (*Recht*)' means the same kind of thing when referring to natural law or to positive law, albeit that the former is illusory – and he struggles to fit legal conceptions of custom into that company. Kelsen nevertheless leaves his theory seriously incomplete: it continues to lack secure understandings of how a legal norm is an 'objective meaning' and 'binding'. Then to admit self-contradiction in the keystone of the theory looks like an admission of failure.

[339] SL Paulson, 'On the Puzzle Surrounding Hans Kelsen's Basic Norm' (2000) 3 *Ratio Juris* 279.

There is no failure, however, if the theory has been displaced from being the observation frame to functioning as an observed frame. Then the self-contradiction is moved from an observation frame to an observed frame. The displacement is motored by two deeper 'turns' in the theory, introducing the Independence Principle and a radical concept of closure. This has been to shift the pure theory – in Kelsen's eyes, legal science – towards becoming social-scientific. Kelsen is beginning to reinvent legal science, again.

C. Law as Closure

Within this prospect of a reinvented science of law emerges – as a further modern hypothesis – a new type of concept of law. Kelsen himself does not propose such a concept, but it appears to lie in the direction of his thinking. This concept may be defined briefly thus: *the legal character of a legal norm is that it is closed*; or, on a more linguistic plane, *a norm that is presented as 'law' is a closed norm*. Having offered bare bones of this concept, I shall clothe it with a few very general remarks.

The concept is proposed as a modification of the pure theory, albeit a dimension of 'modification' that extends to every element of it, including the stairway theory. On a philosophical plane, the concept shares the pure theory's relativism, although it may require a relativism of a deeper kind.[340] An observer using the concept would identify closure as a socio-historical practice – a use of an observed frame, although this feature of the frame might not be explicit or, if explicit, might even appear to its bearer as liberation. Following the closure turn, closure is a dimension of a legal norm, not a feature additional to it that might be given deferred attention; legal norms will always have to be approached from their 'outside'. Currently existing legal science, so far as it is dogmatic or rests upon legal-dogmatic assumptions, would be found on the 'inside' of legal thinking. It would come to appear as part of the object of knowledge, 'law', for 'external' legal science.

Under this concept of law, natural law (belief that there are norms with a transcendent ground) would not appear as merely illusion. A belief really held may contain illusion, but is itself a socio-historical reality.[341] Observation is to relate in the first place to the fact the belief is held and socially operative, and thereafter to the illusory ground of the belief. Natural law would appear as a range of observed frames. The pure theory would now count a natural-legal order as existing in the same way as an order of positive law: that is, through being by and large effective.

A natural-legal order can be effective indirectly and directly. It can be effective indirectly through human law that it is considered to validate. It can also be effective directly: (a) through belief that it is binding – that is, that there are no admissible alternatives; (b) through comfort, as an apparent realm of final answers to social and moral questions (a role important to human law, albeit not with complete finality); and (c) through its own sanctions. Its sanctions may be negative, such as the likelihood of an unfortunate fate or of some manifestation of suprahuman displeasure; they may also

[340] See I Stewart, 'Closure and the Legal Norm' (n 311) 916–19.

[341] As in John Austin's conception of law, said to be 'legal positivism'; but a comparison is beyond the scope of the present discussion.

be positive, such as a reward in heaven. Some of these sanctions may be illusory, but (as with human law) what is factually important is that the threat or promise of the sanction is real to the believer. In Salzburg, Kelsen seems to have observed, indeed experienced, closure in natural law belief, both as held and as practised against him; however, he would not have anticipated any natural-legal punishment or reward (nor is he known to have received any).

Similarly, an order of human law will be included as an observed frame even if it is grounded in non-natural illusory belief, such as personification of the state (which the pure theory already includes as nevertheless 'positive law'), a founding myth like a legendary founder and lawgiver[342] or a traditional 'ancient constitution'.[343] And even though the belief might be grounded in self-contradiction or radical inconsistency, as with an 'internally' presupposed basic norm.

Although Kelsen's conceptualisation of 'closure' is rudimentary, it seems to have a feature that contemporaries were to make more explicit – proposing that ideology, in its claim to encompass everything, 'has no outside'.[344] That, with a total closure – as in Aristotelian-Thomist belief[345] – what is acknowledged to remain will appear to be everything, so that there seem to be neither an outside nor, consequently, an inside. To exclude all possibility of alternatives, moreover, is deny an overall historicity to what remains. What remains may instead appear as lifted out of socio-historical reality and to be metaphysically grounded – whether directly in description or as content of norms.[346]

In Salzburg, then, Kelsen was cast 'out'; and he came back at them from what for them was nowhere.

Still lacking here, also, is a concept of the mechanism (as it were) by which an effect of closure is produced. I have suggested that certain utterances commonly have a 'dark performative' use that may produce closure and that among these is the word 'law'.[347]

[342] J Lenoble and F Ost, *Droit, mythe et raison. Essai sur la dérive mytho-logique de la rationalité juridique* (Brussels, Facultés universitaires Saint-Louis, 1980); 'Founding Myths in Legal Rationality', I Stewart trans (1986) 49 *Modern Law Review* 530.

[343] JGA Pocock, *The Ancient Constitution and the Feudal Law. A Study of English Historical Thought in the Seventeenth Century. A Reissue with a Retrospect* (Cambridge, Cambridge University Press, 1987) (originally published 1957).

[344] TW Adorno, *Negative Dialectics*, EB Ashton trans (London, Routledge & Kegan Paul, 1973) 354–58; L Althusser and É Balibar, *Reading Capital*, B Brewster trans (London, New Left Books, 1970) 188–93. Along this line might be brought in Kelsen's posthumously published sympathy with Marx and Engels' critique of religion: Kelsen, *Secular Religion* (n 50) 163–97. Also I Stewart, 'Closure and the Legal Norm' (n 311).

[345] Thus Pope Benedict, about to condemn Kelsen: 'In its self-proclaimed exclusivity, the positivist reason which recognizes nothing beyond mere functionality resembles a concrete bunker with no windows, in which we ourselves provide lighting and atmospheric conditions, being no longer willing to obtain either from God's wide world. And yet we cannot hide from ourselves the fact that[,] even in this artificial world, we are still covertly drawing upon God's raw materials, which we refashion into our own products. The windows must be flung open again, we must see the wide world, the sky and the earth once more and learn to make proper use of all this.': see (n 171). On use of imagery for ultimate control of cognitive determination, see I Stewart, 'Closure and the Legal Norm' (n 311) 916–19.

[346] Closure of a norm may cause its content to misrepresent reality – ideology. This avoids the problem that attempting to identify law directly as ideology involves the logically difficult task of trying to identify directly (Is) misrepresentation by a norm (Ought). Now it can be said that the content of a norm may be ideological owing to closure in its form.

[347] I Stewart, 'The Use of Law' in M Freeman (ed), *Law and Sociology. Current Legal Issues volume 8* (Oxford, Oxford University Press, 2006) (Oxford Scholarship Online 2012); 'Legal Obligation and Exclusion' (n 276); '"Le problème de l'identité du droit rend les juristes perplexes insomniaques"' (n 271). I commence an analogy with JL Austin's idea of a 'performative illocution': JL Austin, *How to Do Things with Words*, 2nd edn (eds) JO Urmson and M Sbisà (Oxford, Clarendon Press, 1975).

Three possible objections to this new concept of law.

- First, it might be objected that this concept is too simple. However, since the term 'law' (or equivalent, such as 'legal') has a meaning that is understood by almost every member of a society sufficiently to make yes-or-no decisions, ranging from the trivial (such as buying a bus ticket) to matters of the greatest consequence (such as marrying), that meaning must be very simple.
- Second, it might be objected that the definition, as it would be applied in conjunction with the stairway theory, is still too narrow: for human law (apart from custom) will still be identified with the state. However, an objection simply of narrowness is never valid: breadth is not an intrinsic virtue of a definition; in scope, a definition should just be adequate to its material.
- Third, it might be claimed that law conceived as closed would be immoral, so that to conceive it as closed would be an immoral act. This objection might be dismissed as merely a hangover from habitual apologetics in legal science. However, the impression that law conceived as closed would be immoral is to be taken seriously. A partial philosophical answer could be that, while closure may be logically regrettable, from that alone it does not necessarily follow that closure is immoral. A rawer answer could be that a closed norm would be like a gun, as moral as its user. Kelsen the technocrat might have been attracted by both answers. At the least, under the new concept a legal norm is not necessarily good; it might only appear so, after it or its order has rubbed out all possible alternatives. Then there is the interesting (descriptive) question: since an absolutistic claim does not have to be accepted, how far might a closed norm be good despite its closure? I shall leave that end loose.

Kelsen's social-scientific shift remained a displacement only in principle, for which delay two good reasons can be found. On one hand, contemporary social science did not offer him a sufficiently developed concept of closure; whether that is still the case may be investigated. On the other hand, ideas of law and legal norms imbue fundamental concepts throughout the social sciences and wider – for instance, concepts of the individual, the social relation, economic value, property, community and polity. A reconstituted legal science could neither ignore those concepts nor accept them as they stand. There would have to be debates, in the care of Kelsen's benignly envisaged younger spirits.

Appendix: Other Reactions to the Fiction Turn

This appendix summarises other 'takes' on the fiction turn that I have been able to find. They are placed in chronological order – not because the years since 1964 display some sort of development but rather to show how, remarkably, they fail to do so.

1966 The fiction turn appears to be as yet unknown to participants in a Round Table on Legal Positivism held in Pavia in May 1966, even though they include Mario G Losano, whose Italian translation of RR2 (RR2it) appeared in that year.[348]

[348] B Leoni (ed), 'Tavola Rotonda sul Positivismo Giuridico' (1966) 31 *Il Politico* 356–68, 539–70 and 822–29; (1967) 32 *Il Politico* 179–90.

1974 Joseph Raz writes an intensive critique of the basic norm concept,[349] but is still unaware of the fiction turn.

1978 Ronald Moore, as has been mentioned,[350] refers to Kelsen as 'insisting that there is in our thinking a "fictive" or "imaginary" will' – apparently found in Kelsen's 1966 article in the *Israel Law Review*[351] although not included in Moore's quotation from it – and concludes: 'in presupposing the basic norm we are really *thinking* a *willing*, and the result is a most curious hybrid – something which is both *Denkakt* and *Willensakt*'.[352] And thus, he finds: 'It is not difficult to see that in the notion of *Grundnorm* Kelsen has expressed his realization of the *limit* of legal positivism. This is the place in Pure Theory where explanations come to an end.'[353] (However, the closure turn has offered to the pure theory a new dimension of explanation.)

1980 Kazimierz Opałek's admittedly selective survey of ATN[354] discusses in detail what Kelsen says there about applicability of logic to norms and mentions at several points the idea of a norm that is the meaning of an act of thought, but there is no reference to the fiction turn.

1981 When Joseph Raz returns to the basic norm concept in 1981, beyond RR2en he is aware only of the *Israel Law Review* article. This is enough for him to conclude that presupposing a basic norm is now a 'pretence', which confirms Kelsen's *moral* 'non-commitment'.[355]

1982 For Ralf Dreier, 'hypothesis' is acceptable but the 'fiction' idea does not seem to be a 'fortunate move'.[356]

1985 Mario G Losano reckons that, with the fiction turn, Kelsen implicitly restores an appeal to God; yet Kelsen's recourse to Vaihinger is ignored.[357]

1986 Richard Tur, responding to my translation FV2en and my commentary on it, thinks that the basic norm concept can be rescued by counting it as a Kantian idea of reason.[358] Now, if a basic norm, or the basic norm concept, is self-contradictory, that would seem to make its faultiness even more acute. However, Tur shifts his attention to Kant's conception of 'as if', leaving self-contradiction out of the scene.

[349] J Raz, 'Kelsen's Theory of the Basic Norm' (1974) 19 *American Journal of Jurisprudence* 94; reprinted with revisions in his *The Authority of Law. Essays on Law and Morality* (Oxford, Clarendon Press, 1979) 122–45; and in Litschewski Paulson and Paulson (eds), *Normativity and Norms* (n 1) 47–67.

[350] Above (n 239).

[351] Above (n 11).

[352] R Moore, *Legal Norms and Legal Science. A Critical Study of Kelsen's Pure Theory of Law* (Honolulu, University Press of Hawaii, 1978) 89.

[353] ibid 109.

[354] Opałek, *Überlegungen zu Hans Kelsens 'Allgemeiner Theorie der Normen'* (n 159).

[355] J Raz, 'The Purity of the Pure Theory' (1981) 138 *Revue internationale de philosophie* 441, 452–53, 457; reprinted in Tur and Twining (eds), *Essays on Kelsen* (n 5) 79–97, 90–91, 95.

[356] R Dreier, 'Bemerkungen zur Theorie der Grundorm' in Hans Kelsen-Institut, *Die Reine Rechtslehre in wissenschaftlicher Diskussion*. SHKI, Bd 7 (Vienna, Manz, 1982) 38–46, 38–39.

[357] MG Losano, 'La dottrina pura del diritto dal logicismo all'irrazionalismo' (n 159), lvii–lix.

[358] R Tur, 'The Kelsenian Enterprise' (n 5), 172–73. Along this way, Tur characterises my argument as 'historicist' in the sense of historical determinism: ibid 150. But I was supposing only that ideas, being historical, are historically conditioned; a particular historical direction in ideas is never inevitable, although it can be hard to avoid.

1998 Antonino Troianiello investigates Kelsen's recourse to Vaihinger's fictionalism but abandons the idea of a basic norm as still shrouded in myth.[359]

2000 Bruno Celano is justified in explicitly focusing solely upon Kelsen's Classical Phase, to see what can be made of its conception of 'authority'; but less secure, in view of Kelsen's own later doubts, is his claim that in this phase Kelsen 'presents us with a basically homogeneous, stable theory'.[360]

Hans Lindahl criticises the functional adequacy of the basic norm concept but does not trace it after RR2.[361]

2001 Hamish Ross claims (mistakenly) to find a different contradiction in the basic norm concept, although referring solely to RR1en.[362]

2003 Jiří Přibáň classifies a basic norm as a fiction *in any case* – a 'legalist fiction', alongside fictions of social contract and the political sovereign, serving to legitimise positive law. Kelsen's fiction turn appears to him as an additional fictionality that makes no difference to his initial contention.[363]

2004 Otto Pfersmann addresses the element of self-contradiction but reasonably questions whether there is actually any kind of 'fiction', since it is already denied that the presupposition of a basic norm has truth value.[364]

2007 Deryck Beyleveld and Roger Brownsword raise the question of something that 'provides the reason for the "basic norm" (which implies that the "basic norm" is no longer basic)'; but they stop there, in view of the fact that Kelsen had said that one must.[365]

András Jakab claims that a 'fiction' version of the concept of a basic norm is one reason why the pure theory fails. Yet, although he cites ATN, he thinks of this 'fiction' only as a fiction in the ordinary sense and does not mention Vaihinger.[366]

Lars Vinx, although discussing the basic norm concept at several points, ignores the fiction turn.[367]

2008 Neil Duxbury, in a focus on the fiction turn, finds in 1962 only a semi-fiction.[368]

2009 Aleksander Peczenik considers that Kelsen 'created the most perfect positivist theory of law': although he would prefer that Kelsen had just stuck with

[359] A Troianello, 'Science, fiction et mythe chez Kelsen' (1998) 23 *Revue de la recherche juridique. Droit prospectif* 1355.

[360] B Celano, 'Kelsen's Concept of the Authority of Law' (2000) 19 *Law and Philosophy* 173, 173, fn 1.

[361] H Lindahl, 'Authority and Representation' (2000) 19 *Law and Philosophy* 223, 230–31, 233.

[362] H Ross, 'Hans Kelsen and the Utopia of Theoretical Purism' (2001) 12 *Kings College Law Journal* 174. Ross continued to work primarily from RR1en, perhaps because it is a much better translation than RR2en: The Pure Theory of Law and Interpretive Sociology – A Basis for Interdisciplinarity?' in Freeman (ed), *Law and Sociology* (n 347) 69–89. He suggests there 'a theoretical jurisprudence embedded in interpretive sociology', in which Kelsen's pure theory would be 'sociologically repositioned' (ibid 70–71). This has been my trajectory for some time: I Stewart, 'Sociology in Jurisprudence: the Problem of "Law" as Object of Knowledge' in B Fryer, A Hunt, D McBarnet and B Moorhouse (eds), *Law, State and Society* (London, Croom Helm, 1981) 107–35; 'Kelsen and the Exegetical Tradition' (n 5).

[363] J Přibáň, 'Legalist Fictions and the Problem of Scientific Legitimation' (2003) 16 *Ratio Juris* 14, 18–20.

[364] O Pfersmann, 'Les modes de la fiction: droit et littérature' in F Lavocat (ed), *Usages et théories de la fiction* (Rennes, Presses universitaires de Rennes, 2004) 39–61, paras 46–49.

[365] D Beyleveld and R Brownsword, 'Methodological Syncretism in Kelsen's Pure Theory of Law' in Litschewski Paulson and Paulson (eds), *Normativity and Norms* (n 1) 113–45, 129.

[366] A Jakab, 'Problems of the *Stufenbaulehre*: Kelsen's Failure to Derive the Validity of a Norm from Another Norm' (2007) 20 *Canadian Journal of Law and Jurisprudence* 35, 41, 43–44.

[367] Vinx, *Hans Kelsen's Pure Theory of Law* (n 37).

[368] Duxbury, 'Kelsen's Endgame' (n 4) 56.

characterising a basic norm as a 'presupposition', for '[n]either the idea of a hypothesis nor the idea of a fiction can be considered as improvements of Kelsen's main theory'.[369]

To Jörg Kammerhofer, in the context of international law it does not matter whether a basic norm is referred to as a tautology, a hypothesis or a fiction. It might be better, he thinks, only to say that none of these characterisations is successful.[370]

2010 Stephen P Turner, one of Kelsen's most vigorous current opponents, targets the fiction turn. He correctly emphasises how the pure theory is weakened by introducing a type of scientific 'fiction' that is both false and self-contradictory. However, he notices Kelsen's turn to fiction only in ATNen and does not examine the events of 1962 and 1964 or, therefore, Kelsen's own consciousness of his 'turn'.[371]

2011 Agostino Carrino (although referring to two of my own writings on it) treats the fiction turn only as a reason to re-examine Kelsen's discussion of Vaihinger's fictionalism in 1919 – when, however, Kelsen had not considered proper fictions.[372]

2013 David Gawthorne mentions Kelsen's 'fiction' view in passing, although is interested mainly in analogising legal discourse to narrative fiction.[373]

Jo Eric Khushal Murkens simply leaves aside changes to the concept of a basic norm 'post 1962', not noticing that the fiction turn identifies contradiction in the basic norm concept as it had stood earlier.[374]

2014 Pierluigi Chiassoni, while vigorously defending Kelsen against current theorists of natural law, reports that Kelsen proposed a basic norm as 'a juristic "hypothesis" or a juristic "fiction"' but does not analyse either of these; for the fiction view, he cites only ATN and without a page.[375]

2015 Frederick Schauer finds Kelsen's 'fiction' view of the concept of a basic norm baffling; he does not address the idea of a proper fiction.[376]

2016 Carlo Invernizzi Accetti addresses the question of regress but ignores Kelsen's Sceptical Phase altogether.[377]

2019 Maris Köpke says that, when presupposing a basic norm, 'one acts *as if* the makers of the first positive link in the chain – the "historically first" constitution – had the power to make it', but only *General Theory of Law and State* is cited in this connection and the fiction turn is ignored.[378]

[369] A Peczenik, *On Law and Reason* (Dordrecht, Springer, 2009) 181, 184.

[370] Kammerhofer, 'Kelsen – Which Kelsen?' (n 12) 240, 242, 247.

[371] SP Turner, *Explaining the Normative* (Cambridge, Polity Press, 2010) 66–94.

[372] Carrino, *Das Recht zwischen Reinheit und Realität* (n 17) 29–39.

[373] D Gawthorne, 'Fictionalising Jurisprudence: an Introduction to Strong Legal Fictionalism' (2013) 38 *Australian Journal of Legal Philosophy* 52, 60–61.

[374] JEK Murkens, *From Empire to Union: Conceptions of German Constitutional Law since 1871* (Oxford, Oxford University Press, 2013) 31, fn 27.

[375] Chiassoni, 'Kelsen on Natural Law Theory' (n 62) 138.

[376] F Schauer, 'Legal Fictions Revisited' in Del Mar and Twining (eds), *Legal Fictions in Theory and Practice* (n 181) 113–29, 115–17.

[377] CI Accetti, 'The Temporality of Normativity: Hans Kelsen's Overcoming of the Problem of the Foundation for Legal Validity' (2016) 42 *Philosophy & Social Criticism* 25.

[378] M Köpke, *Legal Validity* (London, Bloomsbury Publishing, 2019) 8–9.

2020 Reviewing the Olechowski biography, in which the Salzburg workshop and its Viennese aftermath are briefly discussed,[379] Mario G Losano does not mention fiction but refers merely to a 'revision' of the basic norm concept – even though he cites FV1 and FV2 and comments on the logic turn.[380]

Mario García Berger, as well as Arkadiusz Górnisiewicz, address the question of regress but ignore Kelsen's late Sceptical Phase altogether.[381]

2021 Michael S Green gives the fiction view only a passing mention.[382]

Shu-Perng Hwang provides an extensive exposition of Vaihinger's fictionalism and of Kelsen's interest in it both early and late. She contends that, with the fiction turn, the anti-absolutism of Kelsen's scientific arguments becomes fully complementary to that of his political arguments; the self-contradiction now identified in the basic norm concept can be assimilated to the conflicts of democracy, which Kelsen envisaged being resolved through parliamentary debate and compromise.[383]

Alexander Somek's examination of the fiction turn reaches a position with some similarity to what I am suggesting here: 'Perhaps unwittingly, Kelsen thereby abandons his ambitious project. In the format of a self-contradictory fiction, the basic norm is transformed into an enigmatic symbol designating the unfoundedness of law and the groundlessness of the science dedicated to its exposition.'[384] (I argue that Kelsen's outcome is more complex.)

2022 David Dyzenhaus refers frequently to the concept of a basic norm and to several of Kelsen's works in German, but to a basic norm only as a hypothesis and to no work by Kelsen later than second *Reine Rechtslehre*.[385]

2023 Matthew Bolton confines his attention to the basic norm concept in its erstwhile form while discussing the pure theory with regard to the criticisms and alternatives of Schmitt and Pashukanis, but this restriction undermines his hope for continued applicability of the concept.[386]

Natasha Wheatley traces the birth of the basic norm concept and says that, when Kelsen described a basic norm as a 'fiction', he 'did not mean something imagined or made up' but rather a necessary implication when one asks what are the logical preconditions of a legal order; however, she does not refer to any of Kelsen's statements about fictionality.[387]

[379] Olechowski, *Hans Kelsen* (n 30) 895–97.

[380] MG Losano, 'Le opere e i giorni di Hans Kelsen, il giurista del secolo' (2020) 97 *Rivista internazionale di filosofia del diritto* 457, 484.

[381] MG Berger, 'A Kantian Interpretation of Kelsen's Basic Norm' (2020) 33 *Ratio Juris* 35; A Górnisiewicz, 'Totemism of the Modern State: On Hans Kelsen's Attempt to Unmask Legal and Political Fictions and Contain Political Theology' (2020) 33 *Ratio Juris* 49.

[382] MS Green, 'Hans Kelsen's Non-Reductive Positivism' in T Spaak and P Mindus (eds), *The Cambridge Companion to Legal Positivism* (Cambridge, Cambridge University Press, 2021) 272–300, 297, fn 99.

[383] S-P Hwang, 'Ist die Grundnorm demokratisch? Grundnormfiktion und Demokratietheorie bei Hans Kelsen' (2022) 76 *Zeitschrift fur offentliches Recht* 501.

[384] A Somek, *Knowing What the Law Is. Legal Theory in a New Key* (Oxford, Hart Publishing, 2021) 88–89.

[385] Dyzenhaus, *The Long Arc of Legality* (n 89).

[386] M Bolton, 'Three Theories of Separation: Kelsen, Schmitt and Pashukanis and the Historical Development of the Legal Form' (2023) *Philosophy and Social Criticism* (OnlineFirst since 28 April 2023).

[387] Wheatley, *The Life and Death of States* (n 247) 226.

5

Varieties of Validity

CARSTEN HEIDEMANN

I. Introduction

The concept of 'validity' is one of the most basic elements of Kelsen's pure theory of law. In spite of its prominence, the secondary literature is divided about its exact meaning, and there is a widespread suspicion that Kelsen uses the term to cover very different features: the existence of the norm, its binding force, its applicability, its being part of the legal system, or even its efficacy (to name the most prominent candidates). This suspicion, however, is unfounded. What I want to argue for is that there is one central very clear and simple meaning of 'validity' in Kelsen's writings:

> The norm that you ought to φ is valid exactly if you (really) ought to φ, that is, if the assertion 'you ought to φ' is true.

First, I will trace the philosophical genesis of this core concept of validity. Originating in Kant's critique of reason, it was transmitted to Kelsen's theory via the influential theory of values of the mid-nineteenth century philosopher Hermann Lotze and its theoretical descendant, the normativistic philosophy of the Baden school of neo-Kantianism.

Second, the development of the concept of validity in Kelsen's theory will be depicted. I will concentrate on the neo-Kantian phase of Kelsen's writings which lasts approximately from 1920 to 1934, any later texts will not be covered. The reason for this is that neo-Kantianism is arguably the most feasible and, in fact, the only elaborate background philosophy of the pure theory.[1] However, the neo-Kantian foundation is abandoned in the second half of the 1930s, and Kelsen is reluctant to replace it with something else. From 1940 on, he relies on an implausible naive realism, according to which legal norms are objects which are 'given' to cognition,[2] and he couples this view with elements of legal realism. This led Joseph Raz to hold, somewhat helplessly, that

[1] On this topic, see C Heidemann, *Hans Kelsen's Normativism* (Cambridge, Cambridge University Press, 2022) 31–51.

[2] H Kelsen, 'The Pure Theory of Law and Analytical Jurisprudence' in H Kelsen, *What is Justice? Justice, Law and Politics in the Mirror of Science. Collected Essays by Hans Kelsen* (Berkeley, University of California Press, 1957) 266–87, 268.

according to Kelsen, in the realist phase, a norm is valid or exists in the same way as a 'stone' exists:

> Rules, therefore, are not statements nor prescriptions, not even justified or true prescriptions or statements. They are things the content of which is described by some normative statements and such statements are true if the rules exist, i.e. are valid, and not true if the rules do not exist, i.e. are not valid. Hence our original observation that an invalid rule is not a rule: a non-existent stone is not a stone, though we can talk about such stones and describe some of their properties as we can do about invalid rules.[3]

Third, it will be shown that there is an ambiguity in Kelsen's claim that 'validity is the Ought of the norm' which he sometimes fancifully exploits in promoting the thesis of the autonomy of law: he operates with two different concepts of Ought, without making this explicit. On the one hand, the Ought is the modality 'inside' the norm, as part of its meaning. This Ought is peculiar to norms. On the other hand, a different kind of Ought constitutes the validity of the norm – that which makes it a fact that one ought to act in this way, its objectivity. This kind of Ought is a feature of *all* objective cognitive judgements, be they normative or theoretical/empirical ones.

Finally, it will be demonstrated how the different elements seemingly encompassed by the term 'validity' in Kelsen's theory relate to this central concept of validity.

II. Philosophical Sources of Kelsen's Concept of Validity and its Genesis

It is only in his neo-Kantian writings that Kelsen uses a fully reflected conception of validity; therefore, it is reasonable to trace the history of this notion as it is developed in the Kantian tradition, starting with Kant's philosophy itself.

A. The Role of Validity in Kant's Philosophy

Kant's critique of reason is probably the first philosophical theory in which the concept of validity plays a fundamental role. This is at least partly due to the 'Copernican turn' in theoretical philosophy instigated by Kant, ie, to jettisoning the traditional model of cognition according to which a cognitive judgement is true by virtue of agreeing with a given reality. Kant argues as follows:

> Truth, it is said, consists in the agreement of cognition with its object. In consequence of this mere nominal definition, my cognition, to count as true, is supposed to agree with its object. Now I can compare the object with my cognition, however, only by cognizing it. Hence my cognition is supposed to conform itself, which is far short of being sufficient for truth. For since the object is outside me, the cognition in me, all I can ever pass judgement on is whether my cognition of the object agrees with my cognition of the object.[4]

[3] J Raz, *The Authority of Law. Essays on Law and Morality* (Oxford, Oxford University Press, 1979) 148.

[4] I Kant, 'Jäsche logic' in I Kant, *Lectures on Logic*, JM Young trans (ed) (Cambridge, Cambridge University Press, 1992), 521–630, 557–58 (Königlich Preußische Akademie der Wissenschaften (ed), *Logik*, Kant's *gesammelte Schriften*, Vol IX (Berlin, Druck und Verlag von Georg Reimer, 1911) 50).

It follows, for Kant, that a cognition is true not by virtue of agreeing with a reality which is independent from it. Rather, a cognitive judgement is universally or objectively 'valid' if it is constituted correctly according to the rules necessarily guiding cognition in applying concepts to representations. That an object exists in a determinate way can be inferred from a valid cognitive judgement implying its existence – not the other way around:

> Objective validity and necessary universal validity (for everyone) are therefore interchangeable concepts, and although we do not know the object in itself, nonetheless, if we regard a judgment as universally valid and hence necessary, objective validity is understood to be included. Through this judgment we cognize the object (even if it otherwise remains unknown as it may be in itself) by means of the universally valid and necessary connection of the given perceptions; and since this is the case for all objects of the senses, judgments of experience will not derive their objective validity from the immediate cognition of the object (for this is impossible), but merely from the condition for the universal validity of empirical judgments … The object always remains unknown in itself; if, however, through the concept of the understanding the connection of the representations which it provides to our sensibility is determined as universally valid, then the object is determined through this relation, and the judgment is objective.[5]

That a judgement of experience is universally valid in this sense means that 'I, at every time, and also everyone else, would necessarily have to conjoin the same perceptions under the same circumstances'.[6]

In short: even though the notion of validity/*Gültigkeit* is not particularly stressed by Kant, validity is a cornerstone of his metaphysics. The concept of validity is even more fundamental than the notion of object or existence, and it stands in a close connection to truth (which connection is, however, never spelled out by Kant). But while Kant's theoretical philosophy is thoroughly normativistic – after all, understanding is the 'faculty of *rules*' – the notion of validity as such does not seem to have any explicit normative connotations for him. Judgements can be valid, as can be norms (like the categorical imperative), or even the forms of intuition, ie, space and time.[7]

B. The Role of Validity in Lotze's Philosophy

The next step in the development of the philosophical concept of validity as a normative concept was taken by the philosophy of Hermann Lotze. Lotze is comparatively unknown, although in his own times he was recognised and influential even in English-speaking countries. Writing in the middle of the nineteenth century, when German idealism had lost ground and natural sciences progressed rapidly, Lotze exploited the notion of normative validity to secure the autonomy of philosophy and the humanities. These were endangered by the pretensions of psychology to offer a full

[5] I Kant, *Prolegomena to Any Future Metaphysics*, G Hatfield trans (ed) (Cambridge, Cambridge University Press, 2004) 51 (Königlich Preußische Akademie der Wissenschaften (ed), *Prolegomena, Kant's gesammelte Schriften*, Vol IV (Berlin, Druck und Verlag von Georg Reimer, 1911) 298–99).

[6] ibid 52, 299.

[7] I Kant, *Critique of Pure Reason*, P Guyer and AW Wood trans (eds) (Cambridge, Cambridge University Press, 1998) 282 (A 156/B 195).

explanation of what cognition comes to. Even more than Frege or Husserl, Lotze has to count as the instigator of anti-psychologism. His theory had an enormous impact on neo-Kantianism, analytical philosophy, and phenomenology; and he has aptly been called 'the grandfather of the concept of normativity, which has become such a mantra in contemporary philosophy'.[8]

Lotze was not a Kantian, but he adopted a number of Kantian theorems. In his peculiar philosophy of 'teleological idealism', validity is the timeless mode of being of values or ideas which are the *telos* of human acting or thinking. These values direct human cognition and subjectivity and thus – for an idealistic view – the way the world is. While being a mode of reality, validity must not be identified with the 'existence' of objects. It is a basic undefinable concept, and it is metaphysically prior to any existence, because the existence of an object presupposes that there is a true or valid judgement according to which this object exists. The truth of a judgement is a by-product of the judgement's conforming to what we ought to think. Cognition aims at the value of truth; and the norms guiding cognition emanate from this value.[9]

So, what is special about Lotze's theory in the present context? On the one hand, validity gains centre stage in his philosophy. It is a fundamental, undefinable metaphysical concept, and as such it is given pride of place in Lotze's writings. On the other hand, he takes validity to be, other than in Kant's writings, solely a matter of normativity, understood in a broad sense. Originally, it is the mode of being of values; in a derived sense, it is the mode of being of norms; in an even more derived sense, it is the mode of judgements which might possibly best be described as 'we ought to think that way'.

C. The Role of Validity in the Baden School of Neo-Kantianism

Lotze's concept of validity was taken up and further developed by the neo-Kantians. Neo-Kantianism in the sense meant here is a philosophical trend dominating German academic philosophy between about 1870 and 1920. It is characterised by two slogans: 'Back to Kant',[10] and 'To understand Kant is to go beyond him'.[11] What is meant by this is that in order to prosper again, philosophy must both return to the main tenets of Kant's philosophy and revise them. Typical neo-Kantian innovations are the replacement of classical ontology by a theory of cognition understood as a theory of science and, contra Kant, the elimination of the concept of a 'thing-in-itself'– as Windelband formulated it: 'From the standpoint of the theory of cognition, the thing-in-itself is a completely meaningless and useless, confusing and annoying fiction'.[12] Besides, the later neo-Kantians are as a rule strict anti-psychologists; for them, (theoretical) philosophy is theory of cognition, but theory of cognition is not a theory of mental activity, rather, it is theory of the validity of cognitive judgements.

[8] FC Beiser, *Late German Idealism. Trendelenburg and Lotze* (Oxford, Oxford University Press, 2013) 129.
[9] H Lotze, *Logics*, B Bosanquet (ed) (Oxford, Clarendon Press, 1884) 7–8, 440.
[10] O Liebmann, *Kant und die Epigonen* (Stuttgart, Schober, 1865); some version of this slogan emphatically ends every chapter of the book.
[11] W Windelband, *Präludien*, 3rd edn (Tübingen, Mohr, 1907) IV.
[12] Quoted after FC Beiser, *The Genesis of Neo-Kantianism, 1796–1880* (Oxford, Oxford University Press, 2014) 524.

There were two main schools of neo-Kantianism, both of which had an impact on Kelsen's theory, namely, the Marburg School, and the Baden School. The Marburg School, founded by Hermann Cohen, was concerned with the correct pitch for the transcendental analysis; Cohen found it in the 'fact of science', ie, in the judgements of the institutionalised, successfully operating natural sciences. Philosophy's task is to determine those conditions which are necessary to make such scientific judgements possible.[13] The Marburg School is important for the self-conception of the pure theory as a theory of the necessary elements and presuppositions of the judgements of institutionalised legal science, or legal dogmatics. The Baden School, represented foremost by Wilhelm Windelband, Heinrich Rickert and Emil Lask, is important for Kelsen's normativism and his concept of validity. The Baden School defined philosophy, following Lotze,[14] as a theory of values, the basic values being truth, goodness, beauty. Its task is to work out the necessary connections between these values and the instances of culture striving to attain them, ie, science, morality, art.

What is new in the theory of validity of the Baden School, compared with Lotze's conception? On the one hand, like Lotze, Windelband and Rickert take validity to be an undefinable metaphysical concept. Validity is more basic than existence, pertaining, as their special mode of being, to transcendent values, the norms derived from them, and to cognitive judgements. On the other hand, they are more consequent in pointing out and elaborating the ramifications of this view; and they combine it with an interpretation of Kant's philosophy. Windelband makes use of it to distinguish a critical method from a genetical method.[15] This distinction is related to Kant's distinction between the *quaestio juris* and the *quaestio facti* when treating questions of cognition. It is expressive of the dualism of Ought and Is (which was no explicit issue for Lotze). While the genetical method explores the empirical conditions leading to the acceptance of certain values as axioms, the critical method, which is the only true philosophical method, explores what norms follow from taking certain values to be axioms. Rickert is important for the methodological distinction between natural sciences which explain events by pointing to general laws, and cultural sciences which interpret events by relating them to certain values.[16]

And Rickert's philosophy explicitly deals with a question arising from shifting the fundamental kind of normativity from norms, directed at human subjectivity, to transcendent values: how can human subjectivity relate to a transcendent sphere? This problem was, as far as I can see, not touched upon by Lotze. Rickert distinguishes a transcendental-psychological way of analysing cognition from a transcendental-logical

[13] On this topic, see C Heidemann, 'Das Faktum der Rechtswissenschaft bei Hans Kelsen' in M Jestaedt, R Poscher and J Kammerhofer (eds), *Die Reine Rechtslehre auf dem Prüfstand. Hans Kelsen's Pure Theory of Law: Conceptions and Misconceptions. Archiv für Rechts- und Sozialphilosophie*, Beiheft 163 (Stuttgart, Steiner, 2020) 81–98.

[14] In fact, there is even a direct genealogical line from Lotze to the Baden School: Lotze supervised the thesis of Windelband; Windelband supervised the thesis of Rickert. Further academic offspring would be Max Weber, who relied heavily on Rickert, and Jürgen Habermas, who relied heavily on Weber. *Facticity and Validity*, the title of a book by Habermas, might just as well have been a Rickert title, or even a Lotze title.

[15] Windelband (n 11) 318–54.

[16] H Rickert, *Kulturwissenschaft und Naturwissenschaft* (Tübingen, Mohr, 1926). In fact, his distinction was no original invention by Rickert, it is based on Windelband's distinction between 'nomothetic' and 'idiographic' sciences.

way. He takes these ways to complement each other. The transcendental-psychological way starts from an immanent view, from the 'bottom up', ie, from the psychical act of judging, and explores the norms guiding it. The transcendental-logical way starts at the transcendent values, from the 'top down', and derives norms from them.[17] So there seems to be a '*Stufenbau*', a hierarchy, of levels of validity, as it were. The highest level (level-1-validity) is occupied by the validity of transcendent values which are independent from any human subjectivity (and maybe by the validity of the objective or transcendent meaning-contents of judgements). The validity of the norms directed at human subjectivity constitutes the middle layer (level-2-validity). Their validity is of a lower level, because it is derived from the validity of the transcendent values. The lowest level, finally, is that of the validity of actual subjective acts of judging (or, rather, of their meaning-content; level-3-validity); this kind of validity is in turn given if the factual acts conform to the norms guiding cognition. The hierarchy may be depicted somewhat like this:

Table 1 Levels of Validity

	Pertains to:	**Relation to cognition:**	**Means of discovery:**
level-1-validity:	1. value 2. objective meaning of cognitive judgement	transcendent	transcendental-logical method
level-2-validity:	norm	unclear, derived from the transcendent level, guiding the immanent level	unclear
level-3-validity:	subjective meaning of true cognitive judgement	immanent	transcendental-psychological method

An example: level-1-validity is the mode of being of the abstract value of truth, and of singular 'truths' – like the objective meaning-content that gold is heavier than iron. Level-2-validity is the validity of those implicit or explicit rules which anyone has to comply with to arrive at the truth that gold is heavier than iron. Level-3-validity is the validity of the content of any factual act of judging, which is true – like the validity of the meaning-content of anybody's act of judging that gold is heavier than iron.

However, this model does not really solve the problem of the relation between the subjective meaning-content and the objective meaning-content. Is the former a psychological phenomenon, bound to an empirical act of thought, coming into existence with it and vanishing with it, while the latter is a transcendent abstract entity; or is the objective meaning-content simply identical with the meaning-content of a factual act of thinking which complies with the norms emanating from the value of truth? And are the norms which can be found by moving 'upwards' from the subjective acts of judging using the transcendental-psychological method, really the same as those norms which

[17] H Rickert, 'Zwei Wege der Erkenntnistheorie' (1909) 14 *Kant-Studien* 169.

can be found by using the transcendental-logical method, going 'downwards' from the values? How could we possibly know that? And how exactly do we get at those norms? It is perhaps the most pressing unsolved problem of Rickert's philosophy that he was not able to find the point where immanence and transcendence meet – and to explain how it can be the case that the transcendent values are not as inaccessible as the thing-in-itself.

These pre-Kelsenian developments might be summarised as follows: the history of the neo-Kantian conception of *Geltung*/validity starts with Kant's philosophy.

As for Kant, objects are not 'given' to cognition, the 'that and how' of objects, whether they exist and how they exist, can only be inferred from universally, and hence objectively, valid judgements. But validity does not explicitly play a central role in Kant's philosophy.

In Lotze's philosophy, validity is a central metaphysical term. It is, in contradistinction to 'existence', the 'mode of being' of the fundamental metaphysical building-blocks of the world, ie, values/ideas from which norms emanate demanding that one acts or thinks in a certain way.

The neo-Kantians of the Baden School combine the Lotzean approach with their interpretation of Kant's philosophy. For them, the most primitive validity is that of transcendent values; from these values, valid norms directed at human subjectivity (and especially at cognitive acts) can be derived; complying with these norms lends validity to the immanent meaning-contents of cognitive acts, ie, cognitive judgements.

D. The Role of Validity in *Hauptprobleme der Staatsrechtslehre*

Rickert's depiction of the two ways of cognitive theory was published in 1909. Two years later, Kelsen's first major text, *Hauptprobleme der Staatsrechtslehre*, appeared. At this time, Kelsen was still blissfully ignorant of all the complications connected with the concept of validity. Trained as a jurist, and lacking a philosophical education, he was writing for jurists. He regarded his book as offering a methodology of legal dogmatics.[18] And he does not seem to have consciously been adopting neo-Kantian theorems. Yet, the text is pervaded by set-pieces from neo-Kantian philosophy. This is partly due to the fact that academic culture at that time was impregnated by neo-Kantianism; besides, Kelsen had attended seminars by Georg Jellinek – a legal theorist associated with the Baden School – two years earlier. There is, for example, an emphasis on the dualism of Is and Ought and the corresponding distinction between an 'explicative' view, ie, the perspective of the natural sciences which employs the causal principle, and a 'normative' view, ie, the perspective of legal science, according to which legal norms are part of the Ought-sphere.[19] There are, however, two aspects where Kelsen steers a course different from the tradition of Lotze and the Baden School. On the one hand, he does not believe in the possibility of a cultural science which combines the normative and the explicative view by relating events to values.[20] On the other hand, he neither holds that values are fundamental for normativity, nor does he think that the teleological perspective is

[18] H Kelsen, *Hauptprobleme der Staatsrechtslehre* (Tübingen, JCB Mohr, 1911) III.
[19] ibid 6.
[20] ibid.

useful or irreducible. Norms are, for Kelsen, the elementary units of Ought, and values are only a by-product of applying norms: something is valuable if a norm states that it ought to be the case.[21] And the teleological perspective is, for him, only a special case of the explicative view, because it relies on the causal principle.[22]

In this early text, the term 'validity' does not play as important a role as in later publications. On some of validity's features, Kelsen has a decided opinion, on others, he remains opaque. What is certain is that a norm is valid by containing an objective Ought: validity means that the norm ought to be complied with or applied.[23] Kelsen takes this feature to be part of the concept of a norm itself.

This is clear enough, yet matters become muddled when Kelsen explains the specific *legal* concept of validity. In this early phase of his writings, he knows just one level of legal norms, namely, the level of general norms. The 'ideal form' of the general legal norm is a hypothetical judgement about the will of the state;[24] Kelsen describes its relation to validity as follows:

> If the norm drapes itself in the form of a judgement, then it raises a general claim to truth, and it repeats itself in anybody who hears it, like any judgement. As a *judgement*, the proposition: If somebody steals, then the state wills to commit him to prison, is as true and universally – i.e. for any reasonable being – valid as the proposition: The state is powerful, or: The horse is a mammal. But this logical universal validity is of no consequence for the *validity* of the *norm* posited together with the judgment.[25]

It is obvious that Kelsen is talking about two different kinds of validity. The one kind is the validity of any objective cognitive judgement – that which makes the corresponding act of judging 'true'. As long as the legal norm is taken to be identical with the *Rechtssatz* as a hypothetical judgement about the will of the state, it is valid in this sense. But Kelsen seems to distinguish between the 'theoretical' validity of the *Rechtssatz*, and the Ought-validity contained in the norm itself, so that the *Rechtssatz* and the norm which is connected with it seem to be different entities, furnished with different kinds of validity.

This is, at best, confused. As was shown, the Baden school of neo-Kantianism advocated a 'hierarchy of levels of validity': originally, validity is the undefinable mode of being of transcendent values (and, maybe, of the objective transcendent meaning-contents) which are the fundamental building-blocks of any metaphysics (level-1-validity). From these values, norms emanate which are directed at human subjectivity; these norms are valid in a derived sense (level-2-validity). As far as such norms govern the formation of correct cognitive judgements, these factual judgements, or possibly their content, might also be said to be valid (level-3-validity).

After abolishing the highest level – the validity of values – by taking values to be the derivative product of the application of norms, Kelsen seems to conflate and at the same time to keep apart the validity of norms and the validity of cognitive judgements: legal norms are valid simply because they are norms (this kind of validity meaning 'one ought to comply with the norm'); on the other hand, as *Rechtssätze*, they are judgements in a logical sense and valid as such (this kind of validity meaning, 'one ought to think

[21] ibid 65.
[22] ibid 57–63.
[23] ibid 352.
[24] ibid 236–38.
[25] ibid 259 (my translation, emphasis in original).

that way'). And the relation between the norm and the logical judgement is obscure. According to Kelsen, the norm is 'posited together with the judgment', but how can a judgement be 'posited'? And at the same time the judgement is said to be the 'form' of the norm, which adds to the confusion.

E. The Role of Validity in Kelsen's Neo-Kantian Writings

In 1912, *Hauptprobleme der Staatsrechtslehre* was reviewed, from a neo-Kantian perspective, in the *Kant-Studien*. The review spurred Kelsen to explicitly place his theory on a neo-Kantian fundament.[26] This fundament has more or less three elements.

First, Kelsen favours Kant's version of transcendental idealism which he describes as follows:

> It is impossible for cognition to play just a *passive* part in relation to its objects; it cannot be restricted to *reflect* things somehow existing 'in themselves', i.e. in a transcendent sphere. As soon as we can no longer assume objects to have a transcendent, i.e. knowledge-independent existence, cognition has to play an *active, creative* part in relation to these objects. It is *cognition itself which creates its objects from the material given to it by the senses according to its immanent laws.* Cognition's being guided by rules guarantees the *objective validity* of its results. … What takes the place of metaphysical speculation is the task to determine the rules guiding the process of cognition, i.e. the objective conditions of this process.[27]

Second, following the Marburg School, Kelsen designs his theory as a transcendental philosophy of law, starting from the *Faktum der Rechtswissenschaft* – the fact of legal science, ie, he purports to offer an analysis of the presuppositions of institutionalised legal dogmatics:

> [R]eferring to the fact of science is the essential of transcendental philosophy, its only basis from which it – as a theory of scientifical experience – performs its analyses of its only possible object, the synthetic judgments of experience as science.[28]

The importance of this self-appraisal can hardly be overestimated. Kelsen does not present an 'ontology' of law, or presume to analyse its 'essence'; all he does is to scrutinise the ideology involved in a successfully operating intellectual practice of legal dogmatics which raises a claim to objectivity. He shows what intellectual price one has to pay, as it were, if one takes the ideology involved in this practice seriously, by making explicit on what assumptions its possibility rests. In particular, the theory of the basic norm does not make any sense without these theoretical surroundings. Neither is the basic norm part of the legal system, nor does it serve as an external justification of the law. Inside the practice of legal dogmatics, valid law is 'always there'. Kelsen does not arrogate to question its existence, or argue for it. The basic norm is simply the result of making explicit the necessary presuppositions of the possibility of law as embodied in legal dogmatics.

[26] H Kelsen, *Hauptprobleme der Staatsrechtslehre*, 2nd edn (Tübingen, JCB Mohr (Paul Siebeck), 1923) XVII.

[27] H Kelsen, *Die philosophischen Grundlagen der Naturrechtslehre und des Rechtspositivismus* (Berlin, Pan-Verlag, 1928) 62 (my translation, emphasis in original).

[28] H Kelsen, 'Rechtswissenschaft und Recht. Erledigung eines Versuchs zur Überwindung der "Rechtsdogmatik"' (1922) 3 *Zeitschrift für öffentliches Recht ZÖR* 103, 128 (my translation).

Its hypothetical character is due to taking the fact of legal science as given, without questioning or justifying it.

The third neo-Kantian element follows from combining Kantian transcendental idealism with Cohen's enterprise to relate transcendental philosophy to the fact of science: if it is not possible to map out an ontology of the world as it might be in itself, or to explain cognition by psychology, the task of metaphysics is to analyse the only accessible element which might be said to embody objectivity – the scientific judgement. Accordingly, the scientific judgement is 'the cornerstone of transcendental philosophy, which, therefore, can only be critique of science, critique of cognition, because it is restricted to analysing the synthetic judgment'.[29]

The result, which is only on first glance surprising, is that objective judgements are the basic building-blocks of the world as an object of cognition. On second glance, the result is rather compelling, and it is less counter-intuitive if the term 'objective judgement' is replaced by the term 'fact' – which is a legitimate and not unusual move; at almost exactly the same time as Kelsen was writing his major neo-Kantian texts, Frege defined facts as 'true thoughts',[30] and Wittgenstein famously declared that the world was 'the totality of facts, not of things' (*Tractatus*, 1.1), replacing objects by relations as fundamental building-blocks of the world. And the result is in line with Kant's ambitious attempt to replace traditional ontology by an analysis of understanding (*Verstand*).

Infusing this theorem into his theory assists Kelsen in clarifying the relation between the legal norm and the *Rechtssatz*, understood as a cognitive judgement of legal science. To recap: in *Hauptprobleme*, Kelsen deemed these elements somehow to be interwoven, yet to possess different kinds of validity. But he was not able to determine their exact relation. Now, he equates them with each other. The legal norm is identical with the *Rechtssatz* as a cognitive judgement of legal science. In *Rechtswissenschaft und Recht* – a polemic against his former adherent Fritz Sander, which contains Kelsen's most elaborate reconstruction of a neo-Kantian theory of cognition – he maintains that

> legal science may 'create' its object – law as embodied by legal rules [*Rechtssätze*], by judgements – just as natural science may 'create' its object, the nature of natural science, nature as a system of synthetic judgements without in the least running any danger of becoming a 'source' of law … In cognition, i.e. in the judgements of legal science appearing as legal rules, the willing [*Wollen*], which is objectified in the sphere of judgement, expresses itself as an Ought. Only in this sphere can we talk of law as an object of legal science. As the object of legal science, law is a system of judgements about law, just as nature as the object of natural science is a system of judgements about nature.[31]

It follows that the legal system (and the state, which is identical with it), must be 'conceived as a normative order, ie, as a system of norms which are linguistically expressed in Ought-sentences, logically as hypothetical judgements connecting a condition with a consequence by the Ought (if a, then b ought)'.[32]

[29] ibid 128 (my translation).

[30] G Frege, 'Der Gedanke' in G Patzig (ed), *Logische Untersuchungen*, 3rd edn (Göttingen, Vandenhoeck and Ruprecht, 1986) 30–53, 50.

[31] Kelsen, 'Rechtswissenschaft und Recht' (n 28) 181–82 (my translation).

[32] H Kelsen, *Der soziologische und der juristische Staatsbegriff. Kritische Untersuchung des Verhältnisses von Staat und Recht* (Tübingen, Mohr, 1922) 75 (my translation).

Accordingly, the validity of the legal norm is its validity as an objective cognitive judgement.[33] Validity is what distinguishes a mere *claim* that one ought to act in a certain way from the *fact* that one ought to act this way. So the norm, that *a* ought to φ, is valid exactly if *a* (really) ought to φ, or if the sentence '*a* ought to φ' is true, or if every rational being ought to think that *a* ought to φ. It is the same kind of validity which is connected to any objective empirical judgement: the judgement that snow is white, for example, is valid exactly if snow (really) is white, or if the sentence 'Snow is white' is true, or if every rational being ought to think that snow is white. In an analogous way (taking Kelsen's example), the normative judgement 'If somebody steals, he ought to be punished', is valid in exactly the same way as the empirical judgement 'If a substance is heated, it expands' is valid.[34]

As set out above, the legal norm as such a valid normative judgement might possibly best be understood as a fact in the sense of Frege's theory: 'a normative thought, which is true'.

III. Problems, and an Equivocation

Yet the matter is more complicated than it might appear at first sight. There is an ambiguity in Kelsen's thesis that validity is the 'Ought' of the norm. On the one hand, validity is the 'correctness' of the normative judgement *qua* legal norm, it consists in the fact that one *ought to think* that way. On the other hand, validity is what makes it a fact that one *ought to act* in the way the norm prescribes. Accordingly, there are two different kinds of Ought involved in any legal norm: a valid legal norm, that one ought to φ, exists exactly if anyone ought to think that one ought to φ. The second Ought is what one might call 'modal' normativity, peculiar only to Ought-judgements and part of their content which distinguishes them from Is-judgements. The first Ought is the normativity which is a feature of *any* valid cognitive judgement and not part of their content, but – as Kelsen terms it – their 'form'.

Sometimes Kelsen makes use of this ambiguity (probably without being aware of it) to endorse some central point he wants to make. When dealing with the theory of Max Weber, for example, he holds that even a sociological approach to law has to presuppose the notion of valid law-as-norm, because it would otherwise not be possible to understand the antics of those persons engaged with the law. For an obvious objection to this argument would be that in order to understand the ideology involved in the legal process it is enough to presuppose normative *meaning* (not validity). Kelsen retorts:

> What matters is: if the meaning of certain acts is an 'order' [of social activities] (*Ordnung*), then the actor must connect, with his acts, the notion of a norm according to which his acts

[33] To be sure, Kelsen shares the Baden school obscurity concerning the relation between transcendence and immanence. The norm as a valid objective meaning might, on the one hand, be some transcendent abstract entity; on the other hand, it might be the immanent content of factual acts of judging as far as it complies with the rules guiding cognition. On Kelsen's reliance on Windelband for his concept of Ought, see especially Kelsen, 'Rechtswissenschaft und Recht' (n 28) 206–08.

[34] Kelsen, *Hauptprobleme der Staatsrechtslehre* (n 26) VII.

> ought to take place. If the order, as a meaning-content, is identical with 'norm', then the 'validity' of this order is identical with Ought.[35]

Though the argument is not quite clear, Kelsen seems to say that the concept of an 'order' the way it is employed by Weber implies normativity, and normativity implies validity. It seems to follow that validity can be derived from normative meaning – which is, of course, not the case.

In other places, however, Kelsen seems to argue exactly the other way round by holding that the 'Ought' is just the expression of the autonomy of law vis-à-vis morality and natural sciences; and that this autonomy is guaranteed already by law's validity:

> The Ought … in the judgments of legal science, i.e., the legal rule is no more directed at a human being than the law of nature is … Striving for a non-psychological meaning of the legal norm as an Ought-judgment, I am in the same situation as the logicians vis-à-vis the logical norm … The double meaning of the logical norm, its validity per se, that is its 'objective' validity, … and its validity for us corresponds to the objective validity of the legal norm claimed by me, and its subjective validity which might better be called 'efficacy' … The Ought is the suitable expression precisely for this objective validity of the logical law, the validity per se; accordingly, … this Ought expresses the demarcation of logic against psychology.[36]

This seems to amount to quite a different conception according to which the Ought in law is just another expression for its validity (and not part of its content); validity seems to guarantee that law belongs to the sphere of Ought. However, this is again a fallacy based on conflating the two notions of Ought which are involved in any valid legal norm. This can easily be seen by the fact that empirical judgements share this kind of validity without belonging to the sphere of Ought.

In short: holding that the law belongs to the Ought-sphere, because it is valid, is just as much a fallacy as holding that it is valid, because it employs the modality of Ought. However, both theses seem to be endorsed by Kelsen when arguing for the autonomy of law/legal science against sociology and moral theory.

IV. Varieties of Validity

These are complicated matters, and a lot more might be said about them and the metaphysics underlying them. But for the present purposes this is not necessary, for the core of Kelsen's conception of validity is, after what has been discussed above, hopefully clear and simple enough. It is derived from the (neo-)Kantian conception of the validity of a cognitive judgement:

> That a norm 'one ought to φ' is valid means that one (really) ought to φ, or, in other words, that it is a fact that one ought to φ, or that the sentence 'one ought to φ' is true.[37]

[35] Kelsen, *Der soziologische und der juristische Staatsbegriff* (n 32) 162 (my translation).

[36] Kelsen, 'Rechtswissenschaft und Recht' (n 28) 206–08 (my translation).

[37] Note the similarity to Bruno Celano's 'disquotationalist' reconstruction of Kelsen's concept of validity. According to Celano (B Celano, 'Validity as Disquotation' in P Comanducci and R Guastini (eds), *Analisi e Diritto 1999. Ricerche di Giurisprudenza Analitica* (Turin, Giappichelli, 2000) 35–77, 53), the norm 'one ought to φ' is valid exactly if one ought to φ. This captures quite well the drift of Kelsen's theory. Still, there

In the secondary literature, however, this concept is contested. There seem to be two main categories of objections. According to the first, taking this interpretation seriously would mean that Kelsen promoted a notion of 'justified legal normativity', so that his theory yields the result that the law really ought to be obeyed.[38] This is, however, not the case. To see why this is so, the status of the pure theory during its neo-Kantian phase has to be taken into consideration. Kelsen designed it as a transcendental philosophy of law, ie, in the neo-Kantian context, a theory of the presuppositions of legal dogmatics – with legal dogmatics being an institutionalised intellectual practice raising, with its judgements, a claim to objectivity. It is the task of the pure theory to determine the conditions which must necessarily be accepted if this practice is taken seriously. The pure theory does not hold that these conditions have to be accepted independently from this practice. Taking part in this practice obliges one to regard the legal norms as valid. But from a point of view external to the practice, there is no need to do so, and there is no need to take part in the practice. Kelsen's theory does not yield that the law ought to be obeyed, but that *legally*, legal norms ought to be obeyed, as it were.

Objections of the second category deny that there is a unitarian concept of validity in Kelsen's writings at all. Kelsen is alleged to have used the term to cover very different things, namely, the bindingness of the norm, its existence, its being a member of the legal system, its applicability, and perhaps even its efficacy.[39]

This is not the place to deal with these objections in detail, so a short response must suffice. Validity indeed means, as was shown, that the legal norm is binding insofar as, from inside the practice of legal dogmatics, one should accept as true that one ought to act in the way determined by the legal norms. The same applies to the definition of validity as the existence of the legal norm; that a norm is valid means that, in the legal perspective, it exists as a normative fact. So, the validity of a norm might be expressed by saying that the norm 'exists' or is 'binding'.

This, however, does not count for defining validity as 'membership' in the legal system. While a norm is, according to Kelsen, valid only if it is part of the legal system, ie, if it has been posited in accordance with a 'higher' norm,[40] these notions do not

are fundamental differences. Celano's conception is based on Quine's disquotationalist theory of truth which takes truth to be a property of sentences. However a norm, according to Kelsen, is a meaning-content, not a sentence (ie, a series of signs); and taking validity to be a *property* of norms is scarcely compatible with Kelsen's definition of validity as the *existence* of the norm. In short: the neo-Kantian metaphysics behind Kelsen's conception, which was expounded above, is not compatible with the disquotationalist account.

[38] J Raz, 'Kelsen's Theory of the Basic Norm' (1974) 19 *American Journal of Jurisprudence* 94, 105.

[39] See E Bulygin, 'An Antinomy in Kelsen's Pure Theory of Law' in SL Paulson and B Litschewski Paulson (eds), *Normativity and Norms. Critical Perspectives on Kelsenian Themes* (Oxford, Clarendon Press, 1998) 297–315, 306; E Bulygin, 'Das Problem der Geltung bei Hans Kelsen' in SL Paulson and M Stolleis (eds), *Hans Kelsen. Staatsrechtslehrer und Rechtstheoretiker des 20. Jahrhunderts* (Tübingen, Mohr Siebeck, 2005) 80–95; CS Nino, 'Some Confusions surrounding Kelsen's Concept of Validity' in SL Paulson and B Litschewski Paulson (eds), *Normativity and Norms. Critical Perspectives on Kelsenian Themes* (Oxford, Clarendon Press, 1998) 253–62.

[40] H Kelsen, *Introduction to the Problems of Legal Theory. A Translation of the First Edition of the Reine Rechtslehre or Pure Theory of Law*, B Litschewski Paulson and SL Paulson trans (Oxford, Clarendon Press, 1992) 55 (*Reine Rechtslehre* (Leipzig and Vienna, Deuticke, 1934) 62).

mean the same. Membership is a *criterion* for validity, but it is not the same as validity. Neither is it part of the meaning of 'membership' that one ought to act in certain way, nor is membership in the legal system part of the meaning of 'validity'. This also holds true for the relation between efficacy and validity. While a legal system is, for Kelsen, valid exactly if it is effective by and large, because the basic norm is only presupposed by legal dogmatics if it is so,[41] its efficacy is only a condition of its validity from the perspective of the pure theory as a theory of legal science, and not identical with it. And the validity of a single legal norm is, for Kelsen in this phase, not dependent on its efficacy, anyway.[42]

The relation between validity and applicability is a bit more complicated, partly due to the vagueness of the term 'applicability'. If applicability means that in case the antecedent of a general norm is established, one ought to perform the act named in the consequent, then applicability is identical with validity, or follows from it. However, Bulygin, for one, uses the term in a special sense. He holds that even norms not belonging to a legal system, ie, not meeting the criteria of membership, might still be applicable, like the norms of international private law, or norms which have not been posited in accordance with 'higher' norms but which have not been repealed (yet). He reproaches Kelsen for confounding membership, bindingness and applicability in his conception of validity.[43] But Kelsen would probably reply that this objection assumes a conception of 'legal system' which is different from the one he advocates. For Kelsen, any norm which ought to be 'applied' necessarily belongs to the system of valid legal norms, because its creation and content in some way or other meets the criteria for valid law inside the one-and-only legal system.

Finally, one afterthought: the confusions in the interpretation of Kelsen's concept of validity seem to be partly due to neglecting the distinction between a *concept* and the *criteria* for something falling under this concept. Alexy, for example, holds that there are three different concepts of validity (*Geltungsbegriffe*): a sociological one, an ethical one, and a juridical one. According to the sociological concept, a norm is valid if it is, to a certain degree, either complied with or non-compliance is sanctioned. According to the ethical concept, a norm is valid if it can be justified morally. According to the juridical concept (which Alexy ascribes to Kelsen), a norm is valid if it was posited in the prescribed way by an organ competent for doing so.[44] However, it is easy to see that the conditions named in these definitions for the validity of a norm are no matter of the *concept* of validity; they do not define validity, rather, they are *criteria* for a legal norm to be valid. (This does not count for the sociological concept of validity in case it is taken not to include any normative elements; Alexy's text is not quite clear on this point.) Contrary to Alexy's claim, Kelsen does not propagate a juridical concept of validity in this sense, rather, what Alexy calls the juridical and the sociological concepts of validity define, for Kelsen, intra-legal and meta-theoretical criteria or conditions for a legal norm to be valid.

[41] Kelsen, *Introduction to the Problems of Legal Theory* (n 40) 60–61 (*Reine Rechtslehre* (n 40) 69–70).
[42] Kelsen, *Introduction to the Problems of Legal Theory* (n 40) 62–63 (*Reine Rechtslehre* (n 40) 72).
[43] Bulygin, 'Das Problem der Geltung bei Hans Kelsen' (n 39) 90–94.
[44] R Alexy, *The Argument from Injustice. A Reply to Legal Positivism*, B Litschewski Paulson and SL Paulson trans (Oxford, Clarendon Press, 2004) 85–88.

A very short roundup:

In Kelsen's neo-Kantian conception of law, legal norms are identical with the judgements of legal science. Their validity is the validity of cognitive judgements; that the norm 'that *a* ought to φ' is valid means

- that *a* (really) ought to φ,
- that the sentence '*a* ought to φ' is true,
- that it is a fact that *a* ought to φ, and
- that every rational being ought to think that *a* ought to φ.

For any *legal* norm, its validity is relative to the framework of the positive legal system. Validity might well be called the 'bindingness' of the norm and its 'existence' as a normative fact inside this framework. If a norm is applicable, it is valid. The membership of a norm in the legal system is, for legal dogmatics, a criterion of its validity, but not identical with it. The efficacy of the legal order is the condition under which the institutionalised intellectual practice of legal dogmatics presupposes the basic norm, and thus, from the perspective of the pure theory as a theory of legal science, a condition of legal validity.

6

On Force, Effectiveness and Law in Kelsen*

JULIETA A RABANOS

I. Introduction

The relationship between law and coercion is perhaps one of the most controversial topics in legal philosophy – a topic that has made quite a comeback in legal discussion in recent decades after a period of apparent abandonment.[1] On the basis of various analytical criteria, a broad, complex spectrum of positions on this relationship can be reconstructed. For example, if one analyses the necessary or essential conditions of concepts, positions on the question of whether 'coercion' is an essential or necessary element of 'law' range from a strong affirmative[2] to a strong negative,[3] including positions that question the way the question is posed.[4] Furthermore, if one analyses the nature or type of element, the positions range from coercion as an instrumental element (function or use)[5] to coercion as a substantive element (content or object)[6] of law.

* This chapter results from research conducted within the Horizon Twinning project 'Advancing cooperation on The Foundations of Law – ALF' (project no 101079177). The project is financed by the European Union.

[1] For recent books see, eg, F Schauer, *The Force of Law* (Cambridge, MA, Harvard University Press, 2015); K Himma, *Coercion and the Nature of Law* (New York, Oxford University Press, 2020); T Gkouvas, *The Place of Coercion in Law* (Cambridge, Cambridge University Press, 2023). For recent papers see, eg, E Yankah, 'The Force of Law: The Role of Coercion in Legal Norms' (2008) 42 *University of Richmond Law Review* 1195; K Woodbury-Smith, 'The nature of law and potential coercion' (2020) 33 *Ratio Juris* 223; L Miotto, 'Law and Coercion: Some Clarification' (2021) 34 *Ratio Juris* 74.

[2] See, eg, J Bentham, *Of the Limits of the Penal Branch of Jurisprudence* (Oxford, Oxford University Press, 2010); J Austin, *The Province of Jurisprudence Determined* (Cambridge, Cambridge University Press, 1995); H Kelsen, *General Theory of Law and State*, trans A Wedberg (Cambridge, MA, Harvard University Press, 1949); H Kelsen, 'The Law as a Specific Social Technique' (1941) 9 *University of Chicago Law Review* 75 – reprinted in H Kelsen, *What is Justice? Justice, Law, and Politics in the Mirror of Science* (Berkeley, University of California Press, 1957) 231–56; K Olivecrona, *Law as Fact*, 1st edn (Copenhagen, E Munksgaard, 1939); K Olivecrona, *Law as Fact*, 2nd edn (London, Stevens, 1971); R Dworkin, *Law's Empire* (Cambridge, MA, Belknap Press, 1986); Himma (n 1).

[3] See, eg, HLA Hart, *The Concept of Law* (Oxford, Clarendon Press, 1961); J Raz, *Practical Reason and Norms* (Oxford, Oxford University Press, 1999); J Finnis, *Natural Law and Natural Rights* (Oxford, Oxford University Press, 2011).

[4] See, eg, Schauer (n 1).

[5] See, eg, Hart (n 3); Raz (n 3); Himma (n 1).

[6] See, eg, Kelsen, *General Theory of Law and State* (n 2); Dworkin (n 2); N Bobbio, *Studi per una teoria generale del diritto* (Turin, Giappichelli, 2012).

Finally, leaving aside the analysis in terms of essential or necessary conditions, the positions include law as a type of coercion, coercion as the distinctive feature of law *qua* social normative order, coercion as the most prominent or salient feature of law *qua* social normative order,[7] and coercion as one of the central or paradigmatic features of law.[8]

The complexity and number of these positions grow exponentially when one also considers the significant differences in what is understood by 'coercion'. They range from strict or narrow views of coercion (eg, equating coercion generally with force, especially physical force)[9] to broad or wide views of coercion (also equating coercion with arbitrariness[10] or with non-consented interference with the will),[11] and from the association of coercion with only negative legal consequences to the association of coercion with both negative and positive legal consequences. Moreover, coercion can be used to answer all or some of the four main theoretical questions related to law: Identity (how can a 'legal' order or norm be identified?); Efficacy or Effectiveness (what is the criterion or condition for the existence of a legal order or norm?); Efficiency (how can law fulfil its function?); and Normativity (how can law guide human behaviour?).

Within this picture, Kelsen's position on the relationship between law and coercion – famously conceiving law as a coercive order – occupies a very important place at the theoretical, methodological and chronological intersection of several strands of analysis. On the one hand, his position is based on both a strong critique of fact-based theories of law – which mainly regard coercion as an essential property or distinguishing feature of law – and natural law theories – which mainly regard coercion as a non-essential property of law. On the other hand, his position can be taken both as considering coercion to be an essential element of law in terms of function (coercion as a tool of law to achieve its goals) and/or in terms of content (coercion as a characteristic content or object of 'legal' norms). As we shall see, finally, his position was also ambivalent, both considering and rejecting the analysis of coercion as motivation[12] and both considering and rejecting the effectiveness or efficacy[13] of legal systems as the most important fact in the analysis of their existence and validity (and thus the existence and validity of legal norms).

The aim of this chapter is therefore to critically analyse Kelsen's position on the relationship between law and coercion. Here I will show that the connection between law

[7] See, eg, Bentham (n 2); Austin (n 2).

[8] See, eg, Schauer (n 1).

[9] See, eg, Hart (n 3); Raz (n 3); Bentham (n 2).

[10] See, eg, V Rodríguez-Blanco, 'What Makes a Transnational Rule of Law? Understanding the Logos and Values of Human Action in Transnational Law' in K Himma, B Spaić, and M Jovanović (eds), *Unpacking Normativity: Conceptual, Normative, and Descriptive Issues* (Oxford, Hart-Bloomsbury Publishing, 2018) 209–26.

[11] See, eg, J Núñez, 'The Forces in Law: Sanctions and Coercions' (2017) 42 *Australian Journal of Legal Philosophy* 145.

[12] This rejection stems primarily from his desire to preserve the 'purity' of legal theory and his zealous rejection of psychologism, as well as his rejection of fact-based legal theories.

[13] From now on, and for present purposes, I will use the terms 'efficacy' and 'effectiveness' as interchangeable synonyms, as the English translations of Kelsen's works contain both terms to designate the same concept. This is particularly clear in Kelsen, *General Theory of Law and State* (n 2), where 'efficacy' is used (see, eg, 29–30 ff); and H Kelsen, *General Theory of Norms* (New York, Oxford University Press, 1991), where 'effectiveness' is used instead (see, eg, 22 ff, 138 ff).

and coercion in Kelsen's legal theory goes deeper than the first definition of 'law as a coercive order' suggests: the connection has to do not only with the specific content of legal norms, but also with the existence of the legal order itself.

In section II, I will show that for Kelsen coercion is an essential element of law as the criterion that allows distinguishing law *qua* normative and social order from other kinds of social and normative orders (such as religion and morality), ie, coercion of a certain kind. In section III, I will further develop the argument and show that coercion is also the criterion that allows distinguishing legal norms from other norms (like moral norms), ie, coercion as a specific object of norms which are hypothetical formulations with sanction as consequence. In section IV, I will show that, in Kelsen's framework, coercion is also to be regarded as an essential element for the effectiveness of a legal order, thus for its very existence. I will further argue that in this view the most important effect of coercion is not the direct one – the effective application of sanctions or the effective exercise of force – but the indirect one – the psychological pressure that the mere existence of organised violence and sanctions exerts on the individual. Finally in section V, I will offer a brief concluding remark.

II. Law and Coercion: Coercion between Content and Function of Law *qua* Social Order

It is well known that Kelsen understands law as a normative (social) coercive order. It is a normative order in the sense that it is a system of valid norms whose unity is given by the fact that they all have the same source of validity (a basic norm).[14] It is a social order in the sense that it is a normative order that regulates human behaviour when that human behaviour is in a mediated or direct relationship with other human beings.[15] Finally, it is a coercive order in the sense that it establishes coercive acts, ie, acts in which an evil is to be inflicted on a subject against their will, resorting to physical force in the case of resistance.[16] The essential role of coercion in defining law *qua* social order becomes clear when it comes to distinguishing between different social orders.

According to Kelsen, every social order aims to regulate human behaviour through rules: they encourage certain behaviours and discourage others, especially to ensure that members of a society refrain from actions that are considered detrimental to society.[17] There are several ways to achieve this result, using different motivational techniques.

[14] See, eg, H Kelsen, *Pure Theory of Law*, 2nd edn (hereafter PTL2) (Berkeley, University of California Press, 1967) 4 ('The legal order which is the object of this cognition is a normative order of human behavior – a system of norms regulating human behavior'); and 31 ('An "order" is a system of norms whose unity is constituted by the fact that they all have the same reason for their validity; and the reason for the validity of a normative order is a basic norm – as we shall see – from which the validity of all norms of the order are derived').

[15] See, eg, ibid 24 ('A normative order that regulates human behavior in its direct or indirect relations to other human beings, is a social order. Morals and law are such social orders').

[16] See, eg, ibid 26 ('A normative order, which prescribes coercive acts as sanctions (that is, as reactions against a certain human behavior), is a coercive order'); and 33 ('The first characteristic, then, common to all social orders designated by the word "law" is that they are orders of human behavior. A second characteristic is that they are coercive orders').

[17] Kelsen, *General Theory of Law and State* (n 2) 15. From a psychological-sociological point of view, this 'motivation function' is fulfilled by the representation of the norms that oblige, forbid and allow certain

Direct motivation implies that a behaviour is required by the system, but there is no consequence associated with its performance or omission. In this sense, there is no retribution associated with the behaviour, and the effectiveness of the order is based on voluntary obedience.[18] Indirect motivation implies that a behaviour is required by the system by establishing some consequences for its performance or omission. On the one hand, a behaviour may be required, and the system may link its execution or omission to a positive (execution) or a negative (omission) consequence. On the other hand, the system may link a negative consequence to the omission of a certain behaviour, thus transforming this behaviour into one required by the system. In these latter cases, there is a retribution associated with the performance or non-performance of the behaviour.[19]

Kelsen defines 'sanction' as the act that ought to be performed as a consequence of the verification of the conditions established by a social order.[20] For this consequence to be considered a sanction, at least one of these conditions must be a certain human behaviour. For the sanction to be considered as a coercive act, it must be imposed against the will of the subject and physical force must be available in case of resistance.[21] This means that not all sanctions are coercive acts, and not all coercive acts are sanctions. Regarding the former, it can be said that Kelsen understands the term 'sanction' both in a broad sense ('sanction' including all coercive acts) and in a narrow sense ('sanction' including only punitive coercive acts, ie, acts that bring an evil upon a subject).[22] Hence, in a broad sense all sanctions are coercive acts, while in a narrow sense only some sanctions are coercive acts. As for the latter, there are some coercive acts that cannot be considered sanctions because their conditions of application do not involve at least one human behaviour that is legally ascertained and established, and that could be considered socially undesirable. Some examples of such coercive acts are pre-trial detention (where there is no legally ascertained behaviour), compulsory confinement of dangerous mentally ill persons or compulsory confinement of contagiously ill persons (where there is not an actual behaviour involved, but only a factual condition or characteristic of a subject), and expropriation in the public interest (where there is no a socially undesirable behaviour involved).

behaviours. I will analyse the way this 'representation' is interwoven to Kelsen's concepts of effectiveness and validity of legal orders in section IV.

[18] Kelsen, 'The Law as a Specific Social Technique' (n 2) 235.

[19] 'A social order that seeks to bring about the desired behaviour of individuals by coercion is called "coercive order"' (Kelsen, 'The Law as a Specific Social Technique' (n 2) 235).

[20] See, eg, Kelsen, PTL2 (n 14) 41.

[21] ibid 26.

[22] ibid 39, 41; L Duarte d'Almeida, 'Wrongs and Sanctions in the Pure Theory of Law' (2022) 35 *Ratio Juris* 245, 249. D'Almeida also purposes to recognise a third 'intermediate' sense of sanction, which encompasses coercive acts that are linked to a condition where the commission of the human behaviour is yet to be established and/or where there is no actual human behaviour but just a possibility of it. However, in my opinion this is not really another sense of sanction, at least not in the sense d'Almeida is proposing to differentiate between a broad and a narrow sense of sanction based on the generality or specificity in the consequent of the norm. What d'Almeida proposes as an 'intermediate' sense of sanction seems to refer not to the consequent, but to the antecedent of the norm. It has to do with the conditions the norm established for the sanction, where a 'strong' sense of it asks for at least one human behaviour, legally ascertained and established, and that could be considered as socially undesirable. This 'weak' sense allows the absence of the second condition.

Returning to the idea of retribution, Kelsen argues that there is no social order in which some kind of retributive principle does not apply, not even in religion and morality.[23] Thus, coercion in the form of sanctions is an essential element of any social order. The relevant difference between social orders, according to Kelsen, lies in the type of coercion they establish. In this sense, Kelsen distinguishes between two main types of sanction: transcendent and socially immanent.[24] The former are sanctions whose source is a supernatural authority, so they are generated outside society; the latter, in turn, are sanctions whose source is a human authority, so they are generated within society. There are two subtypes of socially immanent sanctions: non-organised sanctions, which are based on mere approval or disapproval by a non-organised source, and socially organised sanctions, which are specific acts performed by specific subjects as established by the system.

Here, then, lies the main criterion for distinguishing law from other social orders such as religion and morality. Religion is a normative order that imposes transcendental sanctions: there are consequences for actions or omissions that go against the will of the subject, but they come from outside society and are imposed by a supernatural authority (such as God). Morality is a normative order that imposes socially immanent, non-organised sanctions (if any): they come from society and are imposed by human beings, but the system does not designate particular subjects or particular actions outside approval or disapproval.[25] Finally, law is a normative order that imposes socially immanent, organised sanctions: they come from society and are imposed by human subjects, and the system explicitly specifies who, when, what and how. If sanctions in religion can be attributed to this supernatural entity and sanctions in morality to no one in particular, sanctions in law can be attributed to the whole community.

We can put this graphically in this way:

Table 1 Kelsen's differentiation between normative orders

	COERCIVE ORDERS	**NON-COERCIVE ORDERS**	
Type of motivation	Indirect motivation	Indirect motivation	Direct motivation
	Punishment	Reward	
Types of sanction	Transcendental/ Socially immanent	Transcendental/ Socially immanent	No (necessary) sanction
Types of coercion	Psychic coercion	Psychic coercion	Psychic coercion
	Physical coercion		
Efficacy	Resting on sanction-coercion	Resting on sanction-voluntary obedience	Resting on voluntary obedience

[23] Kelsen, 'The Law as a Specific Social Technique' (n 2) 231.

[24] See, eg, ibid 232 ff; Kelsen, PTL2 (n 14) 28 ff.

[25] Kelsen also claims that '[c]oercive orders are based on measures of coercion as sanctions and orders that have no coercive character (moral and religious orders) rest on voluntary obedience'. See Kelsen, 'The Law as a Specific Social Technique' (n 2) 325.

And, comparing the three main social orders Kelsen has in mind:

Table 2 Kelsen's differentiation between social orders: a first version

	LAW	MORALITY	RELIGION
Type of motivation	Indirect motivation[26]	Direct or indirect motivation[27]	Direct or indirect motivation
	Punishment		Reward/Punishment
Types of sanction	Socially immanent	Socially immanent	Transcendental
	Organised	Non-organised	
Types of coercion	Psychic coercion	Psychic coercion	Psychic coercion
	Physical coercion		
Efficacy	Rests on sanction-coercion	Rests (mainly) on voluntary obedience	Rests on sanction-voluntary obedience

It is important to point out that the fact that law is a coercive order does not mean for Kelsen that law has a coercive character – if by this is meant that law *enforces* behaviour. For contrary to what approaches as Austin's aim at,[28] law does not aim at forcing subjects to carry out the desired behaviour and thus at forcing legal behaviour: it merely attaches negative consequences to the performance of the undesirable behaviour. In other words, the terms are reversed: law does not (directly) require the performance of a desired behaviour and attaches an evil to its omission, but instead attaches an evil to the performance of an undesired behaviour and thus the desired behaviour is (indirectly) required by the system.[29] In this way, Kelsen can account for the fact that the desired behaviour may be performed for reasons other than the fact that the law prescribes it, and claim that this kind of 'psychic coercion'[30] is in any case not a peculiarity of law, but a common feature of any social order.[31] Thus, when Kelsen says that law is a (distinctive) coercive order, he means that law is a social order that uniquely imposes coercive acts as a consequence of conditions determined by that same order.

Moreover, this unique capacity for determination means that law regulates *all* use of force within a given society. Law not only separates between authorised and

[26] For a caveat regarding this point, see the table at the end of section III.

[27] See n 40.

[28] Austin characterises law as 'compulsive', or as a 'reinforced rule' by a certain authority. The specific method to 'compel' the subjects is the threatened evil in case of disobedience. For him, coercion is therefore 'psychic coercion': obedience (and performance of the desired behaviour) is achieved on the basis of the subject's fear of the sanction. See Austin (n 2) 89 ff. However, Kelsen criticises this approach for three reasons: because it is not possible to know if 'licit' behaviour is truly product of that fear; because psychic coercion is not a distinctive element of law, especially in relation to other social orders; and because the motives of 'licit' behaviour, in any case, are a subject matter for sociology of law – and not for legal theory. See H Kelsen, 'The Pure Theory of Law and Analytical Jurisprudence' (1941) 55 *Harvard Law Review* 44, 54 ff. We will return to this point in section IV.

[29] Kelsen, PTL2 (n 14) 35.

[30] ibid.

[31] However, Kelsen does not deny that sanctions can be regarded as reasons for engaging in desired behaviour (see ibid).

forbidden use of force, but also establishes a communal monopoly of it.[32] However, this monopoly is only about the *regulation* of the use of force: it can be both centralised (when coercive acts are performed by authorised specialised bodies) or decentralised (when coercive acts are performed by authorised non-specialised bodies). This gives rise to the principle that the use of force is forbidden and that the only exceptions of authorised use of force are those expressly set out in the law under explicit conditions: then, '[t]he use of force of man against man is either a delict or a sanction'.[33] Moreover, all possible human behaviours would be regulated either in a positive sense (when a coercive act is associated with their performance) or in a negative sense (when no coercive act is associated with their performance). To this extent, according to Kelsen, the legal order makes use of its monopoly on the use of force and employs it to pacify the community,[34] to protect subjects from other subjects and to guarantee a minimum of freedom for all. Peace, or at least collective security, is then achieved.

For Kelsen, law is a specific social technique for 'bringing about the desired social conduct through threat of coercion for contrary conduct': ie, law is a means to an end – not an end in itself.[35] It is a specific social technique characterised by the regulation of coercion through norms and the establishment of socially immanent, organised sanctions (which include the exercise of physical coercion and the general monopoly of force over the community); its effectiveness is mainly based on coercion as an indirect kind of motivational technique. Coercion is thus an essential element of law in several respects: it is the criterion for distinguishing law *qua* normative social order from other normative social orders, it is the particular subject matter of any norm considered 'legal', and it is the main element on which the efficacy – and consequently the existence – of a legal order is based.

I will come back to this last part about existence in section IV. Now, in section III, let us look in detail at the idea of coercion as the specific subject matter of 'legal' rules.

III. Law and Coercion: The Content of Legal Norms

Following the methodological considerations and principles of his pure theory of law, Kelsen famously conceives norms as 'the specific meaning of acts of will directed at a definite human behaviour. This meaning is: that men *ought* to behave in a certain way'.[36] In this sense, norms function as normative conceptual schemes for understanding or qualifying reality. One of the main tasks of the pure theory of law, as a theory that is supposed to offer the conditions for the possibility of legal knowledge, is thus to offer an ideal linguistic form of the legal norm.[37]

[32] 'Monopoly of force' here means 'monopoly of force over the legal community': ie, that the legal order determines the conditions under which physical force may be employed by the individual so authorised by the legal community. See Kelsen, PTL2 (n 14) 36; see also H Kelsen, *Peace Through Law* (Chapel Hill, University of North Carolina Press, 1944) 3.

[33] Kelsen, PTL2 (n 14) 42.

[34] ibid 21.

[35] Kelsen, 'The Law as a Specific Social Technique' (n 2) 236.

[36] H Kelsen, 'On the Pure Theory of Law' (1966) 1 *Israel Law Review* 1.

[37] See SL Paulson, 'The Weak Reading of Authority in Hans Kelsen's Pure Theory of Law' (2000) 19 *Law and Philosophy* 131, 149.

If coercion is the main criterion for distinguishing law from other social orders, as we have seen in section II, it is also the main criterion for distinguishing between legal norms and other types of norms, in particular moral norms. The main differences lie in their structure, their (main) addressees, and the way they are supposed to guide behaviour. Let us take a closer look.

For Kelsen, a moral norm such as '*Thou shalt not steal*' is an imperative: it is mainly categorical, with the desired behaviour as its main object, and is addressed directly to the subject whose behaviour is to be guided.[38] Other kinds of moral norms, especially those involving a sanction, are considered secondary or dependent on this primary kind.[39] Even if moral orders can be considered psychically coercive, the content of these sanctions does not consist of coercive acts, nor do these secondary moral norms individualise a subject entitled to their imposition.[40] Conversely, a legal norm such as '*Whoever steals shall be punished with imprisonment*' is not an imperative, but a hypothetical formulation with a (specific type of) sanction in its consequent.[41] On the one hand, its main object is not the socially desired behaviour, but the sanction to be imposed. On the other hand, it is not directed at the subject whose behaviour is to be guided, but at the subject who will be authorised to impose the sanction.[42] Finally, the content of these sanctions is a coercive act. Other types of legal norms, especially those that can be understood as imperatives, are subordinate to this primary type.[43]

Furthermore, whereas the notion of duty is the primary notion in moral norms, in legal norms the notion of sanction is the primary one. On this basis, Kelsen first proposed a distinction between primary and secondary (legal) norms.[44] Primary norms are those that set out the conditions under which a sanction 'ought'[45] to be carried out, while secondary norms are those that prescribe the opposite behaviour to that which appears as a condition in a primary norm. Primary norms thus deal with delicts and sanctions, while secondary norms deal with legal duties. In this sense, secondary norms are in fact a mere reflex or correlate of primary norms: for every posited primary

[38] See Kelsen, PTL2 (n 14) 100–01. See also Kelsen, *General Theory of Norms* (n 13) 52 ff.

[39] See Kelsen, *General Theory of Norms* (n 13) 143.

[40] See ibid 143. See also Kelsen, PTL2 (n 14) 62. This can be seen as contradicting the distinctions Kelsen made between law, religion and morality as social orders, as can be seen in section II. As far as moral orders are concerned, Kelsen indeed seems to oscillate between considering them as direct motivational systems (based on purely voluntary obedience) and indirect motivational systems (based on voluntary obedience and socially immanent, non-organised sanctions). In both cases, psychic coercion would be involved, but in the latter some kind of sanction (retribution) associated with refraining from the desired behaviour would also be involved. In my view, this fluctuation can be attributed both to a development of Kelsen's thought (from 'The Law as a Specific Social Technique' (n 2) to PTL2 (n 14) to *General Theory of Norms*(n 13)) and to a difference in the direct object of his main interest in analysing the subject (eg, social orders in Kelsen, 'The Law as a Specific Social Technique' (n 2) and *General Theory of Norms* (n 13); norms in Kelsen, *General Theory of Norms* (n 13)).

[41] See, eg, Kelsen, *General Theory of Norms* (n 13) 140–41.

[42] ibid, *General Theory of Norms* (n 13) 52 ff.

[43] See, eg, ibid 142.

[44] See H Kelsen, *Introduction to the Problems of Legal Theory. A Translation of the First Edition of the Reine Rechtslehre or Pure Theory of Law*, B Litschewski Paulson and SL Paulson trans (hereafter PTL1) (Oxford, Clarendon Press, 1992) 30.

[45] Paulson claims that Kelsen has oscillated between the meaning of this 'ought' – between 'ought' in the sense of duty and 'ought' as a placeholder for something akin to 'empowerment'. See Paulson, 'The Weak Reading of Authority in Hans Kelsen's Pure Theory of Law' (n 37) 147.

norm, a secondary norm of this kind could be devised – if only to better understand the phenomena.[46] In a second moment, Kelsen proposed distinguishing between independent and non-independent norms.[47] The former are norms that establish a sanction as a consequence of an unlawful act; the latter are norms that do not establish any sanction, but merely prescribe a certain behaviour. Here, the non-independent norms are not to be considered as 'correlates' of the independent norms, even if they do not have functional autonomy and depend on the latter for their function.[48] Finally, in his last work, he seemingly went back to the first distinction of primary and secondary norms,[49] highlighting the independent character of the former and the superfluous and implicit character of the latter.[50]

It is interesting to note that Kelsen initially considered norms as having, as Stanley Paulson puts it, a 'double possibility of effect'.[51] In this sense, norms can be both complied with and applied. From the point of view of those who comply with them, ie, ordinary subjects, norms can be conceived as commands: they directly command them to behave in a certain way (norm *qua* command). From the point of view of those who apply them, ie, officials, norms can be conceived as hypothetically formulated sanction norms: they empower them to apply a certain sanction if certain conditions obtain (norm *qua* hypothetical formulae). However, what Kelsen last called the 'complete legal norm' – the ideal linguistic form of the legal norm – focuses only on the latter. In this sense, the complete legal norm is a hypothetically formulated norm that both empowers officials to impose sanctions under certain conditions and to participate in law-making.[52]

Does the idea of coercion as an essential subject matter of legal norms still hold when considering this complete legal norm? It seems so. Coercion still seems to be the central element, especially when the norms are considered from a nomostatic point of view. The idea of nomostatics and nomodynamics accounts for the fact that, for Kelsen, law is a coercive order that regulates its own creation. From a static or *ex post* perspective, law is seen in terms of coercion (empowerment to sanction); from a dynamic or *ex ante* perspective, it is seen in terms of empowerment (empowerment to issue norms).[53] However, the basic structure of the norm is still the same: a hypothetical formulation that links a certain sanction to the occurrence of certain conditions. Both empowerment considerations are inextricably linked to the sanction: either to its application or to the issuing of the authorisation for its application. Moreover, since all non-sanctioning norms are considered dependent on sanction-empowering norms, they are also to be considered as directly or indirectly referring to the content or validity of the latter.

[46] See, eg, Kelsen, PTL1 (n 44) 29–30.
[47] See, eg, Kelsen, PTL2 (n 14) 56–57 and 257.
[48] See ibid PTL2 (n 14) 54–58.
[49] See, eg, Kelsen, *General Theory of Norms* (n 13) 56–57.
[50] See ibid 142.
[51] See Paulson, 'The Weak Reading of Authority in Hans Kelsen's Pure Theory of Law' (n 37) 142.
[52] See ibid 151.
[53] See Kelsen, PTL2 (n 14) 55–59; Paulson, 'The Weak Reading of Authority in Hans Kelsen's Pure Theory of Law' (n 37) 152. These two points of view of the legal norm can be also seen as 'norm *qua* process' and 'norm *qua* product': see SL Paulson, 'A "Justified Normativity" Thesis in Hans Kelsen's Pure Theory of Law? Rejoinders to Robert Alexy and Joseph Raz' in M Klatt (ed), *Institutionalized Reason. The Jurisprudence of Robert Alexy* (Oxford, Oxford University Press, 2012) 61–111, 87.

Interestingly, this conception of the complete legal norm as a hypothetical formulation regarding empowerment to sanction allows for a further (and finer) distinction from other types of norms. It is not just that moral norms are imperatives, while legal norms are hypothetical formulations of this kind: for Kelsen, the very notion of empowerment is also a *legal* notion. This is because the notion of empowerment seems to be inextricably linked to the notion of a dynamic normative system, as well as to the notions of indirect motivational technique and socially immanent organised sanction. As far as the former is concerned, the concept of empowerment seems to have no place in a normative system that does not allow for deliberate change, ie, that does not regulate its own change. Only when the idea of deliberate normative labour is introduced – in particular, deliberative normative issuance – does the idea of empowerment become both necessary and, in a sense, conceivable. As far as the latter is concerned, in turn, the concept of empowerment seems to be intrinsically linked to the need for systemic organisation whenever an indirect motivational technique is used, and especially when the attributed consequence is a certain behaviour of a certain human subject. This situation requires a systemic determination not only of when (the antecedent) and what (the act or event in the consequence), but also and especially of who and how (the determination of the occurrence of the antecedent and the execution of that consequence).[54]

Here we can briefly return to some considerations from section II. There we saw that Kelsen distinguishes law from other social systems with direct or indirect motivation technique but transcendent sanctions (religious systems) and with direct or indirect motivation technique and socially immanent but unorganised sanctions (moral systems). To this distinction we can now add the fact that Kelsen considers religious and moral systems to be static systems, whereas legal systems are paradigmatically or distinctively dynamic systems.[55] This dynamic quality can only exist where there are subjects who are empowered by the norms of the system to deliberately change the existent norms or carry out the consequences that the existing norms determine ought to be applied. Following Kelsen's idea of the complete legal norm, empowerment as a legal concept is thus always directly or indirectly linked to sanctions. Directly, because there is empowerment to create and/or eliminate general norms that establish sanctions under certain conditions, or to issue specific norms that determine that a sanction ought to be applied, or to enforce a sanction. Indirectly, because there is empowerment to create and eliminate general norms which, even if they do not directly impute sanctions, nevertheless refer to those that do so, for example by limiting or changing their conditions or their validity.

[54] Whether the determination of the occurrence of the antecedent is considered a different and separable question from the execution of the consequent is, for Kelsen, a question of the development of the organisation. See Kelsen, 'The Law as a Specific Social Technique' (n 2). What is important here is whether the determination of the event can be regarded as the issuance of a norm, in this case a particular or individual norm. In this case, both types of empowerment that Kelsen seems to consider clearly refer to the same subject. This is the sense in which Kelsen claims that all legal authorities (ie, competent subjects), though not at the top or bottom of the legal system, both create and apply laws.

[55] See, eg, Kelsen, PTL2 (n 14) 70–71, 195. I say 'paradigmatic' because Kelsen himself puts a caveat on this statement. He recognises that legal systems can be both nomostatic and nomodynamic, ie, that their norms are valid both when they are derived from other norms (nomostatic) and when they are created according to other norms (nomodynamic). For Kelsen, a legal system can be purely dynamic, but it is impossible for it to be purely static. In this sense, it would not be a legal system.

We can summarise this as follows:

Table 3 Kelsen's differentiation between social orders: a second version

<table>
<tr><th colspan="2"></th><th>LAW</th><th>MORALITY</th><th>RELIGION</th></tr>
<tr><td rowspan="3">Main norm</td><td>Type</td><td>Hypothetical formulated sanction-norm</td><td>Imperative</td><td>Imperative</td></tr>
<tr><td>Addressee</td><td>Official</td><td>Individual</td><td>Individual</td></tr>
<tr><td>Deontic characterisation</td><td>Ought (empowerment)</td><td>Ought (imperative)</td><td>Ought (imperative)</td></tr>
<tr><td rowspan="3">Other norms (if any)</td><td>Type</td><td>Imperative</td><td>Hypothetical formulated sanction-norm</td><td>Hypothetical formulated sanction-norm</td></tr>
<tr><td>Addressee</td><td>Individual</td><td>Community at large</td><td>God/Supranatural entity</td></tr>
<tr><td>Deontic characterisation</td><td>Multiple</td><td>Ought</td><td>Ought</td></tr>
<tr><td colspan="2" rowspan="2">Types of sanction</td><td>Socially immanent</td><td>Socially immanent</td><td rowspan="2">Transcendental</td></tr>
<tr><td>Organised</td><td>Non-organised</td></tr>
<tr><td colspan="2" rowspan="2">Types of empowerment</td><td>Empowerment to execute sanctions</td><td rowspan="2">'Empowerment' to execute sanctions</td><td rowspan="2">'Empowerment' to execute sanctions</td></tr>
<tr><td>Empowerment to issue norms</td></tr>
<tr><td colspan="2">Main way to guide conduct (main norm)</td><td>Direct motivation (officials)
Indirect motivation (individuals)</td><td>Direct motivation (individuals)</td><td>Direct and indirect motivation (individuals)</td></tr>
</table>

IV. Law and Coercion: The Existence of the Legal Order

So far we have seen that for Kelsen coercion is an essential element of law because it is (1) the criterion that allows to distinguish law *qua* normative social order from other kinds of normative social orders (such as religion and morality) – coercion of a specific kind (section II); and (2) the criterion that allows distinguishing legal norms from other norms (such as moral norms) – coercion as the specific subject matter of norms (section III).

However, for Kelsen, coercion can also be seen as an essential element of law in a third way: as an essential condition for the very existence of law. On the one hand, and drawing from the conclusions of the previous sections, the existence of coercion can be seen as an essential condition for the effectiveness of law. Although it can be well argued that both direct and indirect effects of coercion are relevant, we will see that the indirect effects are those that contribute most to the achievement of effectiveness. On the other hand, and going a little further, coercion can be seen as an essential condition for the validity of law. Two independent arguments can be put forward in this regard. The first is that Kelsen's basic norm, following Bobbio, can ultimately be traced back to the principle of effectiveness. The second is that the content of Kelsen's basic norm – at least in some of its characterisations[56] – is nevertheless based on the notion of coercion. Let us examine both.

A. Coercion as an Essential Condition for the Effectiveness of a Legal Order

What exactly does 'effectiveness' mean, especially when it comes to a legal system?[57] In his reflections on the concept of validity, Kelsen focuses primarly on the effectiveness of individual norms.[58] The effectiveness of a norm is the real fact that the norm is by and large applied (by officials) and followed (by individuals)[59] – in other words, the fact that norm-compliant behaviour occurs in reality.[60] In this sense, a norm such as '*If behaviour X occurs, then sanction Y ought to be imposed*' can be said to be effective if officials by and large actually impose sanction-Y when behaviour-X occurs, and if individuals by and large refrain from doing-X.

This doubled-faced account of effectiveness has interesting consequences. On the one hand, this norm would be effective if no individual refrains from doing-X and officials by and large impose sanction-Y on these individuals. In this case, the norm is effective because it is actually *applied* by the relevant addressees (officials). If, on the other hand, all individuals refrain from doing-X, then no official would actually impose sanction-Y as a consequence of someone doing-X. In this case, the norm is effective because it is actually *observed* not only by the individuals but also by the officials. Individuals comply with the norm by not doing-X, thus achieving the socially desired behaviour; officials, by not imposing sanctions because the conditions for their application are not met.

Kelsen distinguishes between the conditions for the efficacy of sanction-decreeing norms (primary norms) and other norms. In regard to the latter, he claims that 'the effectiveness of a norm commanding a certain behaviour is dependent on the sanction-decreeing norm, the primary norm'.[61] In regard to the former, he claims that they 'do not need sanctions as reactions to their violation or observance, or need such guarantees to a much lesser degree than other norms which have to *command* behaviour because

[56] See Paulson, 'The Weak Reading of Authority in Hans Kelsen's Pure Theory of Law' (n 37).

[57] For an introductory study of efficacy and law see, eg, L Burazin, 'The Concept of Law and Efficacy' in M Sellers and S Kirste (eds), *Encyclopedia of the Philosophy of Law and Social Philosophy* (Dordrecht, Springer, 2019) 1838–44.

[58] See, eg, Kelsen, *General Theory of Norms* (n 13) 139 ff.

[59] ibid 138.

[60] Kelsen writes: 'The validity is a quality of law; the so-called efficacy is a quality of the actual behaviour of men and not, as linguistic usage seems to suggest, of law itself'. See Kelsen, *General Theory of Law and State* (n 2) 40.

[61] Kelsen, *General Theory of Norms* (n 13) 138.

this behaviour is, or can be, contrary to the natural inclinations of human beings'.[62] Kelsen seems to assume that this is so because it is ultimately easier for people to sanction socially undesirable behaviour than to engage in socially desirable behaviour.[63] Moreover, Kelsen recognises two possibilities for the effectiveness of these sanction-decreeing norms. On the one hand, these norms may by and large be applied. This includes both (1) the situation of issuance of an individual norm declaring that a coercive act ought to be performed and the performance of the act, and (2) the situation of issuance of an individual norm declaring a coercive act ought not to be performed because the conditions have not been met. On the other hand, these sanction-decreeing norms may not be applied at all because the specific condition for sanctions has never occurred nor is suspected to occur (even though it is possible that it will do so).[64]

With regard to the legal system *qua* normative social order, Kelsen points out that the usual view is that a given legal system is effective if 'its norms which command a certain behaviour are actually observed and, if not observed, then applied'.[65] Taking the previous paragraph into account, Kelsen's view can be better understood as meaning that a legal system is effective when its norms are by and large *applied*. This is because, as we have seen, there is the possibility that norms can be considered effective even if the subjects authorised to apply them do not do so because no delict is committed. In other words: a legal system is effective when the socially undesirable behaviour present in the condition of application of its norms is by and large not committed (*effectiveness-by-absence*) or, if committed, the corresponding sanction is by and large determined and executed (*effectiveness-by-action*).

What does coercion have to do with effectiveness, especially the effectiveness of legal systems? Well, if one defines effectiveness in the way Kelsen seems to, then the presence of coercion is a necessary condition for effectiveness, both conceptually and empirically. Conceptually, in the sense that the effectiveness of the legal system is entirely defined by reference to norms that involve coercion. Empirically, because the presence of coercion – in particular, its indirect effects – can account for effectiveness, in particular what I have called *effectiveness-by-absence*.

As for coercion as a conceptually necessary condition, the argument seems quite straightforward: the effectiveness of a legal system is defined solely by what happens in relation to sanction-norms. In this sense, and following Kelsen's definitions, the statement 'LS1 is effective' actually means 'the sanction-norms belonging to LS1 are by and large applied'. And this in turn means: 'the socially undesired behaviours, content of the antecedent of sanction-norms belonging to LS1, are by and large not being committed, and thus the sanction in the consequent of those sanction-norms is not being determined and executed' or 'the socially undesired behaviours, content of the antecedent of sanction-norms belonging to LS1, are being committed, and thus the sanction in the consequent of those sanction-norms is by and large being determined and executed'.

[62] ibid.

[63] One can conjecture that it is easier imposing an evil (to an evil) than asking for providing for a good (without a clear good in exchange).

[64] See Kelsen, *General Theory of Norms* (n 13) 141.

[65] ibid 138.

As for coercion as an empirically necessary condition, Kelsen's argument does not seem as straightforward as the previous one, but it could be constructed as follows. Kelsen claims that 'by the efficacy of law is meant that the idea of law furnishes a motive for lawful conduct' and that 'the efficacy of law, understood in the last-mentioned way, consists in the fact that men are led to observe the conduct required by a norm by their idea of this norm'.[66] In this sense, it can be said that the effectiveness of the legal system – especially the *effectiveness-by-absence* – is caused or supported by the (direct and indirect) effects of coercion within the sanction-norms, which influence the ideas that people have about the norms.

According to Olivecrona,[67] the presence and by and large application of sanctions as a consequence of the occurrence of certain behaviours have direct and indirect effects on human behaviour. On the one hand, the direct effect refers to the causation of human behaviour by fear of sanctions. If sanctions are actually and consistently applied as a consequence of a certain behaviour (*effectiveness-by-action*), this motivates people not to engage in that behaviour. Thus, the more plausible the application of sanctions, the greater the motivation not to behave in that way (*effectiveness-by-absence*).

The indirect effect, on the other hand, refers to the psychic or psychological pressure that both the existence of organised violence – ie, the existence of a system of sanction-norms – and the direct application of sanctions exert on the subjects. This psychological pressure does not manifest itself in the form of fear or discomfort, as (if at all) in the case of the direct effect, but in a sense of objective duty and other similarly moral sentiments towards not committing delicts. Olivecrona argues that this is an adaptive mechanism of humans to maintain sanity and function in society, a mechanism that has been supported and maintained over the centuries by things like education.[68] Although he concedes that coercion is not the only element that generates this sense of duty, he nevertheless claims that coercion is a necessary (though not sufficient) condition for it.[69]

The indirect effect of coercion is of particular interest here, for two reasons. The first is that it provides an interesting explanation for the particularities of psychological or psychic coercion of law *qua* social order. As we have seen, Kelsen rejected it as a distinctive feature of law, since it is a feature shared by all normative social orders. However, here it seems to be intrinsically connected with the presence of the specific type of coercion that Kelsen claims as distinctive of law: socially immanent, organised, physical coercion.

[66] Kelsen, *General Theory of Law and State* (n 2) 40.

[67] See, eg, Olivecrona, *Law as Fact*, 1st edn (n 2) 140 ff, especially 141–42. I am primarily guided here by the first edition of *Law as Fact* (1939) in which Olivecrona offers an articulated exposition on the subject. In the second edition of *Law as Fact* (1971), he argued that the study of these issues should be reserved for a future work, but maintained his position that sanctions are central to the explanation of obedience to the law. In a final article, he finally returned to an in-depth analysis of coercion and law, now arguing that the legal system interweaves coercion and psychological power (1976). See also T Spaak, *A Critical Appraisal of Karl Olivecrona's Legal Philosophy* (Cham, Springer, 2014).

[68] 'Fear rises itself as a barrier against law-breaking. But we cannot go on harbouring ideas of law-breaking and at the same time combating them with fear. This would have a disruptive influence on the personality. We simply cannot do so in the long run without endangering our mental health. The internal cleavage would prove too much. Therefore the dangerous wishes must be excluded from our mind. If we do not entirely succeed in doing this, they are at least relegated to the sphere of day-dreams, more or less completely cut off from our every-day activities' (Olivecrona, *Law as Fact*, 1st edn (n 2) 147–48).

[69] Olivecrona, *Law as Fact*, 2nd edn (n 2) 272.

The second reason is that this indirect effect may be related – both conceptually and empirically – to coercion being a necessary feature for effectiveness. The presence of sanction-norms is not only necessary to conceptualise effectiveness, as we have seen, but its indirect effects are also empirically necessary for *effectiveness-by-absence*. Indeed, the indirect effect of coercion can explain in an empirical way the conceptual link that Kelsen first proposed between primary and secondary norms, ie, between sanction-norms and duty-norms. It is not only the direct effect of coercion that causes people not to commit delicts out of fear of sanctions, as the indirect technique of behaviour-guiding would lead one to expect. It is its indirect effect that mainly causes people not to do so, not out of fear, but because they assume that there is a corresponding valid duty not to do-X associated with the sanction-norm that establishes a sanction for doing-X. In other words: where a sanction-norm exists, the indirect effect of coercion causes people to read the situation as if a duty not to commit the delict were also present.[70]

Furthermore, it can be argued that this psychological pressure is also necessary for *effectiveness-by-action*. Indeed, this pressure would also be exerted on the very subjects who are authorised to impose the sanctions and hence generate a 'sense of duty' to apply them, even when – as Kelsen himself points out – the sanction-norms only concede an authorisation and do not impose a duty to do so. More than that, as we shall see in the next point, it is possible to assume that it explains why these subjects attribute validity to these norms and to the legal order as a whole.

B. Coercion as an Essential Condition for the Validity of a Legal Order

We have seen how, for Kelsen, coercion can be regarded (conceptually and empirically) as an essential condition for the effectiveness of law. As I will try to show in this section, coercion can also be seen as an essential condition for the validity of law. There are two independent paths to do so. The first is to consider how Kelsen's basic norm could ultimately be traced back to the principle of effectiveness. The second is to show that the content of (at least some of the characterisations of) Kelsen's basic norm is inherently based on the notion of coercion. Let us explore both paths.

i. The Basic Norm and the Principle of Effectiveness

The relationship between Kelsen's basic norm and the principle of effectiveness[71] can be examined without having to define the exact content of the basic norm. I will devote

[70] I will return to this in point B.ii below.

[71] According to the principle of effectiveness, 'a legal order must be efficacious in order to be valid'. See Kelsen, *General Theory of Law and State* (n 2) 121. Kelsen understands that this principle, in international law, has the status of a positive norm: 'It is this general principle of effectiveness, a positive norm of international law, which, applied to the concrete circumstances of an individual national legal order, provides the individual basic norm of this national legal order'. At the level of individual norms, the principle of effectiveness acts as a limit for the principle of legitimacy, according to which 'a norm of a legal order is valid until its validity is

more attention to it in the following section. For the moment, suffice it to say that the basic norm – regardless of its precise content – is the ultimate source of what Kelsen calls the 'objective validity' of prescriptive acts undertaken in accordance with a given social coercive order.[72] In other words, the basic norm allows these acts to be interpreted as objectively normative – ie, as norms[73] – because they have been authorised by norms of the system. This basic norm is not a positive norm, but a conditional and hypothetical, presupposed one. And – this is the crux of the matter – *it is presupposed only with regard to the most effective coercive order in a given area at a given time.*[74]

This is the famous answer Kelsen ultimately gives to the question of how to distinguish between the command of a robber and that of an authority, and by extension, between the normative order of a gang of robbers and a legal order.[75] Here, all the characteristics of both the individual prescriptions and the normative order *qua* social coercive order seem to be the same. Regarding the former, in both cases there is an act of will which means that someone ought to behave in a certain way. Regarding the latter, in both cases there is a social order that regulates its own creation, uses an indirect technique to guide behaviour, and consists of (alleged) norms that empower some subjects to determine and carry out socially immanent, organised sanctions. It is clear that the previous distinctions Kelsen traced between different types of social orders – between law, morality and religion – do not apply here. So how can we call one a legal order and the other, a different kind of social order? If these two orders exist at the same time in the same territory, how can we distinguish between a legal order and another coercive social order?

The answer is quite simple: only one of them is a *valid* order – only one of them is really composed of norms, ie, has 'objective validity'. Kelsen explicitly addresses this point and gives this answer:

> Why is the coercive order that constitutes the community of the robber gang and comprised the internal and external order not interpreted as a legal order? Why is the subjective meaning of this coercive order (that one ought to behave in conformity with it) not interpreted as its objective meaning? Because no basic norm is presupposed according to which one ought to behave in conformity with this order. But why is no such basic norm presupposed? Because this order does not have the lasting effectiveness without which no basic norm is presupposed. The robbers' coercive order does not have this effectiveness, if the norms of the legal order in whose territorial sphere of validity the gang operates are actually applied to the robbers' activity … in short, if the coercive order regarded as the legal order is more effective than the coercive order constituting the gang.[76]

The relationship between the basic norm and effectiveness is thus twofold. On the one hand, the presupposition of the basic norm is only possible or meaningful with regard

terminated in a way determined by this legal order or replaced by the validity of another norm of this order'. See Kelsen, PTL2 (n 14) 209–11. In this sense, effectiveness (both of the legal order and the individual norm in itself) are, together with the existence of an act of norm-creation, condition for the validity of a norm: 'effectiveness is the condition in the sense that a legal order a whole, and a single legal norm, can no loger be regarded as valid when they cease to be effective'. See Kelsen, PTL2 (n 14) 212.

[72] See, eg, Kelsen, PTL2 (n 14) 8, 202–03, 217–18.

[73] 'The act of will (which is an Is) "has" the Meaning of an Ought. This Ought is the norm' (Kelsen, *General Theory of Norms* (n 13) 26).

[74] See, eg, Kelsen, PTL2 (n 14) 49.

[75] ibid 44 ff.

[76] ibid 47–48.

to a 'lasting effective' order. On the other hand, if two orders are simultaneously effective in the same territory, effectiveness is the ultimate criterion for the basic norm: it can only be presupposed with regard to the 'more effective' order. This seems to mean that the difference between a valid coercive order (authorised, legal coercion – 'legal order') and an invalid coercive order (unauthorised, illegal coercion – 'gang of robbers') is ultimately only the fact that the first is, by and large, more applied (*effectiveness-by-action*) and obeyed (*effectiveness-by-absence*). As a consequence, if the conclusions of the previous point hold – ie, if coercion can be conceived as an essential condition for the *effectiveness* of a legal order – then ultimately coercion is also an essential condition for the *validity* of a legal order.[77]

Norberto Bobbio summarised this difficulty as follows: could the basic norm be an ingenious but ultimately completely useless expedient?[78] Bobbio says that it is understandable that, out of pure formal correctness, it is necessary to close the legal order with an ultimate norm and not with an ultimate power. Indeed, out of pure formal correctness it seems reasonable to have an ultimate norm that authorises – in some way – the first prescriptive acts at the top of the order. However, if this ultimate norm ends up referring to ultimate power – if a social order is a legal order only because it is more effective than that of a gang of robbers – then the ultimate norm seems rather superfluous for such a purpose. According to Bobbio, Kelsen offers no argument in favour of the thesis that this ultimate power derives its effectiveness from the fact that this power is authorised, and if the 'legitimacy' of this power is ultimately derived from its effectiveness, then 'the adoption of a norm that plays the role of a legitimating norm is a superfluous operation'.[79] This is so because validity is ultimately traced back entirely to the principle of effectiveness, and as a result, the foundation does not help to solve the main problem of positivist theories, namely the derivation of law from fact.[80]

ii. The Basic Norm and Coercion as its Specific Subject Matter

Even if one disagrees with the conclusion of the previous section, there is a second independent argument to show that coercion can be regarded as an essential condition for the validity of law: that the content of Kelsen's basic norm – at least in some of its characterisations[81] – is nevertheless inseparably based on the concept of coercion.

Kelsen was not entirely consistent with his definition of the basic norm throughout his prolific academic career. As Paulson has argued,[82] several groups of characterisations

[77] Whether it can be considered as a necessary and/or sufficient condition is, in my opinion, up to debate.

[78] N Bobbio, *Diritto e potere. Saggi su Kelsen* (Turin, Giappichelli, 2014) 145–47.

[79] ibid 146. The translation from Italian is mine.

[80] Bobbio famously asserts that norm and power are two sides of the same coin: the same phenomena can be analysed one way or the other, depending on the interest of the theorist and the field of study (legal theory, political theory). See, eg, N Bobbio, 'Kelsen and Legal Power' in SL Paulson and B Litschewski Paulson (eds), *Normativity and Norms: Critical Perspectives on Kelsenian Themes* (Oxford, Clarendon Press, 1999) 434–49, 435 ff. In analysing this difficulty of the basic norm, Bobbio says that Kelsen's insistence on finding a norm (rather than a power) to close the legal order may reflect a practical preference: the ideal of the Rule of Law. See Bobbio, *Diritto e potere* (n 78) 146–47.

[81] See, eg, Paulson, 'The Weak Reading of Authority in Hans Kelsen's Pure Theory of Law' (n 37); and Paulson, 'A "Justified Normativity" Thesis in Hans Kelsen's Pure Theory of Law?' (n 53).

[82] See Paulson, 'A "Justified Normativity" Thesis in Hans Kelsen's Pure Theory of Law?' (n 53) 85 ff.

can be drawn out from the different definitions Kelsen offered: 'empowerment and legal validity, normativity, the unity of the legal system, definitions of the law, meaningfulness and "normative consistency", and, finally, two groups that bring together characterization of the basic norm addressing the Kantian or Neokantian dimension of Kelsen's legal philosophy'.[83] Paulson further identifies five characterisations of the basic norm that belong to the group empowerment and legal validity: basic norm [1] *qua* authorisation to enact legal norms; [2] *qua* authorisation to impose sanctions; [3] *qua* ultimate basis for legal validity (= membership); [4] *qua* ultimate basis for legal validity (= bindingness); and [5] *qua* precondition for the transition from the purely subjective meaning of an act to its objective or legal sense.[84] For the present purpose, these five characterisations will suffice.

That coercion is an essential part of the content of the basic norm in both characterisations [1] and [2] is quite clear. Characterised in this way, the basic norm greatly resembles any other norm of the legal order – therefore, the considerations and conclusions from section III on coercion as the specific subject matter of legal norms can also easily be applied to the basic norm. The fact that the basic norm, unlike the other norms, is only presupposed and not posited makes no difference here.

That coercion is an essential part of the content of the basic norm is also quite clear with regard to characterisations [3] and [5]. Regarding the former, as Paulson points out, [3] and [1] interlock neatly, since [3] sets up a criterion of validity as membership that recalls the empowerment of a subject to enact norms. Regarding the latter, [5] fits both [1] and [2] as [5] refers generally to prescriptive acts (both the issuance of norms and the imposition of sanctions). According to Paulson, [5] leads to [3], which in turn is explained in terms of [1].[85] Therefore, all these characterisations – in one way or another – are reconstructed with coercion as their specific subject matter.

Finally, even if it might be considered as an erroneous characterisation,[86] the content of the basic norm in characterisation [4] can be also linked to coercion – albeit in a more indirect way. On the one hand, bindingness is directly related to obligations and duties, which in turn are inextricably linked to coercive acts that function as sanctions. This is clear in the version of Kelsen's theory in which he postulates the existence of primary and secondary norms, although this may be disputed in his later versions. On the other hand, although this may not be exactly what the late Kelsen intended to assert, characterisation [4] can easily be read as the basic norm of the active participants within the legal phenomenon, both officials and non-officials. In this sense, characterisation [4] seems to perfectly reflect their main 'working presupposition' (even if it is not considered by them as a presupposition but as a fact): that there is a duty of some subjects to behave or not behave in a certain way, as a counterpart to the right or power of some other subjects to issue sanction-norms and impose sanctions, a right or power conceded by the order in force because ultimately the subjects who established the first historical constitution of that order had the right or power to do so.

[83] ibid 86.
[84] See ibid 86–97.
[85] ibid 90.
[86] See ibid 91–92.

V. Concluding Remark

The resumption of the debate about the relationship between law and coercion may prove extremely fruitful for legal philosophy and theory for a number of reasons, including the examination of methodological and substantive tenets that have been considered consolidated knowledge and truths in recent decades. Kelsen's particular position is particularly interesting as it considers coercion both as a means employed by the legal order and as the specific content of legal norms. This chapter showed that coercion can be understood as an essential element of law in Kelsen's framework because it is (1) the criterion that distinguishes law *qua* normative social order from other kinds of normative social orders, (2) the criterion that distinguishes legal norms from other norms, (3) an essential condition for the effectiveness of law, and (4) an essential condition for the validity of law. For these reasons, an in-depth study and consideration of Kelsen's approach – within the framework of his fully developed theory of law and legal methodology – may be of great value and interest for the continuation of the debate.

PART II

International Law

7

The Pure Theory's Nomomechanics and the Structural Analysis of International Law*

JÖRG KAMMERHOFER

I. Introduction[1]

The pure theory of law is an approach to legal theory significantly, but not exclusively, shaped by Hans Kelsen's writings; it is also an *approach*, rather than the sum total of Kelsen's or his collaborators' writings – it is more than any one person or their scholarly output. This approach is both a theory of legal scholarship and a theory of norms. As a theory of norms, it is a theory primarily, but not exclusively, of *legal* norms, because it contends that all normativity follows substantially the same mechanisms. It purports to be a legal theory of all possible legal orders: domestic, trans-national, supra-national and international, and it seeks to cover not only the tradition of public law scholarship, but also that of private and criminal law.

Yet to a significant degree, the pure theory is a theory of law and norms, particularly of their interaction and structuring. 'The subject matter of a general theory of law is the legal norms, their elements, their interrelation, the legal order as a whole, its structure, the relationship between different legal orders and, finally, the unity of law in the plurality of positive legal orders'.[2] One of the strengths of this approach is precisely to have pioneered research in the area of legal statics and dynamics – and to have clarified concepts such as hierarchy and conflict of norms, norm-creation, derogation, and application and the problem of 'erroneous' decisions of legal organs. I call this theory of the possible interrelationship of norms 'nomomechanics', because norms, in both rest and movement, follow mechanisms somewhat akin to the laws of mechanics. This body of knowledge is not only closer to the concerns of doctrinal legal scholars than

* This chapter is based on my earlier research and borrows from a number of texts, as indicated below.

[1] This section is based on J Kammerhofer, 'Sources in Legal Positivist Theories. The Pure Theory's Structural Analysis of the Law' in S Besson and J d'Aspremont (eds), *The Oxford Handbook of the Sources of International Law* (Oxford, Oxford University Press, 2017) 343–64; J Kammerhofer, 'The Interaction of Doctrine and Theory in (International) Legal Scholarship' in K Gorobets, A Hadjigeorgiou and P Westerman (eds), *Conceptual (Re)Constructions of International Law* (Cheltenham, Edward Elgar, 2022) 9–26; J Kammerhofer, 'Beyond the *Res Iudicata* Doctrine. The Nomomechanics of ICJ Interpretation Judgments' (2023) 37 *Leiden Journal of International Law* 206.

[2] H Kelsen, *General Theory of Law and State* (New York, Russell & Russell, 1945) xiii.

other areas of the pure theory, for example the *Grundnorm* theory, but it is also an area where other members of the Vienna School of Jurisprudence have had a decisive impact on its development. It was foremost Adolf Julius Merkl, Kelsen's oldest and closest student, who laid the foundations for what he called the 'structural analysis of law', with Alfred Verdross and Josef L Kunz in particular applying the theory to international law.

Legal theory can also focus on the concepts and arguments of scholarship. It can in effect be exclusively a theory of legal scholarship as an academic endeavour, how legal scholarship can and cannot operate if it is to be a *Wissenschaft*, an academic, methodologically grounded cognitive endeavour. The pure theory is certainly also that – its eponymous purity refers to legal-scholarly endeavours, not to the content of the law, after all. However, it has primarily become known for its theory of the structure of law and of norms in general. This function, legal theory in a narrow sense, analyses the law as normative order,[3] as an agglomeration of norms/rules. It looks at the daily operations of legal orders, including a morphology (systems analysis) and functional theory (concerning legal operations) of norms and law, what would in German legal parlance be called a *Struktur-, Geltungs- und Funktionstheorie des Rechts*. This includes a theory of normativity and validity, of the relationship of normative orders to each other, of norm-functions/deontology and of legal operations (creation and derogation, norm-conflict).

But why is this a particularly desirable topic for research, why would it be indispensable to the wider field of legal philosophy? Because for one, these tasks should not be left to black-letter, 'doctrinal' legal scholars, who tend to treat the structure of law in an instrumentalist fashion and use theoretical arguments to support their current doctrinal argument. Doctrinal scholarship, particularly of international law, is usually theory-averse and consequently tends to take implicit theoretical stances; these are likely inconsistent. For another, legal philosophers who focus exclusively on analysing the concepts, arguments and language of doctrinal legal scholars and practitioners, rather than the law and legal norms themselves, are already well on their way to reductivism and non-cognitivism. If theory is merely an analysis of the 'legal discourses around fundamental [legal] doctrines',[4] then legal theory is reduced to an analysis not of the law, but of 'law-talk' and it is a small step from there to the denial of the law as anything more than talk.[5]

The foundation for the pure theory's nomomechanics is the 'dynamic turn'[6] of that approach in the late 1910s to early 1920s, occasioned by the development (primarily, but not exclusively by Merkl) of the *Stufenbau* theory, which, in turn, is the precondition for the pure theory's structural analysis of law.[7] The *Stufenbau* is a metaphorical

[3] See J-M Priester, 'Rechtstheorie als analytische Wissenschaftstheorie' in G Jahr and W Maihofer (eds), *Rechtstheorie. Beiträge zur Grundlagendiskussion* (Frankfurt am Main, Vittorio Klostermann, 1971) 13–61, 15.

[4] J d'Aspremont, *International Law as a Belief System* (Cambridge, Cambridge University Press, 2018) 1.

[5] eg, J Kammerhofer, 'Between Pragmatism and Disenchantment. The Theory of CIL after the ILC Project' in P Merkouris, J Kammerhofer and N Arajärvi (eds), *The Theory, Practice, and Interpretation of Customary International Law* (Cambridge, Cambridge University Press, 2022) 3–28.

[6] R Cadore, *'Rechtswidriges Recht'. Die Merkl-Sander-Kontroverse innerhalb der Wiener Schule der Rechtstheorie* (Tübingen, Mohr Siebeck, 2024).

[7] AJ Merkl, 'Prolegomena einer Theorie des rechtlichen Stufenbaues' in A Verdross (ed), *Gesellschaft, Staat und Recht. Festschrift für Hans Kelsen zum 50. Geburtstag* (Vienna, Springer, 1931) 252–94 (WRS 1311–61, I/1 MerklGS 437–92), 252 (WRS 1311, I/1 MerklGS 437); R Lippold, *Recht und Ordnung. Statik und Dynamik der Rechtsordnung* (Vienna, Manz, 2000) 394.

representation of inter-norm relationships in legal orders, a tool for analysing the structure of positive normative orders. While norms could be structured or ordered along a whole host of criteria, only one such hierarchy follows by necessity from their identity as norm, as Ought, categorically separate from Is.[8] No norm is valid (ie, extant as a norm) without its validity being traced back to another norm.[9] This establishes a relationship between these two norms: one norm establishes the validity of another norm and thus its very 'existence' as norm. This validity-relationship can be described in a 'dynamic'[10] sense: 'a norm [is] valid, if and when it was created in a certain fashion determined by another norm. This norm is the immediate source of validity of the first norm'.[11] In finding out where the law comes from, in finding the sources of law, we look to a particular part of the legal order. We look for 'empowerment norms', the type of norm which authorises the creation of norms.[12] This necessary type of relationship enables us to speak of a normative order and allows for the analysis of this structure: 'The legal order is not a system of coordinate legal norms existing alongside each other, but a hierarchical ordering of various strata of legal norms'.[13] This necessary form of ordering is the 'hierarchy of legal conditionality',[14] where *creation* establishes hierarchy and where new law is created if the conditions imposed by the law on law-creation (*Rechtserzeugungsregel*)[15] are met. 'If the chaos of legal phenomena is to be seen as … legal cosmos, then the principle of delegation [ie empowerment] … must be taken as inherent in the common origin [of norms]'.[16] The *Stufenbau* theory therefore allows legal scholars to conduct an analysis of the structure of more or less complex legal orders.

Another principle of ordering is the hierarchy of derogatory force,[17] also developed by Merkl. It, too, is highly relevant in the daily operation of legal orders and for

[8] J Behrend, *Untersuchungen zur Stufenbaulehre Adolf Merkls und Hans Kelsens* (Berlin, Duncker & Humblot, 1977) 61.

[9] H Kelsen, *Reine Rechtslehre*, 2nd edn (Vienna, Franz Deuticke, 1960) 196.

[10] AJ Merkl, *Die Lehre von der Rechtskraft. entwickelt aus dem Rechtsbegriff. Eine rechtstheoretische Untersuchung* (Vienna, Franz Deuticke, 1923) 217; B Stoitzner, 'Die Lehre vom Stufenbau der Rechtsordnung' in SL Paulson and R Walter (eds), *Untersuchungen zur Reinen Rechtslehre. Ergebnisse eines Wiener Rechtstheoretischen Seminars 1985/86* (Vienna, Manz, 1986) 51–90, 55; See also SL Paulson, 'Zur Stufenbaulehre Merkls in ihrer Bedeutung für die Allgemeine Rechtslehre' in R Walter (ed), *Adolf J Merkl. Werk und Wirksamkeit. Ergebnisse eines Internationalen Symposiums in Wien (22.–23. März 1990)* (Vienna, Manz, 1990) 93–105, 95.

[11] Kelsen, *Reine Rechtslehre*, 2nd edn (n 9) 228: 'eine Norm [gilt] darum …, weil und sofern sie auf eine bestimmte, das heißt durch eine andere Norm bestimmte Weise erzeugt wurde, stellt diese den unmittelbaren Geltungsgrund für jene dar'.

[12] H Kelsen, *Allgemeine Theorie der Normen*, K Ringhofer and R Walter (eds) (Vienna, Manz, 1979) 82–84.

[13] Kelsen, *Reine Rechtslehre*, 2nd edn (n 9) 228: 'Die Rechtsordnung ist nicht ein System von gleichgeordneten, nebeneinanderstehenden Rechtsnormen, sondern ein Stufenbau verschiedener Schichten von Rechtsnormen'; see also Merkl, 'Prolegomena' (n 7) 257 (WRS 1317, I/1 MerklGS 443).

[14] *Stufenbau nach der rechtlichen Bedingtheit*: Merkl, 'Prolegomena' (n 7) 276 (WRS 1340, I/1 MerklGS 468); R Walter, *Der Aufbau der Rechtsordnung. Eine rechtstheoretische Untersuchung auf Grundlage der Reinen Rechtslehre* (Graz, Leykam, 1964) 60; Stoitzner (n 10) 55–56.

[15] Walter, ibid, 61.

[16] Merkl, *Rechtskraft* (n 10) 210: 'Soll das Chaos von Rechtsgestalten … als ein rechtlicher Kosmos gedeutet werden können, dann muß … ein delegierendes Prinzip … als Ausfluß eines gemeinsamen Ursprunges erkannt werden'.

[17] *Stufenbau nach der derogatorischen Kraft*: Merkl, 'Prolegomena' (n 7) 276 (WRS 1340, I/1 MerklGS 468–69); Walter, *Aufbau der Rechtsordnung* (n 14) 54–55.

international law, but will not be discussed in depth here for reasons of space.[18] The pure theory has developed a range of theories relating to nomomechanics in order to explain the complex operations within legal orders. The rest of this chapter discusses the benefits and challenges of such a structural analysis specifically of – and for – international law and will do so in two steps. It first describes what the members of the Vienna School who have specialised in international law have had to say about the structural analysis of international law in particular (section II). However, I believe that an exegesis or re-telling of primary literature should not be the primary concern of today's legal theorists/philosophers. Therefore, the second part reports on (my) recent efforts to develop the pure theory's norm theory further and to reapply this theoretical substratum to international law, discussing the question of the precedential force of international judgments and awards (section III).

II. The Vienna School and International Law[19]

The members of the Vienna School were prolific scholars of international law. Kelsen, for one, published one of the most influential commentaries on the UN Charter in 1950 and a widely read and used textbook of international law in 1952;[20] Alfred Rub has penned an encyclopaedic account of Kelsen's writings in this field.[21] Verdross – though by that stage no longer an adherent of the pure theory – and his series of textbooks[22] were able to exercise a decisive influence on entire generations of German-speaking international lawyers after the Second World War. Equally, Kunz published widely[23] and served as an important gatekeeper for post-war scholarship through his membership of the editorial board of the *American Journal of International Law*. All three – and others such as Rudolf Aladár Métall[24] – (at least at some point) applied the pure theory's theory of law and norms to international law.[25]

[18] See, however, J Kammerhofer '*Robert Walter*, die Normkonflikte und der zweite Stufenbau des Rechts' in C Jabloner, D Kolonovits, G Kucsko-Stadlmayer, R Laurer, H Mayer and R Thienel (eds), *Gedenkschrift Robert Walter* (Vienna, Manz, 2013) 237–56; J Kammerhofer 'Fehlerkalkül ohne Fehler. Die Nomomechanik des Derogationsstufenbaus bei IGH Auslegungsurteilen' in C Jabloner and T Olechowski (eds), *Der Stufenbau des Rechts auf dem Prüfstand* (Vienna, Manz, 2022) 135–71; Kammerhofer, '*Res Iudicata*' (n 1).

[19] This section is based on a number of texts, including J Kammerhofer, *Uncertainty in International Law. A Kelsenian Perspective* (London, Routledge, 2010) 195–205, 235–38; J Kammerhofer, 'Kelsen – Which Kelsen? A Re-Application of the Pure Theory to International Law' (2009) 22 *Leiden Journal of International Law* 225.

[20] H Kelsen, *The Law of the United Nations. A Critical Analysis of its Fundamental Problems* (New York, Frederick A Praeger, 1950); H Kelsen, *Principles of International Law* (New York, Rinehart & Co, 1952).

[21] A Rub, *Hans Kelsens Völkerrechtslehre. Versuch einer Würdigung* (Vienna, Schulthess, 1995).

[22] A Verdross, *Völkerrecht*, 1st edn (Berlin, Julius Springer, 1937); eighth, final, edition, renamed and rewritten together with Bruno Simma: A Verdross and B Simma, *Universelles Völkerrecht*, 3rd edn (Berlin, Duncker & Humblot, 1984).

[23] eg, JL Kunz, 'The "Vienna School" and International Law' (1933) 11 *New York University Law Quarterly Review* 370.

[24] eg, RA Métall, 'Skizzen zu einer Systematik der völkerrechtlichen Quellenlehre' (1931) 11 *Zeitschrift für öffentliches Recht* 416.

[25] See J Kammerhofer, 'Josef Laurenz Kunz' in R Walter, C Jabloner and K Zeleny (eds), *Der Kreis um Hans Kelsen. Die Anfangsjahre der Reinen Rechtslehre* (Vienna, Manz, 2008) 243–59; N Bersier Ladavac,

Of course, not all of their international law writings are equally important in the present context: for example, there is plenty of scholarship rather close to the orthodox mould, and clearly, some debates, such as whether international law is 'truly' law in the sense of national (public) law, are far more fascinating to constitutional lawyers than to dyed-in-the-wool international lawyers. Yet it might be interesting to briefly look at two other questions – questions where the application of the pure theory as developed then became relevant to a structural analysis of international law. How are the sources of international law constituted and arranged? Are national and international law necessarily part of the world legal order?

If empowerment norms, norms authorising humans to create norms,[26] enable us to see a structure of positive law (the *Stufenbau*), then the classical concept of sources of (international) law is reimagined: 'The term "source of law" is used only figuratively and has more than one meaning … In fact, however, only the positive basis of validity of a legal norm, ie the higher positive legal norm regulating its creation, is called its "source".'[27] Orthodox theory of sources then tended and still tends towards the view that, first, the sources of international law are 'methods' or 'procedures',[28] rather than themselves rules;[29] second, that they are to be found in one place, rather than potentially scattered throughout the legal order;[30] and third, that the sources of international law are not its source of obligation.[31] The pure theory doubts that any of these notions about international law's sources are true[32] and Kelsen deals with the sources of international law in a number of his writings.

For example, there is the seemingly central issue of whether the norm regulating the creation of customary international law could itself be a norm of customary international law – or whether that is a *petitio principii*. Kelsen at one point in *Reine Rechtslehre*, discussing at that point more generally the relationship of legislation and customary law in legal orders, mentions the following case: what 'if the constitution of a legal community were not created by legislation, but by way of custom'?[33] That is the inevitable conclusion from the application of the *Stufenbau* theory to international law in Kelsen's later writings on international law and is also supported by many orthodox

'Rudolf Aladár Métall' in R Walter, C Jabloner and K Zeleny (eds), *Der Kreis um Hans Kelsen. Die Anfangsjahre der Reinen Rechtslehre* (Vienna, Manz, 2008) 315–24.

[26] Kelsen, *Law of the United Nations* (n 20) 303.

[27] Kelsen, *Reine Rechtslehre*, 2nd edn (n 9) 238: 'Rechtsquelle ist ein bildlicher Ausdruck, der mehr als eine Bedeutung hat … Doch wird tatsächlich nur der positivrechtliche Geltungsgrund einer Rechtsnorm, das heißt die höhere, ihre Erzeugung regelnde, positive Rechtsnorm als "Quelle" bezeichnet'.

[28] eg, GG Fitzmaurice, 'Some Problems Regarding the Formal Sources of International Law' in *Symbolae Verzijl. Présentées au Professeur J.H.W. Verzijl à l'occasion de son LXX-ième anniversaire* (Leiden, Nijhoff, 1958) 154.

[29] P Hulsroj, 'Three Sources – No River. A Hard Look at the Sources of Public International Law with Particular Emphasis on Custom and "General Principles Of Law"' (1999) 54 *Zeitschrift für öffentliches Recht* 219, 234; AJP Tammes, 'Inter-Action of the Sources of International Law' (1963) 10 *Netherlands International Law Review* 225, 22–227.

[30] eg, Fitzmaurice (n 28) 154.

[31] ibid 155–60.

[32] For a critique of the orthodox international legal sources theory, see Kammerhofer, 'Sources in Legal Positivist Theories' (n 1).

[33] Kelsen, *Reine Rechtslehre*, 2nd edn (n 9) 232: 'wenn die Verfassung der Rechtsgemeinschaft nicht im Wege der Satzung, sondern im Wege der Gewohnheit zustande gekommen ist'.

international legal scholars. Surely, to then argue that custom empowers custom would be self-contradictory? Gennady Danilenko consequently ascribes to Kelsen the view that 'a positive customary rule cannot determine custom as a law-creating procedure'.[34] However, Kelsen's argument is slightly, but crucially different. That (for example) international law's constitution is itself made up of customary (international) law 'should not be interpreted in the sense that custom is made a law-making condition [ie is made a source of law] by a … constitution which was itself created by custom. That would be a *petitio principii*'.[35] Rather, in this case, 'that custom is a law-making condition must be presupposed already [before we analyse the sources of law]. This presupposition can only be … the *Grundnorm*'.[36] In effect, Kelsen argues here that, because the constitution would already be made up of customary law, customary law would be integral to the sources of law before we decided on the possibility of a subordinate source called 'customary law'.

But how are the sources of international law arranged within the *Stufenbau*? The members of the Vienna School seem only to have discussed two of three possible options, discounting the option that each source is its own legal order which we are only in the habit of calling 'international law' as a matter of convenience.[37] This is probably due to the unity-of-all-law argument, relevant primarily in the monism–pluralism debate discussed below, which Kelsen, at least, discards in his *Allgemeine Theorie der Normen* (*General Theory of Norms*) (1979).[38] The two unifying options are, first, that one source reigns supreme and the others are subordinate, and, second, that a meta-source – an (ephemeral) 'international constitutional law' – establishes a coordinative, non-hierarchical relationship between the sources of international law.

Members of the Vienna School had proposed, at various times, all three sources mentioned in Article 38(1)(a)–(c) of the International Court of Justice (ICJ) Statute – orthodox international legal scholarship's *locus classicus* for the identification of sources – as supreme source of international law.[39] In his early *Problem der Souveränität* (*Problem of Sovereignty*) (1920),[40] Kelsen makes the following proposal à propos a discussion of the traditional position that international law is not properly law in the domestic sense, because it lacks legislative organs and because international treaties are no more than contracts:

> A contract is a [legal] act only if it has received its legal force not of its own accord, but from a higher norm which empowers it. Of course, not even the so-called *traité-contrat* can be

[34] GM Danilenko, 'The Theory of International Customary Law' (1988) 31 *German Yearbook of International Law* 9, 16.

[35] Kelsen, *Reine Rechtslehre*, 2nd edn (n 9) 232: 'kann man nicht dahin deuten, daß Gewohnheit von der durch Gewohnheit erzeugten … Verfassung als rechtserzeugender Tatbestand eingesetzt wird. Das wäre eine *petitio principii*'.

[36] ibid 232–33: 'muß schon vorausgesetzt werden, daß Gewohnheit ein rechtserzeugender Tatbestand ist. Diese Voraussetzung kann nur die Grundnorm … sein'.

[37] In earlier publications, I called this the 'default' option, eg, Kammerhofer, *Uncertainty in International Law* (n 19) 237–38; Kammerhofer, 'Sources in Legal Positivist Theories' (n 1) 358.

[38] Kelsen, *Allgemeine Theorie der Normen* (n 12).

[39] Rub (n 21) 337.

[40] H Kelsen, *Das Problem der Souveränität und die Theorie des Völkerrechts. Beitrag zu einer Reinen Rechtslehre* (Tübingen, JCB Mohr, 1920) (HKW4, 256).

> valid without an empowerment norm of general international law. It is doubtful whether any norm other than *pacta sunt servanda* can serve as empowerment norm … International law is … characterised by the fact that there is no intermediate stage between the *Grundnorm*, that necessarily hypothetical presupposition, …, on the one hand, and *traités-lois* and *traités-contrats*, which are all law-making to some degree, on the other hand.[41]

Passages such as this have been interpreted to support the view that before 1934, Kelsen held that *pacta sunt servanda* is (at least part of) international law's *Grundnorm*. Quite rightly, Rub is sceptical whether Kelsen held a specific view on that topic this early.[42] Verdross, on the other hand, clearly did hold this view. In his *Die Verfassung der Völkerrechtsgemeinschaft* (*Constitution of the Community of International Law*) (1926),[43] he argues that '"pacta sunt servanda" … is the ultimate foundation of international law, its ultimate source of validity … The norm "Pacta sunt servanda is the *Grundnorm* of international law'.[44] Two things are of note here, however. One, this is Verdross writing (just) after his naturalist turn, where the *Grundnorm* on his interpretation is no longer a juridico-epistemic hypothesis, but 'an objectively valid norm, anchored in the cosmos of values'.[45] Two, on this view, *pacta sunt servanda* is and in effect has to be the basis for both treaties and customary international law, where the latter is construed as tacit agreement (*pactum tacitum*).[46] This is problematic both vis-à-vis the post-Historical School tradition of conceptualising customary international law and vis-à-vis the pure theory's idea of *Grundnorm* as determined by the 'historically first constitution'.[47]

From about the first edition of *Reine Rechtslehre* (*Pure Theory of Law*) (1934)[48] onwards, but particularly memorably in *Principles of International Law* (1952), Kelsen argues that customary international law is international law's highest source, because its *Grundnorm* is: 'The states ought to behave as they have customarily behaved'.[49] *Pacta sunt servanda* is a norm of positive customary law and empowers the creation of international treaty law, which is therefore subordinate in the *Stufenbau*.[50] Verdross, again changing his position, in 1931 argues that general principles of law are

[41] ibid 262–63: 'Rechtsgeschäft ist ein Akt, soferne er seine rechtserzeugende Kraft nicht aus sich selbst, sondern aus einer höheren Norm hat, die ihn einsetzt, delegiert. Natürlich kann auch die sog. "Vereinbarung" nicht auf eine sie einsetzende Norm des gemeinen Völkerrechts verzichten. Und es muß ernstlich bezweifelt werden, ob dies eine andere Norm sein kann als der Satz pacta sunt servanda … Was das Völkerrecht … kennzeichnet, ist der Umstand, daß zwischen die notwendigerweise hypothetisch voraus*gesetzte* Ursprungsnorm … und das auch rechtserzeugende Rechtsgeschäft des Vertrages oder der Vereinbarung kein speziell der *generellen* Rechtserzeugung dienendes Zwischenstadium'.

[42] Rub (n 21) 313.

[43] A Verdross, *Die Verfassung der Völkerrechtsgemeinschaft* (Vienna, Springer, 1926).

[44] ibid 29, 32: '"pacta sunt servanda" … ist die letzte Grundlage, der letzte Geltungsgrund des Völkerrechts … Die Norm "pacta sunt servanda" die völkerrechtliche Grundnorm'.

[45] ibid 31: 'eine objektiv gültige, im Kosmos der Werte verankerte Norm'.

[46] ibid 43–44.

[47] Kammerhofer, 'Sources in Legal Positivist Theories' (n 1) 358–360.

[48] H Kelsen, *Reine Rechtslehre. Einleitung in die rechtswissenschaftliche Problematik* (Vienna, Franz Deuticke, 1934).

[49] Kelsen, *Law of the United Nations* (n 20) 418; Kelsen, *Reine Rechtslehre*, 2nd edn (n 9) 222, 324–25; Métall (n 24) 425.

[50] Kelsen, *Law of the United Nations* (n 20) 314, 417; Kunz (n 48) 403; Rub (n 21) 314.

at least a co-equal fount of all other sources: 'International law's *Grundnorm* would roughly have this content: sovereign and partially sovereign legal communities ought to behave in their inter-relationships according to the general principles of law, unless international relations have created particular valid norms which deviate from these principles'.[51]

Kelsen's strong monist position on the question of the relationship of national and international law remains one of his best-known arguments, all the more memorable because of the purely theoretical grounds on which he concludes that a dualist (pluralist)[52] arrangement is an epistemological impossibility. He starts by asserting that both norms of national and of international law 'should be seen as simultaneously valid norms, as legal norms both',[53] because a logically consistent dualism would have to deny that one or the other of these is valid, which those propounding dualism typically do not.[54] Once we perceive both, we have already adopted a monist construct. 'If one speaks of a relationship of two normative systems, one must presuppose their contemporaneous validity. Once such a "relationship" has been assumed, their "duality" is essentially abandoned'.[55] On the one hand, the Kelsenian 'coercive order paradigm' – law is a special type of normative order, one defined primarily by being a coercive order – can serve to create both a delimitation vis-à-vis non-legal normative orders and criterion for the unity of all legal norms in one legal order. Law is an epistemic unit, no more and no less;[56] law is then typologically different from other norms. Law is one species and should therefore be cognised as one: 'The unity of the epistemic point of view imperiously requires the adoption of a monistic approach'.[57] On the other hand, Kelsen's methodological postulate of logical consistency (*Widerspruchslosigkeit*) in the portrayal of the law – the notion, discarded in his final works, that a normative order, particularly law, is a logical unit which cannot sensibly be described in a manner which contains norm-conflicts[58] – also serves to substantiate his logical monism. From this springs the idea that national and international law must not contain insoluble conflicts of norms between them for unity to be established and that such conflicts do not exist.[59]

[51] A Verdross, 'Die allgemeinen Rechtsgrundsätze als Völkerrechtsquelle. Zugleich ein Beitrag zum Problem der Grundnorm des positiven Völkerrechts' in A Verdross (ed), *Gesellschaft, Staat und Recht. Festschrift für Hans Kelsen zum 50. Geburtstag* (Vienna, Springer, 1931) 362: 'Die völkerrechtliche Grundnorm würde also etwa folgenden Inhalt haben: Souveräne und teilsouveräne Rechtsgemeinschaften verhaltet Euch in Eueren gegenseitigen Beziehungen nach den allgemeinen Rechtsgrundsätzen, soweit sich nicht im internationalen Verkehre besondere, von jenen Grundsätzen abweichende, gültige Normen herausgebildet haben'.

[52] Kelsen, *Law of the United Nations* (n 20) 404.

[53] Kelsen, *Reine Rechtslehre*, 2nd edn (n 9) 329: 'als gleichzeitig gültige Normen, und zwar gleicherweise als Rechtsnormen, angesehen werden sollen'.

[54] ibid 330.

[55] Kelsen, *Problem der Souveränität* (n 40) 111: 'Wenn von einer Beziehung zweier Normensysteme gesprochen wird, muß ihre gleichzeitige Geltung vorausgesetzt sein. Ist aber eine solche "Beziehung" angenommen, dann ist damit schon die endgültige "Zweiheit" aufgegeben'.

[56] Kelsen, *Reine Rechtslehre*, 2nd edn (n 9) 328–329.

[57] Kelsen, *Problem der Souveränität* (n 40) 123 (emphasis deleted): 'Die Einheit des Erkenntnisstandpunktes fordert gebieterisch eine monistische Anschauung'.

[58] eg, Kelsen, *Reine Rechtslehre*, 2nd edn (n 9) 76–77, 209–211.

[59] Kelsen, *Law of the United Nations* (n 20) 419–23; Kelsen, *Reine Rechtslehre*, 2nd edn (n 9) 329–32.

III. Reapplying the Pure Theory's Nomomechanics[60]

The two examples discussed in section II show the promise of the pure theory as a structural theory of normative (legal) orders. They do also, however, demonstrate the limits of restricting ourselves to the Vienna School's international law-themed texts for a theory-centred account of today's international law and legal scholarship. The limits to their usefulness is not so much occasioned by the facts that much academic literature was not yet written, that many treaties had not yet been concluded or that crucial judgments and awards had not yet been rendered. That would not matter much, because the amount of radically new ideas and arguments in this field is limited. Rather, in doing so we restrict ourselves to those debates on international law which Kelsen, Kunz and others found interesting, both *ratione personae* and *ratione temporis*. We also rob ourselves of innovative ways of implementing the pure theory, inter alia, by not being able to take into account the development of general legal theory since then and by restricting ourselves to exegesis, rather than actively pursuing new theoretical ideas on the basis of the pure theory.

In my writings, I have attempted to reapply the pure theory's nomomechanical foundations to current problems of international legal theory in order to advance international legal scholarship. The following example is taken from my recent book *International Investment Law and Legal Theory: Expropriation and the Fragmentation of Sources* (2021), where I have endeavoured to show the relevance of the pure theory's nomomechanics for international investment law. In the following, I will briefly recapitulate a question discussed there, namely whether and how precedents of international tribunals can be 'binding' beyond the parties to the individual dispute.

The theoretical question becomes relevant for expropriation because investment law is fragmented into thousands of (mostly bilateral) international investment agreements and case law is that of *ad hoc* arbitral tribunals deciding on the basis of one or two such agreements. Because case law is as important there as elsewhere in law, investment arbitral jurisprudence is used as a means of generating, in one sense or another, *general* international investment law. Arbitral awards – and the jurisprudence of international courts and tribunals – are of the utmost practical relevance and importance, yet this fact seems to obscure the distinction between the legal and the factual.

A. Precedents in International Law: The Orthodox Position

We will first look at the mainstream debate on precedents in international (investment) law. The debate on the function of precedent for international courts and tribunals is marked by three standard arguments: (1) international law is not a common law and does not have a system of formal precedents; (2) tribunals do in fact rely largely on previous case law; (3) therefore, some sort of system of quasi-precedent is in operation.

[60] The example in this section is taken from an early manuscript of J Kammerhofer, *International Investment Law and Legal Theory. Expropriation and the Fragmentation of Sources* (Cambridge, Cambridge University Press, 2021).

'International law does not recognize a binding force of precedents or the principle of *stare decisis*, nor is a Court decision … a source of international law'; this typical argument is almost inevitably[61] followed by the reminder that '[t]his is correct in legal theory, but the reality is different'.[62] The doctrinal argument against a system of *stare decisis* in international law is impeccable: Article 57 of the ICJ Statute (and very similar texts for other tribunals) is inevitably read as restricting the binding effect of judgments to the parties to a dispute.[63] Sometimes this is justified by pointing to the lack of a hierarchy of courts, the decentralisation of international justice[64] – as if binding rules from judgments could only exist within a court system. The second question is whether judgments are a 'source' of international law in some sense of the word. Doctrinal scholarship points to Article 38(1)(d) of the ICJ Statute, which states that judicial decisions are mere 'subsidiary means for the determination of rules of law'.[65] Yet, given their impact, scholars are unhappy to consign investment awards, for example, to mere evidence: 'awards cannot now be reasonably described as only a subsidiary source of international law, as they have "attained a very influential position"'.[66]

This is where the dyadic reversal sets in, because it seems to be untenable that the law – as formalistic as it is otherwise construed by international legal scholarship – could bear not to reflect 'reality' as they see it. Investment arbitral jurisprudence's 'great impact' is typically asserted without much in the way of empirical evidence and usually takes the following form: tribunals frequently cite earlier awards; the reasoning of tribunals relies heavily on case law; our view of the law in this field is largely shaped by case law and this reliance has strengthened over time.[67] The pressure is on scholars to explain away this apparent contradiction; numerous authors have tried to do so, none more prominent than Hersch Lauterpacht: 'It is not suggested that … the Court has adopted the common law doctrine of judicial precedent. However, while not fettered by the rigidity of the formal doctrine of precedent, it has … largely adopted its substance'.[68] This solution, the one preferred by most, is, in effect, a cop-out: since we cannot prove precedential effect in law, we rely on an imagined argument from necessity and bring the importance of case law loosely into the legal realm. This is done using three avenues:

[61] JP Commission, 'Precedent in Investment Treaty Arbitration. A Citation Analysis of a Developing Jurisprudence' (2007) 24 *Journal of International Arbitration* 129, 132.

[62] R Bernhardt, 'Article 59' in A Zimmermann, C Tomuschat and K Oellers-Frahm (eds), *The Statute of the International Court of Justice* (Oxford, Oxford University Press, 2006) 1244.

[63] Commission (n 61) 134; CS Gibson and CR Drahozal, 'Iran–United States Claims Tribunal Precedent in Investor–State Arbitration' (2006) 23 *Journal of International Arbitration* 521, 525–26; G Kaufmann-Kohler, 'Arbitral Precedent. Dream, Necessity or Excuse?' (2007) 23 *Arbitration International* 357, 360–61; A Reinisch, 'The Role of Precedent in ICSID Arbitration' [2008] *Austrian Arbitration Yearbook* 495, 498–500.

[64] AK Bjorklund, 'Investment Treaty Arbitral Decisions as *Jurisprudence Constante*' in CB Picker, ID Bunn and DW Arner (eds), *International Economic Law. The State and Future of the Discipline* (Oxford, Hart Publishing, 2008) 265–80.

[65] Commission (n 61) 134; Kaufmann-Kohler (n 63) 361.

[66] Commission (n 61) 132.

[67] Gibson and Drahozal (n 63); Bjorklund (n 64) 266–67; Commission (n 61) 131; Kaufmann-Kohler (n 63) 357; DB King and R Moloo, 'International Arbitrators as Lawmakers' (2014) 46 *New York University Journal of International Law and Politics* 875, 883; PM Norton, 'A Law of the Future or a Law of the Past? Modern Tribunals and the International Law of Expropriation' (1991) 85 *American Journal of International Law* 474, 498; Reinisch (n 63) 499.

[68] H Lauterpacht, *The Development of International Law by the International Court* (London, Stevens & Sons, 1958) 13–14.

jurisprudence constante, persuasive precedent and a kind of 'normative force of the factual' argument.

The (continental legal) institution of *jurisprudence constante* is based on the idea of 'the development of doctrine through the accretion of a consistent line of cases, rather than the establishment of a rule by an individual case'.[69] We would therefore expect the arguments in judgments or awards to rely on trends or lines of jurisprudence, or on leading cases as convenient manifestations of such lines, rather than on single precedents,[70] and on the reasonableness of the interpretation of the law, rather than on the *authority* of a line of decisions.[71] This reading is not uncontested; some argue that '[t]his would actually be a *stare decisis* doctrine applied not to a single decision, but to a line of cases'[72] or '[a]n increasingly continuous, uncontested and consistent modern arbitral jurisprudence is part of the authoritative source of international law embodied in "judicial decisions" … and will develop, with an even greater legally binding effect, into "international custom"'.[73]

Persuasive precedent, born of the common law legal culture, is slightly different. Where *stare decisis* does not apply, decisions may be used as persuasive authority.[74] While it is tempting to say that the only difference between these two is that we either follow a line of cases or potentially a single prior decision, persuasive precedent is argued as having a creative effect, whereas *jurisprudence constante* apparently merely uncovers features in pre-existing law it interprets. Persuasive precedent is a popular analogy for international lawyers: being convinced that jurisprudence shapes the law,[75] writers naturally turn to persuasiveness. Prior decisions do not *have* to be followed as a matter of law, they may and will be followed, if and 'to the extent that the prior opinion contains a convincing analysis of the legal problem'[76] – 'if it is convincing'.[77] Where the prior decision is on point and its reasoning is compelling, good countervailing reasons must be given why the later tribunal does not utilise it as precedent.[78] This 'persuasive authority' reading tends to cross the line to binding precedent,[79] for example in the following statement: 'canonical statements are typically considered to be binding in the formal sense, the anthologizing of decisional law that is not formally binding, for example in textbooks, can also be described as canonical'.[80]

[69] Bjorklund (n 64) 272–73.

[70] See, eg, M Taruffo and M La Torre, 'Precedent in Italy' in DN MacCormick and RS Summers (eds), *Interpreting Precedents. A Comparative Study* (Farnham, Ashgate, 1997) 141–88, 160–61.

[71] MG Algero, 'The Sources of Law and the Value of Precedent. A Comparative and Empirical Study of a Civil Law State in a Common Law Nation' (2005) 65 *Louisiana Law Review* 775, 783.

[72] Kaufmann-Kohler (n 63) 377.

[73] *International Thunderbird Gaming Corporation v United Mexican States*, NAFTA-UNCITRAL, Award of 26 January 2006, Separate Opinion Thomas W Wälde, para 16.

[74] eg, Z Bankowski and DN MacCormick, 'Precedent in the United Kingdom' in DN MacCormick and RS Summers (eds), *Interpreting Precedents. A Comparative Study* (Farnham, Ashgate, 1997) 315–54, 323; G Lamond, 'Persuasive Authority in the Law' (2010) 17 *Philosophy of Law* 16, 16.

[75] See, eg, Gibson and Drahozal (n 63) 527.

[76] SA Lindquist and FB Cross, 'Empirically Testing Dworkin's Chain Novel Theory. Studying the Path of Precedent' (2005) 80 *New York University Law Review* 1156, 1162.

[77] FG Sourgens, *A Nascent Common Law. The Process of Decisionmaking in International Legal Disputes Between States and Foreign Investors* (Leiden, Nijhoff, 2015) 350.

[78] Norton (n 67) 501; A Peczenik, 'The Binding Force of Precedent' in DN MacCormick and RS Summers (eds), *Interpreting Precedents. A Comparative Study* (Farnham, Ashgate, 1997) 461–80, 467.

[79] Lamond (n 74) 20.

[80] Sourgens (n 77) 351.

The argument from the normative force of the factual, in contrast, is a bit more complicated to reconstruct. It asserts that a body of jurisprudence *in fact* constrains arbitrators and *in fact* generates a more-or-less coherent body of 'law' and uses decisional constraint and content-generation as argument. Decisional constraint means that where and because prior arguments and decisions are well argued, they deserve respect;[81] countervailing decisions require good reasons and more exhaustive reasoning than simply following precedents. If everybody argues from precedent, one is under pressure to do so to even if one is not formally bound to follow or distinguish.[82] This is no longer an exclusively persuasive authority,[83] as it '*constrains* arbitrators to account for prior published awards'.[84] Content-generation is the productive side of the argument but, for example in investment arbitration, the two sides are connected:

> Arbitrators regularly cite to prior awards, appear to consider themselves cabined by them to some extent, and demonstrate concern about the impact that the awards they render may have on the development of the law … whether they like it or not, arbitrators do in fact 'make law' in the sense of rendering decisions that are likely to influence the behaviour of both future tribunals and economic actors.[85]

'Law' in the sense employed in this type of argument is understood primarily as the likelihood of influencing future behaviour. Some of the proponents of this argument also believe that the growing body of investment jurisprudence generates a 'system of arbitral case law in which tribunals develop the details of … investment standards'.[86] But what does this 'content-generation' entail? Is it no more than the coincidence of similar views of tribunals, an interstitial change of the treaties applied, or is it a new norm of customary international law? Both propositions have their own set of theoretical challenges attached; each requires a basis in law. Has customary law *actually* been created? How can an 'authoritative interpretation' possibly change the law? As scholars, we are not allowed to be content with unspecific claims, for example that precedents provide a 'concretization of rather vague general standards'.[87]

B. Precedents and Customary Law

One of the methods of content-creation from precedents, prima facie the most promising, is their potential role in the process of custom-creation and cognition. Most international lawyers would accord precedents a custom-evidencing function,[88] but 'even if judges and arbitrators are clearly not law-makers (and have no formal role in the creation of customary rules), it is undeniable that they do in fact play

[81] IM Ten Cate, 'The Costs of Consistency. Precedent in Investment Treaty Arbitration' (2013) 51 *Columbia Journal of Transnational Law* 418, 473.
[82] King and Moloo (n 67) 883.
[83] Reinisch (n 63) 499.
[84] T-H Cheng, 'Precedent and Control in Investment Treaty Arbitration' (2007) 30 *Fordham International Law Journal* 1014, 1016 (emphasis added).
[85] King and Moloo (n 67) 877.
[86] Bjorklund (n 64) 269.
[87] Reinisch (n 63) 505.
[88] Y Dinstein, 'The Interaction between Customary International Law and Treaties' (2007) 322 *Recueil des cours* 243, 316–17; Mohamed Shahabuddeen, *Precedent in the World Court* (Cambridge, Cambridge University Press, 1996) 71, 76.

an important role'.[89] Yet if we uphold the idea that customary law is created by the members of a legal community by means of their acting out of the prescribed behaviour, counting judicial pronouncements becomes problematic. Take a norm which prohibits expropriation, the topic of my book: it prohibits states from expropriating without compensation. Therefore, if it were a customary norm, we must prove the presence of the following behaviour: 'states not expropriating without compensation', because that would be the norm-creating *usus*. Arbitral awards finding a violation of a *treaty* norm of expropriation cannot constitute the presence of that behaviour – and in truth cannot prove such a presence either.

Some do argue that a line of cases could turn into a customary norm. 'If a rule developed [in case-law] works and finds support, it will be followed, with broadening support and acceptance. Eventually, when rules and principles are no longer seriously contested and adopted by tribunals as established truth … judge-made law will have become "customary international law"'.[90] This 'would imply not only a well established practice but also an *opinio juris*, namely, the belief among states, investors and arbitrators that, in the absence of compelling reasons to do otherwise, a tribunal must follow the solution arising from a consistent line of earlier cases'.[91] In the final analysis, this argument presupposes a customary law without customs (*usus*) and magically turns judicial opinion into general acceptance of the presumptive norm and thence into law. In the same vein, others argue in favour of judicial decisions as state practice:

> [D]ecisions have their authority because states have agreed to submit the disputes in question to judicial or arbitral resolution and have generally abided by the results. Indeed, by expressly agreeing to have these disputes determined *by law*, states have arguably shown a much greater *opinio juris* than in most forms of state practice.[92]

Does the agreement to have a dispute settled in conjunction with abiding with terms really amount to the same thing as a community-wide behaviour in accordance with the tentative norm? If this is to be something, would it not rather count as an unspecific belief that whatever the tribunal decides upon is law? Is this argument not reminiscent of 'new custom',[93] an approach shamelessly privileging *opinio iuris* over state practice, having little to do with *customary* law as norms created by way of *customs*, by way of a regularity of behaviour?

Two specifically nomomechanical problems arise from conceptualising jurisprudence as custom-generative. First, can jurisprudence really generate a *general* customary international law, in principle binding on all states? Typically, international dispute settlement involves no more than two parties and cases are more often than not adjudged on the basis of treaty law, in investment dispute settlement typically a bilateral investment treaty. Hence, the behaviour adjudged by the tribunal typically was that of one or two states; the *opinio* expressed in a treaty which is now being adjudged is primarily an *opinio iuris conventionalis*, a belief that treaty terms are *treaty* law, binding

[89] P Dumberry, *The Formation and Identification of Rules of Customary International Law in International Investment Law* (Cambridge, Cambridge University Press, 2016) 43.

[90] TW Wälde, 'Specific Nature of Investment Arbitration' in P Kahn and TW Wälde (eds), *New Aspects of International Investment Law* (Leiden-Boston, Brill-Nijhoff, 2007) 42–120, 47.

[91] Kaufmann-Kohler (n 63) 377.

[92] Norton (n 67) 504.

[93] Sourgens (n 77) 259.

(only) *inter partes*. Second, while judgments do usually contain detailed pronouncements of the law – specific decisions of specific disputes, subsumptions of a specific set of facts under rules[94] – it is unlikely that a series of judicial decisions would in any sense of the word produce a single unspecific customary norm. It is much more likely that any customary norm that could *arguendo* be extracted from a judgment would be very specific indeed, like 'punitive taxation at x% is an indirect expropriation'.[95] Yet, customary norm-creation generates unspecific norms, because it works by the accretion of many instances of *usus* which will vary, which makes creation via case law unlikely. Would such general *ratione personae*, but specific *ratione materiae* norms typically exist in customary international law? Could they even be created in the customary mode of norm-generation? This is highly unlikely.

Equally, as an early commentator on international investment law observed, the idea of jurisprudence as 'best available evidence' of customary norms is probably 'doctrinal legerdemain. Even the earliest decisions in expropriation cases fail to cite actual state practice. They either assume full compensation as an a priori rule or invoke the authority of their predecessors'.[96] Using 'x' as evidence or proof of 'y' depends on 'x' being capable of proving 'y' – international case law[97] has seldom to never actually counted instances of state practice and *opinio iuris* and typically does not even point to sources which may have. We cannot expect to get information about these custom-creating elements from judgments if neither it nor the sources cited have actually done the necessary research.[98]

C. Precedents and the Austrian Pure Theorists

But there is another way in which we can employ the pure theory to analyse the problem of the exact legal status of precedents, namely by using the writings of those Austrian public law scholars applying the pure theory. Austrian public law scholarship in the second half of the twentieth century was heavily influenced by the pure theory and a number of texts use the pure theory to discuss the perennial question of judge-made law. We can draw valuable lessons for a reimagination of the situation in international law.

As mentioned in section I, the *Stufenbau* theory requires us to start by looking for an empowerment norm and so it is here: if we want to find out about judge-made law, we need to analyse the structure of empowerment relations. 'Whether judge-made law is a source of law is not a question of legal epistemology, but of the content of a positive legal order'.[99] And indeed, pure theorists have always argued that judgments are a central part of legal orders: 'Judge-made law is not an exception, but part of every single judgment. It is not an accidental, but a necessary part of the law; it is not a

[94] ibid 334–37.

[95] See *EnCana Corporation v Republic of Ecuador*, UNCITRAL, LCIA UN 3481, Award of 3 February 2006, para 177.

[96] Norton (n 67) 504.

[97] See, eg, Dinstein (n 88) 318; S Talmon, 'Determining Customary International Law. The ICJ's Methodology between Induction, Deduction and Assertion' (2015) 26 *European Journal of International Law* 417.

[98] See Dumberry (n 89) 44–47.

[99] C Jabloner, 'Richterrecht als Rechtsquelle?' in C Jabloner, D Kolonovits, G Kucsko-Stadlmayer, R Laurer, H Mayer and R Thienel, *Gedenkschrift Robert Walter* (Vienna, Manz, 2013) 185–202, 199: 'Ob Richterrecht

secondary, but a primary source of law'.[100] Legal orders regularly empower the creation of judgments as binding decisions of specific disputes, ie, as individual norms. These individual norms are part of the law, just as other general and individual norms are. A legal order can also empower the creation of judgments which are both individual and general norms.[101] Yet, a court may create norms of this type only if it is so empowered – as any organ may create norms only if and to the extent it is empowered to do so.[102] Post-war Austrian pure theorists have developed a comprehensive approach to the judiciary which is pertinent here, because the Austrian legal order leaves us in a similar position as international law: there is an indubitable authorisation to tribunals to create individual norms, but no explicit authorisation for tribunals to create general norms, yet great deference *in fact* being paid to jurisprudence.

Bridging the gap between their theoretical approach and that traditional deference has not been an easy task for this group of scholars. Bereft of arguments from natural law, they have had to resort to what must on first glance surely look like pragmatic half-measures. Robert Walter, for example, identifies our reliance on jurisprudence as 'judicial practice, the actual persistent practice of the courts'.[103] He holds out the tantalising possibility that it could be customary law in a wide sense,[104] but withdraws it immediately, as 'judicial practice' is a matter of fact only. Walter finds the argument that such a custom is 'factually binding' to be nonsensical: 'How should the jurist … deal with a binding force which is not legal in nature, but *de facto*? The connection in this case can only be causal, not normative'.[105] For Heinz Schäffer 'if judicial practice is not *contra legem*, it is a persistent interpretation (a *usus* of interpretation)'[106] with more, yet also less bindingness than a norm:

> It is less, because judicial practice is not binding as norm; it is more, because the 'force' of statutes, their importance in the real world depends on the (observable) 'practical bindingness' of the judiciary's interpretation of legal rules … This is not, however, legal bindingness, but a *prognosis of [future judicial] decision-making …*[107]

als Rechtsquelle gilt, ist keine Frage rechtstheoretischer Erkenntnis, sondern Sache einer positiven Rechtsordnung'.

[100] AJ Merkl, 'Gesetzesrecht und Richterrecht' (1922) 2 *Wissenschaftliche Vierteljahresschrift der Prager Juristischen Zeitschrift* 337 (WRS 1615–24, I/1 MerklGS 317–27), WRS 1617, I/1 MerklGS 319: 'Das Richterrecht tritt nicht nur ausnahmsweise, sondern … ausnahmslos in jedem Richterspruche in Erscheinung. Es ist keine bloß zufällige, sondern eine notwendige Erscheinungsform des Rechtes. Es ist nicht eine bloß subsidiäre, sondern eine primäre Rechtsquelle' (emphasis removed; the original publication was not available).

[101] Kelsen, *Reine Rechtslehre*, 2nd edn (n 9) 255.

[102] On the distinction between 'can create' and 'may create', see P Reimer, 'Können und Dürfen. Zur rechtstheoretischen Zentralität eines unterschätzten Begriffspaars' (2017) 48 *Rechtstheorie* 5 – and my solution in Kammerhofer, 'Fehlerkalkül ohne Fehler' (n 18) 160–65; Kammerhofer, '*Res Iudicata*' (n 1) 21.

[103] R Walter, 'Die Gewohnheit als rechtserzeugender Tatbestand' (1963) 18 *Österreichische Juristen-Zeitung* 225, 225: 'Unter Gerichtsgebrauch ist das tatsächliche ständige Vorgehen der Gerichte zu verstehen'.

[104] ibid 225.

[105] ibid 232: 'Aber was soll der Jurist … von einer Bindung halten, die nicht rechtlich, sondern tatsächlich – de facto – ist. Hier kann keine normative Verbindung, sondern nur eine kausale vorliegen' (emphasis removed).

[106] H Schäffer, 'Rechtsquellen und Rechtsanwendung' in *Verhandlungen des fünften Österreichischen Juristentages Wien 1973*, Vol I.1.B (Vienna, Manz, 1973) 68: 'Denn soweit kein gegen das Gesetz gebildeter Gerichtsgebrauch aufzufinden ist, handelt es sich eben um verfestigte Auslegung (Usualinterpretation)' (emphasis removed).

[107] ibid 69–70: 'Geringer, weil der Gerichtsgebrauch normativ nicht verbindlich ist, und größer, weil die "Kraft" des Gesetzes, seine reale Bedeutung davon abhängt, daß sich aller Erfahrung nach die Auslegung der

The most coherent pure theorist on this topic turns out to be Alfred Schramm. He argues that '[p]recedents elucidate the [applicable] norms and state them more precisely, they are … applied until a new interpretation supersedes the old one',[108] but are decidedly not identical to the individual norm contained in a judgment:[109]

> Precedents are something entirely different: they are general statements on the content of norms, *Rechtssätze*. They describe (interpret) norms, which are mostly general and abstract in scope, in general and abstract statements. They are interpretations which elucidate parts of specific norms applicable to a particular dispute in such a way that they [the interpretations] again take the form of general and abstract *Rechtssätze*.[110]

For Schramm, precedents do not appear to be norms: not only are precedents not binding on later tribunals as a norm prescribing the content of future tribunal decisions, they are also not general norms binding on all subjects of law, as proper judge-made law would be. 'Precedents … are not themselves norms nor individual nor specific … A precedent … is a description of how the delegating (empowerment) norm (or a part thereof) is to be understood'.[111] They cannot, therefore, ever become norms on their own terms, because they are statements about norms. Not even a constant tradition of similar decisions can turn a statement into a norm.[112] 'Judge-made law' via precedents is not norm-creation by judges, but an interpretation of a norm within the text of a judgment. 'In making new law, the organ [eg judge] has the freedom (within the margin of discretion) to create the legal act [judgment] according to his own ideas as to what the law requires'.[113]

The question as restated for international law is whether the jurisprudence of international tribunals is empowered to create general norms. While an analysis on the basis of the pure theory affirms emphatically that judgments of international tribunals are binding on the parties – because each award thus contains an individual norm with a narrow scope of application both *ratione personae* (the parties) and *ratione materiae* (the *dispositif*) – the real question is this: is there a *legal* basis for according the status of general norm to certain parts of judgments, can we find an empowerment norm that authorises the creation of general norms? No such norm is apparent for any

Rechtsvorschriften durch die Judikatur als "praktisch bindend" erweist … Allein, es handelt sich um keine Frage der Rechtsverbindlichkeit, sondern um eine Frage der *Entscheidungsprognose*'.

[108] A Schramm, '"Richterrecht" und Gesetzesrecht. Eine rechtsvergleichende Analyse anhand von Merkls Rechtsnormenlehre' (2005) 36 *Rechtstheorie* 185, 197: 'Präjudizien erläutern, präzisieren den Normbestand, sie werden … angewendet, bis eine neue Interpretation die alte ablöst'.

[109] ibid 198.

[110] ibid 198: 'Präjudizien besagen nämlich ganz anderes: sie sind allgemein-abstrakte normative Aussagen, also Rechtssätze. Sie beschreiben (interpretieren) Normen, die zumeist allgemein-abstrakt sind, wiederum in allgemein- abstrakten Sätzen. Sie sind Interpretationen, die einzelne unklare Teile von gegebenen im konkreten Rechtsfall anzuwendenden Normen anhand verschiedener Interpretationsmethoden dahingehend erläutern, daß wiederum allgemein-abstrakte Rechtssätze entstehen' (emphasis removed).

[111] ibid 198–99: 'Präjudizien … sind aber selbst weder Normen, noch individuell-konkret. … Das Präjudiz ist vielmehr die Beschreibung … wie die delegierende (ermächtigende) Norm (oder ein Teil dieser) verstanden wird' (emphasis removed).

[112] ibid 201.

[113] ibid 206–07: 'Beim Rechtsetzungsakt besteht also für das rechtsetzende Organ [den Richter] die Freiheit, den Rechtsakt [das Urteil] innerhalb des Ermessensspielraumes entsprechend seiner eigenen Überzeugung von Rechtsrichtigkeit zu gestalten'.

international court or tribunal. Hence, precedents as general prescriptions do not form part of the law – precedents may be factually important, but they are *legally not general law*: they neither add general norms nor do they modify existing (treaty or customary) law. On a structural analysis based on a re-application of the pure theory, precedents of international tribunals are best understood as statements on the content of the norm applied by the tribunal, 'a description of how the delegating (empowerment) norm (or a part thereof) is to be understood'[114] – and therefore propositions similar to those made by scholarship, possibly learned, but carrying as little legal authority as those of any scholar. The individual norm contained in a judgment, in contrast, is authoritative – and is so irrespective of its rationality or scholarly merit.

IV. Conclusion

The pure theory is probably the most thought-through and consistent approach to conducting a structural analysis of law – whatever its failings may be, even many of its critics will agree on that. But that does not mean that the only legitimate way to concern oneself with the pure theory is to conduct an intellectual-historical or exegetic-philosophical reconstruction of Hans Kelsen's writings – or that these endeavours should be our most pressing priorities. Rather, I have tried to make the case (for international law, but this is merely the example closest to my doctrinal specialisation) that the *application*, the reapplication, of the pure theory to doctrines about law is an even more fruitful endeavour. But why should we accept this contention; what is the advantage of 'reapplying' the pure theory, whatever that means?

An analysis of the structure and nomomechanical workings of a complex normative order can help us to adjudge the 'viability' of arguments advanced by scholarship (and practice), ie, whether the argument proposed will work, given the strictures of structure, or whether the structure allows for more freedom than claimed. In the example analysed in section III, structural analysis helped us to disclaim the argument from empirical necessity: 'case-law impinges upon the law, because we all agree that it is factually important'. It also helped to clearly mark out the method of proof required to be able to decide what precedents are: 'does the empowerment norm authorise the creation of norms with a general sphere of validity'?

In order to be able to achieve this sort of result, we cannot confine ourselves to the topics which Kelsen, Kunz or Verdross had focused on, or the arguments they had developed in their writings. We must explore new topics like international investment law, we must develop new arguments on the basis of a shared theoretical approach and yes, sometimes, we must disagree with our heroes. For example, Kelsen's reconstruction of the international legal order as coercive order may be internally coherent, but I strongly believe that it does not reflect the structure of post-1945 international law, and particularly of Chapter VII of the UN Charter.[115] Norm-theoretically, I doubt that the

[114] ibid 198–99: 'Beschreibung … wie die delegierende (ermächtigende) Norm (oder ein Teil dieser) verstanden wird' (emphasis removed).

[115] Kammerhofer, 'Kelsen – Which Kelsen?' (n 19).

coercive order paradigm in its strong form is correct – law is not a categorically different form of norms, there is only a typical and empirical difference between normative orders.[116]

The pure theory of law has an enormous advantage over many other theoretical approaches: it is (reasonably) philosophically sophisticated, but *prêt-à-porter*, ready to be applied in doctrinal debates about the law. Its head is not so high in the clouds that it prefers essayist musings to getting its hands dirty; its feet are not so deep in the mud that it would be no more than an apology of current legal practice. This is its strength in domestic law and, I believe, also in international law. Its disadvantages are obvious as well, however, for it neither can nor does it want to give an all-encompassing, a holistic explanation of the totality of law-related phenomena. There are tight limits to its respect for 'the reality of law' just as its tolerance of talk about 'absolute values' is non-existent; it also has no patience for pragmatic short-cuts in scholarship: it is a truly *scholarly* approach to legal scholarship.

[116] Kammerhofer, '*Robert Walter*' (n 18).

8

Kelsen and 'Primitive' International Law: Three Solutions and a Problem

PHIL EDWARDS

I. Introduction

Throughout his mature work, Hans Kelsen envisaged international law as a legal system, existing alongside and continuous with national legal systems. The systematicity of international law is not presented as an ideal against which the present state of the world can be critiqued; Kelsen acknowledged the relatively anarchic conditions in which international law found itself, but considered it as a legal system for all that. Nor did he suggest that international law had become a system relatively recently, or that any identifiable event led to its achieving that status: for Kelsen international law was already a system, existing in continuity with national legal systems, when it was first recognised as existing in any form.

This assumption prompts the question of whether this supposed system is an observable entity or only a theoretical construct. It also poses a question for Kelsen specifically: as Kelsen conceived legal systems, the system must be based on a presupposed basic norm, but what could that norm be? Kelsen's direct comments on these two questions are brief and unsatisfactory. Both can, however, be illuminated by reference to Kelsen's concept of a 'primitive' legal system – a category which Kelsen applied both to pre-literate societies and to international law. Using the concept of the 'primitive' set out in a relatively neglected work, 1943's *Society and Nature*, it is possible both to resolve the existence question for international law as a system and to suggest an appropriate candidate for a 'basic norm' of such a system.

The 'primitive' framing solved another, larger question for Kelsen: setting the pure theory in the context of a model of the history of human civilisation secured its ontological grounding, pointing a clear direction for future development of the law, in theory and practice. However, this solution posed a new problem: not every element of a legal system identified as 'primitive' could easily be expunged from the law, even in theory. The challenge of cleansing the pure theory of 'primitive' elements is one that Kelsen only pursued sporadically in the years after the publication of *Society and Nature*. The result was to leave the pure theory intact but ungrounded, setting the stage for the final turn in Kelsen's theoretical journey in the 1960s. This chapter is divided into seven sections. Following this introduction, section II sets out Kelsen's argument that international and domestic law must be seen as forming a single, 'universal' system (the systematicity assumption) and introduces the existence and basis questions. Section III discusses the concept of the 'primitive' legal order, setting *Society and Nature* in its historical and biographical context. Section IV analyses the models of 'primitive' justice and the 'primitive' legal order set out in *Society and Nature*, which are summarised as models of unqualified retributivism and unmediated community justice. Section V returns to the existence and basis questions regarding international law, showing how they can be addressed by reference to Kelsenian concepts of 'primitive' justice and the 'primitive' legal system. Section VI discusses the additional benefit which the 'primitive' model offered for Kelsen's theory and the problem that it posed. Section VII, the concluding section, situates Kelsen's difficult engagement with the 'primitive' in his intellectual career.

II. The Universal System

Kelsen advanced the systematicity assumption with respect to international law in 1934's *Introduction to the Problems of Legal Theory*:

> Since the jurist regards international law, like the state legal system, as a complex of valid or binding norms, and not – or not merely – as a conglomerate of natural facts, he must conceive of these complexes of norms in one non-contradictory system.[1]

This imperative followed from the 'cognitive unity of all law',[2] which in turn was grounded in three baldly stated assumptions: that 'legal cognition' has the same task as 'natural science'; that this task is 'to represent its object as a unity'; and that '[t]he negative criterion of this unity is non-contradiction'.[3] Legal cognition, for Kelsen, constitutes the law as a unified and non-contradictory system, existing within an autonomous sphere of meaning divorced from the real-world processes through which law is made.[4] Legal validity is seen as having 'a field of discourse comparable to that of truth';[5] just as no two true propositions can be mutually contradictory, neither can two valid legal propositions. It follows that legal science can only cognise law as a unity; both international law itself and the 'universal' system uniting it with domestic law must be understood as unified, non-contradictory systems.

Kelsen did not see this international legal order as a modern achievement, however. In both *Principles of International Law*[6] and *General Theory of Law and State*[7] he alludes to a period when 'there was no international law', but the time frame is remote:

> As long as there was no international law, the reason of the validity of national law was not determined by international law … When, however, an international law arose – that is to say,

[1] H Kelsen, *Introduction to the Problems of Legal Theory*, B Litschewski Paulson and SL Paulson trans (originally published 1934) (Oxford, Clarendon Press, 1992) 50b (references are to paragraph numbers).

[2] ibid 50a.

[3] ibid 50a.

[4] SL Paulson, 'The Purity Thesis' (2018) 31 *Ratio Juris* 276, 298.

[5] SL Paulson, 'Some Issues in the Exchange between H Kelsen and Erich Kaufmann' (2005) 48 *Scandinavian Studies in Law* 269, 285.

[6] H Kelsen, *Principles of International Law* (New York, Rinehart & Co, 1952).

[7] H Kelsen, *General Theory of Law and State*, A Wedberg trans (Cambridge, MA, Harvard University Press, 1945).

> when legal norms created by the cooperation of two or more states came into existence … the national legal orders were brought into that relationship to international law which is asserted by the monistic theory.[8]

An earlier formulation goes further: 'if law is the social organization of sanction, the original form of law must have been inter-tribal law, and, as such, a kind of international law'.[9]

In short, Kelsen asks us to envisage the international legal order as a discrete system of norms existing in a conceptually indissoluble unity with national law. He also asks us to bring under the scope of international law not only the relatively modern phenomenon of formal regulation of relations between nation states, but the customary regularities that previously governed those relations, for as long as any such relations existed. But in this case, what meaning can the word 'system' have? Does that system exist in any empirically observable form, or 'only in the minds of the scholars who have the time to muse about the theory of international law'?[10] As critics have charged, Kelsen's model of international law seems 'more than a little unreal'.[11]

One answer is that, once a basic norm has been inferred from the existence of 'a plurality of general and individual norms' with a shared 'basis of validity',[12] a legal system can in turn be inferred from that combination of positive norm and basic norm. However, this merely shifts the emphasis to the related question of the basic norm of international law – and if the international legal system is difficult to observe, its supposed basic norm is even more elusive. Kelsen's suggestions in this regard generally consist of brief formulations such as '[t]he States ought to behave as they have customarily behaved'.[13] Given the enormous range covered by inter-state 'custom' over history, this 'ought' appears to be a normative void.

III. The International and the 'Primitive'

An approach to both these questions is suggested by Kelsen's repeated assertion that international law is a 'primitive' legal order, comparable to the legal orders of pre-literate societies: '[i]nternational law is real law, but it is primitive law';[14] '[i]nternational law is still a primitive legal system … marked by wide-ranging decentralization'.[15]

For Kelsen, describing a decentralised legal order as 'primitive' carried with it the implication that centralised institutions would develop over time; he argued that legal systems developed everywhere 'from blood revenge toward … steadily increasing centralization of the coercive social order'.[16] Similar propositions, deriving a historical

[8] ibid 418–89 (emphasis added).

[9] H Kelsen, *Law and Peace in International Relations. The Oliver Wendell Holmes Lectures 1940–41* (Cambridge, MA, Harvard University Press, 1942) 42; cp Kelsen, *General Theory of Law and State* (n 7) 334.

[10] J Kammerhofer, 'The Benefits of the Pure Theory of Law for International Lawyers, Or: What Use Is Kelsenian Theory' (2006) 12 *International Legal Theory* 5, 52.

[11] R Clark, 'Hans Kelsen's pure theory of law' (1969) 22 *Journal of Legal Education* 170, 195.

[12] H Kelsen, 'The Concept of the Legal Order' (1982) 27 *American Journal of Jurisprudence* 64, 64 (originally published 1958 as 'Der Begriff der Rechtsordnung').

[13] Kelsen, *General Theory of Law and State* (n 7) 369.

[14] H Kelsen, 'The Pure Theory of Law and Analytical Jurisprudence' (1941) 55 *Harvard Law Review* 44, 66.

[15] Kelsen, *Introduction to the Problems of Legal Theory* (n 1) 49b.

[16] Kelsen, *General Theory of Law and State* (n 7) 339.

teleology from a quasi-organic model of law's essential nature, were common among jurists of the mid-twentieth century: in 1923 Frederick Pollock had likened international law to 'customs and observances … which have not fully acquired the character of law, but are on the way to become law',[17] while as late as 1958 JW Brierly argued that, while international law was perhaps 'an immature, little developed system', this was 'what the history of law teaches us to expect'.[18]

Some of these references to inherent developmental tendencies may have been rhetorical. Kelsen for his part seems to have believed in a literal process of social evolution. He drew an analogy with the 'biogenetic law', the (discredited) belief, derived from the nineteenth-century evolutionist Ernst Haeckel, that embryological development recapitulates the process of evolution:[19] 'perhaps the law of … the international community has to pass through the same evolution through which … national law has already passed'.[20] In line with this evolutionary model, Kelsen believed that contemporary law retained vestiges of the 'primitive', and that further development away from the 'primitive' state was both desirable and ultimately inevitable. Study of 'primitive' societies would thus help contemporary reformers to identify 'primitive' traits that had survived into contemporary thinking, the better to supersede them.

> These facts show clearly that the law of the interstate community develops in the same direction as the primitive law of the pre-state community. They also suggest the direction in which a relatively successful attempt may be undertaken to secure international peace by emphasizing and strengthening the given tendency toward centralization … a social reform has more chance of success if it follows the tendencies hitherto exhibited by social evolution.[21]

Kelsen addressed the 'primitive' world-view in works dating back to 1923;[22] it is a recurrent reference point in the context of international law, particularly in *General Theory of Law and State* and *Principles of International Law*. The fullest treatment in English is in 1943's *Society and Nature*,[23] which is an English-language revision of an earlier work, *Vergeltung und Kausalität* [*Retribution and Causality*] (hereafter *Vergeltung*).[24] Since *Society and Nature* in some areas moderates the arguments of *Vergeltung*, it should be read (by Anglophones) alongside 1939's 'The Emergence of the Causal Law from the Principle of Retribution',[25] which – like its German original[26] – follows *Vergeltung* where *Society and Nature* diverges from it.

[17] Cited in O Hathaway and S Shapiro, 'Outcasting: Enforcement in Domestic and International Law' (2011) 121 *Yale Law Journal* 252, 264.

[18] J Brierly, *'The Basis of Obligation in International Law' and Other Papers* (Oxford, Oxford University Press, 1958) 54.

[19] SJ Gould, *Ontology and Phylogeny* (Cambridge, MA, Harvard University Press, 1977).

[20] H Kelsen, 'Essential Conditions of International Justice' (1941) 35 *Proceedings of the American Society of International Law at its Annual Meeting (1921–1969)* 70, 76.

[21] Kelsen, *Law and Peace in International Relations* (n 9) 149–50.

[22] H Kelsen, 'God and the State' in H Kelsen, *Essays in Moral and Legal Philosophy* (originally published 1923) (Dordrecht, Reidel, 1973) 61–82.

[23] H Kelsen, *Society and Nature* (Chicago, University of Chicago Press, 1943).

[24] H Kelsen, *Vergeltung und Kausalität* (originally published 1941) (Wien, Böhlau, 1982) 6.

[25] H Kelsen, 'The Emergence of the Causal Law from the Principle of Retribution' in H Kelsen, *Essays in Moral and Legal Philosophy* (Dordrecht, Reidel, 1973) 165–215.

[26] H Kelsen, 'Die Entstehung des Kausalgesetzes aus dem Vergeltungsprinzip' (1939) 8 *Journal of Unified Science (Erkenntnis)* 424.

To understand the place of this ambitious but idiosyncratic work in the development of Kelsen's theory, it should be seen in its biographical context. *Vergeltung und Kausalität* was completed in 1940 and was to have been published the Netherlands in 1941, but did not appear until 1946. Kelsen had been dismissed from his university post in Köln when the Nazis came to power in 1933; he lived and worked in Geneva from 1934 to 1940, apart from a brief period teaching in Prague between 1936 and 1938. Between 1937 and 1940 he made repeated approaches to contacts in the United States, hoping to find a position there.[27] He secured temporary posts at Harvard in 1940 and in 1942 at Berkeley, where he was when *Society and Nature* was published. In 1945, approaching the age of 64, he gained a permanent position at Berkeley as Professor of Political Science. Thereafter Kelsen remained in California; he retired seven years later, although he continued to write for another 19 years.[28]

While Kelsen's interest in cultural anthropology can be traced back to the 1920s,[29] his active work in this area began in his Geneva years.[30] As well as being at the centre of a 'Viennese School' of jurisprudential colleagues and followers (which he maintained in different forms throughout his European travels), Kelsen had long been on the fringe of the Vienna Circle, an interdisciplinary group animated by a logical-positivist philosophy of science. Multiple Vienna Circle figures are cited in the third section of *Society and Nature*; indeed, in this period Kelsen seems to have seen himself more as a polymath than as a legal theorist. In 1938 he wrote to the director of the Princeton Institute for Advanced Study, introducing himself as 'a scientist working across multiple disciplines … dealing with multifaceted and perspective-rich topics such as the problem of justice and causal thinking in modern science'.[31] Both in Geneva and at Harvard, he was active in the 'unity of science' movement, participating in the Fifth and Sixth International Congresses for the Unity of Science in 1939 and 1941. In 1941 he gave a version of the paper 'Causality and Retribution'[32] to the Harvard Science of Science Discussion Group – a multidisciplinary group including Vienna Circle alumni Rudolf Carnap and Philipp Frank.[33]

The projected unification of science – the application of a single scientific method and set of concepts across multiple disciplines – entailed the elimination of unjustifiable claims to uniqueness and incommensurability, in the social as well as the physical sciences. This was a natural fit with the debunking tenor of Kelsen's writings on the law, state and justice ('[a]ccording to Kelsen, all idealizations that are also unnecessary

[27] R Cadore, '"Good-bye to all that"? Ein österreichisches Schicksal: Wanderungen und Wandlungen im rechtstheoretischen Exilwerk H Kelsens' in M Beck and and N Coomann (eds), *Historische Erfahrung und begriffliche Transformation. Deutschsprachige Philosophie im Exil in den USA 1933–1945* (Wien, LIT, 2018) 249–74, 251.

[28] SL Paulson, 'Metamorphosis in Hans Kelsen's Legal Philosophy' (2017) 80 *Modern Law Review* 860, 860, fn 1.

[29] ibid 889, 887, fn 111.

[30] L Gross, 'Hans Kelsen: October 11, 1886[sic]–April 15, 1973' (1973) 67 *American Journal of International Law* 491, 494.

[31] Cadore (n 27) 252 (author's translation).

[32] H Kelsen, 'Causality and Retribution' (1941) 8 *Philosophy of Science* 533.

[33] C Jabloner, 'Kelsen and his Circle: The Viennese Years' (1998) 9 *European Journal of International Law* 368, 380, fn 54; G Hardcastle, 'Debabelizing Science: The Harvard Science of Science Discussion Group, 1940–41' in G Hardcastle and A Richardson (eds), *Logical Empiricism in North America. Minnesota Studies in the Philosophy of Science XVIII* (Minneapolis, University of Minnesota, 2003) 170–96, 173–74.

are indefensible').[34] *Society and Nature* can be seen as part of a ground-clearing exercise, preparing for nothing less than the unification of natural and social science. Kelsen's specific point of attack was causality. He argued that pre-Enlightenment science had wrongly projected a universal causal law, understood in Kantian terms as a category of the understanding, onto the material world, and that this category of causality was in any case not (*pace* Kant) 'a form of thought necessarily given to human consciousness'[35] but a mental construct with a historical lifespan: it had been unknown to 'primitive' societies, and it was no longer required by contemporary science. To establish this argument, Kelsen traced the development of the concept of causality prior to the Enlightenment period and its supersession by post-Enlightenment scientific developments.

It should be noted that Kelsen's pure theory would also require modification in the light of the unification of science, and the dethroning of universal causality specifically. Kelsen's *Sollen* – the legal 'ought' – had been constructed 'in strict analogy with the (neo-)Kantian category of causality'.[36] The logical corollary of situating Kantian causality as a conceptual relic was that the Kelsenian *Sollen* faced the same fate; this would deprive the pure theory of any claim to logical necessity and reduce it to a 'legal point of view'.[37] In *Society and Nature* Kelsen acknowledged the destabilising implication that the legal 'ought' might be ripe for supersession, but did not develop it. (It may be significant that the foreword to *Vergeltung* presents it as the first part of a two-part critique of concepts of justice;[38] the sequel never appeared, nor is there any reference to a larger project on justice in the introduction to *Society and Nature*).

Society and Nature is divided into three sections: a lengthy ethnographic investigation of the belief systems of pre-literate societies; a substantial overview of ancient Greek religion and philosophy; and a fairly brief discussion of contemporary philosophy of science. Kelsen's thesis was that, in 'primitive' societies, personal responsibility and retribution had substituted for any concept of causation, all events being understood in terms of retribution (literal or supernatural). This confusion of ideas persisted, Kelsen argued, into a conflation of causality and divine retribution which characterised classical Greek religion and philosophy. This in turn influenced the early development of Western science, whose rigidly deterministic model of causation – 'causality as a concatenation of two events immanently connected with one another in an irreversible chronological order'[39] – represented retributivism in scientific clothing. This version of causality had later been called into question by Hume's scepticism and Kant's transcendental idealism (considered by Kelsen as an extension to Humean scepticism, relocating law-like causation from the world to the human mind). Mechanistic causality had subsequently been superseded altogether by the more sophisticated scientific concepts of functional interdependency, statistical regularity and the conservation of energy.[40]

[34] A Somek, 'Kelsen Lives' (2007) 18 *European Journal of International Law* 409, 411.
[35] Kelsen, 'Emergence' (n 25) 166.
[36] C Heidemann, *Hans Kelsen's Normativism* (Cambridge, Cambridge University Press, 2022) 53.
[37] SL Paulson, 'The Neo-Kantian Dimension of Kelsen's Pure Theory of Law' (1992) 12 *Oxford Journal of Legal Studies* 311, 332.
[38] Paulson, 'Metamorphosis in Hans Kelsen's Legal Philosophy' (n 28) 887, fn 111.
[39] Kelsen, *Society and Nature* (n 23) 76 (references are to paragraph numbers).
[40] ibid 76, 77, 74.

In the final section of the book, Kelsen asserts briefly that modern science had now successfully broken with the relics of retributivism, cementing the division between the scientific and normative realms. The social sciences (law included) had yet to make a similar break; this would require 'a critical analysis of the nature of the norm'.[41] (In *Vergeltung* and 'Emergence' Kelsen had gone further, proposing 'a dissolution of the concept of norm').[42] That achieved, the last bastion of retributivism would fall, allowing for a wholly scientific understanding of society. 'After the complete emancipation of causality from retribution in the modern notion of law, society is – from the point of view of science – a part of nature'.[43] Thus the social and natural sciences would be unified, adopting a common vocabulary of cause and effect (correctly understood); while one would abandon rigidly mechanistic causation, the other would be cleansed of retributivism, with its unjustifiable claim to elevate human responsibility above any causal considerations.[44]

This late flourish – and *Society and Nature's* broader ambitions – attracted less notice than the book's first section: devoted to the supposed world-view of 'primitive' peoples, this makes up 70 per cent of the book (185 of its 266 main pages and 84 of 118 pages of endnotes). (*Vergeltung* is a little less unbalanced: the first section accounts for 60 per cent of the book (170 of 284 main pages and 151 of 258 pages of 'Belege und Exkurse' ['Notes and Digressions']).) Kelsen's venture into ethnography displays impressive erudition alongside a single-minded dedication to his thesis and what can seem a wilful lack of methodological sophistication. Kelsen deploys quotations from an extraordinary range of reading: one six-page section cites 20 different nineteenth-century and twentieth-century anthropological sources ranging across five continents, as well as a seventeenth-century missionary and a Roman observer of the 'primitive' Celts.[45] These sources are treated without distinction of region, period or genre; all are taken as providing evidence on a single underlying object, the 'primitive' mindset. Kelsen's thesis is upheld against all possible challenges – including, on occasion, alternative interpretations offered by his sources, with whom lengthy disputes are pursued in the endnotes.

Contemporary reviews were largely negative. Talcott Parsons dismissed the book as 'definitely incompetent' as sociology, charging that '[Kelsen] quotes freely, from sociological and anthropological authorities, opinions and facts which seem to him to bear out his own pre-conceived ideas'.[46] Even the more appreciative C Wright Mills noted that '[Kelsen's] apparently random selection of primitive data and some of the inferences which he draws from them are at times dubious'.[47] Reviewers were scornful of Kelsen's insistence that, in the world-view of 'primitive' peoples, the category of retribution completely substituted for that of causality: '[n]o primitive expects water

[41] ibid 82.
[42] Kelsen, 'Emergence' (n 25) 202.
[43] Kelsen, *Society and Nature* (n 23) 82.
[44] H Kelsen, 'Causality and Imputation' (1950) 61 *Ethics* 1, 7–9.
[45] Kelsen, *Society and Nature* (n 23) 10.
[46] T Parsons, 'Review: Society and Nature, A Sociological Inquiry by H Kelsen' (1944) 58 *Harvard Law Review* 140, 140.
[47] C Wright Mills, 'Review: Society and Nature, A Sociological Inquiry by H Kelsen' (1944) 59 *Political Science Quarterly* 102, 104.

to run up hill, however much its running down hill may be clothed in the evocative imagery of reward and punishment'.[48] Even Kelsen's use of the racially loaded term 'primitive' – with its connotations of childlike innocence and limited mental capacity – is criticised by Mills, who noted that many contemporary ethnologists preferred the term 'pre-literate'.[49] Kelsen's insistence that he was using the term 'in the sense customary among modern ethnologists'[50] can perhaps be qualified by Parsons' assessment that Kelsen's approach was outdated by 'a generation' or more.[51]

Society and Nature, its first section in particular, thus presents an odd combination of erudition, analytical insight and untenable assumptions. It imposes a developmental model of human society on its subjects, who are taken as exemplifying a stage before that development had begun; it deliberately minimises any differences between distinct cultures, or between religious belief and practical consciousness. Its methodological reductivism and exoticising orientalism were recognised as major flaws by contemporary reviewers and certainly cannot be overlooked now.

Society and Nature has attracted constructive scholarly attention more recently, however, with useful discussions of the evolution of law from its 'primitive' beginnings,[52] of Kelsen's evolutionist model[53] and of Kelsen's thesis on the origin of causality in its contemporary context.[54] What Kelsen offered as a scientific description of the mentality of an earlier stage in human social development is increasingly being understood as a set of assumptions inferred from accumulated documentation of a wide range of social and cultural practices, and organised around a conceptual framework which Kelsen was developing for use in his own work. Kelsen's 'primitive' can then be understood as a term of art denoting key characteristics of communities and cultures existing without a centralised authority, and providing a reference point with which the culture and institutions of modern societies can be contrasted.

IV. Anatomy of a Mindset

For Kelsen, 'primitive' societies were characterised by features including a 'social' relationship to the world, including the natural world; a tendency to 'substantialise', understanding good and ill fortune as quantifiable substances; and collective rather than individual subjectivity. Taken together, these characteristics grounded a world-view of unqualified retributivism. The legal order embodying this world-view would be characterised, Kelsen argued, by a reliance on custom as the sole source of law; 'self-help'

[48] E Garlan, 'Review: Society and Nature, A Sociological Inquiry by H Kelsen' (1944) 41 *Journal of Philosophy* 521, 526.

[49] Wright Mills (n 47) 104.

[50] Kelsen, 'Emergence' (n 25) 166, note 4.

[51] Parsons (n 46) 140.

[52] P di Lucia and L Passerini Glazel, 'Hans Kelsen's Philosophy of Revenge' in R Márquez Porras et al (eds), *Vindicatory Justice* (Cham, Springer-Verlag, 2022) 39–53.

[53] M García-Salmones, 'On Kelsen's *Sein*: an approach to Kelsenian sociological themes' (2011) 8 *NoFo* 41; S Sammarco, 'The 'Vendetta System' in Hans Kelsen's Theory of the Evolution of Legal Orders' (conference paper), IVR 2019.

[54] A Górnisiewicz, 'Totemism of the Modern State: On Hans Kelsen's Attempt to Unmask Legal and Political Fictions and Contain Political Theology' (2020) 33 *Ratio Juris* 49.

as enforcement mechanism; and no distinction between the community and its legal system. While the 'law' of such a society would be based on blood revenge, with one group targeting another, Kelsen maintained that this constituted both a legal and a moral institution. Moreover, he argued, this 'primitive' retributivism was the historical source not only of modern concepts of justice and exchange, but also of the (since superseded) mechanistic concept of causality.

Kelsen argues, first, that the 'primitive' world-view assimilates the world to human society: 'there is no such thing as "nature" in the sense of a connection of elements determined by causal laws and distinct from society'.[55] With no conception of 'the endless chain of cause and effect', the 'primitive' observer 'traces events, which he wishes to understand … not to an object but to a subject, not to a thing but to a person',[56] and 'does not investigate beyond the real or imaginary person to whom the event to be explained is attributed'.[57] This 'animistic view of nature'[58] projects a social consciousness onto the natural world. 'The relationship of primitive man to nature is based … upon the assumption of a social relationship',[59] and specifically a retributive relationship: 'the fundamental principle which determines primitive man's behaviour toward nature is the same as that which decides his conduct toward the members of his own and other groups – the social principle of retribution'.[60]

The tendency to substantialise, secondly, involves considering 'mental and especially moral qualities' – in particular the good or bad quality of actions – 'as substances, which in some way stick to, or are inherent in, the body'.[61] Thus, for example, confession of sin entails physical purification, while anticipatory purification rituals lift the danger of punishment and hence bring good luck: '[a]bsolved of sin, [the hunter] will be able to evade that much worse punishment, namely that the animals will not allow themselves to be caught'.[62] If a wrongful deed has been committed, the burden incurred must be discharged by suffering punishment; conversely, if a wrongful deed has been suffered, that burden must be discharged by inflicting punishment. Any adverse event can thus be interpreted either as a wrongful deed that ought to be punished or as punishment for some wrongful deed already committed.[63] The 'primitive' 'never forgets any injury and considers revenge justifiable under all circumstances',[64] and believes more broadly in 'a certain rigidity governing events – no punishment without wrong, no reward without merit'.[65] Moreover, considering the good or evil effects of an act and its reciprocating act as substances enables them to be matched to one another, and in some sense quantified. Thus, the substantialising tendency 'makes man – even civilized man – believe that the evil which one sustains and the evil which one must inflict according to the principle of retribution can and shall be "equal"'.[66]

[55] Kelsen, 'Causality and Retribution' (n 32) 533–34.
[56] Kelsen, *Society and Nature* (n 23) 14.
[57] ibid 15.
[58] ibid 13.
[59] ibid 15.
[60] ibid 17.
[61] ibid 5.
[62] ibid 30.
[63] ibid 33.
[64] ibid 24.
[65] ibid 80.
[66] ibid 23.

Collective subjectivity, thirdly, is grounded in the substantialising tendency, as the social group itself is seen metaphorically as a substance, or as the social counterpart of a literal substance such as blood. The idea of consanguinity as a 'substance which connects an individual to his group'[67] is strong in 'primitive' communities – so strong that 'it is self-evident … that the whole group is responsible for a wrong committed by a single member'.[68] (Kelsen also notes 'the striking lack of any socially organized sanction' against crimes 'committed within the group itself').[69] Moreover, 'collective responsibility is always absolute responsibility since it cannot be based on the fault of the responsible individuals'.[70] Kelsen repeatedly stresses the validity of a morality of collective and absolute liability, pointing out that these conceptions of liability are not entirely absent from contemporary law.[71]

The world-view of a 'primitive' society, as described by Kelsen, is thus one where all events, whatever their actual cause or source, are interpreted as motivated acts by real or imagined agencies and classed as good or evil; where these acts are understood within a retributive framework, either as acts of retribution in themselves or as creating a burden to be discharged through retribution; and where individuals are considered primarily as members of their kin group, to the point where these collective subjects are seen as committing and undergoing actions both good and bad. This last assumption permits retribution to proceed directly from the experience of a wrong done, with no need to identify a responsible individual. Taken together, these assumptions thus add up to a world-view of unqualified retributivism: all events are to be met with quantified retribution against an undifferentiated collectivity.

The unqualified retributivism of a 'primitive' society, Kelsen argues, was expressed through a legal order with distinctive characteristics, in terms of the sources of law, the process of enforcement and law's institutional embodiment. Kelsen links '[the] submission of the individual to the group' to 'the customary character of the formation of law' and 'exaggeratedly scrupulous observation of customs and usages inherited from, and watched over by, the ancestors'.[72] The present-day community is considered as an extension of the ancestral community, which demands conformity: 'the ancestors are offended and punish with failure if their descendants do not act as they themselves acted, but reward with success if they do'.[73] The perpetuation of the past takes priority over innovation; tradition and custom are seen, not merely as the source of law, but as the only possible source. Kelsen stresses that it is exclusive reliance on custom, rather than recourse to custom itself, which differentiates 'primitive' from modern societies: '[t]here are two methods of creating law: custom, that is, the repeated similar conduct of the subject, and legislation in the broadest sense of the word',[74] and law created by both methods is equally valid.

[67] ibid 5.
[68] ibid 42.
[69] ibid 6.
[70] Kelsen, *Principles of International Law* (n 6) 122.
[71] Kelsen, *Society and Nature* (n 23) 55, fn 150; H Kelsen, 'What is Justice?' in H Kelsen, *Essays in Moral and Legal Philosophy* (originally published 1952) (Dordrecht, Reidel, 1973) 1–26, 12.
[72] Kelsen, *Society and Nature* (n 23) 6.
[73] ibid.
[74] H Kelsen, 'The Law as a Specific Social Technique' (1941) 9 *University of Chicago Law Review* 75, 87.

While custom substitutes for legislation in a 'primitive' society, 'self-help' substitutes for adjudication and enforcement. 'The primitive law of self-help is characterized by the fact that the general norm is applied directly to the concrete instance without being individualized by an individual norm'; if a law is violated, the victim is 'authorized by the legal order to react against the violator of the law with the sanction provided by the law'.[75] Thus when members of the victim's group take revenge on the perpetrator's group, revenge is nevertheless carried out by 'organs' of the legal order: '[e]ven the primitive legal order … has organs';[76] an individual is an organ 'because and in so far as he performs a law-creating or a law-applying function'.[77] Kelsen maintains, counter-intuitively, that this type of violence is 'a monopoly of the community', as the act of vengeance is 'undertaken in execution of the legal order';[78] he stresses that 'a social order is considered as law even if it establishes only a decentralized force monopoly'.[79] Indeed, Kelsen takes the antiquity of blood revenge to show that human society 'from the very beginning has the character of a legal and at the same time moral order'.[80]

The third question about the 'primitive' legal order, concerning its institutional location, had been answered *ex negativo* in *Introduction to the Problems of Legal Theory*, where Kelsen challenges the dualism of law and state: 'The state, then, is a legal system … When the legal system has achieved a certain degree of centralization, it is characterized as a state'.[81] He goes on to identify 'primitive' communities as having a legal system which had not achieved the necessary centralisation. Elsewhere he argues that the legal order of a 'primitive' community not only predates the state but develops with the community itself: 'History presents no social condition in which large communities have been constituted other than by coercive orders'.[82] The assumption that the state was an entity distinct from the legal system was, ironically, a product of the animistic thinking characteristic of 'primitive' communities:

> The state as a power back of the law, as sustainer, creator, or source of the law – all these expressions are only verbal doublings of the law as the object of cognition … [akin to] the animistic presentations according to which 'souls' inhabit things; dryads, trees; nymphs, springs.[83]

If the state can be identified with the legal order that regulates a centralised community, then the legal order regulating a decentralised community (with laws based entirely on custom and 'self-help' by way of enforcement) can be identified with the community itself: 'the community consists only in [its] ordering … the order and the community are not two different things but two different aspects of the same thing'.[84]

[75] ibid 88.
[76] Kelsen, *Law and Peace in International Relations* (n 9) 59.
[77] Kelsen, *General Theory of Law and State* (n 7) 192.
[78] ibid 339.
[79] Kelsen, *Principles of International Law* (n 6) 16.
[80] Kelsen, *Society and Nature* (n 23) 21.
[81] Kelsen, *Introduction to the Problems of Legal Theory* (n 1) 48a.
[82] Kelsen, 'The Law as a Specific Social Technique' (n 74) 82.
[83] Kelsen, *Law and Peace in International Relations* (n 9) 70.
[84] ibid 73.

The 'primitive' community's unqualified retributivism involved normative judgement of all events, the infliction of measured retribution and collective subjectivity. To this picture we can now add the features of a 'primitive' legal order: an unmediated community justice, combining customary law, blood revenge rather than state-backed enforcement and the identification of the legal order with the community as a whole. By contrast, contemporary criminal justice is characterised by institutionalised adjudication and centralised enforcement of documented norms, which typically mandate a quantified retributive response against individuals found to have been responsible for one of a defined class of actions. Rather than emphasise these differences, however, Kelsen insists that the 'primitive' order is the modern system's direct forebear, and that the former was both a legal and a moral order: '[e]ven the social community of the most primitive of primitives … is a legal community'[85] – and 'every social order is virtually a moral order'.[86]

One key question remains: given that the beliefs and practices of 'primitive' communities discussed in *Society and Nature* had been documented under the headings of custom, ritual, religion and myth, why should they be considered as forming a single 'order' in each community – and why should this order be recognised as a legal order? As Marmor asks, '[i]f there are no rules of recognition, how can [members of a community] tell the difference between following the law and any other set of norms they follow or think that they ought to follow[?]'.[87]

An initial response would be that Kelsen's subject (here and elsewhere) was not how members of a society recognised law as law, or what role they considered law to play in their lives. Kelsen's aim in defining the law was not to clarify existing usage by 'repeat[ing] in clear language what common sense has known all along'[88] but to analyse the structure and function of law as an entity, irrespective of how it was generally understood. Kelsen saw the law as a normative system, which existed – for an individual observer and for a society – for as long as it was believed to impose obligations: '[f]or Kelsen, if one does not consider the law as normative, one simply does not speak of law at all, but instead one refers to power relations'.[89] Moreover, while '[t]he law *is* normativity',[90] normativity was not law's exclusive property:

> [I]f we interpret definite human behavior according to a moral, religious, or legal law as merit, sin, or crime, we impute the consequences determined by the moral, religious, or legal law … The moral, religious, or legal question of imputation is: Who is responsible for these acts? And that means: Who ought to be rewarded? Who ought to do penance? Who ought to be punished?[91]

The word 'law', Kelsen wrote, 'refers to that specific social technique of a coercive order … which consists in bringing about the desired social conduct of men through

[85] Kelsen, 'The Law as a Specific Social Technique' (n 74) 82.
[86] Kelsen, *Society and Nature* (n 23) 22.
[87] A Marmor, 'How law is like chess' (2006) 12 *Legal Theory* 347, 363.
[88] C Kletzer, 'The Role and Reception of the Work of Hans Kelsen in the United Kingdom' in R Walter, C Jabloner and K Zeleny (eds), *Hans Kelsen anderswo. Hans Kelsen Abroad* (Wien, Manz, 2010) 133–67, 149.
[89] S Delacroix, 'Hart's and Kelsen's Concepts of Normativity Contrasted' (2004) 17 *Ratio Juris* 501, 516.
[90] Kletzer (n 88) 162 (emphasis in original).
[91] Kelsen, 'Causality and Imputation' (n 44) 7.

threat of a measure of coercion which is to be applied in case of contrary conduct'.[92] This is the *differentia specifica* of law: if law 'claims to trump moral and other reasons for action', the reason is not that its right to coerce gives it a superior claim to obedience, but 'that it claims a right to coerce *simpliciter*'.[93] The question of whether the 'primitive' communities discussed in *Society and Nature* were structured as legal orders equates to the question of whether they were ordered by norms whose infraction brought collectively approved punishment. Practices of unmediated community justice, embodying an ethic of unqualified retributivism, represent just such a normative system. 'Primitive' communities can thus be seen as constituted by a legal order – and it can fairly be said that Kelsen's theory 'allows us to perceive a well-functioning legal system where others would … observe a lack of organization or even nothing at all'.[94]

Having identified the legal order of the earliest human communities – the original model from which later orders have developed and whose evolutionary traces they still bear – Kelsen goes further. He notes that a normative interpretation of the natural world not only substitutes social obligation for natural necessity but enables the observer to judge when those obligations have been broken. Consequently, Kelsen argues, when physical laws were later identified, they were seen as weighing on nature with the burden of normative necessity: unqualified retributivism thus underlies pre-modern ideas of natural causality.[95] Unqualified retributivism also lies at the root of the concept of exchange: 'equivalence between the wrong sustained and the wrong to be inflicted … makes retribution appear a kind of exchange, although it is more correct to consider exchange a special kind of retribution'.[96]

For Kelsen, the legal order of 'primitive' communities was thus an epochal cultural achievement. A moral and legal institution dating back to the earliest human societies, it underpinned the emergence of cultural developments in fields ranging from economics to the physical sciences, as well as underlying contemporary concepts of law and justice.

V. The 'Primitive' and the International

Given the caveats made earlier concerning Kelsen's approach to ethnography, the foregoing should not be considered as making factual assertions about pre-literate societies. The interest of the first section of *Society and Nature* lies not in its ethnography but in its elaboration of Kelsen's concept of the 'primitive', representing the minimum conditions of a legal order. This is the larger sense in which international law, for Kelsen, was 'primitive' law.

[92] Kelsen, 'The Law as a Specific Social Technique' (n 74) 79; see also Kelsen, *General Theory of Law and State* (n 7) 19.

[93] T Spaak, 'Kelsen and Hart on the Normativity of Law' in P Wahlgren (ed), *Perspectives on Jurisprudence: Essays in Honor of Jes Bjarup* (Stockholm, Stockholm University Press, 2005) 397–414, 413; see also E Yankah, 'The Force of Law: The Role of Coercion in Legal Norms' (2008) 42 *University of Richmond Law Review* 1195.

[94] Somek (n 34) 414.

[95] Kelsen, *Society and Nature* (n 23) 15.

[96] ibid 23.

Kelsen sees international law as having the key characteristics of 'primitive' law, namely unrestricted but quantified retribution between collective subjects: '[b]lood revenge … is the reaction of one group against another group. It is precisely this principle which characterizes the technique of international law'.[97] Similarly, the international legal system can be seen as an order of unmediated community justice. Historically, international law has lacked both an identifiable institutional location and an enforcement arm; the international legal order has effectively been identical with the community itself, with any penalties imposed by collective subjects of that order on one another. Equally, prior to the historically recent development of statutory international law, international law's obligations were wholly based on custom.

While Kelsen believed in the possibility and desirability of transition from a world of nation states to a World State, he did not see this as (in Hart's terminology) a passage from a pre-legal to a legal world,[98] but merely as a process of increasing centralisation and formalisation. If a 'primitive' coercive order – with informal adjudication and diffuse enforcement of customary norms, mandating retribution against collective subjects for an undefined range of events – could qualify as a legal system, the fact that international law had only recently and unevenly developed beyond that 'primitive' state would plainly not disqualify it.

A number of related objections can be considered. Lauterpacht's argument that to remove the requirement for any kind of centralisation or formalisation was 'to reduce the law to a shadow of its own self'[99] has some force; a Kelsenian response might be that, given the commonalities between 'primitive' and centralised legal systems, what remains is not law's shadow but its essence. Campbell's thoughtful dissection of the components of a 'primitive' legal system[100] succeeds in establishing that Kelsen's model is a poor fit both for actually existing international law and for some of the legal practices found in pre-literate societies; similarly, Rigaux objects that contemporary international law is not 'primitive' at all, but 'the law of a "civilised" community … which has set up a very sophisticated approach to the rule of law'.[101] However, these critiques misapply Kelsen's model, in particular undervaluing its evolutionary component. The argument is not that international law is always and irremediably 'primitive', but that the international legal order began as wholly decentralised – and hence wholly 'primitive' – and has only partially and imperfectly developed beyond that.

The 'primitive' model also suggests a candidate for basic norm of the international legal order, although this argument is more speculative and runs counter to suggestions by Kelsen himself, which will first be reviewed. Having formulated the concept of 'basic norm' – albeit not under that name – as early as 1914,[102] Kelsen suggested in 1920 that the maxim *pacta sunt servanda* was 'the legal proposition underlying international law's

[97] Kelsen, *Law and Peace in International Relations* (n 9) 98.

[98] HLA Hart, *The Concept of Law*, 3rd edn (originally published 1961) (Oxford, Oxford University Press, 2012) 94.

[99] H Lauterpacht, *The Function of Law in the International Community* (Oxford, Clarendon Press, 1933) 433.

[100] A Campbell, 'International Law and Primitive Law' (1988) 8 *Oxford Journal of Legal Studies* 169.

[101] F Rigaux, 'Hans Kelsen on International Law' (1998) 9 *European Journal of International Law* 325, 337.

[102] H Kelsen, 'Reichsgesetz und Landesgesetz nach österreichischer Verfassung' (1914) 32 *Archiv des öffentlichen Rechts* 202; cited in U Bindreiter, 'Presupposing the Basic Norm' (2001) 14 *Ratio Juris* 143, 145.

binding nature'.[103] In *Introduction to the Problems of Legal Theory* he described *pacta* as a norm of 'special significance', but suggested that the basic norm of international law must be 'a norm that establishes custom – the reciprocal behaviour of the states – as a law-establishing material fact'.[104] In later work he reiterated this formulation and offered suggestions as to the proposed norm, notably '[t]he States ought to behave as they have customarily behaved'[105] and the more detailed formulation in 1960's *Reine Rechtslehre* (unfortunately garbled in the 1967 English translation):

> States, i.e. the governments of the states, in their mutual relations ought to behave in a way that conforms – or, coercion of state against state ought to be exercised under conditions that conform and in a way that conforms – with the custom constituted by the actual behaviour of the states.[106]

Some critiques of Kelsen's proposed 'basic norm' for international law can be set aside. Mitchell argues that the invocation of state custom in *General Theory of Law and State* shows Kelsen abandoning *pacta* and embracing customary law in the wake of the Nuremberg trials, which – with their retroactive penalties and invocation of unwritten legal principles – left him 'reeling from the collapse of his previous *Grundnorm*'.[107] The argument is suggestive but cannot be endorsed, implying as it does that *pacta* was Kelsen's proposed basic norm until 1945. Hart's suggestion that the *General Theory of Law and State* formulation is a 'useless reduplication of the fact that a set of rules are accepted by states as binding rules'[108] is less persuasive. The assertion that the statement 'states should continue to act as they do' duplicates the implicit statement 'states act in certain ways' is plainly flawed: in Kelsen's own formulation, '[f]rom the fact that something is or happens, it does not logically follow that it … ought to be or ought to happen'.[109] In any case, the norm in question makes no reference to rules; rather, it is phrased so as to establish customary behaviour as a stable normative reference point to which positive rules could then refer, making it possible to build a rule-based order on a foundation of custom.

Kammerhofer's critique of Kelsen's basic norm of international law is more substantial, and forms part of his argument for pluralism ('[b]ehind Kelsen's … answer that there can "really" only be one "true" law, lies piety more than consistency').[110] Kammerhofer stresses the observable existence of different 'branches' of international law (notably

[103] Quoted in R Mitchell, 'International Law as Coercive Order: Hans Kelsen and the transformations of sanction' (2019) 29 *Indiana International & Comparative Law Review* 245, 254, fn 47.

[104] Kelsen, *Introduction to the Problems of Legal Theory* (n 1) 49a.

[105] Kelsen, *General Theory of Law and State* (n 7) 369. See also Kelsen, *Law and Peace in International Relations* (n 9) 418; H Kelsen, 'Why Should the Law be Obeyed?' in H Kelsen, *What is Justice? Justice, Law and Politics in the Mirror of Science. Collected Essays by Hans Kelsen* (Berkeley, University of California Press, 1957) 257–65, 264; Kelsen, 'The Concept of the Legal Order' (n 12).

[106] H Kelsen, *Pure Theory of Law*, M Knight trans (originally published 1960 as *Reine Rechtslehre*) (translation modified) (Berkeley, University of California Press, 1967) 34h (references are to paragraph numbers).

[107] Mitchell (n 103) 278.

[108] Hart (n 98) 236.

[109] H Kelsen, 'Value judgments in the science of law' (1942) 7 *Journal of Social Philosophy & Jurisprudence* 312, 321.

[110] J Kammerhofer, 'Kelsen – Which Kelsen? A Reapplication of the Pure Theory to International Law' (2009) 22 *Leiden Journal of International Law* 225, 244.

custom and treaty) with no discernible logical or historical priority between them,[111] as well as the difficulty of identifying anything recognisable as international law's 'constitution'.[112]

However, these points are not decisive. No 'positive act of will creating … customary international law'[113] is required; it is the presupposed basic norm that creates international law by rendering established practice into prospective law – or rather, that is retrospectively seen as having done so. What can be traced in history is the first 'positive [acts] of will' which are seen as having been framed in terms of that basic norm and as having set precedents for subsequent such acts; these acts represent the 'constitution' of international law. If this point is granted, the problem of identifying whether the foundational layer of international law was the chicken of treaty or the egg of custom is more tractable: the earliest international treaties seem likely to have rested on a pre-existing body of international custom, rather than the reverse.

Kelsen's proposed basic norm of international law thus seems fit for purpose, at least relative to contemporary international law. However, as we have seen, Kelsen's own understanding of international law ranged much more widely – functionally as well as in time – and in that broader context Kelsen's proposed basic norm is an odd and unsatisfactory formulation. First and most fundamentally, the norm bears on the putative behaviour of states, not individuals. The option of assuming that, because the basic norm governs the interaction of states, it presupposes their existence is firmly closed off by Kelsen's consistent denial that the state had any independent reality: '[a]s a power, the state is the effectiveness of the legal order, and as an order … it is this legal order itself'.[114] Nor can it be argued that the basic norm of the international legal order specifically must presuppose the existence of national legal orders. National legal orders in Kelsen's model are seen as components of a universal system, unified by the overarching international legal system. If the basic norm of the international system were as Kelsen suggested, not only the national legal orders but their relationship with the international system would have to be presupposed – which would amount, absurdly, to presupposing the system as a whole in order to presuppose its basic norm.

Secondly, given the artificiality of collective subjecthood, the foundational basic norm of a system of collective subjects must embrace the establishment of those subjects, one of the functions of international law as Kelsen saw it. However, while the proposed norm appears suitable as a general norm underpinning an existing system of states – mandating predictability from existing constituents and conformity from new entrants – it says nothing about the relation between international legal norms and national legal systems, or the determination of national legal orders in space and time. As such it cannot serve as a foundational norm of the entire system, particularly if (as Kelsen speculated) the system is seen as emerging at the same time as – or even before – its first constituents.

Thirdly, the second part of Kelsen's formulation – the injunction to maintain customary behaviour – is also problematic. Taken on its own terms the norm appears

[111] J Kammerhofer, 'Uncertainty in the Formal Sources of International Law: Customary International Law and Some of its Problems' (2004) 15 *European Journal of International Law* 523, 548–49.
[112] Kammerhofer, 'The Benefits of the Pure Theory of Law for International Lawyers' (n 10) 41.
[113] ibid 49.
[114] Kelsen, *Law and Peace in International Relations* (n 9) 70.

to mandate some form of continuing regularity of behaviour among the states who are collective subjects of international law. But history shows no identifiable regularity; different states and their organs have treated neighbouring communities as friends, partners, enemies, sources of plunder, potential slaves and worse. Any basic norm for the international system must, somehow, be compatible with a history that seems to show no trace of normative regulation.

Kelsen's model of the 'primitive' legal order suggests a possible alternative basic norm for the international legal order. As we have seen, the 'primitive' legal order is an order of unqualified collective retributivism. The implicit subject of such a legal order is a collectivity which reserves the right to interpret any external influence as an attempted setback to its interests and react accordingly: a formulation which could stand as a definition of the sovereign nation state. The basic norm of a 'primitive' legal order might thus be a formulation along the lines of 'Individuals ought to react collectively and retributively to any influence from outside their collectivity', or more succinctly 'whatever they do to us, we ought to repay them in kind'. This norm – the principle that collectivities have a right to respond collectively to external influences, returning good for perceived good and evil for perceived evil – is expressed in some of the best as well as worst experiences of international society: as well as underlying the *bellum justum* doctrine,[115] as a principle of reciprocity it underpins as basic a doctrine of customary international law as *pacta sunt servanda*.

The model of the 'primitive' legal order developed in *Society and Nature* thus illuminates Kelsen's concept of international law in some unexpected ways. The legal order of a 'primitive' community has no institutional embodiment, relying on the unmediated enforcement by community members of norms deriving entirely from custom; to the extent that the international legal order is a 'primitive' order, these characteristics are not disqualifying or even surprising. The basic norm of a 'primitive' legal order, meanwhile, must be such as to ground collective subjectivity and unqualified retributivism; if international law is a 'primitive' legal order, we can infer that its basic norm will take a similar form. Both of these theory-driven arguments are borne out in multiple correspondences to known features of international law.

VI. Beyond the 'Primitive': A Problem for the Pure Theory of Law?

Kelsen's investigations of the 'primitive' were successful in their own terms – and with reference to international law – but created larger problems. As we have seen, the evolutionary model developed in *Society and Nature* offered an (admittedly speculative) account of the origin not only of causality but of the legal 'ought', which Kelsen's theory had previously presupposed in neo-Kantian style. History (or prehistory), understood in evolutionary terms, could replace the neo-Kantian model as the ontological grounding for the pure theory of law. Moreover, the evolutionary model pointed towards the

[115] Kelsen, *General Theory of Law and State* (n 7) 338–41.

future as well as the past: *Society and Nature* concluded by looking ahead to ridding social science of the last vestiges of the 'primitive' – a reform programme to which, Kelsen hoped, the pure theory could contribute:

> [If] the development of social sciences still lags far behind that of natural science it is due, among other things, to the fact that in this field animistic and hence personifying thinking is not completely exterminated. The Pure Theory of Law considers it as one of its main tasks to free the science of law from the relics of animism.[116]

While most of the key characteristics of the 'primitive' legal order had been wholly or partly replaced in the development of modern legal systems – characterised as these are by formality, centralisation, written law and the responsibilisation of individuals – the 'social principle of retribution'[117] had as yet survived, along with the substantialising assumption that matches a quantum of wrongdoing with a quantum of punishment. Reconstructed on a rational basis, the law could shed these last vestiges of the 'primitive'. Instead, sanctions would be calculated to influence a wrongdoer's behaviour so as to prevent further wrongdoing: '[if], in place of retribution, prevention as the purpose of punishment is accepted, then the equivalence of wrong and punishment loses its sense'.[118] With calculation of cause and effect replacing the imputation of responsibility, it would be possible to say that 'society is – from the point of view of science – a part of nature'.[119] (These are the last words of *Society and Nature*.)

As recently as 1941, Kelsen had defined 'the principle of retribution' in terms of 'associating conduct in accordance with the order and conduct contrary to the order with a promised advantage or a threatened disadvantage respectively',[120] effectively bringing the pairing of delict and sanction under the heading of retribution. However, he had also prepared the ground for the more minimal pure theory of law towards which he now gestured; none of Kelsen's main statements of the pure theory (*Introduction to the Problems of Legal Theory*, *General Theory of Law and State* and *Pure Theory of Law*) define sanctions as retributive, or suggest that their severity is proportionate to the severity of the respective delict.

In 1955's *Communist Theory of Law* Kelsen takes a step further, explicitly dissociating the sanction/delict pairing from the pairing of wrongful act and retributive punishment:

> [T]he legal reality … shows nothing else but a coercive act, the sanction, as a reaction against a definite human behaviour considered as undesirable by the legal authority. That this reaction means retribution is an interpretation of this reality in accordance with a certain ideology.[121]

However, Kelsen made no attempt to fully de-ideologise the pure theory along these lines. Uprooting retributivism altogether would have been problematic. If the principle of retributive punishment for proscribed acts were replaced with that of preventing harmful behaviour, there would be no reason to pair any specific preventive measure with a specific harmful act: a single measure – fortifying a public building or

[116] H Kelsen, 'Law, State and Justice in the Pure Theory of Law' (1948) 57 *Yale Law Journal* 377, 377.
[117] Kelsen, *Society and Nature* (n 23) 15.
[118] ibid 74.
[119] ibid 82.
[120] Kelsen, 'The Law as a Specific Social Technique' (n 74) 75.
[121] H Kelsen, *The Communist Theory of Law* (New York, Frederick A Praeger, 1955) 101.

imprisoning a dangerous individual – might be justified in terms of preventing multiple different harms. As such, a preventive rather than retributive legal order would not 'command only specific acts or omissions of acts', even indirectly – and its citizens could not be assured of the 'minimum of freedom' provided (as Kelsen argued) by any positive legal order, consisting of a 'sphere of human existence not interfered by command or prohibition'.[122] Replacing retribution with prevention, in short, would decentre the delict/sanction pairing, along with the individual whose imputed freedom rests on being capable of being ascribed responsibility for delicts and liability to sanctions.

Kelsen's speculations on removing 'primitive' retributivism from the law thus seem to tend, not towards a rationally law-governed society, but towards one whose officials can wield coercive power at their own discretion, and whose citizens are accordingly less free. There are signs that Kelsen was aware of, and retreated from, this implication: in 1957 he argued (echoing his 1941 formulation) that 'the principle of retribution … is at the basis of the social technique we call law'.[123] There was no scope for a purely rational alternative under that name.

VII. Conclusion

Kelsen's model of the 'primitive' legal order is based on a discredited evolutionary model, extended on debatable grounds to a largely unrelated area; its elaboration is supported by scholarship whose accuracy and impartiality was called into question by contemporary reviewers. Nevertheless, the 'primitive' legal order, considered as a theoretical model, has features which merit consideration – not least because it has numerous points of contact with the reality of international law. The 'primitive' model specified a minimum set of characteristics signalling the existence of a legal order, even in the absence of any centralised institutional embodiment; it also offered a developmental model showing how 'primitive' legal orders might achieve the level of development characteristic of contemporary legal systems, and perhaps how existing systems themselves might develop further. For both these reasons, the concept of the 'primitive' legal order was well suited to the task of accommodating international law within the pure theory of law: it offered a simple and logical explanation of how international law could qualify as a legal system even while codification was imperfect and adjudication and enforcement were decentralised, and how the norms of international law could coexist with those of domestic law despite their relative lack of sophistication (eg, their employment of collective and absolute liability).

The 'primitive' made another, more equivocal contribution to Kelsen's theoretical development. The ideal edifice of the pure theory stood in need of a foundation in the real world: if it offered no more than one theoretical framework among others, it would have no exclusive claim to validity but would take its place alongside other models, including Kelsen's detested natural law theories. Such a foundation had been provided by

[122] Kelsen, *Pure Theory of Law* (n 106) 6b.

[123] H Kelsen, 'Aristotle's Doctrine of Justice' in H Kelsen, *What is Justice? Justice, Law and Politics in the Mirror of Science. Collected Essays by Hans Kelsen* (Berkeley, University of California Press, 1957) 110–36.

Kelsen's use of a neo-Kantian conceptual vocabulary. However, Kelsen's faith in Kantian categories such as causality – and consequently in his own extension of the Kantian framework, with the legal 'ought' and the idea of legal cognition – had been shaken by his investigation of the history of science. An alternative foundation was offered by the evolutionary model, which promised not only to explain when the supposedly innate category of causality had developed, but to do the same for legal normativity – and to point the way beyond both, to a wholly rational future.

This was the second, and more problematic, contribution of the 'primitive' to the development of Kelsen's theory. *Society and Nature* left Kelsen with the suspicion that – with its irreducible element of retributivism – the pure theory of law was built not on scientific concepts but ideological survivals from a 'primitive' world-view, which would need to be replaced if the pure theory was to be truly pure. The post-1960 period, with its reversals and contradictions of Kelsen's earlier positions, may show Kelsen finally attempting to build that theory.

9

The Teleology of Peace and Kelsen's Philosophy of International Law

TOMASZ WIDŁAK

I. Introduction

Hans Kelsen is one of the few legal scholars who provided a fully-fledged theoretical account of international law. Contrary to some other influential authors of his times, he never treated the problem of international law as a neglected albeit necessary supplement to the main theory. Kelsen's work on international law is more comprehensive than the analysis of legal order and the thesis on the monism of international and national law. This chapter claims that the picture is complete only by considering Kelsen's answer to what may be called a teleological question, prompting a response to the problem of the law's aim (*telos*) and how it can be achieved. The standard view is that Kelsen does not answer the teleological question or even excludes the possibility of phrasing it since determining the purposes of the law is not the task of legal science. This chapter discusses the relationship between legal theory and philosophy in Kelsen's views on international law. It aims to reconstruct a more comprehensive picture of Kelsen's work on international legal theory. In what follows, this analysis will first expand on the methodological and epistemic limitations of Kelsen's pure theory of law in dealing with the teleological question. Second, it will comment on the differentiation between the theory and philosophy of law from Kelsen's perspective. After these remarks, the analysis will expand on the reconstruction proposal of Kelsen's philosophy of international law, which comprises two parts: explicative and normative. Within the explicative part, Kelsen provides us with two theses. The first claims that international law builds on the teleology of peace. The second explicative thesis rests on the theory of the evolution of legal orders and consists of three claims. The first of them states that legal orders evolve from more primitive to advanced ones by way of legal centralisation. According to the second claim, international law counts as a primitive legal order, which remains in its initial phases of development. The third claim assumes the analogy of international law to national law. It proposes that the possible development of international law will progress with the centralisation of the international legal order. Explicative philosophy is supplemented by its normative part, which consists of two normative theses. The first claims that the most effective way of developing the international legal order is by judicialisation. It entails the centralisation of judicial application of international law through obligatory jurisdiction of international tribunals and their universal cognition. The second normative thesis supports individuals becoming subjects of international law, especially in the context of international criminal liability. In conclusion, this chapter will summarise the character of Kelsen's philosophy of international law in the context of an underlying assumption of the purity of legal science.

II. The Pure Method and the *Telos* of Law

The teleological question is legal-philosophical reflection about the law's goals and how they should be realised by law.[1] For instance, this issue is prominent in natural law tradition, where the idea of just law is usually clearly articulated. However, Kelsen's theory of law is founded on distinct methodological theorems, which effectively bar any meaningful consideration of the law's *telos*. Where the teleological question of the goals of law is considered in legal-philosophical thinking, it usually unfolds in either the normative (axiological) or the factual direction. The former sees the law as aiming at an ideal of just law or justice itself, which may crystallise in the necessity of realising or protecting specific values. One of the most explicit examples is John Finnis' restatement of natural law theory and his central claim that some universal basic values or goods cannot be reasonably denied. Finnis uses practical reasonableness to derive natural law from these basic goods.[2] In other words, the law's aims are expressed in terms of rudimentary moral notions, which become the source of its normativity. The latter, factual, seeks the law's literal *raison d'être*. For instance, Marx believed that law is merely a secondary superstructure to the material base of economic relations and an oppressive class mechanism of the bourgeois state.[3] On the more conservative side, representatives of the 'Law and Economics' movement support the claim that law aims to promote efficient allocation of economic welfare.[4] In the case of these views, the law ought to be what the social facts demand.

Neither teleological explanations – axiological or factual – is acceptable to Kelsen because of his two foundational theorems: the separation of law and morals and the separation of Is (*Sein*) from Ought (*Sollen*). The effects of these claims of his theory of law are twofold. First, normative teleology is impossible since the consequence of adopting the thesis on the separation of law and morality is the separation of law and justice. Kelsen is trying to show that metaphysical attempts to grasp justice in the history of ideas were unsuccessful in revealing the absolute good or some other fundamental value, nor in formulating the principle of justice.[5] The result would be

[1] W Załuski, *Evolutionary Theory and Legal Philosophy* (Cheltenham, Edward Elgar Publishing, 2009) ix.
[2] J Finnis, *Natural law and Natural Rights* (Oxford, Oxford University Press, 2011) 100–27.
[3] See A Vincent, 'Marx and Law' (1993) 20 *Journal of Law and Society* 371.
[4] RA Posner, *The Problems of Jurisprudence* (Cambridge, MA, Harvard University Press, 1990) 353–62; RA Posner, *Economic Analysis of Law* (New York, Wolters Kluwer Law & Business, 2014) 124–43.
[5] H Kelsen, *What is Justice? Justice, Law and Politics in the Mirror of Science. Collected Essays* (Berkeley, University of California Press, 1971) 1–24.

the inevitable ideologisation of law and its objectification as a carrier of allegedly absolute values. Kelsen stipulates that his relativistic position does not deny the 'existence' of morality or justice in general but merely that 'absolute justice is an irrational ideal'.[6] Therefore, aiming at any ideal of (just) law cannot be accepted as an intrinsic property of law. Second, the separation of *Is* and *Ought* bars any rationalist consideration of law's necessary entanglement with social facts and any attempt by legal science to search for law's immanent function as a primary reason for its validity. According to Kelsen, norms are ideals that belong exclusively to the sphere of Ought. They contain or constitute their claim to be obeyed. The sphere of Ought makes sense only if it remains entirely separated from the sphere of Is (*Sein*) or facts. Kelsen reminds us that 'nobody can assert that from the statement that something is, follows a statement that something ought to be, or vice versa'.[7] Therefore, it is impossible to base the justification of the validity of the legal order on the maintenance or change of a factual state (eg, maintenance of a specific social hierarchy or a particular economic system).

The two theses on the double separation of law from morality and norms from facts make Kelsen's pure theory of law radical in precluding the considerations of the *telos* of law in the strong sense, according to which the aim or aims of law (both as values and facts) cannot be constitutive of its normativity. The result is a dissociation of legal science from ethics, understood as knowledge of making moral judgements on the one hand, and from social sciences such as sociology and political science on the other. While this leads to the distillation of the proper area of study for legal sciences, Kelsen's epistemic position further defines the essence of the legal method to reside in the pursuit of the unity of law as an object of cognition. Following methodological Kantianism, Kelsen believes that the scientific method 'creates' its object 'insofar as it comprehends the object as a meaningful whole'.[8] Therefore, using different methods (eg, sociological or psychological alongside normative ones) for the same cognitive object (law) is excluded. For this reason, he opposes the methodological syncretism of jurisprudence and the epistemological multidimensionality of law. In other words, the law as an object of knowledge must be characterised by epistemic unity; it must necessarily make itself cognisable by the same method. If the subject of research in the science of law requires different methods, then, according to Kelsen, it is no longer law proper but a phenomenon that is the object of research in other sciences. In light of these assumptions, the conclusion already reached by the Viennese scholar on the pages of the first of his international legal theory books – *Das Problem der Souveränität* was clear: legal theory deserves the name of science as much as it can fulfil the postulate of the unity of legal knowledge by allowing the perception of the law as a unitary system.[9]

[6] ibid 21.

[7] H Kelsen, *Pure Theory of Law* (Berkeley, University of California Press, 1967) 6.

[8] ibid 72.

[9] H Kelsen, *Das Problem der Souveränität und die Theorie des Völkerrechts. Beitrag zu einer Reinen Rechtslehre* (Tübingen, JCB Mohr (Paul Siebeck) 1920) 152.

III. Theory and Philosophy of Law

According to Kelsen, legal theory is shaped by its method and epistemic purpose. In its pursuit to cognise the legal norms (the sphere of *Ought*), legal theory as science introduces unity and orders the legal system. Since the method creates its object, this discovery process is inherently creative. However, it can never amount to speculation on the *telos* of law because the method precisely separates the normative structure of law from the considerations of justice on the one hand, and the factual relations of cause and effect on the other. Kelsen states this clearly on the first page of the second edition of the *Pure Theory of Law* when explaining the purity of his approach: 'the theory attempts to answer the question what and how the law *is*, not how it ought to be'.[10] Therefore, when Kelsen seeks to systematise and analyse the structure of international law and its place with state law, he engages in legal theory. His theory of international law encompasses three general theses (an argument I develop elsewhere):[11] the unity thesis (of law and state and the monism of national and international law); the common origin thesis concerning the problem of the basic norm and its relation to international law; and the third thesis on the compulsory nature of international law. Kelsen's enquiries within these areas aim at cognising international law, ie, the structure of the international legal order and its norms.

On the face of it, Kelsen is not interested in any speculative considerations about what and how international law ought to be. These questions, dubbed 'legal politics' in the *Pure Theory of Law*, are precisely the matter of the law's *telos* and axiology. To ask what international law should or aims to become is to pursue answers in international justice or the philosophy of international law. The view that the distinction between the theory of law and philosophy could be grasped in analogy to the Kantian differentiation between theoretical and practical reason has taken some hold in jurisprudence.[12] The essence of this view is that the theory of law is a discipline interested in generalising and systematising 'law as it is', while the philosophy of law *qua* ethics of law (*Rechtsethik*) criticises and reflects on 'law as it should be'.[13] Kelsen may be considered one of the forerunners and adherents of this modern view. In 1926, with Leon Duguit and Francis Weyr, Kelsen began editing the journal *Internationale Zeitschrift für Theorie des Rechts*. In the introduction to the first volume, the editors commented on the distinction between the theory and philosophy of law in a similar vein.[14] They saw the theory of law as 'the starting postulate of all scientific research in the matter of a specific legal system or international law'.[15] It is a theory of positive law, which includes 'questions about the essence of law, its relationship to the state and society, about the basic concepts and methods of legal cognition, about the relations between individual orders of state law, as well as between state law and international law'. In contrast,

[10] Kelsen, *Pure Theory of Law* (n 7) 1.

[11] See also T Widłak, 'Polycentric vs Fragmented: a Neo-Kelsenian order of Global Law' (2019) 10 *Transnational Legal Theory* 229.

[12] D van der Pfordten, *Rechtsethik* (München, Beck, 2001) 18–20; D van der Pfordten, 'Was ist und wozu Rechtsphilosophie?' (2004) 59 *Juristen Zeitung* 160.

[13] J Zajadło, 'Filozofia prawa a teoria prawa we współczesnej jurysprudencji niemieckiej' (2011) 3337 *Acta Universitatis Wratislavensis Prawo CCCXII* 225, 239–40.

[14] L Duguit, H Kelsen and F Weyr, 'Préface – Vorwort' (1926/27) 1 *Internationale Zeitschrift für Theorie des Rechts* 1, 1–4.

[15] ibid.

philosophy of law relates to the speculative solution of problems of 'justice, just, fair, natural or absolute law' ('*das Problem der Gerechtigkeit, des richtigen, gerechten, des natürlichen oder absoluten Rechts*').[16] These were the issues that the journal was not interested in, and neither was Kelsen in his project of the pure theory of law. However, his teachings on international law constitute a notable exception.

IV. Kelsen's Philosophy of International Law

In addition to the theoretical theses concerning the monism of national and international law, the claims on the structure (the *Stufenbaulehre*) and the position of international legal order in relation to the *Grundnorm* or the problem of imputation and sanctions in international law, Kelsen makes several distinct arguments of at least partially teleological character. They can be divided into two types. First, there are arguments motivated by critical-reflective attempts to explain the specificity of international law as a legal order against the background of general claims of pure legal science. They will be referred to as the explicative philosophy. Second, there is normative philosophy, which covers normative postulates as to the preferred direction of the further development of international law. These two groups of arguments of a critical and aspirational (if not speculative) character form Kelsen's insight into what international law should become or – a philosophy of international law. In what follows, each of the two parts and their theses will be elaborated.

A. The Explicative Philosophy: On the Uniqueness of International Law

Kelsen puts much effort into clarifying certain features of international law that objectively make it visibly different compared with any established, developed national legal order. This task is carried out using a theory of legal orders, which may be considered integral to Kelsen's project of the pure theory of law. However, his analysis is not restricted to structural theoretical arguments, as it makes its crucial assumptions founded on a dynamic teleological-axiological thesis on peace as a value constituting the aim of legal orders. Taking the peace thesis as a foundation, the theory of legal orders becomes an evolutionary theory encompassing three theses: the centralisation of legal orders, the primitivism of international law, and the analogy between international and national law.

i. The Teleological-Axiological Thesis on Peace

Kelsen straightforwardly takes for granted that the aim of any law, including international law, is to guarantee peace.[17] Although he denies that making this assertion

[16] ibid.

[17] H Kelsen, *The Legal Process and International Order* (London, The New Commonwealth Research Bureau Publications, 1934) 5.

is a matter of 'moral or political purpose' and tries to dismiss it as a plain fact without a political alternative, it is a tangible articulation of an answer to the teleological question.[18] Even though the Austrian scholar denies its axiological (normative) character and attempts to use more real terms, he pursues a political philosophy. Granted, Kelsen tries to keep his argumentation rudimentary or even 'technical' as he defines peace negatively and minimally. Therefore, peace becomes a state of relative non-use of violence rather than a positive ideal to be sought. The author of the *Pure Theory of Law* makes it abundantly clear that law can only ensure peace in a relative, not an absolute sense.[19] The task of the law is to ensure that the political community is free from violence defined as an anarchic, uncontrolled *bellum omnium contra omnes*. Kelsen believes that law is an organisation of violence – a means of pacifying community members.[20] Only the organs of the political community, acting on law, are entitled to coercively interfere in the sphere of interests of its members to the extent necessary to maintain universal peace. The validity of the legal order is tantamount to ensuring the protection of the sphere of individual interests of the political community members and thus sustaining a state of peace. According to Kelsen, this neo-Hobbesian argument from the state of nature applies to national and international legal orders. Although there is no possibility to eliminate war or, more broadly, the use of force in international relations, monopolisation of violence by the community and putting it under judicial control is attainable.

Against this background, the question arises whether Kelsen thus proposes a specific version of axiological absolutism. The Austrian scholar accepts the value of peace and its priority in international law's axiology without further reason and justification. It suggests that peace for Kelsen is an intrinsic value. However, his other writings strongly contradict this interpretation. Both in the second edition of *Pure Theory of Law*[21] and again in the essay *What is Justice?*[22] he puts his weight behind the view of the fundamental moral relativity of law. Kelsen states openly that even 'justice of the peace is only a relative, and not an absolute, justice'.[23] The law cannot embody any absolute moral value since this is possible only in a religious context based on belief in the transcendent authority of a divine being.[24] Kelsen takes the position of quite radical non-cognitivism. For him, legal values adopted within positive law cannot result from the assumption of a shared moral denominator for a given community. Otherwise, their adoption and implementation would have to determine the essence of the law. Therefore, Kelsen clarifies that 'specifically, the peace value is not an element essential for the concept of law'.[25] Peace is merely an instrumental value that legally eliminates

[18] ibid.

[19] H Kelsen, *General Theory of Law and State* (Cambridge, MA, Harvard University Press, 1945) 22; *cf* J von Bernstorff, 'Peace and Global Justice through Prosecuting the Crime of Aggression? Kelsen and Morgenthau on the Nuremberg Trials and the International Judicial Function' in DA Jeremy Telman (ed), *Hans Kelsen in America – Selective Affinities and the Mysteries of Academic Influence* (Cham, Springer, 2018) 85–100, 86.

[20] Kelsen, *General Theory of Law and State* (n 19) 21.

[21] Kelsen, *Pure Theory of Law* (n 7).

[22] Kelsen, *What is Justice?* (n 5) 1–24.

[23] ibid 22.

[24] ibid; *cf* J McGarry, 'Kelsen and the Necessity of God in the Natural-Law Doctrine' in P Langford, I Bryan and J McGarry (eds), *Kelsenian Legal Science and the Nature of Law* (Cham, Springer, 2017) 241–55.

[25] Kelsen, *Pure Theory of Law* (n 7) 65.

war and other forms of arbitrary abuse of violence in relations between states and replaces it with legal coercion in the form of international law sanctions.[26]

However, despite the large dose of pragmatism in Kelsen's discussion of peace, his claim is normative and, at the same time, foundational for his project of a philosophy of international law. Explaining the structural differences between international and national law can be meaningful with the teleology of peace. The fundamental purposefulness of legal orders opens the way to formulating the theory of their evolutionary development, which allows for gradually ever more effective implementation of the assumed goal. This claim rests on three fundamental theses that can be reconstructed as follows: first, legal orders undergo an evolutionary development from primitive to advanced, and the primary measure of progress is the degree of their centralisation. Second, international law should be classified as a primitive legal order in the early stages of development. Third, the development of international law should progress towards centralisation, analogous to the development that modern state law has undergone.

ii. The Centralisation Thesis

Centralisation and the opposite decentralisation are concepts related to the organisational forms of all legal orders, including international law.[27] Kelsen introduces two aspects of the centralisation of legal orders: the static and the dynamic. In the case of the former, the critical aspect rests in the territorial scope of the legal norms. Centralised orders are those in which the law consists solely or primarily of legal norms valid in the entire territory under their jurisdiction. Such norms are called central norms. In contrast, local norms are binding only in the part of the territory.[28] All norms within a given order, both central and local, constitute a comprehensive (or 'total') legal order that corresponds with the broadest legal community. Taken separately, the central and the local norms constitute partial legal communities.[29] Whether a specific legal order is centralised or decentralised will be determined by the predominance of norms of one or the other type, both in terms of quantity and quality (the importance of the substance of regulation).[30] Centralisation and decentralisation of orders is a typology. Every given legal order will consist of both kinds, while their proportion is decisive for placing the legal order on a spectrum of centralisation and decentralisation.[31]

The dynamic aspect of the problem of centralisation and decentralisation of legal orders relates to the creation and application of legal norms.[32] A legal order is centralised strongly or even ideally in the dynamic sense if its norms are created and applied

[26] H Kelsen, *Law and Peace in International Relations. The Oliver Wendell Holmes Lectures 1940–41* (Cambridge, MA, Harvard University Press, 1942) 27.

[27] Kelsen, *General Theory of Law and State* (n 19) 303.

[28] Kelsen, *Law and Peace in International Relations* (n 26) 107.

[29] Kelsen, *Pure Theory of Law* (n 7) 313–17; Kelsen, *General Theory of Law and State* (n 19) 303–08.

[30] ibid; ibid.

[31] *cf* C Leben, 'Hans Kelsen and the Advancement of International Law' (1998) 9 *European Journal of International Law* 287, 293–94.

[32] Kelsen, *General Theory of Law and State* (n 19) 308–16.

by the same legal organ, preferably one person. The degree of centralisation decreases and decentralisation increases, both with the introduction of multiple authorities into the creation or application of law and with the collegial nature of the legal organs. A decentralised order in the dynamic sense is in place when there is a visible pluralism in law-making and law-applying bodies.[33]

iii. The Thesis on the Primitivism of International Law

International law is a legal order that Kelsen considers primitive because it resembles the law of a rudimentary community.[34] Primitivism must be understood colloquially but only to the degree of centralisation and the relative lack of institutionalisation that follows it. Thus, unlike HLA Hart, Kelsen does not need to appeal to a somewhat vague argument that international law is highly developed in terms of 'concepts, methods, and techniques', but its similarity to national law exists only in form and not in content.[35] For Kelsen, the most characteristic feature of a primitive legal order is the institution of self-help. It ensures that community members obey the obligations established in the rules by administering and enforcing sanctions themselves.[36] He refers to the institution of blood revenge during a blood feud as a historical example of self-help.[37] It is characteristic of this rudimentary institution that, from an external perspective, the act constituting the offence (eg, murder) does not differ in any real way from the sanction provided for by the law of the community (blood revenge). Only the objective sense of these two acts differs because of the legal norm. In carrying out a bloody revenge, the community member does not so much follow the impulse but instead exercises the authority conferred upon him by the legal order. Thus, he acts as an organ of the legal community and administers justice reserved for law enforcement authorities in a centralised legal order.[38] Kelsen argues that the same is true for international law, where members of the international community – a state or a group of states – are authorised to apply sanctions against another member in the act of self-help due to the lack of specialised legal bodies. The international community, not having the appropriate organs at its disposal, acts through its member (a state), which uses reprisals or other sanctions on behalf of the community. Kelsen uses the self-help doctrine based on his interpretation of the 'just war' tradition to explain the nature of sanctions in international law.[39] It needs to be emphasised that this thesis is descriptive, not normative. When read in light of the theory of evolution of legal orders through centralisation, the 'just war' or 'legal war' is not a form of sanction that Kelsen endorses or promotes. His conclusions correspond with the state of development of international law as a primitive legal order, decentralised in a static and dynamic sense.

[33] ibid 309.

[34] Kelsen, *Law and Peace in International Relations* (n 26) 49; Kelsen, *The Legal Process and International Order* (n 17) 11.

[35] HLA Hart, *The Concept of Law*, 2nd edn (Oxford, Clarendon Press, 1994) 227.

[36] Kelsen, *General Theory of Law and State* (n 19) 327.

[37] Kelsen, *The Legal Process and International Order* (n 17) 11.

[38] Kelsen, *Law and Peace in International Relations* (n 26) 56–57.

[39] H Kelsen, *Principles of International Law* (New York, Rinehart & Co, 1952) 33–44.

iv. The Analogy between International and National Law

Like many other scholars, Kelsen used an analogy to state law in his characterisation of international law. His theory of the evolution of legal orders from decentralised (primitive) to more centralised (advanced) ones has been constructed, given a background claim that the apparent deficiencies of international law are only temporary. The historically backed argument about the constant development of state legal orders, evolving from the principle of self-help and blood revenge towards a modern bureaucratic state, which effectively centralised the creation and application of the law, is the point of reference for Kelsen's modernist and optimistic projection of international law's future. The Austrian scholar thought there was no reason why the international community, and its law, could not share in this progress and repeat the success story of a European state legal order. He supported the thesis that international law is bound to follow the evolution of state legal orders and to become increasingly centralised. Harbingers of this process were several advances in the development of international law in the mid-twentieth century, such as the emergence of international organisations and the intensified attempts to sanction the prohibition of the use of force. However, this does not mean that the result of this process is or should be entirely analogous to modern state development. Although Kelsen does not rule out the possibility of international law evolving towards a world state (*Weltstaat*), he does not claim that such a result is desirable or inevitable.[40] He limits the analogy to observing a general tendency to centralise primitive legal orders without prejudging the result. He remarks that, in his opinion, the centralisation of treaty regimes cannot exceed a certain degree, beyond which such a legal order acquires the character of a state.[41] Suppose international law is to maintain its fundamental function and essence as a law 'between' nations. In that case, it should not reach a degree of centralisation equal to or higher than the one represented by the state legal order.

Kelsen's argument is unique and stands out from other conceptualisations of international law that use the analogy to state law. The Austrian scholar does not construct a theory and philosophy of international law based on the so-called domestic analogy as a theoretical foundation. This argument, proposed and used in political science and philosophy, assumes that political conditions and social institutions necessary to form a state must be replicated at an international or transnational level for the international community to maintain peace.[42] The legal version of this argument maintains an enthymematic assumption that in the case of international law, progress is hindered by its dissimilarity compared with national law. It follows that the differences, if not deviations or anomalies of international law, must be first identified and overcome, making the state or state law a model or a kind of *étalon* against which international law is inevitably measured. The supposedly constitutive features of 'true' law, modelled after a state law, dictate a verdict as to the nature and even

[40] Kelsen, *General Theory of Law and State* (n 19) 326.

[41] Kelsen, *Law and Peace in International Relations* (n 26) 121.

[42] See H Bull, 'Society and Anarchy in International Relations' in H Butterfield and M Wight (eds), *Diplomatic Investigations. Essays in the Theory of International Politics* (London, George Allen & Unwin Ltd, 1966) 35–60.

validity of international law or any other form of supranational or global law. Kelsen decidedly rejects this line of reasoning. In his opinion, the state legal order and international law do not differ qualitatively or ontologically (both are normative orders capable of monopolising violence),[43] but only in the 'technical' aspect. The difference between them boils down to dissimilarities in methods of law's creation and application, ie, in terms of the degree of centralisation. This thesis is remarkable also because, in this conceptual aspect, it makes a case for the fundamental monism of national and international law. Kelsen's scholarship remains inclusive – it proposes an analysis of the concept of a legal norm or legal order as such, explaining each of its forms, including the international one.

B. The Normative Philosophy: On International Law's Institutional and Moral Progress

Not only does Kelsen claim that the international legal order is heading towards more centralisation, but also that such a process should take place and is welcome. Moreover, the Austrian scholar indicates a specific way to accomplish this task: judicialisation, which entails centralising judicial processes in applying international law. A second important aspect of the development of international law and morality is the growing anthropocentrism of international law, focused on the international criminal liability of individuals. Endorsed by Kelsen, these views were most fully and comprehensively expressed in the book *Peace Through Law*, published after Kelsen emigrated to the United States. The historical context of these political and legal postulates is obvious.[44] Writing at the end of the Second World War, Kelsen aimed to formulate a concrete proposal for institutionalising the new international order. However, any suspicion of academic opportunism or inconsistency on the part of Kelsen should be dismissed since the claims about the need for centralisation of international law through its judicialisation were clearly expressed as early as 1934 in the book *The Legal Process and International Order.*[45]

i. Judicialisation of International Law

In this context, two fundamental issues arise: how did Kelsen justify the need for more excellent centralisation of international law, and why was this evolutionary progress in international law to take place precisely through the growing importance of the judicative?

Kelsen lists several problematic aspects of the present primitive stage of development of international law, which justify the need to progress towards centralisation. First, he sees the fundamental problem in the anarchism of the process of application

[43] Kelsen, *Law and Peace in International Relations* (n 26) 58.

[44] See J von Bernstorff, 'Hans Kelsen on Judicial Law-Making by International Courts and Tribunals: A Theory of Global Judicial Imperialism?' (2015) 14 *Law and Practice of International Courts and Tribunals* 35.

[45] Kelsen, *The Legal Process and International Order* (n 17).

of international law in specific cases. States become judges in their case since they find themselves in a double role of, on the one hand, parties to disputes or entities whose interests may be affected by specific actions or legal qualifications and, on the other hand, they simultaneously act as organs of the community that interpret and apply the law.[46] This ambiguity often leads to a violation of the principle of objectivity, which is fundamental to maintaining the authority of international law. The problem is burning, given that all states are formally equal members of the international community, and the scope and degree of their mutual relations are constantly expanding. Second, centralisation is necessary to preserve the principle of legalism in law enforcement. The primitive technique of self-help not only leads to the maintenance of ethically questionable collectivisation and absolutisation of responsibility, but also makes the authority of law indirectly dependent on the results of forceful solutions.[47] Kelsen asks us to imagine a situation in which a state or group of states performs a military operation acting lawfully as organs of the international community. However, they lose their case in combat on the part of the notorious law-breaking state, capable of efficient defence. The principle of self-help can only be overcome and substituted by first institutionalising the sanctioning process.[48] According to Kelsen, this requires centralisation at the level of the international executive power to eliminate 'rogue' behaviour (using modern jargon) on the part of states that benefit from breaking international law.[49]

Against this background, Kelsen's postulate of the evolution of international law by centralising the international adjudicative processes (rather than by creating world legislature) acquires full significance. Kelsen appeals to the historical argument in which the law application process's centralisation generally preceded its creation by a law-making assembly.[50] The institutionalisation of judicial power happened precisely because the courts have the power to create the law effectively.[51] Kelsen explains that a less developed legal order generally copes well with law creation at the level of general norms through the development of customary law.[52] However, the existence of an independent legal order hinges on its ability to objectify the process of determining the content of individual norms. It requires creating an institution competent to establish legal facts, which constitute premises for imposing sanctions.[53] Conflicts caused by the clashes of interests of states arise more quickly in specific situations rather than when they abstractly consider certain rules during treaty-making. Therefore, taking the principle *nemo iudex in causa sua* seriously is the first step in realising the axiological goal of law in the form of ensuring peace (understood as the antinomy of conflict). The centralisation of the judicial process of law application even precedes the need to

[46] ibid 11.
[47] Kelsen, *Law and Peace in International Relations* (n 26) 96–102.
[48] ibid 147.
[49] Kelsen, *The Legal Process and International Order* (n 17) 17–18.
[50] H Kelsen, 'The Strategy of Peace' (1944) 49 *American Journal of Sociology* 381, 384–85; *cf* H Kelsen, *Peace Through Law* (Chapel Hill, University of North Carolina Press, 1944) 21; *cf* Kelsen, *Law and Peace in International Relations* (n 26) 148.
[51] Kelsen, *The Legal Process and International Order* (n 17) 14.
[52] Kelsen, *Law and Peace in International Relations* (n 26) 145–46.
[53] Kelsen, *General Theory of Law and State* (n 19) 135–36.

centralise the execution of sanctions, which may be efficiently ensured by self-help.[54] Therefore, the centralisation of the judicative should logically precede the need to establish a uniform, organised administrative and police apparatus, ie, the functions of the executive power. Courts, as the community organs guaranteeing the de facto creation of the most critical individual norms from the perspective of a primitive community, are the first to be established and developed. Only after a proper judiciary is in place is the way open to fully developing other functions. According to Kelsen, the legislative is centralised only as the last of all types of authority.[55] He summarises his argument, writing that 'there can be no lawmaker without a judge, but a judge without a lawmaker can do well'.[56]

It is also worth noting that, apart from theoretical and logical arguments, Kelsen invokes an interesting political argument for developing international law by centralising courts and tribunals. The Austrian scholar notes that while unanimity is the primary procedural rule for creating norms under general international treaty law, in the case of decisions of international courts and tribunals, the majority decision is the rule.[57] It may be a manifestation of the unique, supranational position of the adjudicative bodies. However, traditionally it is not seen as detrimental to state sovereignty, or at least not to the same extent as in the case of the administrative apparatus of international organisations. According to Kelsen, the potentially lower political resistance to the increased position of courts and tribunals is an excellent pragmatic prognosis for taking the path of reforming the international order through the centralisation of international judicative. Elsewhere, he raises a related argument, observing that so far, arbitral tribunals operating based on treaties are the most effective of all forms of dispute solution under international law. The states that refer their disputes to these institutions rarely refuse to execute their judgments.[58] However, for the path of centralising international law through the development of international courts and tribunals to be effective, Kelsen correctly perceives those two conditions must be met: the obligatory nature and the universality of cognition of the international adjudicative authority.

Kelsen's proposal requires, first and foremost, the replacement of interstate voluntarism with the compulsory jurisdiction of a world court. For if one accepts the view that violence in international relations can only be legitimised as a form of sanction, then the logical consequence of the compulsory submission of all disputes between states to an independent and impartial judicial body cannot be rejected.[59] Kelsen believes that any state that does not agree to submit disputes to final resolution by international courts and tribunals undermines its credibility in supporting the rule of law and the love of peace in international relations. Therefore, the obligatory nature of the international judiciary is a precondition for advancing international law and

[54] Kelsen, *The Legal Process and International Order* (n 17) 19.

[55] Kelsen, *Peace Through Law* (n 50) 20.

[56] H Kelsen, 'International Peace – by Court or Government?' (1941) 46 *American Journal of Sociology* 571, 575.

[57] Kelsen, *Peace Through Law* (n 50) 20–21.

[58] ibid.

[59] L Vinx, *Hans Kelsen's Pure Theory of Law. Legality and Legitimacy* (Oxford, Oxford University Press, 2007) 196.

the international community, which legitimises itself by implementing the ideal of peaceful coexistence through law. However, the compulsory jurisdiction of a world court can only achieve its purpose if it is accompanied by the requirement to submit to the authority of this tribunal all types of disputes arising between members of the international community. In order to guarantee peace, the legal order must be complete, which means that it necessarily regulates every issue that may be disputed among the members of the international community. Nothing is more dangerous than the emergence of a conflict in case the law does not provide for any obligatory resolution procedure.[60] Kelsen believes that until universal cognition is established, international law is not ready for commitments to renounce violence in international relations.

When writing about the universality of the jurisdiction of the world court, Kelsen alludes to the famous doctrinal division of international disputes into legal and political ones.[61] He sharply criticises this typology and undermines its validity on logical and theoretical grounds. The problem lies not so much in the vague distinction between the categories of 'legal' and 'political' disputes but in their complete inadequacy to determine the scope of jurisdiction of a world court. Kelsen argues that whether the conflict has an economic, political or another origin in any way does not change the fact that it is regulated by international law. It is absurd to claim that the conflict is not legal because it concerns, for example, the economic interests of states.[62] The criterion for such a distinction is purely subjective as it relates only to how the parties to the dispute justify their positions on a purely rhetorical level.[63] A dispute is always legal if the rules of law are applicable to the parties' behaviour.

Both postulates of the universal and compulsory jurisdiction of an international judicial body constitute a premise for perceiving the legal system as complete and coherent. Kelsen argues that there are only two possible legal outcomes to any dispute submitted to the jurisdiction of international tribunals. Either the applicable law requires a party to a dispute to act in a specific manner, in which case the tribunal must rule per that request, or the positive international law does not stipulate such an obligation. The latter case occurs when a state's particular action or inaction remains in the sphere of freedom of decision and entails the other party's demand for a specific behaviour is not legally justified.[64] This situation cannot be interpreted as a lack of regulation in international law because, according to Kelsen, the tribunal also applies international law when it adjudicates that there is no legal norm regulating the given factual situation. The lack of regulation anticipated in given circumstances may cause a negative moral and political assessment of the state of the applicable international law. However, it excludes a conclusion that there is any logical inconsistency or a legal loophole.[65]

[60] Kelsen, *Peace Through Law* (n 50) 32.
[61] Kelsen, *Principles of International Law* (n 39) 380.
[62] Kelsen, *Peace Through Law* (n 50) 24.
[63] ibid 28.
[64] Kelsen, *Principles of International Law* (n 39) 383.
[65] ibid 384–85.

ii. International Criminal Liability

The second pillar of Kelsen's normative philosophy of international law concerns the increasing role of individuals as subjects of international law. The core and most controversial aspect of this line of argumentation concerns the international criminal liability of individuals. Although he began to formulate his views on this matter as early as 1920,[66] the issue of international criminal liability of individuals became one of the main topics of his publications in the 1940s. Ensuring its full implementation under international law becomes, for him, the condition of ensuring peace in international relations, which is equally essential as the compulsory and universal jurisdiction of international courts and tribunals. It is evident in the very structure of the book *Peace Through Law*,[67] which was divided into two parts corresponding to both issues.

In addition to his detailed dogmatic analysis of the topic on the grounds of the contemporary state of international law at the time of his writing,[68] Kelsen proposes a novel and then progressive argument as to the desired direction of the evolution of international law in this aspect. Kelsen sees the need to develop international law towards a significant extension of an individual's responsibility. He expresses it by his support for the formula of individual criminal liability of individuals for the acts of the state (for instance, when the individual is acting as an organ of the state, issuing legal acts or orders that are manifestly criminal).[69] Kelsen argued that the introduction of criminal liability for the acts of the state occurs in the London Agreement establishing the International Military Tribunal (IMT).[70]

In a 1945 article, Kelsen takes a defensive position, focusing on countering widespread criticism of the establishment of the IMT. The main critique of the planned trials of war criminals concerns the retroactivity of the Nuremberg law, which would constitute a case of violation of the principle *nullum crimen sine lege poenali anteriori*.[71] In his analysis, Kelsen argues that the principle prohibiting the enactment of ex post facto criminal penalisation has limited application. This prohibition is only a variation of the general principle that the law should be known to those who are obliged by it and which in turn is limited by another principle – *ignorantia iuris nocet*.[72] However, particularly interesting is Kelsen's novel argument, which asks the reader to differentiate between a situation when the ex post facto criminalisation would concern acts which are deemed as 'innocent' or 'indifferent' in time and those acts which are commonly considered as 'immoral' or contrary to the norm of a higher level.[73] According to this

[66] H Kelsen, 'Der völkerrechtliche Strafanspruch wegen völkerrechtswidriger Kriegshandlungen' in M Jestaedt (ed), *Hans Kelsen Werke, Veröffentlichte Schriften 1918–1920* (Tübingen, Mohr Siebeck, 2013) 573–78, 574–75.

[67] Kelsen, *Peace Through Law* (n 50).

[68] H. Kelsen, 'Collective and Individual Responsibility in International Law with Particular Regard to the Punishment of War Criminals' (1943) 31 *California Law Review* 530, 537.

[69] Kelsen, *Peace Through Law* (n 50) 81.

[70] Kelsen, *Principles of International Law* (n 39) 136.

[71] H Kelsen, 'The Rule Against Ex Post Facto Laws and the Axis War Criminals' (1945) 2 *Judge Advocate Journal* 8.

[72] ibid 9.

[73] ibid.

reasoning, the supposedly widely shared 'immorality' of specific acts at the time of their commission could, at least in the case of international law, allow for the limitation of the application of the principle of *nullum crimen sine lege poenali anteriori*. Such far-reaching arguments were an attempt by Kelsen to support the legitimacy of the IMT and jurisdiction over crimes against humanity. Regarding war crimes and crimes against peace, the Austrian scholar usually refers to arguments based on valid positive international law.[74]

For Kelsen, bringing about individual criminal liability of state officials is merely a secondary criminalisation of acts whose unlawfulness was unquestionable when they were committed. For instance, bringing Nazi state officials to trial does not count as establishing the illegality of their acts ex post facto but counts only as an extension of their responsibility.[75] Since this argument may raise severe doubts from the criminal law perspective, Kelsen is also looking for other ways to support his view. One is an attempt to dogmatically challenge the validity of the prohibition of retroactivity as a general principle of law under international law.[76] Kelsen concludes that the Allies were legitimate in establishing the rules of individual criminal liability to which they agreed. Based on the doctrine of states' negative freedom under international law, the consequence of this reasoning is the possibility for the Nuremberg tribunal to rely on 'general principles of justice' and moral guidelines.[77] Kelsen explicitly recognises the need for the principle of non-retroactivity to give way to another moral principle demanding priority for the universally shared sense of justice.[78] It is difficult not to get the impression that Kelsen is struggling between, on the one hand, strenuous attempts to rely on positivist arguments based on the applicable law and, on the other, a bid to make use of arguments based on fairness freely. The latter technique is fully justified morally in the historical context, although it violates the epistemological non-cognitivism of the pure science of law.

Moreover, Kelsen formulates a critical new view explaining his thinking about individual responsibility under international law without appealing to political motives. He claims that the principle of individual criminal liability represents a more advanced degree of implementation of justice than the primitive technique of collective responsibility.[79] Even if the emergence of individual liability applies only to some specific cases, it generally improves the technique of international law.[80] Although this is a welcome development, Kelsen concludes that the Nuremberg trials were a missed opportunity because there was no success in developing general rules that would have permanently reformed international law.[81] The reason was that they selectively concerned the responsibility for war crimes only of the perpetrators from

[74] H Kelsen, 'Will the Judgment in the Nuremberg Trial Constitute a Precedent in International Law?' (1947) 1 *International Law Quarterly* 153, 155–56.

[75] Kelsen, 'The Rule Against Ex Post Facto Laws and the Axis War Criminals' (n 71) 10.

[76] ibid.

[77] von Bernstorff, 'Peace and Global Justice' (n 19) 94.

[78] Kelsen, 'The Rule Against Ex Post Facto Laws and the Axis War Criminals' (n 71) 11.

[79] Kelsen, 'Will the Judgment in the Nuremberg Trial Constitute a Precedent in International Law?' (n 74) 165.

[80] ibid.

[81] ibid 170.

the states that had lost the war. In Kelsen's view, as a result, only particular *ad casum* rules concerning the specific behaviour of the winning powers towards the defeated were created.[82] Even worse, the adjudication panel consisted only of the representatives of the principal allied powers. In this way, they became the architects of the Nuremberg law and judges in their case, which, according to Kelsen, weakened the authority of the Nuremberg judgments. However, in formulating these critical remarks, Kelsen confirmed that the mechanisms of shaping individual international criminal liability interested him primarily from the perspective of the evolution of international law.

V. Conclusions

As explained in this chapter, Kelsen's philosophy of international law has a specific meaning in the context of established views and divisions in jurisprudence. First, it is not a philosophy of law as a consideration of the nature of law because Kelsen was not interested in answering this fundamental philosophical question, particularly in international law. He expressed his view on this matter as early as 1920 when he wrote in *Das Problem der Souveränität* that the question 'what is law?' is as meaningless (*sinnlos*) to a lawyer as it is to a biologist to enquire about what life is.[83] Kelsen's philosophy of international law is a pragmatic venture. On the one hand, he uses a teleological perspective of an axiological aim of legal orders to differentiate between them in terms of the stages of their development and thus explain specific selected, problematic features of international law.

On the other hand, Kelsen's philosophy of international law concerns itself with a descriptive-normative reflection with a critical element. It adds perspective to the theoretical findings revealed through the normative legal method. Kelsen becomes empowered to critically assess the current state of international law and its contemporary development, represented, for instance, by his appraisal of the Nuremberg trials.

Second, Kelsen would agree with the methodological claim that differentiating between the theory of law and philosophy of law may be construed in analogy to the Kantian distinction of theoretical from practical reason. This parallel would be close to Kelsen's mind, for whom the Königsberg philosopher was – as Jerzy Wróblewski put it – 'a methodological master'. Indeed, Kelsen's considerations, especially concerning how the value of peace determines the solution of problems and shortcomings of international law, resemble the philosophy of law as ethics – practised from the perspective of practical reason. The division of statements about the law as it is (theory) and law as it ought to be (philosophy) resonates well with the pure theory's methodological and epistemic claims. Although Kelsen regards any considerations on the law's ideal, just law or justice as speculative and beyond the interests of the proper legal science, he does not question their purposefulness. Moreover, as his teleological views on international law show, Kelsen does not shy away from engaging in 'philosophical'

[82] ibid 171.

[83] Kelsen, *Das Problem der Souveränität und die Theorie des Völkerrechts* (n 9) 13–14.

reflection (as defined here). He often changes the hats of legal scientist and legal philosopher, almost imperceptibly.

Third, Kelsen's philosophy of international law is to be understood foremost as construed in response to the teleological question. As such, it fills what some consider a gap in the pure theory of law understood as a particular legal-philosophical school of legal thought. Kelsen shows that the answer to the teleological question does not necessarily amount to providing an axiological or factual foundation for the normativity of law. Instead, the author of the *Pure Theory of Law* uses the teleology of peace as an essential axiological tool that allows him to fully explain his theory of legal orders, which belongs to the 'theoretical' part of his theory of law. Even if peace is an instrumental value and does not violate the methodological assumptions of Kelsenian moral relativism, introducing the teleological context is necessary to depict the evolution of legal orders. The explicative power of the philosophy of law based on the teleology of peace is equally important as the normative philosophy projecting more outwardly political and critical arguments on the desired path of development of international law. Although methodologically and epistemically separated within the pure theory of law, the theory and philosophy of international law are simultaneously inextricably linked and dependent on each other for argumentative power.

PART III

Democracy

10

Hans Kelsen's Normativism, the Theory of Democracy and Enlightenment Values*

MONIKA ZALEWSKA

I. Introduction

Although Hans Kelsen gained recognition mostly due to his pure theory of law, he was a much more versatile thinker. His research interests encompassed a wide scope of social sciences: in addition to legal theory, he explored international law, political philosophy, theory of justice, and even anthropology. Kelsen's ideas on these subjects are recorded in 604 items, primarily books and articles. However, the question arises as to how these research fields are connected with one another.

This chapter examines the relationship between normativism and the theory of democracy. Although, it is argued that the theory of democracy is considered as a part of the pure theory of law, it is worthwhile to clarify the relations between Kelsen's normativism, understood as Kelsen's account on law, and the theory of democracy.[1] The chapter aims to identify the common ground for both theories, and attempts to determine the manner in which they are united into a single project. Such an objective involves more than just a reconstruction of Kelsen's thoughts: it attempts to understand Kelsen's convictions and the values which led him to become a legal positivist and supporter of democracy. For this reason, the main focus will be placed on Kelsen's own writings and a charitable interpretation of them. Kelsen's early account on democracy will be outlined, and will be supplemented with his mature approach to democracy characterised by his 'American years'; this latter approach bears some of the keys to the puzzles surrounding his legal theory and its relationship with theory of democracy. In the conclusion, the common ground between Kelsen's legal science and theory of democracy will be identified. Furthermore, this chapter will demonstrate that Kelsen

* This research has been financed by the National Science Centre (Poland) within the framework of the 2021/41/B/HS5/01174 research project.

[1] For the clarity of the argument, I will use description 'normativism' to signify in this chapter Kelsen's account on law, known mostly from his book titled *Pure Theory of Law* in contrast to the pure theory of law, understood as a theory, which encompasses both domains.

constructed theories not only for scientific purposes, but also for reasons stemming from his own perception of social reality, more specifically, the dangers confronting the society he lived in at the time. His theories were intended to support most the best system for a thriving society, which in his view was democracy.

For this purpose, the first part will briefly reconstruct the idea that lies behind normativism in its classical form, known from the first edition of the *Pure Theory of Law* (1934), especially its methodological assumptions focused on the rejection of natural law doctrines. This part will demonstrate that Kelsen has two main purposes when writing *Pure Theory of Law*. The first was the creation of legal science and the second was his conviction that positive law serves the value of peace. To understand the association of peace with positive law and the reasons for rejecting the doctrine of natural law will be explained. The second part will focus on the theory of democracy with regard to the values serving democracy itself, as well as the institutions stemming from and securing these values. It will be demonstrated that the core value of democracy is freedom and that the core institution of democracy is a parliament, which most efficiently secures the value of freedom. After explaining the significance of democracy, the third part of the work will explain the nature of the relation between normativism and democracy by distinguishing and explaining the meaning of categories common to democracy and the doctrine of legal positivism: the category of relativism, peace, and legality.

II. The Idea of Normativism in the Context of the Rejection of Natural Law Doctrines

Normativism's primary aim is to build legal science (*Rechtslehre*). As Ota Weinberger rightly put it, what Kelsen meant by Rechtslehre is 'a system which depicts one aspect of a sphere defined by the questions put'.[2] Such an approach rules out any syncretism of methods.[3] Kelsen's quest was to address how lawyers cognise the law, and how they organise legal concepts in the structural aspect. As Weinberger notes: 'When he [Kelsen] seeks to depict the universal characteristics of law, this must be understood in terms of structural generality, and not in inductively-based empirical generalisation'.[4]

Kelsen tried to explain these processes in objective terms, first by employing a neo-Kantian paradigm, and later turning to an analytical one. His thought is both a critique of the positivistic approach presented by the older generation of legal positivists, as well as a rejection of natural law doctrines. Although the legal positivists shared the same aim as Kelsen, ie, to describe law in a manner conforming to scientific requirements, Kelsen believed that they failed to achieve this goal by introducing the wrong methodology. Namely, the legal positivists identified law in terms of facts, for

[2] O Weinberger, 'Introduction: Hans Kelsen as Philosopher' in H Kelsen, *Essays in Legal and Moral Philosophy*, P Heath trans, O Weinberger (ed) (Dordrecht, D Reidel Publishing Company, 1973) ix–xxv, xii.
[3] ibid xi.
[4] ibid 14.

instance that legal facts are obtained by the virtue of social facts.[5] For Kelsen, such an approach leads to false conclusions about the nature of law. Contrary to the older generation of legal positivists, Kelsen claimed that, for the purposes of legal science, law is not a fact and cannot be treated as such; hence, its nature cannot be revealed by methods stemming from sociology or psychology. Instead, Kelsen claims that law is a normative phenomenon and as such should be examined in the realm of the Ought sphere, instead of the Is. The importance of this postulate can be fully understood only if combined with Kelsen's neo-Kantian conviction that the method constitutes its object, ie, that 'objects of the scientific system are constituted by the perspective, which is itself defined by the statement of the problem and the mode of approach'.[6] Hence, in order to describe the law as pure and free from any alien elements, one must choose the method correctly, and the only proper method is the normative one. What legal positivists created was not correct legal science, but rather law seen from sociological or psychological perspectives. The aim of legal science is to describe law as it is, abstaining from any evaluations of the findings. This leads to the second grand separation in Kelsen's theory which is the separation of law from morality. In this case, Kelsen shared the view of the older generation of legal positivists; however, he also provided some new arguments, which will be presented in more detail in the following paragraphs.

Kelsen's goal to create legal science seems to be clear. The most straightforward answer to the enquiry 'why Kelsen wanted to create legal science' is that he wanted to explain this part of social reality in objective and universal terms. However, when Kelsen's normativism is interpreted in a broader historical context, along with his critique of natural law doctrines and his theory of democracy, a new reason for creating legal science emerges. As Urbinati and Accetti point out in their introduction to Kelsen's *The Essence and Value of Democracy* (1920) Kelsen's purity of his theory was also a political strategy:

> [T]o assert the political independence of the constitutional conception of the legal order in the face of multiple challenges that were raised against it by revolutionary bolshevism, the Catholic movement, and incipient fascist movements, [Kelsen] constituted a way of reasserting its capacity to deal with the mounting crisis in a peaceful and democratic way, since its implication was that it would not be necessary to overthrow the existing constitutional structure for the contending parties to achieve their goals.[7]

Hence, by observing anti-democratic trends in Europe, Kelsen wanted to create a theory which would be able to deal with forthcoming challenges by securing the constitutional conception of a legal order. The exact approach by which Kelsen's pure theory of law was supposed to fulfil this mission will be discussed in the following sections. The first step can be reconstructed in Kelsen's texts concerning the critique of natural law and support for legal positivism. Kelsen provided many arguments against

[5] See T Gizbert-Studnicki, 'The Social Sources Thesis. Metaphysic and Metaphilosophy' in P Banas, A Dyrda, and T Gizbert-Studnicki (eds), *Metaphilosophy of Law* (Oxford, Hart Publishing, 2016) 121–46.

[6] Weinberger (n 2) xi.

[7] N Urbinati and CI Accetti, 'Editors' Introduction' in H Kelsen, *The Essence and Value of Democracy*, B Graf trans (New York, Rowman & Littlefield Publishers, 2013) 1–24, 2.

the natural law doctrine. In this section, I will analyse only the one relevant from the normativistic point of view. These arguments pave the way for the relation between legal positivism and democracy, which is the value of peace. The value of peace is the goal and the outcome of the application of legal positivism, and one that rests at the core of the concept of democracy, which will be discussed in the final section.

Kelsen critiqued natural law doctrines in several texts. One especially relevant account seems to be 'The Idea of Natural Law' from 1928 and *What is Justice? Justice, Law and Politics in the Mirror of Science* from 1957. The structure of these texts is based on the same principle: for Kelsen, the opposition between natural and positive law is essential, as this contrast allows the nature of both orders to be understood. Hence, these texts explain how Kelsen understands the natural law doctrine and legal positivism, and why he rejected the former. Two main reasons can be distinguished here. First, Kelsen rejected natural law doctrines because he claimed that they are unscientific and second, because for him, a conflict existed between absolute justice and peace, and Kelsen foresaw understanding of law in legal positivism terms as essential for peaceful coexistence.

Kelsen begins his argument with an analysis of the meaning of 'natural law'. He notes the paradoxical character of this term. Contrary to natural law doctrines, 'natural' refers to laws of nature, which can be quantified and solidly described. On the other hand, natural law, being more speculative in its quest to address the enquiry 'what is just?', is immune to such concrete analyses.[8] In fact, Kelsen notes, the term 'natural law' is the antithesis of 'artificial law' which describes positive law: something stemming from the arbitrary will of human beings and is forcefully imposed on individuals.[9] Such natural legal order can be derived from two sources: a divine and immanent one embodied by God, and a physical and mental one based on human nature. In the latter case, the objective principle of justice becomes a more subjective one, with the consequence that the idea of natural law attempts to become positive law.[10] By the same token, when natural law is derived from God's will, which is characteristic of the world of values but non-existent in the world of nature, it is just 'divine arbitrariness'.[11] Kelsen concludes that for this reason, the contrast between objective and natural, and subjective and artificial is deprived of force.[12] Being objective, natural law sets the standard for the subjective positive law, which can be evaluated as 'good' or 'bad'. While natural law draws its validity from its content, which is 'just', 'good' or 'right' (ie, the material principle of validity), the validity of positive law stems from formal grounds, namely it was created in an appropriate way (ie, the formal principle of validity).[13] It can be seen here how the meaning of 'objective' and 'subjective' is twisted on the epistemic level. For Kelsen, only legal positivism is able to provide objective

[8] H Kelsen, 'The Idea of Natural Law' in H Kelsen, *Essays in Legal and Moral Philosophy* P Heath trans, O Weinberger (ed) (Dordrecht, D Reidel Publishing Company, 1973) 27–60, 27–28.

[9] ibid 28–29.

[10] ibid 29.

[11] ibid; H Kelsen, *What is Justice? Justice, Law and Politics in the Mirror of Science* (Berkeley, The Lawbook Exchange, 2013) 139.

[12] Kelsen, 'The Idea of Natural Law' (n 8) 30.

[13] ibid 31.

results; as natural law doctrine is subjective, it lacks the capacity to form scientific conclusions. In this context Kelsen notes:

> Positivism and (epistemological) relativism belong together, just as natural law theory and (metaphysical) absolutism do. Every attempt to shatter the purely relative and hypothetical basis of positive law, to get beyond it somehow, whether covertly or openly, to an absolute justification – and for obvious political reasons, this attempt must repeatedly be made – signifies the abolition of the distinction between positive and natural law, an incursion of natural law theory into the scientific treatment of positive law, and – if an analogy with the science is permitted – an intrusion of metaphysics into the field of experience.[14]

The confusion of positive and natural law, and the speculative nature of natural law, make legal science impossible. It is impractical to address the question 'which value is superior?' in a similar manner as to question whether iron is heavier than water.[15] Hence, enquiries concerning values cannot be the subject of science and make sense only if the social order is separated from the natural order.[16] Hence, for Kelsen the major flaws of the natural law doctrine are its subjectivity and arbitrariness, which result in it being rejected within both the scientific and the social fields. Due to its subjective character, the natural law doctrine cannot be reconciled within the scientific sphere, nor in the social sphere, as it might exclude peaceful coexistence in society. Kelsen sums up the issue of justice thus:

> I started this essay with the question as to what is justice. Now at its end I am quite aware that I have not answered it. My only excuse is that in this respect I am in the best company … I must acquiesce in a relative justice and I can only say what justice is to me. Since science is my profession, and hence the most important thing in my life, justice to me, is that social order under whose protection the search for truth can prosper. 'My' justice then is the justice of freedom, the justice of peace, the justice of democracy – the justice of tolerance.[17]

In the context of peace as the purpose of law, Kelsen claims, the legal institutions are more eligible and better equipped to issue just verdicts than the individuals trying to put an end to a dispute based on their perception of natural law. What matters here is that legal institutions do not aim to discover eternal truth but rather put an end to the dispute. In the higher scope, their challenge is to support the order of peace to which the positive legal order aspires.[18] Positivistic legal order is to guarantee peace by prohibiting the use of force, which is monopolised by a state in the form of a sanction. At the same time, for Kelsen, the conflict between natural and positive law is also presented as the choice between justice and peace.[19] Following Pierre Bayle, Kelsen claimed that 'all disorder arises not from toleration but from intolerance'.[20] And this is the common ground of positive law doctrine and democracy. Both of them favour the order – be it legal or be it social – which is governed by the rule of peace, even if this occasionally

[14] ibid 38.
[15] Kelsen, *What is Justice?* (n 11) 140.
[16] H Kelsen, 'Foundations of Democracy' (1955) 66 *Ethics* 1, 16.
[17] Kelsen, *What is Justice?* (n 11) 441.
[18] Kelsen, 'The Idea of Natural Law' (n 8) 45–47.
[19] ibid 57.
[20] H Kelsen, 'What is Justice?' in H Kelsen, *Essays in Legal and Moral Philosophy*, P Heath trans, O Weinberger (ed) (Dordrecht, D Reidel Publishing Company, 1973) 1–26, 23.

occurs at the price of absolute justice. The problems associated with peace will be further elaborated in section III, whose aim is to identify the common ground for normativism and the theory of democracy. However, the concept of democracy in Kelsen's pure theory of law first needs to be outlined.

III. The Concept of Democracy

Kelsen presented his idea of democracy as an ideal type.[21] Such a type does not necessarily correspond with reality, but indicates the features which an ideal democracy should include. Such an ideal type serves at least three purposes. First, it allows democracy and the values surrounding it to be discussed in more objective terms. Kelsen is able to avoid the counter-arguments that the idea of democracy in question is utopian or that he derives normative conclusions from descriptive premises.[22] Secondly, assuming democracy as the ideal type provides a point of reference for actual democracies, one that can be used to evaluate the strong and weak points of current socio-political situation and determine the direction of changes needed to achieve a democratic system as close to the ideal type as possible.[23] Finally, having an ideal type allows democracy to be compared with autocracy, thus allowing us to better understand both of them.[24]

Early attempts to define the elements which constitute democracy were given by Kelsen in his book *The Essence and Value of Democracy* published in 1929[25] and 'State-Form and World-Outlook' from 1933.[26] Although these two texts have different characters, both of them represent a response to the dangerous trends which occurred in Europe that time, and include a number of elements, such as freedom, people, parliament, representation, majority rule, administration, and the process by which a leader is selected. These elements can be divided into two aspects of democracy: values and institutions. The values, especially freedom, serve as the basis of specific institutions, such as parliament or majority rule, and the reasons for their existence. In turn, the institutions secure the proper realisation of democratic values.

A. Values of Democracy

For Kelsen, the primary value governing democracy is freedom. Kelsen notes that 'the Idea of democracy is the Idea of freedom as political-self-determination'.[27] This quote

[21] H Kelsen, 'State-Form and World-Outlook' in H Kelsen, *Essays in Legal and Moral Philosophy*, P Heath trans, O Weinberger (ed) (Dordrecht, D Reidel Publishing Company, 1973) 95–113, 98.

[22] On this matter, see very interesting critique of Kelsen's relativism performed by Torben Spaak. It seems that Kelsen's description of democracy as an ideal type has the potential to avoid some parts of this critique. T Spaak, 'Relativism in the Philosophy of Law' SSRN Scholarly Paper (Rochester, NY, Social Science Research Network, 2019) 5: papers.ssrn.com/sol3/papers.cfm?abstract_id=3333634.

[23] Urbinati and Accetti (n 7) 5.

[24] Kelsen, 'State-Form and World-Outlook' (n 21) 97–98.

[25] Kelsen, *The Essence and Value of Democracy* (n 7).

[26] Kelsen, 'State-Form and World-Outlook' (n 21).

[27] ibid 99.

very nicely indicates the role of freedom in Kelsen's understanding of democracy. The expression of freedom can be found in the state orders created by 'those who are themselves subject to it'.[28] Hence, freedom is Kelsen's main rule, the one on which democracy depends. Kelsen understands freedom as the embodiment of social order and the idea that the rules of coercion are only legitimate if the individuals subjected to them also contribute to their creation. Such social or political freedom can be regarded as the freedom of practical reason; this can be contrasted with natural freedom, which means freedom from society.[29] Kelsen explains: 'Natural freedom negates the social order, while social freedom, as the idea of free will, negates the causal orders'.[30] Social freedom stands also in contrast with an authoritarian regime which is based on the rule of heteronomy and authority. In the context of democracy, the freedom rule is understood as government by the people.

As Urbinati and Accetti note, Kelsen chooses the rule of freedom over two other alternatives: the principle of equality and the principle of epistemic quality of political decisions. These two principles, especially the former, are still present in Kelsen's doctrine but they are secondary to the principle of freedom.[31] What matters for Kelsen is to identify the distinctive feature of democracy. Equality which focuses solely on the fulfilment of the basic needs of human beings – the so-called government for the people – can also be achieved in an autocracy, for instance, in systems such as communism.[32] In spite of this, Kelsen regards equality as being present, but in a limited form, ie, as a rule existing within freedom understood as collective self-government. Namely, in 'State-Form and World-Outlook' Kelsen derives the majority principle from a combination of the principle of freedom with the equality rule.

Freedom alone cannot completely explain the phenomenon of democracy. Freedom should be supplemented and restricted by the principle of equality, which Kelsen understands as '"I" that wills freedoms, also for the "Thou" to be of the same nature as itself'.[33] Such an approach to 'thou' is signified by tolerance, which is a subsequent and necessary value in democracy, enabling debate and compromise.

In 'Foundations of Democracy', written in 1955, Kelsen brings equality and freedom even closer, stating that they express two characteristic instincts of humans as social beings longing for freedom and equality, and as such, both instincts are fundamental for democracy.[34] Both instincts aim to deny another man supreme power, which can be imposed against one's freedom; they beg the question of how a person can bear such power as 'he is a man like me'.[35] However, Kelsen underlines that these two values cannot be realised together, yet this dialectic can be embodied in democracy within the framework of the normative order. The normative order is the catalyst which transforms natural freedom into social freedom. Social freedom is sustained if one participates in the creation of the normative order.[36]

[28] ibid.
[29] ibid 28; Urbinati and Accetti (n 7) 6; Kelsen, 'Foundations of Democracy' (n 16) 18–19.
[30] Kelsen, *The Essence and Value of Democracy* (n 7) 28.
[31] Kelsen, 'State-Form and World-Outlook' (n 21) 102.
[32] Kelsen, *The Essence and Value of Democracy* (n 7) 31; Urbinati and Accetti (n 7) 8.
[33] Kelsen, 'State-Form and World-Outlook' (n 21) 99.
[34] Kelsen, 'Foundations of Democracy' (n 16) 18.
[35] ibid.
[36] ibid 19. Such freedom is contrasted with the metaphysical one, which means exemption from the law of causality, and hence, by having free will, the man can be responsible for his actions and subject to moral or

On the other hand, the principle of epistemic quality of political decisions, which is grounded by the conviction that democracy produces the best political decision, is criticised by Kelsen. He rejects the existence of objective political truth. Kelsen perceives such an approach as a removal of power from the citizens and its transfer to politicians allegedly having access to the objective political truth, resulting in an infringement of the autonomy rule. Instead, Kelsen distinguishes epistemic relativism as the basis of democracy.[37] The notion of relativism will be elaborated further in a following section. For now, it suffices to say that in Kelsen's view, there is no single objective political truth, but rather a plurality of world-views and points of view: freedom and truth are opposites on the political ground.[38]

This idea might sound a little suspicious when Kelsen's famous scientific approach is considered. However, this can be explained by indicating two different levels on which Kelsen operates. When involved in the legal science enterprise, Kelsen needs to achieve objectivity. But when he states that there is no objective truth on the political level, he derives this claim from a critique of natural law doctrine. Legal science can be objective, while the discussion concerning values cannot. Most of the political sphere concerns the social and ethical area, where objective truth is often unattainable. Furthermore, as will be demonstrated in a following section, for Kelsen, rational world-view and relativism are strictly bound together. In such a vision, the pure theory of law serves as a part of social science aimed at objectivity; on a higher level, it also exists in the sphere of politics. Consequently, the form of law described by the pure theory of law should be politics-neutral, and thus objective. What is shaped by politics and by democratic debates is enabled by a relativistic world-view.[39] These debates form the content of law and must be channelled by special institutions of direct or deliberative democracy. Of these, Kelsen favours deliberative democracy, where the Parliament has the greatest potential to sustain as much freedom in society as possible.

B. Democratic Institutions

On the institutional level the core of democracy, governed by the freedom rule, is Parliament. Kelsen defines parliamentarism as follows: 'parliamentarism means government by a collegial organ democratically elected by the people based on universal,

legal norms. Kelsen opposes the view that human will is the exemption from causality and argues that this confusion stems from the absence of differentiation between fact and value. While one's will in the natural sphere is the subject of causality, in the social sphere, human behaviour can be interpreted through the rule of imputation. In such a sense man is free, because he is responsible on behalf on imputation, which binds the condition with the consequence in a normative manner. Imputation does not exclude causality, but rather most of the times presupposes it. (ibid 20.) This aspect of freedom, bound with imputation is characteristic for Kelsen's normativism, however it seems that it differs from freedom, which is essential for democracy. The freedom associated with democracy is rather bound with participation in the law-making process, and the dynamic aspect of law, while the freedom associated with imputation seems to be relevant for the matter of responsibility and static aspect of law.

[37] Urbinati and Accetti (n 7) 8.

[38] ibid.

[39] Democracy itself is founded on values of freedom; later, in 1955, Kelsen associates democracy with human rights, which might seem striking considering it is a part of the pure theory of law. However, these values are revealed in the content of both substantial and procedural law, which is not the subject of normativism.

equal suffrage and the principle of majority'.[40] As a parliament is chosen by elections, and hence is supposed to represent individuals and embody the rule of majority, Kelsen appears to be against unanimity, and in favour of the majority principle. The majority principle ensures that the maximum number of people is free from coercive order.[41] The danger of unanimity is that even a single individual could prevent the decision-making process,[42] and give real power to a minority. In such case, it would be a minority who rules rather than the majority.[43] As Kelsen aptly notes: '(t)he idea underlying the principle of majority is that the social order shall be in accordance with as many subjects as possible and in discordance with as few as possible'.[44]

The will of the majority must be realised, but to avoid an abuse of its power, this realisation must be tempered by the rights of the minority. Such abuse can result in the alienation or political annihilation of minorities, resulting in the dissolution of both the majority principle and any democratic legitimacy. Hence, minorities should be protected and their active participation in democratic processes should be guaranteed. For this reason, direct democracy may be less representative in character than a deliberative one, because majority might exercise their power without regard to the rights of minority. Direct democracy gives exclusive power to the majority and the strongest, thus eliminating minorities from political debate. Consequently, Kelsen perceives the majority rule in a dialectical way and associates it with compromise. The majority rule exists only as long as the minority also has its political space; otherwise, the majority loses its character. From this follows that the minority party is necessary in the recognition and existence of the party which has majority.

This dialectical majority rule is followed by the essential landmark of democracy: a debate in which argument meets counter-argument, thus giving rise to a compromise understood as 'favouring that which binds over that which divides those who are to be brought together'. Without minorities, the democratic process cannot take place, as it would be impossible for any debate based on arguments and counter-arguments to take place and the possibility of compromise would simply vanish. In such a case, the dynamic processes of self-actualisation of the state and society vision would be supplanted by static silent agreement and the assumption of absolute truth. Hence, for Kelsen, democracy is perceived as a dynamic process rather than the 'achievement of some good or correct outcome and not even the unification of the masses in the image of a single "body" that a leader or a vision pretends to embody'. In order to ensure the rights of minorities, a requirement of higher quorum, or special majority, should be established at two-thirds or three-quarters, and a proportionality rule,[45] should be introduced;[46] such a requirement is necessary when fundamental rights are

[40] Kelsen, *The Essence and Value of Democracy* (n 7) 48.

[41] Kelsen, 'State-Form and World-Outlook' (n 21) 99.

[42] Such a scenario happened in 18th-century Poland, where the anonymity rule existed. Any deputy could use the *liberum veto* to paralyse the decision-making process, which too many times was the case. The use of *liberum veto* is considered one of the reasons why the I Republic of Poland eventually fell at the end of the 18th century.

[43] Kelsen, *The Essence and Value of Democracy* (n 7) 31; Kelsen, 'Foundations of Democracy' (n 16) 25.

[44] Kelsen, 'Foundations of Democracy' (n 16) 25.

[45] Understood as a rule that each political faction finds representation proportional with the outcomes of the electoral process within the elected legislative body.

[46] Kelsen, *The Essence and Value of Democracy* (n 7) 72; Urbinati and Accetti (n 7) 18.

being discussed, as this mechanism would ensure that the minority can influence the decision-making process in the most essential debates. Additionally, the proportionality rule ensures that all political groups are represented in Parliament according to their strength.[47] This is only possible if the principle of tolerance is in effect. While Kelsen mentions tolerance only in general terms in his early writings, in 'Foundations of Democracy', he links tolerance with fundamental human rights and freedoms. Namely, Kelsen argues that in modern democracy the government cannot interfere with the spheres of life of its citizens, if they are protected by human rights; in this sense, Kelsen mentions the freedom of the press, religion, opinion and science, which is especially important for minorities, by constituting a safeguard against the rule of the majority.[48]

Although rule by the majority is time-consuming and leads to indecisiveness, this as an advantage of democracy. Since majority rule does not bring any objective truths, but rather a compromise, which in the future might be subject to change and correction, majority rule is more dynamic and flexible than an autocratic truth-oriented approach. Finally, Kelsen regards direct democracy as inefficient in advanced society. Parliamentarism, as 'a compromise between the democratic demand for freedom and the division of labour',[49] is the only realistic option under contemporary social conditions.[50] As Kelsen notes: 'The larger the political community, the less the "people" as such is able to engage directly in the truly creative aspects of government'.[51]

As a result, the Parliament is at the centre of the institutional part of Kelsen's concept of democracy. Parliament serves as a forum where specific points of view and interests are met and peacefully deliberated by the representatives of interest groups. In addition, more importantly for Kelsen, elections give people the power to select and change those who rule, hence, providing control over Parliament. Elections allow the substitution of leaders and for political reorientation to take place in a peaceful way.[52] Such an approach might be reminiscent of the Hobbesian way of thinking about law, where peaceful coexistence is ensured by the legal order. But by adding freedom as the predominating idea of parliamentarism[53] Kelsen maintains more of a Kantian position, one in which the resignation of unchecked subjective will by the adoption of a legal framework resulted in greater freedom, allowing for peaceful coexistence.[54] At this point, he shares common ground with legal positivism, which such peaceful coexistence should ensure. The value of peace alone can also lead to the social order envisioned by Hobbes, where one who rules stands above the law. However, for democracy, additional values are needed, and for Kelsen one of these is the aforementioned 'freedom'.

Within this framework the key role is assigned to parties. This role is highlighted by Kelsen's critique of 'the People' construct. For him, the idea of the People as a unified entity holding political rights is a naive one, because many are excluded from active

[47] Kelsen, *The Essence and Value of Democracy* (n 7) 72.
[48] Kelsen, 'Foundations of Democracy' (n 16) 28.
[49] Kelsen, *The Essence and Value of Democracy* (n 7) 49.
[50] ibid 48.
[51] ibid 49.
[52] Urbinati and Accetti (n 7) 9–10.
[53] Kelsen, *The Essence and Value of Democracy* (n 7) 48.
[54] Urbinati and Accetti (n 7) 10.

or even passive participation in ruling due to their age or mental state, not to mention gender in the times when Kelsen was writing his text.[55] Kelsen concludes that the People do not exist as a political force and in order to gain an impact on decision-making processes, the People must transform into the party.[56] In practice, the concept of the political party is much more important than 'the People'. For Kelsen, democracy is strictly bound with the multiparty system.[57] Since modern societies are characterised by conflicts of interests and different world-views, parliamentary debates between parties allow conflicts to be resolved in a peaceful manner which is satisfactory to the majority but based on compromise.[58] Hence, political parties are perceived by Kelsen as mediating organs for individuals, through which they achieve political goals. The party is the medium that allows an individual to gain political existence as a voter or a member; the party as a whole then has a chance to influence the political shape of the state. This way, the party becomes a bottom-up organisation which requires proportional representation to include the widest spectrum of views.[59] As such, the existence of parties enables both major values: freedom and peace.

With the question now clearly set out, it is time to identify the source from which legal positivism and democracy are derived. The next section will analyse the relationships between democracy and autocracy according to a particular world view.

IV. The Relation between Democracy and Normativism

The principles of democracy and legal positivism in Kelsen's thought were synthesised in his 1955 text 'Foundations of Democracy'. This text differs from his earlier accounts on democracy; in particular, it seems to be more mature. This may be due to two factors: first, Kelsen had spent about 15 years in America, and as a professor at Berkeley, was involved in political philosophy, and secondly, following the experience of the Second World War and the emergence of the 'Iron Curtain', he had a much clearer insight into both fascist and communist ideologies.

In this section, I will examine both perspectives: his early perspective, which lacks any such synthesis, and his more mature approach, where he explicitly indicates a link between democracy and legal positivism. By taking such an approach, it will be possible to trace back the direction of Kelsen's thought and identify the categories and values which allowed Kelsen to position himself in the positivist and democratic camp. These categories and values are common for both domains, and hence determine the relationship between democracy and normativism that allows them to coexist within the framework of the pure theory of law. I have distinguished three such

[55] Kelsen, *The Essence and Value of Democracy* (n 7) 37. At the time when Kelsen wrote this text, the women in Switzerland were still deprived of the right to vote.

[56] ibid 40. Kelsen wrote his text in 1920, shortly after the First World War when the existence of a modern multiparty system was rather a new trend in Europe (with a few exceptions). Nowadays, Kelsen's firm statement about parties seems to be obvious; however, new trends are emerging, such as the influence of NGOs on national and international bodies.

[57] ibid 38–39.

[58] ibid 40.

[59] Urbinati and Accetti (n 7) 13.

categories: first, absolutism and relativism, which are associated with scientific (or not scientific) outlook; secondly, peace; and finally, legality.

A. Absolutism and Relativism

The difference between relativism and absolutism will bring us closer to understanding how normativism and democracy stem from the same root, as is the case for natural law doctrine and autocracy.[60] As will be demonstrated in both cases, Kelsen associates these differences with personality types and eventually world-view. The latter category is decisive for both theory of democracy and legal positivism.[61] Legal positivism comes from the same world-view as democracy, ie, relativism, and the natural law doctrine comes from the same world-view as autocracy, ie, absolutism. When Kelsen writes about philosophical types of world-views, he uses the method of the ideal type again. As he explains:

> [philosophical types] have been constructed from a particular point of view, namely that of the relatedness of a view of the universe and a philosophy of life, of natural and social philosophy. This makes from the outset, for a certain one-sidedness of the scheme.[62]

This time, Kelsen provides a different justification for the use of this method, and with good reason. Although none of the philosophical systems correspond perfectly with the ideal type, this method 'is able to demonstrate far reaching parallels between natural and social philosophy'.[63] As such, it better fits Kelsen's aim, which is to reveal some tendencies and interpret them properly with the ideal scheme.[64] Kelsen's aim here is to understand some processes rather than accurately reconstruct every detail of them.

In order to establish a common ground for legal positivism and democracy, first I will demonstrate how absolutism and relativism influence legal positivism and natural law doctrines, then I will demonstrate the influence of relativism and absolutism on democracy and autocracy.

i. Absolutism, Relativism and the Doctrine of Legal Positivism

For Kelsen, the fundamental division determining later choices between autocracy and democracy or natural law and legal positivism is that of absolutism and relativism. On an epistemological level, these two attitudes, ie, towards science and truth, determine the social and political spheres, particularly the latter. Kelsen devotes a great deal of attention to the problem of the absolutistic world-view stemming from metaphysical dualism in the Appendix to the *General Theory of Law and State* titled: 'Natural Law Doctrine and Legal Positivism', which is the translation of the

[60] H Kelsen, *General Theory of Law and State*, A Wedberg trans (Cambridge, MA, Harvard University Press, 1945) 419–44.

[61] I use here the description 'legal positivism', just as Kelsen did in his texts meaning legal positivism in a broad sense, in which normativism is also included.

[62] Kelsen, *General Theory of Law and State* (n 60) 441.

[63] ibid.

[64] ibid.

'Philosophischen Grundlagen der Naturrechtslehre and des Rechtspositivismus' from 1928. This text consists of two parts. In the lesser known part, Kelsen analyses the dependence of world-view on one's personality. Today, it would be hard to call this analysis scientific, but it provides an elegant explanation for the fact that legal positivism and the theory of democracy share common ground. As such, it can be treated as a reconstruction of Kelsen's way of thinking about law and social order, and as a means of understanding Kelsen's motives as to why legal positivism has the potential to support democratic rule. Later in 1955, Kelsen still regards the division into absolutism and relativism as essential; moreover, he identifies the epistemological and social dimensions of this division as sharing common ground. As Kelsen notes in each case, an aspect of domination is present in the relationship between subject and object. Be it epistemological or political absolutism, the subject tries to master the object, either by 'bringing some order into the chaos of sensual perceptions', by evaluating the object as good or evil, or by gaining absolute power in autocracy. This observation leads Kelsen to the conclusion that these tendencies, their presence or absence, are rooted in the ego of the philosopher or politician and, to Kelsen, this is why these conflicts are so profound and cannot be reduced into a simple clash between powers.

An absolutistic world-view is characteristic of natural law doctrines and autocratic systems. And, as Kelsen explains in 1955, it is associated with the conviction that absolute reality exists, and that it exists independent of human cognition. This in turn leads to the notion of the existence of absolute truth and absolute values. Moreover 'absolute' is followed by perfection, hence reality, and values are not separated from each other. In such a framework, knowledge is only a reflection of the absolute.[65] Kelsen associates such belief with metaphysical dualism and contrasts it with scientific-critical philosophy.[66] He distinguishes several types of metaphysical dualism based around a pessimistic (revolutionary) type and an optimistic (conservative) type, as well as a compromise type which is more relativist. In this sense, the pessimistic and optimistic attitudes concern the present.

A pessimistic attitude results in either a neglectful attitude towards law or a revolutionary one; this attitude stems from the metaphysical and absolutistic conviction that a true, perfect world exists 'beyond', for instance, after death, and that reality is full of dangers and evil, and should be neglected. By analogy, positive law, being the perfect counterpart of natural law, is perceived as superfluous and harmful. Only natural law, which lies beyond positive law and state, is just and nullifies the positive legal order. Such an attitude leads to anarchism and prepares the ground for a revolutionary attitude.[67] The revolutionist is pessimistic towards the past and present circumstances of society and considers them worth destroying; he fears and runs away from the present and attempts to create a perfect, desired future. Alternatively, he has a strong belief in a 'golden age', a lost paradise at the beginning of time, and most importantly, this golden age is separated from the present by an unbridgeable abyss and has nothing in common with the recent past, which is rejected as the cause of present ills.[68]

[65] Kelsen, 'Foundations of Democracy' (n 16) 16.
[66] Kelsen, *General Theory of Law and State* (n 60) 410–44.
[67] ibid 423–25.
[68] ibid 423–26.

It is possible to foster a more optimistic outlook and reject this conviction that the only true, absolute reality and value is somewhere 'beyond' by building the confidence in oneself through the senses and reason. By doing so, such metaphysical dualism, landmarked by the conviction of the existence of two worlds, now attempts to reconcile the world 'beyond' with reality, instead of rejecting it: the earthly things are related to their divine archetypes. Hence, instead of denying reality, he explains it. The unbridgeable abyss between the two worlds has been filled. The individual is able to approximate reality by his sense and reason. This conviction leads to the development of epistemology. Such a world is not only real but also valuable: it is the best possible world. Positive law is regarded as perfectly valid, and natural law supports its existence, that is to say, even if not perfect, positive law is the best possible approximation of the absolute, just, natural order. Such an optimistic attitude leads to conservatism. The conservative affirms the present as long as it is in accordance with his ideal; hence, he will reject the future and be hostile to change, declaring that 'nothing better will follow'.[69] Instead, he is devoted to the past as the source of a noble present.[70]

The next stage gradually turns into relativism, which Kelsen associates with empirical doctrine and the conviction that reality exists only in the framework of the cognition.[71] Kelsen dubs the relativistic world-view the 'compromise type', which neither rejects reality, nor considers it as the best of all possible worlds. As a result, being hostile to revolution also rejects the claim that the present social order is the ideal. Such people are in favour of reforms which could improve social circumstances. They accept the world and positive law as they are. Kelsen writes: 'the empirical and especially social, world is interpreted as relatively good because they are not absolutely bad'.[72] Since the absolute natural doctrine is substituted with a relative version that has been adjusted to particular circumstances, contrary to its absolute counterpart, it does not preclude compromise. Kelsen notes that such relative natural law is able to justify the positive order and the state.[73]

The final stage overcomes metaphysical dualism and fosters a scientific-critical philosophy.[74] Although such a view may reject metaphysical explanation, it does not

[69] ibid 428.

[70] These two ideal types of metaphysical dualism demonstrate how, according to Kelsen, the general outlook on the world is transformed into attitudes towards the state, and how metaphysical dualism inevitably leads to an ideology which either justifies revolution or preserves social order. From the 21st-century perspective, some patterns in rhetoric used by populists can be identified in Kelsen's thought. These patterns can be compelling and sound coherent for many who identify their interests in them. Nowadays, we can also find revolutionists who neglect the social order and promise a utopian future, using the myth of a long-lost golden age. This vision is appealing for those who lack confidence and fear the present or, being confused by the complexity of the world, choose to reject science. On the other hand, a number of politicians glorify the present or promise a great near future as the outcome of the splendid recent past, and justify it based on the proximity of the social order to the ideal desired by God. Those interested in maintaining the status quo use metaphysical dualism to strengthen their position by the notion of natural law, while the weaker minority tend to have a revolutionary outlook, looking for an opportunity for change. But as long as they are the weaker minority, they submit to the rule of the stronger majority, even at the price of 'their' justice. In any case, both types need an absolute natural law doctrine to strengthen their claim.

[71] Kelsen, 'Foundations of Democracy' (n 16) 17.

[72] Kelsen, *General Theory of Law and State* (n 60) 430–32.

[73] ibid 433.

[74] One of the representatives who overcame this dualism was Immanuel Kant, but Kelsen describes such a way of thinking in much broader terms.

deny that there are limits for scientific enquiry. As Kelsen notes, science 'stops before the ultimate enigma'[75] or rather, that the individual resists the temptation to speculate on the ideas or archetypes of things, or the thing itself. Instead, cognition plays an important role by not being passive but by actively influencing the data of experience. An optimistic or pessimistic attitude does not apply here. Instead the process of cognition guarantees to obtain a truth which is relative.[76] As Kelsen notes in 1955, this means that the object of cognition is relative to the subject. Hence, truth and values are also relative and are separated from each other.[77] It follows from this that subjects of knowledge are equal in their *rational* cognition and in mutual relations, which ensures intersubjectivity.[78]

Kelsen's relativistic approach is not amoral or immoral. He claims that the best possibility is to only grasp relative values. From the point of view of rational knowledge, 'there are only human interests and thus conflicts of interest'.[79] Therefore, either one interest will be satisfied entirely at the expense of another, or compromise will be reached. In other words, only if peace is regarded as the highest social value will compromise serve as a just way of handling conflicts of interest. Thus, even peace is a relative value.[80] Relativism is underlined by the principle of tolerance defined by Kelsen as 'the demand, that is, that the religious, or political outlook of others should be understood in a spirit of goodwill, even if one does not share it, and indeed precisely because one does not'.[81] Tolerance linked to the freedom of thought is also connected with peaceful coexistence. As Weinberger aptly puts it:

> Kelsen's value-relativism naturally implies no denial of values or making light of value attitudes: it is simply a matter of regarding them as decisions, as something that cannot be demonstrated in purely cognitive fashion. Kelsen's pure positivism and his relativist theory of value are not unrealistic or neutral in their pragmatic consequences; they lead, rather to a critique of ideology, to an understanding of value-pluralism, to the postulate of tolerance, to a pluralistic democracy based on the free play of ideas in the self-correcting dialectic of clashing opinions within the field of legal development. They do this, however, without the fiction that in the process we shall simply apprehend 'correct' law that has somehow been previously given.[82]

The description of absolutism and relativism recalls familiar categories, such as absolute truth and justice, peace and tolerance. Also, it can be noticed that the dividing line does not lie between legal positivism and the natural law doctrine. For Kelsen, the relative natural law doctrine is closer to legal positivism than to its absolute version; more significantly, Kelsen also claims that the relative natural law doctrine is actually positivistic in its nature.

[75] Kelsen, *General Theory of Law and State* (n 60) 435.
[76] ibid 434.
[77] Kelsen, 'Foundations of Democracy' (n 16) 16–17.
[78] ibid 18.
[79] Kelsen, 'What is Justice?' (n 20) 22.
[80] ibid.
[81] ibid 23.
[82] Weinberger (n 2) xxv.

ii. Democracy and Autocracy in the Context of Relativism and Absolutism

In 'Foundations of Democracy' Kelsen presents a synthesis of his understanding of a 'democratic' personality type. First, such an individual wants freedom not only for himself, but also for others. In order to gain such a perspective, the ego cannot experience itself as unique and special, but rather as equal with others, claiming that the differences with others are not essential. Such conviction can only stem from a relativistic philosophy and is associated with an altruistic type of person, who sees others as his friends, and not as enemies. Such an attitude corresponds with the form of government, which tries not to interfere too much in the life of citizens.[83] Kelsen notes that such an attitude is associated with political forms where dominance is minimised and relativism prevails. As Kelsen puts it in *Essence and Value of Democracy*:

> [T]he man who, when he looks across at another, hears a voice within him saying: That is you. This kind of personality recognises himself again in the other, experiences the other a priori, not as something essentially alien, not as enemy, but as an equal and therefore a friend, and does not feel himself to be something unique, altogether incomparable and beyond repetition.[84]

In contrast, an autocracy operates according to the rule typical for absolutism: 'the stronger the will to power, the less appreciation of freedom'.[85] An autocratic leader is believed to have special qualities, to sometimes be of divine origin and is often believed to have access to absolute truth. In such a political form, the leader stands above all others as being unique and special. He is surrounded by the leadership myth, which is used to account for the force used to sustain the power[86] and represents absolute value; hence, he is not subject to criticism and is not accountable for his decisions. Kelsen dubs such a type as 'exaggerated ego-consciousness'[87] and links it with the rejection of equality as a social ideal. Hence, alongside freedom, equality between the ruler and the ruled is unwelcome. Inequality leads to a desired identification with authority, which 'is the secret of obedience', as Kelsen remarks.[88] As a result, autocracy represses political emotions into the private sphere, trying to dominate the masses, whose role is to be a passive recipient of orders. Characteristic are the words of Louis XIV 'l'etat, c'est moi', in contrast to the slogan 'l'etat, c'est nous'[89] which is better fitting of democracy. By bringing all these puzzles together, it can be seen that the category of peace stems from a relativistic outlook. Only the personality type which embraces relativism, equality and tolerance can bring the value of peace to realisation. Peace is excluded in absolutism, which is conqueror oriented, and excludes anything which is does not agree with an absolutistic doctrine.

[83] Kelsen, 'Foundations of Democracy' (n 16) 26.
[84] Kelsen, 'State-Form and World-Outlook' (n 21) 100.
[85] Kelsen, 'Foundations of Democracy' (n 16) 26; Kelsen, 'State-Form and World-Outlook' (n 21) 100.
[86] Kelsen, 'State-Form and World-Outlook' (n 21) 105.
[87] Kelsen, 'Foundations of Democracy' (n 16) 27.
[88] Kelsen, 'State-Form and World-Outlook' (n 21) 101.
[89] ibid 108; Kelsen, 'Foundations of Democracy' (n 16) 26.

B. Kelsen's Concept of Peace

Kelsen defines peace 'as a state characterized by the absence of force'.[90] Obviously, Kelsen does not mean the absolute absence of force, which would be reserved for anarchistic doctrines. There is an exception from the rule stating that the use of force is prohibited: force exists in a society, but remains under control of the state, in that its use by a state is restricted to certain individuals and under certain conditions, ie, in case a delict occurs. An individual who imposes force as a response to delict acts in the name of the community, as its organ, and such an organ holds the monopoly on the use of force. Hence, peaceful coexistence is ensured by the state, which has monopoly to use force in response to a delict. The emergence of a state results from the monopolisation and centralisation of force, which delegalises self-help, ie, the use of force to defend oneself.[91] Kelsen explains it as follows:

> It is not so much a question of whether a particular good shall be taken from one person and allotted to another, and indeed to just the one and only person 'entitled' to it, whether the natural law of '*suum cuique*' is to be realised in the relationship between them; what matters, rather is that their dispute shall be brought to an end.[92]

Hence, the scope of law is conflict resolution, ie, the successful finalisation of legal cases, by restoring the balance disturbed by the conflict. In such a vision, justice is perceived as a means which can serve the ultimate end, this being peace, but does not represent an end in itself. Justice should not be an end, because of the limits of human nature. It can be derived that Kelsen, probably following Kant, distinguishes values serving as a means to an end from those which represent a final goal. For Kelsen, peace is the latter, while justice is the former.

Such an explanation of peace and its relation to the use of force clarifies its relation to positive law; however, it does seem to be a sufficient condition for peaceful coexistence in society. When defined in such a way, peace explains the relationships between citizens, but not those between citizen and the state. Here Kelsen introduces a second dimension: the tension between peace and justice. Since justice is subjective, and the idea of what is just differs so widely between people, there is no hope in finding a single universal formula of what is just. This would result in society being condemned to make repeated forceful attempts to impose an idea of justice that may be acceptable to only one group. Even if such a law fulfilled one vision of justice, it would leave large parts of society with the feeling of living in a harsh, unjust order with the rules violating their moral system. Such society would be in a state of war without any hope for conflict resolution. The only resolution is to surrender the absolute ideal of justice in favour of a relative ideal of peace based on the rule of tolerance and compromise. For Kelsen, such an ideal of peace requires institutionalisation and the creation of general positive law rules.[93]

[90] H Kelsen, *Peace Through Law* (Berkeley, The Lawbook Exchange Ltd, 2000) 3.
[91] ibid 4–5.
[92] ibid; Kelsen, 'The Idea of Natural Law' (n 8) 57.
[93] ibid.

It could be argued that peace, as the absence of force, does not contradict conceptually the idea of justice. Moreover, as Kelsen notes, a just social order seems to be a necessary condition for peaceful coexistence: if society considers the social order as unjust, they will rebel against it.[94] In fact, Kelsen speaks about two different aspects of justice. The justice which he criticises is the absolute justice that serves as the foundation of the legal order. Thus, by stating what is just and what is not, Kelsen limits his rejection of justice to absolute natural law doctrines which would arbitrarily influence the content of law, ie, without any discussion. In this context, peace is understood as the coexistence of individuals who have different views on what is just: these individuals acknowledge and tolerate the point of view of others, and look to compromise for the sake of the greater good. These components of peace represent some form of justice which probably fulfils the condition of a just social order. Hence, peace itself is some form of justice. What matters here is that this is not absolute justice, one that excludes any other points of view.[95]

Peace can be reconciled with justice, but it does not have to be. Kelsen provides an example where only one group is interested in peace, this group being the one whose interests are secured. The others might try to violate the order but if they decide to maintain it, it is rather due to their weakness, which requires them to accept the minimal protection they receive under the circumstances. In such cases they do not consider the peace just. Kelsen concludes that 'longing for peace means as a rule, a renunciation of the original ideal of justice'.[96] Hence, such an approach to law requires a political system which would enable the creation of legal rules in the spirit of compromise and tolerance.

For Kelsen, these conditions are fulfilled by democracy. In the field of democracy, the dialectical procedure caused by the permanent tension between majority and minority leads to peaceful coexistence. As Kelsen notes: 'Democracy – it has truly been said – is a discussion. And for that very reason, the outcome of the process in which the state's will is formed here is – compromise'.[97] This feature guarantees, according to Kelsen, internal peace.[98] Kelsen also notes that the freedom that he has in mind is not the economic freedom of liberalism, but spiritual freedom, the freedom to express opinions, and last but not least, the freedom of science stemming from a relativistic outlook. In Kelsen's view, the latter corresponds particularly closely with democracy. Democracy based on peaceful discussion is marked by the same tendency as science. Between 'willing and knowing', both democracy and science move towards knowing and understanding the world instead of conquering and dominating it. Both

[94] S Roth, 'The Status of Peace as a Moral Value' (2008) 41 *Tradition: A Journal of Orthodox Jewish Thought* 156.

[95] The problem of the justice and peace dichotomy is multidimensional. In the literature the most discussed problem is the dilemma of how to end a broadly understood state of war and at the same time ensure justice for the perpetrators. It often happens that the peace is only possible if such justice is not served. For instance, the Good Friday Agreement with the IRA contained provisions foreseeing the early release from prison of members of the IRA who were found guilty of terrorist crimes. Such provisions were perceived by many British living in Northern Ireland as unjust. See N Biggar, 'Peace and Justice: A Limited Reconciliation' (2002) 5 *Ethical Theory and Moral Practice* 167, 168.

[96] Kelsen, *General Theory of Law and State* (n 60) 440.

[97] Kelsen, 'State-Form and World-Outlook' (n 21) 101.

[98] ibid.

value a critical approach and constant revisions of their claims. Such an approach requires both the principle of tolerance and the equality rule, which means that 'I am not special, but I am just like you'.[99] This in turn is possible only if the concept of law is ideology-neutral, and scientific in its nature. Only by adopting such a framework can society freely and peacefully participate in the debate about the shape of its social order. The absolutistic world-view, by infusing some values straight into the concept of law, excludes these values from the debate. In this sense, the concept of law stemming from absolutistic natural law doctrines limits freedom by preventing those who are subject to the law from influencing its content; as such, it is essentially anti-democratic. Contrary to democracy, autocracy does not tolerate opposition, nor the compromise and discussions leading to it. This results in the exclusion of freedom of speech and belief. Since there is only one absolute truth, science must submit to it. Science can only sustain power and is tolerated as such. Willing prevails over knowing, and conquering the world is more important than understanding it. As a result, the irrational triumphs over the relational,[100] which ultimately excludes the possibility of peaceful coexistence.

C. The Ideal of Legality as a Framework of Democracy

Finally, Kelsen notes that democracy exists in the framework created by the constitution and the doctrine of the hierarchical structure of law, wherein the higher organ, empowered by the legal act, grants the competence to issue lower legal acts to the lower organ. Only within such procedures and institutions can the democratic ideal be realised.[101] The doctrine of the hierarchical structure of law is strictly bound with the concept of the formal rule of law and as such, is a guarantee that all the elements described above will be updated in the democratic process.[102] The constitution rests at the top of the system. It is the constitution that is supposed to secure the rights of minorities and to which the special majority principle applies. The efficacy of the constitutional provisions should be secured by the guardian of the constitution, which according to Kelsen is the constitutional court.[103] Freedom and equality in democracy results in the lawfulness and legality requirement. Those who rule cannot be above

[99] ibid 102.

[100] ibid. Also, in foreign policy democracy favours peace. Kelsen in 'Foundations of Democracy' claims that the 'democratic type is decidedly inclined to cherish pacifist ideal, whereas the autocratic type shows unmistakable symptoms of imperialism'. In democracy, argues Kelsen, the tendency exists to justify foreign affairs by pacifistic ideology. In its framework the vision of community of states with equal rights prevails, while in autocracy the heroic effort, struggle for life leads to the 'survival of the fittest'. Kelsen, 'Foundations of Democracy' (n 16) 33.

[101] Urbinati and Accetti (n 7) 16–17.

[102] I elaborate on the issue of the rule of law and democracy in Kelsen's doctrine in M Zalewska, 'Does Hans Kelsen's *Pure Theory of Law* Supports Rule of Law and Democracy?' in H Takikawa (ed), *The Rule of Law and Democracy* (Stuttgart, Franz Steiner Verlag, Archiv Fur Rechts- Und Sozialphilosophie Vol Beiheft 161, 2019) 203–16.

[103] The elaborated discussion between Hans Kelsen and Carl Schmitt concerning the guardian of the constitution was edited and brilliantly summarised by Lars Vinx in L Vinx (ed), *The Guardian of the Constitution: Hans Kelsen and Carl Schmitt on the Limits of Constitutional Law* (Cambridge, Cambridge University Press, 2015).

the law: they are as bound by law as the subjects of their rulings. They must respect the hierarchical structure of law, where the validity of the lower act is grounded in the higher act with the constitution at the top. This way, democracy limits its own power and sets control mechanisms.[104] In 'Foundations of Democracy', Kelsen perceives the rationalistic character of democracy, being a legal order consisting of a system of general norms. As such, it is associated with the ideal of legality associated with transparency.

In contrast, those who rule in an autocracy lack any possible bindings or control measures; having access to the absolute truth and justice, they exist above any positive, imperfect law. Furthermore, since absolute justice is above the law, those who rule also cannot be bound by an imperfect legal system.[105] As can be seen, in each case, while the justification of a democratic institution lies in a relativistic world-view, that of an autocracy lies in the absolutistic possession of an ultimate truth or justice. Furthermore, while positive law requires a relativistic outlook, and democracy requires obedience to its rules, natural law takes an absolutistic perspective, thus serving as a solid justification for the leader of an autocratic system by placing him above the law.

As relativism and peace can be perceived as common for normativism and democracy, legality is the landmark feature of normativism, and democracy functions in its framework. When understood in this sense (and pure theory of law itself) legality is a condition *sine qua non* for democracy, but insufficient for democracy to thrive.[106] However, the relationship is mutual: democracy seems to be the most effective embodiment of legality, closest to the ideal of the legal system envisioned by Kelsen.

V. Conclusions

The aim of this chapter is to examine the relation between Kelsen's legal positivism and the theory of democracy. The analysis of the two categories, along with Kelsen's reasons for rejecting the natural law doctrine and autocracy, indicated striking similarities between Kelsen's legal theory and theory of democracy with regard to their values. These similarities are grounded in the Enlightenment tradition and its values, such as rationality, fostering a scientific world-view, tolerance and equality. This observation suggests that for Kelsen, legal positivism and theory of democracy are not two separate theories, but stem from the same set of values and Kelsen's relativistic world-view. The analysis of Kelsen's texts on normativism and on democracy, especially 'Foundations of Democracy' identified three main sources which determined Kelsen's orientation on positivistic and democratic outlook. The first factor, which is associated with personality type, is the distinction between absolutism and relativism. The second, which is associated with the values that Kelsen favours in the social order, is peace. The third is legality, which creates the necessary condition for democracy to thrive and which reveals that democracy is capable of fulfilling Kelsen's ideal of law at its fullest. The first

[104] Kelsen, 'State-Form and World-Outlook' (n 21) 103.
[105] ibid.
[106] I elaborate on this issue in Zalewska (n 102) 207.

two categories exist in the background of Kelsen's pure theory of law, while the latter is an inherent part of Kelsen's concept of law.

Furthermore, the pure theory of law as a project intended to create ideology-free legal science, creates a framework which enables democracy to thrive. The analysis of the text concerning natural law doctrine and democracy indicates that behind the technical and strict language of the pure theory of law, stands the author strongly concerned with the trends which appeared after the First World War. It can be seen that despite his rigorous scientific mind, Kelsen was deeply humanistic and human oriented. He tried to create a powerful intellectual weapon to provide strong arguments for peaceful coexistence and a rational outlook in Europe. Today, Kelsen's theory is perhaps more relevant than it was in previous decades and it provides solid arguments for contemporary scholars to adopt for the study of democracy, rule of law, science and tolerance.

11

Hans Kelsen and the Crisis of Democracy

LARS VINX

I. The Crisis of Democracy: Between Populism and Liberal Democracy

The current crisis of democracy[1] – as evidenced in the global retreat or regression of democracy in recent years[2] – differs from earlier episodes of democratic collapse. It is not characterised by any open repudiation of democracy. Many modern subverters of democracy, unlike the totalitarian dictators or military strongmen of old, have been elected and loudly profess to be democrats, even while they aim to exercise political control unencumbered by constitutional restraints and to deny the opposition an opportunity to contest for power on fair and equal terms. These latter-day authoritarians frequently employ a populist rhetoric. They claim to implement the true will of the people and argue that they have established, or are on the way to establishing, a more authentic form of democracy than exists in liberal democracies of long standing. Liberal democracy, in the populist understanding, is a corrupted instantiation of the democratic ideal. The self-rule of the people has come to be replaced, in liberal democracies, or so populists argue, with the oligarchic rule of unaccountable elites – be they economic, cognitive, administrative, or judicial. To counter such corruption of the democratic process, populist leaders claim, politics must again be made subservient to the will of the people.[3]

Populist rhetoric identifies the will of the people with the will of the majority. But it does not do so simply on the ground that individuals who support the populist leader

[1] Two illuminating overviews, S Levitsky and D Ziblatt, *How Democracies Die* (New York, Penguin, 2018); L Diamond, *Ill Winds* (New York, Penguin, 2019).

[2] See S Haggard and R Kaufman, *Backsliding. Democratic Regress in the Contemporary World* (Cambridge, Cambridge University Press, 2021).

[3] On populism, see JW Müller, *What is Populism?* (Philadelphia, University of Pennsylvania Press, 2016); N Urbinati, *Me the People. How Populism Transforms Democracy* (Cambridge, MA, Harvard University Press 2019); C Mudde and CR Kaltwasser, *Populism. A Very Short Introduction* (Oxford, Oxford University Press, 2017).

and his party currently happen to enjoy a purely numerical advantage in a political game of indefinitely extended democratic competition. The implicit ground of identification, rather, is the idea that those who support a populist movement are the 'real' members of the political community – a group that need not be coextensive with the set of all those who hold citizenship. Populist rhetoric often assumes that one cannot simply choose to be a member of the people. One must possess certain ascriptive characteristics that, in the eyes of the group, confer eligibility for membership: one must be native-born, or speak the right language, or go to church and own a gun, or belong to the right social class or identity-group, or be one of 'the oppressed.' But to be a member of the people one must also, in addition, satisfy a voluntarist criterion of membership, be willing to identify with the group and to sacrifice for it. Those who refuse so to identify with the group, or who lack the ascriptive characteristics that entail eligibility for membership, though they are fellow citizens, are not, in the populist imagination, to be respected as members of the people. They are implicitly characterised as (potential) internal enemies of the political community whose pre-existing will is not to be constructed but only to be properly expressed by the use of the majority rule.[4]

Appeals to the will of the people, so understood, are frequently employed to legitimise attacks, on the part of populist leaders, on the rule of law and the independence of the judiciary.[5] They also serve to justify attempts to compromise the fairness of political competition and, in some cases, to strip individuals of crucially important individual rights. The apparatus of liberal constitutionalism – a written constitution with a bill of rights protected against the legislator, bolstered by judicial review – is denounced as 'juristocracy' in the service of 'hegemonic preservation', as the rule of an unaccountable elite that claims the authority, in flagrant violation of the ideal of democracy, to second-guess and even to overturn the decisions of the people or their representatives.[6] Where a majority has been won, populist leaders often employ it to amend constitutions, stack the courts with their followers, and remodel electoral procedures in ways that make it difficult for the opposition to prevail in elections. Electoral competition is frequently skewed in other ways as well, by the frivolous abuse of the law to persecute political opponents, by attempts to starve the opposition of funding, by the exercise of partisan control over institutions tasked with policing the fairness of elections, and by informal or formal influence on the media.

The standard response to the populist challenge to the institutions of a constitutional democracy is to point out that democracy is more than majority rule: a legitimate political regime cannot allow the majority to ride roughshod over the basic rights of individuals and minority groups. Democracy is not to be confused with the tyranny of the majority.[7] The problem with this response is obvious. It is a commonplace of democratic theory that there is a tension between democracy and liberalism, between the majority rule and counter-majoritarian constitutional restraint, between the democratic

[4] See Müller (n 3) 11–12; and Urbinati (n 3) 77–112.

[5] See W Sadurski, *Poland's Constitutional Breakdown* (Oxford, Oxford University Press, 2019); KL Scheppele, 'Autocratic Legalism' (2018) 85 *University of Chicago Law Review* 545.

[6] See R Hirschl, *Towards Juristocracy* (Cambridge, MA, Harvard University Press, 2007).

[7] For a classical statement of this view, see R Dworkin, *Freedom's Law. The Moral Reading of the American Constitution* (Cambridge, MA, Harvard University Press, 1996) 1–39.

equality of citizens as a legislating collective and claims to a protected sphere of individual liberty. To claim that the populist challenge to counter-majoritarian institutions is an attack on democracy itself is to assume that a proper democracy must be liberal and constitutional, which is precisely what the populist denies. To speak of 'illiberal democracy', a phrase made popular by the American journalist Fareed Zakaria,[8] on the other hand, is to concede that the systems so described are democratic. Talk of a crisis of democracy engendered by the rise of populist majoritarianism, then, might appear to be little more than special pleading on the part of elites that, according to the populist, rely on the language of rights and constitutionalism to thwart the will of ordinary people.

To illustrate the dilemma, consider how two prominent contemporary scholars of populism – Cas Mudde and Cristobal Rovira Kaltwasser – bend themselves into shapes to be able to claim both that democracy is not essentially liberal *and* that populism poses a danger to democracy. Mudde and Kaltwasser define democracy as follows:

> Democracy (sans adjectives) is best defined as the combination of popular sovereignty and majority rule; nothing more, nothing less. Hence, democracy can be direct or indirect, liberal or illiberal. In fact, the very etymology of the term democracy alludes to the idea of self-government of the people, i.e., a political system in which people rule. Not by chance, the most 'minimal' definitions consider democracy first and foremost as a method by which rulers are selected in competitive elections. Free and fair elections thus correspond to the defining property of democracy. Instead of changing rules by violent conflict, the people agree that those who govern them should be elected by majority rule.[9]

Mudde and Kaltwasser go on to point out that the term 'democracy' is often used to refer to liberal democracy, ie, to 'a political regime which not only respects popular sovereignty and majority rule, but also establishes independent institutions specialised in the protection of fundamental rights, such as freedom of expression and the protection of minorities'.[10] Mudde and Kaltwasser accordingly distinguish between a mere electoral democracy and a liberal democracy. The former meets the defining property of democracy, free and fair elections, and differs in this respect from what political scientists call competitive authoritarianism.[11] Still, Mudde and Kaltwasser imply that liberal democracy is a more desirable or more developed form of democratic political system than mere electoral democracy, and they argue that while populism tends to support electoral democracy, it may come to damage liberal democracy.[12]

This framing of the crisis of democracy is evidently problematic. If one admits that democracy, in its essence, is popular self-government, as implemented through the majority rule, one has no basis on which to argue that liberal constitutionalism and the counter-majoritarian institutions that typically go along with it are improvements of democracy. If democracy is the rule of the majority, one cannot reasonably claim, it would seem, that institutions that are deliberately set up to restrain majority rule in the name of liberal values are authentically democratic. It follows that we cannot

[8] F Zakaria, 'The Rise of Illiberal Democracy' (1997) 76 *Foreign Affairs* 22.

[9] Mudde and Kaltwasser (n 3) 80. cp Urbinati (n 3) 30.

[10] Mudde and Kaltwasser (n 3) 80.

[11] See S Levitsky and L Way, *Competitive Authoritarianism. Hybrid Regimes After the Cold War* (Cambridge, Cambridge University Press, 2012).

[12] Mudde and Kaltwasser (n 3) 82–84.

avoid the question whether democracy is to be associated with the rule of the majority or with an institutional framework that aims to ensure that the state will pay equal concern and respect to all subjects of the law. The adaptation of democratic rhetoric on the part of populist authoritarians cleverly exploits an unresolved ambiguity in our talk of democracy. If it is true that democracy is nothing more than majority rule, populist authoritarians will have reason to dismiss the charge that they are threatening democracy. The objection, it will be argued, does not defend democracy but liberalism, the quasi-oligarchic rule of academic, economic, administrative and judicial elites.

Democracy, Mudde and Kaltwasser claim, is the self-government of the people. Popular self-government is to be identified with majority rule, but only on the condition that those who rule are appointed in electoral contests that are 'free and fair', lest we wrongly identify electoral democracy with competitive authoritarianism. The demand for free and fair elections, however, is by no means trivial. That there are elections and that votes are accurately counted does not suffice to make elections free and fair.[13] In describing the difference between electoral and liberal democracy, Mudde and Kaltwassser claim that a liberal democracy provides for institutions that protect fundamental rights, and they name freedom of expression as one key example of such a right. But freedom of expression, clearly, is desirable not merely on liberal grounds, as a right that is valuable because it gives individuals an opportunity for self-expression and for the correction of mistaken belief.[14] Freedom of political expression is a core requirement of the fairness of an election.[15] The rule of a majority that is altogether unencumbered by constitutional constraints is not merely a danger to individual liberty and to cognitive progress. An incumbent government liberated from effective constitutional restraint and claiming to act in the name of the true people may well be tempted to make use of what Carl Schmitt called the extra-legal premium on political power[16] to put the thumb on the scale and deny the opposition a fair chance to compete for power. It would be rather odd to claim that abuses of this sort are violations of liberalism but not of democracy.

Instead of asking whether democracy is essentially liberal, it might be more productive to set off with a different question: what are the conditions – institutional, social and political-cultural – under which the rule of an electoral majority translates into authentic collective self-government? How can the rule of a majority amount to more than the despotic rule of one social group over another? This is the question that animated Hans Kelsen's theory of democracy.[17] The answer Kelsen gave to that question, it will

[13] See J Elklit and P Svensson, 'What Makes Elections Free and Fair?' (1997) 8 *Journal of Democracy* 32. Urbinati (n 3) 10 puts the point as follows: 'A democracy that infringes basic political rights – especially the rights crucial for forming opinions and judgments, expressing dissents, and changing views – and that systematically precludes the possibility of the formation of new majorities is not democracy at all. A minimal (as electoral) definition of democracy thus implies more than merely elections'.

[14] See JS Mill, 'On Liberty' in JS Mill, *On Liberty and Other Essays*, J Gray (ed) (Oxford, Oxford University Press, 1991) 5–130, 20; and CE Baker, 'Harm, Liberty, and Free Speech' (1997) 70 *Southern California Law Review* 979.

[15] See A Meiklejohn, *Free Speech and its Relation to Self-Government* (New York, Harper & Brothers, 1948).

[16] See C Schmitt, *Legalität und Legitimität*, 6th edn (originally published 1932) (Berlin, Duncker & Humblot, 1998) 33–34.

[17] My discussion will focus on the second edition of Kelsen's treatise on the nature and value of democracy. See H Kelsen, *Vom Wesen und Wert der Demokratie*, 2nd edn (Tübingen, JCB Mohr, 1929), reprinted in

be argued here, is relevant to the contemporary crisis of democracy because it is anti-populist and thoroughly constitutional without being liberal. A closer look at Kelsen's democratic theory can give important orientation to contemporary debate. The perception that democracy is in crisis is correct. Kelsen's reflections on democracy allow us to pinpoint the danger of populism more precisely than theories that are framed around the contrast between electoral and liberal democracy. Democracy is threatened by populism because populism tends to undermine the conditions under which majority rule translates into authentic collective self-government.

II. Democratic Freedom: Kelsen on the Majority Rule

Kelsen's analysis of the nature and value of democracy, like many other German-language attempts in the interwar period to theorise democracy, takes its start from Rousseau. The point Kelsen takes from Rousseau, whether rightly or wrongly, is that democracy is to serve the value of freedom, not that of equality, as is often assumed in contemporary theories of democracy.[18] While the individual, in a democratic state as much as in any other, is subject to coercively enforced law, the laws of a properly functioning democracy, Rousseau argued, draw legitimacy from the fact that democratic citizens are the authors of the laws to which they are subject. Democratic rule does not restrict freedom but enhances it. The democratic citizen 'obeys only himself and remains as free as before'.[19]

Rousseau did not deny, of course, that legislative decisions, in a democracy, must be taken by majority vote, and that an individual citizen may, as a result, find themselves outvoted. He argued that, in such cases, the legislative will (assuming it qualifies as a general will) is nevertheless to be regarded as one's own. Where laws proceed from the general will, the outvoted citizen ought to be able to accept authorship of the majority's decision, even if they voted against it. Rousseau famously claimed that 'when … the opinion contrary to my own prevails, this merely proves that I was mistaken, and that what I considered the general will was not so'.[20]

It appears, at first glance, that Rousseau is working with a positive notion of freedom that has it that we are free only if we willingly abide by some predetermined conception of the good society.[21] As a result, Rousseau has at times been accused of illiberalism.[22]

H Kelsen, *Verteidigung der Demokratie*, M Jestaedt and O Lepsius (eds) (Tübingen, Mohr Siebeck, 2006) 149. For an illuminating outline of Kelsen's theory of democracy see S Baume, *Hans Kelsen and the Case for Democracy* (Colchester, ECPR Press, 2012). Further on Kelsen's theory of democracy, see also H Dreier, *Rechtslehre, Staatssoziologie und Demokratietheorie bei Hans Kelsen* (Baden-Baden, Nomos Verlagsgesellschaft, 1986) 249–94; and L Vinx, *Hans Kelsen's Pure Theory of Law. Legality and Legitimacy* (Oxford, Oxford Univesity Press, 2007).

[18] See Kelsen, *Vom Wesen und Wert der Demokratie* (n 17) 154–62. For a contemporary articulation of the view that democracy is based on the value of equality, see T Christiano, *The Rule of the Many. Fundamental Issues in Democratic Theory* (Boulder, Westview Press, 1996) 47–97.

[19] JJ Rousseau, *Rousseau's Political Writings*, A Ritter and JC Bondanella (eds) (New York, Norton, 1988) 92.

[20] ibid 151.

[21] See I Berlin, 'Two Concepts of Liberty' in I Berlin, *Four Essays on Liberty* (Oxford, Oxford University Press, 1969) 118–72.

[22] See JL Talmon, *The Origins of Totalitarian Democracy* (London, Secker & Warburg, 1952).

But the point that he was trying to express is not, under a charitable interpretation, wedded to a potentially totalitarian misconception of freedom. Some passages in the *Contrat Social* suggest that Rousseau is best understood as invoking a notion of republican freedom.[23]

Republican freedom consists in not being ruled by the whims of a small social elite that has managed to grab the reins of power and that uses them in its own factional interest. In a republic one is likely to be ruled, rather, in accordance with laws that express interests shared by all citizens. The promise that Rousseau associates with democracy, then, is not merely that we will, in being compelled to submit to its law, be incentivised not to act on desires to give selfish preference to our personal interest. Democracy's promise of freedom is in the first instance political. Laws that are made by a majority, at least where the interests and convictions of citizens show sufficient overlap, do more than just express the aggregated preferences of a coalition of factions that so happens to form a momentary arithmetic majority. Under suitable social, political-cultural and institutional background conditions, it is likely that democratic laws will be aligned with interests that are shared among citizens.

This does not rule out that an individual may find this or that law burdensome. Neither does it rule out that an individual will find that to be coerced to obey the law conflicts with a preference to enjoy the benefits of the law without making a fair contribution to the cost of the maintenance of public order. What Rousseau claims is that a subject of democratic law will be able to recognise that the law serves an interest in which they share, like everyone else, and that it is better to live under such law than in a state of nature (or under someone's else's despotic rule).[24]

Kelsen acknowledges that the reality of modern democracy fails to live up to Rousseau's promise, even if that promise is understood in the modest way just outlined.[25] This observation, of course, was a commonplace of interwar critiques of the reality of modern, parliamentary party-democracy. In the real world of modern democratic politics, laws are made by small majorities (typically in a parliament) which are not always committed to the pursuit of a common good. The political process is controlled by political parties, which were often presented as organised interest groups devoted to factional goals. Parties, according to standard anti-party rhetoric, turn their members and supporters into mindless foot soldiers of a partial cause, to deploy them in support of policies that frustrate the common good.[26] Though critiques of the party state in the interwar period were often overdrawn, they pointed to a real problem. That problem is not simply a moral problem, as though everything could be set right by getting people and politicians to be more educated and public-minded. The fact that parties frequently act like factions reflects differences of interest and ideological conviction among groups

[23] I use the term in a somewhat less-demanding sense than contemporary neo-republicans like Philip Pettit and Quentin Skinner. Citizens will enjoy republican freedom where political institutions and political culture make it likely (though they may not guarantee) that governance accords with a plausible conception of the common good.

[24] For interpretations of the general will that support this reading, see F Neuhouser, 'Freedom, Dependence, and the General Will' (1993) 102 *Philosophical Review* 363; G Sreenivasan, 'What is the General Will?' (2000) 109 *Philosophical Review* 545.

[25] See Kelsen, *Vom Wesen und Wert der Demokratie* (n 17) 156–59.

[26] See, for instance, C Schmitt, *Die geistesgeschichtliche Lage des heutigen Parlamentarismus*, 8th edn (originally published 1923) (Berlin, Duncker & Humblot, 1996).

of citizens that will unavoidably arise in a pluralist society and come to be expressed in democratic political competition. Members of an outvoted minority, as a result, will often lack adequate reasons to consider the content of the laws made by the majority as expressing shared interests. Despite the democratic form of decision-making, the outvoted citizen is not always governed by a legislative will that is in line with a creditable understanding of the common good. Even democratic law, therefore, is bound to inflict what Kelsen calls the 'torment of heteronomy'[27] on some of its subjects.

Kelsen's theory of democracy is realistic.[28] It does not challenge the critical observations concerning the reality of modern democracy just outlined. But Kelsen argued that Rousseau's promise can be given an even less ambitious reading than I have presented above, one that descriptively fits modern political reality, but still suffices to show that democracy is superior to other forms of government from the point of view of our interest in freedom. Democracy, Kelsen argues, does not make all citizens free. It does not ensure that all citizens are governed by laws they can recognise to express an interest in which they share. But democracy guarantees, unlike any other regime, that a majority of citizens will find their political preferences aligned with the law.[29]

Imagine a community that chooses to adopt *a rule of continuing agreement* as its rule of collective decision. A collective decision, under a rule of continuing agreement, requires everyone's approval to come into force and it remains in force only for as long as everyone continues to endorse it. A rule of continuing agreement, Kelsen argues, is tantamount to anarchy. It does not constitute a social order as Kelsen understands the term. A social order, for Kelsen, must be objective, in the sense that its demands will continue to apply (and to be enforced) even where some group members come to reject them. Avoidance of a state of nature requires collective decisions to be made binding against the dissent of potential defectors.

Consider, next, a rule of unanimity. A *rule of unanimity* does not run afoul of the requirement of objectivity. Under a rule of unanimity, a collective decision requires everyone's agreement to come into force and remains in force until it is repealed by a later, equally unanimous decision. A decision that is taken under the rule of unanimity continues to bind individuals who change their mind, as time goes on, and come to prefer a different arrangement than the one initially adopted, at least as long as there are those who wish to stick with the original decision. The laws generated by a rule of unanimity therefore possess objectivity. They may come to bind members of society in ways that go against their present will; and it would be wrong to think that the rule of unanimity assures a very high degree of conformity between the content of the law and the political preferences of its subjects. The rule of unanimity may come to bind the majority of members of society against their present will. A widely shared desire for legislative change might, in the most extreme case, come to be frustrated by the veto of a tiny minority of one.

[27] See Kelsen, *Vom Wesen und Wert der Demokratie* (n 17) 154.

[28] On Kelsen as a political realist, see R Schuett, *Hans Kelsen's Political Realism* (Edinburgh, Edinburgh University Press, 2021).

[29] See, for the following, Kelsen, *Vom Wesen und Wert der Demokratie* (n 17) 156–62. Further analysis in E Lagerspetz, 'Kelsen on Democracy and Majority Decision' (2017) 103 *Archiv für Rechts- und Sozialphilosophie* 155.

Any rule of collective decision that requires a super-majority has a similar effect: under such a rule, laws will come into force only if most members of a group agree and they will stand unless they are repealed by another, later super-majority, which makes it possible for a minority to hold a majority hostage. As should be evident, any rule of collective decision that puts the power to enact binding laws into the hands of an autocrat or an aristocratic minority will likewise carry the potential to frustrate the wishes of the majority of members of a group. Where legislative decisions are taken by one person or by a small group, there can be no assurance that the resulting norms will reflect the political preferences of a significant number of addressees of the law. While it is certainly conceivable that a benevolent despot might make laws that align with the wishes of a large majority of citizens, an autocratic rule of decision can easily lead to the enactment of laws rejected by all but a tiny few of the subjects of the law.

These reflections show, Kelsen argues, that the *majority rule* possesses a unique virtue. Under the majority rule, a decision will come into force if and only if it is approved by a majority and it will remain valid and binding only for as long as it is not repealed by a later majority. The majority rule thus gives assurance that any collective decision, while it is binding, will continue to be in line with the political preferences of a majority of norm-addressees. The decision will always be supported, at the very least, by a majority of 50 per cent plus 1. This assurance, Kelsen argues, can neither be provided by an autocratic rule of collective decision nor by a rule that moves closer towards unanimity.

Kelsen's defence of the majority rule, like Rousseau's theory of the general will, aims to show that outvoted citizens have sufficient reason to consider themselves bound to democratically enacted law. But Kelsen does not rely on the assumption that a democratically enacted law can be expected to be aligned, in content, with the shared interest of all. The key claim, rather, is that rule by majority is to be accepted as legitimate because it guarantees, unlike any other rule for taking binding collective decisions, that a majority of citizens will see their political preferences aligned with the content of the law and in that sense be free.

Kelsen's argument for the majority rule, though undoubtedly ingenious, invites two rather obvious critical replies. First, it is unclear why the fact that the majority rule guarantees that a majority of citizens will be free should suffice to reconcile an outvoted citizen with their subjection to democratic law. Suppose it is indeed likely that more people will be free – will find their own political preferences to be aligned with the law – in a democracy than in any other political regime. Why would that fact provide an outvoted citizen with a reason to regard the law to which they are subject against their will as legitimate? If I happen not to be free under democratic law, if my political preferences are not aligned with the content of the law, what difference does it make that the realisation of my conception of the common good is frustrated by a democratic rather than an autocratic law? That a majority of fellow citizens enjoy alignment between their political preferences and the law does not provide me, the outvoted, with any reason to accept my heteronomy. My political preferences have no less of a claim to the support of the law than anyone else's.

The second problem with Kelsen's argument for the majority rule is that it seems to lead Kelsen into conflict with his advocacy for a formal constitution protected by constitutional review.[30] A formal constitution protects certain legal norms against repeal by an ordinary legislative majority by means of a rule of amendment. A constitutional court, what is more, is given the authority to enforce the resulting limitations of legislative authority against the ordinary legislator, by striking down ordinary laws that violate a constitutional norm protected by the amendment rule. But any special procedure of amendment would appear to undermine the assurance, afforded by the majority rule, that no fewer than 50 per cent plus 1 of subjects of the law will be free. Where a super-majority is needed to amend or repeal a norm, a minority has the power to frustrate the preferences of a majority that falls short of a super-majority. Constitutional democracy may preserve legal content that fails to be aligned with the political preferences of a majority and thus make a majority of citizens unfree.

III. Democratic Equality: The Temporally Extended Demos

Kelsen's rhetorical emphasis on the claim that the value of democracy is to be explicated by reference to the value of freedom and not by reference to the value of equality is infelicitous in one crucial respect. It conceals the unacknowledged but important role that the value of equality plays in Kelsen's argument for democracy. That Kelsen recognises the relevance of the value of equality to an analysis of democracy is evident enough from passages such as the following:

> The burden of an alien will, imposed by social order, is felt to be all the more stifling, the more immediately the primary feeling of one's own value expresses itself in the human being, in the rejection of any surplus value of the other, the more strongly the experience of the person who is forced to obey, when faced with the ruler, the commander, is that: 'He is a human being, just like myself, we are equal! Whence, therefore, derives his right to rule over me?' The negative and deeply antiheroic idea of equality, in this way, puts itself into the service of the equally negative demand for freedom … It is precisely the synthesis of the two principles which is characteristic of democracy.[31]

Freedom, for Kelsen, consists in not seeing the realisation of one's political preferences thwarted by laws whose content reflects the political preferences of another. Unfreedom is an affront to our dignity as beings who are naturally equal to those who rule over us. Nevertheless, social order, in all its conceivable forms, requires our subjection to a potentially alien collective will, to a will that may turn out not to be aligned with our own preferences. How, then, can social order ever be legitimate?

The use of the majority rule, as we have already seen, provides part of Kelsen's answer. Where collective decisions are taken by majority rule, the content of the law will assuredly align with the political preferences of a majority of citizens. But this does not

[30] See H Kelsen, 'The Nature and Development of Constitutional Adjudication' in L Vinx (ed and trans), *The Guardian of the Constitution. Hans Kelsen and Carl Schmitt on the Limits of Constitutional Law* (Cambridge, Cambridge University Press, 2015) 22–78. For a defence of Kelsen's argument for constitutional review, see L Vinx, 'Kelsen's Argument for Constitutional Review – A Reappraisal' in S Baume and D Ragazzoni (eds), *Kelsen on Democracy. Genesis, Theory, Legacies* (Cambridge, Cambridge University Press, forthcoming).

[31] Kelsen, *Vom Wesen und Wert der Demokratie* (n 17) 154.

explain why a majority's claim to be entitled to rule over an outvoted minority, to make laws that thwart and frustrate the will of members of the minority, should fail to be an insult to the equality in moral status of those who find themselves among the outvoted. Why should a member of the group of the outvoted recognise the will of the majority as a general will, as the will of a collective of which they form a part and to whose decisions they can, accordingly, give reasonable deference?

To reconstruct Kelsen's answer, it is helpful to distinguish between different dimensions of democratic equality. The first of these dimensions is constitutional and concerns equality of political rights. Suppose you find yourself in the position of an outvoted citizen, in a democratic state, and you ask yourself whether you have reason to assume authorship of the laws. The laws to which you are compelled to submit do not merely guarantee that a majority of citizens will find their preferences aligned with the law. The laws, what is more, were enacted in a free and fair process of political competition. All citizens were afforded an equal right to advocate for their views, individually and in organised groups, without having to fear any disadvantage for expressing their opinion. All social groups were given equal access to the public sphere to make themselves heard. All individual citizens enjoyed an equal vote in the procedure of collective decision. The decision that has been taken, though it is binding for now, is open to revision. It may come to be repealed at a later stage if a new majority so decides. All citizens have the right to work, as individuals or groups, towards convincing their fellow citizens to repeal the offending law. Democratic procedure honours the equality in moral status of all citizens by according to each equal and, ideally, equally effective rights of political participation.

Kelsen recognises that this first dimension of democratic equality, the right to equal and equally effective participation in the process of collective decision-making, may not be sufficient to provide reasonable grounds to all for identification with and deference to the will of the current majority. He accordingly emphasises the openness of the democratic process to future legislative change.[32] A citizen who is now among the outvoted is not regarded as a permanent subject of those who now form the majority. Rather, the outvoted is to be considered as a member of a (potential) future majority. That the currently outvoted can hope to be members of a legislative majority in the future affirms the view that they are as entitled to determine the content of the law as members of the present majority. Individuals who are now outvoted can identify with and reasonably defer to the legislative will of the collective once it is seen as indefinitely extended in time, at least if the outvoted can reasonably expect that they will be part of a future majority.

The chance to be a member of a future majority would be compromised, needless to say, by any infringement of the first dimension of democratic equality – by a restriction of the franchise, for instance, or by restrictions of the freedom of political speech that make it impossible for an outvoted group to advocate for their goals. The chance would likewise be compromised by constitutional constraints that impose material limits on the content of the law which are not justifiable by appeal to the integrity of democracy. What is more, the outvoted must be in a position to assume that a current majority will

[32] See ibid 193–204.

be willing to relinquish power should it lose the next election. But even where constitutional constraints have not been imposed and where equal and equally effective rights of political participation are firmly recognised, members of an outvoted group may find that they lack any realistic prospect of ever becoming part of a legislative majority that will cater to their preferences. Consider, for example, a society divided along a deep religious or ethnic cleavage, or divided into regions with sharply divergent political cultures, but with one of the two opposing groups or regions containing a clear numerical majority of voters. The outvoted, even if their equal right to political participation is scrupulously honoured, may not enjoy any real prospect of winning a future election.

There is thus a second, factual dimension of democratic equality, which may be described, to borrow a term of Hermann Heller's, as a requirement of 'relative homogeneity'.[33] For the outvoted to be able to identify with the collective will, the community must not be too polarised. At least some voters must be willing to switch from one political camp to another, to generate a regular alternation in power between centre-left and centre-right. The prospect that a party-system will take this benign shape presupposes that the voters and the parties that aggregate their individual preferences show a degree of willingness to compromise, to give some consideration to the other side's interests, and to recognise each other as legitimate contestants for power. This willingness, in turn, is more likely to come forth in a society characterised by a certain degree of cultural and ideological cohesion and by the presence of significant shared interests.

Talk of a requirement of relative homogeneity may, at first glance, appear sociological and therefore un-Kelsenian. But Kelsen, who did not hesitate, in his political writings, to don the hat of political sociologist, clearly acknowledged it as a precondition of the proper functioning of a democratic political system:

> It is quite permissible to reject the democratic form of state for a group of individuals who are separated by unbridgeable differences of interest. The democratic form of state is perhaps not suitable for a multitude of human beings who are connected only by the order of their state, but separated, as a matter of fact, by contradictions of language, race, and religion. But such a multitude ought not to be connected into the unity of one state to begin with.[34]

The functioning of democracy, in other words, requires a degree of social homogeneity. Kelsen made sure to add, however, in responding to Marxist critics of electoral democracy, that it would be pointless to demand perfect or absolute homogeneity as a precondition of democracy:

> Whether class conflict, in particular, is difficult to reconcile with democracy is to be doubted. It is of course possible to reject democracy from the point of view of class struggle. It would be meaningless, however, to admit democracy only for a group united in solidarity, that is, for a multitude of individuals whose wills converge, since they are infused with a spirit of community with respect to all relations that need to be regulated by a communal order. Quite apart from the question whether such a group can even exist, we would not, in this case, have

[33] See H Heller, *Staatslehre*, G Niemeyer (ed) (Tübingen, Mohr Siebeck, 1983) 261.

[34] H Kelsen, *Sozialismus und Staat. Eine Untersuchung der politischen Theorie des Marxismus*, 3rd edn, N Leser (ed) (Leipzig, Verlag der Wiener Volksbuchhandlung, 1965) 58. See also Kelsen, *Vom Wesen und Wert der Demokratie* (n 17) 202–03.

> any need for a principle of majority. The problem to which any form of state responds, to bring opposing wills to unity, would not even exist here, since that unity would already be in existence.[35]

Kelsen's demand for relative homogeneity, accordingly, is not to be confused with a theory of constitutional identity.[36] Relative homogeneity is a mere factual precondition of functioning democracy, and the overlap in interest and conviction to which the notion refers can and should transform in content over time. In a democracy, no particular account of what citizens must agree on that goes beyond the demand of respect for the rules of the democratic game can legitimately be enshrined in constitutional law. To do so would be to give constitutional preference to one factional view as to what a good society would look like and to stunt the openness of democratic law to future change.

Where the first two dimensions of democratic equality – equality of rights of political participation and relative homogeneity – are present, however, an outvoted citizen can regard themselves as a member of a potential future majority. Kelsen's full conception of democracy combines the freedom-based argument for the majority rule with a thin account of democratic equality, safeguarded by the legal, sociological and political-cultural conditions of the existence of a temporally extended legislative will that, by way of regular alternation in government induced by free and fair political competition, includes both the current majority and the current opposition.

This is admittedly a rather austere interpretation of Rousseau's claim that democracy preserves our freedom by subjecting us to a general will with which we can reasonably identify. Those who currently find themselves outvoted are faced with a collective will the present content of which is opposed to their understanding of the common good. The opportunity to contest a majority's policies and its power in electoral competition and the promise that one will have the opportunity to govern in the future do not eliminate one's temporary subjection to the will of others. Given its austerity, it is unsurprising that Kelsen's conception of democracy had to contend, in the interwar period, with another understanding of democratic equality that promised complete deliverance from the torment of heteronomy. There were two versions of this competing understanding of democratic equality, one communist and the other fascist, and both were wedded to the idea that authentic democracy requires absolute rather than mere relative social homogeneity.

Modern society, in either view, is characterised by a structural line of political conflict that does not allow for meaningful compromise between opposing political camps. Capitalist society is structured, in the communist version of the theme, by class conflict that cannot be overcome through mere political emancipation, through the establishment of a democratic political system, but only through a revolutionary change in the relations of material production. As long as that change has not taken place, formal democracy must remain a sham and mere cloak for the capitalist exploitation

[35] Kelsen, *Sozialismus und Staat* (n 34) 58–59.

[36] ie, with a theory that claims that the commonalities that make for relative homogeneity are themselves to be regarded, as in Carl Schmitt's talk of a 'positive constitution', as fundamental constitutional principles impervious to democratic change within an existing constitutional framework. See C Schmitt, *Verfassungslehre*, 8th edn (originally published 1928) (Berlin, Duncker & Humblot, 1993) 20–36.

of the working class.[37] In the fascist variation of the view, associated with Carl Schmitt, a pluralist society is divided by a distinction between friends and enemies who cannot coexist in the same political community – whether it is drawn in economic, ethnic, religious, or cultural terms.[38]

Either view has it that the mechanisms of formal democracy – elections, free and fair political competition, parliamentarianism – are fated to remain meaningless and empty formalities unless and until society has been homogenised by dictatorial means. The majority rule will generate legitimate decisions only where societies already exhibit absolute homogeneity. Its results will then manifest or express the underlying convergence of interest and ideological outlook that is to be demanded of a true political community. The claim, in other words, is that Rousseau's original promise, that one will be subject only to laws that express a shared understanding of the common good, can be realised, but only in a society that has been cleansed of deep political conflict. Under conditions of pluralism, by contrast, the outcomes of the democratic process will be little more than instances of arbitrary despotism. Electoral democracy not grounded in a sufficiently homogeneous society will simply give the whip hand to the group that so happens to command a slim majority of votes. The formal apparatus of collective decision-making that we associate with democracy, therefore, is suitable for fair political weather only. It cannot legitimately deal with profound conflict, and it must not stand in the way of extra-legal action that might be needed to create or maintain absolute homogeneity.

According to proponents of absolute homogeneity, democratic citizens are equal not so much in comparison to one another, as individuals endowed with equal rights of participation that flow from the idea that all human beings are naturally equal in moral status, which in turn entails that those who must live together are to participate on equal terms in running their collective affairs. Equality, rather, is understood as a politically salient substantive similarity among the members of a political community, to be defined in terms of a contrast with an out-group. All proletarians are equal in being exploited by capitalists. All those who are true members of the nation are opposed to those who, even while they are citizens, do not qualify as true members of the nation because they do not exhibit the ascriptive characteristics of a true member, or because they do not identify politically with those characteristics. Talk of 'the people', accordingly, refers not to the assemblage of all those who must live together under the same government. Rather, the term is employed to mark a contrast between different groups within one and the same society that are seen to be implacably opposed. Democratic equality, in the words of Carl Schmitt, 'can only be grounded in a specific and substantial concept of equality'.[39] Democratic self-government is not to be understood as the ordered coexistence of groups and individuals with different interests and ideological visions who repeatedly compete for time-limited positions of political authority under fair rules for collective

[37] For a version of this theme that provided a foil for Kelsen's theory of democracy, see M Adler, *Die Staatsauffassung des Marxismus. Ein Beitrag zur Unterscheidung von soziologischer und juristischer Methode*, 2nd edn (originally published 1922) (Darmstadt, Wissenschaftliche Buchgesellschaft, 1964).

[38] See C Schmitt, *Der Begriff des Politischen. Text von 1932 mit einem Vorwort und drei Corollarien*, 2nd edn (originally published 1932) (Berlin, Duncker & Humblot, 1963).

[39] Schmitt, *Verfassungslehre* (n 36) 226.

decision-making. It is the self-assertion of one or another faction that identifies itself with the political whole. The purpose of the majority rule as a method of collective decision, in this picture of democracy, is not to arbitrate political difference but to reveal and confirm that those who vote with the majority are the real people.[40]

Kelsen's theory of democracy opposes such identification of a part with the whole. Political competition between a current majority and a current minority, according to Kelsen, is essential to democracy.[41] If the challenge is to establish a framework for taking binding collective decisions, under circumstances of pluralism, which will render decisions that all citizens can regard as their own, then no faction can rightfully claim to occupy the place of the people. If there is such a thing as a will of the people, it is constructed in the democratic process, and not merely expressed or made visible by the majority rule. Kelsen, as we have seen, understood social groups with conflicting interests and political visions might come to blows. The democratic process is not the only way in which political conflict can be resolved. It is the only way, however, that can create an inclusive collective will under conditions of pluralism. As Kelsen emphasised, it has the further merit of being peaceful, even while it allows for differences of political opinion to be openly articulated. Democracy, for Kelsen, is the indefinite deferral of civil war.

This deferral opposes the promise of liberating violence that was made, in the interwar period, by proponents of absolute homogeneity. Max Adler, one of Kelsen's Marxist interlocutors, derisively referred to Kelsen as a 'Friedensonkel',[42] as an avuncular proponent of peace who was altogether too concerned to avoid violent conflict and who thus delayed the advent of true democracy. Kelsen himself thought that the project pursued by Marxist proponents of absolute homogeneity, to create a general will aligned with the preferences of all citizens through a change in the relations of production, was utopian – not because he doubted the injustice of capitalism but because he agreed with Carl Schmitt that political conflict was ineliminable.[43] But Kelsen, given his preference for the peaceful resolution of political conflict, did not endorse Schmitt's further conclusion that political conflict ought to be relegated to a community's external relations with non-members, with internal or external enemies.

In contrasting his own account of the general will and of collective self-government with the expressive account of the proponents of absolute homogeneity, Kelsen made it clear that his sympathies were with the constructive approach. That preference was not itself justifiable, in Kelsen's view, through scientific argument. But this is no weakness of Kelsen's analysis of the nature and value of democracy. That analysis was concerned, first and foremost, to highlight the contrast between the expressive conception of democracy, built on a notion of absolute homogeneity antecedent to the organised political process, and a constructive account of democracy that allows an inclusive common will to emerge in temporally extended free, fair and peaceful political competition. Someone

[40] See, for further discussion, L Vinx, 'Carl Schmitt and the Authoritarian Subversion of Democracy' (2021) 47 *Philosophy & Social Criticism* 173.

[41] Kelsen, *Vom Wesen und Wert der Demokratie* (n 18) 195–97.

[42] See H Kelsen, 'Demokratie' in H Kelsen, *Vom Wesen und Wert der Demokratie*, 2nd edn (Tübingen, JCB Mohr, 1929) 115, 148. On the centrality of peace in Kelsen's legal and political theory, see M Notermans, 'Peace as *conditio tacita* for the Validity of the Positive Legal Order' (2015) 34 *Law and Philosophy* 201.

[43] See Kelsen, *Sozialismus und Staat* (n 34) 92.

who claims that the expressive version of the idea of collective self-government is the authentic form of democracy does not violate any linguistic rule. It is important, nevertheless, to be alert to the fact that the term 'democracy' is used, in common parlance, to refer to fundamentally different political regimes. A political regime built on an expressive conception of the general will turn out to have little in common, once we give an account of the values which it is meant to serve, with a regime that aims to settle political conflict through recurring free and fair electoral competition. If we value the latter over the former, we must resist an equivocating use of the language of democracy that endows political authoritarianism with a false veneer of respectability.

IV. Democratic Assurance: Kelsen's Defence of Formal Constitutionalism

We have yet to address the second of the two challenges to Kelsen's defence of democracy outlined above at the end of section II. Kelsen argues, to recall, that the majority rule, in contrast to any other rule of collective decision, guarantees that a majority of citizens will find their political preferences to be aligned with the law. Kelsen was also a committed defender of constitutionalism, in advocating for constitutional restraints of legislative authority to be enforced by a constitutional court. At first glance, this stance does not sit well with Kelsen's argument for the majority rule. A written constitution will usually be protected against legislative change by a rule of amendment that requires a super-majority for the repeal or modification of a constitutional norm. A super-majoritarian requirement of this sort may come to frustrate the preferences of a majority of citizens, in case a majority wishes a constitutional norm to be changed, but a minority large enough to prevent the super-majoritarian threshold from being met is determined to preserve the contested constitutional norm – precisely the scenario that the majority rule, according to Kelsen, is meant to prevent.

Kelsen developed several mutually supporting lines of reply to this charge of inconsistency.[44] To begin with, it needs to be stressed that the question whether constitutional entrenchment will stunt democracy depends on the content of the constitutional norms protected by an amendment rule. Suppose that a written constitution contains a norm that creates an established religion and endows its adherents with certain legal privileges. Perhaps it has been written into the constitution precisely because the framers feared that such establishment would come to be rejected by a future majority. Suppose as well that a majority of citizens, in the present, but one not large enough to meet some super-majoritarian threshold, have indeed come to desire that the norm be repealed. The conclusion that its constitutional protection thwarts democracy seems inescapable.

It would nevertheless be premature to conclude that any constitutionally entrenched norm ought to be regarded as suspicious from the democratic point of view. Suppose there is an entrenched norm that protects an equal and inclusive franchise, but that

[44] For further elaboration, see Vinx, *Hans Kelsen's Pure Theory of Law* (n 17) ch 5.

a majority of citizens, though one not large enough to meet the super-majoritarian threshold, wishes to disenfranchise the members of some religious minority. Imagine, for instance, that the members of said religion are pacifists and refuse, on grounds of principle, to perform military service, and it is argued that those who are unwilling to participate in the defence of the community against external enemies ought not to enjoy equal political rights. It is much less clear than in our previous example whether democracy is compromised if the majority does not get its way. One can draw a distinction between constitutional norms that serve to protect the integrity of a democratic system of collective decision-making, of a temporally extended general will, and constitutional norms that serve to maintain the factional interests of a minority. The content of a formal or written constitution, Kelsen suggests, would ideally be limited to norms that constitute and protect a democratic political system.[45]

Kelsen's second line of reply to the charge of inconsistency is to point out that constitutional entrenchment might be required as a result of the complexity of a polity.[46] There are two forms of complexity that Kelsen was especially interested in. Kelsen assumed, plausibly, that a democratic state need not be unitarian but can be federal. A federal state will need a formal constitution that delimits the spheres of competence of the central government and the several constituent states. And this order of competence cannot be subject to the decisions of a legislative majority at the federal level if federalism is to differ meaningfully from a unitarian constitutional set-up.[47] A federal set-up accommodates regional difference, which may lead, in a unitarian system, to the undue and structural neglect of the interests of inhabitants of certain regions. Such neglect would make it difficult for citizens in a disadvantaged region to identify with the unitary legislative that will be formed by a national minority. The problem of representation that might make a federal set-up advisable is thus an instance of the problem of insular minorities, ie, of groups that are likely to be permanently excluded from membership in a governing coalition and thus require special constitutional protection. In response to this problem, Kelsen acknowledges that constitutional protection of minority rights may be called for.

The core function of constitutionally protected minority rights, for Kelsen, and this takes us to the third line of reply, is to incentivise political compromise.[48] A minority whose core interests are constitutionally protected possesses additional political leverage. Policies that affect its constitutionally protected interests can be enacted only with its consent, and this leverage is likely to make a legislative majority more willing to adopt policies that cater to a range of interests wider than that of its own constituency. Such incentivisation of political compromise is desirable from the point of view of democracy,

[45] See Kelsen, 'The Nature and Development of Constitutional Adjudication' (n 30) 59–61. Kelsen's argument bears a resemblance to the view presented in JH Ely, *Democracy and Distrust. A Theory of Judicial Review* (Cambridge, MA, Harvard University Press, 1981).

[46] See Kelsen, 'The Nature and Development of Constitutional Adjudication' (n 30) 69–75.

[47] For the importance of federalism to the development of formal constitutionalism and judicial review see SL Paulson, 'Constitutional Review in the United States and Austria: Notes on the Beginnings' (2003) 16 *Ratio Juris* 223.

[48] See Kelsen, *Vom Wesen und Wert der Demokratie* (n 17) 195–97. For the problem of compromise in Kelsen's theory of democracy, see D Ragazzoni, 'Political Compromise in Party Democracy: An Overlooked Puzzle in Kelsen's Democratic Theory' in C Rostboll and T Scavenius (eds), *Compromise and Disagreement in Contemporary Political Theory* (Abingdon, Routledge, 2017) 95–112.

understood as a means to assuage the torment of heteronomy which is bound to arise from our necessary coexistence under objectively binding social rules. Political compromise reduces the likelihood of catastrophic conflict between the content of the law and the political preferences of the members of a minority group. It is of course true that constitutionally protected minority rights may come to frustrate the will of a political majority. But Kelsen assumes, plausibly enough, that it will often be the case that the frustration of a majority's political preferences as to how some insular minority is to be treated will be a more tolerable infringement of freedom than the complete disregard of a minority's vital interests.

Formal constitutionalism, if properly designed, that is the common core of Kelsen's replies to the challenge of inconsistency, facilitates the identification of all citizens with the temporally extended collective will by protecting the integrity of the democratic process. Kelsen would not have denied, I take it, that it is possible for a democratic polity to work without a formal constitution and a constitutional court. He would have conceded that formal constitutionalism can be abused for ends inimical to democracy. But the option of political constitutionalism – ie, for a democratic system stabilised by conventions and a suitable political culture alone – is available only under favourable and contingent historical and social circumstances. The model of political constitutionalism is very likely to be inapplicable under circumstances of increased political complexity – it could not work in any federal state, for instance – and it will function best where there is a fairly high degree of ethnic, linguistic, religious and cultural homogeneity. It is not to be regarded, therefore, as the paradigm of properly functioning democracy. Where circumstances are not favourable to political constitutionalism, formal constitutionalism and constitutional adjudication, properly configured, can offer a publicly visible manifestation of the polity's commitment to the indefinite continuation of free and fair democratic political competition. They will safeguard the temporal extension of the people's will.

V. Kelsen and the Crisis of Democracy

Kelsen's theory of democracy is an attempt to spell out the conditions under which majority rule will translate into authentic self-government, ie, the conditions under which decisions taken by majority can be regarded as manifestations of a collective will even by those who are outvoted and whose political preferences are, at least for the moment, thwarted. There is some overlap between Kelsen's approach to democracy and theories of liberal democracy. Some rights that stand in need of constitutional protection, if the will of the majority is to translate into an authentic collective will, are likewise supported by a liberal vision of the good society. But this overlap is incomplete, as there are some liberal rights that are not directly supported by Kelsen's account of democracy, and what rights are given constitutional standing receive that position on a justificatory ground that does not implicate a liberal conception of the good society. Kelsen's theory of democracy thus invites us to reconfigure our understanding of the contemporary crisis of democracy. This crisis, I would like to suggest, is best understood in terms of the contrast, drawn from Kelsen's reflections on democracy, between what I have referred to as the expressive and the constructive conception of the collective will, and not by reference to the more familiar distinction between mere electoral and liberal democracy.

Populist rhetoric and political practice are committed to an expressive understanding of the will of the people, and that understanding of the will of the people stands in implicit tension with respect for the conditions under which the collective will can remain temporally extended and thus be truly inclusive. A political faction that claims to speak in the name of the people as a whole, and that portrays its political opponents as lackeys of a corrupt elite that oppresses the people, has little reason to preserve free and fair political competition and to provide its adversaries with the opportunity to take power. The character of the political system will have undergone a fundamental change, what is more, where populist autocrats (who may have come to power in free and fair elections) succeed in rewriting the rules of the political game to make sure the opposition are deprived of any realistic chance to win a future election. The promise of equal freedom for all will have been replaced with the permanent and despotic ascendancy of one social group over the other. Defenders of democracy should therefore refuse to concede that the resulting political regime amounts to an authentic form of collective self-government only because it continues to hold elections, and they should not allow populists to get away with dismissing concerns about democratic backsliding as mere special pleading by liberal elites.

12

Kelsen and the Problem of Democratisation of the Administration

THOMAS OLECHOWSKI

I. In the Monarchy

The Habsburg monarchy was a product of absolutism. In the eighteenth century, strong rulers, such as Maria Theresa and her son Joseph II in particular, had formed a unified state from a large number of countries with different legal systems. Their most important support was the bureaucratic apparatus.[1] On this was based a very special sense of class, a professional ethos of the civil servants, which in a certain way still has an effect today. Joseph II had demanded strict obedience from officials. Their own volition had to take a back seat; the civil servants, who at that time also included the judges, were always considered apolitical. And by and large, they met this high standard. Not only the judges but also many administrative officials, even in subordinate departments, had a legal education at university. The bureaucracy was strictly hierarchical, and every civil servant had a superior, right up to the emperor, who liked to see himself as the 'first servant of the state'.[2] Each superior body could issue instructions to the subordinate bodies, so that the will of the state leadership penetrated down to the bottom. Only civil and criminal justice had been excluded from this since the beginning of the nineteenth century. For various reasons, which need not be discussed here, constitutional law doctrine has considered it inadmissible since the late eighteenth century to issue directives to judges in areas of civil or criminal law. It should be remembered that both Hans Kelsen and his disciple Adolf Merkl, the real 'inventor' of the '*Stufenbau der Rechtsordnung*',[3]

[1] H Dreier, *Hierarchische Verwaltung im demokratischen Staat* (Tübingen, Mohr Siebeck, 1991) 36; W Ogris, 'The Habsburg Monarchy in the Eighteenth Century: The Birth of the Modern Centralized State' in A Padoa-Schioppa (ed), *Legislation and Justice* (Oxford, Clarendon Press, 1997) 313–34.

[2] T Olechowski, 'Josephinismus' in A Cordes, H Lück, D Werkmüller and C Bertelsmeier-Kierst (eds), *Handwörterbuch zur Deutschen Rechtsgeschichte*, 2nd edn, Vol II (Berlin, Erich Schmidt Verlag, 2012) 1396–1402; C Schmetterer, 'Die Rechtskultur in Cisleithanien' in A Gottsmann (ed), *Die Habsburgermonarchie 1848–1918, Vol X: Das kulturelle Leben* (Vienna, Austria Academy of Sciences Press, 2021) 1081–1120.

[3] AJ Merkl, *Die Lehre von der Rechtskraft. Entwickelt aus dem Rechtsbegriff. Eine rechtstheoretische Untersuchung* (Vienna, Springer, 1923). cp T Olechowski, 'Legal Hierarchies in the Works of Hans Kelsen and Adolf Julius Merkl' in U Müßig (ed), *Reconsidering Constitutional Formation II: Decisive Constitutional*

the 'hierarchical structure of the legal system', had themselves started their careers as civil officials of the Habsburg monarchy and were therefore used to thinking in hierarchical structures.

Absolutism ended in Austria in 1848 and the era of constitutionalism began, in which the emperor and Parliament had to work together in matters of all of the three powers: legislative, executive and judicial power. The dogma of the separation of powers became the guiding principle of various constitutions that passed at that time. And it must be noted here that in the German-speaking world, 'judicial power' was equated with 'judiciary' and 'executive power' with 'administration'. This gave Montesquieu's dogma a thoroughly new meaning.

In 1920, in his book *Vom Wesen und Wert der Demokratie* [*The Essence and Value of Democracy*], Kelsen explained in retrospect that the separation of powers had been seen as a 'guarantee of freedom' in the era of constitutionalism. 'However', Kelsen wrote, 'it was meant to provide the monarch, who had been pushed out of absolutism into the restriction of Constitutionalism, a final preponderance over the power of the people concentrated in parliament'.[4] The people were fobbed off with participation in legislation, so to speak, while the executive (administration) remained in the hands of the monarch. 'Only theoretical short-sightedness or political intent could pass the principle of the separation of powers as a democratic one',[5] Kelsen judged.

But what theory was behind this system of separation of powers? For Kelsen the answer was clear: it was the theory that the three powers were three essentially different functions of the state. Legislation, and it alone, creates law; the judicial power, the judiciary, on the other hand, is mere application of the law. As far as the executive power, the administration, is concerned, traditional doctrine did not see it as a legal function at all, but as a function of the state. The state pursues its own purposes with it, and the administration can exist independently of the law.

As is well known, Kelsen developed the thesis of the identity of state and law.[6] With this the doctrine of the essential difference between judiciary and administration had to collapse. For him, both were just specific ways of enforcing the law.[7]

Incidentally, this is not as revolutionary as one would initially assume. John Locke, the father of the idea of the separation of powers, only distinguished between a legislative power and an executive power.[8] Montesquieu then named three powers. However, the two powers, which he compared to the '*puissance législative*' [legislative power], initially referred to as '*puissance exécutrice des choses qui dependent du droit des gens*' [executive power in matters concerning international law], the other as '*puissance*

Normativity (Cham, Springer, 2018) 353–62; C Jabloner, T Olechowski and K Zeleny (eds), *Der Stufenbau des Rechts auf dem Prüfstand* (Vienna, Manz Verlag, 2022).

[4] H Kelsen, *Vom Wesen und Wert der Demokratie*, reprint of the first edition of 1920 in M Jestaedt and O Lepsius (eds), *Hans Kelsen. Verteidigung der Demokratie* (Tübingen, Mohr Siebeck, 2006) 1–33, 15–16.

[5] Kelsen, *Vom Wesen und Wert der Demokratie* (n 4) 15. See also, E Czerwick, *Demokratie und Bürokratie* (Berlin, Duncker & Humblot, 2001) 34.

[6] H Kelsen, *Allgemeine Staatslehre* (Berlin, Julius Springer, 1925) 17.

[7] H Kelsen, 'Justiz und Verwaltung' (1929), reprint in HR Klecatsky, R Marcic and H Schambeck (eds), *Die Wiener rechtstheoretische Schule. Schriften von Hans Kelsen, Adolf Merkl, Alfred Verdross*, 2nd edn (Vienna, Franz Steiner/Verlag Österreich, 2010) 1459–83, 1461.

[8] J Locke, *Two Treatises of Government* (1690), reprint in *The Works of John Locke*, Vol V (Aalen, Scientia Verlag, 1963) part II, § 143.

exécutrice des choses du droit civil' [executive power in matters concerning private law]. For the sake of simplicity, Montesquieu named the first in the broader context of his *Esprit des Lois* quite as '*puissance exécutrice*' [executive power] and the other as '*puissance de juge*' [judiciary power]; the basic similarity was also recognised by him.[9] Here, too, I want to refer to Kelsen, who was involved in the creation of the Austrian Federal Constitution between 1919 and 1920 and in particular proposed its structure. This Constitution had a chapter, named 'Federal Execution', which is divided into a section named 'Administration' and a section named 'Judiciary'. The legislator Kelsen was faster here than the theoretician Kelsen, who only wrote in detail on this problem in his writings that appeared after 1920.

What is the difference between administration and judiciary? On the basis of the Austrian Federal Constitutional Act, this is clearly a question of the organisation of these two state functions: while the administration is carried out by officials who are bound by instructions, the judiciary is independent. According to Kelsen, there is no theoretical justification for why some matters, such as civil law and criminal law, are carried out by independent judges and the remaining matters by officials who are bound by instructions. The distinction has grown historically. Kelsen suspects that in matters such as finance, military, or the school system, the public interest was much more pronounced than in civil or criminal law.[10] He would have found his confirmation if he had dared to look across the Austrian borders into countries such as England, for example, where the borders between judiciary and administration are by no means so, but rather large areas of what counts as administration on the continent are carried out by courts of justice. Another connection that Kelsen points out is noteworthy, and it cannot be explained theoretically, but only historically: precisely because the courts are independent, the laws to be enforced by them are extremely detailed. In contrast, the administrative authorities have a much greater degree of free discretion, their actions are much less determined by laws – but by the instructions of their superior authorities.[11]

As Kelsen also emphasises, however, the activities of the administration are only partly judicial and thus comparable to judiciary. Rather, he divides the administration into two areas and calls the part in which the administration acts like a judiciary as 'indirect state administration'. The state only pursues its goals indirectly by issuing bans and authorising them, for example by issuing a driver's licence or imposing a traffic fine. However, there is the area of 'direct administration', in which the state takes direct measures to achieve certain goals, for example by building a school or building a hospital.[12] He could also leave this to the private sector and authorise them to do so, but chooses the way of doing this through its own state organs – 'civil servants', as Kelsen deliberately calls them here – and thus enters into a certain 'competition' with the private sector. But also in this second function, in which the administration does not appear sovereign, with 'imperium', but 'simply acts', the action of the state organs is a legal action, which

[9] C de Montesquieu, *De l'esprit de loix* (1748), reprint in *Œuvres compètes* (Paris, Gallimard/Bibliotheque De La Pleiade, 1951) Vol II, 396–97.

[10] Kelsen, *Allgemeine Staatslehre* (n 6) 260; Kelsen, 'Justiz und Verwaltung' (n 7) 1467.

[11] Kelsen, *Allgemeine Staatslehre* (n 6) 261.

[12] Kelsen, *Allgemeine Staatslehre* (n 6) 238; Kelsen, 'Justiz und Verwaltung' (n 7) 1479.

in a developed constitutional state can happen only on the basis of the laws, or at least within the framework of the laws.

This brings us to legislation, which in traditional political theory is seen as a power alongside executive and judicial power. Merkl and Kelsen contrasted this traditional image with the doctrine of the hierarchical structure of the legal system, according to which the legislature has its place not alongside but above the executive and judiciary. According to this doctrine, none of the powers mentioned have only a legally creating or only judicial function. Rather, all three powers have both functions: according to Merkl, the emergence of law takes place so that an organ called upon to legislate takes note of the law of the higher level and then creates new law in a process of 'will and thought'.[13] The creation of law – be it the creation of a parliamentary decision, a court judgment or an administrative acte – is therefore a two-stage process. As a first step (Merkl: 'process of thought'), the organ must reflect on what possibilities the higher-ranking law grants it, figuratively speaking, what framework it can fill. At this first step, the organ almost never arrives at a single possible outcome, but at a plethora of possibilities, a framework, so to speak, from which a choice has to be made. This choice is the second step (Merkl: 'process of will'). This means: the legislature must interpret the constitution before enacting a law; the judge must interpret the law before giving a judgment, and likewise a civil officer must interpret the law before making an administrative act.

Kelsen's pure theory of law thus rejects the traditional dogma, according to which courts and administrative authorities merely enforce the law, rather they also shape it themselves.[14] The 'act of will' is not regulated by law; rather, non-legal elements flow here, which could be described as 'political'; Carl Schmitt would speak of a decisive element here.[15] It is only in the light of this doctrine that it becomes clear that the monarch, when he retained extensive influence on the administration under constitutionalism, also ensured a great influence on politics. 'Only theoretical short-sightedness or political intent could pass the principle of the separation of powers as a democratic one', I have to repeat Kelsen's judgement. And he goes on as follows: 'It is almost an irony of history when a republic like the United States of America believes in the dogma of the separation of powers and drives it to extremes, especially in the name of democracy'.[16] Kelsen wrote these lines in 1920 in his book *The Essence and Value of Democracy*. In those months when he was working on the creation of the Austrian Federal Constitution, he turned out to be a vehement opponent of the separation of powers.

The description of the legal situation in the monarchy would be incomplete without mentioning that democratic elements existed in the administration even before 1918. First of all, the administration of the local communities is to be mentioned: the population entitled to vote elected community councils and these elected a mayor. And in a similar way, the provincial state parliaments also elected a state committee, which was headed by a state captain (*Landeshauptmann*) and which – in addition to competing

[13] AJ Merkl, 'Prolegomena einer Theorie des rechtlichen Stufenbaues' in A Verdross (ed), *Gesellschaft, Staat und Recht. Festschrift für Hans Kelsen zu dessen 50. Geburtstag* (Vienna, Springer, 1931) 252–94, 280.

[14] Kelsen, *Allgemeine Staatslehre* (n 6) 234; Dreier, *Hierarchische Verwaltung im demokratischen Staat* (n 1) 167.

[15] C Schmitt, *Gesetz und Urteil. Eine Untersuchung zum Problem der Rechtspraxis* (Berlin, Liebmann, 1912).

[16] Kelsen, *Vom Wesen und Wert der Demokratie* (n 4) 16.

with the imperial governor – performed certain administrative tasks in the states.[17] However, it is typical of the monarchy's constitutional law doctrine that these organs were not perceived as state organs, but as organs of a different body. 'It is the democratic community that does not want to be understood as an organ of the autocratic state', Kelsen judged in retrospect.[18] For him this doctrine of a 'dualism of two systems of norms' was highly 'contradictory', but at the same time it was typical of traditional political theory.

II. The October Revolution in Russia

For what follows, we have to take a look at Russia. Without going into details here, it can be said in general that the tsarist administration was structured similar to the administration in the Habsburg monarchy. It was also based on a hierarchically structured administrative apparatus with specially trained officials. Lenin's famous demand was directed against them: 'All Power to the Soviets!' This meant the worker's and soldier's councils (in Russian: *soviets*), some of which went back to the Revolution of 1905 and had increased its importance since the February Revolution of 1917. With the October Revolution, they became bearers of the new state authority.[19]

The soviets can be described as 'proletarian self-government organs'. In every factory, in every troop unit, workers, peasants and soldiers elected soviets from among them, who performed tasks at the lowest level of administration. This also was true for all higher bodies, up to the all-Russian Soviet.[20] It is noteworthy what Kelsen writes about these workers' and soldiers' councils in *The Essence and Value of Democracy*:

> The short terms of office, the possibility of recalling the people's delegates to the various soviets at a moment's notice and the resulting absolute dependence on the voters, the intimate contact with the primal will of the people – this is democracy in its truest form.[21]

The 'democratisation of administration', as it had happened in Russia and was now also being discussed in Austria, was in principle welcomed by Kelsen.[22] However, he pointed

[17] T Olechowski, *Introduction to Austrian and European Legal History* (Vienna, Facultas, 2021) 146.

[18] H Kelsen, 'Demokratisierung der Verwaltung' (1921), reprint in *Die Wiener rechtstheoretische Schule*, 2nd edn, 1295–1303, 1296.

[19] O Anweiler, *Die Rätebewegung in Russland 1905–1921* (Leiden, Brill, 1958) esp 49, 151, 241, 274. See also for an overview of the political background, G Erler, H Groß, H Haumann, G Schramm and T Steffens (eds), 'Zwei Umbrüche im Ersten Weltkrieg: Vom zaristischen zum bolschewistischen Russland (1914–1918)' in M Hellmann, G Schramm and K Zernack (eds), *Handbuch der Geschichte Russlands*, Vol III (Stuttgart, Anton Hiersemann, 1983) 475–622, 567–622. Czerwick (n 5) 121, clearly summarises the characteristic goals of council (soviet) democracy.

[20] Anweiler (n 19) 151 f.

[21] Kelsen, *Vom Wesen und Wert der Demokratie* (n 4) 13. See also H Kelsen, *Sozialismus und Staat*, 2nd edn (Leipzig, CL Hirschfeld, 1923) 188: 'perfect democracy' (*vollkommene Demokratie*). According to Anweiler (n 19) 198, Lenin also repeatedly emphasised the democratic character of the soviets.

[22] W Pircher, 'Der umkämpfte Staatsapparat. Hans Kelsen und Max Adler: zurück zu Lassalle oder vorwärts zu Marx?' in SL Paulson and M Stolleis (eds), *Hans Kelsen. Staatsrechtslehrer und Rechtstheoretiker des 20. Jahrhunderts* (Tübingen, Mohr Siebeck, 2005) 276–301, 291. Russian-style councils were also established in many other European states, and the question of whether it should be a complement or an alternative to Western-style democracy was widely debated; cp V Arnold, *Rätebewegung und Rätetheorien in der Novemberrevolution*, 2nd edn (Hannover, Soak Verlag, 1985); A Weipert, *Die Zweite Revolution.*

out that the Russian experiment to replace the tsarist bureaucracy with councils had basically failed after just a few months. More than that: Kelsen described the situation in Russia as an 'administrative disaster'.[23] The reason for this was initially that this administrative model 'from the bottom up' had led to complete fragmentation, since the central power owed its existence to the local soviets. In addition, the people elected to councils were completely inexperienced in administration and did not have the professional knowledge that was necessary to manage companies or entire governorate districts. More and more often, the old tsarist officials were called back to their offices and the councils were simply put to their side as a control body. But such control was hardly possible because of the one-party system, which prevented any effective opposition.[24]

III. The Project of Democratic Administration in Austria

As in Russia, workers' and soldiers' councils came into being in many other countries during the war. However, the Austrian council movement was never able to achieve great political importance, as the Austrian Social Democratic Party had observed developments in Russia with great scepticism.[25]

The Austrian head of government, Karl Renner from Social Democratic Party, was also an important legal theorist and theoretician of Marxism. In 1919, he commissioned Hans Kelsen to draw up a federal constitution; however, he reserved the problem of democratisation of the administration for himself.[26] In a paper presumably drawn up in the summer of 1919, the '*Leitsätze*' (guiding principles), Renner suggested dividing the Austrian provinces into smaller districts. These districts were evidently to be headed by an official, but to be provided with representatives of the individual professions, who were to participate in the administration in individual, precisely defined agendas. 'In this form', Renner said, 'the soviet idea is to be exploited and also to be restricted to the permissible level'.[27] Although this was a very moderate form of democratisation of the administration, the conservative Christian Social Party vehemently opposed such plans. The question of the democratisation of the administration became one of the most controversial issues in the constitutional process.[28] Corresponding provisions

Rätebewegung in Berlin 1919/20 (Berlin, be.bra wissenschaft verlag, 2015). cp also the review essay by U Bermbach, 'Das Scheitern des Rätesystems und der Demokratisierung der Bürokratie 1918/19' (1967) 8 *Politische Vierteljahresschrift* 445.

[23] Kelsen, 'Demokratisierung der Verwaltung' (n 18) 1298. cp also RF Kneucker, *Bürokratische Demokratie, demokratische Bürokratie. Ein Kommentar zu Struktur, Gestalt und System der Bürokratie in Europa*. Studien zu Politik und Verwaltung, Vol 117 (Vienna, Böhlau, 2020) 289.

[24] Anweiler (n 19) 305.

[25] H Hautmann, 'Die österreichische Rätebewegung 1918/19' (2007) 102 *Politicium* 37; T Olechowski, *Hans Kelsen. Biographie eines Rechtswissenschaftlers*, 2nd edn (Tübingen, Mohr Siebeck, 2021) 257.

[26] K Renner, *Demokratie und Bureaukratie* (Vienna, Universum Verlag, 1946) 30; G Schmitz, *Karl Renners Briefe aus Saint Germain und ihre rechtspolitischen Folgen* (Vienna, Manz, 1991) 82; H Miehsler, 'Demokratisierung der Bezirksverwaltung in Österreich' in AJ Merkl, R Marcic, A Verdross and R Walter (eds), *Festschrift für Hans Kelsen zum 90. Geburtstag* (Vienna, Franz Deuticke, 1971) 141–97, 155.

[27] K Renner, 'Leitsätze', quoted after Schmitz (n 26) 58.

[28] H Kelsen, G Froehlich and AJ Merkl (eds), *Die Bundesverfassung vom 1. Oktober 1920, Die Verfassungsgesetze der Republik Österreich*, Vol V (Vienna, Leipzig, Deuticke, 1922) 229 f.

were included in the Federal Constitution of 1 October 1920, but their entry into force was made dependent on a law still to be passed, which never came about.[29]

It is crucial to acknowledge these circumstances in order to more fully comprehend Kelsen's thoughts on 'democratisation of administration' in his book *The Essence and Value of Democracy*. Like the Social Democrats, Kelsen was also convinced that the introduction of democracy required structuring administration in a democratic way. And as already pointed out, he was also fundamentally positive about the Russian council system. Not theoretical, but practical reasons made him doubt the usefulness of such a model: especially against the background of Russian developments, he emphasised the necessity, even inevitability, of a professional civil service and declared that 'the abolition of the professional civil service [means] simply the abolition of the division of labour and thus every progressive development, every cultural differentiation within political life'.[30]

IV. Kelsen's Rejection of a Democratised Administration

A few months later, Kelsen wrote a whole essay on the problem of 'democratisation of administration'. This essay was published in a legal journal, edited by Kelsen's disciple and friend, Adolf Merkl, in 1921. Here, too, Kelsen referred to the 'Russian administrative disaster' and that it was 'the anti-bureaucratic spearhead of the Soviet system' that 'broke off first'.[31] The competent officials had been called back to their offices; but wherever professional officials and untrained councillors met, the councils never had a chance to succeed. Kelsen therefore rejected this model of administration. Kelsen also suggested the advisability of dividing the administration into elected and appointed bodies, each with their own areas of activity.[32] This model had already existed in Austria at the time of the monarchy, when, in addition to the imperial governor, there was the state captain, I have mentioned before. And it was precisely here that experience had shown that this 'dual track' was extremely complicated, time-consuming and expensive. So Kelsen rejected this system too.

Finally, there was a third option. The provinces should be subdivided into districts with an elected district captain, and each district captain should be assisted by appointed officials. This model was close to the ideas Karl Renner had had in 1919 and existed in the province of Styria from 1862 to 1924/1934.[33]

But here, too, Kelsen had reservations, and a closer look reveals that he now had doubts about the entire idea of democratising the administration.[34] In contrast to what

[29] Miehsler (n 26) 146.

[30] Kelsen, *Vom Wesen und Wert der Demokratie* (n 4) 20.

[31] Kelsen, 'Demokratisierung der Verwaltung' (n 18) 1298. See also Kelsen, *Sozialismus und Staat* (n 21) 186; Kneucker (n 23) 109.

[32] Kelsen, 'Demokratisierung der Verwaltung' (n 18) 1296.

[33] MF Polaschek, *Die Bezirksvertretungen in der Steiermark zwischen 1918 und 1938. Demokratische Selbstverwaltung oder überflüssige Behörde?* (Graz, Verlag des Steiermärkischen Landesarchives, 1997).

[34] Kelsen, 'Demokratisierung der Verwaltung' (n 18) 1301.

Kelsen had written earlier, he now states that administration was first and foremost law enforcement, and the best guarantee that laws are properly enforced is provided by officials who are bound by instructions. Experience has shown that elected bodies have completely different interests. They look first and foremost to their constituents, to whom they must account for their actions and by whom they wish to be re-elected. If an elected governor gave instructions to a district governor who was also elected, this would run into difficulties. This means that several democratic levels are in competition with one another. Which one takes precedence? Kelsen gave a clear answer to this question: the democracy of the whole must take precedence over the democracy of the parts. In the interests of democracy itself, the administration should therefore not be democratised.[35]

At this crucial point, it is difficult to see what Kelsen's real motivations were. We only find a very hidden reason: Kelsen was concerned with the 'democracy of a higher whole [*Demokratie des Ganzen*]'.[36] His preference for 'democracy of the whole' was simply a political preference directed against federalism. His rejection of a 'democracy of the parts [*Demokratie der Teile*]' arose out of a fear that the whole state could fall apart. However, with his writings Kelsen made a significant contribution to the fact that the project of democratising the administration in Austria was not pursued any further and that the administrative structures of the monarchy continued to exist for decades. The hierarchical bureaucracy in particular should now be the best guarantor of democracy, and the means of instruction were given a key position in this model of democracy.[37]

Merkl later wrote a whole monograph concerning the problem of 'democratisation of administration'.[38] And he, too, was of the opinion that it was best for democracy if the democratic government handed issues over to the bureaucratic apparatus. In this way, the democratic will can penetrate from the top of the administration to the bottom. This model became typical for Austria for decades and was named the 'Kelsen–Merkl-model of administration'.[39]

By contrast, Kelsen's considerations on a democratic administration fell into oblivion. When Kelsen published a second edition of his book *The Essence and Value of Democracy* in 1929, the sections on soviet democracy were some of the few parts that he completely rewrote.[40] There was no longer any sign of his former affection for the Soviet system.

[35] Dreier, *Hierarchische Verwaltung im demokratischen Staat* (n 1) 123.

[36] Kelsen, 'Demokratisierung der Verwaltung' (n 18) 1301.

[37] Czerwick (n 5) 35. Kneucker (n 23) 290, rightly speaks of a 'paradox' that must be accepted.

[38] AJ Merkl, *Demokratie und Verwaltung* (Vienna, Moritz Perles, 1923); see also, AJ Merkl, *Allgemeines Verwaltungsrecht* (Vienna/Berlin, Julius Springer, 1927) 336; Czerwick (n 5) 30; H Dreier, 'Merkls Verwaltungsrechtslehre und die heutige deutsche Dogmatik des Verwaltungsrechtes' in H Dreier, *Kelsen im Kontext. Beiträge zum Werk Hans Kelsens und geistesverwandter Autoren* M Jestaedt and SL Paulson (eds) (Tübingen, Mohr Siebeck, 2019) 135–75, 152–54; Kneucker (n 23) 110.

[39] T Öhlinger, *Der Stufenbau der Rechtsordnung* (Vienna, Manz, 1975) 34; K Weber, 'Das Gesicht der Verwaltung im 21. Jahrhundert' in P Bußjäger (ed), *Moderner Staat und innovative Verwaltung* (Vienna, Braumüller, 2003) 107–27, 109; P Pernthaler, *Österreichisches Bundesstaatsrecht* (Vienna, Verlag Österreich, 2004) 170.

[40] H Kelsen, 'Vom Wesen und Wert der Demokratie'. Reprint of the second edition of 1929 in Kelsen, *Verteidigung der Demokratie* (n 4) 149–228, 182.

V. Conclusion

The chapter has shown how much knowledge of the legal-historical background is important for understanding legal-theoretical and democratic-theoretical texts.[41] At the same time, it shows how closely Kelsen's statements on democratic theory and legal theory are interrelated and complement each other. The basic legal concepts that Kelsen carefully analyses are used by him to identify the democratic or anti-democratic tendencies of a state. Finally, the text is an example of how difficult it is to make Kelsen's terminology, which is based on the German legal tradition, understandable to an English-speaking audience. For Kelsen and German-speaking jurists, 'administration' is synonymous with 'executive power', and Kelsen sees in it a function of law-making, very similar to the 'legislative power' of Parliament. Therefore, he first calls for the democratisation of the 'administration' as well. However, it is not the theoretical insights but the practical experiences from the Russian October Revolution that move him to turn away from this demand. In later works, for Kelsen, the hierarchical bureaucracy, which stems from absolutism, is now the best means of implementing the will of the democratic legislator.

[41] Recently, Stephen Turner and George Mazur have attempted to explain Kelsen's theory of democracy against an American background. However, this shows just how European Kelsen's theories really are. S Turner and G Mazur, *Making Democratic Theory Democratic: Democracy, Law and Administration after Weber and Kelsen* (New York, Routledge 2023).

PART IV

Kelsen's Legacy

13

'A Monument More Lasting than Bronze, Higher than the Pyramids' Regal Structures'? The Vienna School of the Pure Theory of Law as the Work and Legacy of Hans Kelsen

RODRIGO CADORE

exegi monumentum aere perennius
regalique situ pyramidum altius,
quod non imber edax, non Aquilo inpotens
possit diruere

(Horace, Odes III: XXX, lines 1–4, published 23 BC)

With these words, the economist Ludwig von Mises (1881–1973) reported in 1939 in two different letters from Geneva to the political scientist Erich Voegelin (1901–85), who had recently been 'exiled' to the United States, on the prevailing situation in Europe:

> What you smell and hear here every day is apocalyptic and horrific. Everything has come to pass as ... Jakob Burckhardt ... and Herbert Spencer saw it coming. The 'terrible[s] simplificateurs'[1] ... really rule now. The worst thing is that there is no intellectual resistance anywhere.[2]
>
> I would have loved to go to America in the summer, if only to be able to breathe the spiritual air of the old 'Vienna Circle' once again. But unfortunately it is not possible.[3]

Mises nostalgically regretted the disintegration of the intellectual milieu in which his Viennese Circle, which included Voegelin, had been active. But what was meant by this 'Vienna Circle'? Specifically, it was the so-called Mises Circle, which met regularly at

[1] 'Letter from Jakob Burckhardt to Friedrich von Preen of 24 July 1889' in A Dru (ed), *The Letters of Jacob Burckhardt* (New York, Pantheon Books, 1955) 218, 220.

[2] 'Letter from Ludwig Mises to Erich Voegelin of 5 March 1939' in Stanford University, Hoover Institution Archives, Eric Voegelin Papers, Box 25, Folder 23.

[3] 'Letter from Ludwig Mises to Erich Voegelin of 18 July 1939' in Stanford University, Hoover Institution Archives, Eric Voegelin Papers, Box 25, Folder 23.

the Chamber of Commerce from 1922 onwards – at the latest – and discussed primarily methodological questions of the social sciences, but which was not alone in the Viennese cultural landscape of the interwar period. This special Viennese landscape also included, among others, the circle around Hans Kelsen (1881–1973).

The circles around Mises and Kelsen formed the basis for two of the numerous so-called Austrian Schools and were each nothing other than the economic and jurisprudential manifestation of that avant-garde cultural constellation that one tends to call 'Viennese Modernism' ('*Wiener Moderne*'). Perhaps their most famous manifestation can be found in the form of the logical-positivist circle around Moritz Schlick (1882–1936), which called itself the 'Vienna Circle' and was in some ways – typical of the time – as constantly as informally interwoven with the circles around Kelsen and Mises.

The embedding of each of these circles in the overall framework of Viennese Modernism as well as their interconnections with each other shaped the production of knowledge within each circle and conditioned the circulation of knowledge between the different circles. The Vienna School of Jurisprudence as a collective of thought, which grew organically out of the circle around Kelsen in the midst of Viennese Modernism and stands for the pure theory of law, is in a certain – unspectacular – sense nothing more than one of these numerous circles. For legal theory past and present, this circle, which is to a large extent the product of Kelsen's own efforts and genius, represents a legacy that has not been explored to its fullest potential.

Kelsen did not build pyramids and – in contrast to the legal-theoretical Vulgate – nor did he consider the legal order as such: but his contributions to the history of legal theory include the fact that he gathered around him a circle of like-minded people who together developed a unique style of legal-theoretical thinking that has endured for generations and is far from exhausted. After a lot of academic digging, there is still a *monumentum aeres perennius*[4] out there waiting to be rediscovered.

I. A Turning Point in Kelsenian Studies

A. On the Shoulders and under the Shadows of a Giant

When speaking of the pure theory of law or even legal positivism, the association with Hans Kelsen's name is – at least among Civil Law jurists – immediate. There are several widely disseminated labels which indicate the relevance of the 'Kelsen' trademark. For an example, the designation of a whole genre of researchers is built upon Kelsen's name – they are the 'Kelsenians'[5] or the 'Kelsenites'.[6] Commonly, legal theoretical discourse

[4] Horace, 'Carmina' in CE Bennet (ed), *Horace. Odes and Epodes* (Boston, Allyn and Bacon, 1934) 92 (Liber 3, 30).

[5] eg, N Hoerster, 'Hans Kelsens Grundnormlehre kritisch betrachtet' (2008) 63 *JuristenZeitung* 1023, 1025. 'Kelsenianism' is also frequently mentioned, eg, V Frick, *Die Staatsrechtslehre im Streit um ihren Gegenstand. Die Staats- und Verfassungsdebatten seit 1789* (Tübingen, Mohr Siebeck, 2018) 202.

[6] eg, J Stone, *The Province and Function of Law: Law as Logic Justice and Social Control. A Study in Jurisprudence* (Cambridge, MA, Harvard University Press, 1946) 20, fn n 62, 108, 111, fn n 59; L Fuller, 'The Place and Uses of Jurisprudence in the Law School Curriculum' (1949) 1 *Journal of Legal Education* 495, 496.

refers to a 'Kelsen School' ('Kelsen-Schule')[7] of Jurisprudence. In these different formulations, the figure of Kelsen emerges as central and intends to denote, by itself, a specific theoretical inclination and style of legal thinking. It should be mentioned that adjectives and nouns derived from 'Kelsen' often have a pejorative connotation.[8]

However, even the frequent discursive invocation of a 'school' does not generally attest to a great interest in Kelsen's pupils and collaborators. The focus almost always seems to be on Kelsen and not on the school as such. Those who in their time stood on the shoulders of a giant, of the 'gran maestro de Vienna',[9] today remain eclipsed by Kelsen's brilliance, relatively forgotten under his shadow. The dominant image of Kelsen largely covers up the rich legacy of an authentic school of legal theory. The structure and dynamics of the Vienna School of Jurisprudence remain largely uncharted.

B. Tensions: The 'Official' Image of the Vienna School of Jurisprudence

Among initiates and experts, working within the research programme of the pure theory of law, or among scholars who are familiar with it, the situation is not usually different. The 'official' image[10] of the Vienna School privileges Kelsen and ignores – to a greater or lesser extent – not only other characters, but also the contributions of the other adherents of a shared research programme to the development of this programme.[11] Scholarship dealing with the concepts of Kelsen's pupils and collaborators is often limited to the question of how Kelsen himself received their occasional theoretical schemes and solutions; the members of the Vienna School are perceived as satellites orbiting in the Kelsenian field of gravitation and the pure theory is reduced to his version of it.

While the centrality of Kelsen's name is justifiable, the fixation with the Kelsenian version of the pure theory of law comes at a price. Access to other modes of articulation of the research programme of the Vienna School becomes more difficult as the alternative routes to it are reduced. The pure theory is not seldomly understood and treated as a monolithic block of theses to be accepted or rejected all together. Kelsen's formulations

[7] eg, H Heller, *Staatslehre*, edited by G Niemeyer (ed) (Leiden, AW Sijthoff's Uitgeversmaatschappij, 1934) 185.

[8] eg, F Leal, 'O formalista expiatório: Leituras impuras de Kelsen no Brasil' (2014) 10 *Revista Direito GV* 245.

[9] JL Kunz, 'Was ist die Reine Rechtslehre?' (1948) 1 *Österreichische Zeitschrift für öffentliches Recht* 271, 290.

[10] At most, only superficial consideration is regularly given to the contributions of Adolf Julius Merkl (1890–1970) and Alfred Verdross (1890–1980), presented together with Kelsen as part of the 'Great Trio' ('die Drei Großen') of the pure theory of law, eg, T Elsner, *Das Ermessen im Lichte der Reinen Rechtslehre. Rechtsstrukturtheoretische Überlegungen zur Rechtsbindung und zur Letztentscheidungskompetenz des Rechtsanwenders* (Berlin, Duncker & Humblot, 2011) 89. Commenting critically on this narrow and selective interpretation of the pure theory of law, see previously RA Métall, 'Hans Kelsen und seine Wiener Schule der Rechtstheorie' in Hans Kelsen-Institut (ed), *Hans Kelsen zum Gedenken* (Vienna, Manz Verlag, 1974) 15–26, 21.

[11] See, however, the initial efforts of the Hans Kelsen Institute in Vienna: R Walter, C Jabloner and K Zeleny (eds), *Der Kreis um Kelsen. Die Anfangsjahre der Reinen Rechtslehre* (Vienna, Manz Verlag, 2008). See also W Ebenstein, *The Pure Theory of Law* (Madison, University of Wisconsin Press, 1945); C Jabloner, 'Kelsen and his Circle: The Viennese Years' (1998) 9 *European Journal of International Law* 368.

are taken as the only possible execution of the postulates of the pure theory; deviations or rearrangements in the interpretation of the original score are catalogued as something quite different and the label 'Kelsenian' is commonly denied to them. Kelsenian 'orthodoxy' often does not recognise models that offer solutions to problems of legal theory other than Kelsen's as variations of the pure theory; these models are not seen as developing internally from common starting points, but rather as substitutes or abdications; the critics, for their part, do not seem to admit that the pure theory can be a theory in constant development, and exclude the possibility of readjustments in its research programme – the pure theory begins and ends with Kelsen. Thus, it loses nuance and refinement which reduces its historical plurality. The theoretical potential of the Vienna School is arbitrarily confined to the canonical 'Kelsenian' variant of the pure theory, often treated as an archival piece within a museum-oriented approach.

This chapter aims at restoring complexity by tensing the predominantly static academic vision of the pure theory of law. If, on the one hand, it is true that the Vienna School of Jurisprudence is to a large extent the product of the agglutinative efforts and creative ingenuity of Hans Kelsen, on the other hand, it must be asked to what extent the pure theory of law is the product of a school as a research collective ('*Denkkollektiv*').[12] In the following, I first offer a reconstruction of the Viennese years of the Vienna School of Jurisprudence by presenting the formation of the School as a result of Kelsen's initiatives and inspiration and outlining the structure and dynamics of the research network within which the *Reine Rechtslehre* developed (section II). I then address the common research programme developed by the Vienna School, elaborating on the core tenets of theses that was shared by different members of this School, thus characterising a unique style of legal thinking referred to as the pure theory of law (section III). Essentially, disregarding the pure theory's development within the Vienna School entails a significant loss of standing for legal scholarship. This first attempt at implementing this idea, if well executed, should serve as a stimulus for a turn in 'Kelsenian' studies: from Kelsen to the Vienna School of Jurisprudence; from musealisation to aggiornamento, albeit through rediscovery.

II. The Vienna School as the Work and Legacy of Hans Kelsen

The then so-called 'Young Austrian School'[13] emerged from the combination of factors as diverse as improbable. Some of these factors are indelibly linked to the dynamics of the socio-cultural fabric of Vienna in the first decades of the twentieth century, others resulted from Kelsen's personal engagement. The analytical juxtaposition of these factors makes it possible to understand the various operative dimensions of the Vienna School,

[12] L Fleck, *Entstehung und Entwicklung einer wissenschaftlichen Tatsache* (Frankfurt/Main, Suhrkamp, 1980) 146–64.

[13] The designation 'jungösterreichische Schule' emerged originally from the debate between Alfred Verdross (A Verdross, '[Review] Bernhard Stark: Die Analyse des Rechts [1916]' (1917) 41 *Schmollers Jahrbuch* 477, 478, 479) and Bernhard Stark (B Stark, 'Die jungösterreichische Schule der Rechtswissenschaft und die naturwissenschaftliche Methode' (1918) 26 *Juristische Blätter* 301).

which was formed around the young Kelsen and from the theoretical impulses offered in his habilitation writing ('*Habilitationsschrift*'). It is within this school that the 'pure theory' project will become viable.

A. Initial Spark: *Main Problems in the Theory of Public Law*

In 1911, the year of his thirtieth birthday, Kelsen published the work with which he qualified as *Privatdozent* at the Law Faculty of the University of Vienna:[14] a monograph of 736 pages, entitled *Main Problems in the Theory of Public Law*,[15] which could well have been titled ***My*** *Main Problems* ***with*** *the Theory of Public Law*. Kelsen calibrated his academic trajectory by identifying innumerable fractures in the theoretical corpus of public law doctrine and denouncing scientific deficits in legal scholarship. This work laid down the 'cornerstone'[16] of a theoretical building later baptised as the *Pure Theory of Law* (*Reine Rechtslehre*).[17] There, we already find a sharp critique of the 'methodological syncretism'[18] prevailing in German-language public law scholarship, as well as a manifesto proposing a revolt against hypostases and essentialisms, as these would impair the rigour of analysis in describing legal phenomena and prevent an adequate understanding of them. In a dialogical manner,[19] Kelsen subjected the central dogmas of early twentieth-century constitutional jurisprudence to revision by elaborating – mainly *ex negativo* – a distinctive and characteristic way of thinking about legal problems.

The pure theory of law began in this work, as well as in the works immediately following it, as a methodological reflection. In Kelsen's view, it was important to find a specific focus for the legal studies. If something like an autonomous 'legal science' (legal scholarship properly so-called) could come into existence, then it would be necessary to individualise its own methodology and object, and to demarcate its field of research. Without this, *legal* scholarship would have no reason to exist, and legal studies would be the responsibility of other already sufficiently differentiated fields of scientific knowledge, such as history and psychology, ethics and philosophy – or even sociology, which was emerging at the time. The early years of the pure theory of law were therefore years of intense discussions about the epistemological status of 'legal scholarship', which

[14] The documents relating to Kelsen's habilitation are preserved at Österreichisches Staatsarchiv [ÖStA], Allgemeines Verwaltungsarchiv [AVA], Unterricht Allgemein, Universität Wien, 4 Jus, Personalakt Hans Kelsen, Z. 30728/1911.

[15] H Kelsen, *Hauptprobleme der Staatsrechtslehre entwickelt aus der Lehre vom Rechtssatze* (Tübingen, JCB Mohr, 1911) (HKW2, 21–878).

[16] H Kelsen, 'Vorrede' in H Kelsen, *Hauptprobleme der Staatsrechtslehre entwickelt aus der Lehre vom Rechtssatze*, 2nd edn (Tübingen, JCB Mohr (Paul Siebeck) 1923) V–XXXIII, XXIII (HKW9, 324–50).

[17] The expression 'pure theory of law' will be used prominently for the first time to designate the theoretical project of the Vienna School in 1920: H Kelsen, *Das Problem der Souveränität und die Theorie des Völkerrechts. Beitrag zu einer Reinen Rechtslehre* (Tübingen, JCB Mohr (Paul Siebeck), 1920) (HKW4, 235–572). See also, F Kaufmann, 'Wahrheit und Wert in der reinen Rechtslehre. Eine Studie über die Systemprobleme des Rechts' (Vienna 1920) – unpublished doctoral thesis, preserved in Sozialwissenschaftliches Archiv Konstanz, Nachlass Felix Kaufmann.

[18] eg, Kelsen (n 15) V, 184 (HKW2, 53, 294 f).

[19] eg, Kelsen (n 15) XI f (HKW2, 59 f). See also, M Jestaedt, 'Wiener Summe: Die "Allgemeine Staatslehre" als Kelsens vollständigstes Werk' in H Kelsen, *Allgemeine Staatslehre*, Studienausgabe, M Jestaedt (ed) (Tübingen, Mohr Siebeck, 2019) XI–LXXXIV, XLVII.

should be structured as a 'normative science', ie: a science of norms.[20] A singular disciplinary cut-out was sought for this kind of normative knowledge of law: the pure theory developed initially as a theory of the *Eigengesetzlichkeit der Rechtswissenschaft*, ie, as a theory of 'legal scholarship'.

From the outset, perhaps the fundamental theorem of this theory was established: the impossibility of cognising legal phenomena except in their relation to positive legal norms.[21] Thus, legal thinking acquired a relational character – there is no more and no less law than what can be cognised or constructed through the use of positive legal norms as schemes for the interpretation ('*Deutungsschemata*') of reality.[22] The basic category for shaping this specific way of thinking will be found in the concept of 'imputation' ('*Zurechnung*')[23] as the proper normative way of connecting certain factual hypotheses to their legal consequences; a connection which will always be contingent on the authorised decisions (acts of will) of the competent authorities in a concrete legal experience.

Therefore, Kelsen's habilitation thesis already bears his own signature, a special and recognisable style. According to this, the scientific knowledge of law requires the tracing of the analysed phenomena to a set of positive norms; the object of this knowledge is positive law as the product of human decisions, or more precisely of certain individuals who function as legal organs.[24] Hence, all law is man-made law. It is the task of a specific *legal* scholarship to describe and reconstruct normative relations, taking into account the specificity of law as the object of an individualised form of scientific knowledge. What exactly this specificity of law is supposed to be, the young Kelsen had not yet found out. The pure theory emerged as a meta-theory of legal knowledge, which presented intuitions about the *Eigengesetzlichkeit* (specific mode of operation) of law that were still vacillating. This theory developed at first from a set of theses on the structure of positive legal norms (legal proposition theory), which sought in this structure – statically observed – the distinctive feature of law vis-à-vis to causal phenomena and other kinds of normativity.[25] The 'creation', 'application' and 'derogation' of law were perceived as meta-legal phenomena, that could not be addressed by an exclusively normative approach.[26] These phenomena remained outside the scope of legal scholarship.

[20] See Kelsen (n 15) VII (HKW2, 55).

[21] 'Relation zum Rechtssatz' (Kelsen (n 15) 494, 496, 497; (HKW2, 641, 644, 645)).

[22] See the canonical formulations in H Kelsen, *Reine Rechtslehre. Eine Einführung in die rechtswissenschaftliche Problematik* (hereafter RR1) (Vienna, Franz Deuticke, 1934) 4 f/M Jestaedt (ed), Studienausgabe (Tübingen, Mohr Siebeck, 2008) 18 f; H Kelsen, *Reine Rechtslehre. Mit einem Anhang: Das Problem der Gerechtigkeit* (hereafter RR2) (Vienna, Franz Deuticke, 1960) 3 f/M Jestaedt (ed), *Studienausgabe* (Tübingen, Mohr Siebeck, 2017) 25 f (hereafter the pages of the original and of the 'Studienausgaben' (study editions) will be indicated in the following format 'original pp/pp Studienausgabe').

[23] On the concept of imputation in the pure theory, see eg, SL Paulson, 'Hans Kelsen's doctrine of imputation' (2014) 14 *Ratio Juris* 47; C Heidemann, 'Der Begriff der Zurechnung bei Hans Kelsen' in SL Paulson and M Stolleis (eds), *Hans Kelsen: Staatsrechtslehrer und Rechtstheoretiker des 20. Jahrhunderts* (Tübingen, Mohr Siebeck, 2005) 17–34.

[24] 'There is no law in the absence of adjudicators' (Kelsen (n 15) 35 (HKW2, 120)).

[25] Kelsen will deal with what he calls the 'ideal linguistic form of legal propositions', see Kelsen (n 15) 237 (HKW2, 353).

[26] See, eg, Kelsen (n 15) 334 (HKW2, 461); F Weyr, 'Zur Frage der Unabänderlichkeit von Rechtssätzen' (1916) 45 *Juristische Blätter* 387, 387.

B. Crossroads: Kelsen and Weyr

It was precisely that facet of the pure theory of law as a meta-theory of legal knowledge, betting on a normative 'legal science', that attracted the attention of the Czechoslovak jurist František Weyr (1879–1951). An extraordinary professor at the 'Technische Hochschule' of Brno, Weyr saw in Kelsen's *Main Problems* an attempt at a 'critique of purely juridical reason'.[27] On Weyr's reading, it proposed to demythologise the language of jurists and provoke an awareness of the epistemological limitations of legal scholarship, trying to bring it to the level of rigorous, scientific knowledge. Essential to this project of scientificising academic legal discourse would be the conceptual distinction between cognition and volition, between knowledge and the creation of the law:[28] the sole task of legal scholarship would be to cognise its object rather than shaping it, ie, to normatively guide legal practice – a task incumbent on political debate.

Weyr's fascination with Kelsen's habilitation work was followed by a first personal meeting, probably by 1912;[29] and from this meeting and of the intellectual affinities they could infer, a solid friendship resulted, which lasted Weyr's entire life and significantly marked the academic trajectory of both.[30] Weyr soon became the key figure of the so-called Normative School of Brno,[31] which functioned as a kind of resonance board for the theses of the Vienna School. Members of both Schools engaged in intensive scientific exchange, which led to mutual enrichment and shaped the identity of these two different research formations. The Vienna and Brno Schools shared the 'hard-core' of the same research programme[32] and came to be structured in a very similar way, being organised around a nucleus formed by the participants of the (private) seminars of Kelsen and Weyr respectively.

However, the intertwining of the paths of Kelsen and Weyr took place at a time when neither one nor the other were heads of any school. Neither of the theses they propounded were widely disseminated, nor were there young students around them willing to embrace the iconoclasm of the pure theory of law – or the 'Normative Theory', as Weyr called it.[33] This theory was still in a state of incubation. The *Privatdozent* Kelsen and the Extraordinary Professor Weyr[34] shared worries and dissatisfactions regarding

[27] F Weyr, 'Über zwei Hauptpunkte der Kelsenschen Staatsrechtslehre' (1914) 40 *Zeitschrift für das Privat- und Öffentliche Recht der Gegenwart* 174, 178.

[28] eg, F Weyr, 'Zum Problem eines einheitlichen Rechtssystems' (1908) 23 *Archiv des öffentlichen Rechts* 529, 544.

[29] See F Weyr, *Paměti*, Vol 1: Za Rakouská (1879–1918) (Brno, Atlantis, 1999) 283; M Večera, *František Weyr* (Brno, Nadace Universitas Masarykiana, 2001) 32.

[30] See P Hungr, 'Weyr und Kelsen – Geistesverwandte Persönlichkeiten' (1992) 23 *Rechtstheorie* 161.

[31] On the Brno normative school, see V Kubeš and O Weinberger (eds), *Die Brünner Rechtstheoretische Schule* (Vienna, Manz, 1980); A Bröstl, '20th-Century Legal Philosophy in Czechoslovakia, the Czech Republic, and the Slovak Republic' in E Pattaró and C Roversi (eds), *A Treatise of Legal Philosophy and General Jurisprudence*, Vol 12: Legal Philosophy in the Twentieth Century: The Civil Law World (Cham, Springer, 2016) 615–26.

[32] On the notion of 'research programmes', see I Lakatos, 'Falsification and the methodology of scientific research programmes' in I Lakatos, *The Methodology of Scientific Research Programs. Philosophical Papers*, Vol 1, J Worral and G Currie (eds) (New York, Cambridge University Press, 1978) 8–101, 48.

[33] See F Weyr, *Základy filosofie právní (Nauka o poznání právnickém)* (Brno, A Píša, 1920).

[34] Weyr obtained the *venia legendi* for 'Administration Sciences and Czech Administrative Law' at the 'German University of Prague' ('Deutsche (Karls-)Universität zu Prag') on 30 December 1908 – the University's

the usual way of thinking and teaching law, finding in each other fundamental encouragement and stimulus to carry out a bold project of reformation. From the very beginning, it was their concern to put legal knowledge in touch with the philosophy of science, in order to modify the current scenario in which 'legal scholarship' was considered a province way too distant from the centre of (the theory of) scientific knowledge.[35]

If among academic peers the pure theory of law did not find more receptivity, so that Weyr remained initially a more or less isolated 'prophet',[36] reverberating the creed that linked him to Kelsen to almost always closed ears, it was his own characteristic attitude of openness to methodological and epistemological discussions that soon attracted a first wave of students, coming mostly from the first courses offered by Kelsen at the University of Vienna. Drawn from the ranks of the university benches of courses taught by a 30-something untenured lecturer, the first generation of the pure theory was to emerge – and the Vienna School of Jurisprudence was to be built.

C. From Kelsen's Circle to the Vienna School of Jurisprudence

i. *Wickenburggasse 23: The Private Seminar as 'Cognitive Niche'*

By early 1914 at the latest, Kelsen began to offer a private seminar for selected colleagues and students.[37] The seminar took place once a month on a Sunday afternoon in the office of Kelsen's flat where he lived with his wife Margarete (born Bondi, 1890–1973).[38] In this forum, various manuscripts of texts that Kelsen would publish in the second and third decades of the twentieth century will be discussed. The seminar will become a safe space for experimentation, in which ideas were tested, criticisms expressed frankly, and informal debates established, without attention to titles or academic positions.[39]

Although Kelsen acted to some extent as regent, guiding and organising the Sunday colloquia, the other participants took turns in presenting papers submitted for peer review. Articles, monographs and even habilitations theses were often developed, contested and refined in the atmosphere of intellectual exchanges in the private seminar. It was not just works by the members themselves that were discussed since a concerted effort was made to keep current developments in legal philosophy, legal theory and state

decision was confirmed by the competent ministry on 17 March 1909; subsequently he was still granted the *venia legendi* for 'Statistics', see Archiv der Karls-Universität Prag, Deutsche Universität, Juristische Fakultät, Personalakt František Weyr. In the winter semester 1911/1912 Weyr was hired to teach as an Extraordinary Professor at the 'Technische Hochschule' in Brno.

[35] Kelsen, RR1, V/4.

[36] P Goller, *Naturrecht, Rechtsphilosophie oder Rechtstheorie? Zur Geschichte der Rechtsphilosophie an Österreichs Universitäten (1848–1945)* (Frankfurt am Main, Peter Lang, 1997) 172.

[37] See, on the subject of private seminars, the records of the disciplinary investigation concerning the controversy between Kelsen and Fritz Sander (1889–1939), which offer a reconstruction of the formative period of the Vienna School through the testimony of several of the seminar participants between 1913/1914 and 1923: Universitätsarchiv Wien [UAW], Akademischer Senat, Disziplinarfall Hans Kelsen (1923).

[38] See, eg, the first-hand accounts by L Pitamic, 'Hans Kelsen zum 90. Geburtstag' (1971) 21 *Österreichische Zeitschrift für öffentliches Recht* 261, 261–262 and H Silving, *Memoirs* (New York, Vantage Press, 1988) 90–99.

[39] Kelsen's private seminar has not yet received sufficient scholarly attention; see, however, T Olechowski, *Hans Kelsen. Biographie eines Rechtswissenschaftlers*, 2nd edn (Tübingen, Mohr Siebeck, 2021) 146–50; J Busch, 'Hans Kelsen im Ersten Weltkrieg. Achsenzeit einer Weltkarriere' in R Walter, W Ogris and T Olechowski (eds), *Hans Kelsen: Leben – Werk – Wirksamkeit* (Vienna, Manz Verlag, 2009) 57–80, 73–74.

theory on the radar of the participants.[40] There was also no lack of interdisciplinary curiosity. Philosophical, sociological and political theory works were collectively examined, from time to time even in the presence of their illustrious authors, as in the case of Max Weber (1864–1920).[41]

Participation in the private seminar will generate a strong feeling of belonging to a research group, without implying the unrestricted adoption of Kelsen's beliefs. In contrast to university courses, the private seminar was characterised by personal continuity. Over time, professors, postdoctoral researchers, doctoral students, undergraduates and even curious non-academic parties joined in. Wickenburggasse 23 became a kind of centre or engine room of a theoretical movement, which would soon consolidate as a school of thought.[42] It functioned as a link between the academic microcosm and the creative extra-university *milieu* in Vienna. A circle of interlocutors stabilised around the private seminar, and gradually a research formation crystallised out of this circle that was to be responsible for Pure Theory of Law in the academic public sphere. The maturation and refinement of this theory became a collective enterprise, which was to take advantage of the circulation of the members of the private seminar among others of the so-called Vienna circles.

ii. Kelsen's Circle Among Vienna Circles

The circle around Kelsen's private seminar was neither unique nor pioneering in early twentieth-century Vienna. The plurality of circles constituted a solid institution of Viennese Modernism and often aggregated interlocutors from different areas of knowledge or the arts around central figures, in formats similar to working groups, mobilised for the discussion of topics of common interest.[43] In a certain sense, these circles often sheltered marginalised characters, who had not found adequate space in formal academic careers, but who formed an authentic intellectual avant-garde:[44] the juridical expression of this Viennese avant-garde was Kelsen's Circle.

As a university professor, Kelsen enjoyed Vienna's cultural effervescence from a privileged position. On the one hand, he could use his constant contact with motivated

[40] In the summer semester of 1914, for example, Carl Schmitt's (1885–1988) book *Der Wert des Staates* was discussed from a presentation by Verdross, see 'Letter from Alfred Verdross to Carl Schmitt of 27 July 1914' in E Hüsmert and G Giesler (eds), *Carl Schmitt. Die Militärzeit. 1915 bis 1919* (Berlin, Duncker & Humblot, 2005) 498; C Schmitt, *Der Wert des Staates und die Bedeutung des Einzelnen* (Tübingen, JCB Mohr (Paul Siebeck), 1914).

[41] On 6 July 1918 (on a Saturday!) Weber delivered a lecture on the concept of the state ('Staatsbegriff') at Kelsen's private seminar (see 'Letter from Max Weber to Mina Tobler of 3 July 1918' in *MWG* II/10–1, 209–10, 210; 'Letter from Max Weber to Marianne Weber of 3 July 1918' in *MWG* II/10–1, 211–12, 211).

[42] See K Zeleny, 'Die Wiener rechtstheoretische Schule' in R Walter, W Ogris and T Olechowski (eds), *Hans Kelsen: Leben – Werk – Wirksamkeit* (Vienna, Manz Verlag, 2009) 137–149; K Zeleny, 'Die Wickenburggasse 23: Das Zentrum der "Wiener Schule"' in M Ettl and G Murauer (eds), *Hans Kelsen und die Bundesverfassung. Geschichte einer Josefstädter Karriere* (Vienna, Bezirksmuseum Josefstadt, 2011) 41–47.

[43] On 'circles' as institutions in the Viennese socio-cultural fabric of the early 20th century, see, eg, E Timms, *Dynamik der Kreise, Resonanz der Räume. Die schöpferischen Impulse der Wiener Moderne* (Vienna, Verlag Bibliothek der Provinz, 2013); E Timms, 'Die Wiener Kreise. Schöpferische Interaktionen in der Wiener Moderne' in J Nautz and R Vahrenkamp (eds), *Die Wiener Jahrhundertwende: Einflüsse, Umwelt, Wirkungen* (Vienna, Böhlau Verlag, 1993) 128–43.

[44] See, eg, T Ehs, 'Das extramurale Exil. Vereinsleben als Reaktion auf universitären Antisemitismus' in E Adunka, G Lamprecht and G Traska (eds), *Jüdisches Vereinswesen in Österreich im 19. und 20. Jahrhundert*

university students as a kind of headhunter to recruit new talent for his legal theory cause. On the other hand, he himself travelled through the practically overlapping Viennese circles. In addition, he could count on the stimuli emanating from the other participants in his private seminar, who were active in spaces to which he had no direct access, and who brought new impulses to his juristic circle.

Between 1911 and 1930, with greater intensity in the period from 1911 to 1912,[45] Kelsen opportunely attended the 'Wednesday Seminar' of the 'Viennese Psychoanalytic Society', a key part of the 'psychoanalytic movement'[46] headed by Sigmund Freud (1856–1939). He also flitted about in the salons and soirées occasionally organised by Eugenie Schwarzwald (1872–1940).[47] He was in contact with the Austromarxists in the circle of Otto Bauer (1881–1938), his close friend, as well as with at least some members of the (decidedly anti-Marxist) circle of Ludwig von Mises, of whom he was a gymnasium classmate (at the 'Akademisches Gymnasium') and best man – although he did not personally participate regularly in the activities of Mises' Circle. In addition, Kelsen was very much involved in popular education projects throughout the 1910s.[48]

Several members of Kelsen's private seminar assiduously frequented other circles. For instance, Felix Kaufmann (1895–1949), one of the students whom Kelsen habilitated as a *Privadozent*, not only took part in the meetings of the circle of the logical positivists around Moritz Schlick,[49] but was also a prominent member of the Mises Circle[50]

(Vienna, Studien Verlag 2011) 15–29; J Feichtinger, 'Wissenschaftliche Innovationen durch kulturelle Marginalität: Jüdische Intellektuelle im Österreich der Zwischenkriegszeit' in J Feichtinger and P Stachel (eds), *Das Gewebe der Kultur. Kulturwissenschaftliche Analysen zur Geschichte und Identität Österreichs in der Moderne* (Innsbruck, Studienverlag, 2001) 311–33.

[45] See '[154. Protokoll] Sitzungsprotokoll der Wiener Psychoanalytischen Vereinigung vom 13. Dezember 1911' in H Nunberg and E Federn (eds), *Protokolle der Wiener Psychoanalytischen Vereinigung*, Vol 3: 1910–1911 (Frankfurt/Main, Fischer Verlag, 1979) 331–38, 331; '[156. Protokoll] Sitzungsprotokoll der Wiener Psychoanalytischen Vereinigung vom 3. Januar 1912' in H Nunberg and E Federn (eds), *Protokolle der Wiener Psychoanalytischen Vereinigung*, Vol 4: 1912–1918 mit Gesamtregister der Bände I–IV (Frankfurt/Main, Fischer Verlag, 1981) 1–6, 1; '[160. Protokoll] Sitzungsprotokoll der Wiener Psychoanalytischen Vereinigung vom 31. Januar 1912' in H Nunberg and E Federn (eds), *Protokolle der Wiener Psychoanalytischen Vereinigung*, Vol 4: 1912–1918 mit Gesamtregister der Bände I–IV (Frankfurt/Main, Fischer Verlag, 1981) 26–31, 26; '[172. Protokoll] Sitzungsprotokoll der Wiener Psychoanalytischen Vereinigung vom 8., 15., 22. und 29. Mai 1912' in H Nunberg and E Federn (eds), *Protokolle der Wiener Psychoanalytischen Vereinigung*, Vol 4: 1912–1918 mit Gesamtregister der Bände I–IV (Frankfurt/Main, Fischer Verlag, 1981) 94–96; '[176. Protokoll] Sitzungsprotokoll der Wiener Psychoanalytischen Vereinigung vom 30. Oktober 1912' in H Nunberg and E Federn (eds), *Protokolle der Wiener Psychoanalytischen Vereinigung*, Vol 4: 1912–1918 mit Gesamtregister der Bände I–IV (Frankfurt/Main, Fischer Verlag, 1981) 104–107, 104.

[46] For the first mention of a 'movement' in Freudian psychoanalysis, see 'Letter from Sigmund Freud to Carl Gustav Jung of 18 February 1908' in W McGuire (ed), *The Freud/Jung Letters. The correspondence between Sigmund Freud and CG Jung* (New Jersey, Princeton University Press, 1974) 121–22, 122 [Letter 71F].

[47] See D Holmes, *Langeweile ist Gift. Das Leben der Eugenie Schwarzwald* (Vienna, Residenz Verlag, 2012) 285, 297–98; D Holmes, 'Die Schwarzwaldschule und Hans Kelsen' in R Walter, W Ogris and T Olechowski (eds), *Hans Kelsen: Leben - Werk - Wirksamkeit* (Vienna, Manz Verlag, 2009) 97–109.

[48] See T Ehs, *Hans Kelsen und politische Bildung im modernen Staat: Vorträge in der Wiener Volksbildung* (Vienna, Manz Verlag, 2007).

[49] On Schlick's circle, which met from 1924 onwards on Thursdays, see, eg, M Geier, *Der Wiener Kreis* (Hamburg, Reinbek, 1992) 68–72; F Stadler, *The Vienna Circle. Studies in the Origins, Development, and Influence of Logical Empiricism* (Cham, Heidelberg, 2015) 44–57.

[50] On Mises's private seminar, which had already started in 1919 and was held regularly from 1922 onwards on Fridays every fortnight, see, eg, G von Haberler, 'Mises's Private Seminar: Reminiscences' (1981) 4 *Wirtschaftspolitische Blätter* 121; MS Browne, 'Erinnerungen an das Mises-Privatseminar' (1981) 4 *Wirtschaftspolitische Blätter* 110.

and of the so-called *Geistkreis* founded by Friedrich Hayek (1889–1992) and Herberth Fürth (1889–1995) in 1921.[51] Another of Kelsen's *Habilitanden*, Eric(h) Voegelin,[52] also participated in the circles of the economists Hayek and Mises, and beyond that in the sociological circle of Othmar Spann (1878–1950),[53] who rivalled Kelsen within the law faculty. Something similar could be said about the trajectories of other members of Kelsen's private seminar such as Emmanuel Winternitz (1898–1983)[54] or Elisabeth Ephrussi (1899–1991);[55] the former participated in Mises's circle and the *Geistkreis* and the latter delivered the inaugural lecture of Mises's Circle, still in 1919.[56]

The nearly continuous participation in various circles brought a considerable pace to the schedule of the members of the Kelsen Circle, so that several meetings accumulated in a single week. In their extracurricular activities, there was no lack of input coming from the Viennese avant-garde. Above all, it was the individuals with rather 'weak ties'[57] to the different circles who – through participation in several of these circles without greater adherence to the respective research programme or loyalty to the respective leading figure – eventually fostered theoretical receptions and disciplinary entanglements: concepts, methods and models 'travelled'[58] along with the people between the circles. The personal overlaps between them ensured the transfer of knowledge between the groups and disciplines and provided sufficient incentive for creative problem solving in a process of 'cross-fertilization'[59] – just think of the recalibration that the pure theory of law will make of the conceptual pair static/dynamic, commonly used in scholarly economic debates of the time.[60]

[51] On the meetings of the *Geistkreis* – which did not admit women – every two or four weeks from 1921 onwards, see '[Interview with Friedrich Hayek conducted by Axel Leijonhufvud]' in Oral History Program – University of California (ed), *Nobel Prize-Winning Economist Friedrich A von Hayek* (Los Angeles, [s.n.] 1983) 33–37; IK Helling, 'Felix Kaufmann in Perspective: An Introductory Essay' in RS Cohen and IK Helling (eds), *Felix Kaufmann's Theory and Method in the Social Sciences* (Cham, Springer, 2014) 1–102, 41–53 [Interview with Herbert Fürth] and at 53–57 [Interview with Gottfried von Haberler]. See also O Reiss-Sorokin, 'Thinking Outside the Circle: The Geistkreis and the Viennese "Kreis-Culture" in America' (2021) *Modern Intellectual History* 1; B Caldwell and H Klausinger, *Hayek: A Life 1899–1950* (Chicago, University of Chicago Press, 2022) 149–55.

[52] See E Voegelin, *Autobiographical Reflections*, rev edn, E Sandoz (ed) (Columbia, University of Missouri Press, 2011) 31–34, 48–50.

[53] On the Spann Circle see, eg, Anonymo, *Der Spannkreis. Gefahren und Auswirkungen* in Deutsches Bundesarchiv Berlin, R. 558, Nr. 497; J Wasserman, *Black Vienna. The Radical Right in the Red City 1918–1938* (Ithaca, Cornell University Press, 2014) 74–105.

[54] Winternitz's personal impressions of early twentieth-century Vienna can be found in E Winternitz, *The luggage of an immigrant* [typescript and manuscript] in Graduate Center of the City of New York, Research Center for Music Iconography.

[55] One of the first women to be admitted to the study of Political Science – in 1919 – at the Law Faculty of the University of Vienna, Ephrussi was probably the first woman to actively participate in Kelsen's private seminar. See, eg, C Jabloner, 'Frühe Autorinnen der Zeitschrift für öffentliches Recht' (2014) 69 *Zeitschrift für öffentliches Recht* 637.

[56] *cf* JG Hülsmann, *Mises: The Last Knight of Liberalism* (Auburn, Ludwig von Mises Institute, 2007) 365 ff.

[57] MS Granovetter, 'The Strength of Weak Ties' (1973) 78 *American Journal of Sociology* 1360.

[58] See M Bal, *Traveling Concepts* (Toronto, University of Toronto Press, 2002).

[59] E Creaver, 'How ideas migrate' in HM Kramer, HDK Kurz and HM Trautwein (eds), *Macroeconomics and the History of Economic Thought. Festschrift in Honour of Harald Hagemann* (London, Routledge, 2012) 158–64, 162.

[60] cp H Schumpeter, *Theorie der wirtschaftlichen Entwicklung* (Leipzig, Duncker & Humblot, 1912) 93–102; A Amonn, 'Die Probleme der wirtschaftlichen Dynamik' (1914) 38 *Archiv für Sozialwissenschaft und Sozialpolitik* 83 with H Kelsen, *Allgemeine Staatslehre* (Berlin, Julius Springer, 1925) 93 ff.

iii. University Microcosm: The Pure Theory of Law in Austrian Legal Education

The pure theory soon also gained space within the university. Kelsen's lectures at the Faculty of Law, which were initially sparsely attended, were held in large lecture halls and by the early 1920s had already attracted a large number of students. In a short time – not least because of his prominent role in drafting the Federal Constitution of 1920[61] – Kelsen advanced from shooting star to the leading authority on public law and legal theory in Austria. Soon, Adolf Julius Merkl and Alfred Verdross, students of Kelsen's first classes, became Extraordinary Professors and shared the teaching stage with their former academic supervisor.

In addition to Merkl and Verdross, who were habilitated in 1919 and 1921 respectively,[62] Kelsen led – as first examiner in the corresponding procedures – six other members of his private seminar to habilitation. In this way, members of the Vienna School would end up occupying strategic positions within the framework of the academic system. In State Theory and Constitutional Law the school was represented by Fritz Sander (habilitated 1920)[63] and Walter Henrich (1888–1955, habilitated 1922),[64] who, together with Felix Kaufmann (habilitated 1922)[65] and Fritz Schreier (1897–1981, habilitated 1924),[66] also received a *venia* for Philosophy of Law. Josef Laurenz Kunz (1890–1970, habilitated 1927)[67] and Verdross covered Public International Law, while Merkl lectured in the field of Austrian Public Law (mainly Administrative Law). Eric(h) Voegelin (habilitated in 1928),[68] who moved away from the research programme of the pure theory early on as an assistant to Kelsen and Merkl, was concerned with social theory.

With the habilitation of various members of the private seminar, a scenario emerged in which Kelsen's students became his teaching colleagues and supervisors of new generations of seminar participants: Kelsen's future students will thus be students of Kelsen's former students. Emblematic of this phenomenon is the summer semester of 1928, at which time Kelsen appears alongside Henrich, Kaufmann, Kunz, Merkl and Verdross in the course catalogue of the Vienna Law Faculty. Even if not in a coherent and concerted manner, the approach of the pure theory was incorporated in 15 of the courses offered

[61] eg, R Cadore, 'Editorischer Bericht' in *Hans Kelsen Werke*, M Jestaedt (ed) (Tübingen, Mohr Siebeck, 2020) Vol 8, 505–73; T Olechowski, 'Der Beitrag Hans Kelsens zur österreichischen Verfassung' in R Walter, W Ogris and T Olechowski (eds), *Hans Kelsen: Leben – Werk – Wirksamkeit* (Vienna, Manz Verlag, 2009) 211–30.

[62] See ÖStA, AVA, Unterricht Allgemein, Universität Wien, 4 Jus, Personalakt Adolf Julius Merkl, Z. 27385/1919; ÖStA, AVA, Universität Wien, Jus 4, Personalakt Alfred Verdross, Z. 1627-I/1921.

[63] See ÖStA, Archiv der Republik [AdR], Bundesministerium für Unterricht [BMU], Personalakt Heinrich Demelius, *02.11.1893, Teil 2 Z. 13.322-I/1920.

[64] See ÖStA, AVA, Unterricht Allgemein, Universität Wien, 4 Jus, Personalakt Walter Henrich, Z. 15175/1922.

[65] ibid, Personalakt Felix Kaufman, Z. 15174/1922.

[66] ibid, Personalakt Fritz Schreier, Z. 3137-I/1925.

[67] ibid, Personalakt Josef Kunz, Z. 23733-I/1927.

[68] ibid, Personalakt Erich Voegelin, Z. 29159-II/1928.

at the Faculty of Law, which added up to a total of 33 hours per week in that semester.[69] In the winter semester of 1922/23, Kelsen had already taught a seminar on the 'Theory of (Pure) Legal Scholarship', while Kaufmann offered a regular workshop with 'Exercises from the perspective of the pure theory of Law' (for advanced listeners!) that would be nearly unthinkable today.[70]

In a rapid ascent, the pure theory became a trademark of the University of Vienna as early as the 1920s; it ceased to be a weekend hobby exceptionally pursued by a dozen interested people and became an integral part of legal education itself. Its role in the broader marketplace of legal ideas, ie, in academic debate, will increase – the Vienna School would shake up the scene of legal (and state) theory (and philosophy) not only in Austria but in the rest of continental Europe.

iv. The Vehicles of the Vienna School

The *Zeitschrift für öffentliches Recht* (*ZöR*), founded in 1914 and edited by Kelsen from 1919, functioned as the publication organ of the Vienna School and is in a way still associated with it today – at least in a historical sense.[71] Kelsen used to refer to this journal as 'mine', supporters and critics spoke of it as being 'Kelsen's Journal'. In the *ZöR*, some members of the Kelsen Circle made their academic debut; there, the debates that took place in the controlled environment of the private seminar were also made public and exposed to the scrutiny of the wider scientific community. The journal functioned as a kind of 'megaphone'[72] of the Vienna School, enlarging the scope of the internal discussions within the Kelsen Circle and offering itself as a privileged platform for criticism, correction and further development of the pure theory, while at the same time being open to authors from other theoretical dispositions.

In the early 1920s, Kelsen took over, alongside Spann and Friedrich von Wieser (1851–1926), the direction of the renowned series 'Wiener Staatswissenschaftliche Studien' (from 1929 'Wiener Rechts- und Staatswissenschaftliche Studien'), edited by the Austrian publisher Franz Deuticke; Kelsen had published his first scientific work there in 1905.[73] He joined the editorial board of the series after the death of his academic mentor, Edmund Bernatzik (1854–1919), whom he would succeed as professor at the University of Vienna and, to some extent, as a judge at the Austrian Constitutional Court. This series, which was relaunched and redesigned under the direction of the trio

[69] See Öffentliche Vorlesungen an der Universität zu Wien, Sommersemester 1928 (Rechts- und staatswissenschaftliche Fakultät) 8–13.

[70] See Öffentliche Vorlesungen an der Universität zu Wien, Wintersemester 1922/1923 (Rechts- und Staatswissenschaftliche Fakultät) 10.

[71] See M Jestaedt, '"Kelsens-Zeitschrift". Die Reine Rechtslehre im Spiegel der Zeitschrift für öffentliches Recht' (2014) 69 *Zeitschrift für öffentliches Recht* 655; U Spörg, 'Die Zeitschrift für öffentliches Recht als Medium der Wiener Schule zwischen 1914 und 1944' in R Walter, W Ogris and T Olechowski (eds), *Hans Kelsen: Leben – Werk – Wirksamkeit* (Vienna, Manz Verlag, 2009) 149–67.

[72] AJ Merkl, 'Der Vater der Verfassung 80 Jahre. Eine Würdigung Hans Kelsens zu dessen Geburtstag am 11. Oktober' *Die Presse* (10 October 1961) 4 (Merkl-GS III/2, 501–03, 502).

[73] H Kelsen, *Die Staatslehre des Dante Alighieri* (Vienna, Franz Deuticke, 1905) (HKW1, 134–300). See O Lepsius, 'Die Staatslehre des Dante Alighieri in der Sicht Hans Kelsens' (2015) 37 *Zeitschrift für Neuere Rechtsgeschichte* 80.

Kelsen/Spann/Wieser, published dissertations, post-doctoral theses and monographs by members of the Vienna School,[74] many of which were reviewed and discussed in the *ZöR*.

In 1926, Kelsen joined the French jurist Léon Duguit (1859–1928) and Weyr in founding the *Revue Internationale de la Théorie du Droit/ Internationale Zeitschrift für Theorie des Rechts* (*RITD*). This new vehicle will give voice to the research programme of the Brno and Vienna schools beyond the borders of the German-speaking world.[75] The journal, published in German and French, was the first in Europe devoted exclusively to legal theory[76] – deliberately excluding the philosophy of law. Unlike the *ZöR*, the *RITD* will not primarily welcome young researchers, but already renowned international adherents and critics of the *Pure Theory*, serving during the 13 years of its uninterrupted publication – until 1939, when it was forcibly terminated – as a platform for a theoretical conversation of transnational range.

v. The Vienna School in the Marketplace of (not only) Legal Ideas

Through the publishing houses JCB Mohr (Paul Siebeck) in Germany and Franz Deuticke in Austria, the *Pure Theory* entered the German-speaking legal market via renowned publishers. However, Kelsen and his collaborators were also interested in going beyond the legal sphere. In the late 1910s and early 1920s, the Vienna School's efforts to build interdisciplinary bridges of communication are remarkable. For example, the publications of Kelsen and Sander increasingly deal with philosophical, sociological and theological topics,[77] while Kaufmann and Schreier devote themselves to Husserlian phenomenology.[78] Kelsen's most intensive interactions with the Freudian circle are known to date from this period.[79] Also in the 1920s, Kelsen and some of his doctoral students such as Salo Baron (1895–1989) will become involved in debates on political

[74] The following are worthy of note because of their relevance to the development of the pure theory's research programme: F Sander, *Staat und Recht. Prolegomena zu einer Theorie der Rechtserfahrung* (Leipzig, Franz Deuticke, 1922); AJ Merkl, *Die Lehre von der Rechtskraft entwickelt aus dem Rechtsbegriff* (Leipzig, Franz Deuticke, 1923).

[75] See S Ziemann, 'Internationale Zeitschrift für Theorie des Rechts/Revue Internationale de la Théorie du Droit (1926 bis 1939)' (2007) 38 *Rechtstheorie* 169.

[76] See L Duguit, H Kelsen and F Weyr, 'Vorwort' (1926/1927) 1 *Revue Internationale Internationale Zeitschrift für Theorie des Rechts* 1.

[77] See, eg, H Kelsen, 'Zur Theorie der juristischen Fiktionen. Mit besonderer Berücksichtigung von Vaihingers Philosophie des Als Ob' (1919) 1 *Annalen der Philosophie* 630–658 (HKW4, 209–34); H Kelsen, *Der soziologische und der juristische Staatsbegriff* (Tübingen, JCB Mohr (Paul Siebeck), 1922) (HKW7, 69–350); H Kelsen, 'Gott und Staat' (1923) 11 *Logos. Internationale Zeitschrift für die Philosophie der Kultur* 261 (HKW7, 435–58); F Sander, 'Rechtsdogmatik oder Theorie der Rechtserfahrung? Kritische Studie zur Rechtslehre Hans Kelsens' (1921) 2 *Zeitschrift für öffentliches Recht* 511.

[78] See F Kaufmann, *Logik und Rechtswissenschaft. Grundriss eines Systems der reinen Rechtslehre* (Tübingen, JCB Mohr (Paul Siebeck), 1922); F Schreier, *Grundbegriffe und Grundformen des Rechts. Entwurf einer phänomenologisch begründeten formalen Rechts- und Staatslehre* (Leipzig, Franz Deuticke, 1924). On the phenomenological attempts of Kaufmann and Schreier: G Stella, *I Giuristi di Husserl. L'Interpretazione Fenomenologica del Diritto* (Milan, Giuffrè, 1990).

[79] See, eg, H Kelsen, 'Der Begriff des Staates und die Sozialpsychologie. Mit besonderer Berücksichtigung von Freuds Theorie der Masse' (1922) 8 *Imago. Zeitschrift für Anwendung der Psychoanalyse auf die Geisteswissenschaften* 97 (HKW7, 27–68).

theory, especially on the thematic axis of 'socialism & democracy'[80] – a movement partly catalysed by the introduction of the doctoral programme in political science as an independent degree within the Law Faculty of the University of Vienna in 1919.[81] The Kelsen Circle positioned and presented itself as a school and never missed an opportunity to spread the constantly adapting and refining research programme beyond the boundaries of legal discourse: they sold themselves to other disciplines as *the* interesting movement in the field of jurisprudence.

A series of intellectual polemics will give great visibility to the pure theory of law; polemics which, on the one hand, took place within the Kelsen Circle and involved discussions on certain points of the common research programme and, on the other, represented disputes between supporters of the pure theory and its critics who questioned the plausibility of the theoretical model developed by the Vienna School. In the first group of debates, one can distinguish between more or less heated debates of Kelsen with his own students, and such controversies that were carried out among the students themselves without Kelsen being directly involved. One may mention the virulent controversy between Kelsen and Sander,[82] the school's *enfant terrible*, and the debate between Kelsen and Voegelin,[83] on the one hand and, on the other, the controversy between Merkl and Sander about the primacy of legal scholarship or of legal praxis determining what is legal – a debate that would eventually mobilise almost the entire school.[84] Falling into the second group are Kelsen's successive polemics with Eugen Ehrlich (1862–1922), Erich Kaufmann (1880–1982), Alexander Hold von Ferneck (1875–1955), Ernst Schwind (1865–1932) and Carl Schmitt (1888–1985), which go beyond the limits of the Viennese School and confront the pure theory with alternative theoretical models and propositions; all these disputes lead to the school becoming even more prominent in the attention economy of the scientific community.[85]

At the turn of the 1930s, the pure theory of law became an unavoidable theoretical model, and gradually the discourse on legal theory began to organise itself around

[80] See, eg, H Kelsen, 'Vom Wesen und Wert der Demokratie' (1920/1921) 47 *Archiv für Sozialwissenschaft und Sozialpolitik* 50–85 (HKW6, 122–57); H Kelsen, 'Sozialismus und Staat. Eine Untersuchung der politischen Theorie des Marxismus' (1920/1921) 9 *Archiv für die Geschichte des Sozialismus und der Arbeiterbewegung* 1 (HKW6, 358–525); S Baron, *Die politische Theorie Ferdinand Lassalles* (Leipzig, CL Hirschfeld, 1923).

[81] See T Ehs, 'Die Staatswissenschaften. Historische Fakten zum Thema "Billigdoktorate" und "Frauen- und Ausländerstudien"' (2010) 37 *Zeitgeschichte* 238.

[82] On the behind-the-scenes, personal and academic, aspects of the controversy, see: Olechowski, *Hans Kelsen* (n 39) 321–41; TS Tannous, *O Aluno do Aluno: A controvérsia entre Hans Kelsen e Fritz Sander* (São Paulo, Quartier Latin, 2018).

[83] See the comprehensive work by F Lecoutre, *La controverse entre Hans Kelsen et Eric Voegelin en théorie du droit et en théorie politique* (Paris, LGDJ, 2020).

[84] See T Hochmann, 'Welche Rolle für die Rechtswissenschaft? Zu einer Debatte innerhalb der Wiener rechtstheoretischen Schule' in M Jestaedt, R Poscher and J Kammerhofer (eds), *Die Reine Rechtslehre auf dem Prüfstand. Hans Kelsen's Pure Theory of Law: Conceptions and Misconceptions, Archiv für Rechts- und Sozialphilosophie*, Beiheft 163 (Stuttgart, Steiner, 2020) 161–76; A Somek, *Wissen des Rechts* (Tübingen, Mohr Siebeck, 2018) 19–25. On the controversy between Merkl and Sander, virtually unknown even among specialists, see R Cadore, '*Rechtswidriges Recht*': *Die Merkl-Sander-Kontroverse innerhalb der Wiener Schule der Rechtstheorie* (Tübingen, Mohr Siebeck, 2024).

[85] See AJ Korb, *Kelsens Kritiker. Ein Beitrag zur Geschichte der Rechts- und Staatstheorie (1911–1934)* (Tübingen, Mohr Siebeck, 2010).

the Vienna School as a kind of 'Greenwich Meridian'.[86] The pure theory was not only perceived as a characteristic of the '*modus austriacus*'[87] of legal scholarship, but also evolved to become the 'dominant theoretical phenomenon'[88] in Central Europe and its surroundings.

vi. Internationalisation of the Pure Theory of Law and of the Vienna School

As early as the mid-1920s, the growing relevance of the pure theory and the fascination exerted by Kelsen's charismatic figure attracted a number of young international researchers to Vienna, which itself still acted as a magnet for the European intelligentsia of the time. These young scholars, who were later to become central players in the legal discourse within their respective countries of origin, wrote their dissertations or monographs (at least in part) under Kelsen's guidance. They were later to act as hubs for the dissemination of the pure theory in the international debate – even though some of them, such as Luis Recaséns Siches (1903–77) or Alf Ross (1899–1979), were to develop their own theoretical models that more or less diverged from the research programme of the Vienna School.

In the 1920s, translations of works relating to the pure theory of law also started to multiply; in some cases, the translations were to some extent orchestrated by Kelsen himself and executed by members of the Vienna School and close interlocutors. The internationalisation of the pure theory was boosted by the foundation of international institutes in which Kelsen and his students and collaborators participated, as in the case of the 'Institut International de Droit Public', grounded in 1927 in Paris.[89] The strategy of internationalisation also included the aforementioned publication of the bilingual *Revue Internationale de la Théorie du Droit*. With the courses held by Kelsen (1926, 1932) and Verdross (1927, 1929, 1930 and 1931) in The Hague, the Vienna School would expand its reach even more.[90]

Between his fortieth and fiftieth birthdays, Kelsen was to establish himself internationally as the leader of a theoretical movement known worldwide and referred to as such in various languages and cultures as the Vienna School of Jurisprudence.[91]

[86] M Losano, 'Hans Kelsen: Una biografía cultural mínima' (2006) 14 *Derecho y Libertades* 113, 114.

[87] See E Wiederin, 'Denken vom Recht her. Über den *modus austriacus* in der Staatsrechtslehre' in H Schulze-Fielitz (ed), *Staatsrechtslehre als Wissenschaft*, Die Verwaltung, special issue 7 (Berlin, Duncker & Humblot, 2007) 293–317.

[88] M Stolleis, *Geschichte des öffentlichen Rechts in Deutschland*, Vol 3: Staats und Verwaltungsrechtswissenschaft in Republik und Diktatur 1914–1945 (Munich, Beck Verlag, 1999) 164.

[89] See 'Première séance du 26. Juin 1927' (1929) *Annuaire de l'Institut International de Droit Public* 43; Anonymo, 'Internationales Institut für öffentliches Recht (International Institute of Public Law)' (1928) 7 *Zeitschrift für öffentliches Recht* 321.

[90] See C Hoss, 'Kelsen in den Haag. Die Haager Vorlesungen von Hans Kelsen' in H Brunkhorst and R Voigt (eds), *Recht-Staat* (Baden-Baden, Nomos, 2008) 148–65; J Busch, 'Alfred Verdross – Ein Mann des Widerspruches?' in FS Meissel, T Olechowski, I Reiter-Zatlouka and S Schima (eds), *Vertriebenes Recht – Vertreibendes Recht. Zur Geschichte der Wiener Rechts- und Staatswissenschaftlichen Fakultät zwischen 1938 und 1945* (Vienna, Manz Verlag, 2012) 139–69, 153.

[91] In the Anglosphere, the 'Austrian School' was already spoken of in the 1920s: J Mattern, *Concepts of State, Sovereignty and International Law. With special reference to the juristic conception of the State* (Maryland, John Hopkins Press, 1928) 121–39; in France, one spoke of 'École Viennoise' and in Italy of 'Kelsen' and

vii. The Blueprint of the Vienna School as Research Formation

The notion that the pure theory of law is not the product of a single mind was something Kelsen stressed on several occasions.[92] It is the result of the interaction and synergy of a group of people who shared theoretical concerns and agreed on the premises of the same research programme; a group that, at least until 1930, was constantly expanding and acted as an organised network of researchers.[93] The members of the Vienna School articulated the same style of thinking and approach to legal problems, but often disagreed vehemently about the consequent implementation of the basic postulates of a purely legal theory. At no time did they abandon their own theoretical convictions in the name of commitments to the project of the School,[94] but even in divergence they presented themselves as members of the same movement, each with different emphases and responsible for different themes and aspects of the common research programme.[95] There was no need for concessions and the driving force was the joint search for the best formulation of a specifically legal theory of law. Perhaps it is precisely in this practice of open discussion and the airing of differences of opinion that the strength of the Vienna School as a research formation lies: mistakes were pointed out bluntly, directions were corrected, hypotheses were abandoned, and the members were not expected to show theoretical deference to the ideas of the central figure Kelsen.[96]

As a result, an intellectually non-hierarchical research network was formed, which was organised on an (informal) division of labour and continuously developed on the 'basis of trusting scientific cooperation'.[97] The actors of this network:

- Saw themselves predominantly as Kelsen's pupils and as members of a kind of 'working community' (self-perception).
- Were perceived and addressed in academic discourse as members of a distinct academic (legal) movement (external perception).
- Shared the hardcore of one and the same research programme (scientific identity).
- Devised, refined and revised this programme together in constant interaction, debate and controversy (scientific dynamism).

Putting all the pieces of this mosaic together, in its initial formation, the Vienna School is, to a significant extent, the product of Kelsen's efforts and skills as an encourager of

'sua scuola' (R Bonnard, 'La théorie de la formation du droit par degrés dans l'œuvre d'Adolf Merkl' (1928) 45 *Revue du Droit Public et de la Science Politique en France et à l'Étranger* 668, 670; TA Castiglia, 'La Filosofia dell "Als-Ob" nel Diritto' (1928) 6 *Rivista Internazionale di Filosofia del Diritto* 98, 111).

[92] See, eg, Kelsen, 'Vorrede' (n 16) XXIII.

[93] This is the definition of a school of thought offered by Haferkamp: 'a network of research(ers) organized by means of division of labour' (H-P Haferkamp, *Die historische Rechtsschule* (Frankfurt/Main, Vittorio Klostermann, 2018) 11).

[94] See H Kelsen, 'Autobiographie (1947)' in *Hans Kelse Werke*, Vol 1, M Jestaedt (ed) (Tübingen, Mohr Siebeck, 2007) 29–92, 62; F Weyr, 'Zum Geleit' in W Ebenstein, *Die Rechtsphilosophische Schule der Reinen Rechtslehre* (Prague, Taussig & Taussig, 1938) 5–7, 6.

[95] See F Schreier, 'Die Wiener rechtsphilosophische Schule' (1922/1923) 11 *Logos. Internationale Zeitschrift für die Philosophie der Kultur* 309–28.

[96] AJ Merkl, 'Professor Hans Kelsen zu seinem Abschied von Wien' *Neue Freie Presse*, No 23751 (26 October 1930) 7 (Merkl-GS III/2, 363–65, 364).

[97] W Henrich et al, 'Erklärung' printed in H Kelsen, 'In eigener Sache' (1922/23) 3 *Zeitschrift für öffentliches Recht* 499, 502.

younger colleagues and gatherer of talents – after all, he was the one who primarily sewed together a network of researchers[98] interested in similar themes and willing to improve the research programme whose foundations were laid by himself in his *Main Problems*. However, the Vienna School is also – in a significant way – the result of the avant-garde spirit of a time and place, *Vienne fin de siècle*, from which the first generation of the pure theory is nourished. The Vienna School developed from an organisational dynamic that formed a privileged forum for the discussion and exploration of ideas that are hardly replicable, as this group of jurists was not closed in itself, but rather in close contact and exchange with other avant-garde circles. From a large circle of interlocutors, a group stabilises, which between 1913 and 1930 (more or less) eagerly participates in private seminars and gives identity to a school. In this forum, the research programme of the pure theory was elaborated, tested and repeatedly readjusted.

III. The Research Programme of the Pure Theory of Law: *In a Nutshell*

The pure theory of law offers both a model for grasping and understanding legal reality and a metatheory of how to structure legal theory and legal doctrine. The research programme[99] advocated by the pure theory presents propositions in both the realm of legal theory and of legal epistemology (a theory of legal knowledge) that configure a distinctive form of access to the juridical – in its canonical version: to *legal normativity*. These two dimensions of the research programme are strongly intertwined and the theses in these two different levels are mutually dependent. Nevertheless, it is advisable to present them as analytically separate in their respective core tenets.

A. On Legal Epistemology: '*Eigengesetzlichkeit der Rechtswissenschaft*'

i. A Theory of Knowledge for Jurists

The pure theory was conceived by Kelsen – even before it was called as such[100] – first and foremost as a critical reflection on what he considered the methodological cardinal problem of legal knowledge:[101] the individualisation of this knowledge as a specific form of (normative) scholarship concerned with the study and structural analysis of

[98] Besides the already mentioned Elisabeth Ephrussi (see above (n 55)), Margrit Kraft-Fuchs (1902–94), Gysela Rohatyn (1906–?) and Helen Silving (1906–93) actively participated in the private seminar and made relevant contributions to the development of the research programme of the pure theory.

[99] On Kelsen's research programme, without further consideration of the contributions of the various members of the Vienna School, see H Dreier, 'Hans Kelsens Wissenschaftsprogramm' in H Schulze-Fielitz (ed), *Staatsrechtslehre als Wissenschaft*, Die Verwaltung, special issue 7 (Berlin, Duncker & Humblot, 2007) 81–114.

[100] See above (n 17).

[101] Kelsen (n 15) VII (HKW2, 55).

positive law. In this context, Kelsen, Weyr and their first students were interested in the debates inherent in epistemology (philosophy of science). It was necessary to update the vocabulary, grammar and way of thinking of legal scholarship according to the state of the art of the theory of knowledge.[102] In this sense, Kelsen and Sander will draw upon 'neo-Kantian' models, while Kaufmann and Schreier will seek support in the phenomenology of Edmund Husserl (1859–1938).

It was not so much a matter of rigour and consistency in the 'application' of philosophical schemes and theorems to legal thought, but rather of overcoming substantialisms and methodological confusions in legal theory and doctrine towards a functionalisation and relativisation of legal categories. These categories should be placed in a contingent relationship with the various systems of validation represented by the various 'legal systems' and thereby demythologised. If legal scholarship was to be taken seriously as a scientific (academic) enterprise, there was a lot of homework to be done. The members of the Vienna School imagined that it should at least be possible to bring jurists and their scholarship up to the current standards of scientific thinking. Hence, epistemology was placed in the service of reformulating the language of legal scholarship in relation to real existing legal problems.

By updating the conceptual and methodological tools of legal scholarship, the dialogue with other disciplines should also be promoted, to whom the jurisprudential debates finally would have something to offer or with whom one could at least try to communicate at eye level. However, the reception of the conceptual apparatus of epistemology was oriented towards the needs of legal scholarship itself.[103] In this respect, it makes sense to consider this facet of the pure theory as legal epistemology – ie, as a theory of how to do 'legal scholarship'[104] – as an epistemology for jurists, (re)elaborated by jurists. Following the distinction formulated by Norberto Bobbio (1909–2004) between the 'philosophy of philosophers' and the 'philosophy of jurists',[105] the epistemological efforts of the pure theory can be seen as a philosophical exercise made by jurists, for jurists. The focus was not on the adequate interpretation of a philosophical system, but on the refinement of the interpretation and explanation models of the 'legal sciences' through recourse to the most solid epistemological foundations available. One of their ambitions was also to expand the translatability of legal debates and problems into non-legal disciplines.

ii. The Postulate of Methodological Purity

The entire methodological reflection of the pure theory of law is guided by one key question: what specific contribution can 'legal scholarship' make to the understanding of the complex social phenomenon 'law' in the first place? This question makes sense

[102] See F Sander, 'Das Faktum der Revolution und die Kontinuität der Rechtsordnung' (1919/20) 1 *Zeitschrift für öffentliches Recht* 132, 134.

[103] See AJ Merkl, '[Review] Kelsen, Hans, o. ö. Universitätsprofessor in Wien, Das Problem der Souveränität und die Theorie des Völkerrechts, Beitrag zu einer reinen Rechtslehre, Tübingen 1920, Verlag J.C.B. Mohr (Paul Siebeck), 320 S.' (1922) 27 *Kant-Studien* 215, 216 (Merkl-GS II/2, 609–13, 610).

[104] See R Lippold, *Reine Rechtslehre und Strafrechtsdoktrin. Zur Theorienstruktur in der Rechtswissenschaft am Beispiel der Allgemeinen Strafrechtslehre* (New York and Vienna, Springer, 1989) 149–77.

[105] N Bobbio, *Giusnaturalismo e positivismo giuridico* (Milan, Edizioni di Comunitá, 1965) 43–46.

considering the credo of the Viennese School, widespread at the end of the nineteenth and beginning of the twentieth century, according to which an academic discipline only has a raison d'être if it can sufficiently differentiate itself in terms of method and object of investigation. The notion of purity will represent the very idea of scientificity: scientific, scholarly knowledge requires methodological individualisation and a clear delimitation of the field of research.[106] Each discipline will necessarily cut reality in a characteristic way and work within a singular and limited validation system; otherwise it is not an autonomous scientific discipline. Hence the attempt to find out the specificity of law as a social phenomenon and to develop from it a particular kind of access to the juridical world. The main objective was to conceive an autonomous legal scholarship that could produce findings that could not be confused with those of other disciplines that also deal generally with certain aspects of the legal phenomenon. In short, the members of the Vienna School will find themselves grappling with the question: under what conditions is an autonomous 'science of law' possible?[107]

a. Anti-Syncretism and the Turn Towards Law

The postulate of purity will manifest itself in the struggle of the pure theory against methodological syncretism.[108] The method of legal scholarship would have to be designed in such a way as to distinguish itself from causal knowledge – typical of the natural sciences – and from other forms of normative scholarship; legal scholarship, in order to be considered autonomous scientific knowledge, would have to be free of unwanted methodological oscillations. There would have to be clarity about what can be understood and explained with recourse to the cognitive arsenal of a specifically *legal* science and what cannot be: legal science is not a science of everything; legal scholarship cannot be a holistic enterprise.

Since law is considered a normative phenomenon, it must be methodologically isolated from other similar phenomena in order to be studied for what characterises and distinguishes it. This is the so-called battle of the pure theory on two fronts,[109] conditioned by the ambitions (and assumptions) of this theoretical model itself. On the one hand, it is a matter of avoiding naturalistic fallacies and eliminating the rationality inherent in the causal sciences from the field of normative legal scholarship – historicisms, sociologisms and psychologisms would have to be removed. On the other hand, it is important to clean up ideological interference and the (con-)fusion of law with other forms of normativity, such as morality or religion.

Both fronts are about denouncing the same error. Both sociological or psychological reductionism, which identifies law with a set of raw facts, and the politicising

[106] See SL Paulson, 'The Purity Thesis' (2018) 31 *Ratio Juris* 276.

[107] See, eg, JL Kunz, *Völkerrechtswissenschaft und reine Rechtslehre* (Vienna, Franz Deuticke, 1923) 16.

[108] Weyr will speak of 'methodological anarchism': F Weyr, '[Review] Stark Bernhard, Dr., Die Analyse des Rechts, Eine Beschreibung der Rechtsdinge auf Grund der Psychophysiologie des Organismus (1916)' (1918) 38 *Archiv des öffentlichen Rechts* 471, 477; Henrich, in turn, will speak of 'confusion of methods': W Henrich, *Theorie des Staatsgebiets. Entwickelt aus der Lehre von den lokalen Kompetenzen der Staatsperson* (Vienna, Hölder-Pichler-Tempsky A-G, 1922) V.

[109] H Dreier, *Rechtslehre, Staatssoziologie und Demokratie Theorie bei Hans Kelsen*, 2nd edn (Baden-Baden, Nomos, 1990) 27–56.

or ideological approaches in the narrower sense, which make the legitimacy of legal normative practices dependent on parameters that are external to positive law, commit the error of seeking an explanation (or justification) for law outside itself.[110] These approaches are either taken hostage by methods and explanatory parameters peculiar to other sciences, or they depart from law as such to dive into explanations of the ultimate legal foundations or of how law should be framed and practised; they therefore fall into falsifications consisting in presenting ethical and political *aspirations* as legal *realities*. Methodological purity, counterintuitive as it may seem, will serve to reconnect legal scholarship with its own object, to save legal science's adherence to the (normative) reality of positive law ('turning to the things themselves').[111] A specifically juridical theory of law would have to deal with nothing but legal processes and look at their inner workings without getting lost in the search for the explanation or reason for the existence or validity of law in non-legal phenomena – it would be a 'theory of positive law'[112] and of positive law alone.

b. A Descriptive Project: 'Defending' the Law against Jurists

The notion of scientificity underlying the research programme of the pure theory requires the abstention of legal policy judgements within the 'legal scholarship' or at least transparency in the enunciation of these judgements as to what they are, without concealment and smuggling of these judgements, which tend to be sold as a product of the mere cognition of positive law. The proposal of the pure theory consists in the programmatic distinction between description and prescription, which it purports to achieve by limiting the task of jurists as legal scholars (here understood as legal theoreticians) to the structural analysis[113] of positive law and the unveiling of the inner workings of the legal machinery itself. The insights resulting from these investigations and the categories developed to convey them could then be incorporated into the work of legal dogmatics, which consists of addressing the norms in force in different legal experiences and the corresponding procedures.

Legal theory should explain how positive law actually works. To grasp law in its specificity, one would have to observe what individuals do with the normative provisions they use to interpret and legally shape reality. One does not start from an idea or a supposed essence of law that lies outside practice or real phenomena,[114] but rather seeks to describe the normative practice of the legal authorities, formulating appropriate

[110] See C Kletzer, 'Absoluter Positivismus und Normativer Monismus. Zur Idee einer Reinen Rechtslehre' in C Jabloner, D Kolonovits, G Kucsko-Stadlmayer, R Laurer, H Mayer and R Thienel (eds), *Gedenkschrift Robert Walter* (Vienna, Manz, 2013) 257–70.

[111] See, eg, E Husserl, 'Philosophie als strenge Wissenschaft' (1910/11) *Logos. Internationale Zeitschrift für die Philosophie der Kultur* 1 289, 305.

[112] Kelsen, RR1, 1/15; Kelsen, RR2, 1/21.

[113] See Sander, 'Rechtsdogmatik oder Theorie der Rechtserfahrung?' (n 77) 536; AJ Merkl, 'Prolegomena einer Theorie des rechtlichen Stufenbaues' in A Verdross (ed), *Gesellschaft, Staat und Recht. Untersuchungen zur Reinen Rechtslehre. Festschrift Hans Kelsen zum 50. Geburtstag gewidmet* (Vienna, Julius Springer, 1931) 252–94, 252 (Merkl-GS I/1, 437–92, 437); Kelsen, RR1, 61/72; Kelsen, RR2, 112/206.

[114] See C Kletzer, 'Decentralization and the Limits of Jurisprudence' in M Jestaedt, R Poscher and J Kammerhofer (eds), *Die Reine Rechtslehre auf dem Prüfstand. Hans Kelsen's Pure Theory of Law: Conceptions and Misconceptions, Archiv für Rechts- und Sozialphilosophie*, Beiheft 163 (Stuttgart, Steiner, 2020) 63–79, 64.

categories for this description from an observation that presupposes an internal point of view. That means an observation that decides to look at law as normative 'structure and process': what after all can be done and in fact is done with legal norms? It would be up to jurists, as theoreticians, to systematically reconstruct the basic (normative) gears of positive law, which is itself responsible for its own constitution ('creation') and overcoming ('derogation'), in so far as legal bodies, charged with the (re-)production of law, appear themselves to legal scholarship (primarily) as nothing but normative relations.[115] It is positive law itself which, through the legal bodies, determines what counts as law and not legal scholarship or any other social theories.[116]

By locating the constitution of law within itself, ie, in legal processes, the pure theory disempowers jurists as legal scholars, as it were, of the conformation of legal phenomena. Accordingly, their task is to know and explain the law and not to shape or transform it.[117] The Vienna School advocates, to a degree, the self-limitation of 'legal scholarship' as an antidote to the ideological distortions of positive law by legal doctrine – by combating doctrinal activism ('dogmactivism'), the pure theory imagines itself acting in 'defence' of law's autonomy – as the object of a properly legal and rigorously scientific knowledge – against the jurists themselves.[118] It insists on the study of the basic structures and actual functioning of legal processes as the main task of legal scholarship, which in this sense will take on rather modest features. As members of the Vienna School see things, legal scholarship can do much less than jurists normally ask of it, but at the same time it is faced with a gigantic task that has not even begun to be fulfilled: to provide a plausible and realistic description of the legal processes as social processes of resignification of reality through legal norms. It is not in a position to replace the legal authorities in the creation and derogation of law, and it (often) lacks grounds for discourses with a corrective claim with regard to the decision-making practice of the competent authorities.

iii. Demythologising Legal Thought: A Minimalist Proposal

The epistemological presuppositions with which the members of the Vienna School operated gave the research programme of the pure theory a challenging, even inconvenient character from the perspective of mainstream jurisprudence. It was not a matter of providing theoretical comfort to the common understanding of 'legal scholarship'

[115] See H Kelsen, 'Eugen Hubers Lehre vom Wesen des Rechts' (1921) 34 *Schweizerische Zeitschrift für Strafrecht* 217, 246 (HKW6, 261–89, 289).

[116] See H Kelsen, 'Was ist ein Rechtsakt?' (1951) 4 *Österreichische Zeitschrift für öffentliches Recht* 263, 265. It is precisely on this point, however, that the controversy between Merkl and Sander will arise, since Merkl will defend the primacy of legal scholarship in determining what counts as legal under certain circumstances: see above Cadore, '*Rechtswidriges Recht*' (n 84) for references.

[117] Presenting the pure theory as a kind of 'narcissistic wound' (*Kränkung*) of legal scholarship, see M Jestaedt, 'Das Postulat einer streng wissenschaftlichen Erkenntnis des Rechts' in N Aliprantis and T Olechowski (eds), *Hans Kelsen: Die Aktualität eines großen Rechtswissenschafters und Soziologien des 20. Jahrhunderts* (Vienna, Manz, 2014) 3–12, 11; H Dreier, 'Der Preis der Moderne – Hans Kelsens Rechts- und Sozialtheorie' in E Özmen (ed), *Hans Kelsens Politische Philosophie* (Tübingen, Mohr Siebeck, 2017) 3–27, 21 ff. See also, S Freud, 'Eine Schwierigkeit der Psychoanalyse' (1917/19) 5 *Imago. Zeitschrift für Anwendung der Psychoanalyse auf die Geisteswissenschaften* 1, 3–7.

[118] See O Pfersmann, 'The Only Constitution and its Many Enemies' in A Sajó and R Uitz (eds), *Constitutional Topography: Values and Constitutions* (The Hague, Eleven, 2010) 45–68.

and law in established legal doctrine, or of substantiating certain disseminated beliefs with philosophical aphorisms. The ultimate concern[119] of the pure theory is translated into an attitude of demythologisation of legal thought.[120] Legal theory would have the task of including in its description of law what legal actors actually do with the legal norms in the legal processes, refraining from idealisation or romanticisation. From the outset, the Vienna School will wholly reject the question of the ultimate foundation of law,[121] and of legal institutions in particular, to focus on the internal functioning of legal-normative operations. It is a theory that refuses to invoke miracles in its framing of the legal world.[122]

The pure theory will confront essentialisms that are quite deeply rooted in the language and 'theoretical common sense'[123] of jurists and attempt to functionalise the conceptual apparatus of legal scholarship.[124] Following what Kelsen had already formulated in his habilitation thesis, legal phenomena will be set in function to existing normative provisions and always interpreted in relation to these provisions, which in turn also require interpretation. Consequences are not derived from concepts, but it is the concepts used by legal scholarship that must be guided by the observed normative practices – without overlooking the fact that some methodological choices inevitably determine what can and cannot be observed. Amongst the results of this therapy of legal language and thought is the dissolution of the traditional dichotomies with which dogmatics operates, which will no longer be treated as qualitative differences given in advance.[125]

In particular, the pure theory will strive to make law appear as a product of human decisions without concealing their fallibility – the indeterminacy of legal rules, for example, will not be conceived as a problem to be overcome, but as data to be integrated into the description of legal processes.[126] The conceptual scheme used to describe the structure of law and legal processes is then minimalist.[127] No requirements are imposed on

[119] M Jestaedt, 'Rechtstheorie ohne Metaphysik: Die "Reine Rechtslehre" als jüdische Rechtstheorie?' in T van Rahden and M Stolleis (eds), *Emanzipation und Recht. Zur Geschichte der Rechtswissenschaft und der jüdischen Gleichberechtigung* (Frankfurt/Main, Vittorio Klostermann, 2021) 246–65, 258.

[120] W Ebenstein, 'The Pure Theory of Law: Demythologizing Legal Thought' (1971) 59 *California Law Review* 617.

[121] See J Kammerhofer, 'Positivistische Normbegründung' in E Hilgendorf and JC Joerden (eds), *Handbuch für Rechtsphilosophie* (Stuttgart, JB Metzler, 2017) 200–08.

[122] C Kletzer, 'Custom and primitivity. On the unity of the legal technique' in E Frezet, M Goetzmann and L Mason (eds), *Spaces of Law and Custom* (London, Routledge, 2022) 13–26, 15.

[123] LA Warat, 'Saber Crítico e Senso Comum Teórico dos Juristas' (1982) 3/5 *Seqüência. Legal and Political Studies* 348.

[124] On the demystifying ambition as a common feature of the different variants of legal positivisms, see A Somek, 'The Demystification Impasse: Legal Positivism Divided Against Itself' in M Jestaedt, R Poscher and J Kammerhofer (eds), *Die Reine Rechtslehre auf dem Prüfstand/Hans Kelsen's Pure Theory of Law: Conceptions and Misconceptions, Archiv für Rechts- und Sozialphilosophie*, Beiheft 163 (Stuttgart, Steiner, 2020) 45–62.

[125] See H Brunkhorst, 'Critique of Dualism: Hans Kelsen and the Twentieth Century Revolution in International Law' (2011) 18 *Constellations* 496; F Menezes, 'Hans Kelsen's Ideas on Public and Private Law and their Applicability to a Critical Analysis of the Theory of Administrative Law' in M Jestaedt, R Poscher and J Kammerhofer (eds), *Die Reine Rechtslehre auf dem Prüfstand. Hans Kelsen's Pure Theory of Law: Conceptions and Misconceptions, Archiv für Rechts- und Sozialphilosophie*, Beiheft 163 (Stuttgart, Steiner, 2020) 245–56.

[126] See, eg, A J Merkl, 'Das doppelte Rechtsantlitz. Eine Betrachtung aus der Erkenntnistheorie des Rechts' (1918) 48 *Juristische Blätter* 425, 444–47, 463–65, 464 (Merkl-GS I/1, 227–52, 249).

[127] eg, O Pfersmann, 'Is the Pure Theory of Law a General Theory of Law: The Case of the Common Law?' in C Jabloner, A Jakab, L Kirchmair, O Pfersmann and E Wiederin (eds), *Scharfsinn im Recht. Liber Amicorum Michael Tahler zum 70. Geburtstag* (Vienna, Jan Sramek Verlag 2019) 19–34, 24 ff.

reality, the non-fulfilment of which would imply the non-classification of the observed phenomena as legal. Part of the demythologising efforts of the pure theory is expressed in the attitude of 'letting the law be (valid)' as it is constituted in legal processes.[128]

B. On Legal Theory: '*Eigengesetzlichkeit des Rechts*'

i. The So-Called Gegenstandsproblem: *The Positivity of Law*

Taking into account the conditions arising from the specific epistemological orientation that Kelsen propagated in his early writings, the Vienna School was concerned with determining what constitutes legal experience as a human experience that differs from other social practices. It should be possible to clarify what law is by looking at what is regularly made with the norms considered legal and how the normative communication of individuals acting as legal officials works in the legal process. The success of the attempt to establish the foundations of an autonomous legal scholarship would depend on the identification of the specific characteristic of juridicity:[129] it was necessary to find an aspect of reality that could become the object of a specifically legal form of cognition (*Gegenstandsproblem*).[130] Kelsen's original project, which was to individualise the structure of legal norms and to seek in them the distinguishing feature of juridicity, has gradually been pushed into the background. The focus is now on the relationships between legal norms, moving from isolated elements to the 'legal system' or 'legal order' itself and its internal processes.[131]

The more or less classical discussion on the positivity of law, ie, the specific way in which legal norms refer and relate to facticity as interpretative schemes, will mark a relevant part of the School's debates at the turn of the 1910s and the 1920s. The outcome of these internal debates will be a sophisticated theory on the functioning of law, reconstructed as a more or less centralised normative process of assigning meaning to reality, in the course of which legal power is distributed in an organised way and the exercise of violence is re-signified. Hence the lapidary definition of law, as the subject of legal scholarship, as a by and large effective normative *coercive* order of human behaviour.[132]

It is in the course of these explorations of the relations between legal normativity and facticity that the Vienna School will arrive at a dynamic conception of law. The specific distinctiveness of law will be found not in the structure of legal norms, but in

[128] See C Kletzer, *The Idea of a Pure Theory of Law* (Oxford, Hart Publishing, 2018) 134.

[129] See Kelsen (n 17) 12 (HKW4, 235–72, 282); Kelsen, 'Zur Theorie der juristischen Fiktionen' (n 77) 96; Kelsen, RR1, III/3; Kelsen, RR2, 108/200. Also M Jestaedt, 'Die Eigengesetzlichkeit des Rechts. Normativität, Kausalität und die Antwort der Verfassung' in J Rückert and L Raphael (eds), *Autonomie des Rechts nach 1945* (Tübingen, Mohr Siebeck, 2020) 1–24.

[130] See E Winternitz, 'Zum Gegenstandsproblem der Rechtstheorie. Kritische Bemerkungen zu Fritz Sanders "Kampfschrift wider die normative Jurisprudenz: Kelsens Rechtslehre"' (1922/23) 3 *Zeitschrift für öffentliches Recht* 684; C Kletzer, 'Kelsen, Sander and the *Gegenstandsproblem* of Legal Science' (2011) 12 *German Law Journal* 786.

[131] See N Bobbio, *Teoria Generale del Diritto* (Turin, G Giappichelli, 1993) 160.

[132] See R Thienel, 'Der Rechtsbegriff der Reinen Rechtslehre – Eine Standortbestimmung' in H Schaeffer, W Berka, H Stolzlechner and J Werndl (eds), *Staat – Verfassung – Verwaltung. Festschrift anläßlich des 65. Geburtstages von Prof. DDr. h.c. Friedrich Koja* (New York, Springer, 1998) 161–200.

the particular mode of relationship between them. It is by this route that the pure theory will establish itself as a theory about the positivity of law in the sense of a theory about what distinguishes the functioning of law from the functioning of other normative social systems or practices. This theory will find a way to enhance its explanatory potential by focusing on the particular ways in which law normatively intends to regulate its own reproduction.[133] It abandons the legalistic fixation of the mainstream approaches of the late nineteenth century in favour of a multidimensional conception of law, which considers the meaning of different decisions and acts of authority as legal.[134] The great insight here was the realisation that the 'creation', 'application' and 'derogation' of law are also governed by legal rules and can be described by legal scholarship conceived as a kind of normative knowledge.

ii. Competence Thinking

That law is a coercive normative order means, first and foremost, that law functions via successive authorisations (empowerments)[135] both to create and derogate legal norms and to give power of sanction to specific persons acting as legal officials. It was precisely in this special structuring of legal processes through the distribution of competences – ie, of normative powers – that the Vienna School saw the special feature of the juridical: law would be characterised by the fact that it (partially) regulates its own 'creation', 'application' and 'derogation'.[136] In an uninterrupted series of self-referential operations, aspects of reality are reinterpreted as legally relevant in legal processes. The specifically legal qualifications of reality find their expression in the decisions of the competent legal bodies. In the continuous realisation of law, there is a constant tension between the normative claim of the delimitations/assignments of competences by legal provisions and the decisions these provisions purport to programme. At the latest since the adoption of a dynamic perspective in the late 1910s and early 1920s, the pure theory has developed less as a theory of the separability of *Sein* and *Sollen*, and more as a theory of the referability of one to the other.[137]

The particular nature of the self-referential relationship of legal norms is disputed and polemicised within the Vienna School.[138] However, with different emphases and

[133] This is what Pfersmann calls *Selbststrukturierungsthese*: O Pfersmann, 'Hans Kelsens Rolle in der gegenwärtigen Rechtswissenschaft' in R Walter, W Ogris and T Olechowski (eds), *Hans Kelsen: Leben – Werk – Wirksamkeit* (Vienna, Manz, 2009) 367–87, 375.

[134] See G Nogueira Dias, *Rechtspositivismus und Rechtstheorie. Das Verhältnis beider im Werke Hans Kelsens* (Tübingen, Mohr Siebeck, 2005) 155.

[135] On the centrality of *Ermächtigung* (empowerment) as a structuring category of legal thought and of the functioning of the legal machinery according to the *Reine Rechtslehre*, see SL Paulson, 'Ermächtigung. Grundmodalität der Reinen Rechtslehre' in E Schweighofer, M Handstanger, H Harald, F Kummer, E Primosch, G Schefbeck and G Withalm (eds), *Zeichen und Zauber des Rechts. Festschrift für Friedrich Lachmayer* (Bern, Editions Weblaw, 2014) 21–34.

[136] Kelsen, RR2, 73/140; Kelsen, RR1, 74/84.

[137] See H Aufricht, 'Die dialektische Methode und der Stufenbau der Rechtsordnung' in *Zeitschrift für öffentliches Recht* 13 (1933) 68–103; J Kammerhofer, 'Hans Kelsen in today's international scholarship' in J Kammerhofer and J D'Aspermont (eds), *International Legal Positivism in a Post-Modern World* (Cambridge, Cambridge University Press, 2014) 81–113, 87–94.

[138] See on this point, Cadore, '*Rechtswidriges Recht*' (n 84).

perspectives, the pure theory model of law is built on the centrality of the figure of the competent bodies in charge of legal decisions. From this perspective, legal thinking would be characterised by being structured on the basis of the question of decision-making competence: *quis iudicabit* would be the key question that distinguishes purely legal reflection from a lay approach to law.[139] In this way, the institutional dimension of positive law is strengthened, as law can only be produced and reproduced through communications within certain procedural and 'jurisdictional' arrangements.[140] With this seemingly simple step, pure theory takes on contours that move it away from the conventional approach to legal problems, which was primarily interested in the question of 'what ought to be done in accordance with the law'.

iii. Legal Dynamics: A Theory of Legal Processing

The traditional theories at the time of the elaboration and development of the pure theory, in the early years of the Vienna School, viewed law – as most dominant contemporary legal theories do today – as a set or system of norms intended to guide human behaviour by providing 'reasons for action'.[141] Law competes or cooperates with morality and religion in the same market as the latter: it tells norm addressees what to do (by law) and demarcates an area of legally correct or compliant behaviour that is distinct from illegal misconduct. Legal scholarship, especially in the form of legal doctrine and methodology, would then have the task of interpreting the normative claims expressed in the various sources of law and clarifying what is ultimately due, ie, what the law would demand of the norm addressees' conduct. This is a way of thinking about law that can be called a 'demand model'.[142] Law is theoretically modelled in a similar way to the usual account of morality: both would be normative sets of demands on individuals that also prescribe consequences for deviant behaviour. Law, like religion and morality, would be there to guide people's conduct; legal scholarship would in turn guide legal practice itself.

The dynamic theoretical model of the Vienna School, usually presented in (not so) specialised scholarship with recourse to the image of a (legal) pyramid,[143] moved away

[139] See H Kelsen, 'The Law as a Specific Social Technique' (1941) 9 *University of Chicago Law Review* 75, 94; Kelsen, RR2, 244/427; F Sander, *Kelsens Rechtslehre. Kampfschrift wider die normative Jurisprudenz* (Tübingen, Mohr Siebeck, 1923) 136.

[140] See Jestaedt, 'Eigengesetzlichkeit des Rechts' (n 129) 11.

[141] This is what Sander calls the 'dogma of normativity of law', see, eg, Sander, 'Rechtsdogmatik oder Theorie der Rechtserfahrung?' (n 77) 557 ff, 562, 564; Sander, *Staat und Recht. Prolegomena zu einer Theorie der Rechtserfahrung* (n 74) 472 ff.

[142] The term is from Kletzer, *The Idea of a Pure Theory of Law* (n 128) 16–20.

[143] eg, L Fuller, *The Morality of Law*, rev edn (New Haven, Yale University Press, 1969) 110. Among textbooks on legal theory, see: G Bardazzano and R Marquisio (eds), *Introducción a la teoría del derecho* (Montevideo, Universidad de la República, 2022) 165; AL Mascaro, *Introdução ao Estudo do Direito*, 6th edn (São Paulo, Atlas, 2018) ch 9, 'O Ordenamento Jurídico'; A Squella Narducci, *Introducción al Derecho* (Santiago, Editorial Jurídica de Chile, 2000) 327; ER Aftalión, J Vilanova and J Raffo, *Introducción al Derecho*, 3rd edn (Buenos Aires, Abeledo Perrot, 1999) 475–81; P Dourado Gusmão, *Introdução ao Estudo do Direito*, 20th edn (Rio de Janeiro, Forense, 1997) 101; M Miaille, *Une introduction critique au droit* (Paris, F Masper, 1976) third part, ch II, A.2. Admittedly, the pyramid-metaphor also appears in the work of experts, eg, E García Máynez, *Algunos Aspectos de la Doctrina Kelseniana. Exposición y Crítica* (Ciudad de Mexico, Porrua, 1978) 127.

from this 'moral(istic) attitude' towards law.[144] Without denying that individuals can find reasons for their actions in legal norms, the pure theory is primarily interested in the basic cogs of the legal machinery. Law is not out to provide morally – or even only legally – 'right answers' to social problems: this is not its business. Dynamically, the law is perceived as a normative social process in constant restructuration: 'Positivity [of law] is never, it is always in the process of becoming'.[145] This continuous restructuration takes place as a function of the allocations of power for the 'creation' and 'derogation' of law; law primarily refers to itself by structuring chains of transmission of normative powers. Positive normative provisions formulate claims to the mode of creation and derogation of other norms by the competent authorities – claims that these authorities can, however, largely ignore.[146] Moments of cognition and decision, of definiteness and indeterminacy, of bindingness and discretion, are present in every normative operation of the law. Through the allocation and limitation of decision-making powers, even if the extent of these limits is always more or less indeterminate, law presents itself as an order of power (and violence).[147]

The pure theory is about describing the way in which the legal machinery processes information and communication, interprets aspects of reality as legally relevant, and organises and distributes power in society; legal scholarship cannot substitute itself for the legal bodies in their task of determining what counts as (valid) law. In the dynamic model, legal norms function primarily as interpretative schemes used by legal bodies when they make binding decisions: the meaning of the legal norms depends very much on authoritative decisions. These decisions – with the exception of the activity of the final enforcement bodies – produce new norms that can serve as interpretative schemes for structuring new legal operations. It is this process of normative self-structuring that should be adequately described by proper legal scholarship according to the pure theory. This theory takes up the challenge of not usurping the competences of the legal process, ie, letting law be (valid) and trying to reflect its self-constitution process. This self-constituting process, in the course of which law constantly reinvents and reshapes itself through new (albeit routinised) authoritative decisions, can hardly be reconstructed accurately with the help of the limited recourse of a pyramid.[148]

[144] Reconstructing the static perspective as a moral(izing) approach to law, see R Lippold, *Recht und Ordnung.* Statik und Dynamik der Rechtsordnung (Vienna, Manz, 2000) 445–52.

[145] AM Solon, *Teoria da Soberania como Problema da Norma Jurídica e da Decisão* (Porto Alegre, Sergio Fabris, 1997) 191.

[146] This is the problem that Merkl and Kelsen intended to integrate into the description of the operation of law through the theories of Fehlerkalkül and Alternativermächtigung, respectively. On this issue, see P Hilbert, 'Fehlerkalkül oder Alternativbestimmungen – zu den Strategien der Geburtshilfe im Stufenbau der Rechtsordnung' (2017) 72 *Zeitschrift für öffentliches Recht* 549; L Samonig, *Fehlerkalkül, Alternativermächtigung, Revolution. Zur Geltung fehlerhafter letztinstanzlicher Entscheidungen* (Vienna, Jan Sramek Verlag, 2022). For an investigation of the different models conceived internally to the Vienna School for dealing with the 'fallibility' of legal decisions, see Cadore, '*Rechtswidriges Recht*' (n 84).

[147] eg, F Sander, 'Merkls Rechtslehre' (1924) *Prager Juristische Zeitschrift* columns 16–31, 16; Kelsen, RR2, 221/387. The relationship between law and power occupies the centre of the description of legal processes by the pure theory, see eg, N Bobbio, 'Law and Force' (1965) 49 *Monist* 321.

[148] See G Gotsbacher, 'Der Stufenbau als Ordnungsstruktur. Wie zyklische Bedingtheitsverhältnisse im positiven Recht die Stufenbaulehre herausfordern' in C Jabloner, T Olechowski and K Zeleny (eds), *Der Stufenbau des Rechts auf dem Prüfstand* (Vienna, Manz, 2022) 39–60.

C. The Proprium of the Pure Theory of Law as a Research Programme

It is precisely the conscious and reflected connection between the theories of *Eigengesetzlichkeit* of legal science and law that will constitute the identity of the pure theory as a research programme.[149] On the one hand, this theory will present itself as an epistemologically enlightened theory of law, in a constant effort to keep abreast of modern theory of knowledge. On the other hand, it will articulate itself as a theory of legal knowledge, ie, legal scholarship, that is aware of the challenges and problems inherent to legal experience. The task of theoretically investigating and describing the specific functioning of law remains in the hands of jurists as legal scholars, whereby they cannot hide behind philosophical theorems. The bet on the *Eigengesetzlichkeit*, ie, on the singularity and specificity of legal science and law, will characterise the particular way of thinking of the pure theory, which in this respect will try in a radically realistic way and with demystifying ambitions to present law as it is,[150] without ideological falsifications.

IV. The Vienna School and its Pure Theory as a Legacy of Hans Kelsen

If one looks at the emergence and development of the pure theory in the context of the Vienna School, one recognises a constant reworking of theses and arguments on the basis of a common research programme. Kelsen provided the initial spark since he was the designer of a new style of thinking about legal problems, which focuses on the singularity of law as the normative meaning of a social phenomenon or practice that is sufficiently different from other phenomena and that should be studied and reconstructed through theoretical models that pay attention to this singularity. Without Kelsen, there would certainly be no pure theory in this sense and no Vienna School as an organised network of researchers pursuing a common research programme. In his habilitation years, when he did not yet have any followers around him, Kelsen established fundamental theorems on how to do legal science (epistemological dimension) and presented forceful intuitions about the inherent lawfulness of law (*Eigengesetzlichkeit des Rechts*). However, in the intra-school debates that arise from the private seminars, the pure theory will unfold its explanatory power as a legal theory by offering descriptive models about the specific functioning of the legal machinery itself. Without the Vienna School as a cognitive niche, the pure theory would lack a theory of legal processing, ie, a theory of the dynamics inherent in positive law as a process of creation and derogation of legal norms, in the course of which worldly phenomena are (re)interpreted as legally relevant. The development of a theory of the inherent lawfulness of positive law

[149] See M Jestaedt, *Das mag in der Theorie richtig sein* (Tübingen, Mohr Siebeck, 2004) 31–32; Nogueira Dias (n 134) 258.

[150] See A Verdross, 'Die gesellschaftswissenschaftlichen Grundlagen der Völkerrechtstheorie' (1924/25) 18 *Archiv für Rechts- und Wirtschaftsphilosophie* 413, 422.

is a distinctly collaborative work of the Vienna School. This dynamic approach to the legal world, which emphasises the ephemeral qualities of law in its processuality and – contrary to what is claimed by the legal-theoretical Vulgate – bears little resemblance to a pyramidal model of the legal order, will ensure for the pure theory the perpetuity of a royal pyramid.

The Vienna School, formed by a large number of Jews, was hit hard by the rise of National Socialism and the outbreak of the Second World War. Many of its members, including Hans Kelsen, were forced to migrate in order to escape Nazi persecution. With Kelsen's departure from Europe to the United States in 1940, this School was dissolved as a research formation or collective of thought. In 1950, Kelsen commented to Mises in New York on their shared fate: 'You know, Mises, one thing bothers me already … That after your death the Austrians will define you in all their biographies as one of theirs!'[151] It is impossible to know what direction the pure theory would have taken if the School had stayed together and been active as a discussion forum for many more years. In any case, the (unfinished and development-worthy) product of this school, the pure theory of law, can be better understood by taking into account the contributions of its various members. Without this, without taking into account the internal debates and even polemics that led to the formulation of certain theses, it will be difficult to 'decipher' and assimilate the version of the pure theory (that has become canonical) conveyed by Kelsen's works: there one finds answers to questions that remain largely hidden if one ignores the inner dynamics of the Vienna School.

What is more: rediscovering the richness and complexity of the Vienna School allows us to continue the tradition of the pure theory, in so far as it brings to light the existence of solutions to problems of legal theory that are different from those proposed by Kelsen and that can still be imagined to be inserted into the same research programme, revealing a hitherto unexplored potential. At this point, updating and revitalisation can be achieved through efforts of contextualisation and re-engagement; rediscovering the contributions of other members of the School can mean promoting advances in legal theory … in good Viennese fashion, going beyond Kelsen with Kelsen, without hesitating to go one's own way.

The turn in Kelsen studies proposed here has at its core the aim of keeping the challenging results of the Vienna School alive. It is an attempt to reconstruct the *Reine Rechtslehre* as a product of the Vienna School in all its complexity, without '*simplifications terribles*', and to give it an intellectual home again. For all contextualisation and even with due relativisation, Kelsen's place in this whole story remains largely undisputed: the Vienna School is to a considerable extent his own work and legacy and without the Vienna School, there would also be no pure theory of law as it stands.

[151] M von Mises, *My Years with Ludwig von Mises* (New York, Arlington House Publishers, 1976) 149.

14

'Kelsen in the Grenada Court': Simeon McIntosh's Contribution to the Understanding of Kelsen's Theory of Revolutionary Legality

ASYA OSTROUKH*

I. Introduction

Hans Kelsen's legal theory is undoubtedly one of the most important contributions to world jurisprudence of the twentieth century. His reflections on the theory of international law, on the European model of judicial review, and on the foundations of constitutional law have become an integral part of European legal science. However, it is Kelsen's modern legal positivism and his theory of norms that have made him a world-known legal theorist. Kelsen's jurisprudence was the first internationally significant legal positivist theory created by a jurist from a civil law country. Prior to Kelsen, common law legal positivists – Bentham and Austin – dominated global jurisprudence. Although Kelsen would have probably considered his jurisprudence as universal and general, in the Austinian sense, applicable in any specific political, economic and cultural context (and such an understanding would fit his idea of 'purity' of the legal theory), it seems that in many aspects his theory is remarkably civilian and that it introduced into legal positivist theory important adjustments reflecting the major features of the civil law tradition.

Another important contribution that Kelsen made to global jurisprudence is that his legal positivist theory was adjusted to the realities of the twentieth century: the worldwide spread of constitutionalism, the separation of one sovereign power into several and the depersonalisation of the concept of sovereignty, the growth of international law and of its influence on national legal systems as well as successive changes or simultaneous coexistence of different legal orders in many countries across the globe.

* The author would like to express her gratitude to Dr Jorge Emilio Núnez, Dr Jorge Fabra-Zamora and Gonzalo Villa-Rosas for their valuable comments on the draft of this chapter.

These phenomena were either not known to or not addressed by classical legal positivists such as Bentham and Austin.

Given these important contributions that Kelsen made to the development of global jurisprudence in the twentieth century, it is natural that his theory of law in general and its various aspects in particular were adopted, extensively quoted, analysed, and criticised by legal academics in various countries.[1] Moreover, not only did legal scholars develop a profound interest in Kelsen's ideas, but courts in some countries have even used his legal theory as a doctrinal authority that would justify their decisions.

These courts are the courts of a significant number of postcolonial common law countries, and the part of Kelsen's jurisprudence that has become instrumental for these courts is his theory of law and revolution ('revolutionary legality' as it is called by some scholars) that addresses the question of the validity of a new political and legal order established through methods not provided for by the current constitution and the *Grundnorm* of the country in question.[2] This theory became influential in analysing revolutionary changes in political and legal regimes in postcolonial countries that, in the aftermath of acquisition of independence in the twentieth century, were undergoing a turbulent process of change in political orders and legal systems and of the quest for political, legal and cultural identity.

Courts in countries such as Pakistan, Uganda, Cyprus, South Africa, Grenada and Fiji have applied or considered applying Kelsen's theory of revolutionary legality to legitimise newly established political and legal orders.[3] Not only have the courts in these countries used Kelsen's theory, but they have also created a kind of transnational case law dealing with the validity of revolutionary regimes. Once the first cases dealing with the validity of new governments were decided, judges in subsequent cases started making reference to previous decisions and sometimes used them as authorities, even though those decisions were from other jurisdictions and not binding.[4] However, in the judges' reasoning, Kelsen's theory of validity also competed with the doctrine of necessity that had been applied by courts in various common law jurisdictions since

[1] See, eg, P Amselek, 'Kelsen et les contradictions du positivisme juridique' (1981) 138 *Revue international de philosophie* 460; R Bobbio, 'Kelsen et les sources du droit' (1981) 138 *Revue international de philosophie* 474; H Cohen, 'Kelsen's Pure theory of Law' (1981) 26 *Catholic Lawyer* 147; L Duarte d'Almeida, J Gardner and L Green (eds), *Kelsen Revisited. New Essays on the Pure Theory of Law* (Oxford, Hart Publishing, 2013); P De Visscher, 'Observations sur la contribution de Hans Kelsen au droit international positif' (1981) 138 *Revue international de philosophie* 530; H Klenner, 'Kelsen's Kant' (1981) 138 *Revue international de philosophie* 539; J Raz, 'The Purity of the Pure Theory' (1981) 138 *Revue international de philosophie* 441; M Troper, 'Kelsen, la théorie de l'interprétation et la structure de l'ordre juridique' (1981) 138 *Revue international de philosophie* 518; L Vinx, *Hans Kelsen's Pure Theory of Law. Legality and Legitimacy* (Oxford, Oxford University Press, 2007); J Wroblewski, 'Kelsen, the is–ought Dichotomy and the Naturalistic Fallacy' (1981) 138 *Revue international de philosophie* 508.

[2] H Kelsen, *General Theory of Law and State*, A Wedberg trans (New York, Russell & Russell, 1961) 117.

[3] *Valabhaji v Controller of Taxes* [1980] Civil Appeal No 11, Court of Appeal of the Seychelles, Unreported, summarised in (1981) 7 *Commonwealth Law Bulletin* 1249; *Mokotso v King Moshoeshoe II* [1989] LRC (Const) 24 (Lesotho); *Matanzima and Another v President of the Republic of Transkei and Another* [1989] (4) SA 989 (Transkei); *Reference by His Excellency Governor-General* [1955] PLD Federal Court 435 (Pakistan); *Bhutto v The Chief of Staff Pakistan Army and the Federation of Pakistan* [1977] PLD SC 657 (Pakistan); *Madzimbamuto v Lardner-Burke* [1968] 3 All ER 561; *Attorney-General of the Republic of Cyprus v Ibrahim* [1964] Cyprus Law Reports 195.

[4] See, eg, *Mokotso v King Moshoeshoe II* (n 3) or *Jilani v Government of Punjab* [1972] PLD SC 139 (Pakistan).

the nineteenth century and that is based on the idea that courts may validate unconstitutional acts of the state, taking into account the emergency situation and the common good in the interests of which the state acts.[5]

These reflections by postcolonial courts were not an aberration, but rather the deliberate development of a new judicial approach to the resolution of cases concerning the legitimacy of revolutionary political regimes. Courts in countries, quite remote from each other culturally, but having similar colonial and postcolonial histories, were addressing the same question (whether a new political regime is valid and legitimate) and were using the same formal and doctrinal sources of law (case law, Kelsen's writings and doctrinal writings explaining the concept of necessity) to answer this question.

One of the relatively late cases that thoroughly analyses Kelsen's theory of the validity of revolutionary regimes and discusses case law from other postcolonial jurisdictions is a 1985 case from the Commonwealth Caribbean country of Grenada – *Andy Mitchell et al v Attorney General and Director of Public Prosecutions* (the Mitchell case).[6]

In this chapter I will analyse an attempt made by the High Court of Grenada to apply Kelsen's theory of revolutionary legality to validate the new political regime and the rejection of this theory by the Court of Appeal in favour of the doctrine of state (public) necessity. Then, after having exposed certain biographical facts of the Caribbean legal philosopher Simeon McIntosh, as one of the most significant Caribbean legal philosophers in general and as a scholar who provided the most extensive analysis of the Mitchell case, I will look at this jurist's criticism of the appellate court's reasoning. McIntosh reproached the appellate court for failing to acknowledge that a court can never decide the question of a legal regime's legitimacy as a non-justiciable, 'meta-legal' question and to distinguish between the validity and the legitimacy of a legal regime. I will also explain McIntosh's own proposal to complement Kelsen's 'source-based' and 'formal' criterion of validity with the criterion of moral justification of a revolutionary government. Finally, I will explain the significance of McIntosh's analysis of the Mitchell case for Commonwealth Caribbean and global jurisprudence.

II. 'Kelsen is not Law in Grenada':[7] The Theory of Revolutionary Legality Examined but Rejected by the Court

On 7 February 1974, Grenada became independent from the United Kingdom (being the first country in the West Indies Associated States to do so),[8] adopted what later

[5] See, eg, *Reference by His Excellency Governor-General* (n 3) or *Attorney-General of the Republic of Cyprus v Ibrahim* (n 3).

[6] *Mitchell and Others v Director of Public Prosecutions and Another* [1986] LRC (Const) 35, 56 (Grenada).

[7] SCR McIntosh, *Kelsen in the 'Grenada Court': Essays on Revolutionary Legality* (Kingston, Ian Randle Publisher, 2008) xxiii.

[8] For the history of this association that was later transformed into the Organisation of Eastern Caribbean States, see T Robinson, A Bulkan and A Saunders, *Fundamentals of Caribbean Constitutional Law* (London, Sweet & Maxwell Ltd, 2015) 57–59.

came to be known as the 'Independence Constitution',[9] and established a new system of government.[10] However, this Constitution was short-lived since on 13 March 1979 the elected government was overthrown in a coup d'état by the New Jewel Movement, a leftist political party, that established what became known as 'The People's Revolutionary Government' (PRG) headed by Maurice Bishop. Thus, Grenada became the first English-speaking country in the Caribbean to change its government by means of an armed coup d'état.[11] This new government suspended the Independence Constitution and issued a series of proclamations that were supposed to stay in force until the promulgation of a new Constitution. The PRG also repealed the Courts Order of 1967 and the Courts Act of 1971 that provided for the judiciary system of the country. As a result of these reforms, Grenada was no longer subject to the jurisdiction of the West Indies Associated Supreme Court and the Judicial Committee of the Privy Council. In their place, the new government established a Supreme Court that consisted of the High Court and the Court of Appeal.[12] However, the PRG still recognised the British monarch as the Head of State with the Governor-General continuing to discharge his functions as the representative of the Crown.[13]

This revolutionary government ruled the country until 19 October 1983 when an internal palace coup lead by head of the army Hudson Austin took place, establishing the so-called 'Revolutionary Military Council' that consisted of the ideological opponents of Prime Minister Bishop who, along with several other ministers, was assassinated.[14]

On 25 October 1983, a US military contingent, in collaboration with armed forces from Jamaica and Barbados, invaded Grenada, gained effective control over the country, and arrested the leaders of the palace coup.[15]

As a result of the American intervention, on 31 October power was handed over to the Governor-General of Grenada who established an Interim Advisory Council, assisting him in the discharge of his functions, and reinstated the Independence Constitution by issuing the Constitution of Grenada Order on 9 November 1983. However, the Governor-General kept in place the court system established by the revolutionary government, and the relevant section of the Independence Constitution was not reinstated.[16]

In August 1984, the leaders of the palace coup were charged with the murder of the Prime Minister and the other ministers and tried in the High Court of Grenada. The accused challenged the legal existence, constitutionality and validity of the High

[9] Promulgated as Schedule 1 to the Grenada Constitution Order 1973 SI 1973 No 2155 [UK].

[10] F Alexis, '*Grenada Goes Grundnorm*' in G Kodilinye and PK Menon (eds), *Commonwealth Caribbean Legal Studies: A Volume of Essays to Commemorate the 21st Anniversary of the Faculty of Law of the University of the West Indies* (London, Butterworth & Co, 1992) 59–79, 60.

[11] HA Fraser, 'Grenada: The Sovereignty of a People' (1979) 3 May *West Indian Law Journal* 3, 3.

[12] Alexis (n 10) 65–66.

[13] F Phillips, *Commonwealth Caribbean Constitutional Law* (London, Cavendish Publishing, 2000) 183.

[14] ibid 185.

[15] For more information on the US invasion of Grenada and the legality of the actions of the US government from an international law perspective, see M Waters, 'The Invasion of Grenada, 1983 and the Collapse of Legal Norms' (1986) 23 *Journal of Peace Research* 229 and J Quigley, 'The United States Invasion of Grenada: Stranger than Fiction' (1986) 18 *University of Miami Inter-American Law Review* 271.

[16] Alexis (n 10) 70.

Court, the Court having been established by an unconstitutional revolutionary government that acted against the Independence Constitution. From their perspective, the Governor-General did not have any authority to retain such an unconstitutional court either. They believed that the only court that could legally try them was the High Court that operated in Grenada before the revolution of March 1979.[17] The irony of the situation is in the fact that four of the applicants who challenged the constitutionality and validity of the High Court were the very people who, as members of the PRG, participated in the establishment of that same Court.[18]

The applicants' motion to the High Court was unsuccessful. While deciding the case, the trial judge Chief Justice Archibald Nedd explored and partially applied Kelsen's concept of the *Grundnorm* and his analysis of revolutionary changes of a legal order. Kelsen's concept of law and revolution addresses the question of the validity of a new political and legal order that was established through methods not provided for by the current constitution and the *Grundnorm* of the country in question.[19] This concept also links the validity of a legal order to its effectiveness by emphasising that 'a legal order as whole, and a single legal norm, can no longer be regarded as valid when they cease to be effective' and that 'a legal order is regarded as valid, if its norms are by and large effective (that is actually applied and obeyed)'.[20] However, Nedd's understanding of Kelsen's theory is quite superficial and inconsistent, creating the impression that the judge learned it rather from judgments coming from other jurisdictions than from Kelsen's own writings. In my view, certain interpretations given to this theory by Chief Justice Nedd are even incompatible with Kelsen's original theory. Thus, the judge equates the *Grundnorm* with the Constitution ('Accepting that the Constitution was the grundnorm in pre-revolutionary times').[21] He is indecisive about whether the new government has created its own *Grundnorm* ('it seems to me that the PRG in suspending the Constitution took the first step towards replacing it with something else whether or not it could be called a grundnorm').[22] Nedd also speaks about a separate 'judicial' *Grundnorm*, being uncertain of whether the PRG managed to establish its own 'judicial' *Grundnorm* ('in so far as the judicial system was concerned the PRG was deviating only slightly from what I would call the judicial grundnorm of the regime which preceded it in power in a manner which makes it difficult to say whether or not its acts resulted in the establishment of a grundnorm of its own in place of the former').[23] PSJ Smart has justly criticised the inconsistences and contradictions in Chief Justice Nedd's application of Kelsen's theory to the Grenada case, more specifically Nedd's recognition of the partial validity of the *Grundnorm* and his dividing the *Grundnorm* into legislative, executive and judicial *Grundnorms*.[24]

[17] *Mitchell v DPP* [1986] (n 6) 95–96.

[18] Alexis (n 10) 71.

[19] Kelsen, *General Theory of Law and State* (n 2) 117.

[20] H Kelsen, *The Pure Theory of Law*, 2nd edn, M Knight trans (Berkeley, University of California Press, 1967) 212.

[21] *Mitchell and Others v Director of Public Prosecutions and Another* [1985] LRC (Const) 127, 145 (Grenada).

[22] ibid.

[23] ibid 148.

[24] PSJ Smart, 'Revolutions, Constitutions and the Commonwealth: Grenada' (1986) 35 *International & Comparative Law Quarterly* 950, 954.

Probably sensing that such quasi-Kelsenian rhetoric is not very convincing, Chief Justice Nedd also ruled that it was a matter of public necessity that the PRG should create its own system of courts and that the Governor-General should retain it after the fall of that government.[25] Thus, the judge decided that the High Court had the jurisdiction to try the case.

The accused appealed the decision of the High Court to the Grenada Court of Appeal, claiming that the trial court erred in law having decided that it was legally established and was competent to hear their case.[26] The case was decided by the President of the Court of Appeal JOF Haynes and justices NJO Liverpool and N Peterkin on 17 June 1985. The majority of the judges of the Court of Appeal agreed with the appellants that the PRG was an illegal government and that the courts of that government were unconstitutional. Only Liverpool sided with the High Court judge and recognised the revolutionary regime as a valid regime, in Kelsenian terms, that had created its own *Grundnorm*[27] being an efficient political regime that enjoyed popular recognition.[28]

Having discussed all the cases from other jurisdictions that applied Kelsen's theory of revolutionary legality, presented by the appellants' counsel, the Court of Appeal justices ruled that such cases could have only persuasive authority in their country:

> True it is that a number of Commonwealth cases were cited by counsel. And discussed helpfully. But we must bear in mind that they are not binding on this court. They can be persuasive only. We must satisfy ourselves that they are right and acceptable to Caribbean jurisprudence. For an approach and result acceptable in Pakistan or in Uganda or in Cyprus or in Rhodesia or in the Seychelles might well not be socially acceptable to our regional society. Caribbean political interests and public policy might well be involved and affect judicial conceptualisation when an appellate Caribbean tribunal has to determine for the first time what is the law to be applied to a package of facts such as this is.[29]

Thus, the Court of Appeal in Grenada, although admitting the existence of a body of transnational case law that covers the issue of law and revolution and uses Kelsen's theory of revolutionary legality, was cautious in applying this law uncritically to local social and political circumstances. Eventually, the Court of Appeal refused to apply Kelsen's theory to validate the PRG regime, arguing that there was not enough evidence before the justices that the revolutionary government became a de jure government in the Kelsenian sense.[30]

Having decided, on the one side, that the revolutionary government and its courts were illegal and unconstitutional and, on the other side, that Kelsen was not law in Grenada,[31] the Court of Appeal however recognised that the court system established by the PRG was valid based on the doctrine of state (public) necessity that has been known since Henry Bracton's *De Legibus et Consuetudinibus Angliae* and Hugo Grotius'

[25] *Mitchell v DPP* [1985] (n 21) 129.
[26] *Mitchell v DPP* [1986] (n 6) 95.
[27] ibid 116.
[28] ibid 109–16.
[29] ibid 50–51.
[30] ibid 75.
[31] McIntosh, *Kelsen in the 'Grenada Court': Essays on Revolutionary Legality* (n 7) xxiii.

De Jure Belli ac Pacis[32] and that was applied in many cases from various common law jurisdictions[33] as a legal mechanism to justify illegal actions of the government in cases of public emergency.[34] Under this doctrine, the courts may validate unconstitutional acts of the state, taking into account the extraordinary circumstances and the good of society that the state defended.[35]

After exploring the history of the application of the doctrine of necessity by courts from various common law jurisdictions and the doctrinal writings discussing this concept, the appellate judges agreed with the reasoning of the High Court that the decision of the PRG to establish its own system of courts and the decision of the Governor-General to retain it could be validated on the ground of public necessity.[36]

The appellate court thus confirmed the decision of the High Court that validated the PRG court system using the doctrine of necessity while rejecting the applicability of Kelsen's theory of revolutionary legality to the case. More specifically, the High Court ruled that since the West Indies Associated States Supreme Court was no longer functioning in Grenada in the aftermath of the 1979 revolution, it became a matter of public necessity that the PRG establish its own judicial system.[37] The Court of Appeal confirmed this reasoning, ruled that the Governor-General acted in the best interests of Grenada at a time of crisis, and found the retention of the courts of the revolutionary government temporarily valid under the doctrine of state necessity.[38] Consequently, the appellate court confirmed the decision of the trial court that the latter had the jurisdiction to try the perpetrators of the internal coup.[39]

The accused later filed a petition on special leave to appeal to the Judicial Committee of the Privy Council that dismissed it on 25 July 1985, stating that their court was deprived 'clearly and unambiguously' of any jurisdiction to try that case.[40] Thus, the decision of the Privy Council left unchallenged the decision of the Grenada Court of Appeal.

In August 1991 the court system of the PRG was abolished, and the new system of courts similar to the one that existed before the revolution was established. It consisted of the High Court, the Court of Appeal, the Eastern Caribbean Supreme Court and the Judicial Committee of the Privy Council.

Such judicial reform created for the perpetrators of the internal coup an opportunity to challenge the decisions of the courts made in the 1980s. On 28 June 2001, three of the convicted persons (Andy Mitchell himself, Cosmos Richardson and Vincent Joseph) filed a motion to the Grenada High Court, claiming that their continued imprisonment

[32] For more on the doctrine of necessity see L Wolf-Phillips, 'Constitutional Legitimacy: A Study of the Doctrine of Necessity' 1 (1979) *Third World Quarterly* 97 and MM Stavsky, 'The Doctrine of State Necessity in Pakistan' (1983) 16 *Cornell International Law Journal* 341.

[33] See, eg, *Texas v White* [1868] 74 US (7 Wall) 700, 733; *Reference by His Excellency Governor-General* (n 3) 520–22; *Madzimbanuto v Lardner-Burke* [1969] 1 AC 645, 726.

[34] Stavsky (n 32) 342.

[35] S McIntosh, 'Legitimacy, Validity and the Doctrine of Necessity: The Case of Andy Mitchell and others Considered' (1986) 10 *West Indian Law Journal* 127, 157.

[36] *Mitchell v DPP* [1986] (n 6) 76–88, 109, 116.

[37] ibid 146.

[38] ibid 94.

[39] ibid 38.

[40] ibid 125.

or detention beyond the period of the first sentence was unconstitutional and illegal and that the decision of the trial judge in 1986 to impose two or three periods of 15 years to be served consecutively was also unconstitutional and illegal. In February 2002 the trial judge agreed with the applicants and ruled that their imprisonment was indeed illegal and unconstitutional. However, the Court of Appeal reversed the decision of the trial court and ruled that the applicants should continue to serve the remainder of their sentences.[41] In 2002 the applicants filed an application to appeal to the Judicial Committee of the Privy Council through the Eastern Caribbean Supreme Court (ECSC). Their argument this time was that their case involved an interpretation of the Constitution and, because of this, an appeal to the Privy Council should be as of right. The ECSC ruled that the case involved only an interpretation of the relevant provisions of the Criminal Code of Grenada and not of the Constitution and, because of this, the ECSC did not allow the appeal to reach the Privy Council.[42]

Thus, we can we see that the decision of the Grenada Court of Appeal in 1985 remained unchanged and did not provoke any further serious judicial discussions about the validity of the PRG regime. The judges of the new court system fully acknowledged the jurisdiction of the courts of the revolutionary regime and their exclusive right to try the accused.

Legal scholars from the Commonwealth Caribbean have thoroughly studied the Mitchell case and the judges' reasoning.[43] One could argue that this case has acquired a symbolic significance for Commonwealth Caribbean constitutional lawyers and legal theorists, becoming the most well-known jurisprudential case in the region that discusses a whole range of legal-philosophical questions in the Caribbean context and that tests the applicability of Western legal theories to the regional context.

The most famous Caribbean legal philosopher who analysed the Mitchell case, the judges' reasoning in this case, the legal theories that are appropriate for its resolution as well as its socio-legal significance for the region was Simeon McIntosh. It can be justly said that most contemporary Commonwealth Caribbean lawyers perceive the Mitchell case and the Grenadian revolution through the prism of McIntosh's approach and that McIntosh's analysis of the case raised a number of jurisprudential questions that still remain topical for West Indian society.

III. Simeon McIntosh as a Legal Philosopher

Simeon Charles Randolph McIntosh was born on 14 July 1944 in the village of Mount Pleasant on the island of Carriacou, Grenada, then a British West Indian territory.[44]

[41] *Richardson and Others v Attorney General* [2004] ECSC J0126-6 1, 6 (Grenada).

[42] ibid 46.

[43] See, eg, Alexis (n 10); McIntosh, *Kelsen in the 'Grenada Court': Essays on Revolutionary Legality* (n 7); Phillips (n 13) 179–96; Smart (n 24); M Tayyab, 'Jurisprudence of Successful Treason: Coup d'état and Common Law' (1994) 27 *Cornell International Law Journal* 49, 84–89.

[44] D Berry, 'Tribute to Professor Simeon C. R. McIntosh from the Faculty of Law' as quoted by A Ostroukh in 'Simeon McIntosh's Contribution to the Solution of the Chattel-House Problem in the Commonwealth Caribbean' (2015) 4 *Zeitschrift für Rechtsphilosophie* 393, 396.

He studied law at the Howard University School of Law and later received an LLM degree from the Columbia University School of Law.[45]

As for his employment, McIntosh worked for many years at the Howard University School of Law in the United States (1976–91) and at the Faculty of Law at Cave Hill Campus of the University of the West Indies in Barbados (1991–2013), teaching constitutional law, constitutional theory, jurisprudence and civil procedure.[46]

McIntosh died in 2013. According to the recollection of his colleague Stephen Vasciannie, McIntosh was joking about going in his afterlife 'to a heaven in which Hegel, Kelsen, Frankfurter, Dworkin, HLA Hart and other Monarchs of Jurisprudence would be arguing about the nature of law at dinner time'.[47]

McIntosh published extensively on jurisprudential problems in various fields of law: constitutional law, human rights, criminal law and land law. His most famous writings are three books: *Caribbean Constitutional Reform: Rethinking the West Indian Polity* (2002); *Fundamental Rights and Democratic Governance: Essays in Caribbean Jurisprudence* (2005); and *Reading Text and Polity: Hermeneutics and Constitutional Theory* (2012).

In his works McIntosh engaged in jurisprudential debates with the most famous Western jurists of the nineteenth and twentieth centuries: Hegel, Austin, Kelsen, Hart, Finnis and Rawls.[48]

In light of his prolific and profound scholarship, Simeon McIntosh is considered to be the most famous legal philosopher in the Commonwealth Caribbean, acclaimed by Vasciannie as 'a giant in the field of jurisprudence and a Caribbean scholar of rare distinction'.[49] Indeed, McIntosh's writings have exercised significant influence especially in the fields of constitutional law, constitutional theory and human rights scholarship in the Commonwealth Caribbean. This scholar is well known for his analysis of legal problems of Caribbean society from the perspectives of European and North American legal philosophy. While discussing the most important social problems of the Caribbean region, McIntosh always tried to provide possible theoretical and practical solutions to these issues.

Considering Grenada as his birthplace and constitutional law as his specialism, we should not be surprised that one of McIntosh's major interests was the Grenadian revolution as well as the legality and legitimacy of the governments that ruled the country in its aftermath. This subject matter is thoroughly studied in his articles 'Legitimacy, Validity and the Doctrine of Necessity: The Case of Andy Mitchell and Others Considered';[50] 'Continuity and Discontinuity of Law: A Reply to John Finnis';[51] 'Kelsen in the 'Grenada

[45] 'Caribbean Legal Luminary Simeon McIntosh Dies' *Trinidad and Tobago Guardian* (Port of Spain, 30 March 2013): www.guardian.co.tt/article-6.2.398331.daefbee7ef.

[46] Ostroukh (n 44) 396.

[47] S Vasciannie 'Professor Simeon McIntosh: a Tribute' (2012) 37 *West Indian Law Journal* 25, 28.

[48] For instance, his article 'The "Chattel-House Case": A Reading in Hegelian Jurisprudence' ((1995) 5 *Caribbean Law Review* 432) is an attempt to apply Hegelian philosophy to the law of real property in the Commonwealth Caribbean, while his other article 'Controversial Propositions of Law and the Positivist Embarrassment: The Hart/Dworkin Debate Reconsidered' ((1983) 26 *Howard Law Journal* 699) is his own original contribution to the Hart–Dworkin debate.

[49] 'Caribbean Legal Luminary Simeon McIntosh Dies' (n 45).

[50] McIntosh, 'Legitimacy, Validity and the Doctrine of Necessity' (n 35).

[51] S McIntosh, 'Continuity and Discontinuity of Law: A Reply to John Finnis' (1988) 21 *University of Connecticut Law Review* 1.

Court': Revolutionary Legality Revisited';[52] and 'In the Case of Yasin Abu Bakr and Others: A Dissenting View'.[53] These four articles were later collected and published in a book *Kelsen in the 'Grenada Court': Essays on Revolutionary Legality* (2008, republished in 2014).[54] The book also includes an introductory chapter 'Revolutionary Legality' in which the author discusses the main points of Kelsen's theory of revolutionary changes in legal and political orders and several cases from various jurisdictions that applied this theory. This book has become the culmination of McIntosh's long reflections on the events of the Grenadian revolution, on the applicability of Kelsen's theory to the Grenadian context and on the reasoning of the judges in the Mitchell case.

IV. McIntosh's Analysis of the Mitchell Case

McIntosh, while upholding the decision of the Court of Appeal to recognise the High Court of Grenada as a valid court that has the jurisdiction to try the accused, criticises the arguments of the Court of Appeal and the application of the doctrine of necessity to the case. In his analysis of the Mitchell case, McIntosh firmly rejects the doctrine of necessity in favour of Kelsen's theory of revolutionary legality, arguing that the latter – rejected by the Court of Appeal on the grounds that Kelsen was not law in Grenada and that the de jure status of the PRG was not proven – provides a better argument in support of the decision.

The case, according to McIntosh, addresses the question of the legitimacy of two administrations: the PRG that was established in Grenada after a successful revolution in 1979 and the government established in the aftermath of the American invasion on 26 October 1983 (the Governor-General's regime).[55]

While addressing the issue of whether the PRG was a legitimate government, McIntosh stresses the necessity of the distinction between legitimacy and validity (ie, legal validity) of a political regime. According to him, 'legitimacy is a broader concept and entails validity; it deals with the question of the "justness" of the State or the legal order as a whole, while validity applies more to particular laws, whether they have been enacted in a manner prescribed by the basic law of the State'.[56]

The Caribbean philosopher believes that an important weakness of the appellate court's opinion in the Mitchell case is precisely that it failed to recognise this distinction between legitimacy and validity so that when the judges discussed the question of the de jure status of the PRG, they were addressing 'the question of the legitimacy of the State couched in the language of legal validity'.[57]

[52] S McIntosh, 'Kelsen in the 'Grenada Court': Revolutionary Legality Revisited' (1995) 5 *Caribbean Law Review* 1.

[53] S McIntosh, 'In the Case of Yasin Abu Bakr and Others: A Dissenting View' (1992) 2 *Caribbean Law Review* 1.

[54] It is the title of this McIntosh's book that I have incorporated into the title of this chapter. I believe that it perfectly reflects McIntosh's vision of Kelsen's theory and the way it can be used to assess the events of Grenadian revolution.

[55] McIntosh, 'Continuity and Discontinuity of Law' (n 51) 3.

[56] McIntosh, 'Legitimacy, Validity and the Doctrine of Necessity' (n 35) 134.

[57] ibid.

For McIntosh the question of the legitimacy of the state is primarily what he calls a 'moral-political' and not a legal issue. It is a question about 'the justificatory reasons why a citizen must and should obey the State'.[58] Consequently, a court never has jurisdiction or competency to decide such a question. Considering the court to be an agency of this state, Mcintosh believes that in such a case the tribunal only explains to the parties why the state is legitimate and why its laws should be followed, but the court does not validate this state and, moreover, cannot validate it. From this perspective, no court could have the jurisdiction to decide 'whether the State it serves as an agent is legitimate' as that would be 'tantamount to the court creating itself' and contravene 'an irrefutable logic of principal-agent relationship'.[59] Thus, the courts being agents of the new political regime lack the power to decide the question of the validity of that state, since this state cannot derive its validity from its own agents.

Having recognised that a court can never have a justificatory jurisdiction over the question of the validity of a legal order, McIntosh still believes that the court can look at this question from an explanatory perspective. And under this approach, for McIntosh the question of the validity of a revolutionary state is a question of its legitimacy and not of its legality. There can be no question of legality because the revolutionary state is already an illegal regime and the very expression 'revolutionary legality' for the Caribbean philosopher is a 'serious contradiction in terms' as the revolution is by definition an illegal act.[60]

Consequently, for McIntosh it is important to decide what are the criteria for the legitimacy of a political regime that courts should consider. To answer this question, he starts with an exposition of Kelsen's theory of revolution and law.

Throughout his writings McIntosh routinely calls Kelsen's views on revolution and law the 'theory of revolutionary legality'. Moreover, it is McIntosh who has popularised the expression 'revolutionary legality' in discussions concerning the Kelsenian approach to revolutionary changes of legal orders. But the way McIntosh explains it gives an erroneous impression that it was Kelsen himself who coined the expression: '[t]he concept has been given its most thorough exploration in the works of the Austrian legal philosopher, the late Hans Kelsen'.[61] It should be noted that Kelsen himself never used such and expression and most likely would not even consider his views exposed on a few pages of *Pure Theory of Law*[62] and *General Theory of Law and State*[63] as a distinctive theory of 'revolutionary legality'. Courts and scholars that address issues of the validity of newly established unconstitutional regimes refer to such sections of Kelsen's books as 'Legitimacy and Effectiveness'; 'Validity and Effectiveness';[64] 'The Principle of Legitimacy'; 'Change of Basic Norm'; 'The Principle of Effectiveness as Positive Legal Norm (International and National Law)'; and 'Validity and Efficacy'.[65]

[58] ibid.

[59] ibid 135.

[60] McIntosh, *Kelsen in the 'Grenada Court': Essays on Revolutionary Legality* (n 7) xii.

[61] McIntosh, 'Revolutionary Legality' in McIntosh, *Kelsen in the 'Grenada Court': Essays on Revolutionary Legality* (n 7) xli.

[62] Kelsen, *General Theory of Law and State* (n 2) 117–23, 368–70.

[63] Kelsen, *The Pure theory of Law* (n 20) 209–14.

[64] ibid.

[65] Kelsen, *General Theory of Law and State* (n 2) 117–22.

Basically, this is the part of Kelsen's jurisprudence that addresses the problem of changes in a legal order by means not provided for by the existing constitution and the *Grundnorm* (revolution).[66] Scholars such as McIntosh[67] and Tayyab,[68] most likely inspired by Eekelaar's essay 'Principles of Revolutionary Legality',[69] started to label this part of Kelsen's jurisprudence the theory of revolutionary legality. The expression was even used by judges in some cases.[70] Such an elevation of just one (albeit important) aspect of Kelsen's monolithic legal philosophy to the status of a stand-alone 'theory' is revealing. It gives the impression that scholars and judges in postcolonial jurisdictions needed a tool with the important practical function of analysing and, if needed, of justifying newly established unconstitutional legal orders, and this aspect of Kelsen's legal philosophy turned out to be very helpful.

After a brief exposition of the theory of 'revolutionary legality' taken from *Pure Theory of Law* and *General Theory of Law and State*, McIntosh arrives at the conclusion that Kelsen's 'source-based' and 'formal' theory of validity 'would consider any effective regime as a legal system and, by implication, a legitimate one'.[71] Furthermore, a theory in which legitimacy is linked primarily to effectiveness, says McIntosh, leaves open the question of the difference between law and naked force.[72] However, the Caribbean scholar admits that Kelsen's theory of validity offers some advantage because if the new regime has successfully established itself, judges cannot rule that it is invalid because it did not come to power in accordance with the constitution but must face the reality and acknowledge the new source of their authority to decide cases.[73]

This, however, is where McIntosh goes beyond Kelsen's theory and makes an important contribution to the legal-philosophical and judicial discussion of the legitimacy of revolutionary regimes. To Kelsen's criterion of effectiveness, McIntosh adds another criterion – the moral justification of a revolutionary regime – arguing that the PRG regime was legitimate not just because it was efficient, but also because it was morally justified. At this point McIntosh incorporates into his reasoning two other legal theories that, in his view, complement Kelsen's test of effectiveness and are indispensable for the legitimisation of a new legal order.

First, McIntosh accepts Lon Fuller's notion of fidelity to law and states that Kelsen's theory of legitimacy remains inadequate and incomplete as it is not concerned with the question of what would make 'meaningful the obligation of fidelity to law'.[74] Second, the Caribbean scholar explains his own understanding of the nature of law which can be used to address the question of the legitimacy of revolutionary governments. This understanding follows that of Thomas Aquinas who defined law as an 'ordinance of

[66] ibid 117.

[67] In McIntosh's case 'revolutionary legality' has even become a part of the title of his major book on Kelsen – *Kelsen in the 'Grenada Court': Essays on Revolutionary Legality* (n 7).

[68] Tayyab (n 43).

[69] JM Eekelaar, 'Principles of Revolutionary Legality' in AWB Simpson (ed), *Oxford Essays in Jurisprudence*, 2nd edn (Oxford, Clarendon Press, 1973) 22–43.

[70] eg, *Matanzima and Another v President of the Republic of Transkei and Another* (n 3).

[71] McIntosh, 'Legitimacy, Validity and the Doctrine of Necessity' (n 35) 137.

[72] ibid.

[73] ibid 141.

[74] ibid 137.

reason for the common good, made by him who has the care of the community'.[75] However, McIntosh does not explain why he chose specifically Fuller's and Aquinas' ideas over many other jurisprudential theories dealing with the problem of the moral justification of governments. Neither does McIntosh explain how this test of moral justness of a political regime can be applied as a matter of fact so as to produce reliable evidence for the court. Nonetheless, by testing the actions of the PRG against these two legal theories, McIntosh arguably concludes that 'it cannot be denied that the PRG claimed as its principal objective the eradication of injustices and the reduction of the class struggle as well as proposed its own model of distributive justice'.[76]

Thus, adding to Kelsen's theory of effectiveness the notion of the moral justification of a new regime helps the Caribbean legal philosopher to legitimise the revolutionary administration that was clearly illegal but nevertheless a legitimate government.

Then, in a largely similar way, McIntosh addresses the issue of the legitimacy of the regime established by the Governor-General, who assumed power after the American intervention in Grenada on 31 October 1983 and retained the court system established by the PRG. The philosopher does not accept the appellate court's ruling that the Governor-General's acts were unconstitutional vis-à-vis the Independence Constitution and, similarly to his reasoning on the validity of the PRG, applies Kelsen's theory of revolutionary legality to the Governor-General's regime as well. This leads McIntosh to the conclusion that the Governor-General assumed power in 1983 not under the 1973 pre-independence constitutional order but as the Governor-General of the new state that was established in the aftermath of the American intervention in 1983. Even if we argued that his acts were unconstitutional, they could only be unconstitutional with respect to the constitutional enactments of the PRG.[77] It is true that the same person served as the Governor-General for the Independence government and for the PRG. However, in 1983 that person acted in his own name and not in the name of the independence regime that did not exist any more. Neither was he, at that time, a representative of the PRG but rather an individual who established a new political and legal regime on 31 October 1983.[78]

This reasoning leads McIntosh to the conclusion that the appellate court's ruling that the Governor-General's actions were unconstitutional was based on an erroneous assumption of the continuity of all the three consecutive legal orders (that of independent Grenada, of the PRG, and of the Governor-General) and that the Governor-General 'was a constitutional functionary who acted outside the scope of his constitutional powers',[79] which was not the case. Consequently, the Governor-General's authority and decision to reinstate the 1974 Constitution was independent of that Constitution and neither contrary to nor in accordance with it.[80] The Caribbean jurist applies the same reasoning (assumption of the discontinuity of the three legal regimes) to the preservation of the court system of the revolutionary administration by the Governor-General:

[75] As quoted by McIntosh, 'Legitimacy, Validity and the Doctrine of Necessity' (n 35) 138.
[76] ibid 150.
[77] ibid 151–56.
[78] ibid.
[79] ibid 154.
[80] ibid 154–55.

it was done neither in accordance with nor in contradiction with any enactment of any previous regime but in the Governor-General's own right, under his new 'Constitution'.[81] From this follows that the judges were mistaken in the question of the status, the decisions and the actions of the Governor-General's administration as a constitutional issue while it would have been more appropriate to look at this question from the Kelsenian perspective of revolutionary legality.

Thus, according to McIntosh, the Governor-General's regime passed Kelsen's test of effectiveness and established a new *Grundnorm*, a new Constitution and a new legal order.

However, just as with the PRG, the Caribbean scholar does not accept mere effectiveness as evidence of legitimacy and raises the same question of moral justification as with the revolutionary government: whether the Governor-General's decisions and actions were morally justified and whether he acted for the common good and general welfare of the people of Grenada. McIntosh answers in the affirmative to these questions, arguably calling this answer 'virtually self-evident'.[82]

McIntosh also criticises the reasoning of the appellate court that, although qualifying the PRG's and the Governor-General's actions as unconstitutional, decided that those actions nonetheless could be temporarily validated under the doctrine of necessity.[83] The Caribbean legal philosopher firmly believes that the doctrine of state (public) necessity 'primarily applies to the actions of the constitutional state whose validity is already a settled issue, where such actions, though unconstitutional, might still be said to have been "within" the legal system'.[84] Thus, the justices of the High Court and of the Court of Appeal, in his view, misinterpreted the doctrine when they applied it to the acts of the PRG and of the Governor-General with respect to the establishment and retention of the system of courts. In McIntosh's view, a possibility of the application of this doctrine may arise only where a legally valid constitutional rule has been violated, and the court is looking for a moral justification for such violation.[85] Based on his previous rejection of the continuity of the three consecutive legal regimes and his belief that each of them established its own *Grundnorm*, Constitution and legal order, McIntosh logically concludes that it is pointless to declare the enactments of the PRG unconstitutional with respect to the suspended Independence Constitution and the Governor-General's decisions and actions as unconstitutional with respect to the revolutionary 'Constitution'.[86] Thus, for the Caribbean philosopher the doctrine of necessity remains an inadequate ground for the legitimisation of the actions of both the PRG's and the Governor-General's regimes.

From this perspective, McIntosh also argues that it was indispensable to retain the court system of the PRG for the specific purpose of trying the case of Andy Mitchell and others as they had committed a crime against that revolutionary regime and in violation of its laws, and it was the court of that very regime that had the jurisdiction to try their case.[87]

[81] ibid 155.
[82] ibid 153.
[83] ibid 157.
[84] ibid.
[85] ibid.
[86] ibid 161.
[87] ibid 163.

Thus, McIntosh is convinced that the appellate court's argument in the Mitchell case is wrong for more than one reason. First, according to the scholar, the court cannot make legal decisions on the validity of the legal regime that it represents. Affirming that it can do so is illogical as 'the very fact that the court sits to decide such a question and expects its decision to be valid and binding, confirms its validity as only a valid court could render a valid judgment'.[88] Second, unlike the Court of Appeal, McIntosh finds it evident that both the PRG and the Governor-General created their own effective and legitimate legal systems within which they operated. The Caribbean legal scholar insists that there was no continuity of the consecutive legal regimes, and each of them (except for the short-lived regime established by the perpetrators of the internal coup and overthrown during the American intervention in 1983) established a new *Grundnorm*, a new Constitution and a new legal system in the Kelsenian sense. The court that tried the accused was established in accordance with the *Grundnorm* of the PRG regime and was retained in accordance with the *Grundnorm* of the Governor-General's regime, and that court did have the competency to try the accused as it was the court in force when they committed their crime. Third, the idea of the discontinuity of the consecutive legal regimes in Grenada led McIntosh to the conclusion that the doctrine of public necessity was wrongly applied by the Court of Appeal. Neither the actions of the PRG nor of the Governor-General could be considered unconstitutional in terms of the Independence Constitution as it was no longer the fundamental law of the legal system of the two respective political regimes.

Finally, an important contribution that McIntosh made, while analysing the Mitchell case, is that he retained the strongest part of Kelsen's theory of law and revolution that was applied by courts in many postcolonial countries (the test of effectiveness) while adding to this test of mere effectiveness a moral criterion of justification – Aquinas' and Fuller's understanding of law – used to test the justness of the PRG's and the Governor-General's legal regimes. The unexplained choice of these two specific jurisprudential thinkers as well as the lack of sufficient empirical proof that the PRG and the Governor-General were acting in the best interests of the Grenadian people constitute weak points in McIntosh's theory. Nonetheless, such reasoning helped the Caribbean scholar to overcome the circular logic of the Grenada Court of Appeal when this very court admitted that it was an unconstitutional court that had no jurisdiction to try the case, but at the same time expected its decision to be valid and enforceable.

V. Conclusion

The questions that McIntosh discusses, while analysing the Mitchell case, transcend the Grenadian and the Commonwealth Caribbean context. In fact, they are part of the broader discussion on the questions of the validity of political regimes, the application of Kelsen's theory of law and revolution to the actions of new governments, and of the role of courts in the process of legitimisation in various postcolonial jurisdictions.

[88] ibid 165.

It is very interesting that in the twentieth century Kelsen's theory has been used to justify the emergence of new legal regimes by illegal means in postcolonial jurisdictions, most of which were former British colonies. The courts in such countries had to decide the question of the legitimacy of these legal regimes by discussing the validity of their laws, decisions and actions. The two most popular competing theories that were used to justify the newly established political regimes were the doctrine of necessity, well known to the common law tradition, and the relatively new Kelsen's theory of revolutionary legality. The cases that applied Kelsen's theory are, for example: the Pakistani case *State v Dosso*;[89] the Ugandan case *Uganda v Commissioner of Prisons, Ex parte Matovu*;[90] *Valabhaji v Controller of Taxes*[91] from the Seychelles; *Mokotso v King Moshoeshoe II* from Lesotho;[92] and *Matanzima and Another v President of the Republic of Transkei and Another* from the unrecognised territory of Transkei (now a part of the South African Republic).[93] Some twentieth-century cases that were decided on the basis of the doctrine of necessity are: *Reference by his Excellence the Governor-General (under section 213 of the Government of India Act 1935)*;[94] and *Bhutto v The Chief of Staff of the Pakistan Army and the Federation of Pakistan*[95] from Pakistan; *Madzimbamuto v Lardner-Burke*[96] from Southern Rhodesia (now Zimbabwe); and *Attorney-General of the Republic of Cyprus v Ibrahim*[97] from Cyprus.

The use of the doctrine of necessity as a justification of the validity of rules promulgated by a revolutionary political regime is not new to common law countries as the doctrine had been applied by courts since the nineteenth century. What is new is that in the twentieth century common law courts started to actively use Kelsenian terminology and arguments for validating newly established political orders. Consequently, in a significant number of cases Kelsen's theory was preferred to the doctrine of necessity.[98]

One can agree that the application of the doctrine of necessity is not an adequate explanation of the validity of the legal rules of new political regimes. In the first place, as McIntosh aptly explains, this doctrine applies best in a situation where a lawful and constitutional government violates its own laws in a situation of emergency for the sake of public good. However, this doctrine fails when it is used to justify the actions of a completely new revolutionary government as this government's actions cannot be considered unconstitutional or unlawful with respect to the old constitution. Besides, the notion of necessity is open to judicial interpretations and political biases and can be used for justification or legitimisation of oppressive dictatorial governments by courts.

However, the fact that the concept of state necessity is flawed does not imply that Kelsen's theory of revolutionary legality, as it was applied by the courts in the Commonwealth, is free from legitimate criticism and constitutes a better alternative.[99]

[89] *State v Dosso* [1958] PLD 533 SC.
[90] *Uganda v Commissioner of Prisons, Ex parte Matovu* [1966] EA 514.
[91] *Valabhaji v Controller of Taxes* (n 3).
[92] *Mokotso v King Moshoeshoe II* (n 3).
[93] *Matanzima and Another v President of the Republic of Transkei and Another* (n 3).
[94] *Reference by His Excellency Governor-General* (n 3).
[95] *Bhutto v The Chief of Staff Pakistan Army and the Federation of Pakistan* (n 3).
[96] *Madzimbamuto v Lardner-Burke* (n 3).
[97] *Attorney-General of the Republic of Cyprus v Ibrahim* (n 3).
[98] For the analysis of these cases, see Tayyab (n 43).
[99] To what extent Kelsen's theory as interpreted and applied by courts in the Commonwealth really reflects Kelsen's own thinking is a very good question that deserves a separate discussion.

Basically, postcolonial courts rather simplistically applied Kelsen's test of effectiveness by deciding that, if a new political regime was functional and effective, the court should rule that its legal order is valid, even though Kelsen himself did not fully equate effectiveness with validity.[100] As a result of this, the fact that in a number of postcolonial jurisdictions courts recognised as valid new political regimes and their legal systems, considering only the criterion of effectiveness, turned out to be an important socio-legal and jurisprudential problem.

It seems that McIntosh's legal-philosophical reflections represent an attempt to address this important issue and constitute a significant original contribution to legal philosophy in more than one way.

In the first place, McIntosh has detected circularity in courts' reasonings and has highlighted that a court cannot decide whether a new political regime is valid or invalid because in such a case the court serves as an agent of this very regime and cannot validate itself. If the court expects that its decision is valid and binding (and this is certainly the case in all trials), this already implies that the political regime represented by the court is valid by default. According to McIntosh, courts in such cases do not validate the new regime: rather they explain why the regime is valid, ie, they simply justify it. Such a justification is not a question of law but rather a moral and political issue which cannot be decided within the strict confines of legal positivism.[101] This circularity in courts' reasoning is not just a logical or legal-theoretical problem but has very important practical implications. Being agents of a new state and being allowed to adjudicate within the confines of a new legal order, courts can hardly be considered as unbiased and objective arbiters in such disputes. While analysing their judgments, we should always keep in mind possible political biases as well as career interests of the judges.

Moreover, McIntosh firmly rejects mere effectiveness as the only ground for the legitimacy of a new political and legal order. Even though the philosopher does not deny that effectiveness is a very convincing factual argument that contributes to the legitimisation of a new regime, it should never be considered as the sole ground for the legitimacy of a new government. The Caribbean philosopher adds to the criterion of effectiveness a test of moral justification by incorporating Aquinas' and Fuller's understanding of law and applying it to the PRG regime in Grenada. This idea of moral justness of a new order is something that was missing from certain cases concerning the validity of new regimes in postcolonial countries. This criterion can also be the subject of legitimate critique (namely, the choice of legal theories made by McIntosh and the need for factual evidence of the new regime's justness rather than someone's personal perceptions), but the very denial of the 'might is right' principle and the articulation of the need for moral reflections on the role of the new order in society constitute an important contribution to legal philosophy.

Finally, Mcintosh rejects the application of the doctrine of necessity used in some Commonwealth judgments and bases his reasoning on Kelsen's theory while recognising its limitations and complementing it with other relevant legal-philosophical

[100] Kelsen discusses in some detail the relationship between validity and effectiveness and criticises the view, that he considers extreme, according to which 'validity and effectiveness are identical' (*The Pure Theory of Law* (n 20) 211–14). Whether Kelsen's attempt to distinguish validity from effectiveness within his own theory is convincing is a separate matter.

[101] McIntosh, 'Legitimacy, Validity and the Doctrine of Necessity' (n 35) 135.

considerations. Other legal scholars have also extensively criticised the courts' reliance on this doctrine.[102] However, what constitutes McIntosh's important contribution to the discussion is that he emphasises the fact of discontinuity between the consequent legal regimes in the case of a revolution and insists that the doctrine of necessity can only be applied in a situation of continuity of legal regimes and is not needed to justify the retention of legal rules and judicial bodies of previous political regimes when there is no such continuity. If the new order turns out to be successful as a matter of fact, such a regime creates a new *Grundnorm* and a new legal system and simply disregards some provisions of the old law in its own right rather than on the basis of necessity.

Thus, we can observe that the Mitchell case from Grenada has joined the body of transnational case law from various, predominantly common law, jurisdictions that discuss possible grounds for the legitimisation of new political regimes or their legal orders by applying Kelsen's theory of law and revolution or the doctrine of necessity. Even though the Grenada Court of Appeal rejected Kelsen's theory in favour of the doctrine of necessity, Caribbean legal philosopher McIntosh has skilfully criticised the applicability of this doctrine and discussed a possible application of Kelsen's approach complemented by a criterion of moral justification of the new government. Although McIntosh's own views are not immune from criticism, his reflections on law and revolution, on the role of judges in the legitimisation of governments as well as on the appropriateness of Western legal theories and judicial approaches to the Caribbean political and legal context constitute an important original contribution to regional and global jurisprudence.

[102] Tayyab (n 43) 113.

15

Hans Kelsen and Soviet Law

MIKHAIL ANTONOV

I. Introduction: Much Ado about Nothing?

Kelsen's ideas provoked much criticism among legal philosophers, and many scholars were and are still seeking to challenge his pure theory of law for its real or supposed vices. Such interest does not come as a surprise given the immense role of this 'lawyer of the century'[1] in the development of the legal philosophy of the twentieth century. Critical interest in Kelsen's work can be compared, as he puts it himself, to 'an impassioned resistance rarely seen in the history of legal science'.[2] Such resistance, in its turn, is due to his relentless and merciless attacks against rival legal conceptions and to his incessant attempts to uncover the ideologies behind the established dogmatic schemes of legal and political sciences.[3]

Kelsen's critical exchanges with the leading Western legal and political philosophers of the twentieth century are thoroughly examined in the scholarship. Nonetheless, one aspect still mainly remains in penumbra. The critical assaults of the Soviet legal theoreticians[4] against Kelsen's legal conception and his responses to these assaults have so far attracted only marginal attention,[5] compared with a huge amount of literature dedicated to Kelsen's exchanges with such prominent Western thinkers as Carl Schmitt or HLA Hart.

[1] H Dreier, 'Hans Kelsen (1881–1973): Jurist des Jahrhunderts?' in H Heinrichs, H Franzki, K Schmalz and M Stolleis (eds), *Deutsche Juristen jüdischer Herkunft* (München, CH Beck, 1993) 705–32.

[2] H Kelsen, *Introduction to the Problems of Legal Theory. A Translation of the First Edition of the Reine Rechtslehre or Pure Theory of Law*, B Litschewski Paulson and SL Paulson trans (originally published 1934) (Oxford, Clarendon Press, 1992) 1.

[3] R Schuett, *Hans Kelsen's Political Realism* (Edinburgh, Edinburgh University Press, 2021) 8–35.

[4] The term 'Soviet legal theory' refers here to an ideal type describing the principal ideas of the leading Soviet lawyers. One cannot deny that not rarely various Marxist-Leninist legal conceptions diverged from each other, including the ways they dealt with Marx and Lenin's ideas. Surely, it would have been more appropriate to study apart each Soviet legal theoretician and his ways to deal with the pure theory of law, but this would require a rather monographic research. Anyway, it was not the approach of Kelsen that is the focus of this chapter.

[5] eg, M Gassner, 'Hans Kelsen und die sowjetische Rechtslehre' in C Jabloner, T Olechowski and K Zeleny (eds), *Das internationale Wirken Hans Kelsens*. Schriftenreihe des Hans Kelsen-Instituts 38 (Vienna, Manz, 2016) 141–68; A Lukina, 'Opening the Pandora's Box: Kelsen and the Communist theory of law' (2020) 4 *Jurisprudence* 530.

Pragmatically, this lack of interest is explicable. On the one hand, Soviet social science was and still is considered by many researchers to be merely a reflection of Communist ideology. From this standpoint, almost everything that Soviet scholars said on various topics in social sciences, including their critical assessments of Kelsen's legal positivism, can be easily written off as determined by ideological biases. Given the political servility of these authors, why examine their writings of days long past in which they blasted Kelsen or other 'bourgeois' scholars?

Kelsen's main book on Soviet legal philosophy, *The Communist Theory of Law* (1955),[6] was not based on a careful analysis of sources, most of which remained unavailable to the Austrian legal philosopher because of his inability to read in Russian. One of the reviewers of Kelsen's 1955 book admitted: 'I do not believe that the author's inability to read the original Russian sources has caused any serious deficiency; at any rate, however, it is only through their translation that those Russian sources have assumed international importance'.[7] However, such an excuse is hardly valid for such a diligent scholar as Kelsen.

Evaluating Kelsen's criticism against Soviet lawyers, Hart found that 'much less than justice has been done to these writers by Kelsen's criticism', Kelsen made them 'appear as fools, but only by methods of argument which do not bear close scrutiny'.[8] In Kelsen's 1955 book Hart finds many flaws, 'most unexpected in such an author', while the book itself 'gives the impression that the author has been overcome by impatience and distaste for his subject'.[9] In the same vein, Hazard finds in Kelsen's 1955 book only an attempt to promote his own pure theory of law, while intentionally misinterpreting the ideas of his Soviet antagonists,[10] although this misinterpretation did not confirm anything except the fact that 'Kelsen lived in quite another world from theirs'.[11]

Along the same lines, one of the reviewers admits having 'the impression that *The Communist Theory of Law* is a kind of *Streitschrift* which involves not only Soviet writers but lumps together with them all others "in the bourgeois camp who disagree with him"',[12] so that 'no coherent picture of Soviet legal theory ever emerges from this book'.[13] Another reviewer contends that the 'basic intention of the book is in fact not anti-communist, but the book attacks the communist legal theory as a paragon of the prevailing, i.e. impure theory of law'.[14]

The style of this discussion on both sides is reminiscent of cherry-picking: collecting some citations from the scarcely available sources[15] that were utilised to confirm prejudices already formed in advance. As a result, the Soviet scholars saw Kelsen as someone

[6] H Kelsen, *The Communist Theory of Law* (New York, Frederick A Praeger, 1955).
[7] R Parker, 'The Communist Theory of Law by Hans Kelsen' (1956) 8 *Western Reserve Law Review* 104.
[8] HLA Hart, 'The Communist Theory of Law by Hans Kelsen' (1956) 4 *Harvard Law Review* 775.
[9] ibid 777.
[10] JN Hazard, 'The Communist Theory of Law by Hans Kelsen' (1956) 4 *Soviet Studies* 417.
[11] J Plamenatz, 'The Communist Theory of Law by Hans Kelsen' (1956) 304 *Annals of the American Academy of Political and Social Science* 182.
[12] HA Hammelmann, 'The Communist Theory of Law by Hans Kelsen' (1956) 2 *Modern Law Review* 220, 221.
[13] ibid 222.
[14] U Drobnig, 'The Communist Theory of Law by Hans Kelsen' (1957) 3 *Zeitschrift für ausländisches und internationales Privatrecht* 563, 565.
[15] Few selective English translations of Soviet authors accessible to Kelsen or few Russian reviews of Kelsen's books available to Soviet lawyers.

who isolated law from any connection with social reality in order to hide the fact that every law protects social injustice and class exploitation. For Kelsen, Soviet legal theory was inimical to individual freedom and favourable to authoritarianism – quite in line with the ideological bias that characterised many of the American publications on the Soviets in the McCarthy era.

Based on his earlier research from the 1920s, Kelsen *ex ante* associated metaphysical speculations about absolute values with authoritarian ideology,[16] and interpreted Soviet theory as a kind of natural law in accordance with the general pattern he applied to sundry conservative philosophers from Plato to Hegel.[17] In general, his explanation scheme was akin to how Karl Popper understood 'the enemies of open society' and their philosophical conceptions. According to Popper's reconstruction of these conceptions, only the few who are able, through a mystical *Wesenschau* (the intuition of essences and essential structures), to understand the ultimate truths, have the right to govern the rest of the population which is devoid of this mystical capability and is therefore doomed to full obedience.[18]

Kelsen and Popper agreed that this scheme is applicable to Marx's political philosophy too. By way of analogy, Kelsen also applied it to the Soviet lawyers who claimed themselves to be Marxists. Famously, the disparity between Marx and Marxism had already been underscored by Marx himself.[19] In reality, there was a considerable distance between Marx's writings and how they were interpreted by Soviet authors. So, Lenin revised Marx's utopian political ideals immediately in the days following the 1917 Revolution, and argued that the Soviet state and its dictatorship would not die away any time soon after the socialist revolution[20] – contrary to Marx's prophecies who did not envisage any long duration for the proletarian dictatorship. The distance grew even larger in the 1930s, when the utopian ideal of the state's dying away 'withered' itself away from the Soviet ideology. In fact, Soviet jurisprudence had very little to do with Marx's political and legal ideas, except the title 'Marxist-Leninist theory of law' that it proudly bore.

Kelsen could be quite right in his earlier critical assessment of Marx's writings on the state and their ideological implications for political theory.[21] But he was apparently wrong in transposing this criticism onto Soviet legal theory, especially after the 1930s. In the early 1950s, Stalin or Vyshinsky would readily subscribe themselves to Kelsen's statement that no developed society can exist without a well-organised and efficient state. The naive dream of Marx about the leap to the kingdom of freedom[22] that had

[16] H Kelsen, 'Absolutism and Relativism in Philosophy and Politics' (1948) 42 *American Political Science Review* 906.

[17] H Kelsen, *What is Justice? Justice, Law, and Politics in the Mirror of Science. Collected Essays by Hans Kelsen* (Berkeley, University of California Press, 1957).

[18] K Popper, *The Open Society and its Enemies* (Princeton, Princeton University Press, 2013).

[19] According to Marx's famous remark, quoted by Engels in his letter to Eduard Bernstein: 'What is certain is that I myself *am not a Marxist*'. K Marx and F Engels, *Selected Correspondence* (Moscow, Progress Publishers, 1975) 11.

[20] VI Lenin, *State and Revolution* (first published 1917) (London, Aziloth Books, 2017).

[21] H Kelsen, 'Die ökonomische und politische Theorie des Marxismus. Eine Selbstanzeige' (1920) 12 *Der österreichische Volkswirt* 560, 560–62.

[22] A Walicki, *Marxism and the Leap to the Kingdom of Freedom: The Rise and Fall of the Communist Utopia* (Stanford, Stanford University Press, 1995).

inspired the Russian revolutionaries in 1917, had little to do with Stalin's real policies from the 1930s onwards.[23]

Willingly or unwillingly, Kelsen overlooked the cardinal shift in Soviet political and legal theories in the late 1930s when the ideology dispensed with the Marxist utopian ideal. The leading Soviet legal scholar, the general prosecutor Andrei Vyshinsky, and the entire cohort of Soviet lawyers who had no choice but to follow him, denied that the socialist state could wither away in the foreseeable future, if ever. Their argumentation was absolutely compatible with the point that Kelsen had made in the second edition of his *Sozialismus und Staat* – the annihilation of antagonist classes and cancellation of private property would require there being the state also in Communist society.[24] This was exactly the point made in 1929 by Joseph Stalin: class struggle will inevitably be intensified under the socialist conditions because of harder resistance from the enemies and, consequently, the socialist state will grow stronger than ever before, utilising socialist law for securing more effective control over the society.[25]

And indeed, the Bolshevik Party came back to the standard methods of governing, in what Nicholas Timasheff called 'The Great Retreat': the state and its law regained their crucial importance for keeping up the system of social control.[26] This was a resolute farewell to the stateless utopia of Engels' *Anti-Dühring*. It became clear that socialist society as every other civilised society is unable to exist without the state. Even if Vyshinsky and other Marxist authors had somehow to reconcile this evident truth with the classical Marx-Engels teaching about the stateless future,[27] this reconciliation resulted only in adding some insignificant decorations to hide the discrepancy, but did not change anything substantially. As a matter of fact, Soviet jurisprudence came back to the statist theory of law that had been prevalent before the 1917 Revolution.

Regardless of this ideological development, Kelsen exposed the ideas of Soviet lawyers as if they followed Marx *à la lettre*, as if Marx's texts could give insights into what Vyshinsky and other Soviet lawyers thought and wrote about state and law in the 1950s.[28] This evidently was not the case. One may ask whether such a keen thinker as

[23] A Lukina, 'The Semenchuk Case of 1936: Storytelling and Propaganda above the Law in the Soviet Criminal Trial' (2016) 2 *Review of Central and East European Law* 63.

[24] H Kelsen, *Sozialismus und Staat. Eine Untersuchung der politischen Theorie des Marxismus*, 3rd edn, N Leser (ed) (Leipzig, Verlag der Wiener Volksbuchhandlung, 1965).

[25] 'The dying classes are resisting, not because they have become stronger than we are, but because socialism is growing faster than they are, and they are becoming weaker than we are. And precisely because they are becoming weaker, they feel that their last days are approaching and are compelled to resist with all the forces and all the means in their power. Such is the mechanics of the intensification of the class struggle and of the resistance of the capitalists at the present moment of history' (IV Stalin, 'The Right Deviation in the C.P.S.U.(B.)' in IV Stalin, *Works*, Vol 12 (Moscow, Foreign Languages Publishing House, 1954).

[26] The title that Nicholas S Timasheff introduced for description of the backward evolution of the Soviet legal systems under the rule of Stalin to the pre-revolutionary patterns (NS Timasheff, *The Great Retreat: The Growth and Decline of Communism in Russia* (New York, EP Dutton & Co, 1946)).

[27] The signs of this bright future were described by Engels as follows: 'State interference in social relations becomes, in one domain after another, superfluous, and then dies out of itself; the government of persons is replaced by the administration of things, and by the conduct of processes of production. The state is not "abolished". It withers away' (F Engels, 'Anti-Dühring' in K Marx and F Engels, *Collected Works*, Vol 25 (London, Lawrence and Wishart, 1987) 268.

[28] FG Homan Jr, 'Soviet Theory of Jurisprudence' (1965) 14 *Cleveland State Law Review* 402.

Kelsen was unable to understand it. And if he understood it, why did he undertake this unpromising intellectual enterprise of investigating something that was doomed to remain (because of the language and other practical barriers) the *terra incognita* for him?

Everyone who is familiar with Kelsen's scholarly diligence, will not avoid noticing there the striking difference with his other research projects.[29] The 1955 book on Soviet legal theory appears as an evident exception to the high standard of scientific scrupulosity which characterised Kelsen's writings. Why did Kelsen care to write and publish it at all? And why did his Soviet opponents spend their time and ink criticising Kelsen's works that most of them had never seen? This is what the present chapter attempts to elucidate, summing up and evaluating some possible clues to this enigma.

II. The Objectivity of Legal Science

This investigation can start from one of the most controversial and emotional issues in the debate between Kelsen and his Soviet opponents – what for legal scholars objectivity shall mean and how it can be secured. The pure theory of law required that legal science 'recognizes the postulate of an objective science, and that means of a science independent of political value judgments mandates, and therefore does not consider the vindication, legalization, justification of any social phenomenon described by it as its legitimate function'.[30] Both sides were convinced that legal knowledge cannot be considered as independent from social, economic, political and other conditions, that the legal schemes and concepts inevitably reflect these conditions and the ideologies that justify or challenge them.[31] Professor Koskenniemi keenly observes that 'Kelsen intervened in politics in the way a critique of ideology did: by revealing the political content of theories that had been thought of as neutral', making no secret of 'his democratic and left-liberal preferences or of his cosmopolitanism'.[32]

Kelsen, like his Soviet opponents, did not think to deny the evident political fact that 'the existing law is more in the interest of one class than in the interest of the other'.[33] Kelsen's criticism of the pretendedly eternal schemes of legal science (public and private law, sovereignty, rights, etc) and Marx's enquiry into the bourgeois class consciousness behind these schemes evidently hit one and the same nail. Both denied that there could be any ideal source of legal validity beyond posited norms and rules, that this source can be found in human nature or in practical reason. The Austrian legal

[29] To illustrate Kelsen's diligence, one can refer to how rigorous he was with publication of his manuscript *Secular Religion*. After getting notice of the newest literature on the topic, he took the book away from the publisher and left it unpublished, because he wanted to deepen his research. (See IM Stewart, 'Kelsen, the Enlightenment and Modern Premodernists' (2012) 37 *Australian Journal of Legal Philosophy* 251.) That Kelsen feared that his positive account of Marx could result in political difficulties for him, is another version of his leaving that manuscript unpublished which is also relevant for this chapter.

[30] Kelsen, *The Communist Theory of Law* (n 6) 75.

[31] E Topitsch, *Sozialphilosophie zwischen Ideologie und Wissenschaft* (Neuwied, Luchterhand, 1966).

[32] M Koskenniemi, *The Gentle Civilizer of Nations: The Rise and Fall of International Law 1870–1960* (Cambridge, Cambridge University Press, 2001) 245.

[33] Kelsen, *The Communist Theory of Law* (n 6) 73.

scholar wrote: 'Ideologies are not aimed at deepening cognition, but at determining the will',[34] and his Soviet opponents could not but sign up to this statement.

In this critical perspective, one could ask furthermore: can a legal scholar be free from his subjective biases that are imposed by the conditions under which he exists? Kelsen and the Soviet scholars took 'ideology' in the Marxian sense of false consciousness – this implied that truth and objectivity are unattainable for those scholars whose judgements are ideologised. With this, the discussants were led to the conclusion that each scientific conclusion informed by ideology is false; it distorts reality. Kelsen concluded that

> [s]cience can only describe and explain; it cannot justify reality. It has the immanent tendency to be independent of politics and, as a rational and comprehensive cognition of reality, cannot presuppose in the description and explanation of its object the existence of a transcendent authority beyond any possible human experience.[35]

Basing their *Ideologiekritik* on the assumption that all constructions of legal science run the risk of being informed by ideological biases, both parties in this debate responded to this question negatively. But this critical perspective, in its ultimate conclusions, would make senseless their own conceptions. Being consequent, they had to admit that not only their adversaries but also themselves can be subject to political conditions, to ideological biases and therefore unable to ensure the objectivity of their own conclusions. With this result, their conceptions would be as fallible to ideologies as those of their opponents: bourgeois legal conceptions will be as ideologised as socialist conceptions, and the other way around. This argument about ideologies behind each and every legal conception was persuasive, but at the same time was extremely dangerous. It followed that law *en tant que* science is not possible at all. Neither Kelsen, nor his Soviet opponents, would be happy with such a rigoristic conclusion.

While both Kelsen and his Soviet opponents failed to provide any satisfactory solution to this problem of objectivity, they were keen enough to see trickeries behind the solutions proposed by their adversaries. Kelsen condemned as a pure trickery Marx's pretension that his conception was able to uncover objectivity, 'social truth' in objective reality. In Kelsen's words, his objectivity of reality is 'his [Marx's] own socialist ideology projected into it. His reality, like the top-hat of a magician, has a double bottom, out of which anything you want can be produced by magic'.[36] In their turn, Soviet theoreticians did not spare ink to prove that their bourgeois antagonists, among them Kelsen, were under the spell of bourgeois values. In the words of Professor Strogovich: 'It is political motives that determine Kelsen's attitude towards the Soviet legal science',[37] so that his analysis had nothing to offer except 'a distorted and falsified description of this science'.[38]

[34] H Kelsen, *Pure Theory of Law*, M Knight trans (Berkeley, University of California Press, 1967) 286.

[35] H Kelsen, *Secular Religion. A Polemic against the Misinterpretation of Modern Social Philosophy, Science and Politics as 'New Religions'*, R Walter, C Jabloner and K Zeleny (eds) (Vienna, Springer, 2012) 267.

[36] Kelsen, *The Communist Theory of Law* (n 6) 20.

[37] MS Strogovich, 'Bourgeois theories of legality and personal rights' [Burzhuaznye teorii zakonnosti i prav lichnosti] in MS Strogovich, *Problems of General Theory of Law. Selected Works* [*Problemy obshchei teorii prava. Izbrannye sochineniia*] Vol 1 (Moscow, Nauka, 1990) 293.

[38] ibid.

At the same time, Strogovich and other Soviet lawyers were reluctant to admit that their own theories stood on the protection of the interests of the Soviet political regime. This, certainly, would be an open secret, but absolutely intolerable for the ideology. The response of Soviet legal scholars to this objection was given in the form of an awkward implication that their conceptions reflect the objective regularities of social development and constitute an objective description of these regularities.[39] Kelsen also defended objectivity of his conception and resorted to a similar argumentation that 'science is not, as the Marxists pretend, a mere intellectual superstructure over political reality'.[40]

Portraying the pure theory of law as an objective knowledge of law, Kelsen accused his opponents of ideological blindness and political servility which led them to 'the shameful decline of a social science that is not able to emancipate itself from politics'.[41] He insisted that his theory refuses to serve any political interests and corresponds to the standards of scientific objectivity as a strictly descriptive science.[42]

Was Kelsen sincere in these statements? His legal theory had too evident connotations with his political commitment to democracy[43] and favoured one kind of value (stability, predictability), while struggling against other values (as is demonstrated by his diatribes against natural law and justice that pretendedly support authoritarianism) exactly for the sake of defending democracy.[44] Kelsen apparently had to fall prey to his own criticism, as was noticed by many scholars, among them Barna Horvath who found that 'Kelsen eliminates the ideological flavour of vindicating some values of civilization, such as "free" or "objective" science, without vindicating others instrumental to the former, by including in existing law, as a norm, the connotation of justice'.[45]

One has the impression that Kelsen and the Marxists attempted to unmask the ideological biases of each other in order to save their own face by discrediting their

[39] This position was represented in two volumes of works of the Soviet authors translated and published by Hugh W Babb after the Second World War: *The Law of the Soviet State* (New York, Macmillan, 1948) and *Soviet Legal Philosophy* (Cambridge, MA, Harvard University Press, 1951).

[40] Kelsen, *Secular Religion* (n 35) 271. Kelsen's account of the basis-superstructure relationship in Marxism – in the sense that economic basis fully determines how people think and behave themselves – was oversimplified. Marx did not admit such predetermination. Quite on the contrary, on the example of the conflict between property relations and the material productive forces he demonstrated that the superstructure can exert reverse effects, changing and reshaping the basis. See I Sabo, 'Hans Kelsen and the Marxist theory of law' in *Against the Contemporary Legal Ideology of Imperialism* (Moscow, Inostrannaia literatura, 1962) 297–341; N Poulantzas, 'A propos de la théorie marxiste du droit' (1967) 12 *Archives de Philosophie du Droit* 145.

[41] Kelsen, *The Communist Theory of Law* (n 6) viii.

[42] In the preface to the second edition of *The Pure Theory of Law*, Kelsen defends his theory as an objective, solely descriptive science of law that 'hurled against the stubborn resistance of all those who, misunderstanding the borderlines between science and politics, in the name of the former prescribe a particular content for law – that is, "right law" – and thereby suppose that they have been able to establish a set of values to which positive law must conform' (the English translation according Stewart (n 29) 269).

[43] See, eg, CM Herrera, *Théorie juridique et politique chez Hans Kelsen* (Paris, Éditions Kimé, 1997); S Baume, *Hans Kelsen and the Case for Democracy* (Colchester, ECPR Press, 2012).

[44] 'The rationalistic character of democracy manifests itself especially in the tendency to establish the legal order of the state as a system of general norms created by a procedure well organized for this purpose. There is a clear intention of determining, by a pre-established law, the individual acts of the courts and administrative organs in order to make them – as far as possible – calculable. There exists an outspoken need for rationalizing the process in which the power of the state is displayed' (H Kelsen, 'Foundations of Democracy' (1955) 66 *Ethics* 1, 29).

[45] B Horvath, 'The Communist Theory of Law by H. Kelsen' (1955) 4 *American Journal of Comparative Law* 629, 633.

opponents. After all, this strategy turned out to be sterile on both sides. It stands to reason that no one can be absolutely objective in his judgements and observations. Every scholar is inevitably influenced by the *Zeitgeist*, by political, economic and other conditions of his existence, by language and culture, by his academic position, and so on. In terms of *Ideologiekritik*, Kelsen or his Soviet opponents could be equally disparaged for being transmitters of class interests as any other 'bourgeois' or 'socialist' scholar.[46]

In Kelsen's description, Soviet legal science will have no scientific value as long as it remains dependent on politics: 'the very function of the Soviet doctrine of law is not to describe and explain social and especially legal reality in an objective way, but to form this reality by destroying an existing social order and replacing it by another, considered to be better'.[47] But were his own 1948 and 1955 books much better, if one critically examines them against the same background?

The Soviet authors had good grounds to accuse Kelsen of having made his political choice ex ante in favour of democracy and liberalism,[48] so that his pure theory of law only sought to justify ex post the relevant political principles resulting from this choice. His democratic and liberal convictions transpire in all his writings where

> he combines an ethical and a sociological analysis of democracy, and acknowledges the complexity of mass democracy by developing an eloquent 'ideology' centred on the controversial relation between institutions and ethical ideals, which seems to be explicitly meant to meet the collective disillusionment about a democratic system unable to match its ethical standards, and yet equally unable to do without them.[49]

Fighting for purity of legal science, Kelsen could not deny that there are certain values that determine binding force of law. This aspect of the Kelsenian conception was dubbed by Professor Raz as the thesis of justified normativity.[50]

III. Justified Normativity and Natural Law

The methodological principles of the pure theory of law were, at the first glance, irreconcilable with the idea of binding force which frequently implies ethical or religious justification of law. In Eugenio Bulygin's opinion, the use of a normative concept of validity in the pure theory contradicted Kelsen's positivistic programme of value-free legal science, and led to an antinomy in his conception.[51]

It was in order to avoid such justification that Kelsen tried to exclude ethical values and social facts from discussions about legal validity. But these attempts could not hide

[46] G De Angelis, 'Ideals and Institutions: Hans Kelsen's Political Theory' (2009) 30 *History of Political Thought* 524.

[47] Kelsen, *The Communist Theory of Law* (n 6) viii.

[48] J Cohen, 'The Political Element in Legal Theory: A Look at Kelsen's Pure Theory' (1978) 88 *Yale Law Journal* 1.

[49] De Angelis (n 46) 543.

[50] See on this thesis and debates around it, SL Paulson, 'A Justified Normativity Thesis in Hans Kelsen's Pure Theory of Law? Rejoinders to Robert Alexy and Joseph Raz' in M Klatt (ed), *Institutionalized Reason. The Jurisprudence of Robert Alexy* (Oxford, Oxford University Press, 2012) 61–111.

[51] E Bulygin, 'An Antimony in Kelsen's Pure Theory of Law' (1990) 3 *Ratio Juris* 29.

the ethical background of his theory.[52] In the eyes of Kelsen's critics, the entire hypothetical construction of legal order topped by the impersonal, transcendental *Grundnorm* implied the values of freedom, peace, democracy and tolerance.[53] From this standpoint, Alf Ross, Eugenio Bulygin and a number of other prominent legal positivists qualified the pure theory of law as a camouflaged natural law doctrine that relied on ethical arguments.[54] The justified normativity of law looked like a genuinely ethical conception, so that 'Kelsen's theory must be understood as a genuinely normative strand of thought'.[55]

Indeed, one cannot overlook that in Kelsen's theory, *Grundnorm* works as a guarantor of objectivity of law: 'The basic norm, therefore, is not the product of free invention. It is not presupposed arbitrarily in the sense that there is a choice between different basic norms'.[56] *Grundnorm* as the necessary presupposition of legal cognition assumed certain principles around which this cognition had to be organised.[57] According to Kelsen's thesis of minimal efficiency, legal validity is dependent on the factual level of rule-obedience in a given society. The next question comes as to why certain standards of behaviour are followed, and this leads to ethical and ideological principles behind them. Kelsen was not that naive not to see that legal normativity implies value judgements: 'To present law as norm is an elusive ideology only if the law is in truth not just; if the law is just – and the answer to this question depends on the definition of justice – it is correctly presented as something that ought to be'.[58]

But admitting that values influence legal validity also in the pure theory of law would undermine the principle of *Wertfreiheit* (freedom from values). Kelsen tried to avoid this problem by recurring to relativism. He proclaimed that 'a legal theory cannot be formalistic and at the same time define law as an eternal category'[59] and conceded that presupposing objective legal norms might be 'senseless or merely ideological fallacy'.[60] Although, without this presupposition thousands of statements in which the law is expressed daily would become senseless.[61] Seemingly, there was no way to escape from the regressive transcendental argument – in order to explain law, we cannot but make judgements about objective legal norms.[62] This was a hard problem that Kelsen faced investigating the sources of justified normativity of law. In terms of the Pandora's Box objection, 'Kelsen's surprising notion that connecting law's validity to its conformity

[52] E Fechner, 'Ideologie und Rechtspositivismus, ideologische Elemente in positivistischen Rechtsanschauungen, dargestellt an Hans Kelsens Reiner Rechtslehre' in W Maihofer (ed), *Ideologie und Recht* (Frankfurt/M, Klostermann, 1969) 97–120.

[53] As Kelsen admitted himself in Kelsen, *What is Justice?* (n 17) 24.

[54] A Ross, 'Validity and the Conflict between Legal Positivism and Natural Law' in SL Paulson and B Litschewski Paulson (eds), *Normativity and Norms. Critical Perspectives on Kelsenian Themes* (Oxford, Clarendon Press, 1998) 147.

[55] L Vinx, *Kelsen s Pure Theory of Law: Legality and Legitimacy* (Oxford, Oxford University Press, 2007) 57.

[56] Kelsen, *Pure Theory of Law* (n 34) 201.

[57] L Vinx, 'Hans Kelsen and the Material Constitution of Democracy' (2021) 12 *Jurisprudence* 466.

[58] Kelsen, *The Communist Theory of Law* (n 6) 66.

[59] ibid 72.

[60] ibid 101.

[61] ibid 104.

[62] SL Paulson, 'The Great Puzzle: Kelsen's Basic Norm' in L Duarte d'Almeida, J Gardner and L Green (eds), *Kelsen Revisited. New Essays on the Pure Theory of Law* (Oxford, Hart Publishing, 2013) 43–61.

with natural law opens a way for inadvertently morally justifying all kinds of legal systems regardless of their adherence to norms of morality'.[63]

Why Kelsen calls for ethical neutrality of law is quite clear and explicable. But it is still hard to deny that before he formulated the task of the purification of legal science, Kelsen had already made his choice in favour not only of Kantian epistemology, but also of Kantian ethics. Making our moral beliefs depend on the legislator's ethical choice can potentially deprive subjects of their moral freedom. To save this autonomy, Kelsen defended ethical non-cognitivism that guarantees the freedom of moral choice,[64] criticising his Soviet opponents for sacrificing moral autonomy to Communist ideology.[65] He apparently hits the nail on the head, suggesting that the ultimate goal of Soviet ideology – doing away with capitalism and securing the victory of the proletariat in class struggle – is taken for granted as if it were a factual statement. But, as a matter of fact, it is a value judgement pretendedly derived from the regularities that determine historical development. This method of universalisation of values is proper to philosophical idealism in general: 'Soviet writers from the social relationships of a socialist society work out the ideal norms of socialist law'.[66]

As often happened in this discussion, the accusations brought by Kelsen against Soviet legal theory merely mirrored the accusations against the pure theory of law that the Soviet lawyers had formulated before. For his numerous opponents amongst Soviet legal theorists, Kelsen hypocritically covered values and interests of the capitalist class making them appear as if they were value-neutral.[67] Both sides accused each other of utilising such conceptual schemes that intentionally set out to justify and eternise certain political programmes.

The discussion found itself in a stalemate. Soviet legal theorists rejected Kelsen's positivism considering it as an example of bourgeois hypocrisy, while Kelsen criticised the positivism of the Communist theory of law for the same trickery: presenting public interests and communitarian value-preferences as if they were objective. In fact, both doctrines could be equally accused of justifying their political and moral preferences. Having nothing to refute this accusation, the opponents tried to neutralise it by claiming it to be worthless based on the anti-scientific paradigm of a natural law doctrine.

Applying this strategy, Kelsen and the Soviet scholars treated each other as false positivists claiming respectively that Kelsen's *Grundnorm* and the Communist teaching about a bright future axiomatically presupposed absolute values. Clutching on the

[63] Lukina, 'Opening the Pandora's Box (n 5) 530.

[64] J Raz, 'Kelsen's Theory of the Basic Norm' (1974) 19 *American Journal of Jurisprudence* 94.

[65] 'The deplorable status of Soviet legal theory, degraded to a handmaid of the Soviet government, should be a grim warning to social scientists that true social science is possible only under the condition that it is independent of politics' (Kelsen, *The Communist Theory of Law* (n 6) 193).

[66] ibid 120.

[67] 'Thus, normativism does not see the material content of social relationships, does not admit of the class structure of society, the struggle of social classes and does not acknowledge the state as an organ of domination and repression. It excludes all this as meta-juridical lying outside juridical categories and normative ideas. Normativism shows completely and logically the vacuity of neo-Kantian methodology which struggles only to disguise by juridical norms and legal formulae the class antagonisms destroying bourgeois society and the capitalist order' (AY Vyshinsky (ed), *The Law* of the *Soviet State* (New York, Macmillan, 1948) 33). Here, by 'normativism' Vyshinsky describes Kelsen's pure theory of law.

principles of legal positivism, Kelsen and his Soviet opponents found themselves in an impasse. On the one hand, they could demonstrate that their rivals were subject to ideological biases but, on the other, were unable to deny having such biases themselves.

Kelsen found in the Soviet legal ideology the absolute justification of law: 'The prediction of a stateless and lawless society of perfect justice is a utopian prophecy like the Messianic Kingdom of God, the paradise of the future'.[68] From this perspective, he viewed Soviet legal theory as 'a natural law doctrine thinly disguised as a prediction of the Utopia bound to emerge from the class struggle'.[69] The eschatological perspective of the bright future provides a tool for metaphysical justification of one, socialist legal system, and for criticism of other, ideologically opposed legal systems. These other systems were evaluated depending on whether they help bring the Communist future closer or impede it and, in this sense, correspond or contradict the laws of historical development. Finding the social truth is possible in so far as this truth is immanent to the social reality: '[T]he just social order of communist society is immanent in the social reality of production and, hence, can be discovered by an examination of this reality. This is genuine natural-law doctrine'.[70]

Professor Strogovich put forward similar counter-arguments against Kelsen:

> Every bourgeois legal theory serves to protection and reinforcement of the bourgeois social orders. So does Kelsen's theory too, albeit he denies it. His theory plays this role in a specific form and by specific methods: by removing from the sphere of jurisprudence all social, political and moral moments and by reducing legal analysis solely to legal form. This allows to bourgeois lawyers to make appearance they are not concerned by the acute political struggle.[71]

In his opinion, Kelsen's teaching is much more dangerous than natural law doctrines. For Strogovich, Kelsen intentionally obscures his ideological preferences and, by doing so, lures positivists into the trap of bourgeois ideology which is cunningly represented as best fitted to the methodology of legal positivism.

The argument about natural law was for both sides a kind of philosopher's stone. For legal positivists, someone who relies on natural law stands on knowingly false ground, so that his critical arguments are, by definition, devoid of sense. This explains why both Kelsen and his Soviet critics did not find it appropriate to respond to critical accusations about natural law elements in their own conceptions. In this strange game, one had only to diagnose the adversary as a natural lawyer in order to skip substantial discussion with their counterpart.

For Kelsen, every natural law doctrine implied three claims: law is an objective normative order with absolute validity, independent from human acts; men are able to cognise this order; and law cannot be valid unless it meets certain ethical criteria.[72] The methods of the Soviet scholars seemed very similar to natural law doctrines:

> Just as the natural-law doctrine asserts – as a consequence of its presupposition – that it is possible to deduce from nature the just, i.e., the natural law and attributes to science,

[68] Kelsen, *The Communist Theory of Law* (n 6) 38.
[69] Hart (n 8) 774.
[70] Kelsen, *The Communist Theory of Law* (n 6) 21.
[71] Strogovich, 'Bourgeois theories of legality and personal rights' (n 37) 292.
[72] P Chiassoni, 'Kelsen on Natural Law Theory. An Enduring Critical Affair' (2014) 23 *Revus. Journal for Constitutional Theory and Philosophy of Law* 135.

> the science of law, the task of discovering this natural law somehow hidden in nature, so Marx affirms that out of social reality the justice of socialism as the social truth can be developed.[73]

This Kelsen strategy was not new: again, it was a replication of the critical arguments thrown by Pashukanis and other Soviet scholars against his pure theory of law. As early as the 1920s, Pashukanis accused Kelsen of being a natural law scholar. For the first time this argument was voiced in 1923, in Pashukanis' review of Kelsen's writings on state and sovereignty (*Problem der Souveränität und die Theorie des Völkerrechts* and *Der soziologische und der juristische Staatsbegriff*).[74]

For Pashukanis, Kelsen's constructions were 'artificial and paradoxical to the extent that they will hardly find any application even in the narrow field of dogmatic legal science, let alone the authentically scientific understanding of law and state – Kelsen's method leads in the absolutely opposite direction'.[75] The right place for the application of this method, for Pashukanis, is in an insane asylum,[76] because 'it does not want to have anything to do with facticity'.[77] Pashukanis stresses what he considers Kelsen's sheer logical contradiction and absurdity:

> Legal positivism grew due to its struggle with natural law in order to eradicate the last remnants of this doctrine. And Kelsen, who considers himself as a continuator and terminator of this struggle in the defence of positive law, in his end-conclusions falls back to the same natural law … and drops his anchor in peaceful waters of the natural-law doctrine … in one leap from the formal and official understanding of law he flies into the conception of natural law.[78]

This criticism was repeated in Pashukanis' *opus magnum* published in 1927 (the third edition).[79] In this opus, the Soviet lawyer characterises the pure theory of law as an idealist abstraction, a kind of a chess game, finding that 'the excessive formalism of the normative school evidently is a part of the general decadent trend in the bourgeois science of the recent years – the science that exhausts itself in fruitless methodological, formal and logical tricks and plays in a full disassociation with the reality'.[80]

[73] Kelsen, *The Communist Theory of Law* (n 6) 20.

[74] EB Pashukanis, 'To the review of the literature on general theory of law and state' (1923) 5 *Vestnik sotsialisticheskoi akademii* 227.

[75] ibid 231.

[76] Here, Pashukanis utilises the Russian colloquialism 'yellow house'. This language use can serve as one of the proofs of the strategy described above – to classify the adversary as a natural lawyer would equate to the diagnosis of his mental insanity. Here, long before Alf Ross' argument about 'pseudo-positivism' of Kelsen, for the first time sounds the allusion to 'split personality' that allegedly is proper to those legal positivists who, as Kelsen, are in fact disguised natural law scholars trying to hide this discreditable fact from others and from themselves.

[77] ibid 232.

[78] ibid.

[79] EB Pashukanis, *The General Theory of Law and Marxism* [*Obshchaia teoriia prava i marksism*] (Moscow, Izdatelstvo Kommunisticheskoi akademii, 1927). Kelsen makes use of the same language when he characterised the methods of his adversaries who project values into reality and then take them back, 'just as a circus magician pulls out of his top hat doves and rabbits which he had put into it beforehand' (H Kelsen, 'Naturrechtslehre und Rechtspositivismus' in HR Klecatsky, R Marcic and H Schambeck (eds), *Die Wiener rechtstheoretische Schule* (Vienna, Europa Verlag, 1968) 817–32, 821).

[80] EB Pashukanis, *The General Theory of Law and Marxism* (n 79) 29.

In his 1928 review of Kelsen's *Allgemeine Staatslehre*, Pashukanis goes even further and accuses Kelsen of plotting against the Soviet state by his contrafactual description of the legal order.[81]

These accusations were not completely groundless. Kelsen's *Weltanschauung* indeed relied on certain political ideals that were formed in the interwar period in the Austrian and Weimar contexts and remained more or less stable throughout his life. His plaidoyers in the defence of democracy were often drafted in the style proper to natural law doctrine. Kelsen actively utilised ethical arguments to justify the impersonal rule of law (*Rechtsstaat*)[82] axiomatically preferring it to collectivism and authoritarianism.

In 'Foundations of Democracy', Kelsen admits that his 'anti-ideological, rationalistic, and relativistic political theory corresponds to that intellectual type which has been described as democratic'.[83] When one reads further that '[f]reedom and equality are the fundamental ideas of democracy and the two basic primitive instincts of man as a social being',[84] one would guess there is a partisan of natural law behind this statement. But this statement belongs to Kelsen. Earlier, in 'Vom Wesen und Wert der Demokratie', Kelsen spoke about certain 'fundamental human needs and aspirations' that determine political values in society and are, in this sense, objective.[85] Here, he unconditionally accepted the Kantian principle of moral autonomy and proclaimed the intrinsic ethical value of democracy which 'leaves the decision about the social value to be realized to the individual acting in political reality',[86] making them appear as objective foundations of legal order.

These Kelsen statements do not substantially differ from the classical theories of social contract. His argumentation runs mainly outside any social or historical contexts, basing them on transcendental assumptions which, in the last resort, are informed by his ethical convictions. Paradoxically, Kelsen's principal intention to liberate scientific analysis from its dependency on facticity led him to the argumentation sounding very similar to the natural law doctrines which he wanted to put before the tribunal of science.[87] The Austrian lawyer criticised absolutism in political philosophy, but his own political works were abundant with a priori statements about political virtues.[88]

His doctrine of international law gives illustrative examples of such apriorism. Thus, choosing between the international and national versions of monism, Kelsen endorsed the former. He treated this version as objectively preferable to 'state subjectivism', admitting at the same time that both were theoretically possible and that his own choice was

[81] EB Pashukanis, 'Review of H. Kelsen, General Theory of State [Obshchee uchenie o gosudarstve]' (1928) 2 *Revoliutsiia prava* 149.

[82] H Dreier, *Rechtslehre, Staatssoziologie und Demokratietheorie bei Hans Kelsen*, 2nd edn (Baden-Baden, Nomos Verlagsgesellschaft, 1990) 278; M Jestaedt and O Lepsius, 'Der Rechts- und der Demokratietheoretiker Hans Kelsen: Eine Einführung' in H Kelsen, *Verteidigung der Demokratie*, M Jestaedt and O Lepsius (eds) (Tübingen, Mohr Siebeck, 2006) VII–XXIX.

[83] Kelsen, 'Foundations of Democracy' (n 44) 34.

[84] ibid 3.

[85] H Kelsen, 'Vom Wesen und Wert der Demokratie' in H Kelsen, *Verteidigung der Demokratie*, M Jestaedt and O Lepsius (eds) (Tübingen, Mohr Siebeck, 2006) 149–228, 154.

[86] Kelsen, 'Foundations of Democracy' (n 44) 40.

[87] Kelsen, *What is Justice?* (n 17) 137.

[88] Kelsen, 'Vom Wesen und Wert der Demokratie' (n 85) 158.

influenced by his democratic convictions.[89] It is not by chance that one of Kelsen's former students evaluated Kelsen's theory of international law as 'the most sophisticated natural law theory which has been developed during this century in the field of international affairs'.[90] Haesaert also found a natural law doctrine in Kelsen's theory and concluded that Kelsen's book on principles of international law was 'speculation in the disguise and semblance of law'.[91]

His Soviet opponents did not fail to notice this *ius*-naturalist footing of the pure theory of law, mocking Kelsen's inconsistency about his claims of objectivity. Putatively, this discussion was not free from rivalry, as Kelsen at that time was the main opponent of Soviet jurisprudence in the field of legal positivism. Perhaps, this competitive context can better explain why 'Hans Kelsen has been in the centre of Soviet attack upon the Western legal philosophers'.[92]

The uncontested leader of Soviet jurisprudence from the mid-1930s onwards, Andrei Vyshinsky, the founder of what in Soviet jurisprudence was called 'normativism' or 'the narrow conception of law',[93] insisted that values are irrelevant for the definition of law which is nothing more than a system of coercive norms. He held that any theory that denies that, is unscientific and inimical to the socialist legal consciousness. As a result, in the 1930s, all competing theories (such as Pashukanis' commodity exchange theory, Reisner's psychological theory or Stuchka's class interest theory), were rejected as flawed and counter-revolutionary. Fighting for purity of legal science in his own way, Vyshinsky condemned these and other non-positivist theories for their inability to distinguish between law and other social phenomena.

Apparently, he could have found in Kelsen an ally for this scientific enterprise. But for Vyshinsky, the pure theory of law was not pure enough – the USSR general prosecutor accepted the argument of Pashukanis about Kelsen's conception being contaminated by natural law and other remnants of idealism. Kelsen's criticism of the 'communist theory of law' in his eponymous book was based on the same argument of impurity of Soviet theory and its proximity to natural law thinking.

These mutual accusations implied that a sensible scientific (read – positivist) theory of law had nothing to do with natural law doctrines, so that accusing an opponent of being a natural law lawyer equated to a statement of his insanity and allowed one to just get rid of substantial discussion with him – a discussion for which both parties were anyway not prepared because of lack of sources, ideological controls, etc.

[89] H Kelsen, *General Theory of Law and State* (originally published 1945) (Clark, Lawbook Exchange, 2007) 386. Also the Kantian ethics exerted a strong influence on Kelsen's conception of international law. See J Kammerhofer, 'Kelsen – Which Kelsen? A Reapplication of the Pure Theory to International Law' (2009) 22 *Leiden Journal of International Law* 225.

J Kammerhofer, 'Kelsen – Which Kelsen? A Re-application of the Pure Theory to International Law' (2009) 22 *Leiden Journal of International Law* 225.

[90] JH Herz, 'The Pure Theory of Law Revisited: Hans Kelsen's Doctrine of International Law in the Nuclear Age' in S Engel (ed), *Law, State, and International Legal Order: Essays in Honor of Hans Kelsen* (Knoxville, University of Tennessee Press, 1964) 107–18, 108.

[91] JP Haesaert, 'Review of Hans Kelsen's Principles of International Law' (1953) 2 *American Journal of Comparative Law* 576.

[92] Hazard (n 10) 412.

[93] This was the mainstream theory imposed by Professor Vyshinsky from the mid-1030s onwards, that coincided with the command theory of John Austin on almost all counts. This 'narrow conception' had prevailed in the Soviet jurisprudence until Stalin's death; only in the years of Khrushchev's Thaw there appeared a number of 'broad conceptions of law' that asserted that law is not reducible to a set of coercive norms.

IV. Intentional Misunderstanding?

Why did Kelsen and his Soviet opponents initiate this discussion to which both were unprepared? They belonged to the positivist camp, they described law and its machinery more or less similarly and their discord in many respects looked like a rivalry but not as a principled disagreement. Exactly because of the common methodological ground, the parties knew each other's weak spots and masterly utilised them in mutual critical remarks. Apart from the rivalry, there were other quite prosaic problems that fuelled the reciprocal misrepresentation. These problems concerned the practical conditions under which the discussants were eking out their existence on both sides of the Iron Curtain, namely: availability of sources, language problems and political vulnerability.

For contemporary scholars who have the opportunity to read almost all scholarly sources online without being censored while reading, the problem of censorship is scarcely understandable. Not only was the availability of sources from the 'alien camp' limited in the years of the Cold War but also access to them; not only writers but also readers were censored. Only a few Soviet scholars with special permissions had access to the *Spetskhran* – the special repositories at the few biggest Soviet research libraries where the newest Western books on social sciences were kept. Not only were these sources barred for all other readers, but those selected few who could get access to the sources of bourgeois propaganda, ran imminent risks of being suspected of interest in this propaganda. There is no need to explain what such suspicion could cost in the years of Stalin's purges when millions of 'enemies of the people' perished under less significant accusations.

A less dangerous strategy for those who ex officio had to write against the 'bourgeois legal ideology' was to follow the few book reviews published in the 1920s by Pashukanis and other 'intellectual leaders' of Soviet jurisprudence, repeating their ideologically distorted descriptions. Due to these conditions, for most of Kelsen's opponents in the Soviet Union, his writings were quasi-inaccessible. They snatched citations for their critical analysis not directly from his works, but from some sparse book reviews where these citations had already been incorporated into specific ideologic contexts and interpreted accordingly.

As a result, Kelsen's critics in Soviet Russia mostly attacked not his writings and the ideas contained in them, but the accounts of these ideas made by Pashukanis and other reviewers. These reviews were made of his old books published from the 1920s,[94] while Kelsen's newer publications that appeared in the 1930 to 1950s, were seldom mentioned in the Soviet critical literature of that time. Only when political terror slackened during Khrushchev's 'Thaw', did reading and discussing foreign scholarly literature become not so life-threatening. There began to appear publications where the second edition of *The Pure Theory of Law* and other newer writings of Kelsen were examined.[95]

[94] After the 1920s, there were many fewer reviews of foreign books in law and other social sciences – even for 'intellectual leaders' requesting them at a library repository would be a risky undertaking. Among all other proofs for Pashukanis' guilt, his accusers listed his 'ideological blindness' which resulted in his attempts to throw 'false light' on the Soviet law by relying upon bourgeois authors.

[95] In 1957, the new leader of the Soviet theoretical jurisprudence, Vladimir Tumanov, published his voluminous research on the bourgeois legal ideology in which Kelsen's theory was exposed there in a very detailed manner. This book has become the main citation source for the current and following generation of the Soviet

Over the years, one more problem was added. There remained lesser Soviet scholars who spoke foreign languages and were able to read original books, while almost all Western books in legal philosophy published after the 1917 Revolution remained untranslated.[96] This happened with Kelsen's works too, none of them had been translated before the *Perestroika*.[97]

Things were not much better on the other side of the Iron Curtain during the McCarthy era, when leftist sympathies or even an interest in what was happening in Soviet Russia could provoke distrust and create problems for public employees. Even having an interest in or sympathy towards the Soviets could be dangerous in these years, quite in the same way as a suspected interest in Western propaganda could easily bring Soviet scholars to the GULAG.[98] In the preface to the 1955 volume, Kelsen avertedly made the reservation that he did not examine Soviet law or Soviet politics but the Communist theory of law and its political sources.[99] Apparently, he was tormented with fears similar to those experienced by his Soviet opponents – to be suspected of sympathies to a hostile ideology. It is another question whether Kelsen had really abandoned his socialist sympathies or just was forced to disown them publicly.

Being employed at a US university in the years of witch-hunting, Kelsen had to be careful in expressing an interest in Soviet legal theory. Perhaps, under other circumstances he would never have written on such subjects. But his situation was anyway not irreproachable in the eyes of the US secret services because of his former leftist sympathies. In Professor Losano's words: 'All his life long, Kelsen was accused from the right-wing people of being a communist, while the left accused him of being a reactionary'.[100] Probably, Kelsen had the practical need to show his loyalty to his host country and antipathy to its sworn enemy, the USSR and its ideology.

In his earlier works from the 1920s and in his political engagements of that time, Kelsen was politically close to Renner and other Austrian social-democrats. He even

lawyers. In 1974, its second edition (1971) was even translated into English: VA Tumanov, *Contemporary Bourgeois Legal Thought: A Marxist Evaluation of the Basic Concepts Theories and Critical Studies* (Moscow, Progress Publishers, 1974). Another important source was the book on *The Legal Doctrines of Imperialism* published in Polish in 1957 and translated into Russian in 1959: GL Seidler, *Doktryny prawne imperializmu* (Warszawa, Państwowe wydawnictwo naukowe, 1957). These and other publications that appeared after 1955 are not examined in this chapter as they fall outside the context of Kelsen's book on the Communist theory of law.

[96] With exception of Maurice Hauriou, Leon Duguit and several other institutionalists whose works were translated and published in the late 1920s.

[97] The first partial translation of the 1960 *Pure Theory of Law* appeared only in 1987. Other Kelsen writing remained unpublished in Russian until the mid-2010s. Prior to these first translations, Soviet scholars criticised Kelsen's work relying mainly on Tumanov's volume, eg, ES Komarova, 'H. Kelsen and legal philosophy [Kelsen H. i filosofiia prava']' (1984) 3 *Problems of the bourgeois theory and philosophy of law* [*Problemy burzhuaznoi teorii i filosofii prava*] 104.

[98] The abbreviation for the Head Directory of Lagers – the Soviet system of lagers for enemies of the people.

[99] Kelsen, *The Communist Theory of Law* (n 6) xxiii.

[100] MG Losano, 'Hans Kelsen "criptocomunista" e l'FBI. In margine al suo libro postumo Religione secolare' (2017) 1 *Sociologia del diritto* 148. Further, Professor Losano explains the motives that allegedly incited Kelsen to writing his books on the political theory and legal theory of Bolshevik: 'Being aged already over seventy, he probably was reluctant to provide explanations before the parliamentary committee which dealt with the anti-American activities' (ibid).

praised the first political experiments with Soviets (self-governing collectives) in the first years after the 1917 Russian Revolution.[101] In terms of his political orientation, Kelsen could be identified as an Austro-Marxist;[102] at least he sympathised with their programme, and remained favourable to socialist ideas all his life.[103] In the atmosphere of anti-Communist hysteria, one could easily suspect him of sympathies to Soviet ideology.

This identification of Austrian Marxism and Russian Bolshevism would be evidently wrong, but the US secret service people were hardly well prepared to understand nuances between different versions of socialism. The FBI dossier on Kelsen contains, among other materials, protocols of several interrogations during which he was intensively interviewed on his socialist sympathies.[104] It is revelatory that at one of such interviews Kelsen has found nothing better to say in his defence that he published a book against the Communists – meaning his 1948 opus.[105] The FBI dossier was closed in 1955. One cannot but notice that this was the year of publication of Kelsen's book on Soviet legal theory. Although, there is no evidence that the FBI's suspicions were cleared exactly due to the publication of this book.

Kelsen used this publication also to criticise, along with the Communists, those who disagreed with the pure theory of law in the West. On the one hand, 'by proving that Soviet scholars engaged in natural-law thinking, Kelsen aimed to show the natural-law theory's unreliability in securing a particular type of – Western – moral ideal'.[106] On the other, he sought to demonstrate that the Communist theory of law was 'only a variation of sociological jurisprudence widespread in non-communist countries'[107] and did not spare his opponents from obfuscating their theories with hints at their intellectual kinship with Communism.

Can it be that Kelsen's *The Communist Theory of Law* was written without real intention to engage in a serious discussion exactly with the Soviet authors he criticised? As explained above, one of the arguments in favour of this thesis is that the 1955 book was characterised by such astonishing carelessness to details, by the penury of the employed sources and by such superficiality of analysis that were highly untypical for his research. It does not seem implausible that in order to clear himself from his doubtful intellectual past, Kelsen published in 1948 and 1955 two superficial (for his intellectual level) volumes.

Kelsen's haste is already apparent in the selection of the political prophecies of Marx as the main object for his criticism in *The Political Theory of Bolshevism*. As these prophecies had already been analysed in 1923, in his *Sozialismus und Staat*, he did not need to spend much intellectual effort – this time, putting his analysis in a form better digestible

[101] H Kelsen, 'Demokratisierung der Verwaltung' (1921) 1 *Zeitschrift für Verwaltung* 5.
[102] GH Wielinger, 'Hans Kelsen' in W Mantl (ed), *Politik in Österreich. Die Zweite Republik: Bestand und Wandel* (Vienna, WUV, 1992) 766–86.
[103] T Ehs, *Hans Kelsen und politische Bildung im modernen Staat. Vorträge in der Wiener Volksbildung* (Vienna, Manz Verlag, 2007).
[104] O Rathkolb, 'Hans Kelsen und das FBI während des McCarthysmus in den USA' in R Walter, W Ogris and T Olechowski (eds), *Hans Kelsen: Leben – Werk – Wirksamkeit* (Vienna, HKI, 2009) 339–49, 347.
[105] ibid.
[106] Lukina, 'Opening the Pandora's Box (n 5) 535.
[107] Kelsen, *The Communist Theory of Law* (n 6) 193.

for the American readership. Miriam Gassner in her profound publication has persuasively demonstrated that the 1948 book was 'a mere English compendium of the ideas that Kelsen had already expressed'.[108]

In his 1923 book, Kelsen cunningly uncovered the evident inconsistency in Marxist political philosophy: it called for the elimination of the state, and at the same time planned to keep up the coercive system of economic and, inevitably, legal and political organisation that would be impossible without the state – the dictatorship of proletariat or whatever other name one gives to the Communist political system, it will exercise the same functions as states elsewhere. The same line of argumentation was reproduced in his 1948 opus.

In the 1955 book, Kelsen focused his critical remarks on the anarchical elements of Communist theory. But this criticism was quite outdated. As shown above, in the first years after the Bolshevik revolution, there indeed appeared a number of theories alternative to legal positivism. The most known and influential were Mikhail Reisner's theory of revolutionary consciousness and Evgenii Pashukanis' commodity exchange theory. But gradually, these projects fell into oblivion; those who dared think otherwise and criticised the narrow conception (the command theory) of law were added to the list of enemies of the people.[109] From the 1930s onwards, there was no serious discussion about the elimination of the socialist state and abolishing its law – this occasionally would constitute a *corpus delicti* of counter-revolutionary activity punishable by death. Even paying lip service to the intellectual legacy of Marx and theoretically admitting the idea that state and law can someday wither away,[110] Vyshinsky and other legal scholars evidently did not consider this option seriously.[111] Kelsen overreacted with his criticism of the anarchical trends in Bolshevik legal theory, these trends in the 1950s being in the long-forgotten past.

As with the methods of his Soviet opponents, in these books Kelsen did nothing but comment on several extracts from the outdated works of the Soviet authors. By the time Kelsen's book was published in 1955, many of these authors were no longer alive (Reisner and Stuchka died in 1928 and 1932, and Pashukanis perished in a prison around 1937), while Vyshinsky and the others who were still alive, had considerably revised their conceptions by then. As a result, Kelsen criticised the Communist legal theory that at that moment did not exist any longer and, rather, had never existed in the form he represented it. There were many conflicting conceptions and theories of Soviet authors which were artificially brought together by Kelsen in a kind of a coherent whole for the purpose he did not conceal – to show that his version of legal positivism is free from the flaws he imputed to Soviet scholars.

[108] Gassner (n 5) 154. She further explains that 'As the pure theory of law did not quite match the US legal thinking where prevailed case law, Kelsen tried to establish himself, on the one hand, in the province of posited international law and, on the other, in the province of political science' (ibid).

[109] LL Fuller, 'Pashukanis and Vyshinsky: A Study in the Development of Marxian Legal Theory' (1949) 8 *Michigan Law Review* 1157.

[110] Vyshinsky and other Soviet legal scholars did not formally deny the perspective of withering away, but projected this utopic ideal in the unforeseeable future when people will freely follow, without the need for coercion, the moral rules necessary to social order.

[111] GC Guins, 'Law Does Not Wither Away in the Soviet Union' (1950) 9 *Russian Review* 187.

V. Conclusion: Antipodes or Doppelgangers?

Were their ideas and ideals antagonistic to the extent Kelsen and the Soviet scholars described it? There can be two ways of approaching the discussion between Kelsen and his Soviet opponents. Placing them at opposing poles in what concerns their methodological, philosophical or ideological orientation is one way to resolve this conundrum.[112] The first impression is that ideologically the pure theory of law and Soviet legal theory defended diametrically opposing values: those of liberal democracy and *Rechtsstaat*, and those of collectivism and authoritarianism, accordingly, standing on methodologically different positions. However, this black-and-white picture is not entirely correct.

Kelsen and his Soviet contenders were methodologically close to each other, perhaps closer than they wanted. Paradoxically, this closeness is confirmed by the criticism that Kelsen and his Soviet opponents unleashed against each other, repeating basically the same main arguments about lack of objectivity and about natural law. By belittling and mocking each other, Kelsen and his Soviet antagonists pursued the same strategic goals of survival.

On the other hand, both Marxists and Kelsen pursued the same project of critical analysis of bourgeois legal science. This project was aimed at revealing the hidden value preferences and interests behind seemingly perpetual theoretical schemes. Symptomatically, the author of the first textbook on Marxist legal theory, Mikhail Strogovich, spoke of Kelsen's method rather laudably:

> Certainly, Kelsen cannot be viewed as one of the most reactionary bourgeois lawyers like American pragmatists or right-wing French Catholics. Accounting to his ideas and his entire *Weltanschauung*, he is a quite moderate bourgeois liberal who is very far from the extremities of the most vigorous apologists of the reaction.[113]

This favourable characterisation does not come as a surprise if one considers that Kelsen sympathised with socialist ideals, especially during his Austrian years, and had never fully given up these sympathies, remaining a 'liberal socialist'. He insisted that stability should be prioritised over freedom; he denied that one may disobey rules following one's individual ethical judgements; he admitted individual freedom only within posited legal order. All this brings him quite far away from classical liberalism in the style of Smith or Hayek, who saw human freedom as a natural fact.[114]

Undoubtedly, ideology played a major role in the discussion between Kelsen and his Soviet critics. But apart from ideology, both Kelsen and his opponents belonged to legal positivism, and undeniably shared many common methodological principles. There were no principal disagreements about the main principle of legal research that had to remove from the province of jurisprudence everything except legal norms.[115]

[112] C Jabloner, 'Kelsen als Feindbild' (2022) 2 *Juridicum* 164.

[113] Strogovich, 'Bourgeois theories of legality and personal rights' (n 37) 293.

[114] RA Posner, 'Kelsen versus Hayek: Pragmatism, Economics, and Democracy' in R Posner, *Law, Pragmatism, and Democracy* (Cambridge, MA, Harvard University Press, 2003) 250–91.

[115] Kelsen put the main idea of his pure theory as follows: 'to develop those tendencies of jurisprudence that focus solely on cognition of the law rather than on the shaping of it, and to bring the results of this cognition as close as possible to the highest values of all science: objectivity and exactitude (Kelsen, *Introduction to the Problems of Legal Theory* (n 2) 1).

Equally accepting this principle, Kelsen and his Soviet opponents faced the same problems and vividly discussed whether legal positivism is reconcilable with the axiomatisation of political values and how scholars can ensure the objectivity of their analysis. Here, political values, be they liberal or socialist, were only secondary variables in the formula to which both sides signed up.[116]

The Marxist-Leninist authors were apparently wrong in picturing the pure theory of law as a kind of ivory castle that considers legal norms as fully independent from social conditions and isolated from them. This analysis was already outdated in the 1930s when Kelsen abandoned the strong Neo-Kantian Ought–Is distinction, and in the first edition of *The Pure Theory of Law* (1934) admitted that the social 'Is' can in many respects substantially influence the legal 'Ought'.[117] Already in the 1940s Kelsen had defined the ability to exercise organised coercion as the main element of legal order, so that the legal and the political coincide: 'the specifically "political" element consists in nothing but the element of coercion',[118] while political power is understood as 'the efficacy of the coercive order recognized as law'.[119] This statement is one which Vyshinsky and other Soviet legal positivists would readily accept.

Professor Römer seems to be right in his conclusion about their pragmatic proximity:

> Pure theory of law can be utilized not only instrumentally for the Marxist critic of the established bourgeois legal theory, but can also secure the results to which arrives the Marxist theory basing in its dialectically historic analysis; with this, the Pure theory of law would even become a part of the Marxist legal theory.[120]

In his indirect discussion with Pashukanis, Kelsen even acknowledged that the results of his criticism of bourgeois ideology in legal science fits quite well with the tendencies of the materialist philosophy of history and could eventually become a part of it.[121]

After all, in spite of the seemingly insurmountable ideological contradictions, there was a certain proximity of political attitudes. On the one side, they were brought together by the same aversion to political conservatism, philosophical idealism, moral absolutism and religious ethics. On the other, Kelsen had a certain inclination towards leftism that triggered a number of personal problems for him. His demission from the Austrian Constitutional Court or FBI control in the post-war United States can be cited as examples of such problems. Kelsen's anti-Catholic, laic position in the matter of divorce was evidently informed by his social-democratic, leftist convictions. Should his Soviet critics have wanted to know about it, they would certainly applaud him for this 'anti-reactionary' position, at least in this respect.

[116] G Brunner, 'Naturrecht und Sowjetideologie' (1971) 1 *Anales de la Cátedra Francisco Suárez* 47; SL Paulson, 'Kelsen as Political Theorist' (1990) 17 *Cahiers de philosophie politique et juridique* 97.

[117] SL Paulson, 'The Neo-Kantian Dimension of Kelsen's Pure Theory of Law' (1992) 12 *Oxford Journal of Legal Studies* 311.

[118] H Kelsen, 'The Law as a Specific Social Technique' (1941) 9 *University of Chicago Law Review* 75, 82.

[119] Kelsen, *General Theory of Law and State* (n 89) 191.

[120] P Römer, 'Die Reine Rechtslehre Hans Kelsens als Ideologie und Ideologiekritik' (1971) 4 *Politische Vierteljahresschrift* 579, 596.

[121] H Kelsen, 'Allgemeine Rechtslehre im Lichte materialistischer Geschichtsauffassung' in Hans Kelsen, *Demokratie und Sozialismus: ausgewählte Aufsätze*, N Leser (ed) (originally published 1931) (Vienna, Wiener Volksbuchhandlung, 1967) 69.

INDEX

NB–page number in **bold** denote information in tables

www.ingramcontent.com/pod-product-compliance
Ingram Content Group UK Ltd.
Pitfield, Milton Keynes, MK11 3LW, UK
UKHW020232290926
15470UKWH00002B/487

9 781509 965809